W9-BPJ-023

The New York Times

SUNDAY CROSSWORD OMNIBUS

VOLUME 4

Edited by
Eugene T. Maleska

TIMES BOOKS

SOLUTIONS TO THE PUZZLES ARE FOUND AT THE BACK OF THE BOOK

Copyright © 1995 by Random House, Inc.

All rights reserved under International and Pan-American Copyright Conventions. Published in the United States by Times Books, a division of Random House, Inc., New York, and simultaneously in Canada by Random House of Canada, Limited, Toronto.

All of the puzzles that appear in this work were originally published in *The New York Times* Sunday editions throughout 1980, 1981, 1982, 1983, and 1984. Copyright © 1980, 1981, 1982, 1983, and 1984 by The New York Times Company. All rights reserved. Reprinted by permission.

ISBN 0-8129-2480-0

Manufactured in the United States of America
9 8 7 6 5 4 3

Preface

Welcome to our fourth omnibus volume of 200 Sunday crosswords from the pages of the *New York Times*. You may be interested to know that this omnibus series of collected volumes from our regular Sunday *Times* series is our biggest seller – thanks to the combination of the *New York Times* name and a great price. So you're in good puzzling company.

For your information, you will find a listing of our newest crossword books opposite puzzle #200; this listing will now be updated on a regular basis. You can find these books at your local bookstore (which can order for you any title that may be out of stock), but you may order them directly from us if you wish.

There's one new book that we'd particularly like to call to your attention: *Random House Masterpiece Crosswords* – it's unlike any other puzzle book you've ever seen. With superb all-new crosswords by America's best-known puzzlemakers (photographs and profiles of each are included) and an elegant, hardcover hidden-spiral binding, *Masterpiece* is the "crown jewel" of our crossword line. It's at your bookstore now.

Your comments on this or any of our books are most welcome. The address: Times Books Crosswords, 201 East 50th Street #11-1, New York, NY 10022. We'll be happy to respond personally if you enclose a self-addressed stamped envelope.

Best wishes for happy solving!

Stanley Newman
Managing Director, Puzzles & Games
Times Books

High Spirits

By Joy L. Wouk

ACROSS

1 Chorus in "The Green Pastures"
7 Volcanic emissions
13 Least attentive
20 Lark or eagle
21 Paid (up)
22 Hurriedly
23 Assignations
24 River to Hecate Strait
25 Office, in Santander
26 Lace tag
27 "Balloon Hoax" author
28 Comic-strip pilot
30 Early car
31 P.S. 6 Man., e.g.
35 Press
36 Sommer
37 Po River city
39 Song syllable
40 Teller's place
41 "Mr. Republican"
42 Pigments for Gainsborough
44 Ann Ronell's command to a willow
45 Certain jockey's concern
47 Game, such as rounders
48 Lend —— (help)
49 Crab shells
52 Ulithi, e.g.
54 Patriotic org.
55 Vedic sky dragon
56 Browning's "—— Duchess"
57 Poet St.-John, 1960 Nobelist
58 Rainbow goddess
60 Seat for Burger
62 Barbarian
63 ". . . —— spacious skies"
64 Did some decorative stitching
66 Oar parts
68 Tybalt, to Juliet
72 Bergamot, e.g.
73 U.N. arm
74 Augury
76 Saarinen
77 Obtund
80 Mogadishu resident
83 Stingo, in Soho
84 Muffler mangler
85 Ouida
86 Becoming communicative
88 Mesta
90 D.C. agency under Miller
91 Occlude
93 Heller hero
94 Used a rosary
95 Pongo and wou-wou
97 "—— volat propriis" (Oregon motto)
99 Ass, in Tours
100 Flora and fauna
101 Ford's running mate: 1976
102 Moroccan district
103 Kentucky Derby winner: 1956
105 Game played with counters
108 Buccaneers' black banner
111 Aria area
112 G.I.'s "sky pilot"
114 Spanish philosopher: 1864-1936
115 Swatch
118 Christie's "The —— of Chimneys": 1925
119 Covered with tin or steel
120 Creates a jam
121 Part of a rosebush's hip
122 Arranges beforehand
123 Kaufman quips
124 —— prunes

DOWN

1 "—— Is Born"
2 Neighbor of Sverige
3 ". . . haughty gallant, ——?": N. Rowe
4 Gaelic
5 Possessed of learning
6 Grads-to-be
7 British spa or college
8 Card
9 Paris-to-Reims dir.
10 Co., in Metz
11 Sawbucks
12 He wrote "The Native's Return": 1934
13 Conversation writer
14 Donkeys on shipboard
15 "Two owls and ——": E. Lear
16 Kind of aircraft
17 Reversible machine
18 Measures of set type
19 Vessel on the range
27 Implement for flights of fancy
29 Sultanic say-sos
32 Fleur-de-——
33 Quintessence
34 Opper creation
38 Inspiration for Keats
42 Bedouin's goal, at times
43 Allure
44 Farm wagon
46 Poultry treat
49 Its capital is N'Djamena
50 Astringent
51 Provencal love song
53 Pithy
55 Slayer of Eric IV
59 A quick bread
61 Region, to Byron
63 Choice
65 Sharpers
67 Buck heroine
68 Iodine source
69 Buffoon
70 "Any fool can make —— . . .": Thoreau
71 Eminent
75 Whittier's Miss Muller
77 Decathlon item
78 Satirist
79 Like plants of the carrot family
80 Grits and chitlins
81 Choosing
82 "—— swell foop"
87 Campus group
88 Broad view
89 Erode
92 Snood
94 Flan
96 Lagerlöf et al.
98 Mexican institution
100 Wheat, in Colmar
104 Abysses
106 Drama by S. Johnson
107 Apportioned
109 Time of "comfort and joy"
110 Foray
113 Yearn
116 Brooks
117 "—— Love You," 1934 song
118 His Most Serene Highness: Fr. abbr.

Field Lark

By Caroline G. Fitzgerald

ACROSS

1 Coating or film
6 On Old Ironsides
12 Frolic
16 Churchill's "—— Country"
20 Start over
21 Thurified
22 Unlucky
23 Largest country in Africa
25 Originate
26 Apostles' and Nicene
27 Tarzan's swing
28 Moslem scholars
29 Memorial Stadium
31 Riverfront Stadium
33 Observe
34 Suffix with diction
35 Ham it up
37 Rumpled
38 Hog fat
40 Metallic disks
42 High, waterproof boot
43 Meadowlands stadium
46 Shea Stadium, once
51 City ENE of Indianapolis
52 Suffix with suffer
53 Drudge
55 Ericsson
57 Baba the woodcutter
58 Bullet
60 Eight-time Norris Trophy winner
62 Capital of Southern Yemen
63 Piscivorous flier
64 Veterans Stadium
67 Starfish
71 Noted ref. book
72 Spurt
73 Trouble
74 Year in reign of Otto I
75 Mounted police
77 Eye sore
79 Estelle from Lynn
82 Part of Can.
83 False claim
88 Central Park producer
89 Key letter
92 Undercover cop
95 Linden or Holbrook
96 Isolated
98 Louisiana Superdome
101 Great Barrier Island
103 Operatic prince
104 Islanders' org.
106 Undiluted
107 Kier or keeve
108 Compact
109 Make bubbly
111 Egg-shaped
113 Doe, to a fawn
115 Pontiac Silverdome
117 Orange Bowl
120 —— Canals, St. Marys River
121 Roman officials
122 Suit to ——
123 Ex-Dodger manager and family
127 Kind of remark
128 N.Z. tree
129 Bill
132 Metropolitan Stadium
134 Raiders' Cave, once
139 ". . . —— and silver beam": Shelley
140 Asian desert
141 Unworthy idol
142 Dimmer
143 Moore's "—— Rookh"
144 Persea or wicopy
145 Witch in TV's "Bewitched"
146 Nautical direction
147 Loom reed
148 Orange-red ring stone
149 Taws, often
150 Tithe part

DOWN

1 Favor
2 "Bad" Mr. Brown
3 Old-womanish
4 Gusto
5 Togolese group
6 Harmonies
7 Bird's morsel
8 Person who is sui generis
9 On a cruise
10 Memorable, as a day
11 Deg. for one who cares about caries
12 Faces, as an embankment
13 Like bighorns
14 Type of porcelain
15 Skirt feature
16 "Business ——"
17 All-out
18 "Lets Make ——"
19 Nettle
24 Plant or ointment
30 Trusts
31 "Treasure Island" pirate
32 Drooping
36 Ferrer or Tormé
38 Varnish base
39 Cordials
40 Roast or roaster
41 Tie for a groom
43 Solzhenitsyn's "Archipelago"
44 Architect Jones: 1573-1652
45 Like gnus in zoos
46 Broken-down horse
47 She married a Lloyd
48 Drift
49 Great-grand-child, in Glasgow
50 Forty-——
51 Busch or Marsh
54 Quarter type in Paris
56 I.R.S. agents
59 —— boat, for sailing
61 Memorial Coliseum
65 Irving Stone's "—— for Life"
66 Bribe
68 Dr. in "Tristram Shandy"
69 Charged atom
70 Southern New York, e.g.
74 Demo follower
76 Egyptian god
78 Chemical suffix
80 Notwithstanding
81 Place to get fit
83 Unit of illumination
84 Amount of assessment
85 Ink resin
86 Emulated Caleb
87 Bore hated by sailors
90 Official language of India
91 Suffix with opal
93 Poe's one-word bird
94 Sharp metallic sound
97 Bookbinder's sheepskin
98 Spot for a snow bunny
99 One of many behind bars
100 Four-time N.L. home-run champ
102 Marginal note
105 Outlet for fans
109 "I Feel —— Comin' On": 1935
110 Arcaro or Stanky
112 Letters on a chasuble
114 "Norma ——"
116 Lunchtime for many
118 Like: Suffix
119 —— a jaybird
121 Committed a deadly sin
123 Of grandparents
124 Certain beans
125 Carpentry, for one
126 Some noncoms
127 Temperate
128 Antonym for abhor
129 Leftovers in solitaire
130 Prevent
131 Slip for a ship
133 J. F. Cooper heroine
135 Lick ——
136 "—— promise Rhythm": 1930
137 Young oyster
138 Elizabeth is one
141 Boston jetsam: Dec. 16, 1773

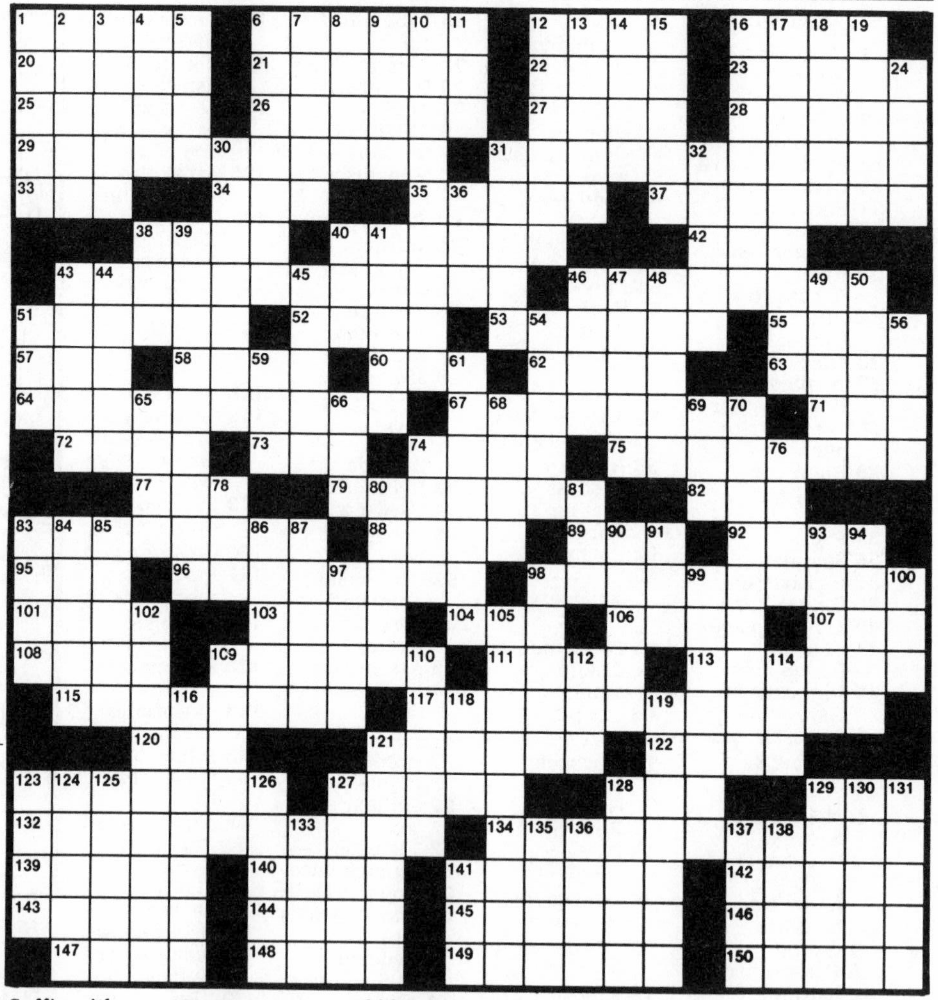

3

Mind Your P's and Q's

By C. J. Angio

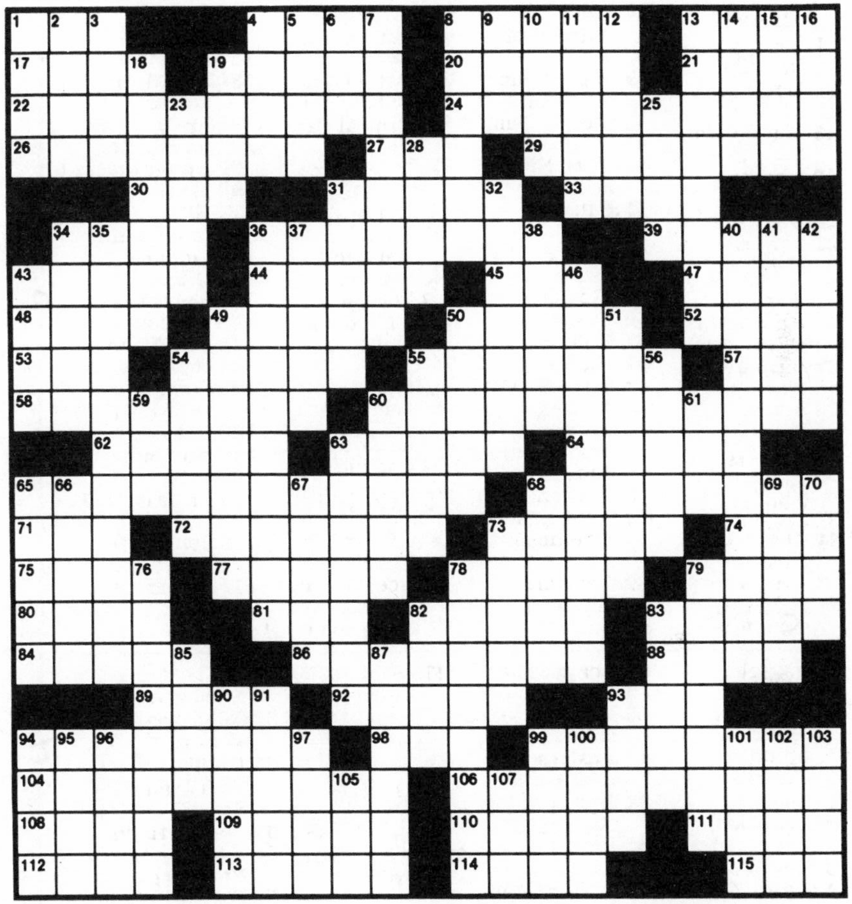

ACROSS

1 Mournful
4 Jai ——
8 Man of Manche
13 Trevi tidbit
17 Star in Pegasus
19 Entomb
20 Epic translated by Pope
21 Turgenev's birthplace
22 Dowitcher
24 Lampoon
26 Comes down, like Hillary
27 Mercatorial device
29 Follows
30 Foulard
31 Trees or monkeys
33 Suffixes with Jersey and Wisconsin
34 Meas. of area
36 Basketball teams
39 Form of croquet
43 Perkin's purple
44 Writer Sinclair
45 Mont Buet is one
47 Famous Spartans' coach
48 Seaman's word
49 Miasma
50 Long leg
52 Packy —— (Bob Hope)
53 Hwy.
54 Movie shots
55 Himalayan cedars
57 Weight in Calcutta
58 Solaced
60 Required beforehand
62 Project; plan
63 Hitler's father
64 Expend or exhaust
65 Japanese varnish tree
68 Demolish
71 Emulate Lot's wife
72 Apportion
73 D.S.C. receiver
74 Lingerie item
75 Furniture style
77 Fuliginous
78 Mails a letter
79 Sit down heavily
80 Squash, e.g.
81 Sum, esse, —— . . .
82 Ethan of fiction
83 Actor in "Get Carter": 1971
84 Bergen puppet
86 Where hounds go round and round
88 Head of a tale
89 Sounds in rounds
92 Below, to Blake
93 Under: Prefix
94 Having a wide range
98 Peak in Nepal
99 Most sentimental
104 Water-skier's next of kin
106 Redoubles
108 Buck's Wang ——
109 Use artgum
110 Ruined
111 Madame Bovary
112 Cheat on a check
113 Wet
114 First place
115 Haggard's title

DOWN

1 Logician's abbr.
2 "Requiem for ——"
3 "Buenos ——!"
4 Author Tyler
5 Firpo
6 French Dadaist
7 Tchaikovsky's Symphony No. 5 ——
8 Hobohemian's cousin
9 Biographer Winslow
10 "Little —— Marker"
11 Chilean evergreen shrub
12 Inference
13 Adjective for Gobel
14 Dies ——
15 Comedian Foxx
16 English country festivals
18 Imaginary
19 Man, for one
23 Label on a French garment
25 Champagne bucket
28 Envelope abbr.
31 Singers Schipa and Gobbi
32 Parts of turbines
34 City in Uruguay
35 Myrtle used for timber
36 Like some buildings in S.F.
37 Raised the bet
38 Kind of rule
40 Like railroads, gas companies, etc.
41 Loose, as a diamond
42 —— nous
43 Chagall
46 Small decorations on books
49 British appraisers
50 Murrow's "—— Now"
51 Ties
54 Add
55 Idler
56 Seis plus uno
59 Continuation of a bk.
60 Tropical aquarium fish
61 Châlons- —— -Marne
63 State of having wings
65 Bounds' partner
66 Locale for Rosalind
67 Tarquin the ——
68 Dime of 1792
69 Beldam
70 Sprinter's goal
73 Kin of the belly dance
76 Pledge
78 Postquarantine permission to use a port
79 Mouth organ
82 Tighten, as drum cords
83 S.A. rodent
85 Tackle
87 Equipped
90 Had the flu
91 Springe
93 Famed painter of ranch hands
94 Columbo
95 Here, in Honduras
96 Litter Lilliputian
97 Emulate beavers
99 Radio's "Vic and ——"
100 Host at Valhalla
101 End of an O'Neill title
102 Trucking rig
103 Autocrat
105 Compass dir.
107 "Hansel —— Gretel"

4

Board Members

By Louis Baron

ACROSS

1 Astringent
5 Glower
10 Puppeteer Lewis
15 Con job
19 Except
20 Blake of jazz
21 Moslem judge
22 Disyllabic sigh
23 Gardner's "The Case of the ——"
26 What bêtes noires inspire
27 Hard-to-hold type
28 Author Kingsley
29 Asks for
30 Spinachlike plant
32 Apprentice
34 Director of "The Servant": 1963
35 He wrote "Uhuru"
36 Poe's "The Angel of the ——"
37 Promenade
38 Most sharp-witted
41 Write back
44 Hit musical of 1951
46 Hugo's "—— Blas"
47 Kazan
48 Use 'baccy
49 Oval segments
50 U-boat's sea
51 Burrows
52 Vernon Blythe's dancing partner
56 Amerind group
57 Certain settlers
59 Wolf-whistle accompaniment
60 Proust or Marceau
61 Undo
62 Interweave
63 Admiral Andrea
64 This can be Cannes
66 Mil. training unit
67 Fast and dazzling
70 Without help
71 Carroll character
74 Vowel for Euripedes
75 Not like a sure thing
76 Courts
77 Oxalis plants
78 It once cost 5 cents
79 One place to get an E.E.
80 Slangsters' uncles
84 Actor Hagman
85 Like an igloo
87 Defective: Comb. form
88 Rooks, e.g.
89 Sidled
90 Anglers' delights
91 Top of the ladder
95 More foresighted
97 Edible tubers
98 Middle: Comb. form
99 Mini-question
100 Center of Q.E.D.
101 She played a maid in "G.W.T.W."
105 Icy coating
106 Commercial willow
107 Old district of Asia Minor
108 Plod
109 Made oneself scarce
110 Junk and Scotland
111 Butter melter
112 Sand's "—— et Lui"

DOWN

1 Plus item
2 Staller's promise
3 Tonsil's neighbor
4 Conjoined
5 Appeared
6 One of two Nobelists: 1903
7 Ginza purchases
8 Beat the game
9 Reporter's routine
10 Order to a "Harvest Moon": 1908
11 Precipitate
12 Spirits, in Egyptology
13 Sugar Loaf's city
14 Seizes legally
15 Veld entourage
16 Rake's progress
17 Eastern nana
18 Like a pittance
24 Jessica of the stage
25 Pinza and Hines
31 Rajah's lady
33 City in SE Kansas
34 Lerner's collaborator
35 Sheriff in a Puccini opera
37 Oland, Toler et al.
38 Composer Orff
39 Glove-in-the-raw
40 Yodeler's turf
41 Decode a primer
42 River to the North Sea
43 "But helpless —— He plays": FitzGerald
44 "Hey" or "Over" follower
45 Like many fences
48 Peak
50 Puzo or Lanza
52 "Fain would I, but —— not"
53 "Pastorale" painter: 1873
54 Type size
55 Smooth-talking
56 "Add here" mark
58 Speaker's device
60 Millers
62 Cap. of Queensland
63 Artist Edgar
64 Jules Muraire of French cinema
65 Pixie
67 Prefix with scope
68 Caesar's way
69 Author Joyce
71 Had 'em in the aisles
72 Neighbor of Guat.
73 Seasonal songs
76 Song of 1922
78 Judicial seat
80 Trainbearer
81 Those who vituperate

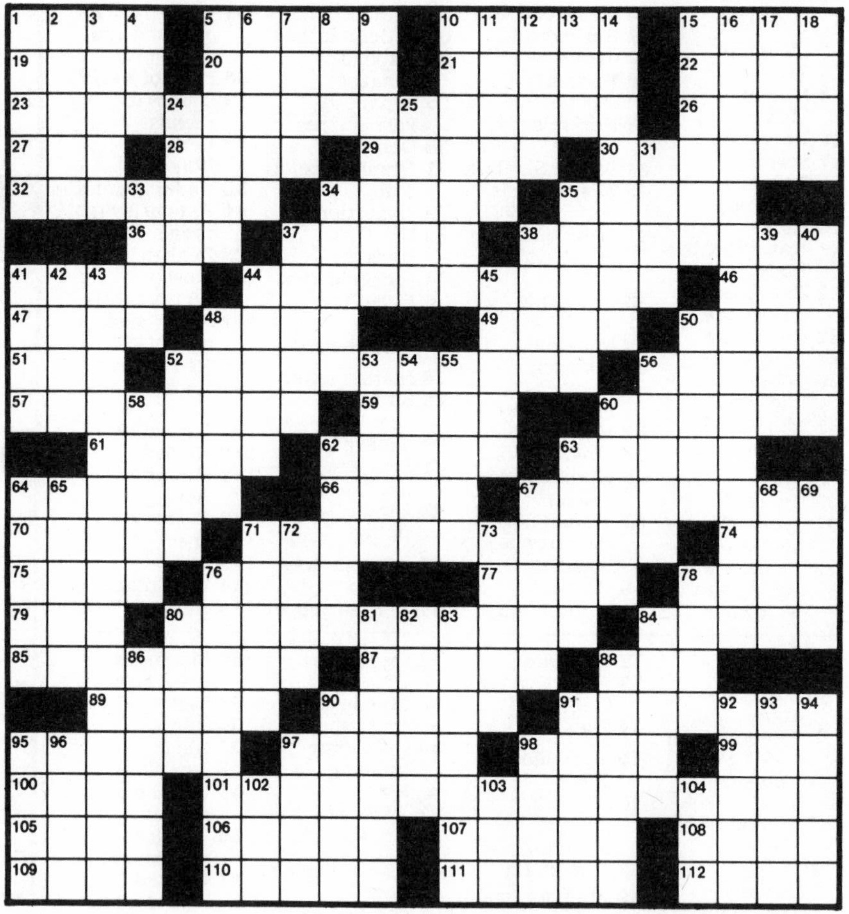

82 Web-footed mammal
83 Do exercises
84 Gaboriau's gumshoe
86 Made publishable
88 Oman's capital
90 Like some breaths
91 Game rounds
92 Tom of "The Seven Year Itch"
93 Underworld, O.T. style
94 Irish Renaissance dramatist
95 Anthologist Bennett
96 Seed envelope
97 Show life
98 Parrot's rival
102 Kyushu town
103 Richard ——, Oriental actor
104 "What's the ——?"

5

Reverse English

By Herb L. Risteen

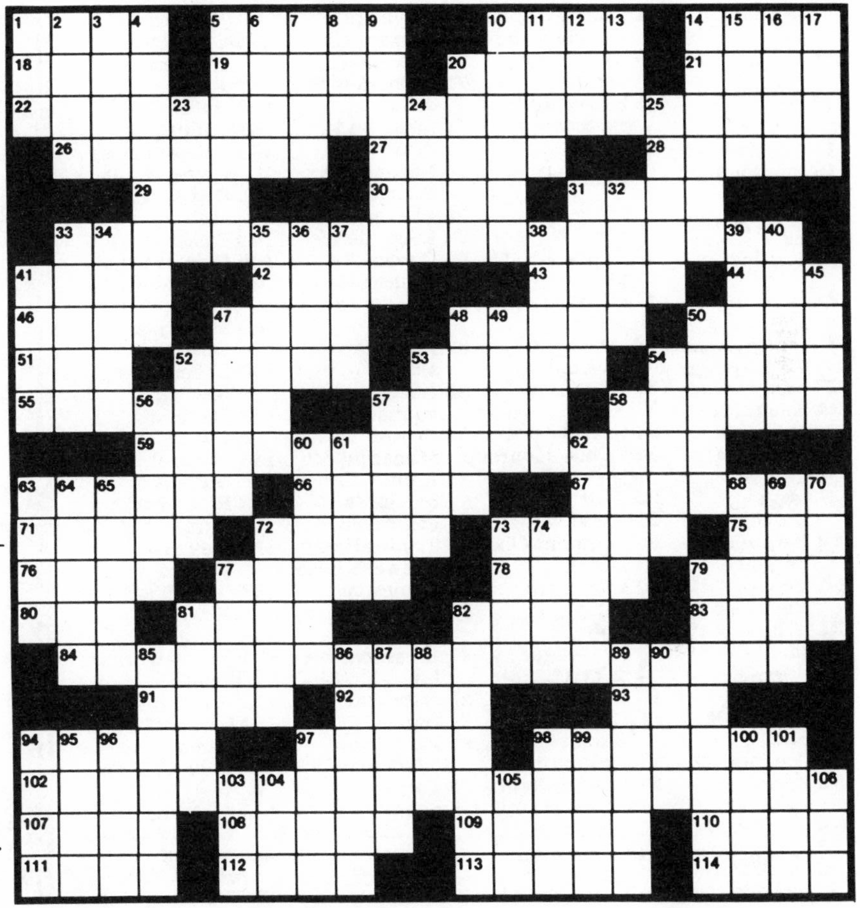

ACROSS

1 Leaping lights
5 Casts off
10 Founder of Lower Slobovia
14 Ill composed
18 Opinion
19 Sound of Washington
20 Big book
21 Cupid
22 "Christabel" poet
26 Five Nations group
27 Departer from Orly
28 Came about
29 Early sixth-century date
30 Places for loafers
31 Split-lipped mammal
33 "Invictus" poet
41 Whip mark
42 Companion of Enyo
43 Kind of ant or brat
44 Soho swell
46 Electrical units
47 On the house
48 Deck posts
50 Unadorned
51 Lobster coral
52 He wrote "The Cheats"
53 Giotto subject
54 Analyze grammatically
55 Twist the meaning of
57 Threnody
58 Equivocate
59 Mayor of Plymouth: 1581
63 Goose-pimply
66 After, in rouge et noir
67 Treated a lawn
71 Officiates at a tea
72 Culloden Moor fighters: 1746
73 Minds
75 Harem room
76 Pop singer Gibb
77 Arbuckle
78 At another time
79 Stiffly precise
80 Far East tongue
81 Flippant
82 Alaskan island
83 Water current
84 Ambassador at Paris: 1814-15
91 Layers
92 Arabic letter
93 Pro ——
94 Houston athlete
97 Fragrant seed
98 Missionary priest
102 Philip Stanhope
107 Like certain controls
108 Window type
109 Hawk's weapon
110 —— avis
111 Betray
112 Hit hard
113 Soft-soaps
114 Warren

DOWN

1 Prayer
2 Manipulates
3 Grant
4 Cons
5 Coined money
6 Mimetic dance
7 Parts of psyches
8 Calendar abbr.
9 Machine-guns
10 Prairie preyer
11 King or Bates
12 Alveolus
13 Eur. land
14 Victory emblem
15 War supplies, for short
16 Bygone birds
17 Gaelic
20 Swift kangaroo
23 Check
24 Calcar
25 C.S.A. commander
31 Ah Sin's creator
32 Intentions
33 Uncouth person
34 Gantry
35 Novelist Lee
36 Dryad's home
37 Hide's companion
38 Topic
39 ". . . shut yourself up —— . . .": Flaubert
40 Less desirable
41 Herbaceous plant
45 Ginger ——
47 Unit of capacitance
48 Potential playhouses
49 Actress Swenson
50 Raft material
52 Gherkins, for short
53 Cuts up
54 Poker holdings
56 Comics hero
57 —— tricks
58 Dress up
60 Metrical foot
61 Maculation
62 King of Egypt: 1936-52
63 Young oyster
64 Literary middle name
65 TV sound equipment
68 The Pentateuch
69 Rescript
70 Knight's wife
72 Agra attire
73 Quaestor under Scipio
74 Stake
77 Twain hero
79 Lévesque, Peckford et al.
81 "The —— Innocence": Wharton
82 Moves
85 Cause to vibrate
86 Malayan tree
87 Architect Gottlieb —— Saarinen
88 Thought's "father"
89 Motoring maneuvers
90 Walter —— Mare
94 Augments
95 Pivot
96 Greenwing
97 Monkshood
98 Water ——
99 Down, to a skipper
100 Pledge
101 Done, for short
103 Rifle
104 Christian or Caesarean
105 Stir up
106 Head covering

Guess Who!

By Raymond F. Eisner

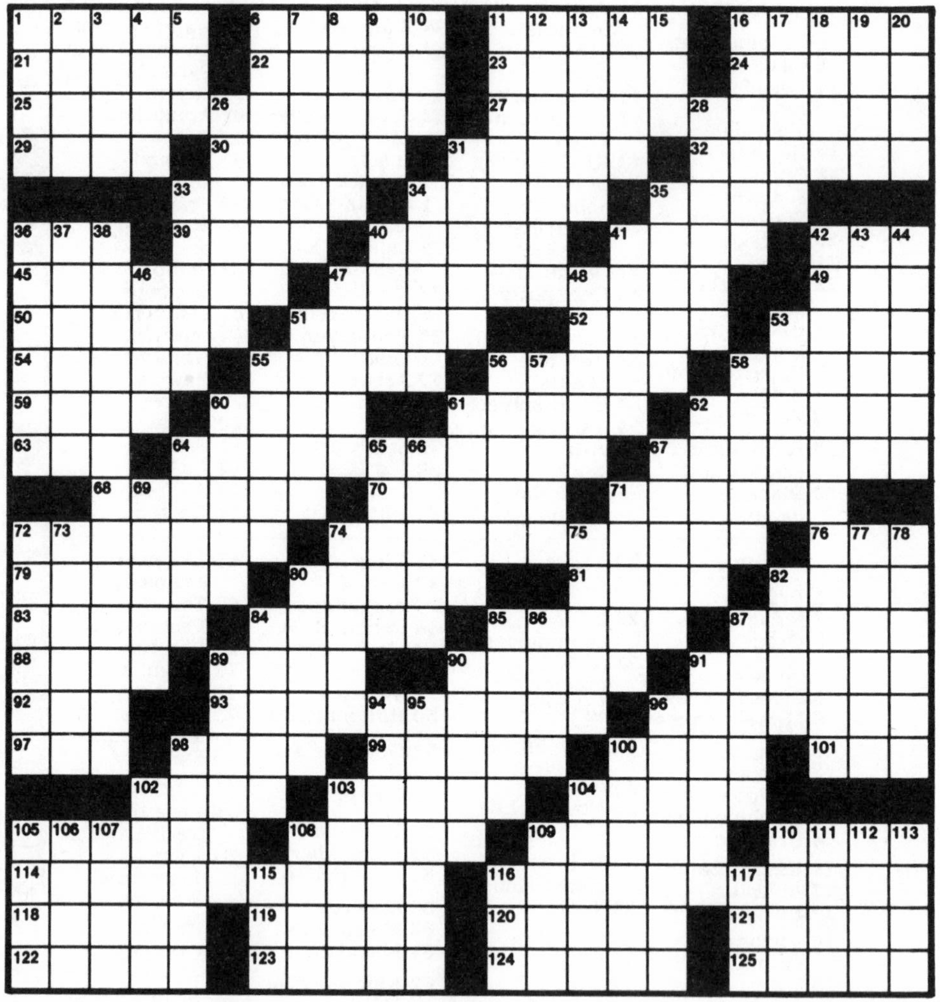

ACROSS

1 Chamber ensemble
6 Bowler's problem
11 "And why the —— boiling hot"
16 ——-Powell (Sir R. S. Smyth)
21 U. of Maine site
22 Marie Louise de la Ramée
23 Sam or Tom
24 Anoint, old style
25 Ann Myrtle Swoyer
27 Issur Danielovitch
29 Hershfield's "Agent"
30 Ends of churches
31 "The —— of sin . . ."
32 Parts of structures
33 Meccawee, e.g.
34 Companies
35 Brontë pen name
36 Unit on a space vehicle
39 Relative of a via
40 Heavenly sustenance
41 Dance's partner
42 Liberian native
45 To startle, in Savoie
47 Richard Starkey
49 —— Palmas
50 Diverse
51 Oracle site
52 Vallee
53 Campus org
54 "Once upon —— . . ."
55 Twirling rod
56 Yaks
58 Contralto Glaz
59 Depend
60 Elaborate party
61 Piggy
62 Two-edged sword
63 Fool follower
64 Charles Farrar Browne
67 Charles Henry Smith
68 Elephant grass
70 Grand backer
71 Onion-flavored rolls
72 Small hand drum
74 Nathan Birnbaum
76 Peaked
79 Loved dearly
80 City in Afghanistan
81 Word with while
82 Hawaiian shark
83 Horne and Nyman
84 "—— Macabre"
85 Latin teacher's command
87 Tropical fruit
88 Brewer's yeast
89 Orifice
90 Plein-air painter
91 Is responsible for
92 Nebraska Indian
93 Karoline Blamauer
96 Express sympathy
97 Pipe joint
98 City of the Huguenots
99 Vice ——
100 Bathe
101 Cain's land
102 Lobes in moss leaves
103 On a large scale
104 Classified
105 Fidel's friends
108 Old: Comb. form
109 Signorina Scicolone
110 Laboratory medium
114 Mary Ann Evans
116 Michael Gubitosi
118 Nine: Comb. form
119 Meat, in Madrid
120 "—— With Me"
121 Spent
122 Krupp Works locale
123 Eire's first family: 1938-45
124 Luciano Pavarotti, for one
125 Signified

DOWN

1 Chaplin's widow
2 Master-tailor
3 Tennille
4 Suffix with differ
5 Haydn's —— Symphony
6 More unctuous
7 Celestial source of radio waves
8 Draw a parallel
9 When Brutus struck
10 Ralph Rackstraw, e.g.
11 Indonesian statesman
12 Mysteries
13 Lots of land
14 Kinds
15 Conjunction for Cato
16 Gewgaw
17 Seraph
18 Rue —— Paix
19 Media was its neighbor
20 Much-studied lake
26 Was prodigal
28 William Sydney Porter
31 McCartney group
33 Actress Anouk
34 Papal vestment
35 Creepers and rollers
36 Molière drama
37 Snapping beetle
38 Norma Jean Mortenson
40 Grain sorghum
41 Intimidate
42 Josephine Swenson
43 Swinger in Fenway Park
44 Steep slope
46 Frosted
47 O.T. juniper
48 Chord of three tones
51 Librarian's device
53 Acknowledge an R.S.V.P.
55 Climbing pepper
56 Baby linked with Eng
57 Batu Khan's Golden ——
58 Aula and odeum
60 Squiffed
61 Dark-colored
62 Laughing
64 After, in Avignon
65 Consumers
66 Greek porticoes
67 Bristle, in Bute
69 Garfield's middle name
71 Cloud or sun follower
72 Lyle from Pittsburgh
73 Preconceive
74 Janet Flanner
75 City near Cleveland
77 San ——, spa in western Texas
78 Caught in a springe
80 TV couple
82 Poem by Tennyson
84 Blackmore's Lorna
85 Heartsease
86 Novelist Seton
87 Like stallions
89 Crosby hit
90 Bluish-gray
91 London's famed Garden product
94 Satan
95 Envoys
96 Wedding figure
98 Catch phrase
100 City on the Rio Grande
102 Consent to
103 TV pioneer
104 Actor Williams
105 Author James: 1909-55
106 "—— sana . . ."
107 Free electrons
108 Pinter
109 It's often pierced
110 River in Poland
111 Festival
112 Consanguineous
113 Take a lease on
115 Flight formation: Abbr.
116 Bandicoot
117 Socko!

7

Jumping Jehoshaphat!

By Tap Osborn

ACROSS

1 Beaver or Angel
6 Finery
13 Invention of the 1830's
19 —— of quinine
21 Tuesday chore
22 Last
23 Start of a verse
26 Abuse
27 Août's saison
28 Southpaw's stat
29 Charge
30 Prepare for action
31 Sorrow
33 Red-carpet recipient
34 Hot Mediterranean wind
37 "Iron pumper"
38 Secured
39 Farm animal
42 Greek letters
43 Boxer's garment
44 Learned role on TV
45 Careless
46 Second line of verse
53 Nürnberg article
54 Young conger
55 Seine tributary
56 Drill
57 Abased
59 Like a heliogram
60 Father
61 Protest
62 Kitchen aid
63 Balm for a rash
64 Addict's pill
67 Viscous
68 Practiced horticulture
72 Toss out
73 Foal producer
74 —— the good
75 Hogg
76 Third line of verse
81 Bar order
82 Shell
83 Refuse
84 Airhole
85 Yo-yo, for one
86 Severe wound
87 Penned in
89 Pageboy, e.g.
91 Giant of fame
92 Boxing is his job
93 Bivouac
94 Evian, for one
97 Wine: Comb. form
98 U.S.N.A. grad.
99 Panaceas
103 Last line of verse
108 Throw open the windows
109 Child born early in Nov.
110 Sailboat
111 L.T.A. craft
112 Damselfish
113 Emulate Juliet

DOWN

1 Compose
2 Jai ——
3 Garlands
4 At the —— (just before the end)
5 Recipe phrase
6 Estrangement
7 Bungle
8 Stickum
9 Lansbury
10 Loser to Clay: 1964
11 Read into
12 Past
13 Avenger's act
14 Spellbound
15 Hassle
16 Variety of pastry
17 Canal finished in 1825
18 Network
20 Madrid month
24 Rove idly
25 Overhaul
31 Exclude
32 Augur
34 Glimpsed
35 Actor Davis
36 Old Peking weight
37 Sharpened
38 Celebrated
39 R.I.P. speech
40 Arouses
41 Strive
43 Place for birling
44 Molière's Harpagon
47 Bequeath
48 Rot-resistant wood
49 Hotel employees
50 Journalist Hugh
51 Nobleman's domain
52 Electricity
58 Estancia
59 City of about 6,000,000
60 Ex —— (one-sided)
62 Floorboard
63 Garrulous
64 Make skim milk
65 Convex molding
66 Lean and supple
67 Boffo
68 Thymus, for one
69 ". . . miner, forty- ——"
70 Correct
71 "Good —— you": W. S. Gilbert
74 Arab chief
77 Bric-a-brac holders
78 Usage
79 Advantage
80 Producing eggs hatched outside the body
86 Ascends
87 Grand ——
88 Arrange
89 Preminger's "In —— Way"
90 Don of late shows
92 Shelley subject
93 Hoppe's "weapon"
94 Mop
95 Bandleader Harris
96 Air: Comb. form
99 Half a toy train
100 Parrotfish
101 Finn's neighbor
102 —— terrier
104 —— de plume
105 Viper
106 "Conning Tower" monogram
107 Pewter metal

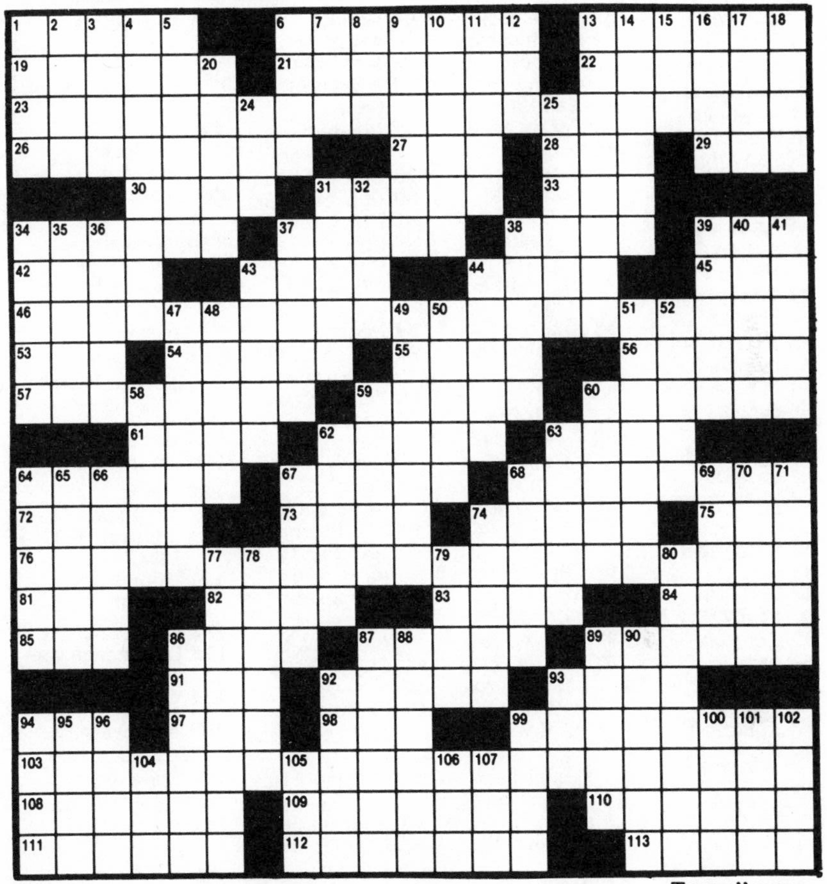

8

Buried Cities

By Jim Page

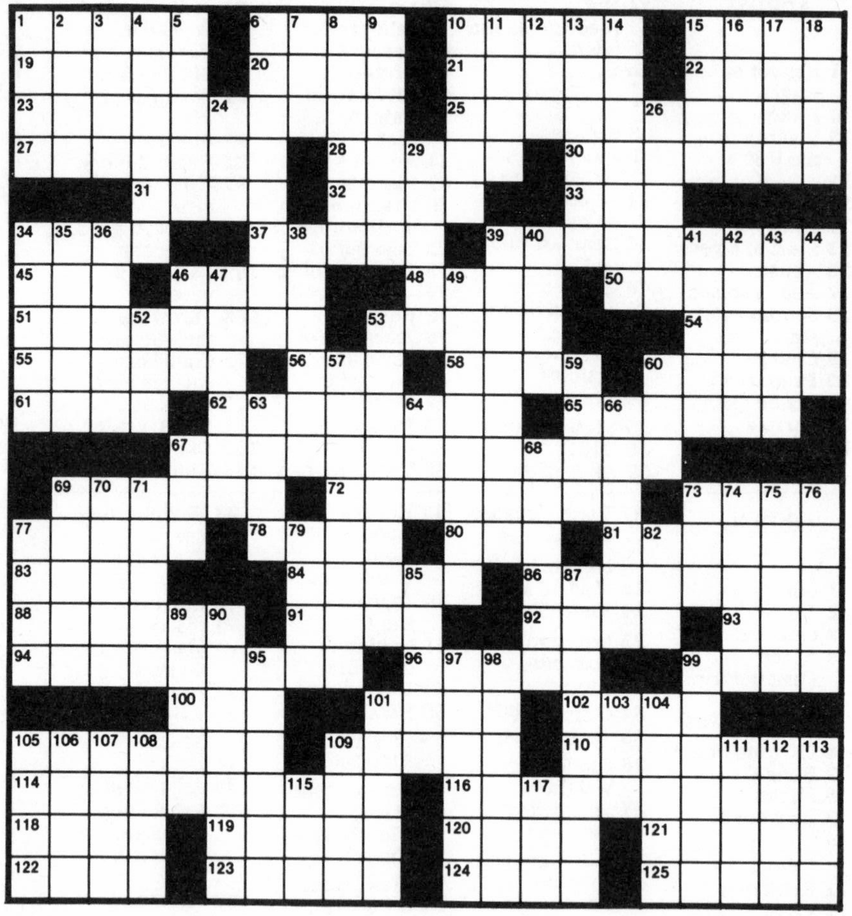

ACROSS

1 Org. for Berlin and Rome
6 —— bien
10 Kind of stores
15 Lady Hamilton
19 Headliner in April 1909
20 "—— soit . . ."
21 Pal, in Palermo
22 Where cows browse
23 Pa. city is involved in unforgettable event
25 City taken in by sackers
27 Surgical instruments
28 Quiverleaf
30 Rain repellent
31 Being
32 Deneb or Procyon
33 Her mate is a ruff
34 Mercatorial items
37 Hindmost
39 Alaskan city gets into some bad name-calling
45 Habitat: Comb. form
46 Order to Gridley
48 Domestic
50 Ugandan pest
51 French city features decorative strips
53 Like the Charleston today
54 Except
55 Bring about
56 "—— sea is calm . . .": Arnold
58 E.R.A., for one
60 River in Kan. and Neb.
61 Capp of comics
62 More supercilious
65 Yellow flags
67 German city comes across with top grades
69 Endure patiently
72 Most loutish
73 Bugs is his bane
77 Incubator newcomers
78 Williams team
80 Opp. of WNW
81 F.B.I. man, at times
83 Wylie's "Jennifer ——"
84 Peaches
86 Indian city has a hot-rod event
88 Zed's Greek cousins
91 Hawaiian goose
92 Swan's mythical mate
93 —— Palmas
94 Italian city takes on a forecaster
96 City that finishes a Holy City
99 "—— well . . ."
100 Chemical ending
101 Beaujolais, e.g.
102 Former British colony
105 Movie producer-director
109 "Our —— Havana"
110 Peregrinations
114 Swiss city visited by a tourist
116 Ecuadorean city has lots of stingers
118 Matinee ——
119 Bridal path
120 Noted Japanese admiral: 1854-1937
121 Gemstone weight
122 Sawbucks
123 Commence, as winter
124 Withered
125 Autocrats

DOWN

1 Summit
2 Erotic
3 Balaclavas
4 High ridges
5 Combustible heaps
6 "—— the times that try . . ."
7 Actor Glass
8 Crate
9 Postlunch snooze
10 Ralph or George
11 Orison finis
12 Force
13 Cotten and Woolley
14 Important French port
15 Culbertson et al.
16 Proverbial heirs
17 Spouse, in Savoie
18 Y.M.C.A. or N.A.A.C.P.
24 Apl. collectors
26 Spreads not for beds
29 Type of violet
34 Place attracting crowds
35 Kind of squash
36 Lucubrated
38 Famed columnist
39 Marvell's was coy
40 Impression
41 Kin of lomas
42 Storehouse
43 Letters on invitations
44 "—— pin . . ."
46 Transient mood
47 Calls for defrosting
49 Levies a fine
52 Legislative vote
53 Noted German philosopher-educator
57 "King of the Hill" author
59 Obsessions
60 Sonny's sibling
63 "Rock On" author
64 "Life —— jest": Gay
66 Backward
67 Euclidean abbr.
68 Tease
69 Spicy odor
70 Brown Betty preparer
71 Brazzaville location
73 Evergreen
74 Morris or Stewart
75 Transfer of a kind
76 Cure, as skins
77 Splotch of color
79 Corncake
82 Begum's mate
85 Plastics ingredient
87 "Spark of Life" author
89 Vestment
90 Mesdames, in Cádiz
95 —— -weenie
97 Feeling of hatred
98 Bürger ballad: 1774
99 Bryant and Gillette
101 What some clocks do
103 Dutch painter: 1613-75
104 Oust
105 Glassmaker's mixture
106 Makeshift
107 Black
108 Mixed matches: Abbr.
109 Year in Louis VII's reign
111 Writer Ephron
112 Duffel-bag contents
113 Some jets
115 Superlative ending
117 Letter opener

9

It's a Woman's World!

By Elaine D. Schorr/

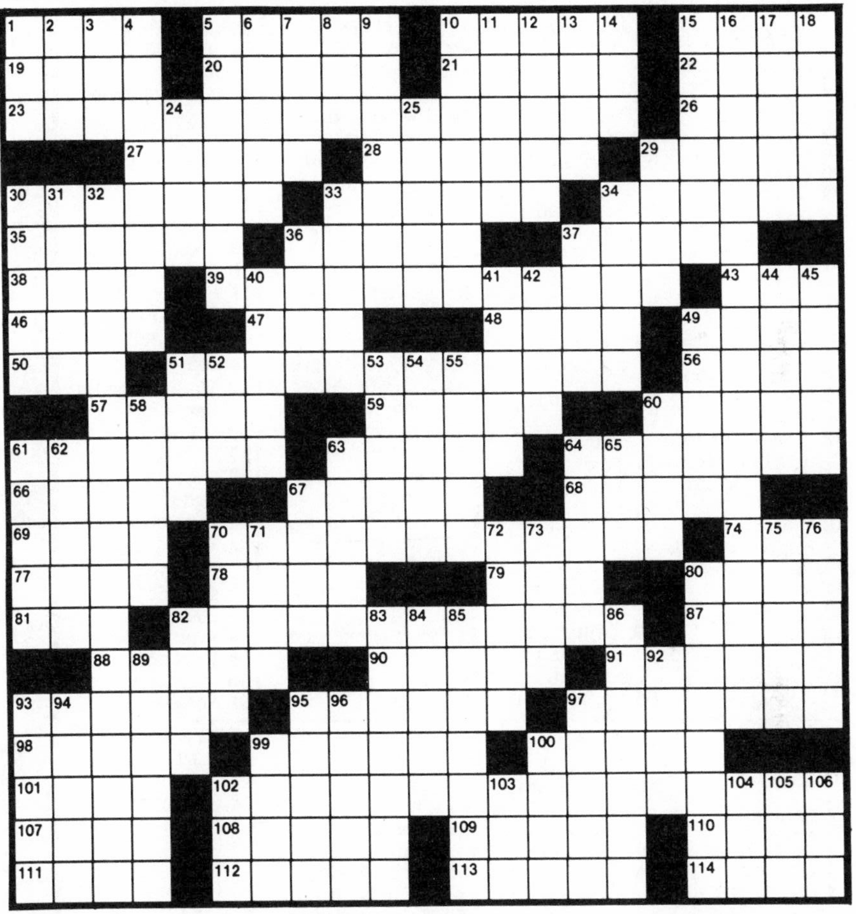

ACROSS

1 Auricular
5 Expeditious
10 Reduce in rank
15 Competitive setting
19 Togetherness for leftovers
20 Be devious
21 Part of U.S.N.R.
22 —— cloth
23 Carmen in Herrera's country
26 Lady of Limerick land
27 Kind of activity
28 Demesne
29 Practice halieutics
30 Implement for Hawkeye
33 Company lover
34 Doll babies
35 Start of a speech
36 Ulan ——
37 A discovery of Gene Kelly
38 Arrow poison
39 Ellen of Big Sky country
43 Doxy
46 Flappers, e.g.
47 Resinous substance
48 Heraldic wreath
49 Fierce Hawaiian shark
50 Biographer Winslow
51 Tennyson lass in a hit musical
56 The Tentmaker
57 Culvert entry
59 Like some rules
60 Ball-gown fabric
61 Fashion fashioner
63 Gemstone surface
64 Honeyed phrases
66 Sharp spur
67 Fey
68 Up and about
69 Glacial ridges
70 Stone maiden of the Nile
74 Rheine's river
77 Profligate
78 Boundaries: Lat.
79 Hunters' org.
80 Waterlogged
81 Officeholders
82 Georgia girl in pine country
87 "—— creature was . . ."
88 Cantankerous
90 Then: Fr.
91 Used the aerie
93 Actress Fisher
95 Desultory
97 Like a corduroy fabric
98 George Eliot's real name
99 Precursor of the feminist movement
100 Stockholm's Hasso
101 Apologue, e.g.
102 English queen in Ahmadou Ahidjo's land
107 Les Etats- ——
108 Grenoble's river
109 An Alexander
110 Smooth sailing
111 E.R.A. is one
112 Stuck in the mud
113 Pueblo Indians
114 Take in tow

DOWN

1 Electrical unit
2 Asian language
3 Rep. bordering Lebanon
4 "—— Angels"
5 Most rubicund
6 Profit
7 Peacock constellation
8 Orfe
9 Dullness
10 —— - Sudzhensk, U.S.S.R. city
11 Hank ——, ex-Yankee
12 —— Fisher Hall, N.Y.C.
13 Kind of closeout
14 Guidonian note
15 "—— the public"
16 One of the Mayos in the Land of Lakes
17 Old-womanish
18 Rural rights of way
24 Place for a clasp
25 —— Downs
29 Distinctive air
30 Irish port
31 Sight from Buzzards Bay
32 A leading lady Down Under
33 Polo
34 Crete's capital
36 Nail variety
37 Storm's predecessor
40 Flower of the flock
41 Like very few baseball games
42 Walked on
44 Dragnet
45 Amsterdam
49 Poet Marianne
51 It precedes where
52 It precedes work
53 Tough wrapping paper
54 Aboveboard
55 Rocket stage
58 Saltpeter in Soho
60 Food for hogs
61 Soprano Kiri Te Kanawa is one
62 Bean raised in Vermont
63 Turns tail
64 Three-time also-ran
65 Outer edge
67 Genesis brother
70 A way to go
71 Caligula specialty
72 Equip for the fray
73 Like ashes in Amiens
75 Touring stop
76 One of a top suit
80 Honored an R.S.V.P.
82 Take-it-or-leave-it phrase
83 Performed, as the Castles
84 Cabinetwork wood
85 Like Saracens' architecture
86 Hard nuts to crack
89 Wilde hero
92 Nine: Comb. form
93 Equatorial constellation
94 —— - garde
95 Bonneville contestant
96 Cavern, poetically
97 Emil Gilels plays it
99 Porkfish
100 Give the once-over
102 Ginger
103 Cry of triumph
104 Rower
105 Explorer Johnson
106 Unessayed

10

Nickname Dropping

By George Rose Smith

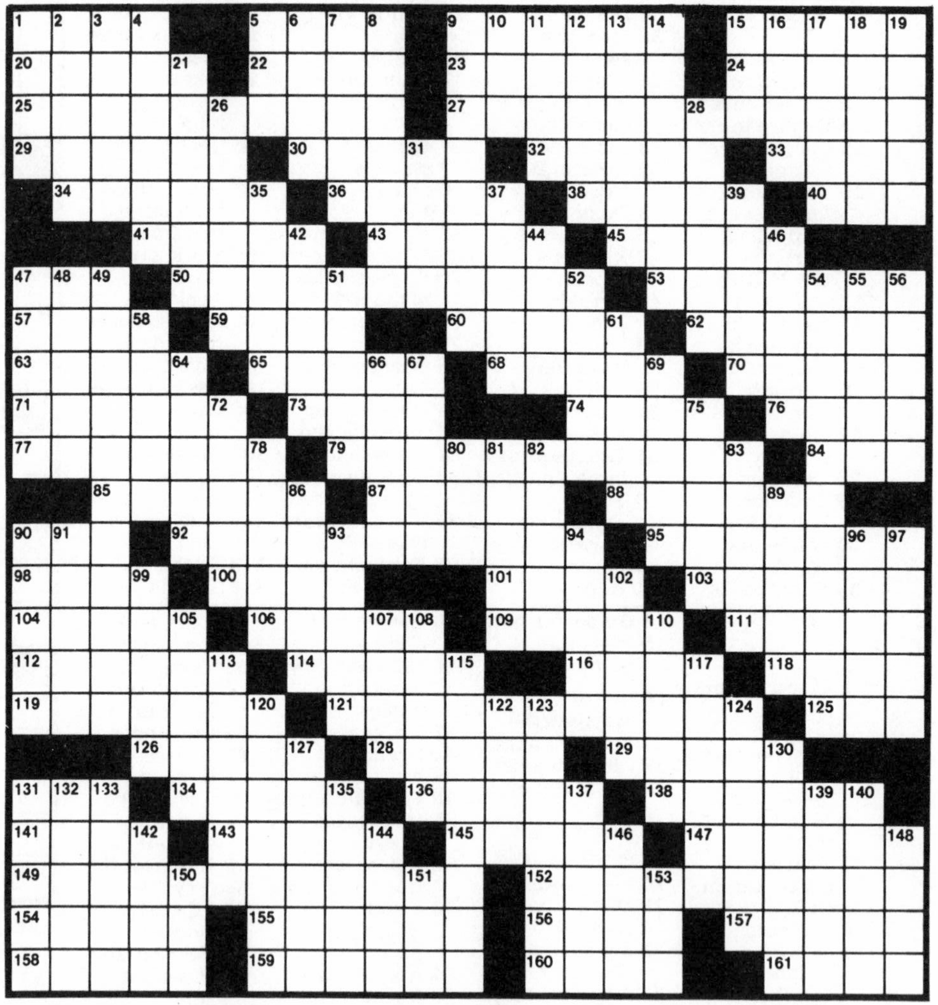

ACROSS

1 Arabic letter
5 Egyptian Christian
9 Lay away
15 Was solicitous
20 Fanaticism
22 —— fixe
23 Power for a jinrikisha
24 Coeur d' ——, Idaho
25 The end
27 Like aged Beethoven
29 Deliverance
30 Moroccan capital
32 "Josh" is his autobiography
33 Bone: Prefix
34 Snaps
36 Vichy prime minister: 1942-44
38 Certain murals
40 Poet's contraction
41 Printers' marks
43 Metric quart
45 O.T. word
47 Like Mr. Dick
50 Sarcastic
53 Testified
57 Spartan king
59 Cuchulainn's wife
60 Barbizon painter
62 Breakfast serving
63 A pastry, for short
65 Insect appendages
68 Omphalos
70 Metric measure
71 Taws
73 Think
74 Ancient country
76 Drag, as logs
77 Became a keener
79 Emulated Babilonia or Fleming
84 Legal point
85 Crocs' kin
87 Rootstock
88 Popular appetizer
90 The horned horse
92 Fickle, à la M. R. Rinehart
95 Savors
98 "The Years with ——": Thurber
100 Antibodies
101 One of the Aesir
103 Yellowish pink
104 —— salt (delicate wit)
106 Smears
109 Fortification
111 Defunct defense org.
112 Goth, for one
114 Cassandra's father
116 Dutch cheese
118 Tie
119 Fictitious, as a name
121 Medicine-chest item
125 Culbertson
126 Natural, at Reno
128 Con man who duped 114 Across
129 Made public
131 Biblical king
134 The filthy weed, in Nice
136 Spoils
138 Remain aloof
141 Forearm bone
143 Of a dowry
145 Fates, for instance
147 Mediterranean fish
149 V.I.P.
152 Goblet
154 Perfect
155 Square accounts
156 Man, in Milano
157 Remove stannic coating
158 Pomme de ——
159 Part of H.S.H.
160 Recluse
161 Soaks

DOWN

1 Cupid
2 Fernando or Lorenzo
3 Asinine
4 Sports triumphs
5 Approx.
6 River to the Baltic
7 Flower part
8 Perforated sphere
9 Beside oneself
10 Part of a jury verdict
11 Saw, e.g.
12 Bread spreads
13 No-see-ums
14 Was circumspect
15 Benny's Maxwell
16 Moro or Ray
17 A.F.B. in Texas
18 Growing out
19 Yield precedence
21 S.A. rodent
26 Famed French physicist
28 Horn
31 Cupidinous
35 Jazz dance
37 Lycée event
39 Former cough-cures
42 Three-time P.G.A. champ
44 —— avis
46 Communion wafers
47 "——, I'm Adam"
48 Galore
49 Thingamajig
51 City on the Rhone
52 Rodgers-Hart hit: 1933
54 Energy-saving way to go
55 Mysterious
56 Sediment
58 Sermon by Buddha
61 Purposive
64 Dress types
66 Kind of tea
67 Chichi
69 Wrinkled
72 Strives for
75 Soupy
78 Cut's companion
80 Relative of tetra
81 —— miss
82 Play byplay
83 Parisian artist
86 Part of a slip
89 Held sway
90 Persona ——
91 Lecture material
93 LaPlante or Baugh
94 Staff group
96 Universal
97 Like Kilimanjaro
99 Position
102 Gymnast Comaneci
105 Kohoutek, e.g.
107 Snaffles
108 Sir, to Din
110 Hakenkreuzler
113 Battle Born State
115 A species constituting a genus
117 White sheep
120 Prepares to dice chicken
122 Anchor
123 Front porch
124 Like certain Hawthorne tales
127 Autochthonous
130 A Christmas reindeer
131 C.P.A.'s task
132 Lab item
133 Wrath
135 Supply food
137 A subject of the Houyhnhnms
139 Combine
140 Understood
142 Showing a crack
144 Miler's path
146 Execrate
148 Lacrosse teams
150 Caucho
151 Streamlet
153 Soldier at Seoul

11

Acceleration

By Bert H. Kruse

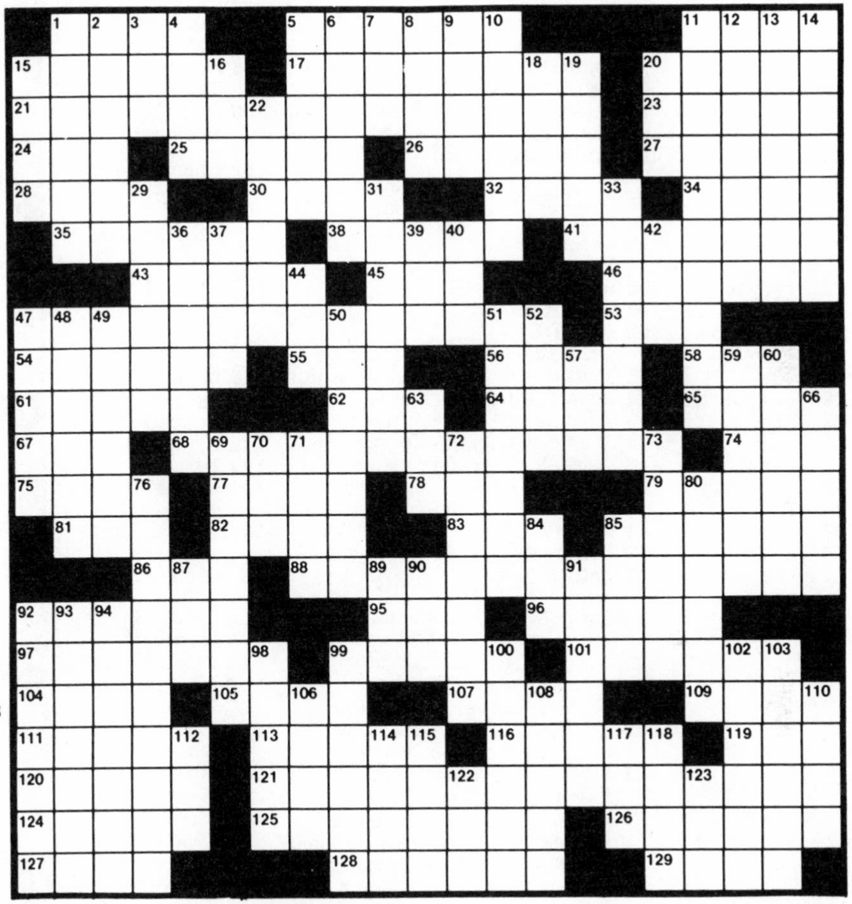

ACROSS

1 Presently
5 —— Belt or Sword
11 Actor Parker
15 Charm piece
17 Expedient
20 Judge's rapper
21 Best seller published in 1936
23 Rhone tributary
24 Rainbow
25 Wild plums
26 Shoulder movement
27 Narrow ravine
28 Island garlands
30 Campus figure, for short
32 Piperlike
34 Kind of work
35 Ultra
38 Usual situations
41 Snappy comeback
43 Humorist Bennett and family
45 Arctic explorer
46 Kitchen appliance
47 Long-run Broadway play, with "The"
53 A hammer-head
54 Liabilities' opposites
55 Devil's-bones
56 Pertaining to grandparents
58 Mack or Williams
61 Frighten
62 Mates of pas
64 U.S. or English poet
65 English county, for short
67 Skater Babilonia
68 Dismissal, as from a job
74 Greek letter
75 Of a historical time
77 Shipshape
78 Asian holiday
79 Perfect
81 Haggard novel
82 Philippine island
83 Snooze
85 Come out
86 Australian native
88 What Roosevelt and Truman were
92 Pilgrimage-church site near Naples
95 Novelist Levin
96 Lost color
97 Quagga, wou-wou et al.
99 Emulate Duccio
101 What speeders may hear
104 Italian river
105 Biblical country
107 Rackstraw's colleagues
109 Slangy refusal
111 Borders on
113 Guard on a helmet
116 Standing rib, e.g.
119 Essex contemporary
120 Hymn ascribed to Zoroaster
121 "The ——" (Wagner opera)
124 Willow
125 Showing cessation of growth
126 Secateurs
127 Close
128 Ebullient
129 Fulmars' kin

DOWN

1 Old love token
2 Papal representative
3 Comedian Olsen
4 Intelligence
5 Tryon's "The ——"
6 Squeals
7 "—— bin ein Berliner": J.F.K.
8 Inhabitants: Suffix
9 At hand
10 Steep declivities
11 "On a —— China"
12 Scaler's dream
13 Arranged in succession
14 Monoski user
15 Arab's head cord
16 Sesame
18 His, to Henri
19 Influential French artist: 1881-1955
20 Dogfaces
22 Add frosting
29 Teamen's forte
31 Shop boss
33 Transplanting machine
36 Vacillate
37 Gold ornaments, in Spain
39 Fall call
40 —— culpa
42 Coal size
44 Hampshire's dwelling
47 Spacious, to Stéphane
48 Duo for de Havilland
49 O.T. book
50 Chew the scenery
51 Knocking sound
52 Disappear: Abbr.
57 Ingested
59 Authority
60 Medicinal unit
63 N.C.O.
66 McKinley's Ohio birthplace
69 Straightens out a hose
70 Wedding-news word
71 Seizes
72 Burgee
73 Ferment or poach
76 Cinderella's was mean
80 Blunt or obscure
84 Humdinger
85 He, in Roma
87 Actress Arthur
89 Inlet
90 South Korean city
91 Cruise port
92 Perfect diamond of 100 or more carats
93 —— hit (single)
94 Trivial details
98 Island off Norway
99 Flans and frangipanes
100 Butt
102 Author Mailer
103 Asparagus shoots
106 Bugs or Max
108 McDowall
110 Mind-boggling ages
112 D.A.R.'s relative
114 To —— (on the mark)
115 Soprano Della Casa
117 Aves.
118 Small Asian tree
122 P.M. periods
123 L.B.J. beagle

Verbal Hi-Jinks

By Alfio Micci

ACROSS

1 Mar
7 Complain
13 Drains
17 —— and excursions
19 Was fearful
20 Oregon, for one
22 ꓕՈꓤNS
24 Reindeer, to René
25 Irish patriot
26 Plural ending
27 Reply: Abbr.
28 Worked on socks
29 "—— Fideles"
32 Mystery writer Josephine
33 Algonquian
34 AIR
39 Bow
40 Roofed passageway
41 Full of fury
42 Brilliantly colored fish
43 Belfry denizen
46 Shows pleasure
47 An old ruse: Colloq.
48 Argillaceous rock
49 Christian or Roman
50 Roof feature
51 Proscribes
52 DE DE AL AL
55 Scuttle
56 Royal family of Scotland
57 Double quartet
58 Lose
62 Sound of laughter
64 Actress Balin
65 Flammable hydrocarbon
66 Foreigner
67 Taproom
69 Crude abode
70 AP ES
72 French wives: Abbr.
74 Terminate
78 "—— Alone": Romberg
79 Rudimentary seed
80 Robin of balladry
82 "The Wreck of the Mary ——"
83 Palindromic name
84 In a high degree
85 Procure or secure
86 Liquified by heat
87 Beautician Westmore
88 1,000,1,000
91 Takes the helm
95 Actress Tanguay
96 Maroon
97 Decanter
98 Linguist Mario A. ——
99 Agcy. succeeded by N.R.C.
100 Peep show
105 Stradivari's teacher
106 WORL
110 Chief ingredient
111 Annexed
112 Bring to a total
113 Torn
114 Crystal-lined rocks
115 Compound similar to another

DOWN

1 Boy-meets-girl event
2 Cle——, city in Washington
3 Old MacDonald had one
4 Composer of "Comus"
5 Desserts
6 Ostrich's cousin
7 Serling or Steiger
8 Ram's dam
9 Footed: Comb. form
10 Mangle user
11 Given to gossip
12 Bulldog or final: Abbr.
13 O U T
14 Common contraction
15 Zoo attraction
16 Tendon
18 Triple agents
19 Artificial reservoirs
21 Mother of Helen of Troy
23 Part of a seminar
28 Esprit de corps
30 Sandra or Ruby
31 Site of Sagan's dragons
34 Target for Trottier
35 Odd, in Scotland
36 Year in the reign of Henry IV
37 Oriel part
38 Scorched
39 Separated
42 Flicka's creator
43 Blessed Roman Catholic woman
44 "Stormy Weather" composer
45 Discernment
47 Bounder
48 —— pan (Chinese abacus)
51 Dandiprat
53 One of the Dionnes, for short
54 Outside: Comb. form
55 APPLAUSE ☞
56 Cordwainer's creation
58 City in Georgia
59 One of the Masseys
60 Enchantress
61 The quiet side
62 By chance
63 Everyone, in Essen
65 Charabanc
67 Reject
68 Orange or Indian
69 Part of H.R.H., sometimes
71 Disinclined
72 Aver
73 Sofia sight
74 Order to a broker
75 Actor Jacques
76 Mountain: Comb. form
77 Robert —— Warren
81 Speaker's milieu
82 Becalmed state
86 Andy Gump's wife
88 Exaggerate
89 Did carpentry
90 Jet speed units
91 Picket-line crosser
92 Devonshire river
93 Expunge
94 Dine at home
95 Horatian verse form
101 Prefix for sphere or meter
102 Paper quantity
103 Being, in Barcelona
104 Large German dam
106 Joker
107 H.S.T.'s successor
108 Certain servicemen: Abbr.
109 French assent

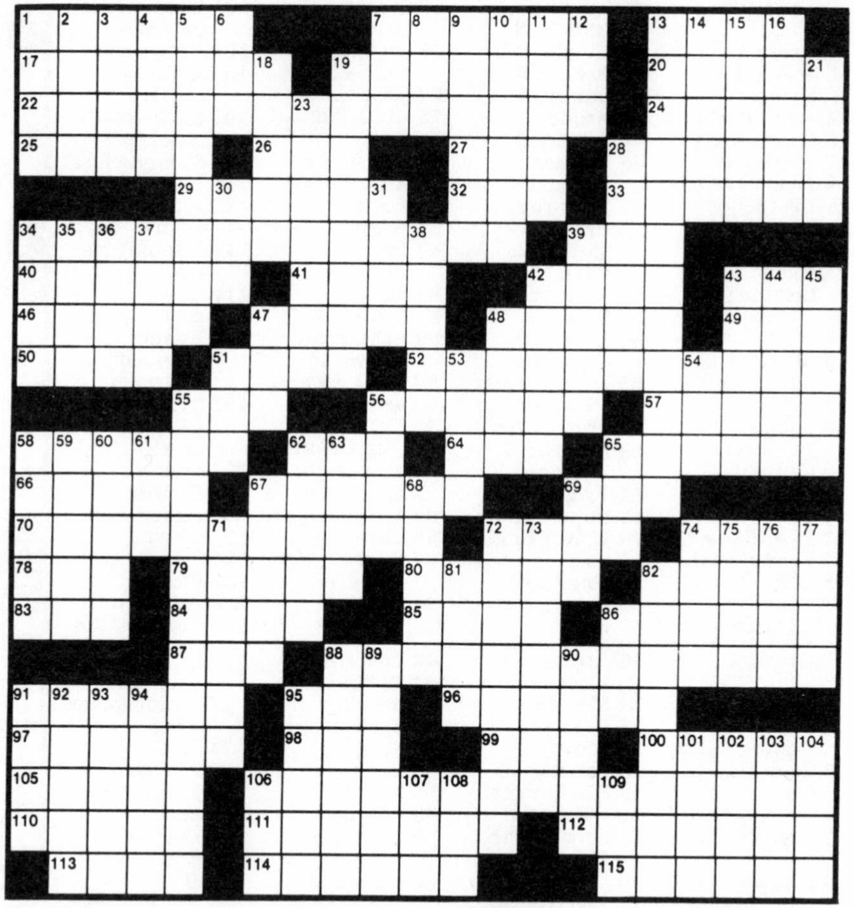

13

Typecasting

By John M. Samson

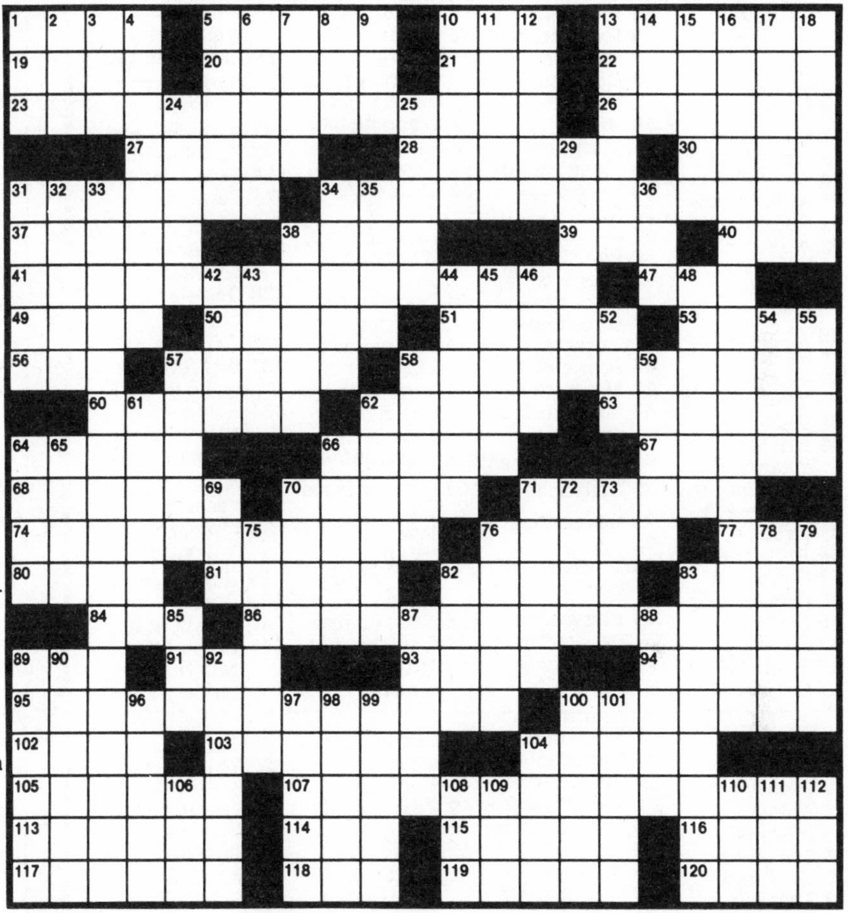

ACROSS

1 Sins
5 What jabberers do
10 Pod
13 Mix
19 Debauchee
20 Irritated
21 Instead of: Abbr.
22 Reveres
23 Musical starring Billy Graham?
26 Abhor
27 Big books
28 Libel
30 Container
31 Crazy ——
34 Movie starring Tatum O'Neal?
37 Diversions
38 Star at a French film festival?
39 Belgian resort town
40 Entity
41 Movie starring a Venus?
47 Kind of office
49 Minerva's mind
50 Zola
51 Defeated Spassky
53 Church part
56 Sound from Sandy
57 Affected
58 Musical starring Ann Sothern?
60 Rossini works
62 Mex. misses
63 Fire god
64 Hourly
66 Item for transplanting
67 Davis or Midler
68 Divine revelation
70 Kind of photo
71 Cantaloupe's cousin
74 Movie starring Wilt Chamberlain?
76 Prides of lions
77 Chinese pagoda
80 She, in Savoie
81 Cape Cod resort
82 Seed coating
83 Hair treatment
84 B'way sign
86 Film starring Dinah Shore?
89 New Guinea port
91 Excavators' org.
93 Bank (on)
94 First prime minister of U.S.S.R.
95 Play starring Margaret Mead?
100 Favorable factors
102 "—— darn shame!"
103 Needlefish
104 Swoon
105 Electron tubes
107 Movie starring Evel Knievel?
113 Flowery
114 Actress from Montana
115 Joshua's friend
116 Lamb
117 Settled down
118 Obj. of protest
119 Yonder
120 Baseball part

DOWN

1 Stage in history
2 "Vive le ——!"
3 Retreat
4 Roanoke Island group
5 In the first place
6 Gone skyward
7 Reverends' robes
8 Palmer's peg
9 O.E. letter
10 Fixed
11 Arabic A's
12 Zoospore
13 Fictitious
14 Orfe
15 Indent
16 Movie starring Bob Hope?
17 Belittle
18 Glycerides
24 Bull ——
25 Major Joppolo's post
29 Star who draws a crowd?
31 Small lizard
32 Less dangerous "60 Minutes" star?
33 Vehicle starring Zsa Zsa Gabor?
34 Assemble
35 Eucalyptus
36 Chatter
38 Curtails
42 Withstand
43 Soprano Eames
44 TNT explosive
45 —— Gan, city in Israel
46 High spots: Abbr.
48 Famed sharpshooter
52 Org. for certain ex-G.I.'s
54 Capital
55 Serf
57 Certain strings
58 Waggish
59 Sudanese tribe
61 An N.F.L. player
62 Battle site: 1862
64 Elias or Sir William
65 Spoken
66 Square one
69 Tolkien creature
70 Flabbergast
71 Pallid
72 Stake
73 Anjou or Tyson
75 Gain in one's affection
76 Farinaceous
78 Play starring 48 Down?
79 Mil. commands
82 Shrill note
83 Bridge supports
85 Ump's call
87 Max ——, German painter
88 Hurled
89 What Macduff did
90 Array
92 Disarranged
96 He wrote "In Search of Identity"
97 Gallinaceans
98 Santa's sunny sounds
99 Gives the nod to
100 Standardbred
101 Love, to Luther
104 Quannet, e.g.
106 Après printemps
108 %: Abbr.
109 Booster's call
110 Kin of 109 Down
111 Creek
112 Camote

14

Pouring It On

By A.J. Santora

ACROSS

1 Of the soft palate
6 N.F.L. scores
9 Where Bradley is
15 Hebrew bushel
20 —— fell swoop
21 Kind of pads
22 Commuters
23 Weather-stripped
25 Lay away now; use later
28 Three-bagger
29 Verily
30 Personnel head's task
31 Recoils
33 Kind of steamer
34 —— alone (do by oneself)
35 Grape seed
36 Preserved
38 Cottontail
39 Gannet's kin
40 Hellene
41 Favorites
42 Route for Geronimo
44 Piece of land
46 Pasty cement mixture
49 Daisy cutter's cousin
50 One of Margaret Mead's topics
52 Robert ——
53 Rotated
55 —— Lama
59 Beard of grain
61 Logger's activity
63 Some textile workers
64 Proficient
66 Slaving away
67 Maladjusted person
68 Singer James
69 Bellyache
71 Where Puno is
72 Jitney
73 Truth, in Confucianism
74 Plunges into the limelight
78 Omega, in Oxford
81 Cool drink
82 Stulm
83 In —— (correctly timed)
84 Chipping tool
88 Allow
90 Appease
93 Children's game
95 Kind of wave
96 What many tests test
98 Ceramic-floor material
99 Anagram for abode
100 Word with while
101 Joss
102 Stares intently
103 Of an Arizona tribe
105 Road sign
107 "Fighting Bob" of ring fame
108 Colorful fish
111 Govt. worker
113 Prussian lancer
115 Fond du ——, Wis.
118 Hebrew letter
119 Reign of ——: 1793-94
121 Make beloved
123 Hindu writings
124 Give a decision
126 Town of Kaiser's exile
127 Break a promise
128 On —— (equal)
129 Latitude
131 Wet forecast by Louis XV?
134 Ancient ascetic
135 Bridal wreath
136 A kind of "easter"
137 "Sweet —— O'Grady"
138 Hat material
139 Flips
140 Trio in fluff
141 Crime by one carrying a torch

DOWN

1 Appearance
2 Charm
3 Snow-in-summer
4 Concerning
5 Gridiron off.
6 Twice and again
7 Pepys's and Evelyn's books
8 "Let-us-spray" device
9 Puritanical ones
10 One, in Berlin
11 Homeric epic
12 Cardinal's topper
13 Trolley tracks
14 Up to now
15 N.Y. time
16 Impudent
17 These keep waves wavy
18 Woolly fabric
19 Actor Dantine from Austria
24 Strong bench
26 Chicago airport
27 Babylonian god
32 Dorcas society's activity
37 Rather or Cupid
40 Rasp
41 No bar to the postman
43 A bit ruddy
45 Rib
47 Ending for pend or sept
48 Slots spot
49 Pearl Buck's Wang ——
50 Equivalent
51 What the suspicious smell
53 Moves about
54 Dolls on the walls
56 Portside
57 Melody
58 That —— say
60 Roofed passageway
61 Old Phoenician port
62 What hurriers shake
65 Louise or George
67 White grape
70 Biblical 150
72 Deadly poison
74 Aural ossicle
75 Suit (to)
76 Blue hue
77 Sparky of baseball
78 Greek letter
79 Chisholm Trail town
80 Slotted groove
84 Musical key
85 Hail-fellow-all-wet
86 Region
87 Roe
89 A little bit of rain?
90 X-rated, for short
91 Bessell and Nugent
92 Organic compound
94 —— a blanket
96 Terminated
97 Part of seventh heaven?
104 Where divas reign in N.Y.C.
105 Accumulates
106 —— fortune
107 Got along
108 Spouter at sea
109 Grotto
110 Certify
111 Too much, to Toscanini
112 Poet who popularized a chair
114 Light beers
116 Graceful tempo
117 Heel over
120 Barbecue
121 Bombeck et al.
122 Modernist
123 Courage
125 Nursemaid, in Nottingham
130 Evergreen
132 Bishopric
133 Time of "Good Feeling"

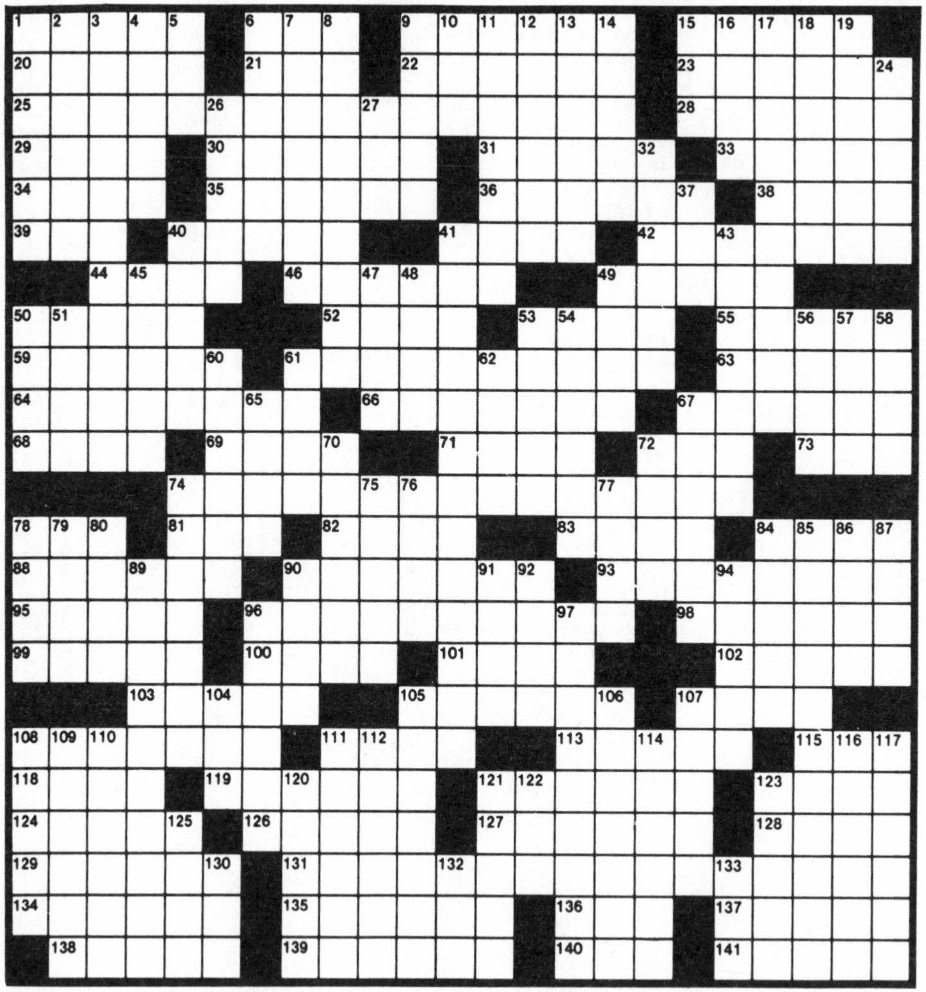

15

Exotic Aviary

By Jordan S. Lasher/Puzzles Edited by Eugene T. Maleska

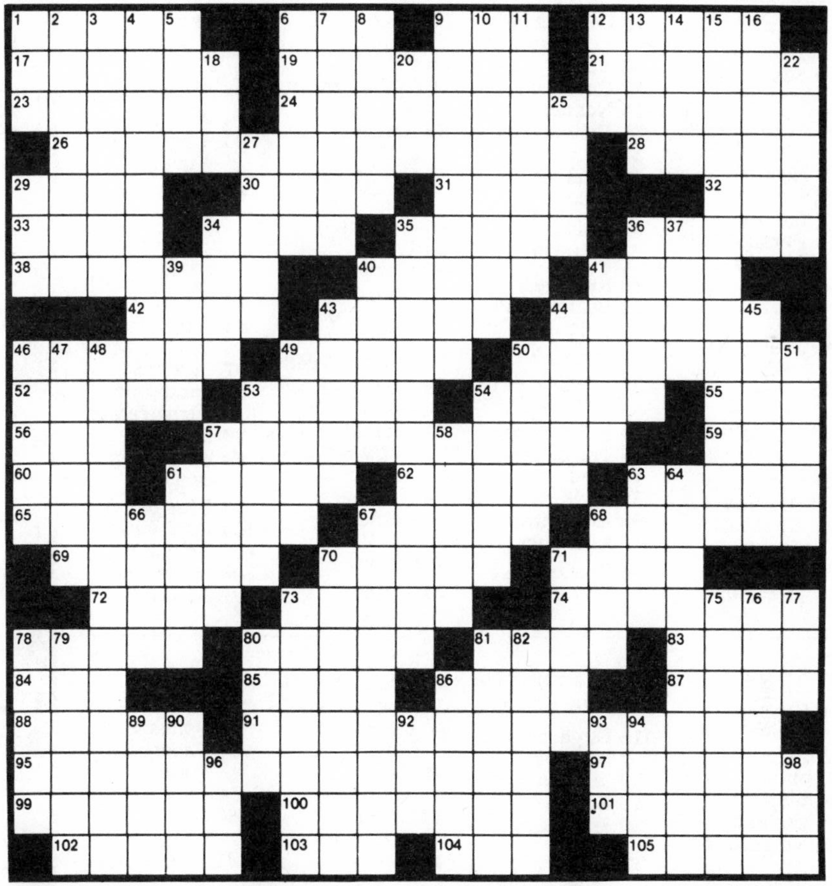

ACROSS

1 Plaster painting surface
6 Air-rifle ammo
9 NBC's ex-parent
12 Far from being a birdbrain
17 Tiny interstice
19 Breakfast dish
21 Harold Robbins or Robin Cook
23 Love song
24 Woodcock
26 Loon's relative
28 Used a strop
29 Subatomic particle
30 "Step ——!"
31 Black cuckoos
32 River to Gorki
33 Snug as a bug in ——
34 Sources of peat
35 Sojourns
36 Complex silicates
38 Portend
40 Protozoan
41 Buster Brown's dog
42 Henley team
43 "Frozen rope," in baseball
44 Paparazzo's meal ticket
46 Visits unexpectedly
49 Worked in a colliery
50 Buildings in Boston and Boise
52 A Green Mountain Boy
53 Roast meat serving
54 Tourn. round
55 Dine
56 Porta ——, Roma
57 Cousin of a plover
59 Physician's org.
60 Bird: Comb. form
61 Siamese fighting fish
62 Sister of Calliope
63 —— bird (bobolink)
65 Nestlings' appendages
67 Queeg's ship
68 Snap
69 Tired
70 Crusty
71 "Amscray!"
72 Actor Devine
73 —— bird (ostrich)
74 Durable yellow fabric
78 Matchmaker in Anatevka
80 Cotton packer
81 Dribble or gush
83 Author Seton
84 The birds —— the bees
85 Khachaturian
86 Quay
87 Très ——
88 Angler's basket
91 Feathered chatterer
95 Anhima; kamichi
97 —— Avon (Anthony Eden)
99 —— line (conform)
100 B-52's place
101 Without adulteration
102 "Les —— Mousque-taires"
103 Perched
104 —— Jeanne d'Arc
105 Fraught

DOWN

1 M.C.'s "gift"
2 Obliteration
3 Turn traitor
4 Large white gannet
5 Oslo monarch
6 Making a grand salaam
7 Members of a certain worldwide religion
8 Tour of duty
9 Taught an old dog new tricks
10 Desk or wall piece
11 Made excuses
12 Slump
13 Mawkish sentimentality
14 Physics abbr.
15 Razorbill's kin
16 Home of some Jayhawkers
18 Hubble-bubble
20 S O S is one
22 "—— a rose is she": Coleridge
25 Famous Fed
27 Day bisectors
29 Shelley's "Queen ——"
34 City on the Aar
35 Giant petrel or osprey
36 Benzell and Sheraton
37 "—— Ideas," 1951 song
39 Malayan sarong
40 North Dakota city
41 Animal with a snout
43 "Shores of Tripoli" site
44 Bit part for a star
45 They reune
46 Fleshy fruit
47 Newton-John
48 Button quail's look-alike
49 Brewery supply
50 —— nuit (tonight, in Tours)
51 "And God —— unto Israel . . .": Gen. 46:2
53 Sea gull, for short
54 Remain in force
57 Quite cautious
58 Bay window
61 Cutter
63 Posthaste
64 Down Under kingfisher
66 Bloke
67 A soft cheese
68 Tobacco wad
70 Reggio ——, Italian seaport
71 Contemptuous sound
73 Bolívar's birthplace
75 On Alcatraz, e.g.
76 Mask feature
77 Masefield heroine
78 The Courageous, e.g.
79 Plant firmly
80 Eleanor, to F.D.R.
81 New York's —— (police)
82 Cruelty personified
86 Lightweight cottons
89 Within: Comb. form
90 City on Utah Lake
92 R.P.I. room
93 With it
94 Actor Julia
96 —— Prés, Flemish composer
98 Island of Denmark

16

Clued-In People

By Alex F. Black

ACROSS

1 Easy gait
6 Something special
11 Raphaelle or Rembrandt
16 Nestor's father
18 Starr of a foursome
19 Persian Gulf measurements
21 Mediumistic miss
23 Sends par avion
25 Bowlers and dicers
26 Opposite of disassociate
27 Others, in Orizaba
28 Rhythmic dance
29 Tierra del Fuegian
30 Leading lady in a pastorale
32 Yucca
33 Outer coat
35 Not neg.
36 British pokey
37 Sat
38 Ramses I's successor
39 Cravat material
40 Rumple
41 Bretons and Britons
42 Outback cry
44 "Angela ——," 1928 song
45 U.S.S.R. sea
46 Tali or tarsi
48 Stadium event
51 Mythical beast
55 Also-ran at Aqueduct
56 Draper or Potter
57 Decorative strip
58 Call it ——
59 "—— Jimmy Valentine"
60 Amorous author
62 Runner or racer
63 Undiluted
64 Hunt
65 Word with poem
66 Takes both sides
67 Within: Prefix
68 Ney and Foch
70 Not so cheap
71 Violent protest
73 Canaday's subject
74 Numbers game
75 Stick
77 Grant
79 Triton
80 Yen
84 U.S. painter: 1871-1951
85 Hit rock musical
86 Biographer Winslow
87 Antitoxins
88 Sliding bolt
89 Senior citizen
93 "Pourquoi ——?"
94 Circle segment
95 Separates
96 Kitchen utensil
97 Crooked
98 Computer measurement
100 Backslider
102 Kind of legs or pockets
103 Orange variety
104 Fur hunter
105 No-nos
106 In reserve
107 Ruhr city

DOWN

1 Grapnels
2 Ashley's wife
3 Offensively obtrusive
4 Waikiki garlands
5 Neighbor of Afr.
6 "Phineas Finn" author
7 Money in Saudia Arabia
8 Mother's sister, e.g.
9 D.C. dropout: 1973
10 Bit of rum
11 Matched
12 Solecism
13 Estuaries
14 He wrote "The King Ranch"
15 Oligarch's relative
17 Montenegrin
19 Anticlimax
20 Schedules
22 Prexies' understudies
24 Fokker fighter
27 Giant slain by Apollo
31 Balanced
32 Multi-husbanded helpmate
34 Arbitrary fellow
37 Pod occupant
39 Vlodrop's river
40 One of the Waves
41 Early Manitoban
43 Cheers for Manolete
44 Buffet
45 N.Y.S.E. competitor
46 Destructive hurricane: Aug. 1980
47 Soprano role in "Ariadne auf Naxos"
48 Thwarts
49 Hoods or simps
50 Chill
52 Saw
53 Worthy is one
54 Spuds' buds
55 Sheet of stamps
56 Mole
60 —— Generation
61 Dunce-cap wearer
62 Ballet star Lavery
64 Ecologist's concern
66 Preliminary race
69 One of a common trio
70 Vandal
72 Caravansary
74 Put down

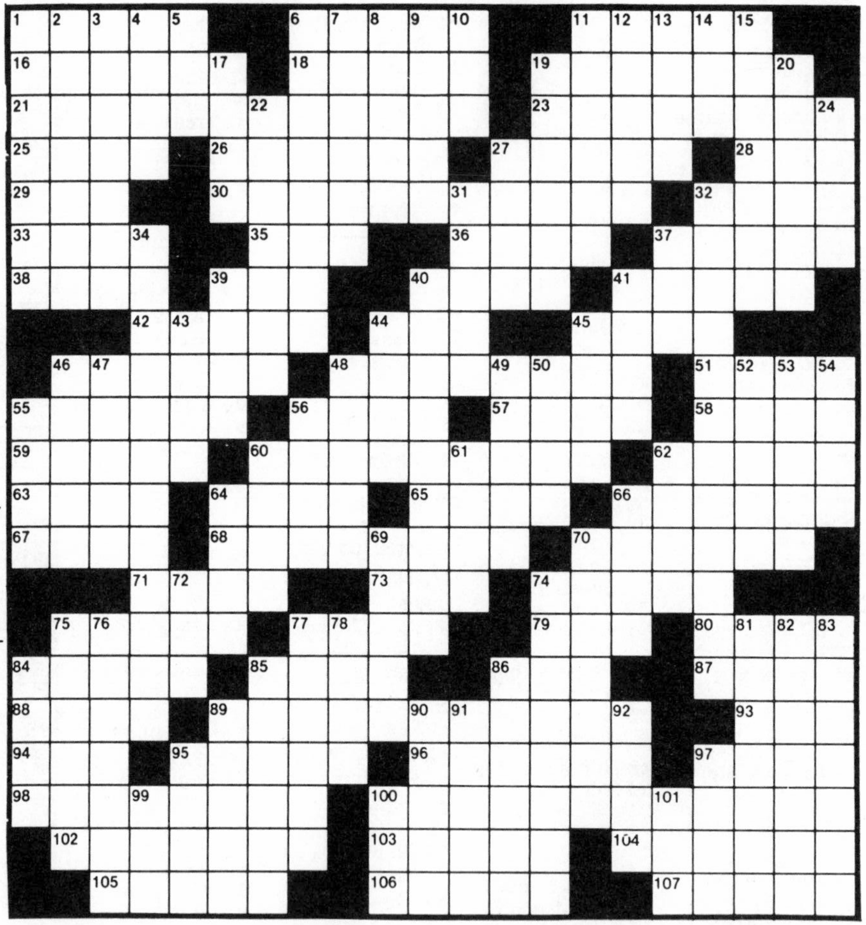

75 Bordeaux product
76 Deuce or trey
77 Jimmy or Nick
78 What some put on
81 Abrogates
82 Spanish nobleman
83 —— Seaboard
84 Box
85 Caduceus carrier
86 Held forth
89 Beam
90 Titled Turks
91 Famed fountain
92 Angels' favorite signs
95 Shock
97 Arm, in Armentières
99 Trevanian's "The —— Sanction"
100 Genetic factor
101 Order to Dobbin

17

Yule Tale

By Anne Fox

ACROSS

1 Writer St. Johns
6 Jumble
10 Swiss theologian: 1886-1968
15 Annie Oakley
19 Saw
20 Palo ——
21 Yale
22 Part of Q.E.D.
23 Words by C. F. Alexander
27 Ibn- ——
28 Climax
29 Of yore
30 Ancient Ethiopian capital
31 Famed muralist
33 U.N. labor agcy.
34 Helm dir.
36 Between bi and quadri
37 Words by G. L. Hill
45 —— Kippur
46 Coats of arms
47 Southwestern gulch
48 Great Barrier Island
50 Celtic Neptune
51 Grads
52 U.S. possession
56 Firmly fixed
59 French colony: 1604-1713
62 Roomy
63 Words by M. E. Coleridge
69 Small bird
70 Fling
71 Relative of coral
72 Malay master
73 Ref. book
74 ". . . Christ our Saviour ——"
79 Indigo dyes
80 Built —— (durable)
81 Apiece
82 Rajah's wife
83 Cartoon
85 Bill, of a sort
87 Court great
91 Electronic devices
93 Mohammedan
97 Powder ——
98 Words by Johann Rist
103 "Faerie Queene" heroine
104 Furrow
105 Center
106 Bagnold
107 All, in music
109 Hautboys
112 Nimbus
115 Fed
118 Words by Johan Franco
122 Frozen: Fr.
123 Santa ——
124 Shoshones
125 Roman emperor: 96-98
126 Heaven on earth
127 Winter hazard
128 Indiana city
129 Kind of attack

DOWN

1 O.T. book
2 Actress Wynter
3 Steve Martin's "Well, ——!"
4 German songs
5 Nice friend
6 Angel's instrument
7 Bitter plant
8 Charon's river
9 "—— Binh," 1971 film
10 Man for whom Miss Liberty's island was once named
11 "When I was —— . . ."
12 Sever
13 ". . . as a seal upon ——"
14 Newman movie
15 Eight quarts
16 East: Comb. form
17 Second-largest planet
18 Thwart
24 Kind of day
25 Lounges
26 Fresh
32 Johnny ——
33 Car part: Abbr.
35 Business abbr.
37 Neighbor of Neb.
38 Kind of air or water
39 Where NaCl is made
40 Suffix with colon or patron
41 Irish girl's name
42 Priests of Mars
43 School skippers
44 Golf great
49 Rearward, at sea
51 Kraits
53 Exhorted
54 Rocket stage
55 "The quality of —— . . ."
57 Dumas swashbuckler
58 Aspersion
60 Go around
61 Hilo greeting
62 Radar navigation system
63 Fighting
64 Climbing plant
65 "—— the bag!"
66 Debate ending
67 Part of Paris, famed for its racecourse
68 "I Remember ——"
75 Balloon's relative
76 Scandinavian
77 Suffix with rend or vend
78 Urial
83 Jacob's brother
84 Of the chest
86 "—— pro nobis"
88 Saratoga Springs college
89 Biddy
90 Kind of cup
92 High home
93 North Sea feeder
94 Eye
95 Mess up
96 Chinese dynasty
98 Power failure
99 New
100 Disconcert
101 Pass —— (beg)
102 "—— on the Keys"
108 There's companion
110 Drill
111 English painter: 1761-1807
112 Dog star
113 Fir pole
114 Optimistic
116 Part of T.A.E.
117 Sen. Burdick's state
119 British V.I.P.'s
120 Harbor need
121 Conceptual being

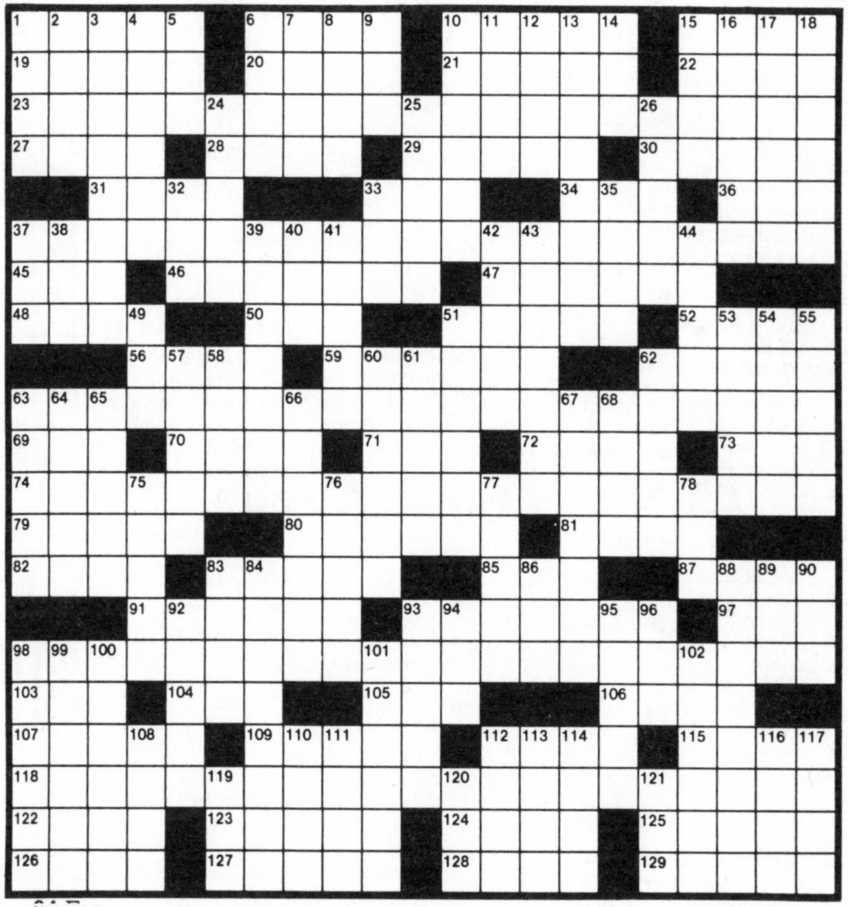

18

Collegiate Collection

By Bert Rosenfield

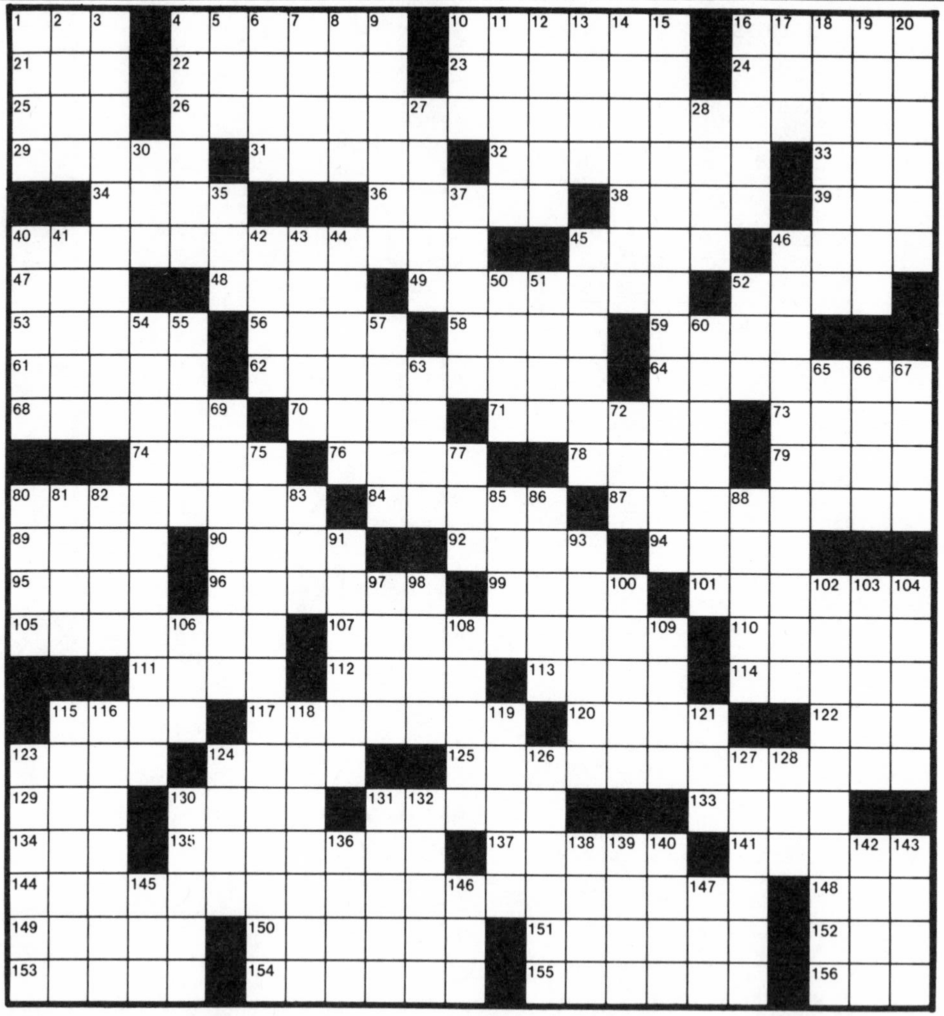

ACROSS

1 Palmer or Wilkinson
4 —— as a ghost
10 Chaplet
16 Underworld figure
21 River to the Channel
22 Purloined
23 Double-cross
24 Vaquero's milieu
25 Remote-control bomb
26 RICE
29 Avian diver
31 Tree yielding boxwood
32 ". . . their tongues —— speak against us!": Shak.
33 Buchwald
34 Northern constellation
36 Closefitting denims
38 Golconda
39 Blobby substance
40 DRAKE
45 Actuality
46 "—— Kampf"
47 Capek play
48 Kind of oil
49 Adjective for pale bluish-gray furs
52 Pack of camels
53 Honshu seaport
56 Grassy tracts
58 Rugby's river
59 Memorable Viennese conductor
61 Join the group
62 CORNELL
64 Sheep or snipe
68 Taken care of
70 Talk-show name
71 Craft
73 Lemur called bashful Billy
74 Hence, in Harfleur
76 Royale and Rivoli
78 Native of Rayong
79 Ululate
80 Marie of movies: 1923-65
84 Comprehend
87 Liliaceous plant
89 St. —— College Choir
90 Forage legume
92 Lumpish mass
94 Peter or Paul
95 Whale groups
96 Lightweight champ after Canzoneri: 1936
99 Side petals, in botany
101 Davis & —— College, W. Va.
105 Source of self-satisfaction
107 DUKE
110 Touch- —— (jewelweed)
111 Ash receptacles
112 Melville's 1847 opus
113 Bombay bigwig
114 Prefix with type or spore
115 Auto pioneer
117 Like some addictives
120 Gordon or Roman
122 Sarcle
123 Liquidate a dragon
124 Rembrandt's "Lady with ——"
125 AUBURN
129 Asner and Figueroa
130 Grad. of R.P.I.
131 Mezzo-soprano Obraztova
133 Japanese general in W.W. II
134 Stat for Seaver
135 Glacial deposit
137 Termagant
141 Yawl's cousin
144 WILLIAM & MARY
148 Paramilitary org.
149 Canadian medical notable
150 Luck, in León
151 Henry, e.g.
152 Dye holder
153 Very small
154 Checked
155 Age of a nonagenarian
156 Merino's dam

DOWN

1 Growler
2 Calpurnia was one
3 Slow down
4 Napoleonic battle: 1809
5 A Udall nickname
6 Pipkins
7 Elder, in Essen
8 Glassmaker's oven
9 Sign up
10 —— Kemal, town in Syria
11 Vamp of the silents
12 Comrade of D'Artagnan
13 Mild oath
14 He wrote "Lot's Wife"
15 YALE
16 Convention decision
17 "The Greatest"
18 Scarlet —— (red robin)
19 Kind of barometer
20 Carney role
27 Score in match golf
28 Rodomontade
30 Scoring play in cricket
35 Be under the weather
37 Of the soft palate
40 Egregious
41 Hall of Fame pitcher Amos
42 Nurse a grievance
43 Structural unit
44 Tiger-hunt aide
45 "Their —— Hour": Churchill
46 SMITH
50 Tel ——
51 Sol is one
52 Charlemagne's dom.
54 BROWN
55 Composer Bruckner
57 —— off (minimize)
60 Geometric figure
63 State for the record
65 Bufo or agua
66 One of five bodies
67 Brooklet
69 Rescheduled
72 TV's "—— Na Na"
75 TUFTS
77 Droop
80 Brood
81 Kind of dance
82 Part of a pedestal
83 Small amount
85 Side dish
86 —— bear
88 Board game
91 End a separation
93 Legendary horse
97 City on the Tevere
98 Photo
100 Weltschmerz
102 Of the beginning
103 Not at all
104 Dutch genre painter
106 B.&O. and B.&M.L.
108 Black, in Blois
109 Beanery sign
115 Grayish red
116 Inst. at Philadelphia
118 Cashew's kin
119 Thurify
121 Loser to R.M.N.
123 "—— they run"
124 Pretty soon
126 Suit material
127 Pieman's headquarters
128 Hwy.
130 Abrasive
131 Stulm or adit
132 Where Tacloban is
136 Fancy; inkling
138 Father of Ahab
139 Kind of shark
140 Adore to excess
142 Bird's crop
143 Love's antithesis
145 Retreat
146 Conducted
147 Decay

19

Coin Toss

By Nancy A. Wood

ACROSS

1 Canon
4 Donnybrook
9 Feeling ennui
14 Party item
19 M.D.'s group
20 Weird
21 A dweller on Parnassus
22 Judge
23 Tail heads
27 Ready
28 The best policy
29 One-fifth of CCLX
30 Rages
31 Strong point
32 The Black Prince
35 Sniveled
38 —— en scène
39 Callas or Tallchief
41 Dromedary features
42 Cleave
43 Golf shot
45 Religious council
49 Body of Kaffir warriors
50 Prefix for typist
51 Tones down
52 Digression
53 Kind of opera
54 Something unique
55 Dodge
56 Builder's material
57 Italian seaport
59 Pure air
60 Dep.
61 Tail and head tails
66 —— de plume
67 Remains
68 Indubitable
71 Slow, musically
74 Oligophrenic
75 Incite
77 Likewise
78 Heeling
79 Succeed
80 Hors d'oeuvre item
81 "And, will you, —— you . . .": Shak.
82 "Tiger" man of poetry
83 Female ruffs
84 French fabric
85 Abbr. on some invoices
86 Bothered
88 Wellington's school
89 "—— upon the midnight . . ."
90 ". . . that worn-out —— idly spoken": Lytton
93 Soil sci.
95 Division word
96 Corroded
97 Moor growth
100 Set apart
104 Head heads
108 Esteem
109 Barbecue
110 "Worn-out" adjective (see 90 Across)
111 Prefix with puncture
112 Rows
113 Evicts
114 Soft
115 Louis XIV, e.g.

DOWN

1 Finn's neighbor
2 Moslem nobleman
3 Pay
4 Is on guard
5 Rose like a horse
6 Van Gogh lived here
7 Frenzied
8 Zodiac sign
9 Prior to
10 Praying figure
11 Rajah's wife
12 Japanese outcasts
13 Wouk's "—— Stop the Carnival"
14 Watch chain
15 Spring mo.
16 Duke Orsino's bride
17 Buoyantly
18 Made over
24 Tail tails
25 "—— woods these are . . .": Frost
26 The vat man
31 Fin
33 Catastrophe
34 Head tails
35 Card game
36 Thurber forte
37 Damage
38 Distance for Coe
39 Common fungus
40 Vaulted projection
42 Start over
43 Punctuation marks
44 Hecate's companion
46 Never, in Bonn
47 Epicede, e.g.
48 Actor Duilio —— Prete
50 Carved emblem
51 "Les Baigneurs" creator
58 Kiddy vehicles
59 Hateful
60 Cordwood measure
62 Pressed
63 Dog's role in "Peter Pan"
64 Sharp
65 —— test, for a race horse
69 Moslem faith
70 —— prosequi
71 Label
72 Tennis term
73 Inlet
74 Nothing but
75 Number 3 wood
76 Distress
84 Openbill
85 Harmonized
87 Cairene's eye shadow
88 Puts up
89 Maniacal
90 German guard
91 H.R.E. ruler: 962-73
92 What alumni do
93 Global supporter
94 Shade
95 Bar at Fort Knox
98 Saarinen
99 Hassan in "The Arabian Nights"
100 Dome-shaped edifice
101 Distant
102 Mexican fare
103 Small case
105 Heart, to Hadrian
106 Old Ger. coins
107 Gr. resistance movement

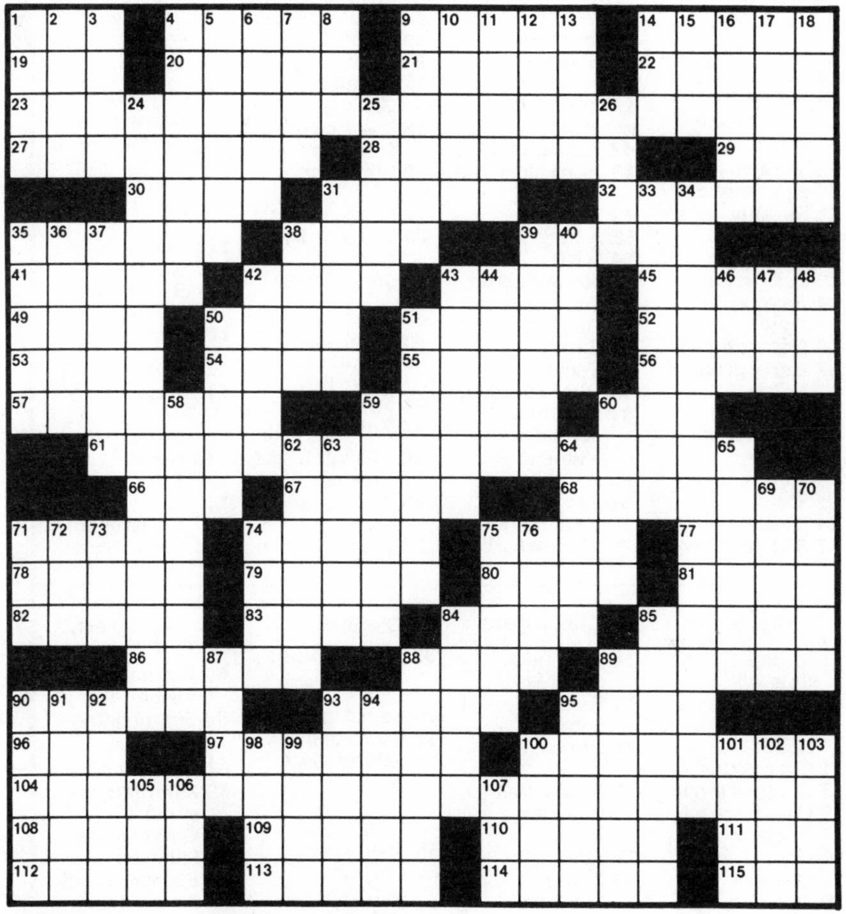

Tutti-Frutti

By Stanley Glass

ACROSS

1 Layers of paint
6 Rain checks
10 Set upon
17 Ex-Redskin chief
18 Turkish inn
20 Apprentice
21 Missing links
22 Names, to Nero
23 Less patient
24 Payola, D.C. style
26 Desert shrub
27 Early gridiron great
28 Dixie dish
30 "Londonderry ——"
33 O'Neill's —— Smith
34 Diet spoilers
42 Radar image
44 Wee bit bigger than wee
45 Ghostley presence
46 Imitation pearl
47 Exceedingly
49 Introduces at court
51 Stealthy
52 A Finger Lake
54 What bindweeds do
55 Dr. J., e.g.
56 Dir. letters
57 Catch
58 Tenor Kollo
59 Pilsen product
61 Capital of Southern Yemen
62 Shills
64 Subject of Swindell's "Screwball"
66 Tight squeezer
69 Iago's forte
70 Hutch
71 Emulated Galway
75 "—— on parle français"
76 Whammy
77 French toast
78 Tragedy by Corneille
79 Jerry-builds
81 Eyes fixedly
84 Incubus, e.g.
85 Broadway play: 1977
86 Mirador
87 Fidel's disciple
89 Pastrami spot, for short
90 Area in eight states
92 Blood: Prefix
94 J.E.C. or E.M.K.
95 Caen's river
96 City on the Somme
98 Henry of ——
103 Song popularized by Fats Domino
110 Thin silk fabric
111 Boat for three rowers
112 Evening bash
113 "Dearly ——"
114 Beneficiary via primogeniture
115 Nonet
116 Zetetics
117 River in a Burns poem
118 Cooper role

DOWN

1 Millay's "Aria da ——"
2 City on the Oka
3 Word on a ticket
4 Cut cuspids
5 Campus group
6 Coal-mine gas
7 Integument
8 Gourmand's interest
9 Anathema to Sam Adams
10 Statue by Phidias
11 "Battle Hymn . . ." phrase
12 Cut
13 Ceremony
14 Actress Markey
15 Clairvoyant
16 Infection suppressants
17 Hack writer's output
18 Phrase in a carol
19 Weak-eyed tunneler
25 Inhibit
29 Aces
30 Lower
31 Lake near Novgorod
32 Laughing
34 Landlocked harbors
35 Coeur d'——, Idaho
36 Lowest pinochle card
37 Beseeched
38 Diamond ——
39 Like Harvard Yard
40 Keyed up
41 Dutch genre painter: 17th century
43 Huey —— Long
48 Sports org.
50 Certain crockery
53 Perfect arrangement
55 Winter mo.
59 Kipling subject
60 Johnson's ordeal: 1868
61 Paid honor to
63 Flicks
64 "—— Street," 1956 song
65 Constantine's vision
66 Sept. 1 baby, e.g.
67 Less friendly
68 Summation symbol
70 Galley mark
72 Subdued
73 French school
74 Z-twist fabric
76 Placed in the Louvre
77 World Series pitcher: 1948
80 Original ——
81 Shortly
82 Adjective for a Lippizaner
83 His and her
88 Rising from water
91 Beliefs
93 "Tennis ——?"
96 French mob's "Down with!"
97 Effulge
98 Apprehends
99 Away from the wind
100 Frost's "In a ——"
101 Berserk
102 Peregrinate
104 "Fiesque" composer
105 Ruin
106 First place
107 Enraged
108 Meadows
109 Shepherded

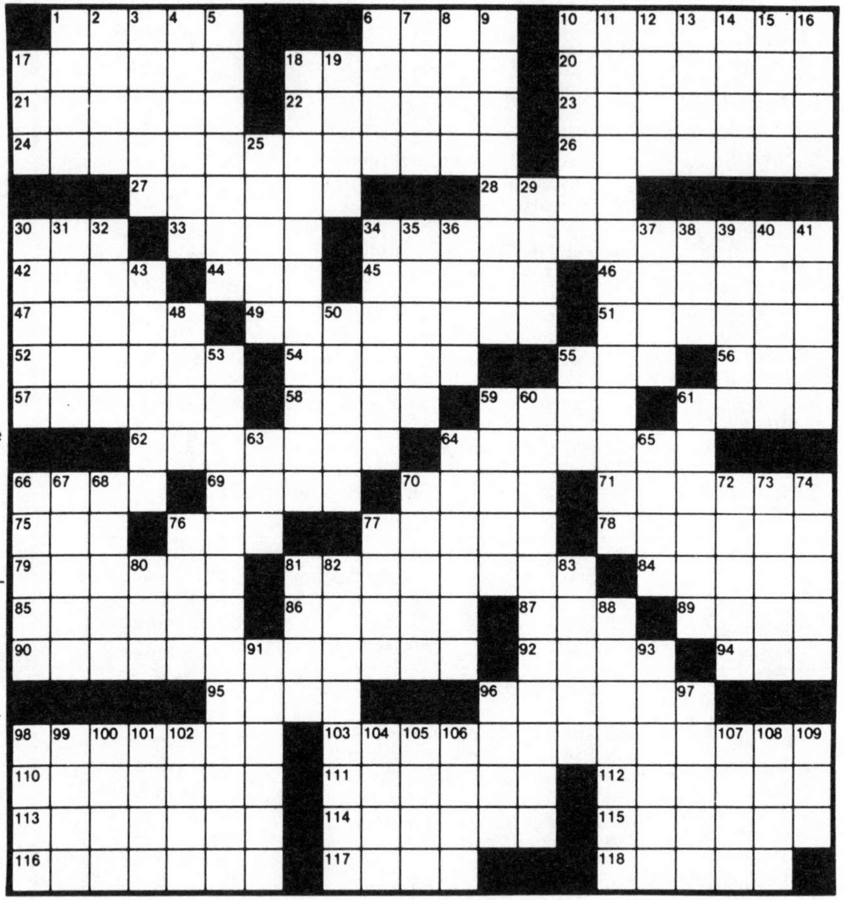

21

Super!

By William Lutwiniak

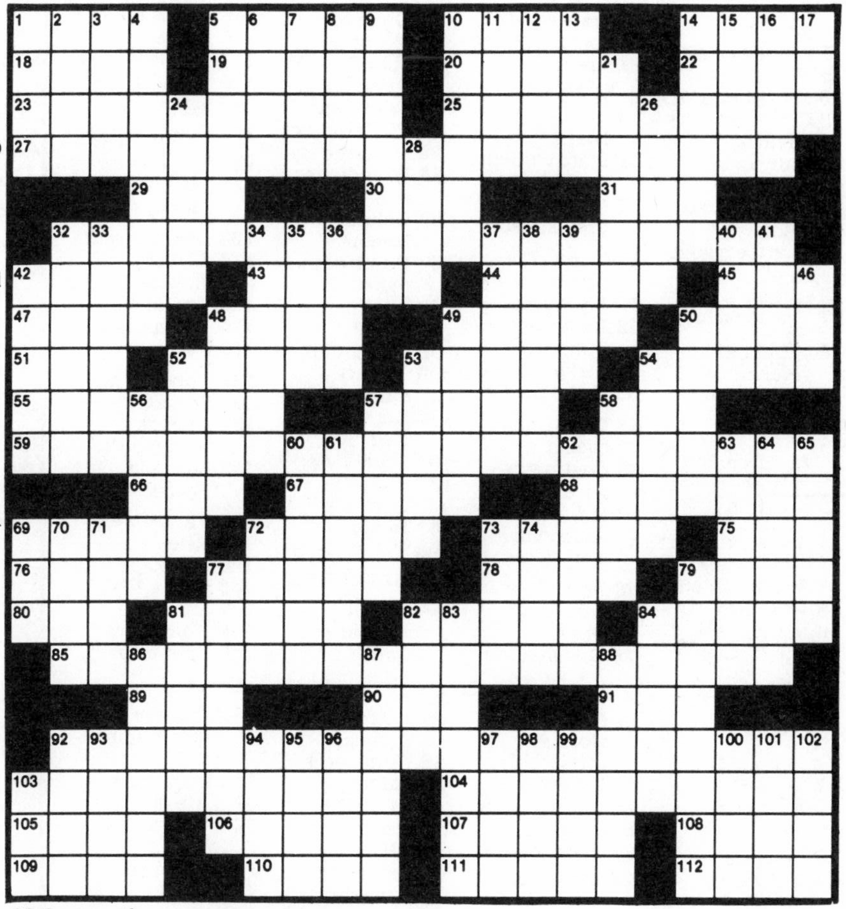

ACROSS

1 Pedestal feature
5 Varnish ingredient
10 Grackles
14 "Industry" is its motto
18 Jannings
19 Idolize
20 Engaged in
22 Neighbor of Java
23 Dart thrust into el toro
25 Punctured
27 Headline subject: 1912
29 "—— Got Sixpence"
30 Free electron
31 Forming a corner: Abbr.
32 Broadway hit: 1937
42 Classical medico
43 Inside vocabulary
44 Mitigates
45 Stately tree
47 Rice team
48 Very well
49 Fastened, in a way
50 Etui or pomander
51 Honshu bay
52 Underworld units
53 Trustworthy
54 See 4 Down
55 Slight
57 Barker's aide
58 Some of us
59 Film of 1965, with "The"
66 Wall St. term
67 Illinois airport
68 Obtrusive one
69 Sewed rapidly
72 Bright
73 Gulae
75 Fr. title
76 Unbalanced
77 Transmission components
78 Car part
79 "—— Lisa"
80 James Jones's heroes
81 Blue shade
82 Count, for one
84 Crude broom
85 Statue of Apollo by Chares
89 Ending with cash or cloth
90 —— -Magnon
91 "—— Belong to Me"
92 Lloyd C. Douglas novel
103 Barge hand
104 A la chinoise
105 ". . . care'll kill ——": Jonson
106 Bay of the ——
107 Correggio lived here
108 El Bahr
109 Nabokov novel
110 Tolkien creatures
111 Arnall of Ga.
112 Center

DOWN

1 Red-ink entry
2 Wuhan nanny
3 Eat out
4 With 54 Across, bits of lore
5 Lurch
6 Lyrical
7 "Young Hickory"
8 Guthrie
9 Turning the pages
10 Opera by R. Strauss
11 Letters before cee
12 Herbaceous plant
13 Moslem mystic
14 Congo border river
15 Famed pantomimist
16 A Waugh
17 Camouflaged
21 Wrecked completely
24 Songwriter Drake
26 Emulates a devil chaser
28 Contretemps upshot
32 Mooring line
33 Offer, as a plea
34 Coruscates
35 Let fly
36 "Snake eyes"
37 Indeed
38 Glib
39 Wielded
40 Fast breaker
41 Lord High Everything ——
42 Departure
46 "Allons, —— enfants . . ."
48 Plane surface
49 Tours's river
50 Dantean division
52 Outfit
53 Unawares
54 U. of Maryland team
56 Go for eagerly
57 Reference marks
58 Baltic port
60 Marinara base
61 Parts of plows
62 Panopticon
63 Diffuse, in a way
64 Kástron's isle
65 Oneiric image
69 Tease
70 Lodged
71 Snack
72 Cachet
73 Numerical prefix
74 "A good walk spoiled": Twain
77 Nimbi
79 Jellyfish
81 Olfactory stimulus
82 Curdle
83 Ionium, e.g.
84 Encouragement
86 Septuagenarian's goal
87 Mielziner designs
88 Veld scavengers
92 Fuchsite, e.g.
93 Source of gelose
94 Untrammeled
95 "—— the Mood . . ."
96 Quitter's word
97 —— Roberts U.
98 Roleo verb
99 Trucker's rig
100 Nastase
101 Casa pot
102 Denial in Dudinka
103 O.T. book

22 Crazy Rhythms

By Maura B. Jacobson

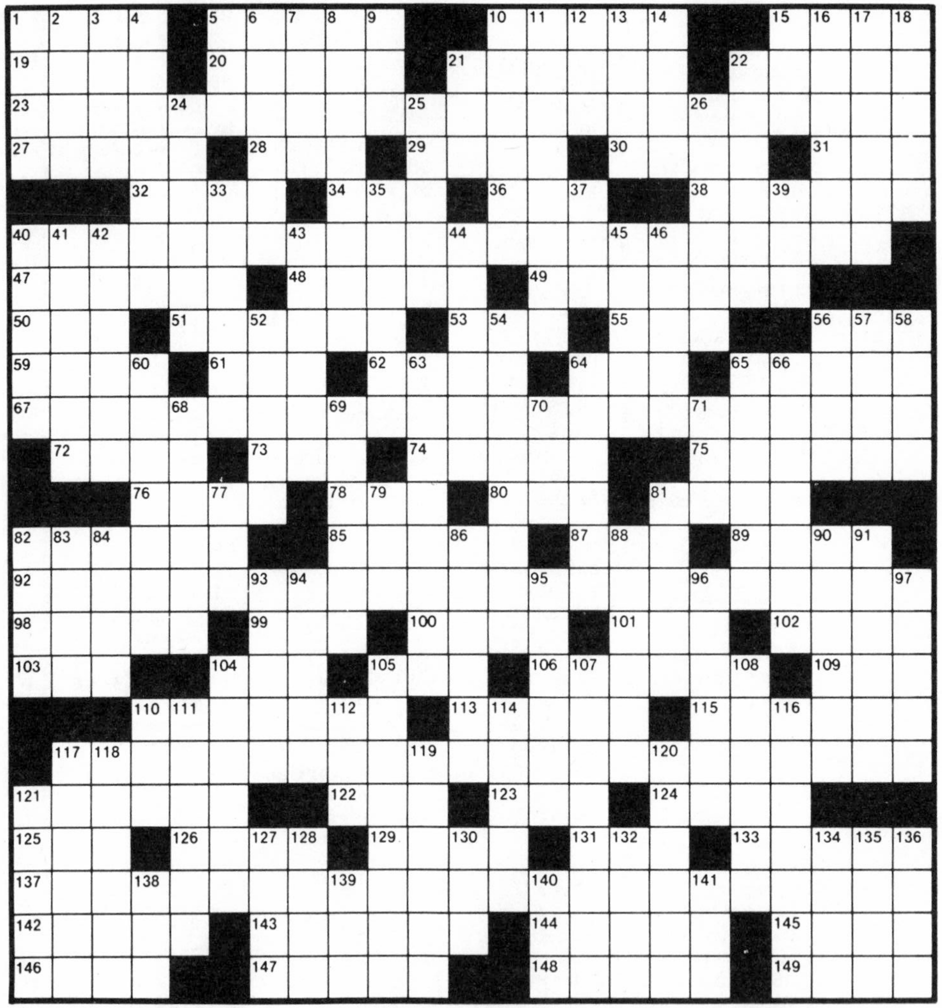

ACROSS

1 Actor's quest
5 Pindar, e.g.
10 Half of MMMD
15 C.S.A. soldiers
19 Rival of Babylonia
20 Nab
21 Bribe money
22 "Bobby Shaftoe's gone ——"
23 Author's song?
27 Trattoria buy
28 Highland refusal
29 Arizona city
30 Equal
31 "Old MacDonald" refrain
32 —— fixe
34 Soft shoe, short style
36 Shade of blond
38 Wee ones
40 Mathematician's song?
47 Scale start
48 Construe
49 Summer quencher
50 Before, to Blake
51 State without proof
53 N.R.C. predecessor
55 Parts of psyches
56 Ivy clump
59 Bando and Mineo
61 Tiriac of tennis
62 Nasal prefix
64 Road runner's cousin
65 Containing good earth
67 Prince's song?
72 Agrippina's son
73 Make a gaffe
74 Innsbruck area
75 Dispossesses
76 Girds up
78 Morning abbrs.
80 After printemps
81 Pirate's take
82 Soporific fly
85 W. Indies fish
87 Holiday in Hanoi
89 Howls at the moon
92 Jazzman's song?
98 Gators' kin
99 Lettuce variety
100 Actress Kedrova
101 Spelldown
102 "—— Old Cowhand"
103 Biddy
104 Cub Scout unit
105 Arafat's org.
106 Arizona political family
109 Zeta's follower
110 Sabra
113 Partisan
115 Rely for support
117 Poet's song?
121 Uri, for one
122 Sky sighting, perhaps
123 Boxing great
124 Slithery slayers
125 Garfunkel
126 Bruins' home
129 Pteroid
131 Nabokov novel
133 Spooky
137 Actress's song?
142 Best and Ferber
143 Tattletale
144 Rife
145 Blockage
146 Morse E's
147 Stockpile
148 Romanovs
149 Poetic dusks

DOWN

1 Lop the crop
2 Spanish jug
3 Resinous substances
4 Hortatory
5 Decide in favor of
6 "Fantasia" creator
7 Quechuan
8 Given to machinations
9 Weatherman's abbr.
10 Kenyan rebel
11 Like Ming rulers
12 Gear tooth
13 Sabot sound
14 Word for Apley
15 Singer Acuff
16 Affari —— (foreign affairs): It.
17 In arrears
18 Aegean island
21 Not sing.
22 Greek region
24 Artist Alma-——
25 French school
26 Argues back
33 One of the Dionnes
35 Bids
37 Hic, haec, ——
39 Dock union: Abbr.
40 I.e.
41 Cleveland neighbor
42 Ultimatum words
43 Wurst
44 Like an egghead
45 "Die Lorelei" author
46 Of Old Norse poetry
52 "Poirot —— a Client": Christie
54 Mezzanine
56 After-shave item
57 Fail to include
58 Anil and eosin
60 Pertaining to rock layers
63 July phenomenon
64 "And no man was —— answer . . .": Matt.
65 Decorative basin
66 Japanese paper-folding art
68 Lippizaners
69 A Musketeer
70 Scottish "not in"
71 Wield an ax
77 Parisian possessive
79 Fleetwood ——
81 Pittsburgh export
82 Cal or Carnegie
83 Unfailing
84 Black: Poetic
86 Lazy
88 Go aboard
90 Native of Sana
91 Fixed part of a motor
93 Cousteau's milieu
94 Ennead
95 Near the tail
96 Greece, to the Greeks
97 —— off (intermittently)
104 Soak
105 Booby traps
107 Scornful ones
108 "—— Fidelis"
110 Adherent: Suffix
111 Strong ales
112 Boudreau of baseball
114 Japanese porcelain
116 Truancy, e.g.
117 Texas border city
118 Rapt
119 Doyle hero
120 Mooring place
121 Congealed
127 "—— Smile Be . . ."
128 Throat-clearing sound
130 Loc. of Mali
132 Far East area
134 Get one's goat
135 Privy to
136 Soufflé ingredients
138 —— de deux
139 Spanish Main wave
140 Bandicoot
141 Con Ed et al.

23 Half a Loaf

By Vincent L. Osborne

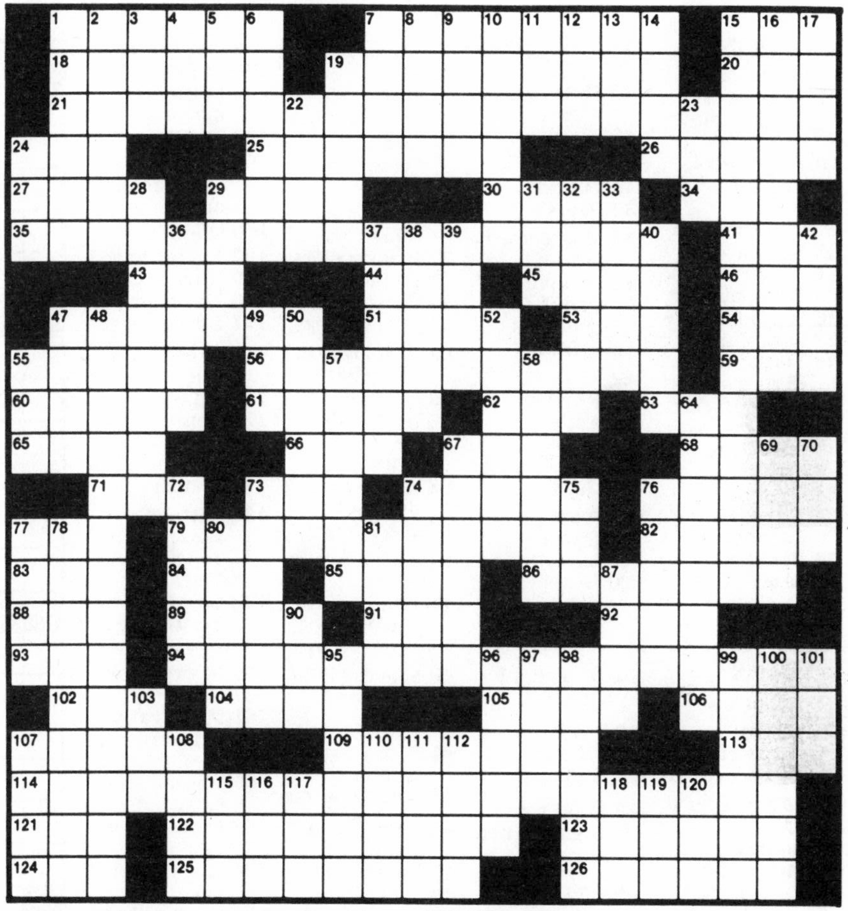

ACROSS

1 Arabian gazelles
7 Relative of Armageddon
15 Toward the poop deck
18 Freight shipment
19 Caustic
20 Word of contempt
21 Thrift-shop book?
24 Pyramidal conifer
25 Epitome of rapacity
26 Master of genre
27 Like a famous office
29 Index
30 Chills
34 Fauvists' forte
35 Almost baffled?
41 Watch over wee ones
43 Stole
44 Qt., e.g.
45 Zeno's "Painted Porch," e.g.
46 Marker
47 Marks for Mark Roth
51 Certain parientas
53 Useful abbr.
54 Wimple wearer, perhaps
55 Vice President before Curtis
56 Furlong sprinter?
59 Federal agcy.
60 Melodramatize
61 Gussets
62 Sixteen make a pt.
63 Brynner
65 Strip of shoe leather
66 Syria-Egypt acronym: 1958-61
67 Tree used for war clubs
68 Opera by Handel
71 Orion's beloved
73 Rather
74 Warwick is one
76 Krait
77 Ex-President of Gabon
79 Interrupted nap?
82 Leno or twill
83 Lummox
84 Robert Burns's birthplace
85 Pythoness
86 Church in a 1945 film
88 Parabola
89 Smart-alecky
91 British thank-yous
92 Symbol of sovereignty
93 Start of Colo. motto
94 Mini-mystery?
102 One on a trike
104 Weather satellite
105 As far as
106 Sturdy cart
107 Fresh
109 Of Hindu incantations
113 Halfway house
114 Unfinished novel?
121 Marin's milieu
122 Estranged
123 Card game for two
124 Sigma
125 Singing family
126 Matters ex cathedra

DOWN

1 Verbal voice
2 Full of school spirit
3 Incensement
4 One of the wahoos
5 Trevanian's "The —— Sanction"
6 "Don't do that!"
7 Lady of the casa
8 U.S. Army branch
9 Straight: Comb. form
10 Angora's pride
11 Lith. or Ukr.
12 Casino cube
13 Angelus prayer
14 Slangy assents
15 Near-great in baseball annals?
16 Jesting
17 There's companion
19 Judy from Northampton
22 Hard by
23 Greek letter
24 Place for a timekeeper
28 Metastasio creation
29 Neighbor of Wyo.
31 Paley's org.
32 Van Gogh's "The Potato ——"
33 Journalism positions
36 Racket
37 Time or Christmas
38 Skips
39 Home of the Uintas
40 Town in Washington
42 Bluefin or yellowfin
47 Unchanged
48 Charms for schlemiels?
49 Brain-waves rec.
50 Omaha, for one
52 Sure thing
55 Kind of line
57 Funds for research
58 Boston Mountains locale
64 Win a business contract
67 Craving
69 Steps on the gas
70 Tinstone or bauxite
72 Mace or crosier
73 Etymologists' interests: Abbr.
74 Drudgery
75 Part of i.e.
76 Edgar, for one
77 Plaint
78 Merrill and Milnes
80 Creator of Jennifer Lorn
81 Himalayan mystery
87 Madeleine ——, cosmetician
90 Foot, to Fabius
95 Monody or threnody
96 Emulated Lorelei
97 R.I.P. statement
98 Was eager
99 Grain bristle
100 City on the Loire
101 Prefix with thesis
103 Mystery writer Josephine
107 Alaskan cape
108 Meads
110 On the horizon
111 "—— creature was stirring"
112 III
115 Ring name
116 "Oysters —— season"
117 Actress Arthur
118 Prefix for system or type
119 Kiosk item, for short
120 The law's is long

24

Homophone Exchange*

By Sandra Gast

ACROSS

1 Sea voyages*
7 Word with laugh or play*
13 Frightens
19 Full of wool
20 Acquire
21 Story installments*
23 British ——*
24 Mouth: Prefix
25 Commotion*
26 Secondhand
27 Jazz pianist
29 Verbal rhythms
31 Grassy field*
32 Letter or river
33 Southern breads
34 Optimistic
35 Astronaut Slayton
36 Banks of baseball
38 St. George was one*
42 Crossed the plate
44 Mucilaginous pods
46 Egg whites*
48 Y's
49 Villain
52 Peers
54 Mus. comedy locale
56 Surviving
57 Campus buildings
58 Affronts*
62 "I —— Rhythm"
63 Authentic
65 Genuflect*
66 —— Stanley Gardner*
67 Alert
69 Dancer Shearer
70 British Columbian group
71 "Swing and ——. . ."
72 Familiar Midwest sight
73 Cantinflas role: 1959
74 In power*
76 —— State (N.D.)*
77 Bright colors
79 Panache
80 Carved poles
82 Anchor rings
83 Employee in an orchard
84 Turkish mountain
85 ——-Mari-times
88 Method of self-defense*
90 B.&O. man
91 Third-largest island
93 Grains, as of corn*
96 —— Downs
100 Swiss canton
101 Study for a quiz
103 Style*
105 Memorable yachtsman's nickname
106 Offs and ——
107 Babies do it
109 Kitchen device
110 Troubles*
111 Decreases*
113 Preserve, as Tut
115 Injure
117 Tercet
118 "Toiler" of comics
119 Charm
120 "Strong Poison" author
121 Supplied with funds
122 Copal and mastic, e.g.

DOWN

1 Scratched*
2 Shaving instrument*
3 Not discovered
4 Did a cobbler's job*
5 Compass point
6 Sixth, in Siena
7 Antagonistic*
8 Dense or dull
9 Iota
10 Aries
11 Gulf of ——
12 Diarists
13 They have the misery*
14 Timothy and Herbert Fairfax
15 Watertight vessels*
16 R.S.V.P., for instance
17 Ruffians
18 Make smooth
22 High-spirited horses
28 Amphora adjunct
30 Ripped
33 Temple of Heaven site
35 Medicinal amounts
37 Hebrides island
39 End of a T. Williams title
40 Space inside Sherwood Forest
41 "Jolly Trio" painter
43 Colombian city
45 Heat and cool again
47 Roman coins
49 Sugar-cane residue
50 Foreign
51 King of the Huns
52 Furnishes
53 Company of singers*
55 Malaysian state
58 More rational*
59 Mooring rope
60 Shock
61 Most crafty
64 Originating in the intellect
65 Unsophisticated
68 Foreshadow
70 Listen
74 Right-hand page
75 Gormandizer
78 Costello and Gehrig*
79 Mean or vulgar*
81 Boat cover, for short
83 Gains*
85 Electromagnetic unit
86 Solitary ones*

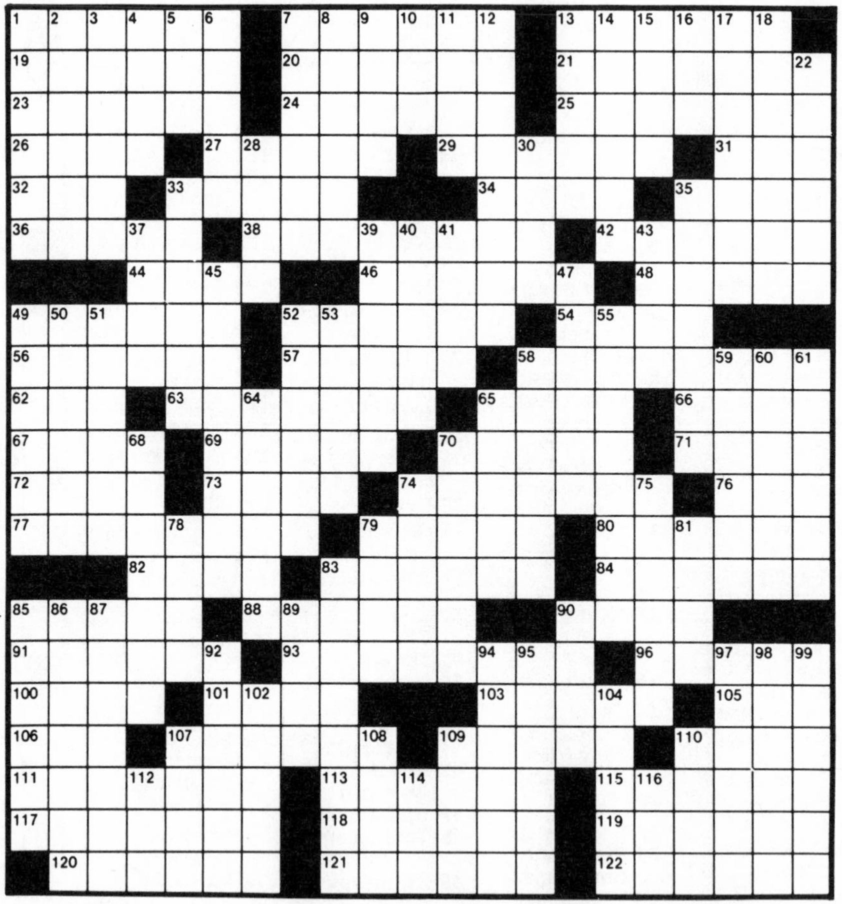

87 European kingdom: 1701-1871
89 Vinegar: Prefix
90 Serf in a fief
92 First bidder
94 One of a famous quintet
95 Gave birth to sheep*
97 Deli purchase
98 Beaver State
99 Skinflints
102 Takes by force*
104 Mandate
107 Tax or duty*
108 Issue
109 Converse
110 León landladies
112 Undercover agent
114 Coll. degree
116 Chemical suffix

Word Feast

By Jeanette K. Brill/

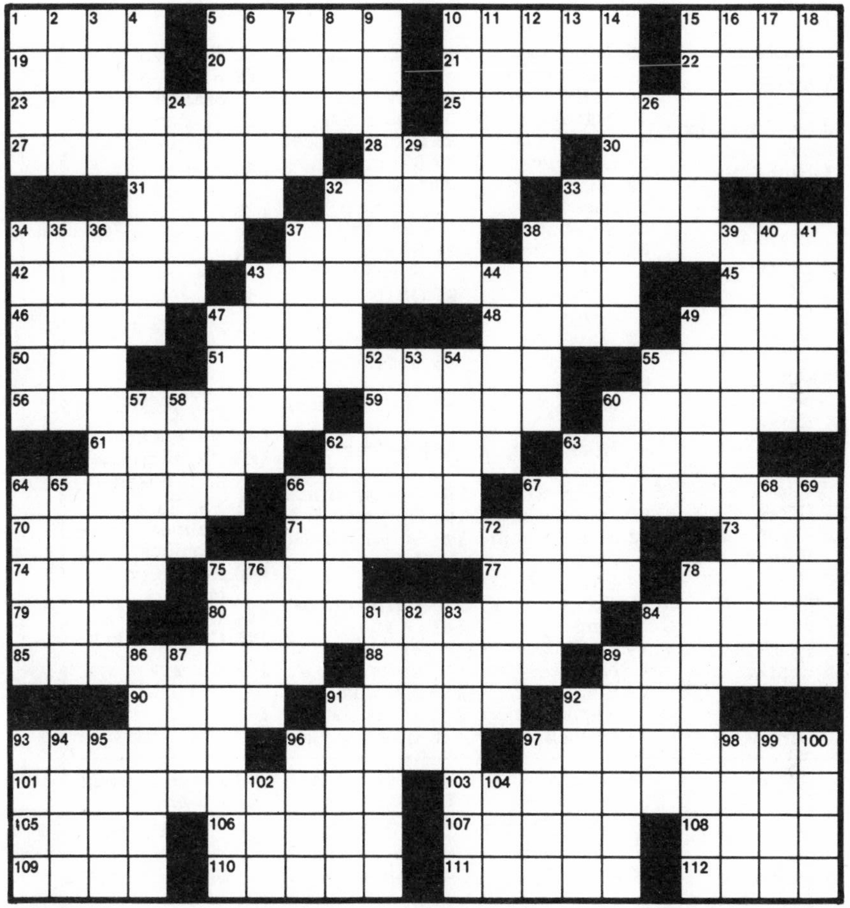

ACROSS

1 Tarry
5 Begat
10 Deadly
15 Horn of a crescent moon
19 Arabic letter
20 Accrue
21 —— Gay
22 One of the Aleutians
23 Yeomen of the guards
25 Skinny one
27 Muscle
28 "Dragonwyck" author
30 Exuberant
31 Gloat
32 Surname in a Broadway musical
33 Canaan deity
34 "Lady Be Good" playwright
37 Freight
38 Piazzas
42 Mirador
43 Dolt
45 Castor, e.g.
46 Hollywood writer-producer
47 Arid
48 Pk. and bu.
49 Birthplace of Galileo
50 Parks' successor at Atlantic City
51 Redhead
55 Crab or snake
56 Cole Porter's "It's ——"
59 Main Line town in Pa.
60 Oyster's enemy
61 Sardonic form of humor
62 Author of "Games People Play"
63 Aptly named novelist
64 Emulate Mamie Stover
66 Caravansary
67 Ship routes
70 Frenchman's awl
71 Dense fog
73 Little, to Sandy
74 Araceous plant
75 Washer cycle
77 Roman historian
78 Bender
79 Follower of Paul or Benedict
80 Leg art
84 Caesar's last word
85 Strange events
88 Hart or Stephen
89 Put paint on
90 Dogfall, in wrestling
91 Burrows
92 Schmidt works here
93 Commination
96 Body in Paris
97 Part of an academic year
101 "Simple Simon ——"
103 Bunk!
105 Explorer Tasman
106 Jug for liquids
107 Culpability
108 Clothed
109 Cape
110 A deadly sin
111 Major followers
112 Heath and Nugent

DOWN

1 Bunyan's blue ox
2 Holly
3 Bantingize
4 Brought about
5 Habituate
6 Under one's guidance
7 One who repents
8 Stray
9 Napoleon, e.g.
10 Swag
11 Composer Bruckner
12 Rent
13 "The Greatest"
14 Pieces passing through deadeyes
15 Occult doctrine or science
16 Ouray's people
17 R.b.i. or e.r.a.
18 Niggling
24 Register
26 Paraphernalia
29 Therefore
32 He wrote "Marius the Epicurean"
33 Belabor
34 Submitted
35 Church vestment
36 Pusillanimous
37 —— favor (fawn)
38 Largo and presto
39 Takes the coward's way
40 Item for Peter Hurd
41 Fixed look
43 Farinaceous
44 Caucasian, in Hawaii
47 Inkling
49 China's gift to Washington Zoo
52 "Billy Budd" is one
53 "—— Bulba," Gogol novel
54 "Pagliacci" role
55 Money in Meshed
57 Site of the U. of Maine
58 Field mouse
60 Pall
62 U.S. dress designer
63 Female sandpiper
64 Proportion
65 Bushbuck's cousin
66 Hale and Hari
67 Thwart a plan
68 Indulge in cabotinage
69 Satisfied
72 Prussian lancers
75 Hip-thigh ailment
76 Dog-days word
78 Negotiate
81 TV device
82 Assam silkworm
83 Rate for transporting
84 Minstrel end man
86 Dreams of youth
87 One-horse carriage
89 Travelers with tails
91 Lend-—— Act: 1941
92 Outlaw Starr
93 Govt. agent
94 A wife of Hercules
95 U.S. 1 and U.S. 66
96 Complacent
97 Barbecue accessory
98 Bulrush
99 Plant form
100 Smith and Barber
102 Sea bird
104 Wall St. term

Title Flaws

By Tap Osborn

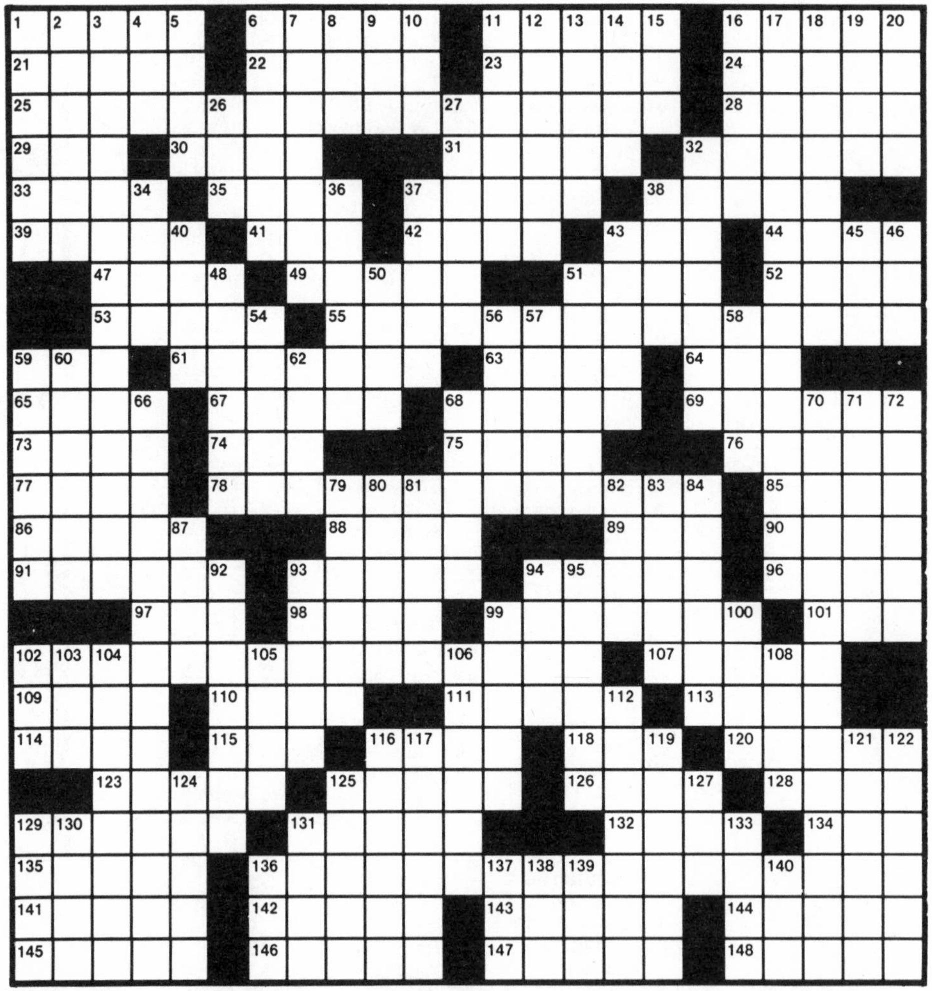

ACROSS

1 Silent performers
6 Sear in an open pan
11 Humiliate
16 Ayn Rand's shrugger
21 Legislate
22 Dickinson from N.D.
23 Kupang's island
24 Met soprano
25 Cut glass
28 Seed integument
29 Rob follower
30 "Two by Two" role
31 Urbane
32 Famed park in Vienna
33 Newspaper publisher
35 Jaunt
37 Episode
38 Conflict zone
39 Ray
41 Hog's want
42 Director Vidor
43 Sales-chart illustration
44 Roller's duo
47 Actress Diana
49 Rabbit fur
51 Gold novel
52 D.C. agent
53 Speedily
55 Kickback
59 Mud: Comb. form
61 Reveling devils
63 Waves, at Málaga
64 Sault —— Marie
65 Stulm
67 Hike
68 Like chalcedony
69 Spill the beans
73 Stone: Comb. form
74 Part of NATO
75 Phone-booth item
76 Neighbor of Nepal
77 Ending for wagon
78 Barbell
85 Race: Comb. form
86 City near Stockholm
88 Groupie's need
89 Bar drink
90 Major Hoople's expletive
91 October offerings
93 On the mother's side
94 Hostile look
96 Bar mitzvah, e.g.
97 —— Gardens, L.I.
98 Eye part
99 More viscous
101 Roman bronze
102 Outgrows
107 Suffer Icarus' fate
109 Obstreperous
110 Farm sounds
111 Of an architectural order
113 Fashion
114 Austen novel
115 Hawk's cage
116 Fastener
118 F.D.R.'s brainchild
120 Moslem mendicant
123 Figure on Jacob's ladder
125 Flourishing
126 Arizona river
128 State tree of Ark.
129 Toot
131 Manufacturer's spoiled paper
132 Louise from N.Y.C.
134 K-O connection
135 Upper crust
136 Strip poker
141 Far East nannies
142 Sea duck
143 Bone: Comb. form
144 Ragged crest
145 Gift recipient
146 Battery terminal
147 Reject
148 Street show

DOWN

1 Subways in Milan, Paris, etc.
2 Pawned
3 Lamb chop
4 Household: Comb. form
5 Stupefy
6 Tuaregs' milieu
7 Busy, congested community
8 Sound of distaste
9 White-collar symbol
10 Slithery one
11 Heisted
12 Camp activity
13 Clerical neckpiece
14 Capuchin, e.g.
15 Work unit
16 National Leaguer
17 Lady-in-waiting with a bad connection
18 Words in a song about Paris
19 Word with bellum or date
20 Desiccate
26 Won
27 Like a shrike
32 Do market research
34 End
36 Runs in the money
37 Hydroplanes
38 Plug a chink
40 Of an epoch
43 Easy mark
45 Calloway
46 Spanish queen
48 Egyptian amulet
50 Hit the books
51 N.Y. island
54 Sister of Terpsichore
56 One of Aristotle's fortes
57 Southern fruit tree
58 Shaky attempt
59 Most washed out
60 Ross or Giroux
62 2.2046 lbs.
66 Drop dead
68 Confuse
70 Skipjack
71 Woolly
72 Disintegrates
79 Home-run king Ralph and family
80 Hersey locale
81 Untrue
82 Small drink
83 Ghastly
84 Sultans' cousins
87 Suit to ——
92 Spitz, for one
93 Rush-hour weapon
94 Novelist Elinor
95 Brake part
99 Inclining
100 Gambrel ——
102 Stout
103 Thumb
104 Native of Ploesti
105 Coward
106 Destiny
108 Fur piece
112 Cow or horse, to a ranch hand
116 Looking saintly
117 Fascination
119 "Miller's Tale" heroine
121 Prisoner
122 Lease signer
124 Graylags or Emdens
125 Child: Comb. form
127 Year, to Pedro
129 Globule
130 Sailor's saint
131 Climb, in a way
133 Yonder
136 Gunpowder, for one
137 Salad item
138 Cerastes
139 One of the Udalls
140 Angelico

Look B-4 U Solve

By Jordan S. Lasher

ACROSS

1 Sunbeams
7 Footnote note
11 Rip off
14 Soliloquy opening
18 —— Avon (Anthony Eden)
19 Doris Day hit: 1956
21 A language spoken in Arizona
22 Early rock-'n'-roll favorite
24 Was beholden to
25 Walk laboriously
26 Nessen or Ziegler
27 Village in Nièvre Department, France
28 Submachine guns
29 Mediterranean ketches
31 Win by ——
32 Popular screen android
33 Play by William Gibson
37 Winnie of fiction
40 French sailors
41 Unspecified number
44 Hawaiian mackerels
45 Grass genus
49 Marry in haste
50 Cross on the red
52 More cuckoo
54 Cod catcher
55 Xanadu's river
58 Pat Boone hit: 1957
61 Ford boo-boo
62 Glacial block
64 City near Brussels
65 Spanish export
66 Farm vehicle, for short
70 "—— the time . . ."
72 Donkey serenade?
74 "So —— to you, Fuzzy-Wuzzy . . .": Kipling
75 Family of composers
77 Actress Lilia
79 Loosen, in a way
81 Negative particle
82 Like heavy fog
84 Crème —— crème
85 "—— e Leandro," Mancinelli opera
88 Upper edge of a ship's side
90 Freshen
92 "—— Rain?": 1937 song
94 Skewer
95 Official proceedings
98 Clockmaker Thomas
99 Deli purchase
100 Youth lodgings
103 Poor alternative to the Devil
105 Normandy city
107 Battle site: 394 B.C.
110 Soprano Rosa
111 Singer Tucker
112 Shallows
113 Theologian who opposed Luther
114 Hideout
118 To join, in Nancy
119 Nursery-rhyme line
122 Garment for Pavlova
123 Tie-breaking periods
124 Actor Tommy
125 Leaf through
126 Visitors to a U.S.O. center
127 Clumsy vessel
128 Hotel populace

DOWN

1 Jiffies
2 The loot
3 Woody's son
4 The Santa Maria, e.g.
5 Infant
6 Electronic detector of storms
7 N.Z. is one
8 River mouth
9 Of a Great Lake
10 Drawing card
11 Captured anew
12 "—— Plata," Montana's motto
13 Piece of candy
14 Gable film: 1938
15 Arcuate
16 —— question (debatable)
17 Disencumbers
19 Big Eight team
20 Señor Panza
23 Fabulous fliers
28 B'way sign
30 Trojan hero
33 ". . . good-will ——!": Longfellow
34 "Do you look —— and cakes . . .": Shak.
35 Pony
36 Smash hit
38 One form of a multiform organism
39 Bear, to Pedro
42 Kind of apple or fly
43 Exile isle
46 Nautical reply
47 Thread a rope, at sea
48 City on the Rhone
51 TV newsman Marvin
53 Former antipoverty agcy.
56 Dawson or Deighton
57 Search for gold
59 Brian ——, Irish king
60 Reasons
63 Italian greeting
66 Pekoe containers
67 Stitched quickly
68 Grape seeds
69 Observation re candidates?
71 Cast aspersions on
73 Part of R.S.V.P.
76 Scottish skiing surface
78 Impersonates
80 Mogul viceroys
83 Chemical suffix
85 A son of Isaac
86 Cold coating
87 Of hearing
89 —— Palmas
91 Itinerary abbr.
93 Edgar ——
96 Bridge holdings
97 Sour brew
99 Base runner's misfortune
101 "Boy —— Dolphin"
102 Young salmons
104 Apiece
105 "Oh, say —— . . ."
106 Bryant or Loos
108 Wind-borne
109 Wind: Comb. form
111 Impatient remarks
112 Role for Channing
115 ——, zwei, drei
116 Tiff
117 Sawbucks
119 Razorback
120 Morning moisture
121 Worthless thing

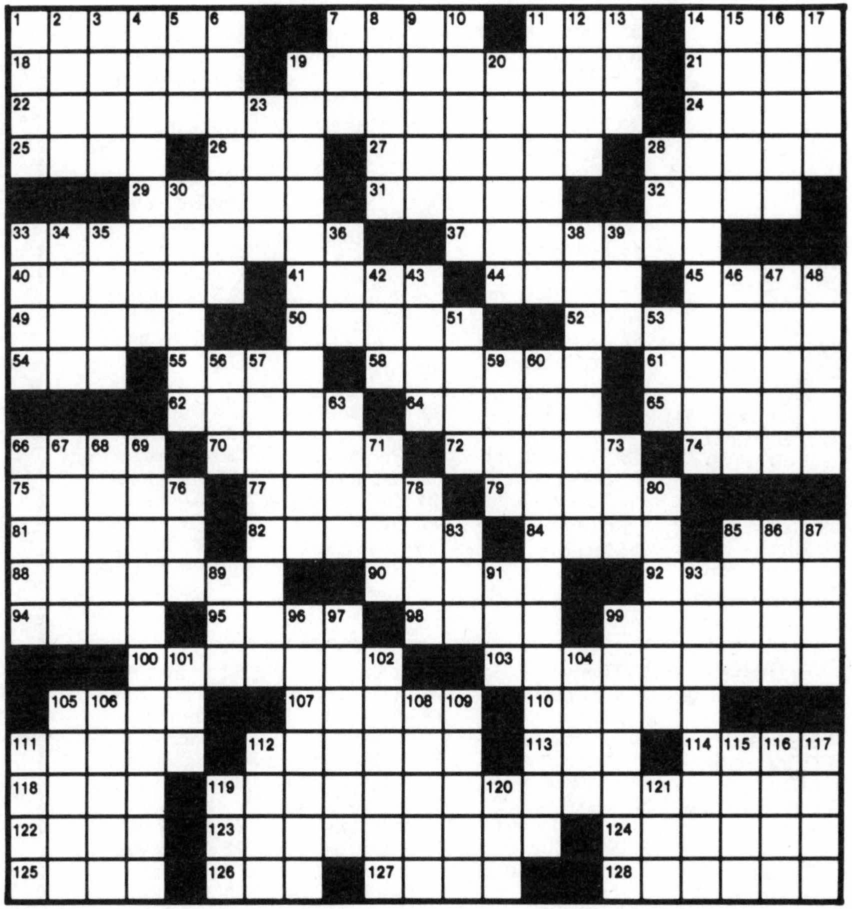

Over the Rainbow

By Mary Virginia Orna

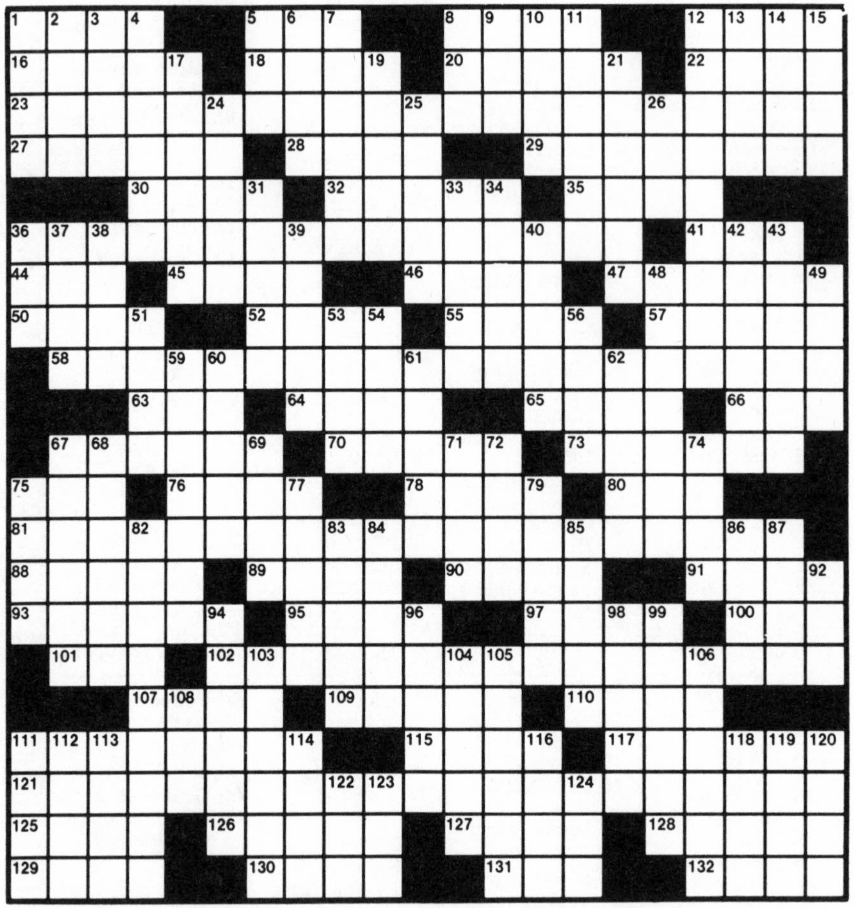

ACROSS

1 Black ——, plant disease
5 Browne
8 Sake source
12 "——, let me clutch thee": Macbeth
16 Buckwheat mush
18 Spirit
20 Belgian violinist: 1858-1931
22 Sharif
23 Nobel Peace Prize recipient: 1944
27 Laurence of literature
28 City in Oklahoma
29 Iron-bearing
30 Biotite
32 Frame for a colorful work
35 Shade of green
36 Kubrick film: 1971
41 This may be blue
44 Monte, but not Blue
45 Province on the Red Sea
46 Barrie "character"
47 Dynamo part
50 Colleen
52 Alençon product
55 N.W., e.g.
57 Honshu seaport
58 She "beat the belles of Tennessee"
63 Guidry or Cey
64 A ratite
65 Pungent humor
66 Red or black follower
67 Uses greenbacks
70 Yellow-white antelope
73 White is their QB
75 Roof piece
76 Tragacanths
78 Nantes negatives
80 Green parrot
81 Reich best seller in 1970
88 Brightly colored fish
89 Become less brilliant
90 Polynesian reef islet
91 Corn container
93 Gully
95 Goof
97 Relative of pres. and fut.
100 Nabokov heroine
101 Aurora, to Aristotle
102 Appalachian scenic route
107 White ——
109 He tests paint colors
110 Graf ——
111 Protract
115 Sch. subject
117 Unpaid debt
121 Grey novel
125 Yellow flag, e.g.
126 Pupil
127 Grill part
128 Plan of action
129 Preserves
130 Alexis, e.g.
131 Evian-les-Bains, e.g.
132 River to the North Sea

DOWN

1 Killy gear
2 Pulsate
3 Elbe feeder
4 Prefix with meter or gram
5 Coral, for one
6 Claudia —— Taylor Johnson
7 He wrote "The White Negro"
8 Kind of rug
9 Greenland is one: Abbr.
10 Balloon parts
11 Observing
12 Do a statistician's job
13 Melville novel
14 Newtonian quantity
15 Gaelic
17 Analgesic tincture
19 Kim of films
21 Vortexes
24 Isthmuses
25 —— flute (organ stop)
26 Sheet for making film cartoons
31 "Where there's —— . . ."
33 A sister of Melpomene
34 Track strips
36 "—— a green willow . . ."
37 Joseph's many-colored garment
38 Fertile
39 Fanon
40 Nose parts
42 Muscular disorder
43 "But —— work is never done"
48 Yellowlegs or redshank
49 Actuarial factor
51 Dried up
53 Lake or Perry
54 Oenochoe
56 "Follow the Yellow Brick ——"
59 "Who touches a hair of —— head . . .": Whittier
60 Invest
61 Penitent's process
62 Paint chip
67 Social stratum
68 Composer Locatelli or Mascagni
69 Relative of a ruddy duck
71 Upsurge
72 Lowdown
74 Secular
75 Judy Canova, née Julia ——
77 Cause of many a blue funk
79 Composer of "Mercure"
82 Lack of refinement
83 Estuary
84 Word form with surgeon
85 Childhood disease
86 Crop
87 Amonasro's daughter
92 Reddish brown
94 Subdivision for the Reds
96 Paint-the-town-red activity
98 Adjective for Wojtyla
99 Jacques et al.
103 Enlarged, as a skirt
104 Chasms in the Black and White
105 Clutches
106 Woolen cloth for uniforms
108 Cabinet dept.
111 The Red
112 Gray coin in Genova
113 Husband of Frigg
114 Salamanders
116 Bag
118 Corrodes
119 Chill
120 Agt.
122 Orange pekoe
123 Pronoun
124 Org. dating from 1897

Word Play

By Lynn Gilbert Lempel

ACROSS

1 Hebrew prophet
7 Exam for some H.S. students
11 Limped
18 December sights
19 "Mother of Presidents"
20 Ankle-joint protuberances
21 Smog?
23 Orozco and Rivera
24 —— Thani, city in Thailand
25 School org.
26 Actress Betty or Lauren
28 —— facto
30 Hangover?
35 Involved
38 Tear jerker
39 Sluggish
40 Pilot
41 Arctic sheets
43 Village: Ger.
46 Anne or Cécile
47 Slow, to Solti
48 Life story, for short
49 ". . . —— gently": Hamlet
51 Ophthalmologist's office?
57 Bungled
62 Northern
63 Sebastian Coe, for one
65 In layers
67 Campaigned
68 The Messiah
71 Upper and lower items
72 Wonderland character
75 ". . . with —— compass'd round": Milton
76 Warning for the fast-food set?
80 Flight
81 Prefix for fix
82 Castigate a text
87 Bedouin group of N. Africa
90 Snack
91 Criticize sharply
94 Astral
95 Alone, in Arles
97 Fixed quantities
99 Hot spot
100 Lethargic leader?
105 Biblical verb
106 Completely
107 Varnish ingredient
108 Raisa or Bonheur
112 Pollutes
114 Cio-Cio-San?
118 Always
119 Excited
120 Dough boy's milieu
121 Pianists Rudolf and Peter
122 Character on the staff
123 Plan of procedure

DOWN

1 Birthright trader
2 Placed
3 Obi accessory
4 Oppose change
5 Chance
6 Cleopatra's undoing
7 —— Alegre, Brazil
8 Quiverful of arrows
9 Rhone feeder
10 "—— own self . . ."
11 Turf and surf?
12 City in Lamb Co., Tex.
13 Hunter's hideout
14 Engineering degrees
15 Salve
16 Passes
17 Expatiate
20 San ——, Calif.
22 Tip
27 Etats - ——
29 Bone: Comb. form
31 Viola, e.g.
32 Omega's counterpart
33 Pursue
34 Chuck Connors role
35 White House nickname
36 Swedish actress Parath
37 Gump's wife
41 Transient mood
42 U.S. philanthropist: 1867-1933
44 Done, to Donne
45 "Norma ——"
48 Wait
49 NATO leader
50 Dishonest
51 Whipstitch
52 Bloomery item
53 Degree hurdles
54 Extend a subscription
55 Woman electee, in Paris
56 Tiresias, for one
57 Agcy. combating price fixing
58 Daughter of Laban
59 Major or Minor
60 Novel
61 Clip
64 Tusitala's monogram
66 Singles-bar frequenters?
69 Gds. for sale
70 Frame within a frame
73 Clemens, —— Twain
74 Curfew for campers
77 Psyche component
78 Prefix for giving or taking
79 N.Y.C. line
82 Being, to Balzac
83 Magician of comics
84 NOW cause
85 A.E.C. successor
86 Batik requirement
87 Author of "Moses"
88 Acts
89 Convincing
91 Crack
92 Footstool
93 Residue
94 Big ——, Calif.
96 Palanquin
98 Item for men who are out to lynch
99 Central points
101 County name in three states
102 Chekhov
103 "Middlemarch" creator
104 Emblem carried on a beat
109 Frank
110 Type of chalcedony
111 A Seton
113 Nettle
115 Gettysburg Address word
116 Org. in which a Bird flies
117 What a barfly might have on

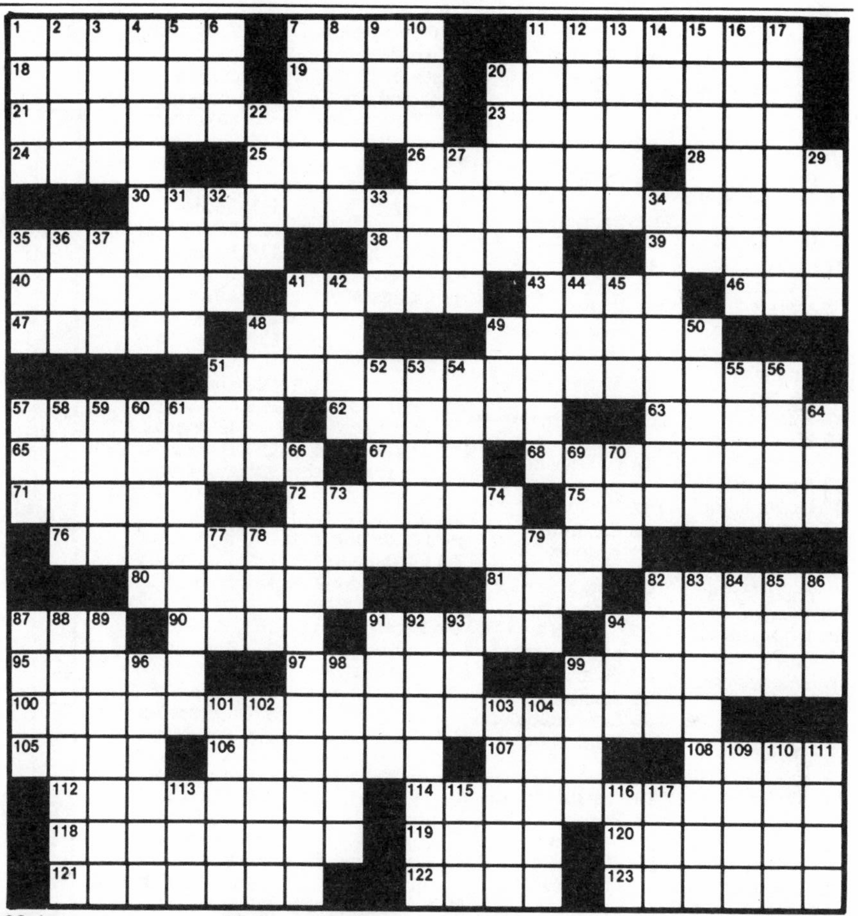

Non-Conveyances

By Bert H. Kruse

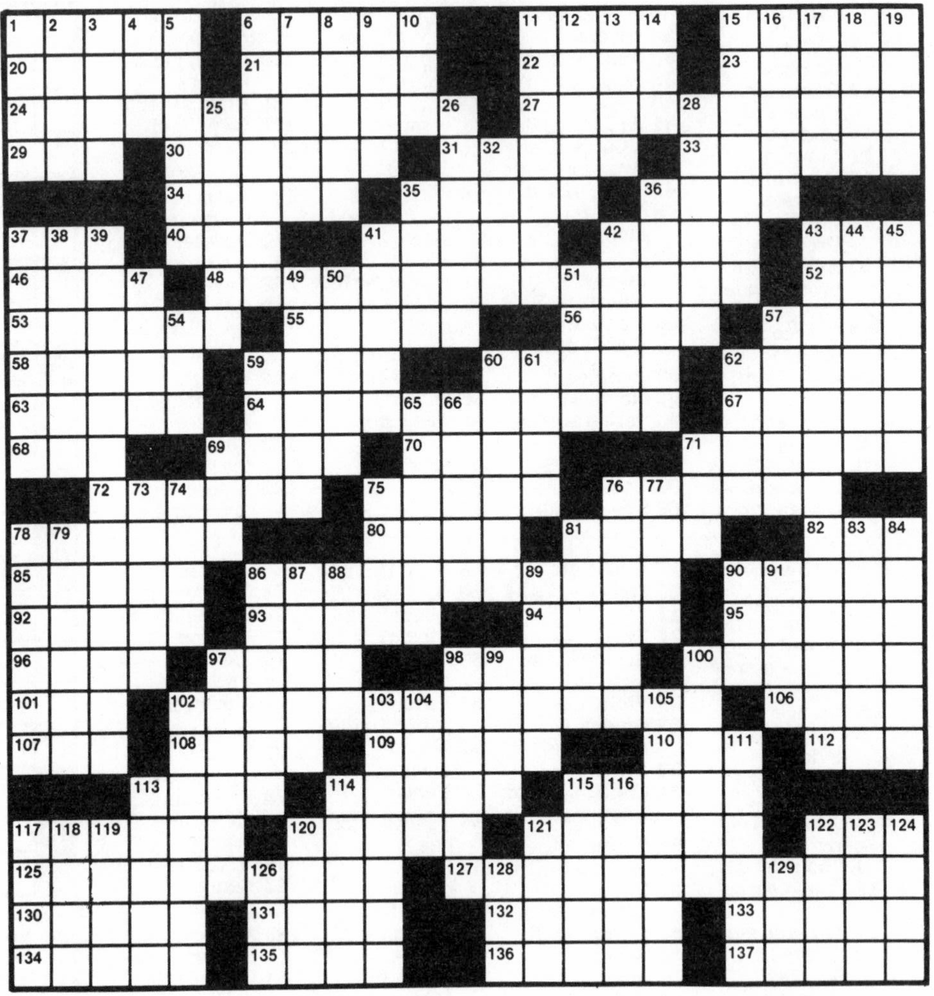

ACROSS

1 Derby drink
6 University in N.Z.
11 Beene creation
15 Part of a chair back
20 Theater signs
21 Showed a video tape again
22 One of the "Amazin' Mets"
23 Whence to view Cotopaxi
24 One who snores
27 Butcher
29 Late shipping tycoon
30 Opportunity
31 Grate sight
33 Repetitive recital
34 Old trade association
35 Tracks
36 Huguenots' city
37 Science ctr.
40 Fate
41 Of wrens, hens, etc.
42 Go after flies
43 Grid ball-carriers
46 Chamber: Comb. form
48 Strong bar orders
52 Kind of grass
53 Particular
55 Bête ——
56 Microscope part
57 Knife resembling a machete
58 Eucalyptus eater
59 Town on the Vire
60 Of hogs and peccaries
62 Dissuade
63 German seaport
64 Container for mandarins
67 "Lolita" playwright
68 Evergreen
69 Becloud
70 Ornithologist's adjective
71 Opposite of maritime
72 Apex
75 Synod site: 15th century
76 Involve
78 English whodunit writer
80 Singer Coolidge
81 Jib guy
82 Gangster's getaway
85 Ruhr industrial center
86 Tobacco addict
90 Russian villa
92 Texas player
93 Tin Man of the movies
94 Market
95 Shade of green
96 Grazing areas
97 Chalcedony
98 —— potatoes
100 Pipes
101 Our lang.
102 Ear part
106 Adolescent's problem
107 Rd.
108 Tiny item
109 As a consequence
110 Priest's garment
112 Grainger's "Shepherd's ——"
113 Stand
114 Looey's aide
115 Kringle
117 Rawboned animals
120 —— cum laude
121 New York island
122 Hades
125 "—— the Hesperus"
127 Ho-hum writer
130 Ballerina Jeanmaire
131 Rickey ingredient
132 Poison
133 Evangelist's name
134 Pledged solemnly
135 Vizier's superior
136 Certain collars
137 Penurious

DOWN

1 Napoleonic victory site
2 Calpurnia, to Caesar
3 Half of CVI
4 French conjunctions
5 She loved Cupid
6 Rosalind's swain
7 Awakening period
8 Source of betel nuts
9 Yawn
10 Popular bill
11 Tried the slots
12 Moldings
13 Follower of foot or men's
14 Proceeds
15 Is strabismic
16 Par allows two per green
17 Chaplin's second wife
18 Egyptian symbol
19 Churchill was one
25 Sterne's "Tristram ——"
26 Improve, usually
28 Exonerates
32 "The —— Love"
35 Wireless word
36 Gershwin tune: 1919
37 Servile follower
38 Comfortable
39 Drama center
41 "—— is in the streets": Proverbs
42 Bloodhound's forte
43 Noll or Bryant
44 Whalebone
45 Put away
47 Hercules' captive
49 False
50 Clayey
51 Essayist
54 —— Quentin
57 Noted lawyer
59 Thenar
60 Protest vigorously
61 Orsk's stream
62 Actor Andrews
65 Like certain wallpaper
66 Orients
69 Army V.I.P.'s
71 Suffix with acid or vapid
73 Equals
74 Yes ——
75 Canapé spread
76 Extensive, in Etampes
77 Ointment
78 Wood finisher's need
79 Agreement
81 Shooting sport
83 Actor Brian
84 Famed impersonator of Lincoln
86 Unsullied
87 Twain collaborator
88 Robert or Alan
89 Woolly and dumb
90 Patriotic org.
91 Inter ——
97 Switzerland, to Pierre
98 Oscar —— O'Flahertie Wills Wilde
99 Derby Type of chair
102 A displaced person
103 Bevel
104 Statue in the form of a square pillar
105 Small fowl
111 Widespread Indian tree
113 Less experienced
114 Finland, to Finns
115 Gregg girl
116 Elvis —— Presley
117 Orch. sections
118 Quid
119 Lake's Crossing, today
120 Read on the run
121 Dele's antithesis
122 Christie was one
123 Glacé
124 Bar on an ox yoke
126 —— Elum, city in Wash.
128 "—— Got Sixpence"
129 Skedaddle

Literally Speaking

By Jim Page

ACROSS

1 Hit the books
5 Dalai ——
9 Taiwan Strait seaport
13 Greek letters
17 Blockheads, in Brest
18 —— -on-Hudson, N.Y.
20 Jay or Kay
21 Pinsetter's place
22 L
24 Cassini
25 Came down
26 Kind of spring
27 R
30 Contralto Nikolaidi
31 Idle
34 Cozy retreat
35 Gram weight
36 Eng. author
37 Quick-fry
38 "Betty ——"
40 In Dutch it's Rijn
42 Decrees
44 Bd. members
45 "Some —— meat . . .": Burns
46 Took 40 winks
49 Mmes., in Cádiz
51 Type of type
55 Bar, legally
56 V
61 Anne or Jeanne: Abbr.
62 Regions
63 Grassland
64 All knotted up
65 El Cordobés bullring foe
67 AL
70 Sonoran Indians
71 Indigo
72 Wine: Comb. form
73 Island near New Guinea
74 Animal pouch
75 O
79 Play about Perón
81 Made the grade
82 Essence
83 Barrymore or Hampton
84 Kin of rds. and sts.
85 "—— Clown"
86 Endurance-race site
89 Vermont ski resort
92 —— War: 1899-1902
93 Uncanny
94 Forming a corner: Abbr.
97 Ear: Comb. form
98 Marsh growth
100 Dairy-company devices
102 Galileo taught here
104 Y
107 Albert Speer book
109 Author Sheehy
110 Carty of baseball
111 Y
114 Prefix for blast or carp
115 Agenda entry
116 Sheathe a blade
117 —— homo
118 Benchley's "The ——"
119 Existence
120 Rim hangings
121 Ending with pun or fun

DOWN

1 Golf great
2 House Speaker Tip
3 City WSW of Paris
4 Ruhr steel center
5 Chaney
6 Panay people
7 Mailer subject
8 Breed of cattle
9 Shortly
10 Stiff, silk net
11 Foretold
12 Safecrackers
13 Land developer's map
14 Deli order
15 ". . . armies clad ——": Milton
16 Sink like a soufflé
18 V.I.P. at tax time
19 Gunnery officer's command
23 Early English money
28 Honeybee's intake
29 Layers
32 Calendar abbr.
33 "—— only a paper moon . . ."
37 Like McCullers's café
39 About
41 Equine ailment
42 Dancer Michio ——
43 Ribbed fabric
45 King of Tyre
46 Replace, as postage
47 Baltic Sea republic
48 Compounds including vitamin D
49 R.b.i. or e.r.a.
50 Sarasota and Palm Springs
52 "And she —— our alley": Carey
53 Go over verbally
54 Sneering
56 Recent: Comb. form
57 —— Good Feeling
58 Saul's grandfather
59 Chip
60 To freeze: Fr.
66 Maxim, redundantly
67 Pays close attention
68 Trilby or tootsy
69 Mail convenience: Abbr.
76 Jimmies
77 Pointed arch
78 "Other Skies" poet
79 Chem. suffix
80 Flemish painter: 16th century
83 New Guinea locale
85 Women's vests
86 He bestrode Traveller
87 Go astray
88 F.D.R.'s secretary et al.
89 Drooped
90 Gridiron's Green Wave
91 Cheap-jewelry alloy
92 Is suited to
93 Refrigerant or fuel
94 Habituate
95 Shade of difference
96 British excise-tax collector
99 Eagle's nest
101 Pallid
102 Roast or roaster
103 Machu Picchu setting
105 Sterne's Dr. ——
106 Seward Peninsula city
108 —— Dee (Carolina river)
112 Pt. of the whole
113 Ballerina's —— seul

Lettermen Uncovered

By John McCarthy Samson

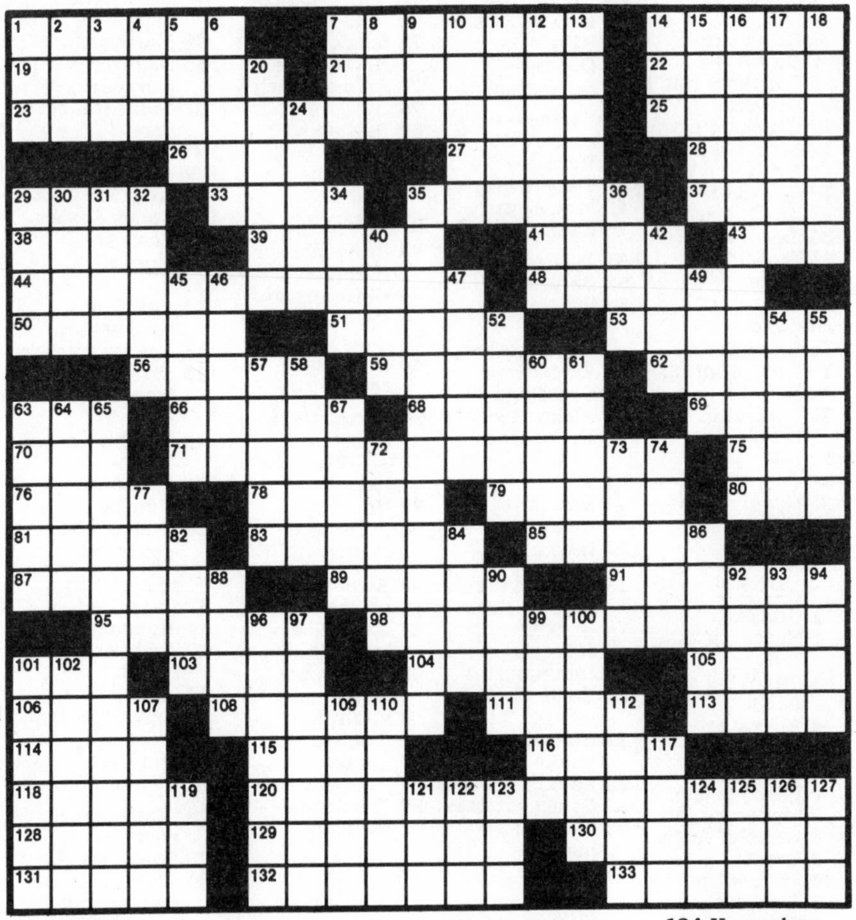

ACROSS

1 Sluggish
7 "Heart of Dixie"
14 Indian ruler
19 Restrains
21 They made a star trek
22 Figure of speech
23 General Stuart
25 Principle of right
26 Sixth Hebrew month
27 Doozy
28 Quechuan
29 Dada
33 Town in Yugoslavia
35 Serial material
37 Young oyster
38 Mythomaniac
39 Ho predecessor
41 Piles
43 O'Neill play
44 Poet cummings
48 Lament
50 Canal Zone district
51 Esteem
53 Like Alice's pool
56 Mrs. Polk
59 Hidden by
62 A famous picker
63 ETV purveyor
66 Play, in a way
68 Actress Anouk ——
69 Writer Ephron
70 Holmes called him "The Oldest"
71 Poet Eliot
75 —— tree (margosa)
76 Foxx
78 Corday's victim
79 Exhaust
80 Cachar, e.g.
81 Landed estate
83 Muppet drummer
85 Grani or Sleipnir
87 Punta ——, Chilean port
89 Oneida Community founder
91 Thin pancakes
95 "Mr. October" was one
98 Poet Housman
101 Type of gen.
103 Blunt
104 Badger's kin
105 Empress Ivanovna
106 Firmness
108 Sour drink
111 Pteroid
113 Fume
114 Comme ci, comme ça
115 "—— corny . . ."
116 Olympic fencing game
118 Court petitioners
120 Novelist Wodehouse
128 Molded entree
129 Scrooge, at first
130 More unkempt
131 "Clo-Clo" composer
132 State socialism
133 Edward Morgan Forster, e.g.

DOWN

1 J.F.K.'s successor
2 Epoch
3 Purpose
4 R.M.N. was his V.P.
5 "Lohengrin" heroine
6 Requisites
7 This can be boring
8 A Gish, for short
9 Fireproofing: Abbr.
10 Uncle Miltie
11 Love affair
12 Like the infant in Jaques' speech
13 Ring-shaped
14 Abbr. for 1 or 81
15 Gilmore, of hoop fame
16 Financier Morgan
17 At the summit
18 Queen of Hades
20 Bandage
24 Iroquoian tribe
29 Frosh at the U.S.M.A.
30 Ghislanzoni libretto
31 Detent
32 Wahabis, e.g.
34 Inside stuff
35 American showman Barnum
36 Polish foregoer
40 Lumpish mass
42 Ooze
45 Meat treat
46 —— Vader, film villain
47 Type of pitcher's dream game
49 Conceited
52 Frosted
54 Like Poe's prose
55 A work by Samuel Nathaniel Behrman
57 Bouquet
58 Not quite angelic
60 Comes close
61 Rid of rodents
63 Toscanini's birthplace
64 Dim; cloudy
65 Humorist Perelman
67 U.S. watercolorist: 1870-1953
72 Island group north of Tonga
73 Caroline, to Ted
74 Wooden comedian
77 Lady from Lisbon
82 Strip of shoe leather
84 Jim Rice's field
86 Chemist's flask
88 Gull-like sea bird
90 Muchacha's title: Abbr.
92 Counter follower
93 Haliaeetus albicella
94 Pierre's loc.
96 Elongated circle
97 Gold or silver
99 Conger catcher
100 Part of the décor
101 Prayer book
102 Excite
107 Water wheel
109 Casque
110 Scottish platter
112 Start over
117 Constantly
119 Text for a dir.
121 Onassis
122 Enero or febrero
123 Metric unit of wt.
124 Homophone for Eydie
125 Kindled
126 Grant of films
127 Bungle

33 Split Personalities

By Elaine D. Schorr

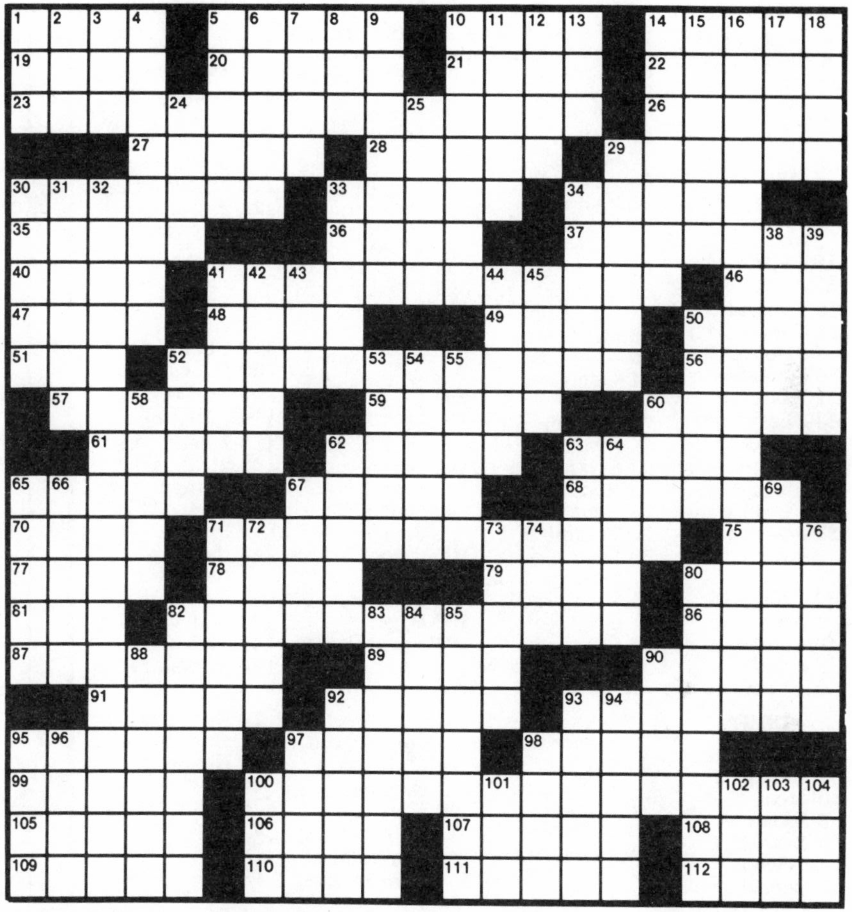

ACROSS

1 Sickle holder
5 —— barrel (helpless)
10 Deliquesce
14 Major port of Iraq
19 —— of Man
20 Lady with a lure
21 One of the Adamses
22 —— -les-Bains
23 Jefferson Davis
26 Ancient rabbi of Palestine
27 Pamphleteer of '76
28 Argillaceous
29 Farm fledglings
30 Stuck
33 Gate in Gallipoli
34 "—— We Dance?"
35 Farm-machine pioneer
36 Exchange premium
37 Chateau roof style
40 Facial woe
41 Lee Grant
46 Gambling tab
47 Pharmaceutical ingredient
48 Horne highlight
49 Kiln for curing tobacco
50 Soviet sea
51 "—— Wednesday," 1966 film
52 Marg(a)ret Mitchell
56 Berlin divider
57 Gauguin's paradise
59 Man's slipper or shoe
60 Give and take
61 Care taker
62 Ruins
63 Potsherd
65 Spoil, as an egg
67 West ——, in New Guinea
68 Controlled oneself
70 Calcutta chief
71 Carroll O'Connor
75 Ring V.I.P.
77 Son of Seth
78 Actress Virna
79 Gay deceiver
80 "The —— that men do . . ."
81 Biblical verb suffix
82 Elliott Gould
86 Carpentry tool
87 Toothed
89 Noblewoman of Lahore
90 Rector's residence
91 Nick of films
92 Rustic roads
93 Tarzan was one
95 "—— of Honey"
97 Notational sign in music
98 Byrd book
99 —— macabre
100 Wayne Newton
105 Kitchen utensil
106 Dies ——
107 Monkeyshine
108 One of Calliope's sisters
109 Inexorable
110 Trading center
111 Kiangs
112 Sailor's saint

DOWN

1 Ten-strike
2 Combustion follower
3 Polly Holliday role on TV
4 Moderated
5 Actor Davis
6 Comestible unit
7 River in Ireland
8 Embarrassed
9 Parallelism
10 Powerful explosive force
11 Tomato blight
12 Turk's cap
13 Caddy's contents
14 Where Jesus revived Lazarus
15 Is utile
16 Lewis Stone
17 Flagrant
18 Collections of quotations
24 River to the Rhine
25 Irrigation device
29 Magna ——
30 Turkish city on the Seyhan
31 Pour port painstakingly
32 James Garner
33 Allotheist
34 Atomize
38 Explorer Amundsen
39 Sans spirit
41 Breeches and britches
42 Pyle or Banks
43 "Yes!" in Roma
44 Walleyed pikes
45 Roman Censor
50 D.S.O. or D.S.C.
52 Leeds's river
53 Deplete
54 Protozoan, e.g.
55 Set to rights
58 Polynesian dances
60 Acomous
62 Quiz kid, e.g.
63 Military headwear
64 Leda's daughter
65 Slender as ——
66 First name of a Rossetti
67 "—— deal!"
69 Oder feeder
71 City in S.D.
72 McPherson
73 Root used in cosmetics
74 King Cole
76 Pooh-pooh
80 Fade from sight
82 Where brine is refined
83 Jack Webb's web
84 Windfall
85 City on the Susquehanna
88 Quoits player
90 Mary Quant style
92 Operetta composer
93 Portion
94 Functions properly
95 Says more
96 Australian honey possum
97 Rail with a tail
98 Bargain-basement sign
100 Backus or Bowie
101 A.M.A. members
102 Kit and caboodle
103 Target-practice order
104 Cote cry

Rhyme and Reason

By Michael Priestley

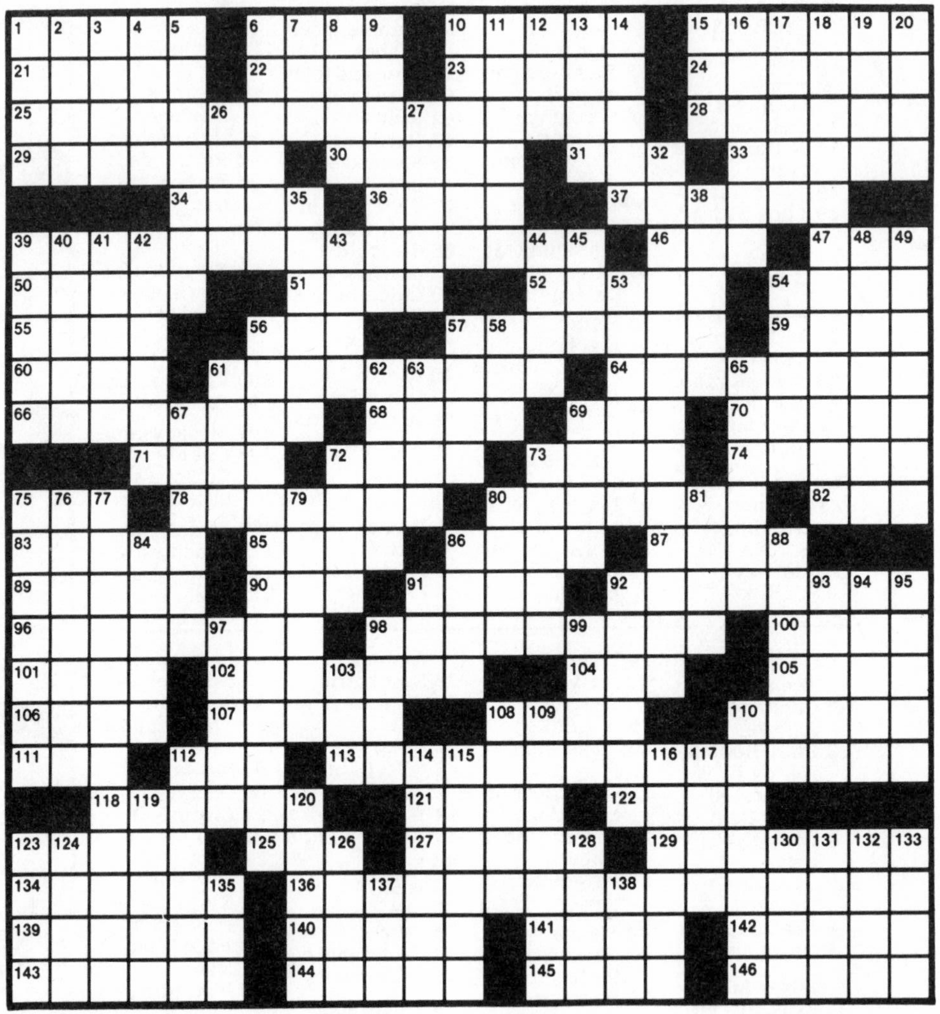

ACROSS

1 Hegel's forte
6 Tuileries, e.g.
10 Railroad switch
15 Henry was one
21 Operating
22 Mad scientist's aide
23 Odin, Thor et al.
24 Inundate
25 Airplane glue?
28 Idolized
29 Character in "No Exit"
30 Squama
31 Possesses
33 These make stakes
34 Relative of a maguey
36 Ferrum
37 —— gentle (trained falcon)
39 Aromatic peripatetic?
46 Confining grind
47 Oosphere
50 Draws water
51 Hawaiian port
52 Nimbi
54 Loire feeder
55 Discordant
56 Enero, e.g.
57 Snoozes
59 Albacore
60 Zola opus
61 Plane curves
64 Rained, e.g.
66 Curtails
68 Taurine complaint
69 Mil. school
70 —— nous
71 Tennyson poem
72 Shrill or tubular
73 God for Radamès
74 Heliacal
75 Tatami
78 Wear in a nursery rhyme
80 Submerged coral reefs
82 Bx. rumblers
83 On the qui vive
85 Start of a counting rhyme
86 Temple enclosures
87 Former president of Chile
89 Veranda, in Waikiki
90 Direction suffix
91 Wind-shielded
92 Greek patron of drama
96 Extra ingredient
98 Winter sight
100 Radio's "Vic and ——"
101 May 15, e.g.
102 Onomatopoeic drumbeat
104 Sound from Sandy
105 "More Pricks —— Kicks," Beckett book
106 Beget
107 Anoint, old style
108 Peer Gynt's mother
110 Simon and Diamond
111 College subj.
112 Keelbill
113 Cause of prickly heat?
118 Actors' group
121 Reconcile
122 Shipshape
123 Cartes before the courses
125 Boisterous laugh
127 Encircled
129 Inning in polo
134 Revise
136 Union vehicle?
139 Zetetic person
140 "Halt, salt!"
141 Nymph pursued by Pan
142 Region of Indochina
143 Part of H.S.H.
144 Wall vaults
145 Tribune
146 Yorkshire city

DOWN

1 Long sentence
2 Burden of proof
3 Squall
4 Caesar's "video"
5 Oenologists' storerooms
6 Columbary denizen
7 Iron or Stone
8 Gypsies
9 Acute
10 O'Neill was one
11 Shakespearean heroine
12 "The Nifty Fifty"
13 In propinquity
14 Wine and dine
15 Concubine's chamber
16 What diaskeuasts do
17 Unaccompanied
18 Chelonian charge?
19 S-shaped arch
20 Ohio nine
26 Actress Nazimova
27 Something to stow below
32 Guardian of angels?
35 Inflammable liquids
38 ——-Japanese War
39 Custard tarts
40 Malay ruler
41 Hersey town
42 Poet Hopkins
43 Border order
44 Turner and Cole
45 Cask for amontillado
48 Mark Clark was one
49 They rate
53 Scaramouch
54 Comb: Comb. form
56 Sea cow's conceit?
57 Kaolin, e.g.
58 Rhine tributary
61 Elfin creature
62 Saline
63 Butterfingers' cry
65 Smith's comrade in arms
67 Small English bird
69 Singer Redding
72 Keystone State eponym
73 Elbowed
75 Discomfort
76 Lamp rubber
77 Females?
79 Cylindrical
80 Cauldron contents
81 Disturbance
84 Bump the bet
86 Scads
88 Formulated theory
91 Compilation of information
92 Most ominous
93 Hindu title
94 Stu or Mo
95 Import or purport
97 Man of Isfahan
98 Suffix with fun or pun
99 Flatten a flat
103 Relative of a dalmatic
108 Addis ——
109 So-called
110 Uncultivated
112 "Persuasion" author
114 "My kingdom for ——!"
115 Is entitled to
116 Chocolate trees
117 Coal region
119 Tremble
120 Arizona Indians
123 Rumple
124 Sword of a sort
126 Australasian pepper
128 Ten: Comb. form
130 Cattle, in poesy
131 Welles role
132 "Horrors!"
133 Quantities in radiology
135 Poetic palindrome
137 London's defenders
138 Greek X

35 Saving Space

By William Lutwiniak

ACROSS

1 ". . . lift dat ——"
5 The end
10 Naldi of the silents
14 Box-score data
18 "Giralda" composer
19 Serviceable
20 Islands off Galway
21 Horn
22 Uprising in Uganda
25 Viscount Templewood
26 Fortify
27 Caper
28 Expert
29 Undo
30 Crowd together
31 —— spumante
32 Layer
33 Slight
34 Fondled
38 Ade book: 1896
41 Canadian land agent
43 Gibbon
44 Leaflet: Abbr.
45 —— Hari
46 Western pact
47 Destine
48 French pronoun
49 Accident in Kansas
53 Currier's partner
54 Maligns
56 Sharif
57 Is trepid
58 Skips
59 Krait
60 Developed ability
62 Wine-bottle size
64 Dust-bowler
65 Immature
68 Bucket
69 Political victory in California
73 —— de vie
74 "—— homo"
75 Habilimented
76 Painter Holbein
77 Adriatic feeder
78 Bee follower
79 Bay State ceramics
83 Give
84 Indonesian volcanic island
86 Pigment for Gainsborough
87 Help!
88 Essential meaning
89 Be nosy
90 Comatose states
94 Copter features
96 Cotton thread
97 Part of E.C.A.
98 Apocopate
99 Uruguayan symbol
101 Runcible ——
102 Former constellation
103 J.R. in "Dallas"
104 Quaker word
105 "—— clock scholar"
106 Benchley's "The ——"
107 Actress-singer Blakley
108 Grit

DOWN

1 Used the oven
2 ". . . Nothing Like ——"
3 Actors' club
4 Sharing another's emotions
5 U.S. inventor
6 Where the Po flows
7 Pleasant
8 O'Neill play
9 Ophidian
10 French-Spanish region
11 Literary device
12 Dialogue
13 Exemplar for a sluggard
14 Perches
15 Czech necklace
16 As to
17 Litigant
21 Bar serving
23 End of a Kilmer poem
24 Gaffe
28 Strand
30 Mount Moses climbed
33 Millers
34 Orch. member
35 Aleutian island
36 What "- vore" means
37 Sheath or shift
38 Proceedings
39 Mayo and Yaqui
40 Law enforcement in Lebanon
41 Symbols of authority
42 Conductor Previn
45 Aerosol output
47 Blue part of Old Glory
49 Legal paper
50 —— bean
51 Exceedingly
52 In the buff
55 M. Zola
57 Do an office task
59 Five centesimi
60 Do very well
61 Small fry
62 Mote
63 Indiana athlete in the N.B.A.
65 Mrs. Luce
66 Lateen, e.g.
67 Dominik's dog
69 Mexican pines
70 Too
71 Judo exercises
72 Acute
77 Frolics
79 Unproductive
80 Airline adjective
81 Pierre's school
82 Unspecified person
83 Of tender years
85 Veld beast
87 Straight man
89 Beauty-shop treatment
90 Vista
91 City on the Missouri
92 Bring to a peak
93 Timetable: Abbr.
94 Relax
95 Wine flask
96 Erudition
97 Dun ——, Scotland
99 Dippy
100 —— Jima

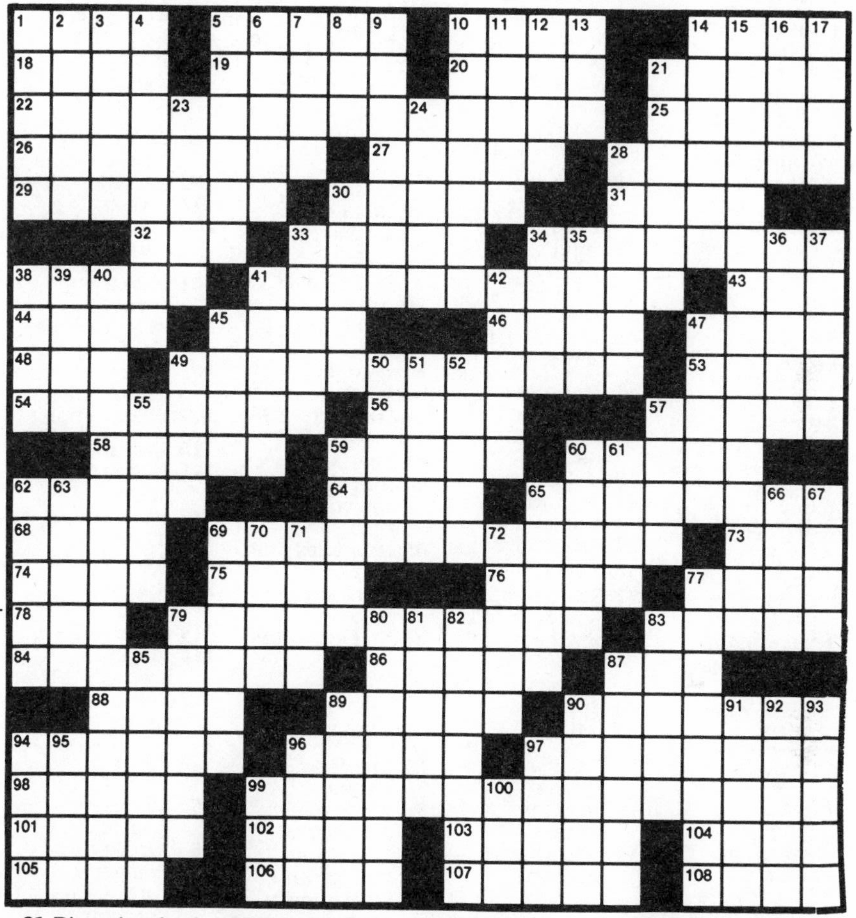

Daffynitions

By A. J. Santora

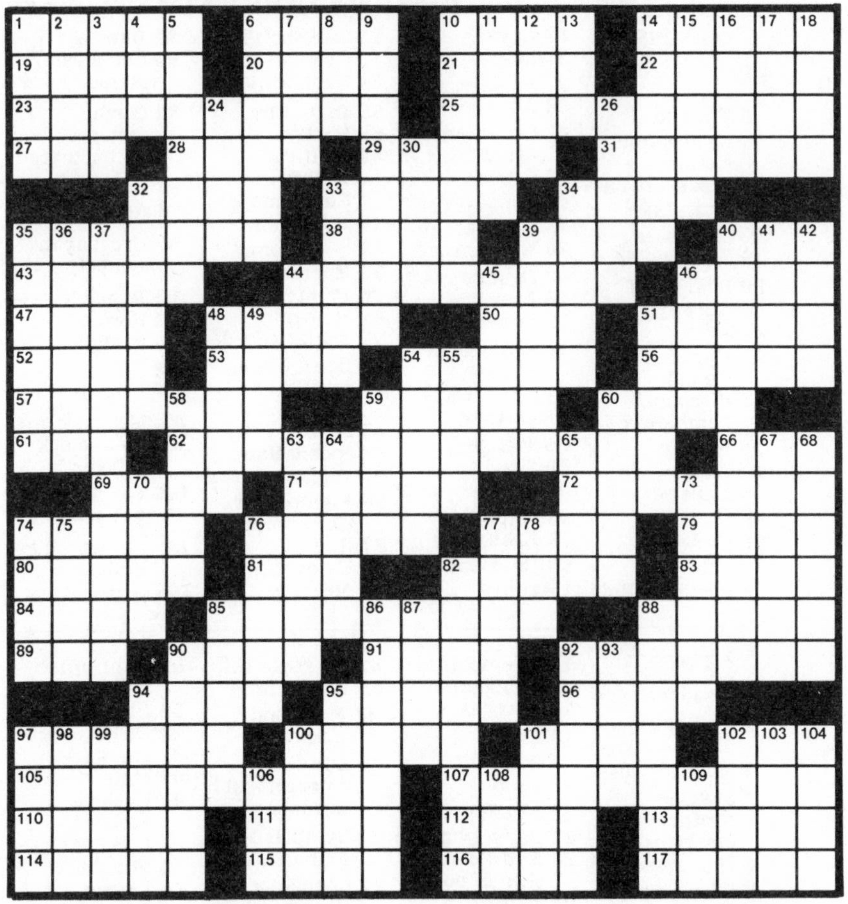

ACROSS

1 Dish served at Rice?
6 What old stogies do
10 Like a MOMA ship
14 Yemeni's neighbor
19 Slip cover?
20 Bird of merit?
21 Part of a main dish
22 Clergyman who got fired?
23 Fashion plate?
25 Rag cheats readership?
27 Sword beater
28 Arm in Armentières
29 Wearies Anka and Lynde?
31 Spot for a plug
32 Big-footed, abominable one
33 Renown for Renoir?
34 It's mimetic, energetic and esthetic
35 His day is 11/11
38 Means-end connection
39 Match involving heats
40 Start of a drum sound
43 —— in the dark
44 Place that once went boom
46 Pupil's protector
47 It's on the watch
48 Something for the record
50 Poetic start
51 —— be tied
52 Like look-alikes
53 Ab follower
54 Describing a young Feller
56 Father of a merry widow
57 Goose-pimply
59 Shield for Zeus or Athena
60 Post-office delivery
61 Bro. or dau.
62 It figures
66 These come from stiff socks
69 Proper Etta
71 Destroyer's "ears"
72 What a winning golfer at Augusta has attained
74 Bonnie associate
76 Dog-tired
77 Serb or Sorb
79 Yalies
80 Went through an "oar-deal"
81 Ewe said it
82 When penitents convene?
83 This is groovy
84 King of the entertainment field
85 He makes a net profit
88 Pittsburgh pillar?
89 Nellie or poet Robert
90 Slush —— (money from a snow job?)
91 Valley that sounds sleepy
92 Logician's proposition
94 Matter conqueror
95 Baton Rouge race?
96 Spotted
97 Scrape
100 Carpel's companion
101 Scorch or parch
102 "The good old U.S. ——"
105 Where to wring out the old
107 Gossip's tidbit
110 Wiry sprite
111 Farmer's place
112 Big apple pitcher
113 Alley denizen
114 His comedy was divine
115 Paper size
116 Virginia creeper: 1587-?
117 Teeny or weeny

DOWN

1 His productions are not for infants
2 Court name
3 Mortgage
4 Covering on the Sahara
5 A European nut
6 Sit tight
7 King of hearts?
8 He may be tight
9 Advice to Hotspur?
10 Graft at the hospital
11 Gave each player a hand
12 Bussing quartet
13 Point for a skipper
14 Like a happy medium?
15 Island of "Knights"
16 Blue dye
17 Yep's opposite
18 Sec.
24 Ambracian Gulf
26 Duckling or French city
30 Dignified "Shucks!"
32 Petty officers
33 Gas for Merman?
34 Made the fir fly
35 One of Smith's sisters
36 Will's subject
37 Cowpath?
39 Having the mulligrubs
40 Where angry drinkers meet?
41 Dog star
42 Early hammer thrower
44 Puzzling beast
45 Subject
46 Twisted tales
48 Open land for an eland
49 Philbrick's "—— Three Lives"
51 Honey's victims
54 Put on a second shift
55 Chinese gelatin
58 Supplied a swinger
59 Lambs, to Lucretius
60 Jack in the deck
63 Long place in N.Y.
64 Homeless Philip
65 "—— Old Cowhand"
67 Earl Weaverbird?
68 Something to beat
70 First place
73 Sixpence for Shakespeare
74 Marine hermit
75 Lounge on the lounge
76 Change a bill
77 Take a tangent
78 Water game?
82 Shocked
85 Pitchman of a sort
86 How Mr. Butterfingers behaves
87 Pedro's parlor
88 Dixon, but not Mason
90 Housetop instrument?
92 Insect that bit Sleeping Beauty?
93 Make sound
94 Painter who made quite an impression
95 Domain for Charlemagne
97 W. S. Gilbert in 1850
98 Theodosia Goodman
99 End of a certain road
100 Character hooked up with Hook
101 Where certain pros become cons
102 Señora's pot
103 Post-trip occurrence
104 Kind of alcohol
106 Type of ball
108 Novelist Levin
109 Avuncular giant

37

Interior Decoration

By Jeanette K. Brill

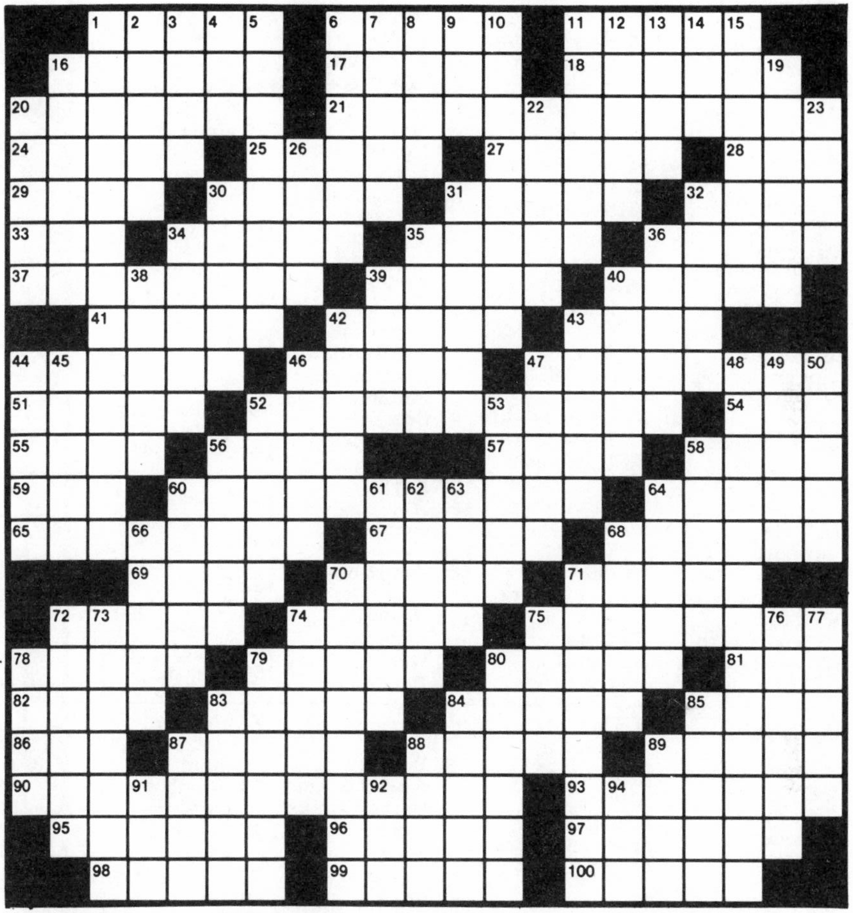

ACROSS

1 Triad, e.g.
6 De Mille films
11 Highest point in Crete
16 Eighth note
17 Tendon
18 Showy
20 Nationality of U Nu
21 Outsiders in the political arena
24 Metric unit
25 River in E France
27 Evergreen shrub
28 Brock or Costello
29 Edible tubers
30 Houston athlete
31 Leaning
32 Coadjutor
33 T'ai ——, Oriental martial art
34 Weather forecast
35 Example of workmanship
36 Pochards
37 Thesmothetes
39 Describe grammatically
40 Kind of beet
41 Reddish-brown colors
42 Forearm
43 Legendary first king of Britain
44 Card game for two
46 "Ici on —— français"
47 Ciceronian classics
51 Choice
52 Reversal of sorts
54 "Both Sides ——," folk-song hit of 1968
55 Jurgen's wife
56 "Dove ——," Mozart aria
57 Broadcasts
58 Second-brightest star
59 Scottish uncle
60 Informer
64 Man of sound mind
65 Abandoned
67 Squash variety
68 Consecrated oil
69 One of the Yalies
70 Flèche
71 Chinese unit of weight
72 Sew or cook
74 Carved stone pillar
75 Plundered
78 Hereditary factors
79 Ward off
80 Fissures
81 Ralph Rackstraw, e.g.
82 Tote-board figures
83 Jaffe and Barrett
84 Bounded
85 Poet Boiardo's patron
86 Stout
87 Gold coins of ancient Rome
88 Trattoria offering
89 Networks of nerves
90 Location of Marycrest College
93 Mathematical quantity
95 Environment
96 Heron
97 Novelist's or publisher's task
98 Shades of green
99 —— Dame
100 Worked for the K.G.B.

DOWN

1 Preliminary skit
2 Harness parts
3 Wireless word
4 In medias ——
5 They tend to the stars
6 Rara avis at a singles bar
7 Softly, in music
8 Regarding
9 Vine-stock, in Champagne
10 Most saccharine
11 Alabama port city
12 Mather product
13 Actress Swenson
14 —— Hammarskjöld
15 Studio
16 —— Lorraine
19 Worn away
20 Voting groups
22 Instant
23 Becomes a litigator
26 Memorable stuttering comic
30 Byrd book
31 More sprightly
32 Valuable violin
34 Condition
35 Picasso
36 "In the Wet" author
38 Anatomical artery
39 Contented sound
40 Rugged rocks
42 Reed of film fame
43 Muscular strength
44 Sniggled
45 Region, to poets
46 Wine grape
47 "With how sad steps, —— . . .": Sidney
48 Musician's gig
49 Prof's props
50 Large group led by a queen
52 Sponge
53 French Alps area
56 Mushroom stalk
58 Poet who wrote "The Holy Fair"
60 Animal tracks
61 Credentials
62 With coldness
63 Skirt panel
64 Massenet opera
66 Snaky shapes
68 Relative of a delundung
70 Hamper
71 Satirizes
72 Scene of confusion
73 "Good —— . . . grow up together": Milton
74 More logical
75 Coin in Kerman
76 Gourmand's preoccupation
77 Great fear
78 Prod
79 Permeable by liquids
80 Interact realistically
83 Money in Karachi
84 Frown
85 Weird
87 Lively: Mus. dir.
88 Larboard
89 Ancient people of Gaul
91 Father of Phineas
92 "—— Ape," Sedaka hit
94 Hack writer's output

Biblical Baseball

By Bert Rosenfield

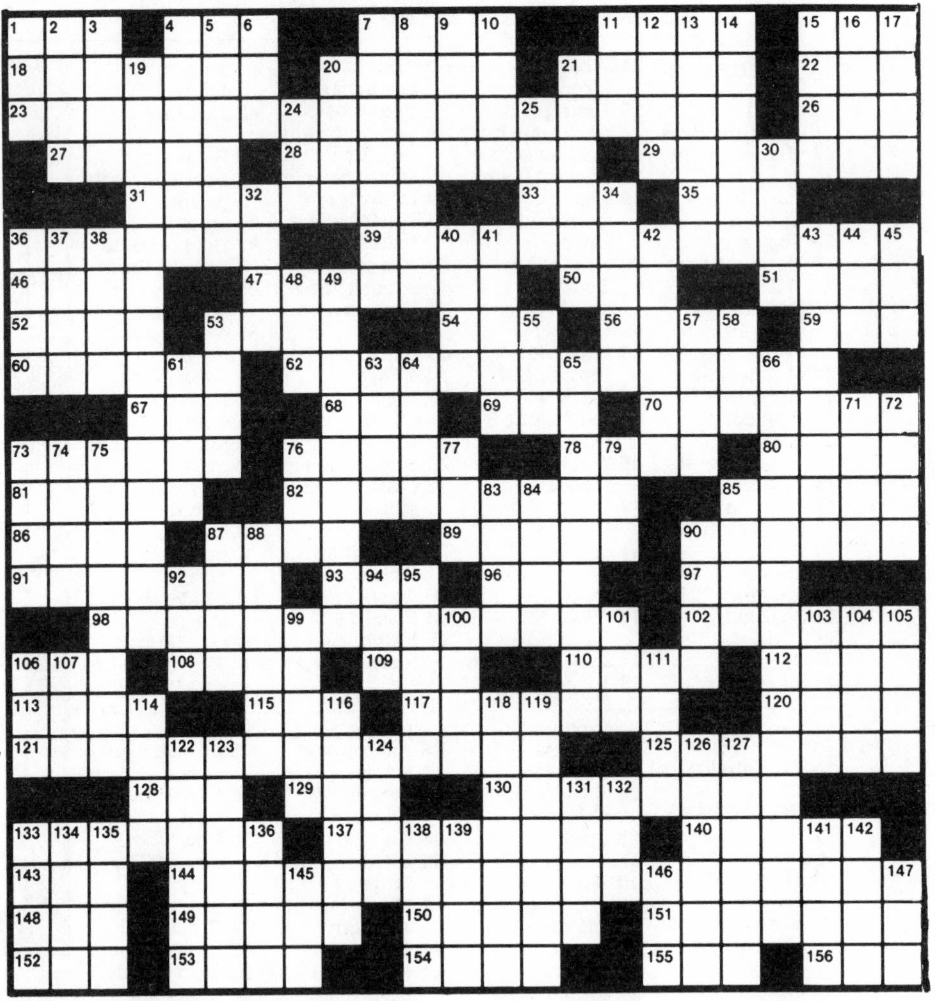

ACROSS

1 —— matter of fact
4 —— bodkins!
7 Police dept. calls
11 Shake —— (get going)
15 Pipkin
18 Fouls
20 Small land mass
21 Italian philosopher-historian
22 "—— Blue?"
23 JUDGES 15:4
26 Select for membership
27 Type of ball game
28 Of a bishop's authority
29 Seven —— (hybrid rose)
31 Water, figuratively
33 Hagen from Gottingen
35 Wedding-report word
36 —— Ike (Cliff Edwards)
39 II SAMUEL 17:26
46 Threshold
47 Former L.A. manager and family
50 Linowitz or Hurok
51 Vagrant
52 Musial
53 Nautical term
54 W.W. II agency
56 —— Hills of India
59 Box-score col.
60 Eclat
62 NUMBERS 13:33
67 Le Duc —— of Hanoi
68 Yugoslav city
69 U.S. missile
70 In a flutter
73 Keep —— (watch closely)
76 Bear Bryant was one
78 Outdo
80 Kin of shamrocks
81 Bedouin headcords
82 NUMBERS 11:32
85 Richter-scale item
86 "—— Marlene"
87 Many-headed missile
89 One of the Cyclades
90 Axis title, with "Der"
91 Diplomatic conflict
93 Bankbook entry: Abbr.
96 Sash for Suzuki
97 Creek
98 LEVITICUS 20:23
102 Rejoin
106 Dit's companion
108 "—— fishin'"
109 Drop a pop
110 Dawnlike
112 Painted metalware
113 When William II died
115 Singer Janis ——
117 Victor at Tiberias: 1187
120 Mediocre
121 II CHRONICLES 33:22
125 Graig of baseball
128 Clink; slammer
129 Subject in H.S.
130 Verdi's Ethiopian king
133 "Lucky" inning
137 Phil of hockey fame
140 Tissue layers
143 Comedian Olsen
144 LEVITICUS 25:35
148 Caucho
149 Aged: Abbr.
150 Black haws
151 Bumblebees
152 Face value
153 Diving duck
154 Clods
155 Mideast rep.
156 Shea player

DOWN

1 Univ. degrees
2 O'Casey
3 Burp-gun fodder
4 Copper-tin alloy
5 —— floss
6 Jacksonville-to-Tampa dir.
7 Home of Tennyson's Elaine
8 Inert medicament
9 Very well, in Verona
10 Norms: Abbr.
11 Indonesia's —— Islands
12 Yule fuel
13 Sea urchins
14 Race-starting words
15 Golfer Jerry
16 Moreno of baseball
17 They're hot at Belmont
19 PSALMS 26:1
20 Amazon dolphin
21 Pound works
24 Stanky and Ott
25 Veneer-shaping sheet
30 Georgia or Texas
32 One of three squares
34 In company with
36 Crimea's locale
37 Cheat on a check
38 Mongolia's —— Bator
40 Fuji's topper
41 Aides to execs.
42 Scotties' garb
43 Trolley's relative
44 Recede
45 "—— Hear a Waltz?"
48 Burdette of diamond fame
49 Part of simian motto
53 Soon
55 "—— Na Na" of TV
57 Canter, for example
58 White —— (termite)
61 "—— on first?"
63 Shensi province capital
64 Author Sholem ——
65 Confused
66 GENESIS 31:26
71 Hogarth's made progress
72 North Sea feeder
73 Steatite
74 Exchange premium
75 Flamboyant puffery
76 Between rg. and lg.
77 Kind of carrier
79 Tee preceder
83 Sound from Grimalkin
84 Island off Corsica
85 A Dafoe charge, for short
87 Portia tree
88 Like Bani-Sadr
90 Tarkenton
92 Savoyard monogram
94 Opp. of 6 Down
95 Artistic trunks
99 Norman and King
100 Farm machine, for short
101 Japanese carp
103 What a ewe grew
104 Otherwise
105 Cars of the 20's
106 Rad. x 2
107 Firing-range word
111 Hammerstein heroine
114 Grimm opener
116 Most precise
118 —— all (lowest)
119 Marvels at
122 Barbara and Clara
123 "O Canada," for one
124 Dace or plaice
126 Fragrant compounds
127 Actor Howard
131 Natives of: Suffix
132 Lon —— of Cambodia
133 Dinner beginner
134 Author Leffland
135 Swerve
136 Table d' ——
138 —— doble, corrida music
139 Sonoran stewpot
141 Throat-clearer's sound
142 Ireland, to a Gael
145 Big Detroit org.
146 March 15, in Milano
147 Colo. time

39

Silly-bus for Pun-dits

By Louis Baron

ACROSS

1 —— Archipelago
6 Pool
10 Mild oath
14 Preserves
19 City on the Mohawk
20 Book after "Typee"
21 Ubangi feeder
22 Hives
23 Course for grid illiterates?
25 Whiz-course in earth science?
27 Veered, as a boat
28 Asset for Godiva
30 Peer's mother
31 "—— du lieber!"
34 Haw's buddy
35 Recumbent
36 Stoop
39 Tin Pan Alley's Irving
41 Irgun Zvai ——
42 Less lenient
44 Like Mr. Milquetoast
45 Know-how for a country druggist?
48 Rocco's "Hurrah!"
49 Khachaturian
50 Doting
51 Met extra
52 Linen marking
53 "Junior"
54 Study of a crooner's lyrics?
58 Eclipse cycle
59 W.W. II craft
61 Street show
62 Refer
63 Meat treats
64 Golden Horde member
65 Ready for the sack
66 Lennon's "I Am the ——"
67 Like an oriel
68 "With . . . your —— your feet . . .": Exodus 12:11
69 Oak-to-be
70 D.D.S. who makes house calls?
72 Hoover, e.g.
74 Place to keep gds.
75 Garden tools
76 Angers
77 V.I.P.'s "wheels"
78 Thou, in Thiers
79 Sage at the gas pump?
83 Wadi
84 Vintage car
86 Anchor position
87 Large stain
88 Stern choices
89 Flynn
90 Foot: Comb. form
91 Pilot's dir.
92 Upward: Prefix
93 Cutter's cousin
94 Code word for T
96 Study of cab-caused pollution?
100 Science of reptilian tissue?
105 Handpicked group
106 Claque exciter
107 Quod —— demonstrandum
108 Venezuelan prairie
109 Poker verb
110 Founder of a state
111 The O'Hara mansion
112 Workable fact

DOWN

1 Moscow's mart
2 Hagen
3 Came to rest
4 Hurting
5 Symbol of purity
6 Indian symbol
7 Surrounded by
8 Army missile
9 Quack's prescription
10 Well-born
11 Brants, e.g.
12 Pub offerings
13 —— volente
14 Not thorough
15 Sacred asp
16 D.C. title
17 Defunct letter
18 —— sauce
24 Washstand item
26 Spot for a sale
29 "Arrivederci ——"
31 Documents, in Durango
32 Some Egyptian practitioners?
33 Doctor for red-blooded machos?
35 Lost, in Lyon
36 Tennis strokes
37 Alumni of Dr. Twinkletoes' classes?
38 Science of estate disputes?
40 Actor Alastair
41 Andrew and Fritz
43 Grizzled civet
45 Type assortments
46 Basket willow
47 Writer-diplomat
50 Edicts
52 Summons to court
54 Ship's petty officer
55 Man from Qum
56 Stuffed
57 Part of F.T.C.
58 Hiemal hazard
60 Wilkes-——
62 Inge's "—— of Roses"
64 Symphonic poem by Liszt
65 Not so bold
66 Use recklessly
67 Decorticate
68 —— throat
70 Functions
71 It was nothing, to Nero
73 Dayan of Israel
75 Man from Bombay
77 Citizen of Vientiane
79 She said "yes"
80 "The Time of Your Life" author
81 Other for José
82 Joel or Amos
83 Dark yellow color
85 Mambas' kin
87 Out of shape
89 —— marbles
90 Ristorante order
93 Tender
94 Bolshevism casualty
95 Mexican stew
96 Thrice: Comb. form
97 Chicken —— king
98 Midnight on Big Ben
99 Sitter's formation
101 Author Levin
102 Rustic pipe
103 African antelope
104 —— tov (Jewish holiday)

Possible Possessives

By Richard Silvestri

ACROSS

1 Hardy heroine
5 Lively dances
11 Tuck and Laurence
17 Send down
18 County in Texas
19 Overwhelm by argument
21 Actor's golf stroke
23 Certain secretaries
24 Sheep in its second year
25 Harmonica virtuoso
26 R.P.I. or F.I.T.
28 Gloomy
29 Transcript item
31 Traveling theatrically
33 Grid flag-thrower
34 Musical sheikdom
35 Educator's passage
39 Mil. decoration
42 Actor Jacques
43 Brooklyn developer
44 Bikini part
45 —— noire
46 It multiplies by dividing
48 Tea holder
49 Place for pins
51 Ludwig
52 Painter's achievement
56 Midway accomplice
57 Free
61 Having rounded projections
62 "Streetcar . . ." cry
63 A bee —— bonnet
64 Toothsome
65 Square dance V.I.P.
66 Dagger
67 January registrant
68 Cannery employees
70 Assume as fact
71 Citizen's foreign coin
73 Slaughter of St. Louis
74 Bombs
76 Mien
77 Kitchen utensil
82 Fissure
83 Promissory note
84 Olive genus
85 Bell attachment
86 Former campus org.
87 Doris's tennis ploy
91 1929 occurrence
92 "—— Mutual Friend"
94 Modern-day gramophone
95 Make straight
96 Axilla
99 Houston and Browne
100 Small American bird
103 W.W. II front
105 Juvenile apparel
107 Mrs. Skirvin
110 Hay-fever symptoms
111 Like Zeno
112 Young eel
113 Collar
114 Forcible restraint
115 Polygraph indications

DOWN

1 Wire
2 Leave home, in a way
3 Oft-bracketed word
4 Unfaltering
5 Beaufort-scale reading
6 Asseverate
7 Beat soundly
8 "Your place ——?"
9 P.D.Q.
10 —— Liberty
11 TV watchdog
12 What buffalo do
13 Hereditary
14 Blazing
15 Director's race
16 Anne and Marie
17 When we "spring ahead"
18 A.F.C. plus N.F.C.
20 Nice time of year
22 Pindar opus
27 Drinking glass
30 Nisan, formerly
31 Accolade for Manolete
32 Slightly cooked
34 —— glance
35 Facing the pitcher
36 Steaming
37 State flower of Utah
38 Con word
40 Partner of Meara
41 Wine stocks
45 Descried
47 Demon, in Arabic mythology
49 White elephant, e.g.
50 Plumbum
53 Orient
54 Natural abilities
55 Russian coin
56 More hackneyed
57 They call a spade a thpade
58 Chanted
59 Actress's sons
60 Muster
62 Analyze verse
64 Rebuff
67 Bottom-line items
68 Killy, e.g.
69 Unit equal to 200 milligrams
72 Presidential pooch
74 Cry heard at Elsinore
75 Lane of comics
78 Dies ——
79 Protect from depletion
80 Apostolic messages

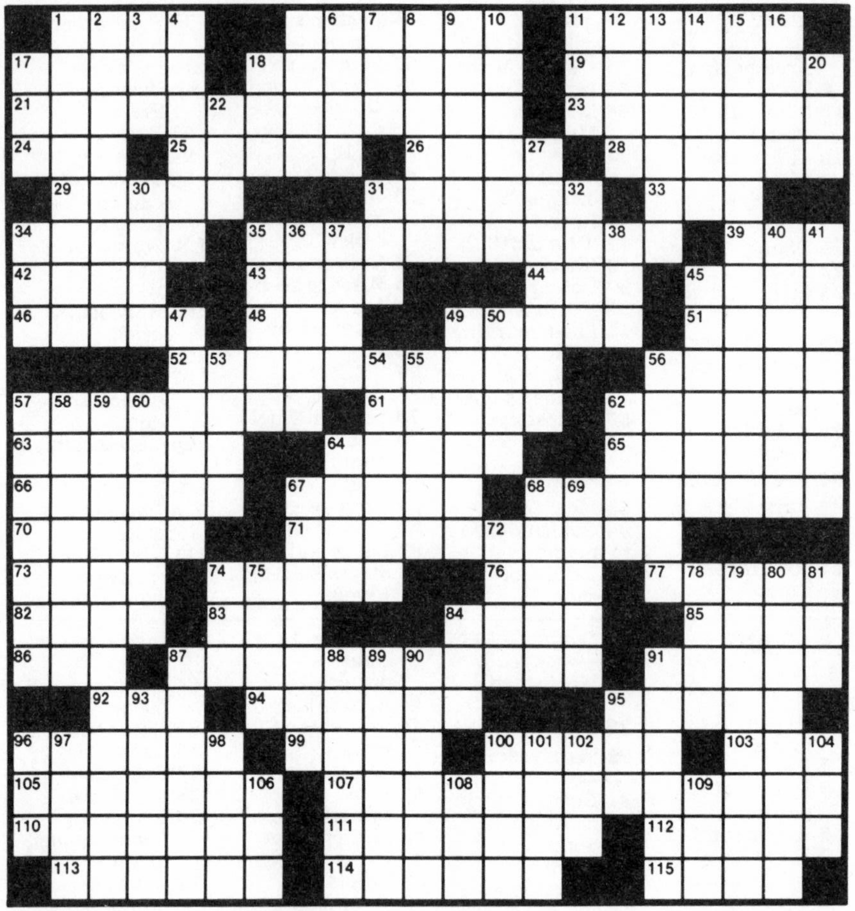

81 Kind of rm.
84 Surprised sound
87 Entablature part
88 Yoked
89 Mosaic gold
90 Rankle
91 Impart motion to
93 Shoe part
95 What this is: Abbr.
96 —— poetica
97 Writer Jaffee
98 After dos
100 D.V.M.'s
101 Rainbow
102 Fabulous bird
104 Atop, poetically
106 Speedy plane
108 Possess, in Edinburgh
109 Father of Phineas

Stepquote

By E.T.M.

ACROSS

1 Start of Stepquote
6 Pinch
11 Angular-measurement units
18 Props
19 Unbent
20 Resilient
21 Any La. county
22 Balzac
23 Stepquote source, for short
24 A neighbor of Ga.
25 Tendon
27 Antithesis of outgo
29 Bright saying
30 Liturgy
32 Stepquote: Part III
35 Scene of the Tell legend
36 Rialto
37 Vitiate
39 Merchandise
40 Associates of the Lincolns
42 Of a battery terminal
44 Send on a detour
46 Former initials at Cairo
47 Malefic
49 Immerse
50 Set of a sort
54 Love poem or song
58 "I cannot —— lie"
60 Facing a glacier
61 "Bullets," in poker
62 Ally of Abraham
64 Casabas
66 Army
67 Small flounder
68 Garnish for pasta
70 Major, in music
71 Furniture style
73 Slippery one
74 Budge
75 Durrell heroine
76 Bogged down
78 Incensed
79 Most rigid
81 Not Occidental
83 Winner at Gettysburg
86 Strike out
87 Noted cartoonist
88 Comply with an R.S.V.P.
90 More expensive
94 Makes a gleeful, snorting sound
97 Feet, to Fabius
99 —— acids
100 Red 1 and Blue 5
101 Sunglo, e.g.
102 Stepquote: Part V
104 "Star Wars" hero
105 A feast —— famine
106 Execration
109 "—— of snow-white horses"
111 Flange
112 Poe's adjective for Lenore
114 League of Nations seat
117 Autochthonous
119 Tidy
120 Los ——, N.M.
121 Not so fresh
122 Speaker of the quotation
123 Librarian's device
124 End of Stepquote

DOWN

1 Comic
2 Hamlet's friend
3 "—— tu," Verdi aria
4 —— up (spill the beans)
5 Stepquote: Part II
6 Gave abundantly
7 Peaked
8 —— Jima
9 Beautiful woman
10 First place
11 Shark's hanger-on
12 About 8 percent of earth's crust
13 Freshwater fish
14 Kabibble
15 Cossack chief
16 Strong smells
17 "Kenilworth" author
18 Capital of Laconia
19 —— of 1812
26 Dir. from Paris to Calais
28 Adjective for a koala
31 Nobelist in Physiology or Medicine: 1954
33 Prefix with plane
34 Stepquote: Part IV
36 Photographer married to Arthur Miller
38 Rikki-tikki-——
40 Dallas and Kowalski
41 Rackstraw and Deadeye
43 Bind up the wounds
45 Plaintiffs
48 Base for cosmetics
50 Liked
51 Note-pad artwork
52 Campaign concerns
53 "Lady Inger of ——," Ibsen play
54 Bovary, for one
55 University in Nova Scotia
56 Interdicts
57 Sifaka or potto
59 Chawbacons
63 Hero desired by Amneris
65 Was adequate
69 Rollers in Robespierre's day
72 Subways on the Continent
75 Soft candies
77 Does
80 Birthplace of Zeno
82 Caned
84 Take-charge person

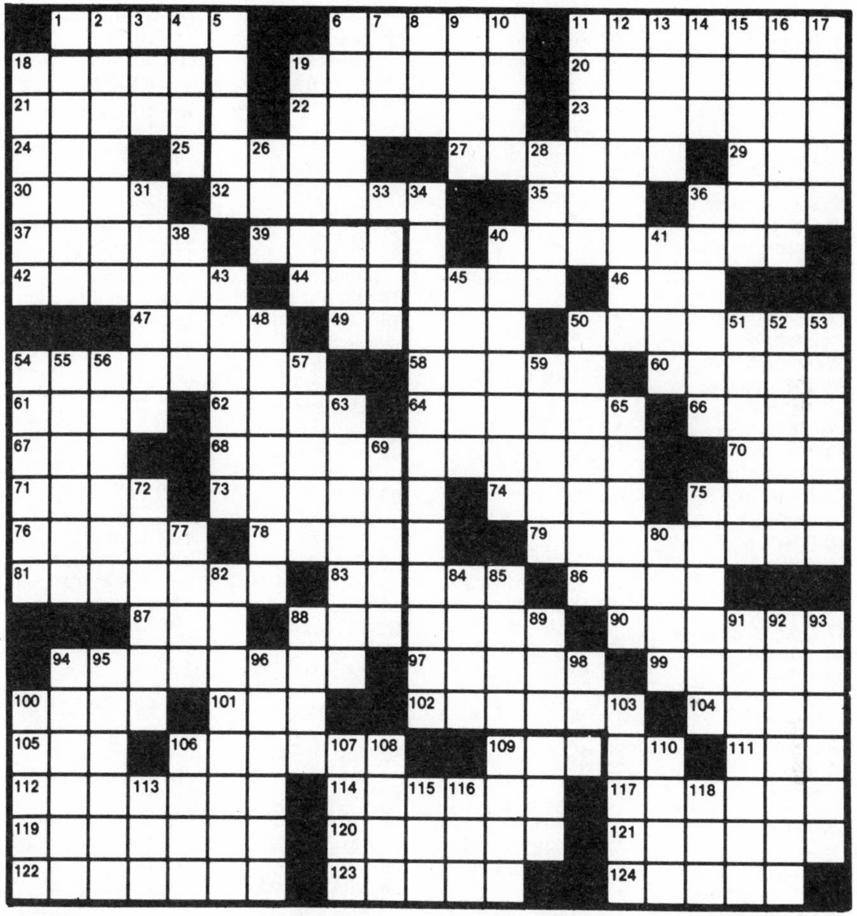

85 Try
88 Erect
89 Triangles
91 Popular song of 1926
92 Animate
93 Hostel patron
94 Role Hampden played 1,000 times
95 Unpleasant way to meet
96 Nice note
98 Sault —— Marie
100 Lincoln Memorial column style
103 Stepquote: Part VI
106 "Mary —— little . . ."
107 Hoople's cry
108 With 110 Down, a poet
110 See above
113 Kind of vb.
115 Cole or Turner
116 Friend, in Aberdeen
118 Comedian Conway

42

All's Swell

By Judith C. Dalton

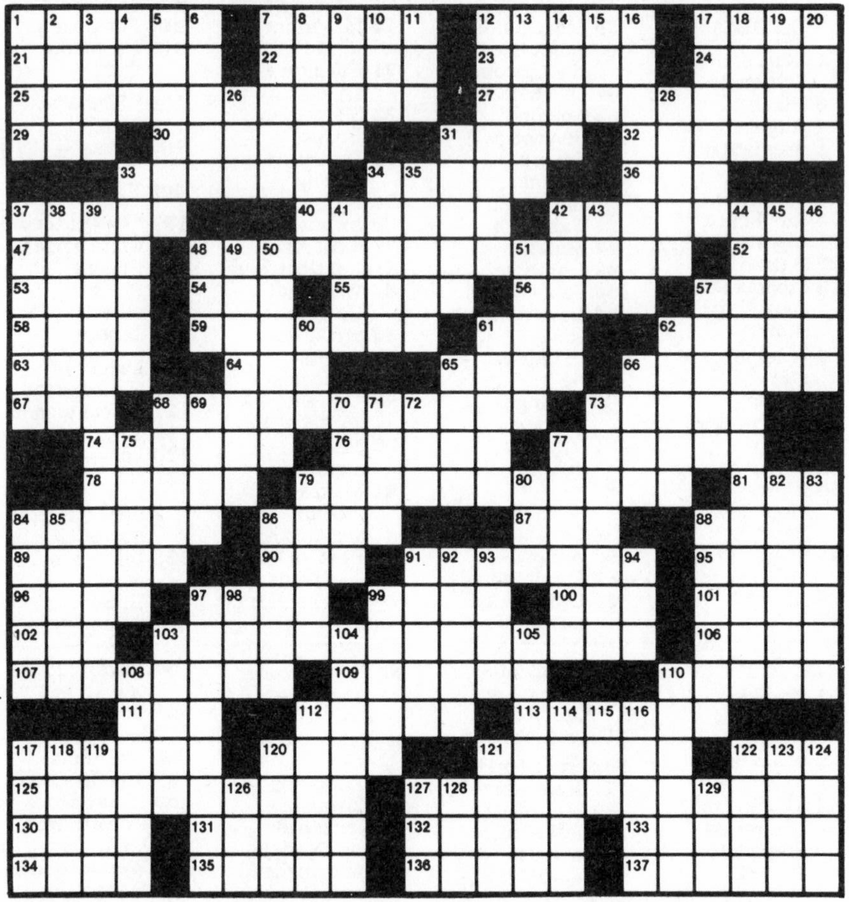

ACROSS

1 Fleet
7 Actress Dickinson
12 Moslem decree
17 Hunk
21 Sung by a group
22 Street show
23 Gets wan
24 Communica-tion prefix
25 Creative origin
27 Copperfield, perhaps
29 Asian holiday
30 G.I. groups
31 Actress Verdon
32 Bluish crystalline mineral
33 Zodiac twins
34 Way up or down
36 Upstate N.Y. school
37 Like a rainbow
40 Imitative
42 —— court
47 Silver salmon
48 Baseball commissioner, e.g.
52 Brit. sea backup
53 Winglike
54 Cost
55 Term papers: Abbr.
56 Decorate again
57 Wee one
58 Zeke's expletive
59 Oils
61 Mom's apple ——
62 Humble
63 Theologian William Ralph
64 Prince Valiant's son
65 Trampled
66 Winos
67 Summer drink
68 Pioneer's problem
73 Italian lawn game
74 Prayer
76 Terrier type
77 Pointillist Georges
78 Burglar, for one
79 Wise French warden
81 Sixth-sense letters
84 Egg or Island
86 Playbill heading
87 Old Sol
88 Italian wine region
89 Hornswoggles
90 —— -relief
91 Marmoset
95 Ballet lake
96 Edomites' leader
97 The Tentmaker
99 Beget
100 Chemical suffix
101 Hue
102 Tic follower
103 Starched camisole
106 Within: Comb. form
107 Item hinged to a gate
109 Himalayan language
110 Clothe
111 Former power agcy.
112 Follows orders
113 Twist, as a wrist
117 Haughty
120 An alum
121 Those apart
122 Here, in Paris
125 Little stem
127 Thomas Paine
130 It's on the watch
131 From head ——
132 Embellish
133 Have more warriors
134 Rigel, e.g.
135 Use up
136 Equanimity
137 Usurps

DOWN

1 Bank rec.
2 Korea's Syngman
3 Blanc or Cervin
4 Skill
5 Moved like a chickadee
6 Frighten
7 Fire crime
8 More shaggy, as a rug
9 Pâté de foie ——
10 Comparative ending
11 Small shriek
12 Wolsey's birthplace
13 Snake or crab
14 Astronaut Bean
15 Rep. antithesis
16 —— Santo (E Brazilian state)
17 Dzhugashvili
18 V.P. Morton
19 Settled
20 Eliot's Adam
26 Law, in Nice
28 Disney dwarf
31 Canters, e.g.
33 Gobel or Gershwin
34 Do sculpting
35 Track tipsters
37 Maine National Park
38 Legendary French hero
39 Movement
41 Middle pts.
42 Set loose
43 Shed
44 Thirsty albino hog
45 Foot joint
46 Three-spot cards
48 Silver cur.
49 Virtue model
50 Merle of movies
51 Diana's beloved
57 Puccini role
60 Raggedy doll
61 Lithograph, e.g.
62 Filthy wealth
65 Mountain lake
66 Clamorous
68 Feminine ——
69 Hebrew zither
70 Flees, as a feline
71 Rikki-tikki- ——
72 Inlet
73 Architect of St. Peter's
75 O.T. juniper
77 Saltwater food fish
79 Neck cloth
80 Juliette Low's org.
82 Podia
83 Piebald horses
84 Chanteuse Piaf
85 Invisible vapors
86 Toward the back of the ship
88 Toward the back of the ship
91 Like a canoe
92 Regions
93 European blackbird
94 Cluster of fibers
97 Invertebrates' sense organs
98 Negative prefix
99 Cruiser's asset
103 Weather period
104 Not yet in the oven
105 Monials
108 Chef, at times
110 French speaker
112 Acrylic fiber
114 Patronize Ma Bell
115 Bowl whistler
116 Toxophilite's item
117 Utah Beach craft
118 Leave out
119 Siamese king
120 Arena take
121 U.S. satellite
122 Beliefs
123 Chesterfield, for one
124 Serais
126 Choicest part
127 Nitwit
128 Fuss and feathers
129 Spenserian hag

Questionable Art

By Bert H. Kruse

ACROSS

1 Child saint
6 Wampum item
10 Professors' world
17 Please
18 Sore
19 Grassy stalks
21 Painter of "Hebrew With Tablet"?
23 Painter of "Potter's Wheel"?
24 Hebrew liquid measure
25 Computer data
26 Painter's need
27 Beachhead boat
28 Skipper's "Stop!"
31 Painter of "Fog Over Scotland Yard"?
33 German composer: 1840-76
34 Jewish festival: Var.
35 Legal right
36 Electrical unit
37 Actress North
39 Tokyo banjo
41 Choice pork cuts
43 Caught, as a dogie
44 —— -doing
45 Wordsworth work
46 Early Irish tenant
47 Lerner-Loewe hit
50 Painter of "Fish Market Purchase"?
53 Obtains
57 Papal garments
58 Harris's Fox or Rabbit
60 Drug plant
61 Level
62 Sails nearer the wind
63 Interrogate
64 Give off
65 White poplar
66 Star in Draco
67 Change
68 Used a hatchet
69 Gladiatorial loci
70 Stitch
71 York portraitist?
73 Have a sauna
74 Informal approval
76 Seat, with 77 Across
77 See 76 Across
78 Less fleshy
81 Pelota requirement
83 Meat slices
86 Elevates
87 Western athlete
88 Japanese measure
89 Came to
91 Steak order
92 He actually painted "Arbor Day"
95 Hudson contemporary
96 Outside: Comb. form
97 Musical key
99 Transfers a house plant
101 Prefix for light or night
102 Painter of "Drugstore Cowboy"?
104 Painter of "Ruth at the Plate"?
107 Musical sound
108 Great range
109 End of a Kansan's motto
110 Contends against
111 Parker of films
112 A time of your life

DOWN

1 Is successful
2 The Alhambra's city
3 Author Anaïs
4 Cousin of a Ph.D.
5 Big truck, for short
6 Journalist Heywood's family
7 Bridge positions
8 Bomb trial
9 —— Plaines
10 Dismays
11 Leave off
12 Together, in music
13 Pickle
14 Luther's foe
15 Lady Chatterley's lover
16 November winner
17 Moslem commanders
18 Confine a canine
20 Took forcibly
22 Time-honored
26 Hired-man Holden
29 Painter of "Telegraph Poles"?
30 Big hits
32 Dramatic spirit
33 Painter of "The Village Forge"?
37 Plumber's tool
38 Kind of down
40 Francisco and Paulo
41 Trini or Vincent
42 What carbon monoxide lacks
46 Glaswegian
47 Drinks
48 "To the mercy / Of —— stream . . . ": Henry VIII
49 Puzo subject
51 Kind of brain
52 Rank
54 Meet unit
55 Bodily tissues
56 Cynical look
58 "Ironside" actor
59 Call
63 Landing spot
64 Newsboy's shout
65 Spaces between veins of leaves
67 Tyrants
68 Med. subject
69 Guardhouse candidate
72 TV's Jones
73 —— reason (was logical)
75 U.S.S.R. river
77 Ashcan, etc.
78 Cunning
79 Thief of a sort
80 Book about CBS, by Gates: 1978
81 Poison-producing plants
82 State, to Mitterrand
84 Workers for William F. Bolger
85 Barbecue tools
88 Thickets
90 Iowa town
92 Ohio Senator
93 Threesome
94 Old Slavic group
97 Plaintive last words
98 Beat
100 Get a fly
103 Brandy measurement
104 Air Force member
105 Div. of Congress
106 Unclose, to Keats

Historic Headlines

By Anne Fox

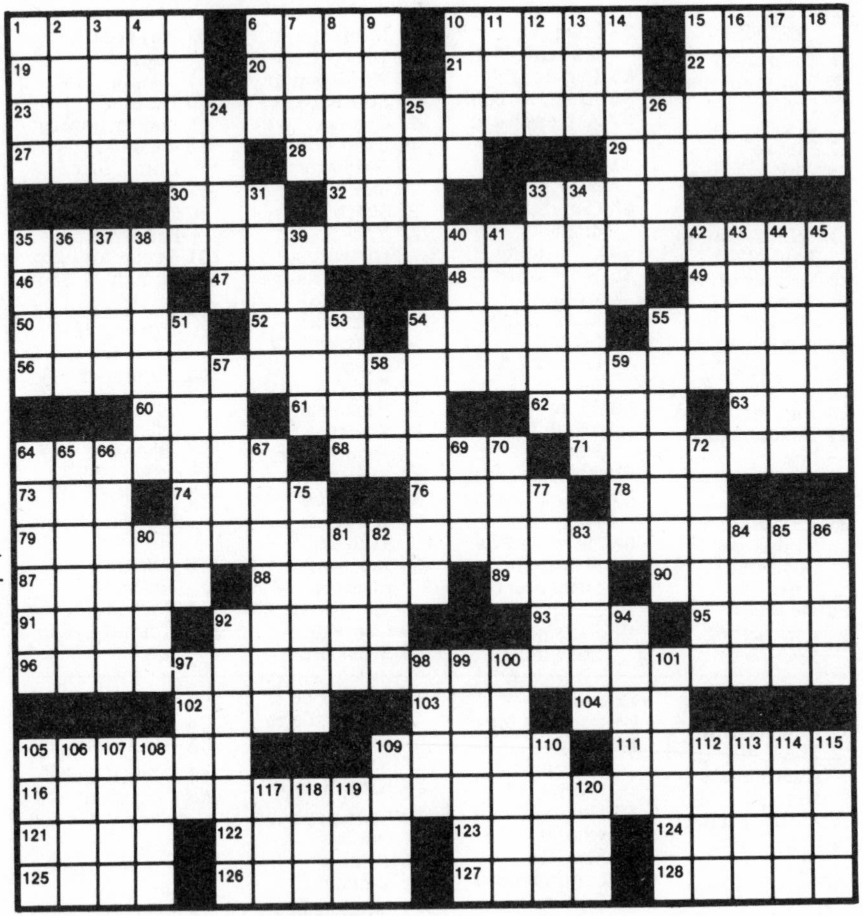

ACROSS

1 March figure, for short
6 Thin nail
10 Cheapskate
15 Storied lioness
19 Writer Segal
20 Aussie kangaroo
21 —— Gay (W.W. II plane)
22 Magician Henning
23 July 3, 1775
27 Globe
28 Egg: Sp.
29 Veranda
30 G.P.'s
32 Ike's command
33 Discordant
35 October 17, 1777
46 Russian sea
47 House wing
48 —— game (pitcher's coup)
49 Of the mouth
50 Stews
52 Thai language
54 Stone marker
55 Part of the arm
56 February 6, 1778
60 Its capital is Altdorf
61 Manx call
62 1922 play
63 "Le Coq ——"
64 Beach of Florida
68 Of Norse poetry
71 Custer busters
73 Word with long or now
74 ——-être (Marcel's maybe)
76 Site of Bryce Canyon
78 Lemon
79 July 16, 1779
87 Texas city
88 Accordion item
89 Arles assent
90 Strength
91 River to the Elbe
92 Nobelist in Chemistry: 1921
93 Cribbage card
95 Lady of Spain
96 September 23, 1779
102 La-di-da
103 Eras upon eras
104 Chosen, in Calais
105 Summing, e.g.
109 "—— beaucoup!"
111 Asian wild sheep
116 October 19, 1781
121 Type of bed
122 —— sanctum
123 Host
124 City on the Arkansas
125 Aleutian island
126 Certain trainee
127 Pottery pail
128 Companion-way

DOWN

1 Stitches
2 Gin
3 Phooey!
4 Hurt
5 Musical intervals
6 Entreat
7 O.T. book
8 Voltaire's real name
9 —— a turn (cooked perfectly)
10 100 centavos
11 Business abbr.
12 "Hitchy-——," Kern revue
13 Slippery ——
14 Bulwark
15 Wife of Skelton or Stengel
16 Polish city
17 Historic waterway
18 City on the Jumna
24 Cheek
25 Novello
26 Grass genus
31 Brooklyn's gift to opera
33 Building stone
34 Game like handball
35 Fishing hook
36 Côte d'——
37 Volume
38 Golf term
39 Demand as a right
40 Con
41 Pigeon follower
42 African antelope
43 California town
44 Boastful one
45 Changes
51 Predicaments
53 Finishing strip
54 Doll stuffing
55 Conclusions
57 Met basso
58 Land of ——
59 "Lone Eagle"
64 Phoebes
65 Mandarin, e.g.
66 N.J. governor: 1954-62
67 Military station
69 Possessive
70 "The Censor"
72 Martin-Preston vehicle
75 ". . . a tale —— an idiot . . .": Macbeth
77 Hecate's companion
80 1933 initials
81 Make over
82 Yucatán Indian
83 Daughter of Tantalus
84 Hep or hip
85 State bird of Hawaii
86 Start of a C. Moore poem
92 Alluring
94 Corporation rule
97 Sheet of stamps
98 Shorten sail
99 Biblical seamstress
100 Bis
101 Magistrates
105 U.S. satellite
106 Part of Q.E.D.
107 Turkish city
108 Asian republic: Var.
109 Cartoonist Walker
110 "La Douce"
112 Cloy
113 —— breve
114 Actress Virna
115 Munich's river
117 Genetic initials
118 Sake
119 Arikara
120 Man. campus

45

Title Search

By John M. Samson

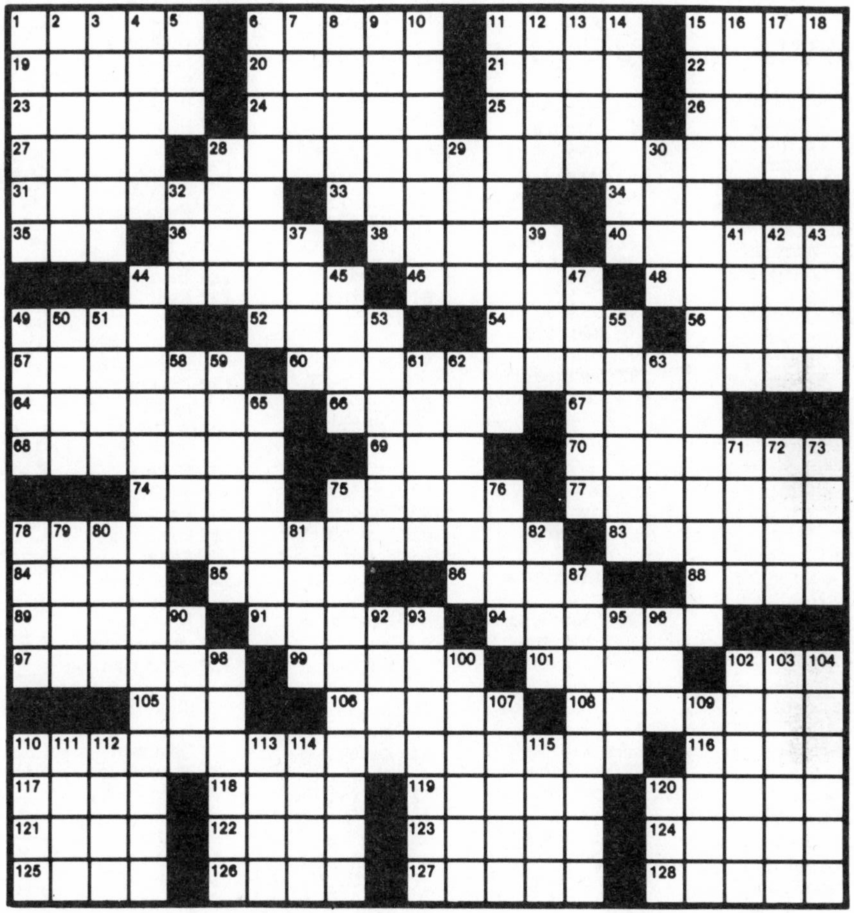

ACROSS

1 Margaret Chase——
6 Reduce drastically
11 Fortifies
15 Vidal
19 Asian capital
20 Some "pearls"
21 Arabian father
22 East German river
23 Cereal plant disease
24 AMPAS award
25 "——do anything better . . ."
26 Actress Simone
27 Cambodian monetary unit
28 Original title: "The Various Arms"
31 Boundless enthusiasm
33 "For—— sake!"
34 At once
35 Colony member
36 Grass cluster
38 Aforesaid
40 Harry's successor
44 Matador
46 ——Hills, former HUD head
48 Longhorn
49 Oriental maid
52 Disaster
54 She, in Somme
56 Hoagy or submarine
57 Deplore
60 Originally "Incident at West Egg"
64 Licoricelike flavoring
66 Swagger
67 Span
68 Underwriter
69 Basket part
70 Counts again
74 Prying
75 Toast or Moore
77 Ship's cargo
78 Originally "The Sea-Cook"
83 Dodgers' all-time h.r. leader
84 Fling
85 Walden, e.g.
86 Moselle tributary
88 Wall St. market
89 "Look Homeward, Angel," originally
91 Puccini opera
94 Timorous
97 Saratoga Springs, e.g.
99 An oil source
101 Fencing sword
102 Horned viper
105 Town in Spain
106 Novosibirsk names
108 Solve
110 Originally "Mag's Diversions"
116 Hawaii's state bird
117 "Trinity" author
118 Smart
119 Hazes
120 A legume
121 Ford's running mate
122 Thought
123 Happify
124 Summons by name
125 Rams' dams
126 Vaudevillian humor
127 Took out
128 Mountain ridge

DOWN

1 Himalayan guide
2 Maid of Sherwood Forest
3 Swallow
4 Instruments
5 "Evita," e.g.
6 Coddled
7 Whip
8 Org. founded by V. Herbert
9 Like some barrels
10 Deviationist
11 Originally "The Village Virus"
12 E antecedents
13 Ancient mariner
14 Resnick's "—— Shadow"
15 Originally "Ba! Ba! Black Sheep"
16 Norse god of war
17 "Biggest Little City in the World"
18 Quod—— demonstrandum
28 Excursion
29 Luzon native
30 Pledges
32 Noted Japanese statesman
37 Jog
39 Earthenware pot
41 Haws' opposites
42 Caraway or dill
43 Type of weight
44 Originally "The Lost Generation"
45 Ahs' associates
47 Saint Peter's has several
49 Russian mountain range
50 Horace, Thomas or David
51 Friends of Jourdan
53 Rhythms, to Shelley
55 Herons
58 Peter and a Wolfe
59 Gets ready to drive
61 Cross-examine
62 Cuban dances
63 Produce an effect
65 Timber disease
71 Knight's wife
72 After meds.
73 Withered
75 Roger Staubach, once
76 Course for a would-be g.p.
78 God of thunder
79 Straightedge
80 Love god
81 A son of Seth
82 Virginia——
87 Driven back
90 Trampled
92 "Fingal's ——"
93 Frightened
95 Remain undecided
96 Suffix with cash
98 Maneuver
100 French commander's order
102 Exact satisfaction
103 Barracuda
104 Crosby hit
107 Cordage plant
109 Keep—— to the ground
110 Dandy
111 In a rank
112 Depraved
113 Mass calendar
114 Buttress
115 Suffrage suffix
120 Bex or Dax

Phony Finales

By Tap Osborn

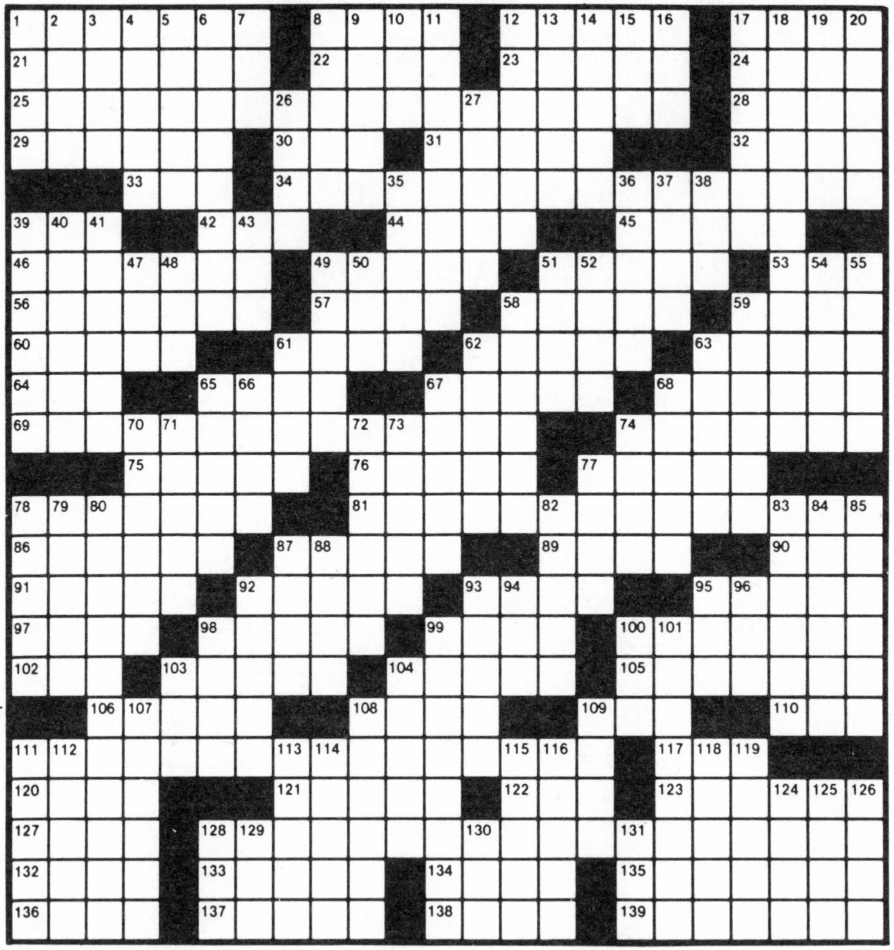

ACROSS

1 Huge
8 Maman's man
12 "Horse designed by a committee"
17 Loggia's cousin
21 Muscle Shoals' state
22 Cassini
23 Overhead
24 Overdo the toast
25 Napoleon's last words?
28 Tibet's "monster"
29 Shoelace receiver
30 Bot. or biol.
31 Spices from nutmeg
32 Boat chains
33 Cenozoic, e.g.
34 Composer's last words?
39 New London sight
42 Word with total
44 Like early press proofs
45 Wire: Abbr.
46 Soup or salad item
49 —— green
51 Chum, in Croydon
53 Joke
56 Caustic critics
57 Quechuan
58 Vacillate
59 Dwarf: Comb. form
60 Lacking guidance
61 Insipid
62 Doomed one
63 Family name of Pope Innocent XIII
64 For shame!
65 Ta-ta, in Tivoli
67 Furnace tender
68 Ornamental braid
69 "Hobo king" Livingstone's last words?
74 Bailsman's activity
75 Drew water
76 Springtime of life
77 Veranda
78 In harmony
81 Trotsky's last words?
86 Type of pigeon
87 Tuck, e.g.
89 A Waugh
90 Blanc or Brooks
91 Proprietor
92 In turmoil
93 Throb
95 Spot for a service pin
97 Ogden or Wallace
98 Decline with disdain
99 Impudent
100 War vessel
102 Corp. officials
103 Wander about
104 Like fruits
105 Celebrant
106 Unisonally
108 Java's neighbor
109 Feel out of sorts
110 Ending for arch or witch
111 Epitaph for Icarus?
117 Fountain order
120 Comedienne from Butte
121 Vichyssoise, e.g.
122 Hoary: Abbr.
123 Irish Cobbler
127 Religious statue: Var.
128 Final tribute to Pavlova?
132 Printer's mach.
133 Writer Michael
134 Bakery worker
135 Pointed out
136 Grant and Cobb
137 Boob-tube, in Brighton
138 Not one, country style
139 Peregrination

DOWN

1 Domesticate
2 "Now —— me . . ."
3 Track handle
4 White poplar
5 Identifier
6 Copycat
7 Preserve
8 Trespass
9 Janis or Ferguson
10 Indian salt mixture
11 Extreme self-conceit
12 Like some tunes
13 Caen clerics
14 Dewy
15 Second person
16 Irish sea god
17 This cuts a swath
18 Posthumous book by Bonnie?
19 "B" western
20 Coup command
26 Villa d' ——
27 Dress-shop fixtures
35 Tree that Frost swung on
36 Aquatic fish-eater
37 —— pressure
38 Not to be trusted
39 Nape
40 Muse for Hipparchus
41 Tank for heating water
43 Conceptual being
47 Latex yielder
48 Do a farm job
49 Test film
50 Memorabilia
51 Ponytail
52 Claim
54 Chekhov
55 On the way out
58 Deteriorate
59 Adjective for a Swede
61 Acomous
62 Conceded putt
63 Name before Doyle
65 One yielding
66 "—— Three Lives"
67 Handbill
68 Shaped like some shells
70 Cleansed
71 Baseball's "Big Poison"
72 Choice
73 Buddhist monk
74 Ignoble
77 Cadence
78 Left of the helm
79 Sears ——, Chicago
80 Rommel's last words?
82 Fine's partner
83 Pin with a stake
84 Seesaw
85 Queen
87 Kin of the twist
88 To laugh: Fr.
92 Loss of breath
93 Former scourge
94 Ski spot for Killy
95 Ullmann
96 Census question
98 Sound
99 Communiqué
100 Pt. of "T.G.I.F." workout
101 Backslid
103 Ape Sutton
104 Polynesian skirt
107 Ct. group
108 Nobleman's domain
109 Shoe part
111 U.S.M.A.
112 Early comic actor
113 Incantation
114 European blackbird
115 Newsman Morley
116 Ingress
118 Soft and fluffy
119 Moral code
124 Islets
125 Family ——
126 Song hit of yesteryear
128 Convened
129 Charlemagne's dom.
130 Edible root
131 Oft-heard vow

47

United They Stand

By Jim Page

ACROSS

1 Wild duck
6 Actor Morris
10 Voiceless sound
14 Wac's cousin
17 Showed more endurance in negotiations
19 Pathway
20 Abstract painter: 1879-1940
21 Hungary's Nagy
23 Annual tax for Hurd and Tracy
25 Hoosier introduces Fox to Fleming
27 Binnacle letters
28 Japanese religion
29 Tops at St.-Tropez
30 Start of the 14th century
31 Author read by Bando and Stevens
33 Common French verb
34 Winning
35 A Lauder
37 Small cavity
39 He played Marshal Dillon
41 Wee
42 Jrs. of yesteryear
43 Grants-in-——
44 Sullivan and Begley
45 Yield
46 L.B.J. pet
47 Sault —— Marie
48 Bartók and Lewis become tardy
52 "In a cavern, in —— . . ."
55 Wolf's threat
56 Arena prelims
58 Bruno Walter, for one
61 Route for Geronimo
65 Make over
66 Kind of angle: Abbr.
67 Dish shared by Byington, Young and Kesey
70 Wrap-up
71 A memorable Cobb
73 Duck, as an issue
74 Some British royalty
76 Mother of Perseus
78 Thrice: Comb. form
79 Answers
81 Surfacing traveled on by Davis and Smith
83 Chopper
85 Sothern or Harding
86 B'way signs
90 Liberian tribe
91 Ring name
92 Pitcher Young et al.
93 N.Z. aborigine
94 Rode the combers
97 Site of Red Square
99 Pointed
100 —— metabolism
101 Astronaut Bean
103 Strauss opera taken in by Parseghian and Abzug
106 Island for honeymooners
107 Billy or Pete
108 Irish statesman Eamon De——
109 Assn. for "Dr. J"
112 Plant sown by Alpert and Helen's abductor
114 Quartz mined by Hudson and Gayle
116 Warriors that sound mischievous
117 Eden throwaway
118 Contemporary of Dashiell
119 Roman conqueror's victim
120 Inquired, in Dogpatch
121 Belles in a fold
122 Ending for fun or pun
123 Straits

DOWN

1 Bribes
2 Rods for "Fats"
3 Bore witness
4 Bring into play
5 Soup garnish
6 Cap worn by Campbell and Moore
7 Kin of ravers
8 Concert bonus
9 Predecessor of aitch
10 Edged along
11 Of the forearm bone
12 Aden-to-Suez waterway
13 "Agnus ——"
14 Rifle used by Elliot and Arthur
15 Ecclesiastical vestments
16 Brawl
18 Gold Coast tongue
22 Bagnold or Markey
24 Fraternity ——
26 Smollett and T. Williams heroines
29 Disguise
32 Classic wanderer
35 Catchall abbr.
36 Bishopric
38 Cereal grain
40 Electrical unit
42 Granada girl
46 Parts of lamps
47 Hidden obstacles
48 Bric-a-——
49 "Gandhi's Truth" author et al.
50 Moslem prince
51 "I —— Know What Time It Was"
53 Parts of dols.
54 Steinbrenner, for one
55 Bellyache
57 Covers with topsoil
58 Gelatin shaper
59 Position on the briny
60 Actress Verdugo
62 G.I. at boot camp
63 "Over ——"
64 Admit
68 Bibliography entry
69 Breed of pigeon
72 Kind of start for Nicklaus and Maranville
75 Attack verbally
77 Lobe weather-protector
80 Pedestrian run over by John and Nancy
82 Postage——
83 Without equal
84 Letters from Greece
87 Sentimental
88 Galena is one
89 Partner for Imogene
91 Accumulates
92 British boat
93 Native of Indonesia
94 Strategic island in the Baltic Sea
95 Seizes, as a throne
96 Scopes trial figure
98 Frolic
100 Fortune, to a gypsy
102 River of France
104 Bird's bill: Fr.
105 Slips up
110 Set of elevators
111 Foamy brews
113 Red Baron, e.g.
114 In medias——
115 Dir. at sea

Typographics

By Maura B. Jacobson

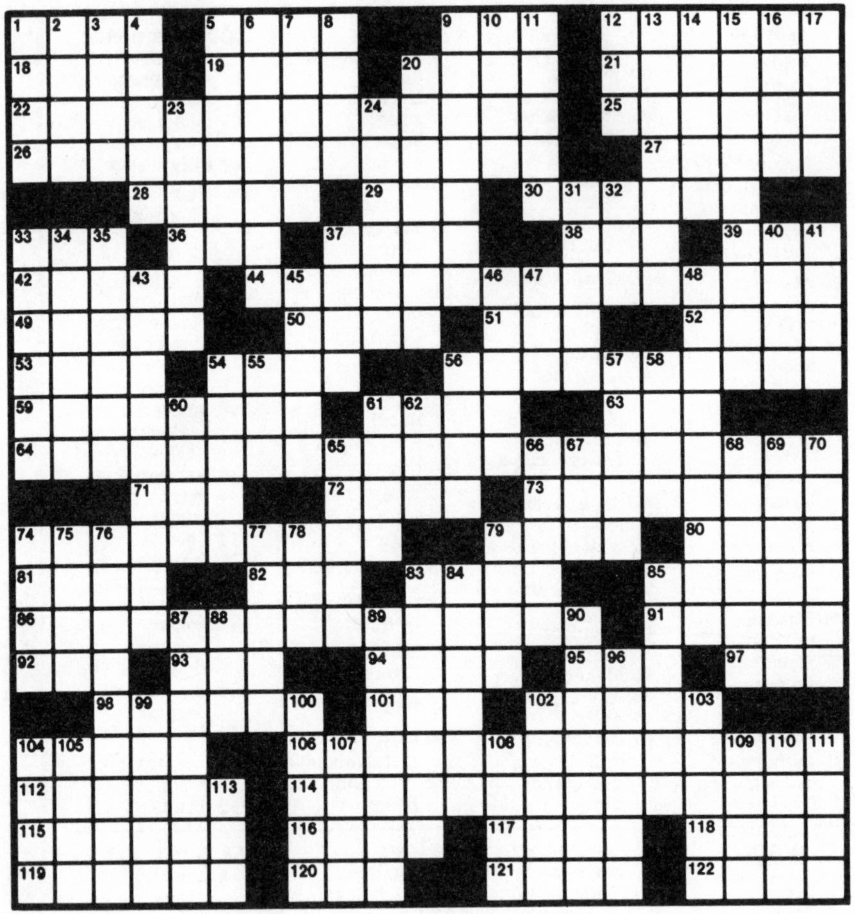

ACROSS

1 Borge is one
5 L. A. problem
9 Literary monogram
12 African tree
18 To —— (unanimously)
19 Muchacha's home
20 "Pretty maids all in ——"
21 Baltimore player
Kit **22**
25 Taft's successor
26 Look
27 Gustos
28 Exclude
29 Haul
30 Kyoto sight
33 Slithery slayer
36 Author Deighton
37 Ocean motion
38 Soprano Merriman
39 Modern: Prefix
42 Shoulder covering
44 1 c. ◊
49 Marner of Raveloe
50 Abbr. in Reykjavik
51 Caviar
52 Roman poet
53 Balin and Claire
54 Fris. followers P
56 Path t h
59 Less shaky
61 Actress Lee
63 Faucet word
64 2 4 1,1 trousers
71 Col. Stoopnagle, for short
72 Greek peak
73 Frigid edifice
74 5,280′ 5,280′
79 Those girls, to Juanita
80 Sky Bear
81 "Play It —— Lays": Didion
82 Be in the red
83 Apache's victim
85 Van Gogh view
86 A M
91 Gregg specialist, for short
92 Bantu, for one: Abbr.
93 Pastoral place
94 Fortune
95 Kind of room
97 Lair
98 Pucci of fashion
101 Carp's kin
102 Vapors
104 Word with well or way
106 80 oz. ♪ ♪
112 Acid salt
114 60′ ——
115 Aspiring doctor's course
116 Moss or Lorenz
117 Old Norse poetry collection
118 Klemperer
119 Step smartly
120 S
121 A proverbial seven
122 Encounter

DOWN

1 Paints quickly
2 Mine, in Monaco
3 Salve
4 Signed off
5 Penman
6 Unhealthy: Sp.
7 Basketry twig
8 Outlaw outfit
9 Farm-club member
10 Autumn pear
11 Chimney or clean follower
12 Archer's need
13 Grand Canyon State
14 Did a grease job
15 Latin dance
16 "Thanks ——!"
17 Hecht and Vereen
20 Lacking a tail
23 Actor Tom and family
24 Former Pacific island group
31 & EE
32 Merry, in Metz
33 Act the aide
34 Samurai's faith
35 Prehistoric: Comb. form
37 Gumshoes
40 Wife of Geraint
41 Bookie's quote
43 Could
45 TNT ingredient
46 Capital of Pas-de-Calais
47 Also
48 Mock trial
54 Between rho and tau
55 Yanks of W.W. I
56 Durrell heroine
57 Rears up
58 Portnoy's creator
60 —— Irae
61 Flubbed the game
62 Entrance signs
65 Composer Ned
66 Buffalo
67 N.Y. skyline letters
68 Practiced pitching
69 Ascetic of old
70 Add spice
74 Name in spydom
75 "Time —— the essence"
76 Graduate of a school for the deaf
77 Yellow Sea gulf
78 Reverence plus fear
79 Musician Satie
83 Circumspect
84 Become an M.A. at Cambridge
85 Climb
87 Played the coquette
88 —— Aviv
89 Cromwell and Twist
90 Andalusian city
96 Book of the Apocrypha
99 Home of the Dolphins
100 Son —— soil
102 —— Maupassant
103 Gomorrah's partner
104 Uses a straw
105 Legal wrong
107 "—— a King in Babylon": Henley
108 Hear ye!: Var.
109 Thames gallery
110 Tasso's patron
111 Close-up, e.g.
113 Arnhem's neighbor

49

Literal Translations

By Bert Rosenfield

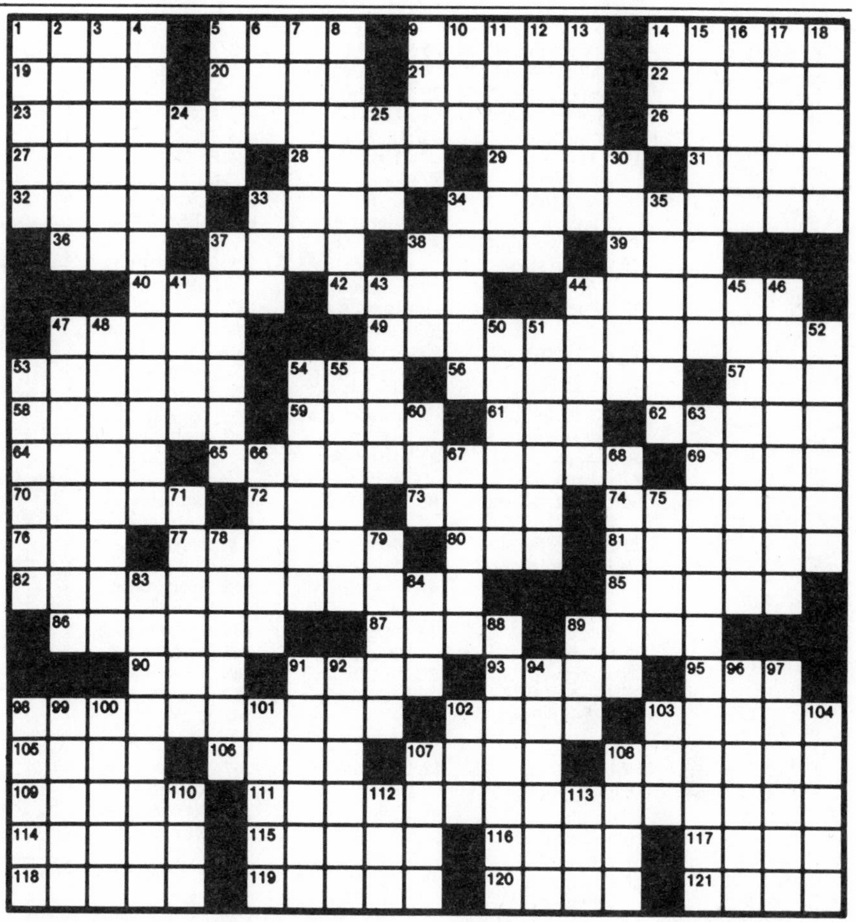

ACROSS

1 Grant from Bristol
5 Twenty quires
9 Slide calculators
14 Seaport in Honshu
19 Cruising
20 Gumbo ingredient
21 God of festive joy
22 Sub detector
23 Swatow supermarket workers
26 Good will
27 Sound of wind chimes
28 Jack of silent westerns
29 Radio time signal
31 Author Kazan
32 "—— Thee Every Hour": Lowry
33 "Te ——," ancient hymn
34 Vert
36 Prior to, to Prior
37 Like the cosmos
38 October quaffs
39 Parts of a cen.
40 Faucet problem
42 End-of-summer event
44 Quaker grays
47 Did a blacksmith's job
49 Fandango and tango
53 "I never hope to ——": Burgess
54 Second follower
56 Fitzgerald song word
57 Lair for Leo
58 Textile machine
59 "Symphonie Espagnole" composer
61 Pop's companion
62 Painting on dry plaster
64 One-sixth drachma
65 Madras masseur
69 Prefix meaning south
70 Scoring plays, in rugby
72 Mid-April letters
73 Neighbor of Ark.
74 Pad for Odin
76 She was also called Aurora
77 Makes out
80 Air: Comb. form
81 Logician's boo-boo
82 Candelae
85 Light refractor
86 Gene and Grace
87 Olympic hawk
89 Warren Beatty film
90 Former Riga coin
91 River in Russia
93 Perpetually
95 Presidential monogram
98 Harry Lauder recording
102 Blackleg in Bristol
103 Marine hazard
105 High-school subj.
106 Soprano Berger
107 Rotated
108 Old Asia Minor region
109 Whence a phoenix arises
111 Perth traffic jam
114 Cubic meter
115 Small role
116 "—— boy!"
117 Sports org.
118 "—— mud in your eye!"
119 "—— Dream," Wagner aria
120 Display behind a bar
121 City of the Huguenots

DOWN

1 Mojave flora
2 Glittering
3 Fritz or Rob
4 Sketch by Sam Adams
5 A Kennedy
6 —— out (supplement)
7 Curves
8 Elephant drivers
9 Bank holding: Abbr.
10 Florida's —— Singing Tower
11 One-celled animals
12 Preservers
13 Japanese immigrant to U.S.
14 Explorer Johnson
15 Author Maugham
16 Old-womanish
17 Porter's "—— Went to Haiti"
18 Indo-European
24 Antiquity, to Poe
25 Ulmaceous tree
30 Soul or self
33 Dip bait lightly
34 Kilt feature
35 Grains for grinding
37 "Esse Quam ——," N.C. motto
38 Zugspitze, e.g.
41 Descartes
43 Places of refuge
44 "—— no questions . . ."
45 Washington's foes
46 Entire extent
47 Controversial nuclear site in N.H.
48 Bravery, in Bayeux
50 What Jack has to be
51 Line on a weather map
52 Hair securers
53 Sea duck
54 Moon man No. 2
55 Reached by radio
60 Pelf for Pizarro
63 Attachments on Rolls-Royces
66 Palm trees
67 Fiat
68 File
71 1066 battle site
75 Cagliari native
78 Implement for Father Time
79 The nominees
83 Rational
84 Historic period
88 Lay
89 Johnny ——
91 Kind of training
92 Bursts of energy
94 "Behold, all is ——": Eccles. 1:14
96 Comfort
97 Its flag is red, white and blue
98 Tennis stroke
99 Varna, for one
100 Colette's "The —— One"
101 Part of a harness
102 Saratoga is one
103 Like Chablis
104 Refrain notes for Figaro
107 Angels' favorite signs
108 Library treasures
110 French possessive
112 Historic Boston jetsam
113 Goddess of infatuation

Military Review

By Herb L. Risteen

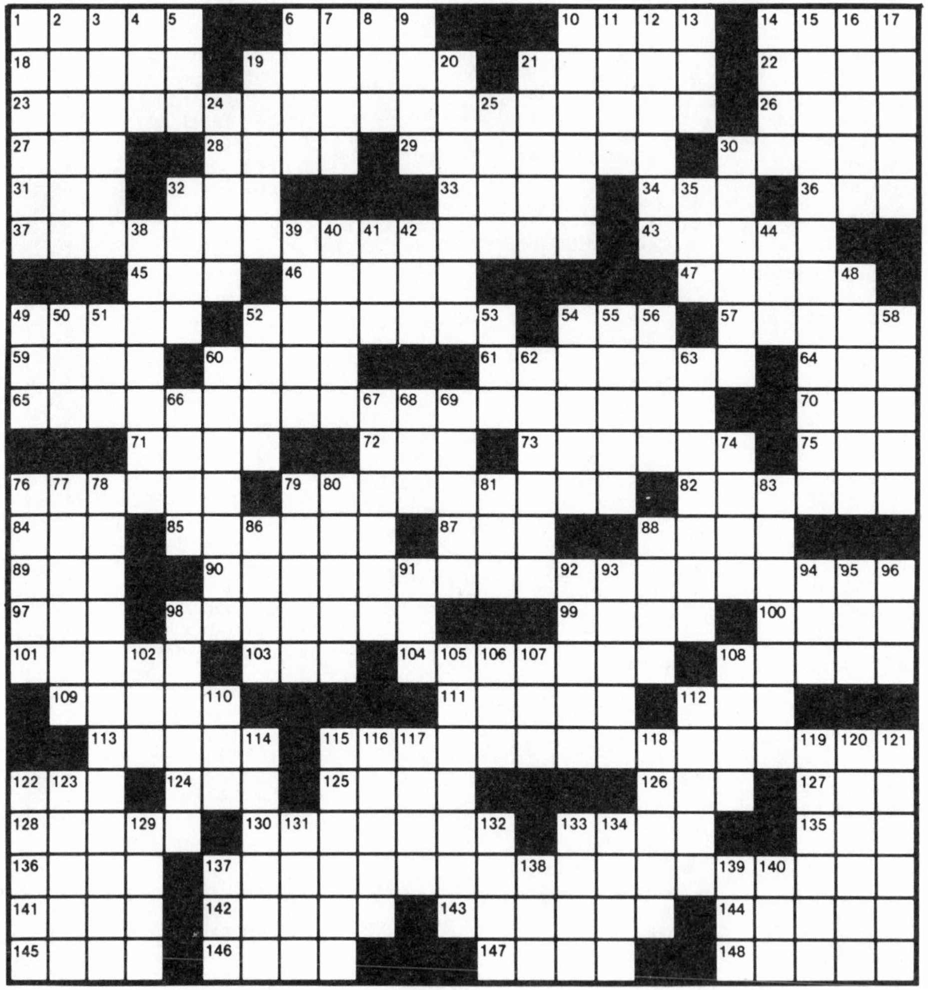

ACROSS

1 Get together
6 Branchling
10 Implore
14 Arabian sultanate
18 Like Lerner's "Day"
19 Devilfish
21 "Oh, give me ——. . .": Higley
22 Biblical trio
23 Kipling classic
26 Siege of Troy hero
27 —— burner
28 Contemporary pact
29 Claims
30 Herd
31 "Three Men —— Horse"
32 Thus
33 Marquand sleuth
34 Albuquerque-Springfield dir.
36 The —— Baron
37 Dixie notable
43 Indian title of respect
45 Mesabi Range product
46 Ray ——, noted manager of boxers
47 Gauchos' gear
49 Custer's last ——
52 Sweet rocket, e.g.
54 Small amount or degree
57 Lyon laughs
59 Fare for Dust Commander
60 —— the dogs
61 Qum native
64 "None —— the brave . . ."
65 State official
70 Heavenly Altar
71 William —— Benét
72 Sweep
73 Shearer et al.
75 Kind of doll
76 Battologize
79 Excite pleasantly
82 Use sonar
84 Attention
85 Singer from Brooklyn
87 —— -leaf cluster
88 Hebrew lyre
89 "—— was saying . . ."
90 Federal officials
97 Gun a motor
98 Agon
99 Graceful tree
100 "Counter-Attack" star: 1945
101 Allay, as thirst
103 Title Drake held
104 Metal urn
108 Righteous
109 —— a march on
111 Consumers' champion
112 Witticism
113 Facilitates
115 They help hizzoner keep order
122 Actor Ferrer
124 "Cap'n ——"
125 Baseball family name
126 Statute
127 Billing time: Abbr.
128 Like campus buildings
130 Servants
133 Be downcast
135 Clock-dial number
136 Source of obsidian
137 Application of the hickory stick
141 Picnic treats
142 Member of an Eastern church
143 Complained bitterly
144 Agra attire
145 Love ——
146 Soy or Roy
147 Equal
148 Lock

DOWN

1 Nebraska city
2 Arthurian lady
3 Go back to the drawing board
4 Roscoe
5 Caesarean or Alexandrian
6 The Army's alpha was one
7 Home of the Baylor Bears
8 Nigerian native
9 Trinket
10 Carbolic-acid source
11 Crucifix
12 Diverts
13 Sycophant's response
14 A famous Bradley
15 G.B.S. play
16 Desert plant
17 Put the kibosh on
19 Not quite a mess
20 Violinist's vibration
21 Quartz variety
24 Pack —— (refrigerate)
25 Egyptian god
30 Do a ranch job
32 Irrational number
35 Collar
38 Haircut for a fra
39 Conference site: Feb. 1945
40 Sing like young Bing
41 Where would-be offs. are trained
42 Bandleader Brown
44 Lake Balkhash feeder
48 French Pointillist
49 Scale note
50 Bangkok dweller
51 Was corrosive
52 Radius or scapula
53 When Henry II invaded Italy
54 Playing card of a sort
55 "Gun" girl
56 Fashion name
58 Put on
60 Relative of Gay-Pay-Oo
62 Transform
63 Asian salt lake
66 Agua or bufo
67 Tribal emblems
68 Merry, on the Marne
69 Flat plinths
74 Before long
76 Puts up
77 Atelier equipment
78 Noel Coward play
79 "Good-bye" composer
80 Prefix with line and section
81 Map line: Abbr.
83 Stradivari's hometown
86 Belgian city
88 Antiquing device
91 U.S. satellite
92 Split
93 Show surprise
94 Capek classic
95 Collection
96 Diamond ——
98 Desisted
102 New Zealand parrot
105 Gaunt
106 Clarke or Murray
107 Harem room
108 Hershfield's Homeless Hector
110 Gaelic sea god
112 Linear units
114 Writer de Beauvoir
115 Oriental boat: Var.
116 Prufrock's creator
117 Cannon sound
118 Flavorful
119 Patriot of '75
120 French friars
121 Strikes
122 Fine straw hat
123 Sidestep
129 "—— Lyne"
131 Silkworm
132 Direct insult
133 U.S.M.A. mascot
134 Unique thing
137 —— Scout
138 Quiche Lorraine, e.g.
139 He defeated T.E.D.
140 Damage

Charger Account

By A. J. Santora

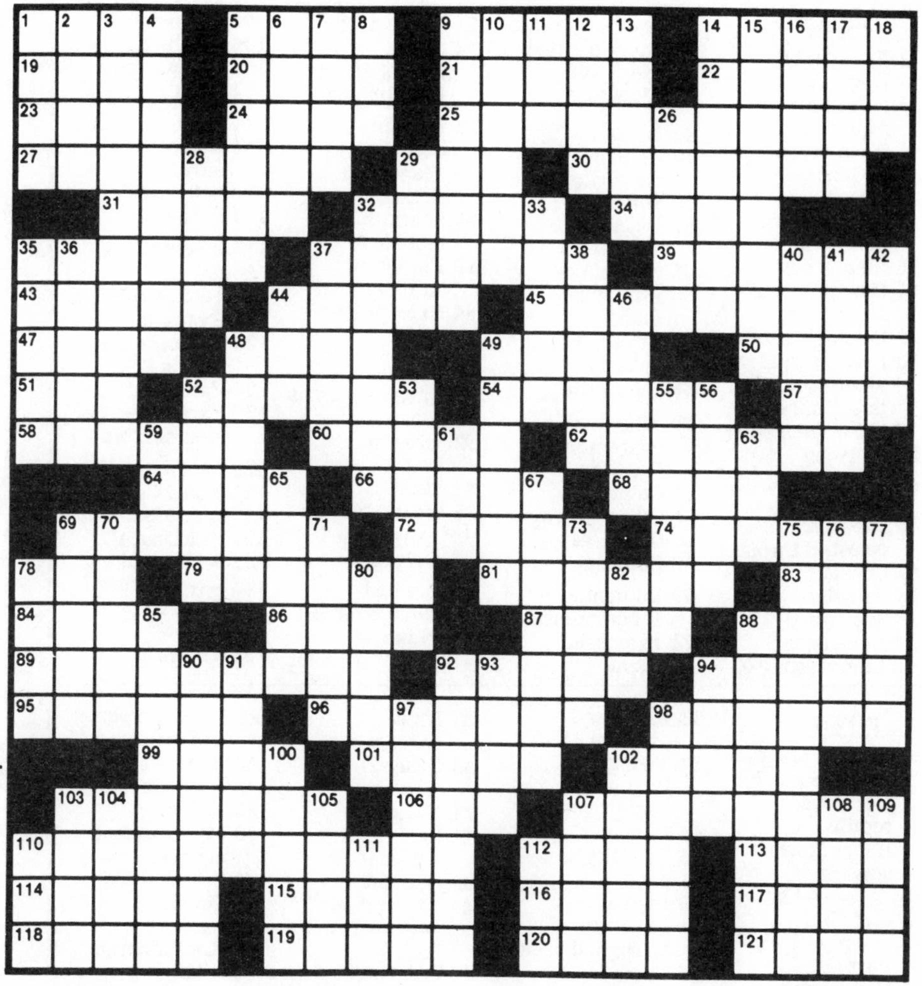

ACROSS

1 Plenty of horn
5 Gold chaser
9 Swiss miss of fiction
14 Horse-drawn carts
19 —— for one's money
20 Golden-rule preposition
21 Per —— (yearly)
22 Famed columnist
23 NATO is one
24 Delaware, to Lafayette
25 Favorite horse of Richard II
27 Odin's eight-legged mount
29 Keelbird
30 Travers winner: 1876
31 Make a call
32 Rings —— (registers)
34 Schoolboy's collar
35 Pallas ——
37 An equine color
39 Ascended
43 Turf
44 Picture puzzle
45 Don Quixote's nag
47 "Aloha" city
48 Trademark
49 Creator of Lena the Hyena
50 Port of Okinawa
51 Old French coin
52 Rinaldo's bay horse
54 Toad or frog
57 "My kingdom —— a horse!"
58 Wise counselor
60 Fortune-teller's card
62 Winged horse of fable
64 Kind of sch.
66 Original first name of John Paul II
68 Chalet feature
69 Black —— (Warwick's horse)
72 Talking bird
74 Mexican liquor
78 Tim —— (1958 Derby winner)
79 "Moonlight ——"
81 At the summit
83 Unclose, to Donne
84 Downfall
86 Horselaughs, in a way
87 Five-time Presidential also-ran
88 On —— (equal)
89 Caligula's equine
92 Accesses
94 Don's January
95 —— d' (headwaiter)
96 Napoleon's white horse
98 Sparse
99 Prison outbreak
101 View halloos
102 Horse's saddle strap
103 Set of open shelves
106 Horsy refusal?
107 Furor
110 Favorite horse of Richard III
112 Swain
113 Equal, in Nice
114 Candy stripers
115 Maquillage item
116 Annapolis sch.
117 Blackbird
118 Ridge on a horse's neck
119 Lee's Traveller
120 Chinese dynasty
121 Devine or Hardy

DOWN

1 Bugler's job
2 U.S.S.R. river
3 Alexander the Great's war horse
4 Protagonist of a sort
5 Chaperone
6 Loosen
7 Dark —— (1953 Derby winner)
8 Infant
9 Kind of racing
10 Anoints, old style
11 Needle —— haystack
12 Importunes
13 Dye; tinge
14 Like the U.S. in 1865
15 Mother Teresa's mother tongue
16 "No man —— island"
17 Myrna Loy role
18 Hale or Hari
26 Asian range
28 Walden, e.g.
29 "—— Ben Adhem"
32 Mohammed's winged horse
33 Navigational aid
35 Blanched
36 Once and again
37 Sired
38 Finish, informally
40 Fouled up
41 Community standards
42 —— beer
44 Rogers or Clark
46 Carousal
48 Horse-opera locale
49 "—— Hot Tin Roof"
52 Dogie entangler
53 "Equus" etc.
55 Lizards
56 Kind of orange
59 —— Aviv
61 Suffix with audit or transit
63 His, in Nice
65 North Dakota city
67 Chihuahuas, e.g.
69 Steam bath
70 Pompey's pals
71 Book of the Bible
73 Sacred: Comb. form
75 Wellington's horse
76 Separated
77 Horse trainer Jolley
78 Svelte
80 That is ——
82 Dan Rather's milieu
85 Fertilizers
88 Curse
90 Most hackneyed
91 Epochs unlimited
92 Slowed up
93 Part of S.R.O.
94 Beige
97 Call a spade a club?
98 Dakota Indian
100 City on the Loire
102 Sigurd's magic mount
103 Fan sound
104 Word with raw or horse
105 Yonkers race
107 Black —— (Dick Turpin's mare)
108 —— Ridden (1958 Epsom winner)
109 —— Sloper (1915 Grand National winner)
110 G.I. Jane
111 Regret
112 Word of protest

Suiting Sound to Nonsense

By Arnold Moss

ACROSS

1 Founder of Dogpatch
5 Nickname for Aqueduct Race Track
9 "¿Quién —— ?"
13 Scorch
17 Longfellow's bell town
18 Manila hemp
20 Houdini's real name
22 London's subway
23 French window
24 Shakespeare's tamed shrew
26 Norwegian river
27 Collision
29 Actor Alan from N.Y.C.
30 Guardians of a celestial throne
32 Cockloft
34 Growlers
36 Sea squirt
37 Nobelist in Literature: 1909
40 Lower or resign
42 Climbing plants
45 Mayan or Mundane
46 Drink noisily
48 English county bordering Wales
50 Staring
51 C.I.A. operatives
53 Kind of tide
55 Philippine mahogany
57 Ariosto's patron
58 Fuliginous
60 "Romola" character
62 Robe for Calpurnia
64 Plural endings
65 On the way
67 Pungent
69 Influential acquaintance
71 Indonesian island
72 Stoneworts
74 "—— Perpetua," Idaho motto
75 Printer's dummy
78 Flanders of fiction
79 Seurat's technique
83 Father, in Arabia
84 Hide the loot
87 Upholstered couches
89 Parts of pippins
90 Glove leather
92 "Slammin' Sam"
94 Betel
95 Starts' partners
96 "Angélique" composer
98 Biblical witch's home
100 "Like ——, all tears": Hamlet
103 Lincoln note
104 —— blanches
106 Rental sign
108 Word game
110 Medicinal plant
112 Defeated narrowly, with "out"
114 Proboscis
115 Indemnify, in law
118 Tonic water, e.g.
120 Evaluate
123 Napoleon won here in 1796
124 Vaterland
127 Exchange membership
128 Cruising
129 Noted Cairene
130 Cuttlefish
131 "La Douce"
132 Wide-awake
133 —— nostrum
134 Some roulette bets
135 Vice prin.

DOWN

1 Moslem judge
2 Mighty mite
3 Decorous reptile
4 Henry Morgan was one
5 ". . . —— I be best": "Henry VI, Part III"
6 Nigerian native
7 Vasco da ——
8 Bitter
9 Roundup rider
10 Org. succeeded by the N.R.C.
11 Prejudice
12 —— Park, Colo.
13 Plumber's problem
14 Young Burmese at home
15 Dugout
16 Quantity of paper
19 Invited
21 Of certain ecological areas
25 Flags
28 Men in front of QB's
31 Ending for margin or Saturn
33 Use an analgesic
35 Lapham of literature
37 Broker's concern
38 Gaseous element
39 Manumit
41 Basis for a civil suit
43 Nahuatl
44 "What thou ——, write in a book . . ."
47 Ziti, e.g.
49 Meetings of McEnroe and Borg
52 Ermine
54 Sacred song
56 Cather's "—— Lady"
59 Christmas-tides
61 Rival of Sparta and Athens
63 Huxley's "—— Hay"
66 Ballyhoos
68 Mythical man of brass
70 "On —— Old Smokey"
73 Puckish
75 Kind of button
76 Addis ——
77 Excellent material for furniture
80 Result of solitary sorrow
81 "—— Eat Cake," 1933 musical

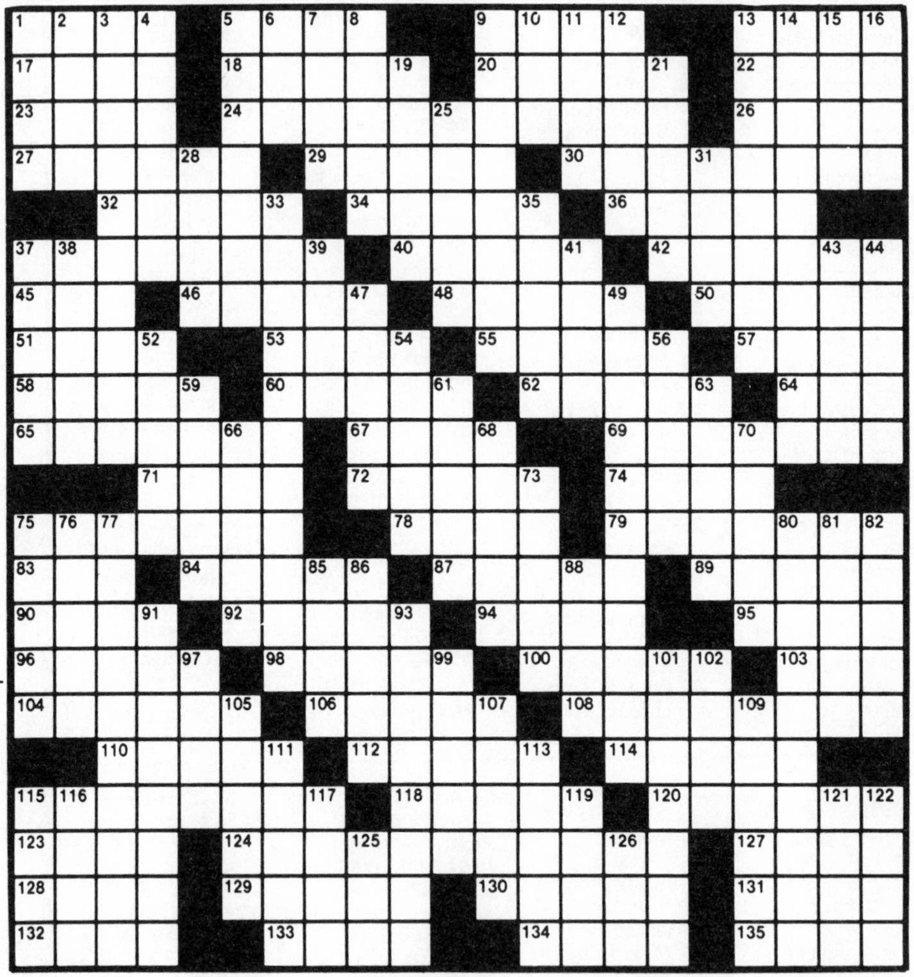

82 Curves
85 Posted
86 Wore
88 Song for Horne
91 —— well
93 Rock-forming mineral
97 Where Achilles sulked
99 Pitch
101 Honduran exports
102 Analysts' concerns
105 Obstructions
107 Tower's territory
109 Where Peter was great
111 ". . . —— of snow-white horses"
113 Inhibit
115 City map
116 Rambler
117 Wagnerian earth goddess
119 Mellow
121 Yorty and Spade
122 Photo or thermo follower
125 Vandalize
126 Resembling: Suffix

53 Gender Bender

By Dorothea E. Shipp

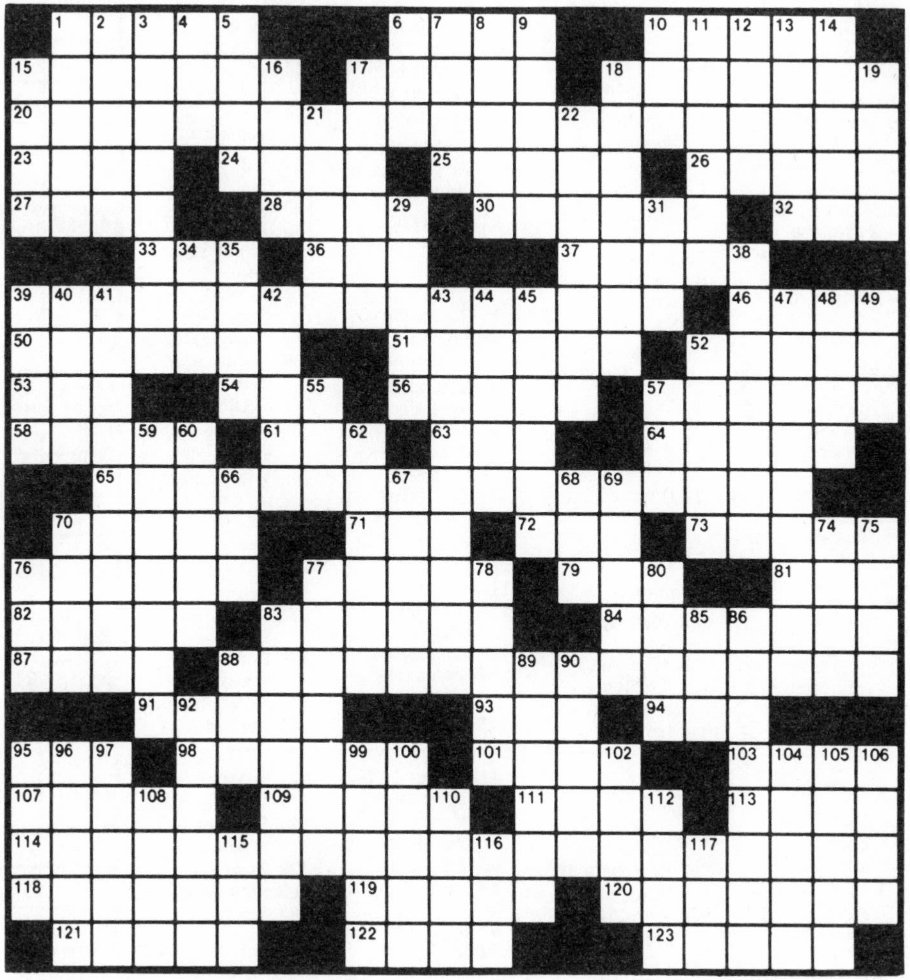

ACROSS

1 Fanatical
6 Year in the reign of Louis VII
10 Rubberneck
15 Item counted by a dieter
17 Very intelligent person
18 Devices for cold feet
20 Queen's group of musicians
23 Lacoste of tennis fame
24 Noted Alaskan politician
25 Cities in Ala., N.Y., etc.
26 Previn's platforms
27 German donkey
28 Sinister
30 Town on Lago Maggiore
32 Meek's partner in comics
33 "Tote —— barge!"
36 That, in Valencia
37 Auguries
39 Ladylike flowers
46 Latin I word
50 Darwin, for one
51 N.M.U. members
52 Hammer parts
53 Gas: Comb. form
54 Character in "Charley's Aunt"
56 Allgood and Teasdale
57 Quint name
58 These might be light
61 Nandu's look-alike
63 Droop
64 Footwear for dancers
65 She wants more proof
70 Position in yoga
71 Musical instrument
72 Sort of sack
73 Grant's portrayer on TV
76 Cold, in Calabria
77 Become prevalent
79 Stocky horse
81 Tokyo, formerly
82 Code name for a French beach
83 Much-photographed word
84 Releases by deed
87 —— Fiord
88 Feminine upstart
91 Thugs
93 Meadow barley
94 Earl Grey, for one
95 —— Anthony Wayne
98 Worsted
101 Automobile pioneer
103 Cobbler's need
107 Heeling at sea
109 Archangel in an epic
111 But, in Brest
113 Division word
114 Handy woman
118 Cassatt and O'Keeffe
119 Rommel
120 Some pitches in horseshoes
121 Roman shades
122 Nostradamus was one
123 They hustle after those who rustle

DOWN

1 Harsh breathing sounds
2 Coeur d'——, Idaho
3 N. American maple
4 Novelist Levin
5 Eat in style
6 Miniver's status
7 Golf conveyance
8 Emulators of Ananias
9 Bar at Fort Knox
10 Levene or Levenson
11 Surgeon's tool
12 Pulpit of a sort
13 Author of "The Cloister and the Hearth"
14 One of the Fords
15 Humane org.
16 Razor's feature
17 Exile
18 Melchior, e.g.
19 Pierre is its cap.
21 Tangle or untangle
22 Family in an O'Neill play
29 Wind-borne deposit
31 His: Fr.
34 Body east of N.A.
35 Bird cry
38 Nation's targets
39 British blackleg
40 Exclamation of elation
41 Otary
42 River feature
43 Anyway
44 Halting place in Exodus
45 Insects in final stages
47 Element used in many alloys
48 Barley features
49 Mao ——-tung
52 Eyelashes
55 —— "Blue?": 1929 song
57 Certain aircraft
59 Highway menace
60 —— Islands, in the Malay Archipelago
62 Sight ——
66 —— Dai of Vietnam
67 Stadium sign
68 Singer Davis
69 Put on a pedestal
70 Coat of ——
74 Biographer of Henry James
75 Optimistic
76 Eggs —— yong
77 Prime Minister of India: 1964-66
78 Prefix for mancy
80 Bible ——
83 Representatives abroad
85 Daisy —— of Logpatch
86 Dante, Gabrielli and Rossetti
88 Namath
89 Wildcatter, e.g.
90 Purple Heart, for one
92 Dull
95 Goya subject
96 Cry wolf
97 Ukases
99 —— Tages (one day): Ger.
100 Farm implement inventor
102 Threshold
104 Where Aconcagua rises
105 Cordwood measure
106 Flip
108 Meas. of area
110 Actor Edmund
112 Short distance
115 French connectives
116 Larch or sapin
117 Noted Indian novelist

Musical Excerpts

By Alfio Micci

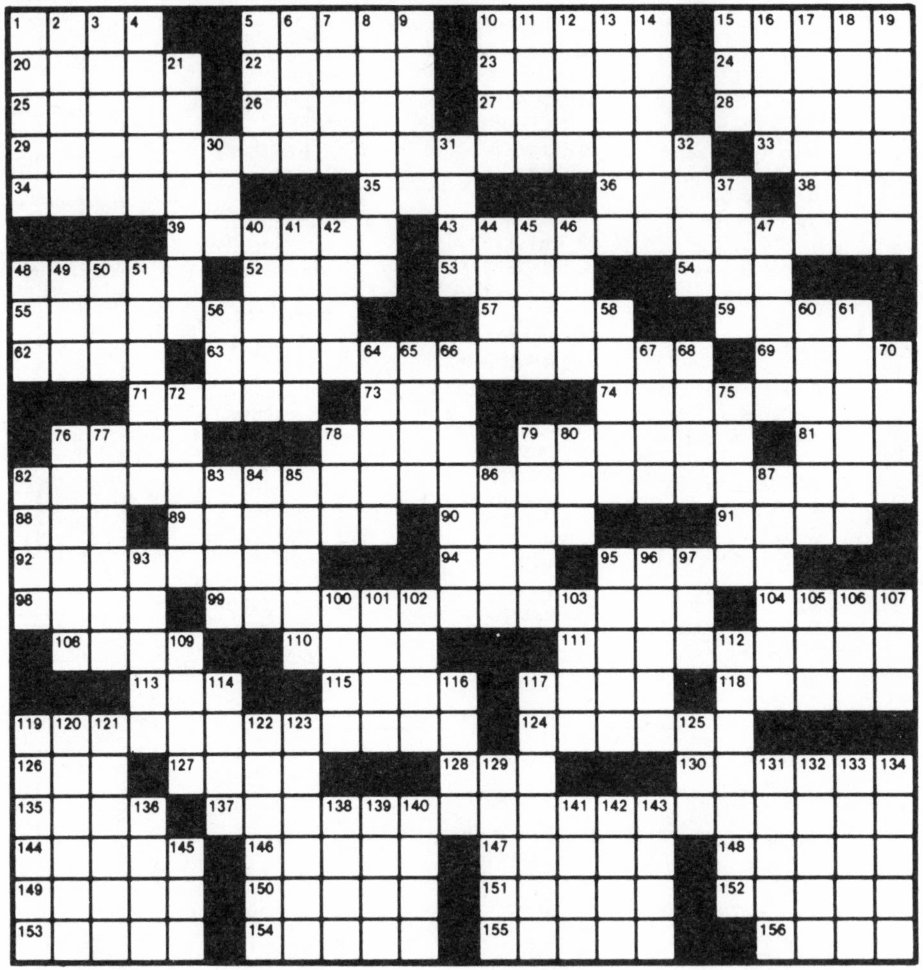

ACROSS

1 Stuff
5 Dull finish
10 Regular guy
15 Goose genus
20 Pertaining to the blood
22 "I want —— just like . . ."
23 Skin ailment
24 Farm-machine pioneer
25 —— Gay
26 Math term
27 News bits
28 Brazilian parrot
29 Air from Borodin's "Polovtsian Dance No. 2"
33 Spoken
34 Taken care of
35 Stabler or Rosewall
36 Reik's "The Secret ——"
38 Corporation initials
39 Make possible
43 Song from Tchaikovsky's "Andante Cantabile"
48 "There Is Nothin' Like ——"
52 U. of Ga. group, e.g.
53 Othello's ensign
54 A cont.
55 Explosive
57 Chanteuse Horne
59 Shankar
62 Campus figure
63 Tune from Tchaikovsky's Symphony No. 6
69 "Caro ——"
71 Acquires
73 Super ending
74 Doctor's instrument
76 "When the frost —— the punkin . . ."
78 Teen-ager's woe
79 "Get thee —— the high mountain": Isa. 40:9
81 Dapper one
82 Pop song from Chopin's "Fantaisie-Impromptu"
88 Speed abbr.
89 Bell portrayer
90 First Chinese dynasty
91 When both hands are up
92 Word differently
94 Gormandize
95 Artist's headwear
98 Dissimilar: Prefix
99 Air from Tchaikovsky's Piano Concerto No. 1
104 Amphibian
108 Villein
110 Salver
111 Illustrative
113 Londoner's nog
115 Retained
117 Mideast region
118 Eldritch
119 Melody from Ravel's "Pavane . . ."
124 He converted Havana
126 Poetic preposition
127 Fed
128 East, in Essen
130 Withstand
135 Big Dipper
137 Borrowing from a Borodin nocturne
144 Piano feature
146 "Adam and Eve" painter
147 Big game
148 Making do, with "out"
149 Winter month in Madrid
150 School for René
151 Use a blender
152 Stupid
153 Williams's Big ——
154 Changed the décor
155 Noted violinist
156 Oboe, e.g.

DOWN

1 Tal's forte
2 French income
3 Love, Italian style
4 La Scala locale
5 Moon feature
6 Culture medium
7 S.A. monkey
8 Ornament
9 Marry in haste
10 Cooking direction
11 Agave plant
12 Wedded
13 Neglectful
14 Mortarboard feature
15 Nabokov heroine
16 Opera by Handel
17 Horizon on the briny
18 Printing boo-boos
19 Landed property
21 G.I. hangout
30 RR car
31 Con
32 Robt. ——
37 Quartet
40 River of song
41 Foreheads
42 Zhivago's love
44 Seraphic symbol
45 City of Hungary
46 Bulwer-Lytton heroine
47 Money for monsieur
48 Continue
49 Cee's follower
50 —— loss
51 Kalmuck
56 Keelbill
58 To have, in Le Havre
60 Certain charm
61 Pledge security
64 Spot for a bust
65 Lady of Spain
66 Sudden inundation
67 Lab burner
68 French roast
70 Poetic times
72 El- —— Sadat
75 Stuttgart sunshine
76 Incites
77 Taste
78 Berliner's expletive
79 Fuse
80 Links org.
82 Soprano Petina
83 Latin I word
84 Gypsum
85 Basset's forte
86 What "vidi" means
87 Kind of neck or nose
93 Of a time period
95 Spars
96 Episode
97 Ad —— (pertinent)
100 Vexes
101 Highlander
102 Stimulate, in a way: Slang
103 Huxley book
105 Scull
106 "Exodus" name
107 Use henna
109 Dwindle
112 Inhabited
114 Goldman or Bovary
116 Braces
117 Does charades
119 Beat
120 Play by Euripides
121 Disintegrated slowly
122 Go-between
123 Persuade
125 Caviar
129 Nitwits
131 Kind of face
132 Sheeplike
133 Wisdom
134 Moved slowly
136 Hospital unit
138 Trampled
139 Prefix for copter or port
140 Angered
141 Sir Thomas ——
142 River in Nord
143 Has- ——
145 Myrna of films

Impish Inferences

By Elaine D. Schorr

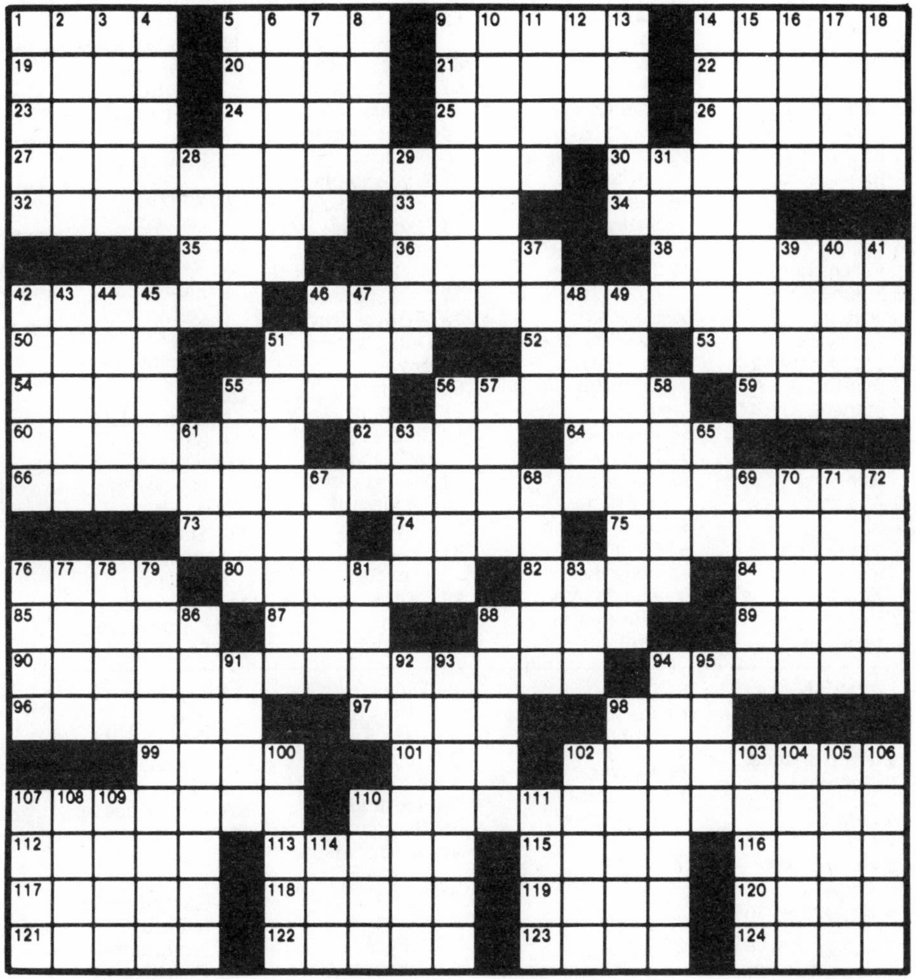

ACROSS

1 Bridge bonanza
5 Wagner heroine
9 Lamb Chop's Lewis
14 City NE of Dortmund
19 Conte
20 Cause to descend
21 Bouncer, usually
22 "South Pacific" hero
23 Gum up the works
24 Aerie dweller
25 Manliness; valor
26 Sycophants' answers
27 Waiters ——
30 Lares' partners
32 Cure-alls
33 Livy's lang.
34 Jog
35 Suffix with Capri
36 Pt. of a monogram
38 Cornell's site
42 Highlight
46 A conductor ——
50 Scandal-sheet info
51 Shavers
52 Ovine sire
53 Worker's goal, often
54 Ottoman officials
55 "Out, damned Spot!"
56 Throw a line to an actor
59 Food for thought
60 Youmans heroine
62 Like a "painted ship"
64 Lamb that wrote about a pig
66 Editors ——
73 Lily plant
74 Suffix with comment
75 Stoopnagle
76 Waist hugger
80 Terrapin
82 Explorer Tasman
84 —— bene
85 With 98 Across, forte
87 Barracks bugaboo: Abbr.
88 Catalufa
89 Symbol of strength
90 Ventriloquists ——
94 Respectable
96 Spuds
97 Ely or Wight
98 See 85 Across
99 Contend with
101 Actor Cariou
102 Go beyond; excel
107 "—— du Printemps": Stravinsky
110 Roofers are ——
112 Honshu metropolis
113 Author Lagerlöf
115 Gourmet's concern
116 One of many in a blind
117 Minstrel Mr.
118 Characteristic
119 Aqueduct of Silvius, e.g.
120 One of Bjorn's rivals
121 Put forth effort
122 Whereas
123 Rock piles at the peak
124 Ants.' opposites

DOWN

1 Hogtie
2 Author Hobson
3 Outlander
4 Altar top
5 Man's lounging slipper
6 Caterpillars
7 "The wages of —— death"
8 Actor Clunes
9 Indian medicine men
10 Torquemada victim
11 Sermon finale
12 Hamelin horde member
13 Malapropos
14 A pianist is a ——
15 A stockyards owner is ——
16 Windshield wetter
17 Robt. ——
18 Famed loch
28 Univ. course
29 Inventor Howe
31 Composer Satie
37 Corrida attraction
39 Samoan port
40 "—— la vie!
41 Neighborhood
42 Turkish city on the Seyhan
43 Smoke producer
44 Bustard's relative
45 And the following: Lat.
46 Five score
47 Zeno follower
48 Fiber of the Philippines
49 Allocated
51 Post-knockdown litany
55 Wading bird
56 Piece of china
57 Civil War general
58 Yodeling country
61 P.I. tree
63 Pigeon pea
65 Part of NATO
67 Crimean seaport
68 Moore or Kelly
69 Column style
70 Night noise
71 Range of the Rockies
72 Virgule
76 Jazz singer's improvisation
77 Scent of roses, e.g.
78 Small barracuda
79 A builder is a ——
81 African antelope
83 —— mitzvah
86 An angler on the links makes a ——
88 Family feud, e.g.
91 Narc's target, at times
92 Of a certain creed
93 Opposite of demote
94 Balzac's "Le Curé ——"
95 Lawman of the old West
98 Slave rebellion leader
100 Touchstones
102 "—— Psyche": Keats
103 Orbit point
104 "Let not poor —— starve": Charles II
105 Tiny bit
106 —— Park, Colo.
107 Earring locale
108 Pike and pickerel genus
109 Compos mentis
110 Joie de vivre
111 Hit, old style
114 Assam silkworm

Uncommon Combos

By Reginald L. Johnson

ACROSS

1 Strikebreaker
5 Useless stuff
10 Item often barked
14 Raison d'——
18 Bye-bye
19 Pierre's income
20 Snivel
21 Foreordain
22 Mannequins posing as divorcées
26 Thanks giving
27 Lustful glances
28 Winds
29 Mideast land: Abbr.
30 And not
31 Mt. sometimes identified as Horeb
32 Horatian creation
33 Part of a TV set
34 Skedaddle
35 "—— Shanter"
37 Twice
40 Trio sharing a guffaw
46 Ruffle
47 Soak, as flax
48 "Agnus ——"
49 Town in the news: 1944
50 Big-city headline after successful antilitter drive
58 Pod occupant
59 During
60 "Look here!" in France
61 Bone: Comb. form
62 Body that sounds scary
63 Plumber's joint
64 Jet-set transportation
65 Makes a call
67 Washington was his sitter
69 Great Barrier Island
70 White Sulphur Springs, e.g.
73 Exciting event at the dock
77 Tale starter
78 Wire measure
79 Dull grayish brown
80 Precinct
81 Training places run by Vigoda
89 Marine raptor
90 Goddess of discord
91 Le ——, French port
92 Faiths, to Fidel
93 Latin paradigm
94 Greek letters
95 This has a no.
96 "Voi, —— sapete," Cherubino aria
99 Kind of law
101 Work in concert
102 Pigweed
104 Result of a hot-corner collision
107 Rajah's mate
108 Hampton ——
109 Earl Campbell is one
110 "The wonderful star"
111 Suffix for room or kitchen
112 Prescribes
113 Christmases
114 Sherbets' kin

DOWN

1 Smokers
2 Keep in stock
3 Perfume
4 Night crawlers, e.g.
5 Having three shapes
6 Happen again
7 Indigo source
8 G.C. or Penn
9 One up to deviltry
10 River to Lake Chad
11 Villain's greeting
12 The electees
13 Thackeray character
14 Cantor
15 Burin or dibble
16 Brawls
17 Printers' measures
20 Yule decoration
23 Fagin, for one
24 Jib overlapping a mainsail
25 An antiseptic
31 Macbeth and Macduff
33 Betray
34 Sam or J.C. of sports
35 Part of a switch
36 Didion's "Play It —— Lays"
37 Copper-mining center
38 Arctic sight
39 Boutique
40 Sand or mouse follower
41 Socks
42 Costa ——
43 A Ford
44 One-eyed god
45 Aides for prins.
51 Viscounts' superiors
52 Mennonite group
53 Spring-practice nine
54 Novelist Cather
55 Moody or Reddy
56 Schlimazel
57 Founded: Abbr.
62 Kind of beaver
64 Sandhurst weaponry
65 Giver
66 Early dweller in Peru
67 Smug ones
68 Fish dish
69 Immature seed
70 Kálmán operetta
71 V.I.P. at D.C.
72 A wife of Esau
73 Division of a leaf
74 Arena at Atlanta
75 Lavender and lilac
76 Blockheads
82 Evil spirit
83 Laundry workers
84 Flimflams
85 Senator from Utah
86 Pavarotti's usual reception
87 Vale——
88 "Your —— Too Big," Waller hit
93 Broadway girl
94 Certain investments
95 Kind of yell
96 Martin or Lewis
97 Viscount Templewood
98 Heaters
99 Partisan: Suffix
100 Margaret, to Charles
101 Blazer
102 Pkg.
103 Apostle of the Franks
104 Modern "art"
105 Lobster coral
106 Brazilian coffee

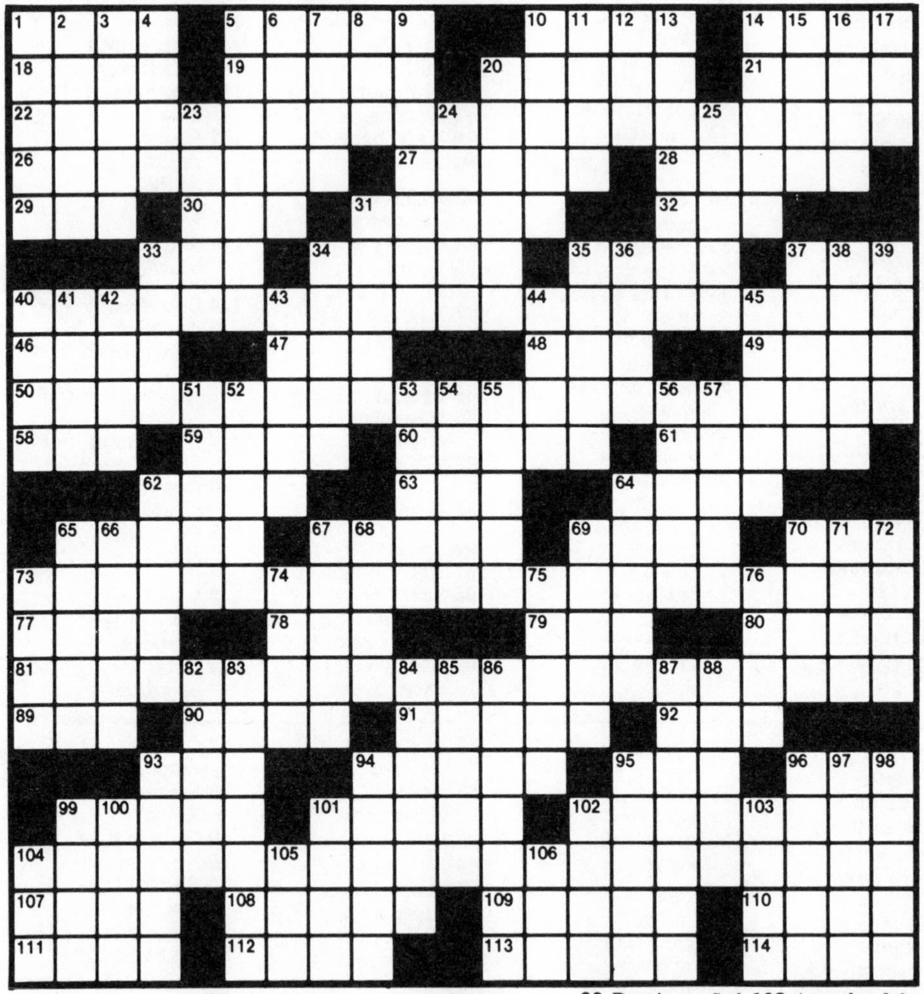

57

Funny Business

By Hume R. Craft

ACROSS

1 Edgar or Obie
6 Kennedy visitors
10 Peacock Throne locale
14 Friend's address
18 Miasma
19 Eye part
20 Cantina fare
21 Regatta sight
22 Bouquet
23 Italian pyrotechnics factory?
26 Oater role
28 Wrathful
29 Knobbed
30 Biblical clip joint?
34 Makes amends
35 Lost a lap
36 Tackle or guard
40 Also-ran
41 Credible
43 Larrigans' kin
44 Cadmus's daughter
45 Bldgs. for bibliophiles
46 Chamberlain of N.B.A. fame
47 Carney and Buchwald
48 Capital of Southern Yemen
49 Rarebit ingredient
50 Specialties at Wilhelm's fruit stand?
54 Upright, e.g.
55 Briny residue
57 Oscar film: 1955
58 Best quality of merchandise
59 Daltons and farads
60 Shinbone
61 Painter's effects
62 Inserts
64 Actress Thomas
65 F.B.I. machine
68 Underground vault
69 Scout's containers for trappers' gear?
71 Compass-card notation
72 "The ——'e knows . . .": Kipling
73 Papilloma
74 Like Albee's Alice
75 Honeymoon spoiler
76 Kind of soil or sail
77 Like Hubbard's cupboard
78 Menu items
81 Mouth: Comb form
82 Spot for an aerialist
84 More rational
85 Cunning one
86 Cotton Belt saloon?
90 Leg covering
93 Arab warrior and poet
94 Best in long bargaining sessions
95 Greek remedies for strained shoulders?
98 Switch words
101 Wattle
102 Skipper's order
103 Highlander
104 Kind of show
105 Tarzan's friends
106 Earl —— Biggers
107 Hurok et al.
108 More crafty

DOWN

1 One of Mickey's exes
2 Sherman's hell
3 Olympic cosmetic resort?
4 Lettuces
5 Extender of vowel sounds
6 Jacob's fourth son
7 Dwight of the Red Sox
8 Sawbuck
9 Glut
10 OB's announcement
11 Used a catamaran
12 Quaker gray
13 Fjord land: Abbr.
14 Carlisle's favorite son
15 Sestos priestess
16 Tooth fanciers
17 Word with who or what
21 Syncopes
24 Flynn or Fauntleroy
25 One of Aristotle's fortes
27 Kettle and Barker
30 Prouty's Stella
31 Prima ballerina
32 N.B.A. targets
33 Capp character
37 Legendary Fort Knox?
38 About
39 Social taboos
41 Sings gayly
42 Troubles
43 Victim
46 Shoe parts
47 Claudia —— Taylor Johnson
48 Broadcast
50 Besmirch
51 Moslem princes
52 Picasso
53 Dovelike petrel
54 Some are knotty
56 Wading bird
58 Life's "beginning"
60 Bakery product
61 Waters
62 Antarctic explorer
63 Misplay
64 Lunar sea
65 Bamboozle
66 Smalto is one
67 Iterate
69 One of the Cavalier poets
70 Welty product
73 West Pakistanis
75 Having endurance
77 "If he ——, he's nothing": Shak.
78 More spiteful
79 Region in Indochina
80 Noblewoman
81 Stimulus-response devices
83 Corolla
84 Transgressor
85 Comedian
87 Selassie
88 Mexican liquor
89 Winds
90 Dippy or dotty
91 Expectant
92 Lenard's "Winnie —— Pu"
96 Shropshire individual
97 He ranks a Pfc.
99 Payment
100 —— -de-lance

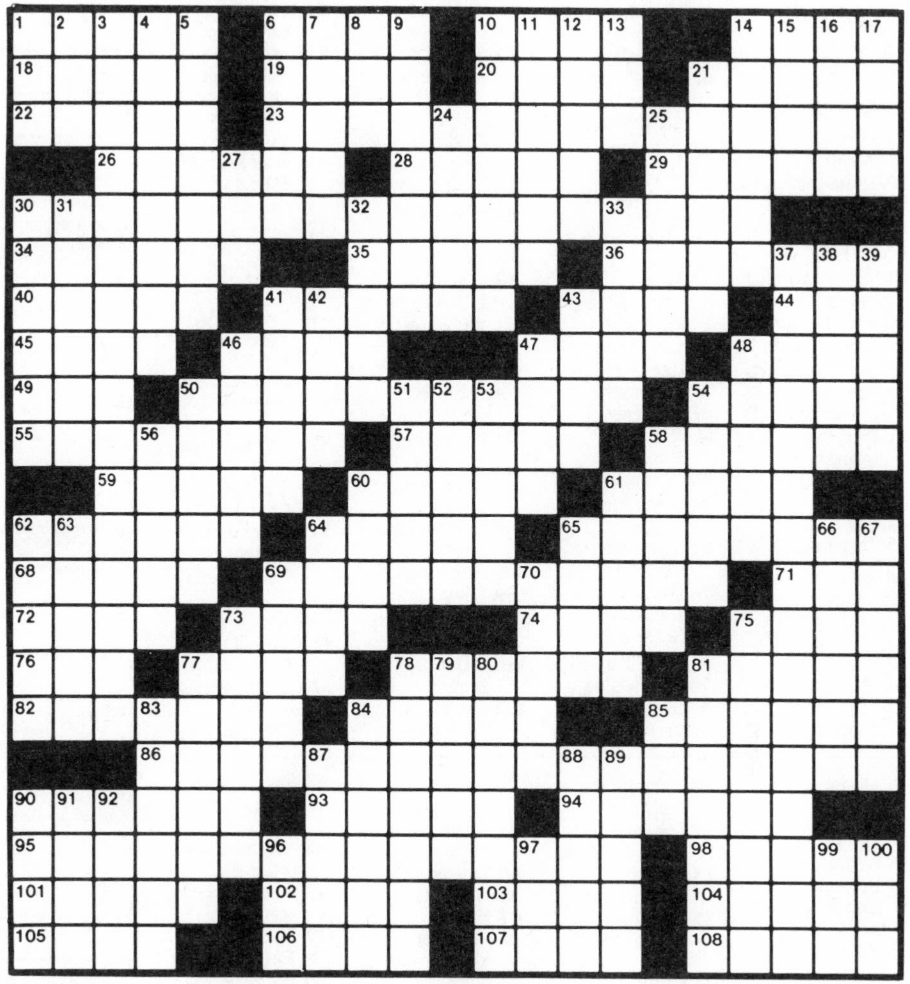

Assembly Line

By Joy L. Wouk

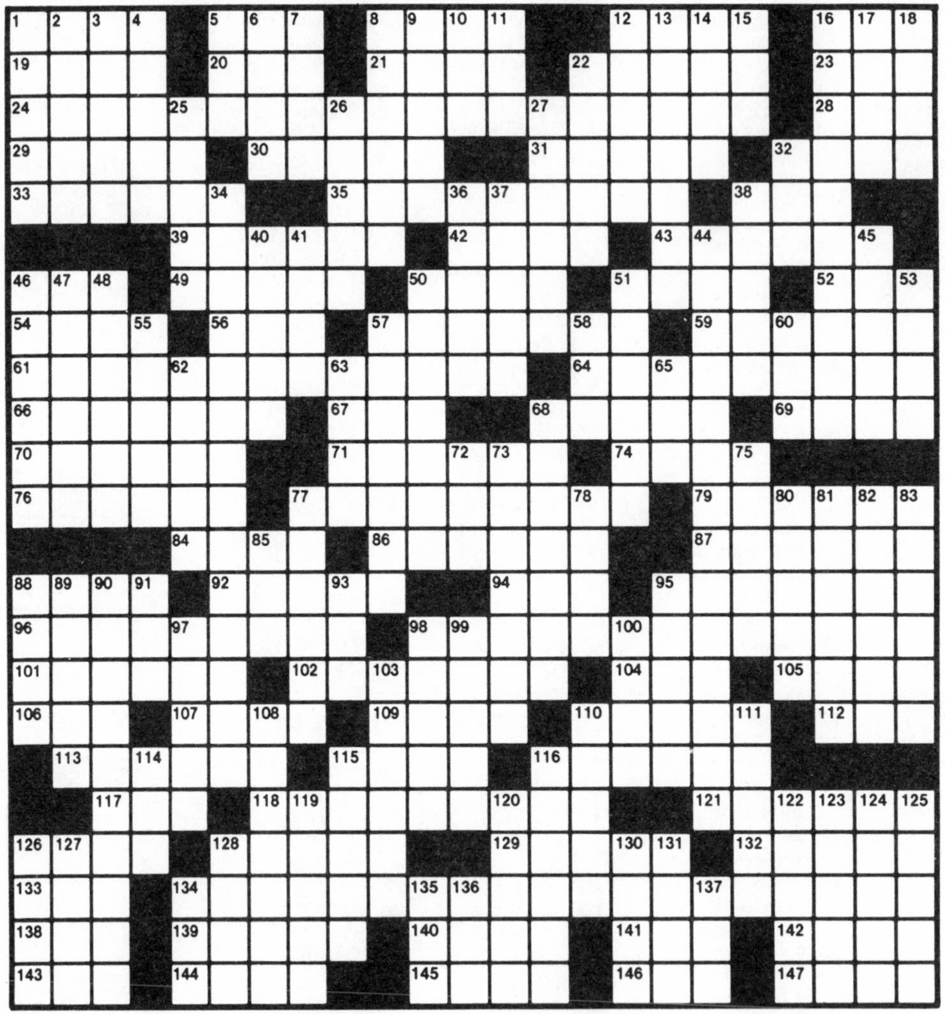

ACROSS

1 Cordial
5 Double agent
8 Bruins' home
12 Humane org.
16 Belfry occupant
19 Russian range
20 Contains
21 Scheme
22 Landed
23 Suffix with indent
24 Wolf's visitor
28 Singer Tillis
29 Before febrero
30 Emulate Columbo
31 Praying woman, in classical art
32 Girasol
33 Forsake
35 Jerry-built
38 Summer quaff
39 Short necklace
42 Trotsky
43 Haves
46 Barrette
49 High-warp tapestry
50 Gladiolus root
51 Court celebrity
52 Secret agcy.
54 Pierre's girlfriend
56 Fall mo.
57 Propose
59 Certain tidal waves
61 "Woodman, ——!": Morris
64 "Black Oxen" author et al.
66 Intersecting lines, in geometry
67 Gr. tense
68 Bailey or Buck
69 Young oyster
70 Redactor's process
71 Trouser feature
74 Quid of tobacco
76 Stand for
77 Brainy group
79 Old fiddles
84 Saragossa's river
86 Coal-gas ingredient
87 Scopes's attorney
88 —— California
92 Tasks, in Taxco
94 Young seal
95 Abélard's lover
96 Issuance
98 Warning on a 1775 Navy flag
101 Take it all back
102 Gamester John and family
104 Kind of painting
105 Granny or bowline
106 Cartoonist's need
107 Nap
109 Levy
110 Goals of forty-niners
112 Balaam's mount
113 Goethe's dreams
115 Noted cosmetician
116 Withdraw
117 Elec. unit
118 Barney Google's mount
121 Black bucks
126 Pamper
128 Cache
129 "—— unattractive old thing . . .": W. S. Gilbert
132 "—— vincit amor"
133 Flow's partner
134 Henry VIII and Victoria
138 Former ring king
139 Shrewd
140 Change
141 Work unit
142 Nobelist in Medicine: 1947
143 Shea player
144 Gaucho's cattle-catcher
145 Corn units
146 Stein
147 Door part

DOWN

1 Ridged
2 Skirt style
3 Appraises
4 British bishop's headdress
5 Haggard novel
6 Parisian oasis
7 North Sea feeder
8 Din
9 Toast sound
10 Youth
11 Cuckoo
12 Bavarian sheep
13 Sudden impulses, in Madrid
14 Simonides' birthplace
15 Append
16 Farmer's delight
17 Space
18 Have an effect
22 Smiling broadly
25 He wrote "Yerma": 1934
26 Crowns of furnaces
27 ". . . there warn't —— like a raft": Twain
32 Verse form
34 "Of Thee I Sing" role
36 Funeral oration
37 Suit material
38 Lend —— (heed)
40 Mus. groups
41 Set of judo exercises
44 Some used-car salesmen
45 Tuscan city
46 Went by
47 Hinder
48 Member of the vitamin-B complex
50 Now in progress
51 Censure
53 Kind of prof.
55 Muse for Marceau
57 Kipling's "Just So ——"
58 Thus, to Burns
60 Wts. of 2,240 lbs.
62 Growing out
63 Buckle clasp
65 Initials for a prince
68 Schulz strip
72 Egyptian spirit
73 London borough
75 Wooded country
77 Muscular
78 Rel. of Jupiter
80 Put up with
81 Author of "Distaff"
82 Carl Sagan's TV program
83 Nougat and caramel
85 Baseball stat.
88 Sudanese native
89 Idiot
90 Western hare
91 Library treasure
93 Aged: Abbr.
95 Spyri opus
97 Sale-sign words
98 Squiffed
99 Successful
100 John Wellborn or Elihu
103 Idolized
108 Piquant
110 ——-mutton sleeve
111 —— Marmara
114 Locksley Hall girl
115 Epernay's river
116 Grapevine growths
119 Ovid was one
120 Light-amplification device
122 Slap
123 Cranial bump
124 Part of TNT
125 Hindu's word for Clive
126 Show delight
127 Qualified
128 Dry, as an arroyo
130 Stanch
131 Done, for short
134 Small flounder
135 Massenet oratorio
136 Cartoonist Gardner
137 Dominique's donation

Urbanites

By William Lutwiniak

ACROSS

1 Small flounders
5 Aides et al.
10 Ice pinnacle
15 —— cry
19 Gelatinous substance
20 Victor Herbert played it
21 —— acids
22 Euphonium
23 Berlin
27 Golf area
28 Phooey!
29 London's —— End
30 Daze
31 Henpecks
33 Kind of terrier
34 QE2, e.g.
35 "Oh, give me ——..."
37 Painter called "The Cornish Wonder"
39 Troubadour
40 Tape-speed abbr.
43 Rochester
49 Circular headgear
50 Come-on
51 Afflict
52 Kind of rocket
53 Pablo's gold
54 Like a bump on ——
55 Jabberwocky adjective
57 Quickly, to Ovid
58 Turncoats
61 Mountain winder
62 Shoe part
64 Albany
68 Subjoin
71 Ship's channel
72 German shepherd
76 He kayoed Carnera
77 Price for Red Chief
80 Nuchal area
81 Orinoco tributary
82 Moving
84 Personalities
85 Humiliate
87 Con —— (vigorously)
88 London
92 Projection
93 Vaunt
94 Sums: Abbr.
95 Whence Chianti comes
96 Thermoplastic
98 Numerical prefix
100 Colorado resort
102 Anthropologist's adjective
104 Source of roughage
105 Civil rights org.
106 Asner and Wynn
109 Paris
114 "This one's ——"
115 Functions
116 Barrage
117 Orison
118 Flatten, in Soho
119 Salad days
120 Shevchenko
121 Famed puppeteer

DOWN

1 Dress detail
2 Malarial woe
3 "Art thou —— and popular?": Shak.
4 Grads-to-be
5 Diving duck
6 Bivouacs
7 Kin of rochets
8 Polly Holliday's TV role
9 Fronts
10 Impudent
11 Indulge in cabotinage
12 "Oysters —— season"
13 Sharp-cornered: Abbr.
14 It builds no nests
15 Wicker's "—— to Die"
16 Like much sci-fi
17 Fortas and Burrows
18 Exceptional
24 "The Lady ——," 1935 song
25 Exposed
26 Interpret
32 Singer Nancy
34 Spare
35 One in a cast
36 Viscount Templewood
37 Catapult
38 —— diem
39 "Illusions" author
41 Napoli gateway
42 Busybody
44 Ellis or Parris
45 Electron-tube element
46 Kind of setter
47 Really goes for
48 Diminish
54 Dramatic conflict
56 Swift, in Siena
59 Female adviser
60 Messina mister
62 Far East capital
63 Quondam
65 Rodeo gear
66 Undersea trackers
67 Lambaste
68 Slacken
69 Turkish V.I.P., once
70 Heavy wool overcoats
73 Song hit of 1919
74 Mirador
75 Lamebrain
77 Actress from Limerick: 1860-1916
78 Eagerly anticipating
79 Pursuer of wealth
83 Gloss
86 Vespertilio
87 —— noire
89 Gothic openwork
90 Catastrophic

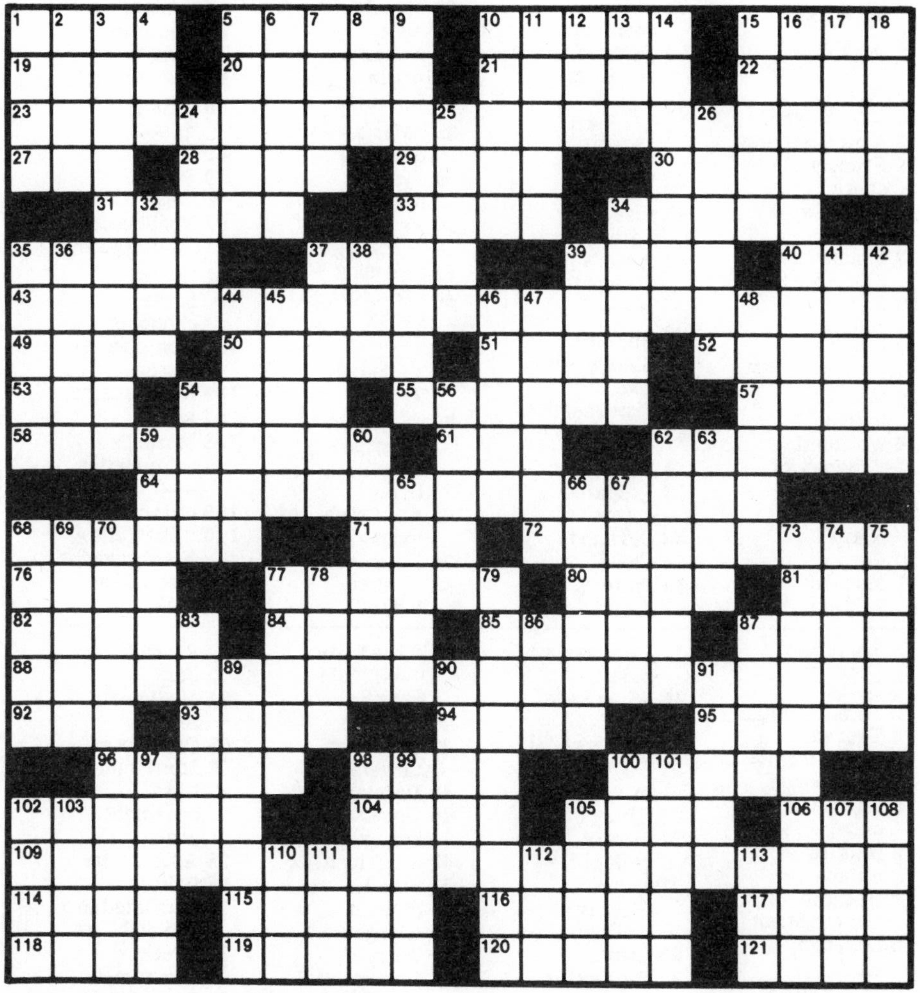

91 Acrobatic feat
97 Pierre's year
98 —— trouvé
99 Pulverize
100 Ghana's capital
101 Clobbers
102 —— effort
103 Singer Turner
105 Suffix with comment
107 Whitetail
108 Part of a hippocerf
110 "—— Ernest ...," 1922 song
111 Achy ailment
112 Greek vowel
113 Boosts

Clues to Amuse

By Louis Baron

ACROSS

1 Gershwin's "—— Again"
5 Pleasant
10 ——-Magnon
13 Aussie leapers
17 Frances of opera
18 Ouida's real name
19 Mount where Aaron died
20 Cab for Holmes
22 "Feel I Pretty"
25 Menotti heroine
26 Was merciful
27 "Thanks for the"
29 Temple, in poesy
30 Record
31 Mona's follower
32 Soviet cooperative
35 Party shunners
37 Tool
41 "Man bites dog"
42 Ohiowa
45 Pisa-to-Verona dir.
46 Ravel's "Gaspard de la ——"
47 Hunter's blind
48 Belligerent god
49 Trite theatrics
50 Connections
51 Bert Bert
55 Prepared cords
56 Old hands
58 Clods
59 Potter's debris
60 Mid-Q.E.D.
61 Nasty remarks
62 Apple, e.g.
63 Obscures
65 "Maria ——," 1933 song
66 Type of headline
70 Egyptian dancing girls
71 Pekolong
73 Chemical prefix
74 Curb
75 River to the Trent
76 —— Blair (George Orwell)
77 O, e.g.
78 All: Comb. form
79 Hotmacs
83 Ovidian "ciao"
84 Spiders' nests
86 Common to many
87 Furrier's pile
88 "Clair de ——"
89 Upshots
90 Pteroid
92 Taset
97 Mini-bombs
101 Paying guest
102 hsilgnE
104 Some choppers
105 Item on a fasces
106 Kin of adagio
107 Byway
108 Mozart's "Coronation ——"
109 42d and 34th
110 "The Yellow Flag" novelist
111 Monoski or luge

DOWN

1 Dotty
2 TV backdrop
3 Thought: Comb. form
4 Gab session
5 Bobby Orr, once
6 Milk, in Milano
7 Island in Taiwan Strait
8 Collector's clock
9 Leave an SST
10 Keystone Kops, usually
11 Army missiles
12 Mountain: Comb. form
13 V.I.P. at Karnak
14 Kind of band or show
15 Christiania today
16 When René dines
20 Berbers et al.
21 Dogwood time in N.Y.
23 Girasol
24 Most of galloped
28 James Galway's collection
30 Come to
32 Big day for Mr. & Mrs.
33 What grads may do
34 Idmn
35 Arms or wings
36 Jolts
38 "White and the Seven Dwarfs"
39 "The Lady ——," 1935 song
40 Imparts
42 Corvettes' targets
43 Parsing word
44 Enclosures in synagogues
49 S. African fox
51 Small amounts
52 Glasgow or Terry
53 Use a pestle
54 Vibes' kin
55 Pumps
57 Devonian division
59 Strauss's "Also —— Zarathustra"
61 Showers icily
63 Ochs, in "Der Rosenkavalier"
64 Medicinal resin
65 Or follower
66 Stern fiddle
67 Nose ornament of India
68 Apotheosize
69 Offices
71 Osculated on a vehicle?
72 Greek communes
75 Pair of jacks, often
77 Shop wear
79 Vigorish collectors
80 "Bringing in the ——"
81 Soeur de mon père

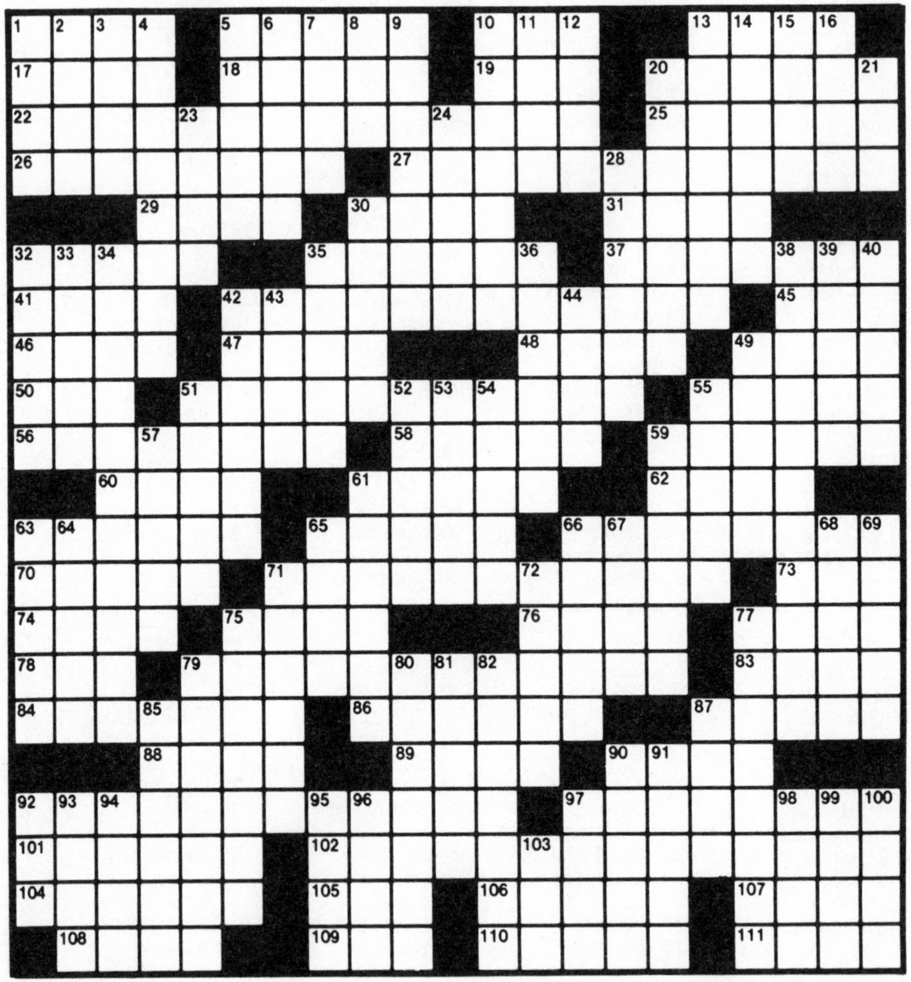

82 Practicing eutaxy
85 Groups of Moslem scholars
87 Throe
90 Virtue
91 Marquisettes
92 Brachium's locale
93 Heddle's place
94 "Welcome ——," Altman film
95 Mex. matrons
96 Quote source
97 Dapper chap
98 Call
99 One freer than a theow
100 Storage place
103 Coral or Arafura

Night Life

By Nancy A. Wood

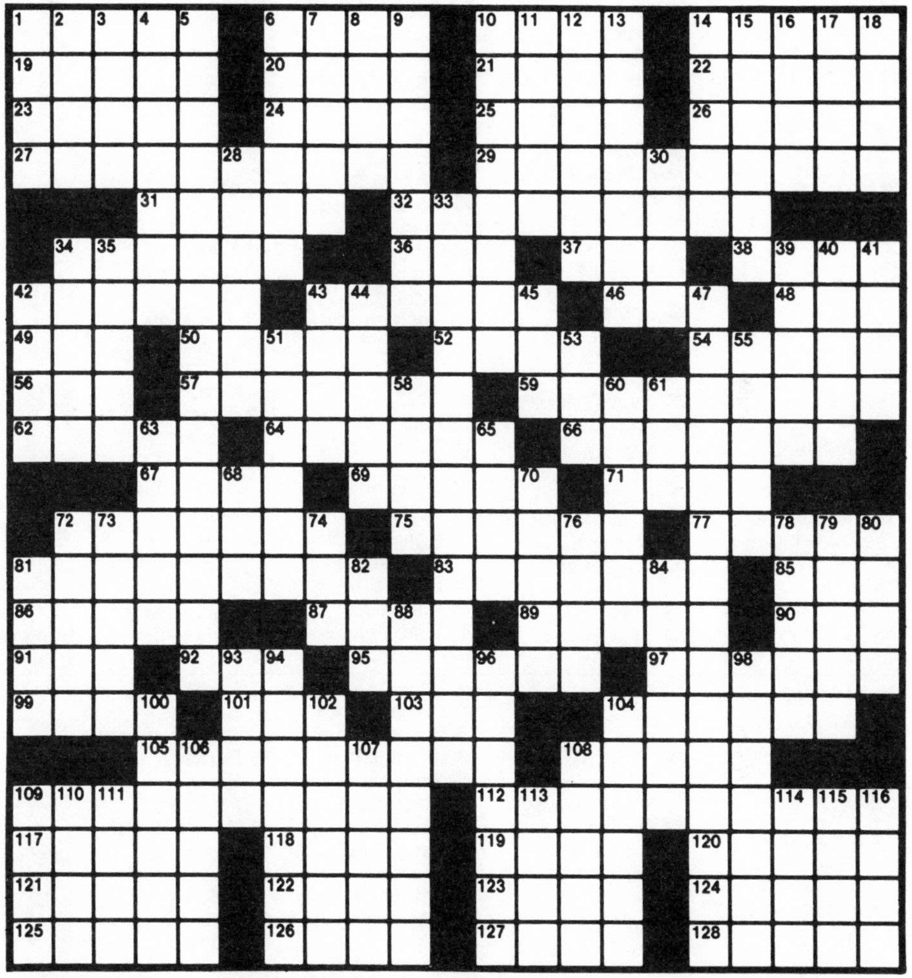

ACROSS

1 Trifling sum
6 Phone attachment
10 Boundless
14 To a colleen, he's a spalpeen
19 Actor Meeker
20 Opposite of apterous
21 Dies ——
22 Terry item
23 Absquatulate
24 Lollygag
25 World Series pitcher: 1948
26 Love in Aquila
27 Nocturnal howlers
29 One with a midnight curfew
31 Buenos ——
32 Housed
34 Share the billing
36 Pinna
37 Work unit
38 Pluto's plaint
42 Imperfection
43 Dreary
46 Douceur
48 Hutch dweller
49 Ouph
50 Deceive
52 Early church lang.
54 What some spirits do
56 Pub offering
57 Early time
59 Golfers' considerations
62 Ponti's wife
64 Connect
66 Turner, e.g.
67 Greek contest
69 Della Casa and Kirk
71 Whit
72 North Carolinian
75 Paton place
77 Allow
81 Like most monsters
83 Star in Scorpio
85 Gold, in Genova
86 A friend of Job
87 Salem, to Essex Co., Mass.
89 What ogres cause
90 Milne character
91 Where a herd might be heard
92 Nocturnal prowler
95 Pigments for Peale
97 Floating
99 One of the Hoppers
101 Roulette bet
103 Hill, to an Arab
104 With wisdom
105 Pen
108 Santander sir
109 Deadly nightshade
112 Nocturnal flier
117 Buoyantly
118 Actress Patricia
119 Landed
120 Architect Jones
121 Cat-——-tails
122 One below a marquess
123 Familiar farewell
124 Histrio
125 Ocean hazards
126 Squirrel's nest
127 Dummkopf
128 Rundown

DOWN

1 Developed
2 Kin of a wheeze
3 Smell, in Toledo
4 Conciliate
5 Midnight
6 Barn-dance official
7 Norwegian kings
8 Destroy
9 Clothes
10 Intuitive
11 Thin as ——
12 Jeanne, for one
13 Auxiliary boats
14 Fixed look
15 Broadway's "Arsenic and Old Lace," e.g.
16 Mil. problem
17 European blackbird
18 Nul tiel record is one
28 Henry, e.g.
30 Therefore
33 Shakespearean ghost
34 One of the strings
35 Present
39 Infer
40 Misanthrope, perhaps
41 Household members
42 "Big ——!"
43 Cape Cod sight
44 "Manner —— . . .": Cowper
45 Terhune canine
47 These may cause screams in dreams
51 Band instrument
53 Gratuity
55 Staked
58 Mother of the Titans
60 Maple seed
61 Niña's uncle
63 A spinner in space
65 Merit
68 Poetic contraction
70 Shankar's instrument
72 Tessellated
73 Meccawee, e.g.
74 "—— Misérables"
76 Dieter's worries: Abbr.
78 Upright
79 Literary device
80 Binge
81 Strike out
82 —— volente
84 Verdi opera
88 In reality
93 Start of a well-known series
94 Like a night owl
96 Produce levitation
98 Roman playwright
100 Under the weather
102 "—— and yet so far"
104 Of a clan
106 Nostrils
107 Kind of drum
108 Cuff
109 Dunce
110 Nine: Prefix
111 Retreat for Simba
113 Word of distress
114 Fall for a trick
115 "Thou art —— . . .": Neh. 9:17
116 Loyalist of '76

Notable Halloween Tale

By Caroline G. Fitzgerald

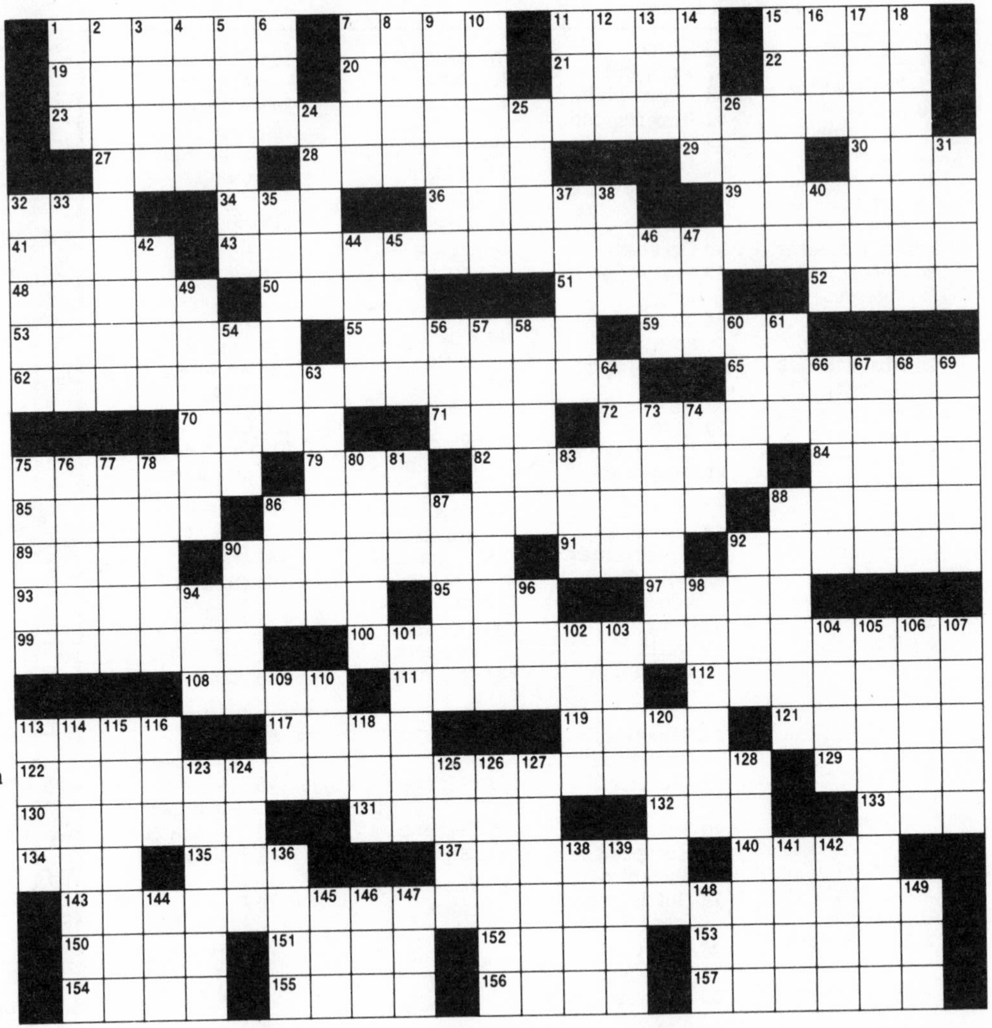

ACROSS

1 Lament
7 Youngman's giveaway
11 Famed street
15 Lhasa —— (canine)
19 "—— of Honey"
20 "... how like ——!": Hamlet
21 Fancy
22 Jack the quipper
23 Departure order
27 "Ah, yes!"
28 Make effervescent
29 Dawber or Shriver
30 Supped
32 Comrade of Chu Teh
34 Concorde
36 Gate fastening
39 Pekingese, e.g.
41 Refs' colleagues
43 Arrival
48 Drudges
50 West German river
51 Siamese
52 Onagers: Fr.
53 Gad about
55 Attached
59 Heavy, for one
62 Invitation
65 Brunch order
70 Laughter, in León
71 Pompey, to Caesar
72 Harry and Bess
75 Harvey, for one
79 Mrs. in Murcia
82 Put on a new front
84 "To —— tale of length ..."
85 Rat Islands native
86 Host
88 Ornamental scheme
89 Letter opener
90 Valuable violin
91 Thread: Comb. form
92 Iris pests
93 "... Dr. Jekyll ——"
95 Darkish
97 Frost or Snow
99 Used-car deal
100 Discovery
108 Sailor
111 Ancient ascetic
112 Negotiator of the night
113 "—— forgive those ..."
117 Zola novel
119 Suffix with inchoative verbs
121 —— Po, eighth-century Chinese poet
122 Plea on the way home
129 Lease leader
130 Misanthropes
131 Pope who became a saint
132 L-P connection
133 Actor-comedian Louis
134 Getaway: Abbr.
135 Solicit
137 Town in Kathiawar
140 Memorable anthropologist
143 Home again
150 Dream, to du Barry
151 Carol
152 Japanese monastery
153 "When Day ——," 1926 song
154 "—— Tod," in a Grieg work
155 Sturdy cart
156 Mine vehicle
157 Obnoxiously hazy

DOWN

1 —— Dai of Vietnam
2 Selassie, for one
3 Plats
4 Douay Bible book
5 Demonstrate
6 Becky Crawley, —— Sharp
7 Engage in
8 The Munsters' pet bat
9 "—— We Know," 1934 song
10 Greeley's process
11 Costume accessory
12 State further
13 Peggy or Brenda
14 Jack-o'-lantern
15 Pithecanthropus
16 Buddy
17 Crusaders' mighty enemy
18 "Like rock —— ...": Wordsworth
24 Seeded in tennis
25 Fishermen's gear
26 Indonesian island
31 Roe
32 Blockheads
33 Love, to Dean Martin
35 Ghost costumes
37 Start of a Williams title
38 R.M.N. aide
40 Org. for golfers
42 Hit home, in a way
44 —— noire (bugbear)
45 Clapton or Heiden
46 Pinna's locale
47 Bravo or Muni
49 Haunted-house occupant
54 Fit of pique
56 Prankster
57 Large-headed studdings
58 Outdoorsy fabric
60 Master
61 Nonflying bird
63 Jumbled
64 Disgrace
66 Turkish title
67 Uhlan's weapon
68 Home of a biblical hag
69 Autocrats
73 Shrimp dish
74 Bridge honor card
75 Airport device
76 Coeur d'——, Idaho
77 Wampum
78 Rangoon's country
80 Convened again
81 Famed French explorer
83 Danish island
86 Essay
87 "Backbone" of S.A.
88 Pipe-tobacco leftover
90 Consider
92 Grizzly one
94 Literary initials (See 93 A)
96 Busch or Marsh
98 Bone part: Comb. form
101 "I —— knocking ...": Shak.
102 Device for collecting plankton
103 Tom's affirmative to Aunt Polly
104 Sora
105 Charmian's activity
106 Former labor leader
107 Flower
109 Bay State cape
110 Pooh-—— ("Mikado" character)
113 Laver's erstwhile rival
114 Sacred scriptures of Hinduism
115 Soarers on brooms
116 Compass point
118 Forty winks
120 Dangerfield, e.g.
123 Rubs out
124 Greek peak
125 St. Jerome's Bible: Abbr.
126 Defender of Gibraltar: 1779-83
127 Come to a boil
128 Conduct based on religious laws
136 Class
138 Theda of the silents
139 Small amount
141 Within: Comb. form
142 Excited
144 Second person
145 Neither's partner
146 Cachar or congou
147 Skillful at trickery
148 Word on a towel
149 Wellington adversary

Expertise

By Margaret Rigby

ACROSS

1 Kind of mask or main
4 —— Moines
7 Humiliated
13 Stale
18 Luxuriant
20 Self-important
22 Suffix for a science
23 Open porch
24 Pale color, to an oologist?
26 Cousin of a via
27 Hamartiologist's topic
28 Strained
29 Anthropologist's interest
30 Hedonist, to a lepidopterist?
35 Female swans
36 Box for eggs or milk: Abbr.
37 Contends
38 Gazes
39 Actress Merkel
40 Lowest level, to a lithologist?
44 Composer Rorem
45 Word on a wine label
46 Key for Grieg
47 Merit ——
50 Laryngologist's interest
53 Escorial's country
54 Place of rustic contentment
57 Having a slightly notched, rounded apex
58 "American Dreams" author
60 Kind of scene or cap
61 Dorothy and Molly
62 Cave salamander
65 Boys in Barcelona
67 Sell to the consumer
69 Make lace
70 Deal with in passing
72 Letters on a TV dial
74 Waiting room
76 What fools do
77 Made a two-base hit
79 Protozoan
83 Finch or lark, e.g.
84 January, to señor
85 Guinness role on TV
86 Meadow
87 Pierre's friend
88 Oenologist's stock
92 Pershing's men in W.W. I
93 "—— the origin of his action": Aristotle
96 Father of Enos
97 Incense
98 Focal points
99 Disappeared, to an anemologist?
103 Acapulco gold
104 Fictional plantation
105 Seraglio room
106 Thought: Prefix
107 Provocative, to a stomatologist
111 Ethnologist's concern
115 Ford or Pyle
116 Noted 19th-century Peruvian historian
117 Potassium, sodium, etc.
118 Gaseous element
119 White House name
120 Brown or Paul
121 Witty remark

DOWN

1 Carey of N.Y., for one
2 Mimic
3 Big ——, Calif.
4 Tooth: Prefix
5 Strive
6 Like a bright night
7 Calendar abbr.
8 Lift
9 Circuits
10 Piano type
11 Long period of time
12 Clean, as a shelf
13 Noted German zoologist: 1817-95
14 Priest's robe
15 Result of a numerologist's field trip?
16 Lizard
17 Colorers
19 Secular
21 Made hermetic
25 Dolls' partners
30 Jazz dance
31 Maltese coin
32 Atlantic City action
33 Servicemen's org.
34 Seemed familiar, to a campanologist?
35 —— Rico
36 Tomorrow, to Tacitus
41 Purl's partner
42 Osteologist's dinnerware?
43 Grad. degree
45 Conchologist's swindle?
48 Navy V.I.P.
49 Fashion name
50 Retinue
51 Traveling on the QE2
52 Course finale
54 Cognate
55 Kind of room, for short
56 Nephologist's bliss?
59 Avignon's river
61 Tennyson poem
62 Another, in Córdoba
63 Brock and Piniella
64 Inflexible, to a myologist?
66 Third-rail contact
68 Word with hold or nail
71 Kansas City 11
73 Kolinsky, e.g.
75 Author Ludwig
78 Sherwood Forest weapon
80 Mrs. Irving Berlin
81 Awn
82 Isle of Man's northern point
84 One that issues forth
85 Timetable
87 Indifferent to right or wrong
89 Ending for self or sheep
90 Catch by stratagem
91 Moral
92 Dawn goddess
93 Ethiopian group
94 "... —— big red rose"
95 Short track
98 "Maine Coast" painter
100 City in Egypt
101 Lawrence and kin
102 Tittle
104 Now's partner
108 Uncle, to Pedro
109 Before, to an elegist
110 Brig. or lt. follower
112 Einstein's birthplace
113 Grande, for example
114 Superlative ending

ID's

By Nancy W. Atkinson

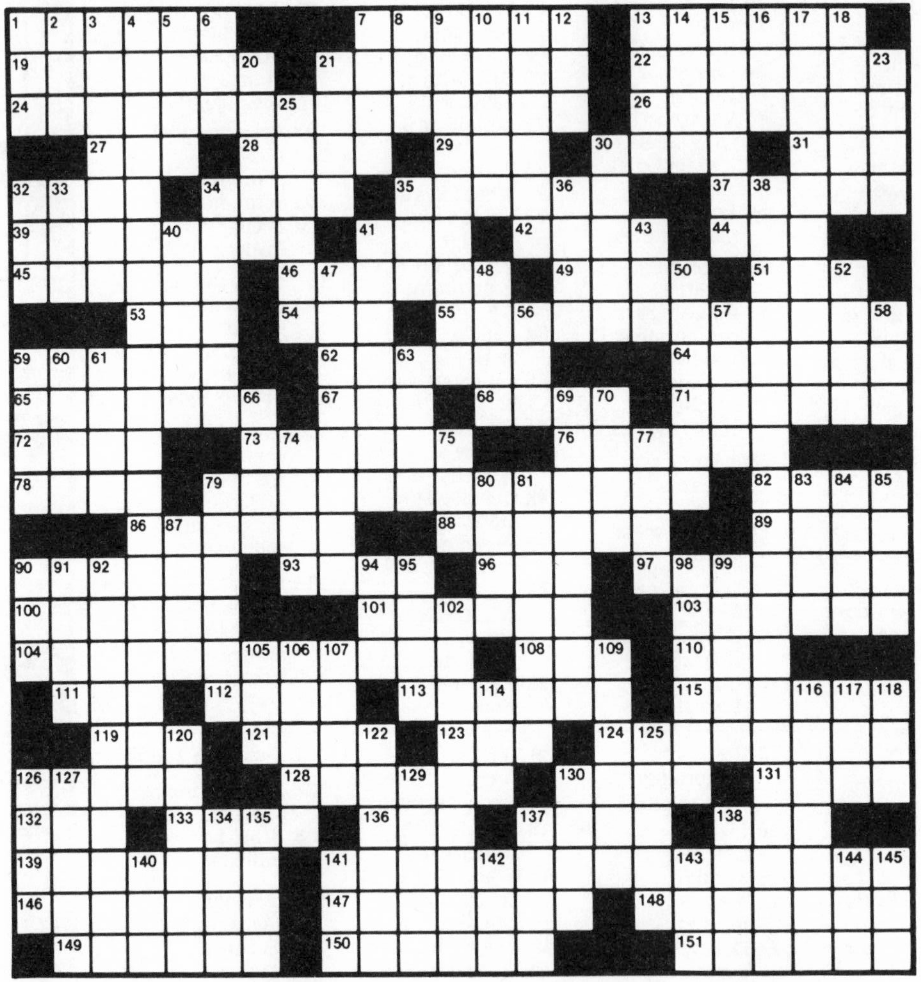

ACROSS

1 Establishes as true
7 Nursery items
13 Author of "De Oratore"
19 Sojourn anew
21 Property recipient
22 Solid ——
24 Invention
26 Film of 1963, with "The"
27 Tpk.
28 Night crawlers
29 Meek's teaser, in comics
30 Vino locale
31 Note from Guido
32 Town on the Vire
34 —— qua non
35 Black and Valentine
37 "—— is an island . . ."
39 Detective
41 Triple, e.g.
42 Stevens of opera
44 Ohio university town
45 "—— Sincere?": 1957 song
46 Ran off
49 Soccer great
51 Do wrong
53 Memorabilia
54 Costello or Grant
55 Theory
59 What Allen and Keaton often do
62 Ukrainian port
64 "—— of horns . . .": John Day
65 Hurriedly
67 Five-eighths of a mi.
68 Dodo and Hogg
71 Casino employee
72 Cambodian coin
73 Short story
76 ". . . —— and not heard"
78 Kin of etc.
79 Cartoon character
82 Bit of news
86 Head: Comb. form
88 Cash for tacos
89 Prado name
90 —— as gold
93 Brahmin
96 E.M.K. is one
97 A kind of gambler
100 —— -café
101 Chipmunk or beaver
103 Hand warmer
104 Statue
108 "Agnus ——"
110 Letter for Sappho
111 Heraldic colors
112 Altman's "Welcome ——"
113 Some New Delhi women
115 Nymph deserted by Paris
119 Part of Can.
121 Annie, for one
123 Scottish pike
124 Professor, at times
126 Duffer's problem
128 Slip by
130 Communion, e.g.
131 Eras upon eras
132 Felt shoe
133 Type of rug
136 Lee Mazzilli, e.g.
137 Desiccate
138 City transp.
139 Connecting device
141 Royalty
146 Novel
147 Like some gems
148 Separate
149 Binges
150 Plain of a sort
151 Place with lots of dough

DOWN

1 Beginning for package
2 Family mem.
3 Rest upon
4 Phrase from a W.W. II speech
5 Tasso's patron
6 Guinness, for one
7 Blind part
8 Play by e. e. cummings
9 Fraudulent voters
10 —— den Linden
11 Goblet
12 Episcopacy
13 Hacks
14 "Lord, —— I?": Matt. 26:22
15 Keellike part
16 European shrew
17 Novel character
18 City in Florida
20 Shinbone
21 "Shall Caesar send ——?"
23 Kublai ——
25 Wipe out
30 Brains or beauty
32 Bad Ems or Bex
33 Craggy place
34 Astronaut Roosa
35 Gymnastic feat
36 Australasian palm
38 Poem
40 Namesakes of Chaplin's widow
41 Erich Weiss
43 Biblical priest
47 Pay a brief call
48 He played Ricky on TV
50 Gave the go-by
52 Scratch out
56 Hood's exit
57 Relative of curare
58 Suffix with racket
59 Glossy finish
60 Step —— (hie)
61 Neighbor of La Guardia
63 Otherwise
66 Hibernia
69 Type of ballot
70 Melampus or Mopsus
74 Cannes cordial flavoring
75 Sci-fi year
77 Cram at Cambridge
79 Achieved success
80 Compiègne's department
81 Not finished
83 Tug's salute
84 Brontë heroine
85 Horace or Thomas
87 —— ha-Shanah
90 Smart as a whip
91 N.Y.C. area
92 Painting
94 Ice name
95 Wild hog
98 Obtrude
99 Japanese-American
102 Place for a hot rod
105 Wooden peg
106 Light for the set
107 "Fatha" Hines
109 O.T. book
114 Born
116 Stub —— (miscalculate)
117 Modernist
118 Pelagic flier
120 SAT participant
122 Wail
125 Fine fiddle, for short
126 Aped an angry cat
127 Kind of man or maid
129 Corps for J.F.K.
130 Foxx
134 Foolish giggle
135 Shaw's "—— and the Man"
137 Dirk of yore
138 The Adamsons' pet
140 Via
141 Lyon lily
142 Viper
143 Child's marble
144 We, in Weimar
145 Curve in a hull

65

Split Personalities

By Mary Virginia Orna

ACROSS

1 West Indian Indian
6 Distress signal
11 Hosp. group
14 Forehead
18 John or Maureen
19 Ephesus's locale
20 Chesterfield
21 Baltic island
22 Communion plate
23 "—— Day," 1929 song
24 Type of mackerel
25 Joint
26 MillWright
30 Classify
33 Carrot feature
34 Krupp's bailiwick
35 Coagulate
36 Chinese monetary unit
38 Collects bit by bit
40 ManDrake
43 Surmises
44 One of the Bobbsey twins
47 Coronet
48 Like Shea
50 Fish repository
52 Ceremony
55 Elated
56 Tons upon tons
58 School of art
60 Hamartiologist's topic
61 War site, to some G.I.'s
62 1 and 66, e.g.
63 Poker stake
64 ChildHood
68 Actor Andrews
69 Sacred image
70 Became a candidate
71 Blemish on the skin
72 Most mature
74 Cheats
77 Vega's constellation
78 Westernmost point in the U.S.A.
79 "I have —— begun to fight": J. P. Jones
80 Split ingredient
82 Plant with fleshy leaves
86 Hesitant sounds
87 Auditorium feature
90 HeadHunter
93 Dragging forcibly
94 Ibsen character
95 River to The Wash
96 Mrs. Schumann
100 A prayer
104 Certain light sources
106 BlackSmith
109 Arab ruler
110 Brooklet
111 City on the Po
112 No way!
117 Cosmos ex-star
118 Inhabitants: Suffix
119 Midas's downfall
120 Tchaikovsky's Black Swan
121 Ski turn
122 Belgian-French river
123 Pips
124 Atoll features

DOWN

1 —— a plea
2 Villain's cry
3 Weasel's prey
4 Rage
5 Type of clock
6 Spad or Fokker
7 Abandoned
8 "—— of robins . . ."
9 Texan's lariat
10 Devour
11 Words on samplers
12 Sioux
13 Reference mark
14 Foundation
15 Country dances
16 Papal vestment
17 Luce subject
20 Sang at a crèche
27 Composer Carl
28 Contended
29 Pinafore, e.g.
30 Jai ——
31 Kind of bean
32 KayO.
35 Where to see a d.a.
37 Tennis necessity
39 —— -do-well
41 Secular
42 Falls to
43 MarshallEd
44 —— a pin
45 Heated
46 Town on the Snake River
49 Creator of Mrs. Battle
51 SnowField
53 —— Mahal
54 Habituate
56 Wheel eccentric
57 Soprano Lucine
58 QE2 accessory
59 Ermines
61 Petroleum derivative
63 Soissons's river
65 —— Palmas
66 A daughter of Cronus
67 Roost
73 His temple appears in "Aïda"
75 Horse's bit
76 Graceful tree
77 More capacious
80 Cincinnati 11
81 Ohio campus town
83 State
84 Highway sights
85 180° from WSW
88 What obfuscators lack
89 Stings
91 Loyalties, e.g.
92 Lapsang souchong, etc.
96 Cowhands' accessories
97 Director Sidney
98 Supple
99 Composer Ned
101 Release

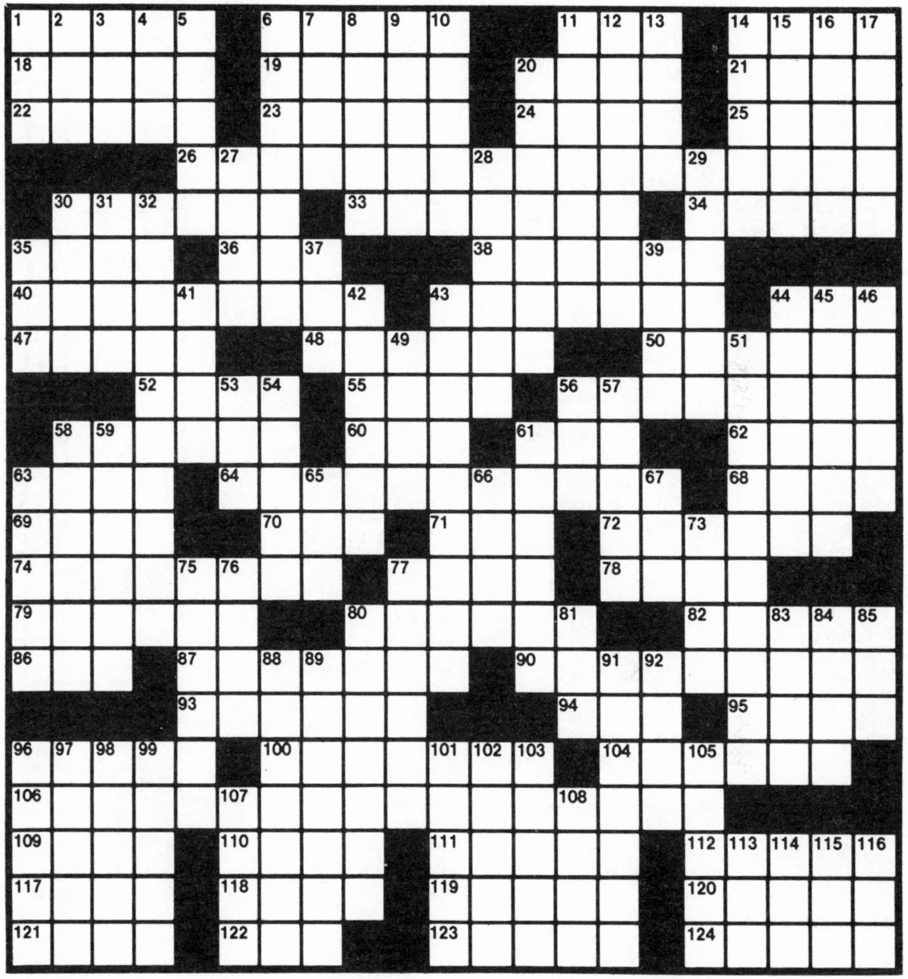

102 Driver's maneuver
103 Landslide debris
105 Caballero's title
107 Integument
108 Herr's "Here!"
113 Noted painter of birds
114 Compete
115 Shoemaker's friend
116 Object, in law

Equid Pro Quo

By Fletcher Ingalls

ACROSS

1 Nag
5 Harness, e.g.
9 Uncle, in Mulegé
12 Jackie's predecessor
17 Pique
19 Camels' watering place
21 Letter from Plato
22 His beast rebuked him
23 Straw mattress: Slang
26 Morning ringers
27 Centennial year electee
28 She was born free
29 Mlle. La Douce
30 Make one's day
31 Globes
32 Singer Laine
33 Martian: Comb. form
34 Earth's apex
36 Reb's government
37 Weapon
40 Teachers' org.
42 —— mein
44 Dactyl or hallux
45 Tintamarre
46 Pale-yellow horse
48 Querists
50 Tolerated
52 Symbol of satiety
53 Rodeo rope
54 Chassepot
55 Bill's follower
56 Soil: Prefix
57 Moderate gallop
58 Not so straightforward
59 Columnist Barrett
61 "—— up, Doc?"
63 Concern of many a carter
64 Neck and neck
65 Montana structure
68 Actor Holbrook
71 —— Park, Cleveland
72 "Follow Me ——": Kipling
73 Dank
74 Taylor nickname
75 Be an also-ran
76 Civil War general
77 Striped heliconian
80 Bombeck
81 —— diem
82 Gawk
83 Knot of wool
84 Famed street in New Orleans
85 Circus group
88 Switch positions
89 Wild Bill Donovan's org.
90 An Astaire
91 Muse with a lyre
92 Groom
94 Hoof coverer
97 Choose
98 Paddock papas
99 Poet Merriam
100 Suffix with Jacob
101 Vessel for café
102 Dir. from Barnstable to Nantucket
103 Old-fashioned
109 Burro
112 He flew the coop
116 Guthrie
117 Heroic poem
118 Salt tree
119 Robes for Pompey
120 He wrote about Private Slovik
121 Mexican's pittance
122 Cinereal
123 A driving horse
125 Black Bess
128 Willows
129 "Nut-brown ——"
130 Specialty of quarter horses
131 Jabirus' kin
132 Fuses
133 Hide —— hair
134 Isle of Man point
135 Fixes the roof

DOWN

1 Small, fast football unit
2 Massinger and Wolfe characters
3 Functions
4 Considerable, in Dundee
5 Snifter
6 —— corn (spikes)
7 In the horse latitudes
8 Creek
9 ". . . a —— snow-white horses"
10 "—— bet!"
11 Feed-bag item
12 Cheekbone
13 Winged
14 Mess
15 "Just As ——" (hymn)
16 Bad —— (spa)
17 —— committee
18 "The Crowd ——," 1932 film
20 Garbed like knights' horses
22 Bundle of hay
24 Hawk successfully
25 Norse god of love
30 Hambletonian, e.g.
32 Muleys
33 Suffix with buck
34 Ponerology topic
35 Josh
37 Kitchen gadget
38 Siouan
39 —— delight (card game)
41 —— patriae
43 City in Montana
46 Buy a horse after a race
47 Tolled
48 A poison: Comb. form
49 Famous horse of radio
50 Tulsans, e.g.
51 Chinese association
52 Encourage
55 Ort of a sort
56 "The Galloping ——" (Red Grange)
57 —— Horse, Sioux chief
60 Brassard
61 —— mule (moonshine)
62 Dissocial

65 Gardeners, at times
66 —— truly
67 Pickles
68 Bunk!
69 ". . . —— on Casey's face"
70 Good throw, in horseshoes
75 Sluggish
77 Ciphers
78 Penitent one
79 Licorice, for one
81 Writer Hamill
84 Singer Manilow
85 Polanski film
86 Emanate
87 Cirrus cloud
92 Giggle
93 Wild cry
94 Aral and others
95 —— War, great race horse
96 Ky. neighbor
97 Close knots of hair
104 Limoges item
105 Actor Estrada
106 Horn
107 Higher part
108 Muscleman
110 Like a well-groomed horse
111 Ships
113 Hid the meaning
114 Ripening agents
115 To Watson, these are elementary
118 Fur merchant
120 Big city in Hawaii
121 Raven
122 Movie pooch
123 Dust-up
124 Simple sugar
125 McGrew
126 —— tree (cornered)
127 Concorde, e.g.

Musical Meteorology

By Bert Rosenfield

ACROSS

1 "—— 'em!"
4 Tax
8 500 lbs. of cotton
12 Forecast: tornado alert
19 V.I.P. at Burning Tree
20 City in Kansas
21 Type of car
22 On a 24-hour schedule
23 Regatta necessity
24 Enlivening
26 Charms
27 Forecast: 20° Celsius
30 Actor Erickson
31 Basketry fiber
32 Lowell and Carter
33 Univ. degrees
36 The Red Raiders
39 Mar. follower
41 Start of the "Aeneid"
42 Island off Copenhagen
44 Forecast: flood watch
50 155-mm. gun
52 —— B'rith
53 Cottonseed residue
54 Hedonist of a sort
55 N.B.A. team
56 Tamarisk salt tree
57 Beth ——, Jewish tribunal
58 Certain pols
59 Suffix with ethyl
60 Openers for documents
62 —— culpa
64 Forecast: drought continues
67 Fleur-de-——
68 Archibald Leach
71 Bon follower
72 Born, in Bourges
75 "—— tu," Verdi aria
76 Virginia City phenomenon
77 Quadragesimal period
78 Immersed
82 Machiavelli
84 Navy warrant officer
85 Handel opus
86 Forecast: precipitation
89 Suppliants
90 Pinza
91 Highway sign
92 Card game
95 Pop
96 Monk's cloak
99 Hindu lute
101 Group of poems
104 Forecast: -20° Celsius
109 President Doe's land
112 "—— cannot be undone": Lady Macbeth
113 Arrowroot
114 Whence Tosca leaped
115 Chaplin's widow
116 Church mem.
117 Prefix for Asian
118 Forecast: smog warning
119 Film ambiances
120 Gypsy gentlemen
121 Want-ad abbr.

DOWN

1 Damage
2 Teed off
3 City SE of Dallas
4 Outer portion of the earth
5 Product of a Spanish pine
6 Malvolio's employer
7 Least feral
8 Synthetic rubber
9 Stage direction
10 Popilius ——, of "Julius Caesar"
11 Raw-nerved
12 Dialect of a people
13 Hop of the 40's
14 Painter —— van Leyden
15 Fay of "King Kong"
16 Hostel
17 Turner or Hentoff
18 Librarian's deg.
25 —— ego
28 Forecast: travelers' advisory
29 Pool for an oread
33 In coarse fashion
34 Appalachian range, popularly
35 Reduces toxic effects
37 Leave intact
38 He has a stable job
39 Mallard genus
40 Hawaiian staple
41 Rainbow
42 Zugspitze, for one
43 Gram weight
45 Evening in Berlin
46 Fit together
47 Emblem worship
48 Starch grain nuclei
49 Plat. or plut.
51 "Me and ——," air for Feb. 2
55 Triton
56 Constellation
60 The Panthers
61 Forecast: clearing trend
62 Countess of a Kálmán operetta
63 Heathlike
65 Waugh's "The Loved ——"
66 Seine tributary
68 Used a thurible
69 Swipe
70 Poly preceder
73 Kind of bath or boat
74 Shakespeare's "Hurry!"
77 Real estate
79 Legendary German musician
80 Stirrup site
81 A.L. tenth men
83 ——-Magnon
84 Cote noise
87 Palermo pronoun
88 Moslem weights
93 Run, British style
94 Tuckered out; mopish
96 Wrist bones
97 Awards for playwrights Breuer and Durang: 1979-80
98 Mother in "Father Knows Best"
99 Not enough
100 Whits
102 Stigma
103 Name on the world's tallest building
104 I or H
105 Bills seldom passed
106 Loafer, e.g.
107 In Gallic harmony
108 Polanski heroine
109 Pelican State inst.
110 Author Fleming
111 Bikini part

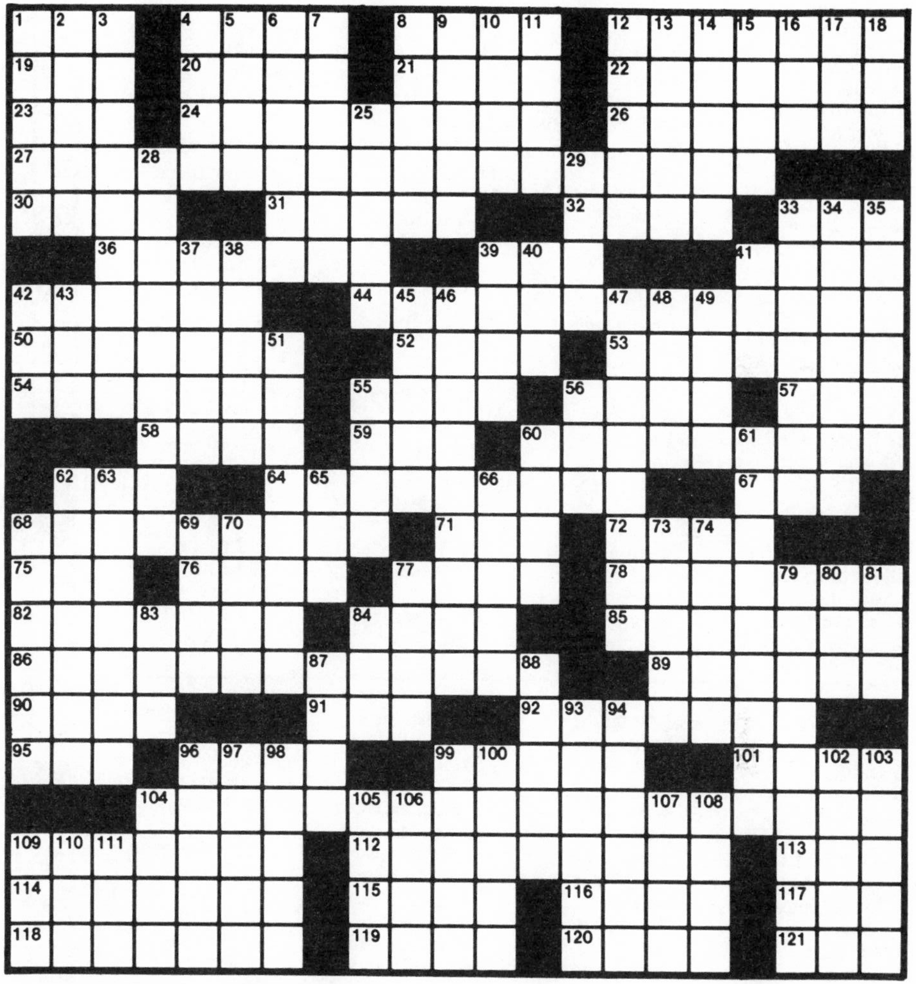

Union Members

By Judith C. Dalton

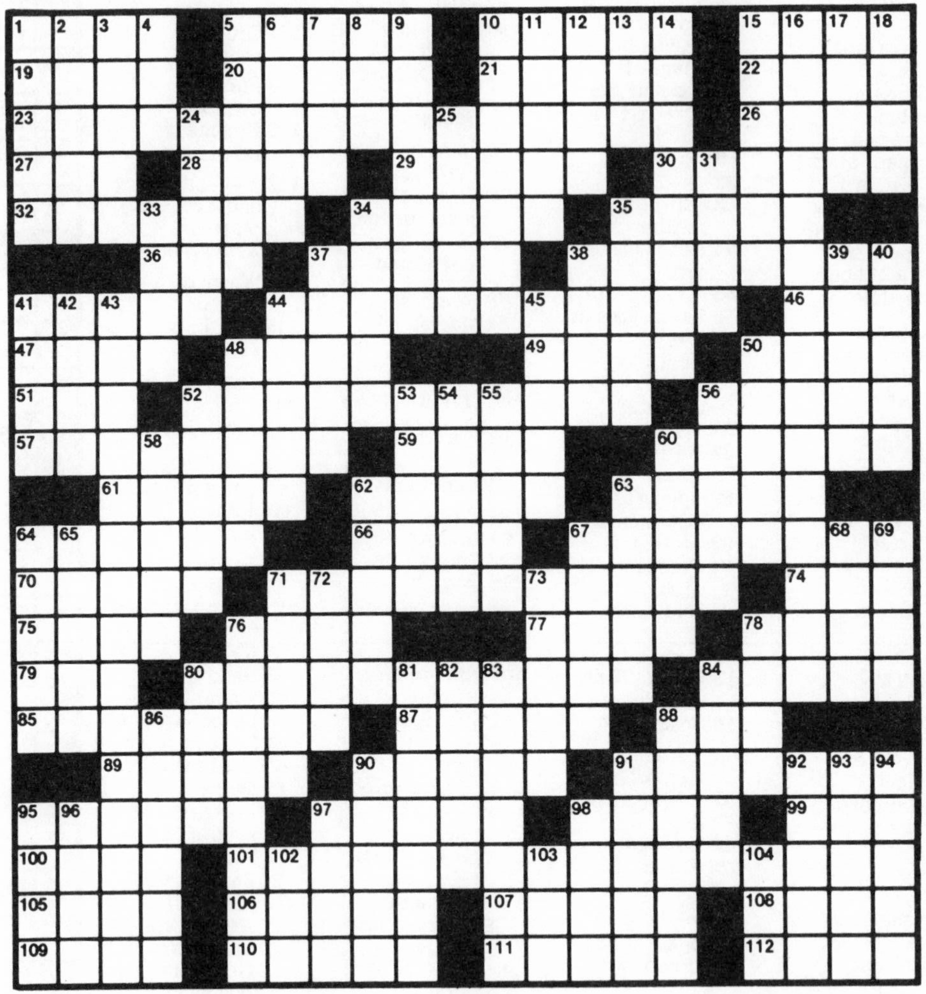

ACROSS

1 Whet
5 Gift for a virtuoso
10 Turkish cavalryman
15 Jazz singing
19 —— Bator, Mongolia
20 Coarse cotton cloth
21 Court dance
22 Young animal
23 Southern musician
26 Tub plant
27 Egg-shaped ornaments
28 Cat's-paw
29 Earls, barons et al.
30 Bars at the bar
32 Memorize again
34 Horse blanket
35 Gallery at D.C.
36 Rochet's relative
37 Craze
38 —— jerk (weight-lifting term)
41 Stale
44 Mining-area examiner
46 "Diga Diga ——," 1928 song
47 Disney's inventive mouse
48 Penalty
49 Painter Mondrian
50 Helix
51 Saint Anthony's cross
52 Austin evaluator
56 Mud volcano
57 Lively
59 Stake of a sort
60 Harangue
61 Farmer, often
62 "Deutschland über ——"
63 Rorschach items
64 Descendants
66 Nourish
67 Baldness
70 Cautious
71 Thankless wretch from Cheyenne
74 O'Neill's monogram
75 Chevalier's strap
76 To's antithesis
77 Sponsorship
78 Shortly
79 Period
80 Dixie dilettante
84 Metric measure in Manchester
85 Eavesdrops, modern style
87 Have —— for news
88 Unite
89 Wooden-soled shoes
90 Well-worn
91 Like some doughnuts
95 Musical key
97 "Beau ——"
98 Gas: Prefix
99 Pinna
100 Reno token
101 Sooner official
105 Polanski film
106 Follower of book or wood
107 "All —— for Christmas . . ."
108 Great Barrier Island
109 Loathe
110 Kefauver
111 Largest asteroid
112 Rhabdos

DOWN

1 Indulge
2 Oil producer
3 Twangy
4 Quartet in "No, No, Nanette"
5 Collect liquid in condensed form
6 Nuclear particle
7 Blue dye
8 Baksheesh
9 Grafted part
10 Native of Laconia
11 Zoo attraction
12 Rara ——
13 "—— Dog": Terhune
14 Personal influence
15 New York island
16 Western teen-ager
17 Surmounting
18 Dactyl and hallux
24 Where Leghorn is
25 Asia Minor region of yore
31 Garment part
33 Engineer James Buchanan
34 Spirits, to Seneca
35 Pamphlet
37 Unit
38 Muse for Thucydides
39 Cacophony
40 Gave out sparingly
41 Conductor Eduardo
42 Middle East land
43 Bayou revolutionary
44 Good party guest
45 Church parts
48 Galas
50 Bill of fare
52 Brownish-yellow
53 Oregon's capital
54 Chou ——
55 Unyielding
56 Range
58 George or Marianne
60 Grooves
62 Bouquet
63 D.C. House
64 Fastener
65 Colette novel
67 Debate
68 Borodin's Prince
69 The best
71 Envelops
72 Soho fellows
73 Gaggle members
76 Schoolyard sight
78 Verdi opera
80 Doer: Suffix
81 Paludous places
82 Philippine idol
83 Like carved emblems
84 On the up and up
86 Slide by
88 Sausages
90 Hector
91 Sight from Pont Neuf
92 Lariat
93 Ingested
94 Great fear
95 Kin of corti one
96 Mets' home
97 Nimiety
98 Kanten
102 Ring events
103 Reverence
104 Tier

69 Jingle, Jingle

By Ruth N. Schultz

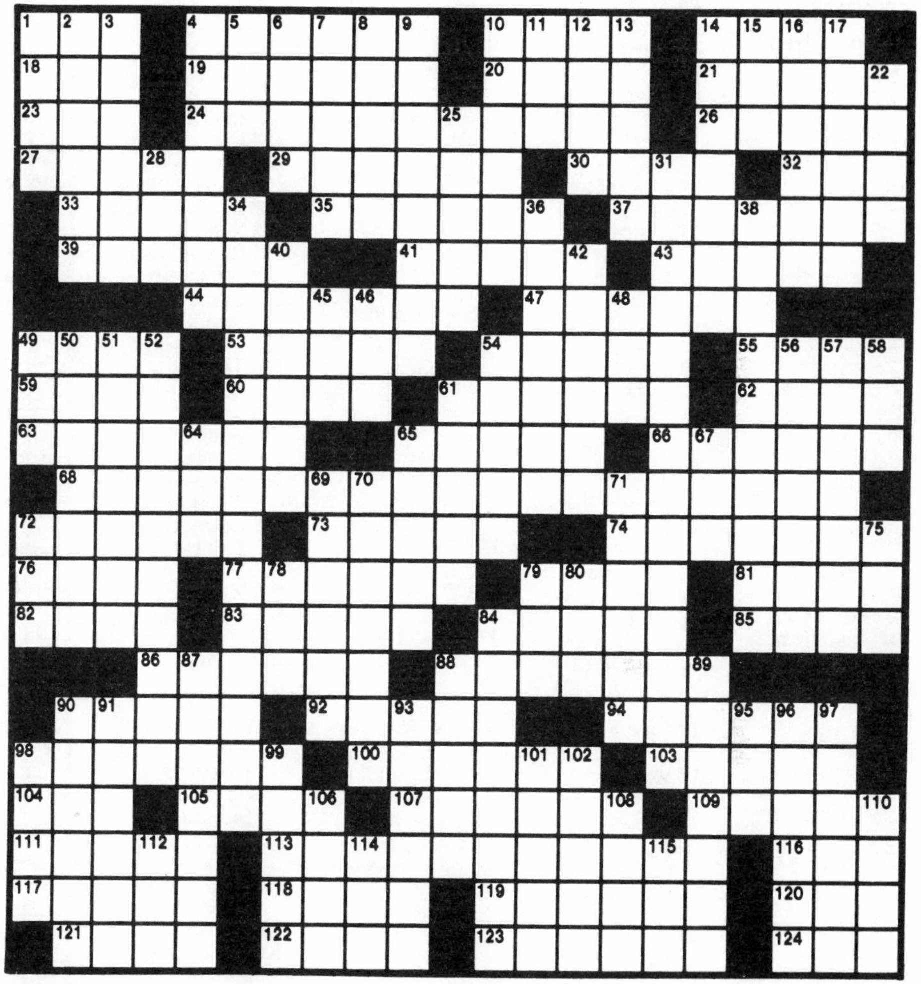

ACROSS

1 Bowl off.
4 Greet the shogun
10 Luxuriate
14 Suffix with canon
18 Fadiman's "Party of ——"
19 Matriarch in "The Glass Menagerie"
20 Author Leffland
21 These are bleeped on TV
23 Suffix for dull
24 Arthur's bewitching sister
26 Consider pros and cons
27 Biblical mother-in-law
29 Not often
30 Pirates' cry
32 Christmas gift
33 King of the "topless towers"
35 Fall fallers
37 Seasoned
39 Kind of acid
41 Pre-Pasch periods
43 Soft-palate sound
44 Erasmus was one
47 Go to mass
49 Saga name
53 Kunta Kinte scion
54 Extorted
55 Vestige
59 Oeillade
60 Sailing
61 Begin to enjoy a feast
62 ". . . gently —— perfumed sea": Poe
63 Gay and family
65 Decree in Canada
66 Penny-pinch
68 Words by Lorenz Hart: 1937
72 Clever imitation
73 Gardner et al.
74 Gift for a gypsy
76 Osiris's crown
77 Taken down several pegs
79 Bad Ems and Bath
81 Henry's second or fourth
82 Offspring: Abbr.
83 He wrote "Rhymes of Childhood"
84 Herod's place
85 North Sea feeder
86 Color of a stormy sky
88 Poppaea in "The Sign of the Cross": 1932
90 Stigma
92 Ready to greet the day
94 Salary hikes
98 Carter
100 OPEC, e.g.
103 Baker's need
104 Ball-park verdict
105 Votes for
107 Like some postcards
109 Cellist Jacqueline
111 Feminine endings
113 Poet's "wonderful" vehicle
116 Skate
117 Golden and slide
118 Type of star
119 Home of the Green Wave
120 Suffix with Bethlehem
121 Withered
122 Influence
123 Percolated slowly
124 Moppet

DOWN

1 Reddish brown
2 On cloud nine
3 Giordano opera
4 Greek islanders
5 Opposite of odi
6 Porsena
7 Crèche figure
8 Allan-—— of legend
9 Road's end for Kipling
10 Hive operators
11 Landon
12 Do in
13 Ring victories
14 Entwined
15 Great miler
16 "Peer Gynt" enchantress
17 More sluggish
22 Lean-to
25 Hero, to Leander
28 Mrs. Gump
31 "All we like sheep ——": Isaiah
34 Diamagnetism discoverer
36 Winters in 1944
38 Stephen Foster song
40 Dance step
42 Fools, to Fabius
45 Comedian Olsen
46 Pasture
48 Explosive
49 Piece of land
50 "Liberté! ——! Fraternité!"
51 Group of clay minerals
52 Idol's disappointing features
54 Emulates Cassandra
56 Gets back
57 Mrs. ——, in "Lady Windermere's Fan"
58 Go, in Scotland
61 "How About You?" lyricist
64 Gen.'s aides
65 Tin Pan ——
67 Jerusalem is its cap.
69 Calf
70 Insecticide ingredient
71 Start of an Adams hymn
72 "It —— to Be You"
75 Neighbor of Aust.
78 Auction action
79 Hurok
80 The "local"
84 Events for puzzle solvers
87 In a group
88 Tail: Prefix
89 Hand-colored, as fabric
90 Famed conspirator
91 Gift for a baby
93 Alteration of 40 Down
95 Belgrade's river, to a Berliner
96 —— de corps
97 Layers
98 Facient
99 Lights on a marquee
101 Result
102 Material for socks
106 White Christmas sight
108 Fellow
110 Like a peacock's feathers
112 Poetic contraction
114 Lehár work
115 Onager, in Oise

70

Seasonal Songs

By Anne Fox

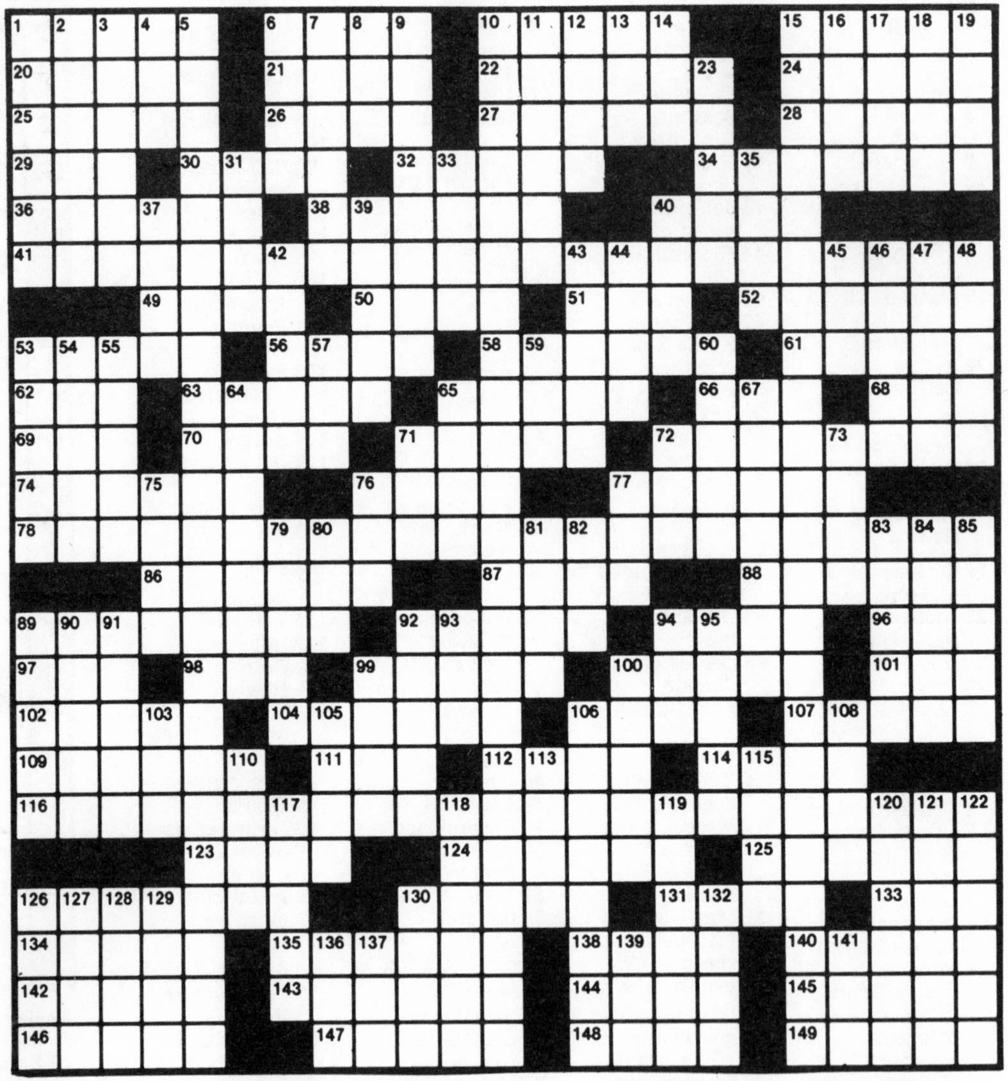

ACROSS

1 Kind of buckler
6 Von —— (German count)
10 Malignity
15 Overwhelm
20 Fragrance
21 Quatre follower
22 Summons
24 —— Soleil (Louis XIV)
25 Obstruct
26 Indic language
27 Seventh largest state
28 De Valera
29 "—— in the Shade," 1963 musical
30 Family member
32 Bellini's sleepwalker
34 Full
36 Goes wrong
38 Close-fitting caps
40 Brilliant stratagem
41 Words from an English carol
49 African antelope
50 Arm of the Black Sea
51 Law of Laon
52 Jerry-built
53 Delicate
56 Meadow mouse
58 Beethoven's Third
61 Illinois city
62 —— cit.
63 Perfect
65 Rubinstein
66 Ruby or Sandra
68 Yoko ——
69 A vote
70 Presley hit
71 Peace Nobelist: 1911
72 Ran wild
74 Petit four, e.g.
76 Ancient Briton's foe
77 Alley item
78 U.S. folk song
86 Manhattan ——
87 Envious ensign
88 Garibaldi's country
89 Some chickens
92 African trade language
94 Chaff
96 Siouan
97 Direction suffix
98 Word with come or go
99 —— one (Indian file)
100 Shrewd
101 Zero
102 Snare
104 Latin poet
106 Voiceless consonant
107 Some roles
109 Smitten
111 Whistler, at times
112 "—— the night before . . ."
114 Black
116 Words from "Wassail Song"
123 Sauce thickener
124 Crepey cloth
125 Amos —— Stagg
126 Feet for Homer
130 Venetian red
131 Crèche figure
133 Gym item
134 Dome-shaped dwelling
135 —— his own
138 Verdon
140 Constructed
142 Terrier
143 Fountain favorite
144 Eugene's daughter
145 Cosmetician Lauder
146 Danish coin
147 Kingdom
148 Comic sketch
149 Memorable Israeli

DOWN

1 Cruel one
2 Visible spirit
3 Honshu port
4 Dallas inst.
5 Words by A. McCreery
6 Food fish
7 Crime at sea
8 Lineman
9 Make even
10 Words from "Adeste Fideles"
11 Nevertheless
12 PBS program
13 River to the Volga
14 Kind of sch.
15 Words by F. A. Gevaert
16 Take away gradually
17 First word of the "Aeneid"
18 Wasteland
19 Like some woods
23 Taste-producing quality
31 Very wet
33 Manner, in Murcia
35 Boxer Firpo
37 Piedmontese wine center
39 In any way
40 Smart
42 Pep up
43 Genesis event
44 Mint
45 Wire: Abbr.
46 Son of Japheth
47 Dye type
48 Church council
53 U.S. illustrator: 1877-1960
54 Princely
55 Vinegar: Comb. form
57 Cereal grass
59 Road map abbr.
60 Hersey town
64 Letter
65 Word with fiend or enemy
67 Derring-do
71 Proper
72 Jewish title of respect
73 Singer Paul
75 Apple thrower of myth
76 Pericarp
77 Company, proverbially
79 Mother ——
80 Wts.
81 Ex-prime minister of Hungary
82 Kind of trip
83 A Massey
84 Bright; lustrous
85 British prisons
89 Back out of: Colloq.
90 "Stein Song" home
91 "There was —— woman . . ."
92 Bollixed up
93 N.R.C. predecessor
94 Container
95 Utah city
99 Mountain: Comb. form
100 Pointed ends
103 Sea call
105 Eland's cousin
106 Hard, green cheeses
108 Greek war goddess
110 Chemical compound
113 Charles's —— (Big Dipper)
115 Tolerate
117 Wipes off
118 Topmost
119 Native of Sana
120 Ill will
121 Garden shrub
122 Spoiled
126 Tec
127 Culture medium
128 Inspiration for Thucydides
129 Actor Rip
130 Actress Thompson
132 Sister of Baal
136 Possessive
137 Compass pt.
139 Chinese cooker
141 Dos Passos trilogy

Stepquote for '82

By E.T.M.

ACROSS

1 Start of Stepquote
7 Propounded
12 Love song
18 Yukon garb
19 Daydream
21 Panay port
22 Safe
23 Diaskeuast's task
24 Principal's kin
25 Haven
26 Indulge in cabotinage
28 Black-belt art
30 Norris Dam agcy.
31 Darrow client
33 Stepquote: Part III
36 Hebrew letter
37 Absquatulated
38 Pandurinas
40 More recent
42 The sandbox set
44 Perfume
46 Lifetime, to Lucretius
48 "Father of French Surgery"
49 Gate
51 Month after Ab
53 "—— Have Broadway," 1906 song
57 Item raised by some sharks
60 German seaport
62 Disposed
63 Affair at a salon
64 "—— Valentine"
66 Jerseys' laments
68 Beatles' Pepper
69 Slews
70 Considerable sum of money
73 Appear
74 "Spring ahead" in N.Y.C.
75 Gypsum
76 Saarinen
77 Mrs. Kowalski
79 Oleoresin
82 Mouth: Comb. form
84 Beating of a drum
86 Scrutinize
88 Aspersion
89 Delitescent
90 "—— little prayer . . ."
92 Inspiration for Pindar
94 Query in I Samuel 17
98 Site of a Bernini baldacchino
102 Accrues
104 Canyon or Carlton
105 Cries of triumph
106 European coal basin
108 Stepquote: Part V
110 Legendary Irish king
111 Suffix with cash
112 Drooped
114 Soothing word
116 Estuary
117 Segovia's companion
119 Issue forth
122 Early center of Christianity
124 Take for granted
125 Naval stores item
126 Dancer-actor Ben
127 Titles in colonial India
128 Headline word in July 1973
129 End of Stepquote

DOWN

1 He named Louisiana
2 Burdensome
3 "And the —— red glare . . ."
4 Actress Joanne
5 Stable belle
6 Stepquote: Part II
7 Place for an idol
8 Egg: Comb. form
9 Coterie
10 Composer Satie
11 Coin in Qain
12 "A —— Thought" (Stepquote source)
13 Nautical term
14 —— cit. (footnote)
15 Popular impersonator
16 "It was —— and his lass": Shak.
17 Catfish
19 Neural networks
20 Showy bird
27 Young hooters
29 Soaking wet
32 Devices emitting signals
34 Printemps follower
35 Stepquote: Part IV
37 ——-de-lis
39 Saw cords in bed
41 Govern
43 Tackle; sack
45 Like a ghost story
47 Pantomimist
50 Certifies under oath
52 "Il Trovatore" heroine
54 TV sportscaster
55 Writer Thirkell
56 Connors is one
57 "And miles to go before ——": Frost
58 Tickle the keys idly
59 Giggle
60 N.Y.C. subway
61 Sine qua ——
65 Burton's co-star in "Becket"
67 Complex of schools
71 In medias ——
72 Cosset
73 Partitioned
78 Ancient Egyptian city
80 Ponders
81 "—— engaged in guessing . . .": Poe
83 Imprison
85 "—— of Honey"
87 Sights that are blights
89 Young and Swit
91 Sea in Turkestan
93 Junior's Saturday evening post
95 Lowered
96 Abroad, to a Londoner
97 Where to get good marks
98 Siberian antelopes
99 Les Etats-Unis
100 Celtics' center
101 Starchy foodstuff
103 Wide blue yonder
107 Pardon
109 Stepquote: Part VI
112 Author of the Stepquote
113 Famed newspaper editor: 1819-97
115 River joining the Fulda
118 Parson bird
120 Cotton knot
121 Spenserian hag
123 Suffix with cook or rook

Employeese

By Jim Page

ACROSS

1 Khayyám
5 Cleric's title: Abbr.
9 Kind of knight or sweeper
15 Attend Exeter, e.g.
19 Deep mud
20 River at Leeds
21 Chicago-fire name
22 Tony of fairway fame
23 "Farewell" and "goodbye," to a stagehand
25 EKG's, to a watchmaker
27 Righted the tenpins
28 —— -anker (Ger. kedge)
30 Wedding-report word
31 "Gunsmoke" et al.
32 Subject of Pope's mock-heroic
33 Ripley's "Believe—— Not"
34 Noted friend of Leonardo
37 Dep.
38 Hawaiian goose
39 Pen name
40 Lodge, as a protest
41 Bolger, Bailar et al.
43 Critic Huxtable
46 Wielded the baton
48 Former campus org.
49 Tucker's partner
52 Special concern of a tailor
57 Ballroom dance
59 Actor Greene
60 Fuliginous
63 Porgy
64 Type of farmer
66 Fairy queen
69 Crystal gazer's opening
70 Prime Oregon land, to a realtor
72 Higgins or Moriarty
75 State of nonexistence
76 Hilo neckwear
77 Strong Greek brandy
79 "Woe——!"
80 Thanksgiving Day: Abbr.
82 Portly
84 Bani-Sadr, for one
86 Exerting influence, as a puppeteer
90 Ending for ethyl
91 Holders of i.o.u.'s
94 Yang's counterpart
95 Mao—— -tung
96 "Fire in the Lake" family
97 "Wiener Frauen" composer
100 Jungfrau, etc.
102 Actor Jannings
104 Hines or Siepi
108 "—— told by an idiot . . ."
109 River of Greece
111 Jane, to Tarzan
112 Televox
113 Poilu
115 Long time span
116 Part of être
117 Book by Read
118 Objective of a Dover fisherman
121 Newspapers, radio and TV, to a Boston ad exec
123 College in N.C.
124 Grayish tans
125 Yucca's kin
126 Titubate
127 Planes once barred from J.F.K.
128 Kraits
129 Its grads are often at sea
130 Scraps for Spot

DOWN

1 Sicilian code of silence
2 Get-togethers
3 Rebels
4 SAT, given again
5 Avril follower
6 Bear market, to a stockbroker
7 Ali, to himself
8 Virginia city
9 Foldaway
10 Type of skirt
11 Grade-schooler's break
12 "Ma and ——," 1949 movie
13 Homophone for air
14 Beginner
15 Typewriter part
16 Is contrite
17 Like some aquatic plants
18 Jaworski and Todd, e.g.
24 O.T.S. grads
26 Poet Nahum
29 "Don't —— me"
35 Ogler
41 Certain G.I.
42 Faces
44 Malicious talk
45 Blyth, from Mt. Kisco
47 —— Plaines
49 Dithers or Tweed
50 Charm
51 Bondi, from Chicago
53 High spirits
54 Mephistopheles, e.g.
55 Lyon product
56 —— the towel (cede)
58 Stepped on the gas
61 Music-hall star O'Shea
62 Petty officer
65 Ham's father, to Italians
67 Parseghian
68 Training tip, to a cigar packer
71 Merchant ship, in Tokyo
73 N.D. city
74 Story by Chateaubriand
77 Fort spread
78 Regards highly
81 Stallone's nickname
83 Purchased: Abbr.

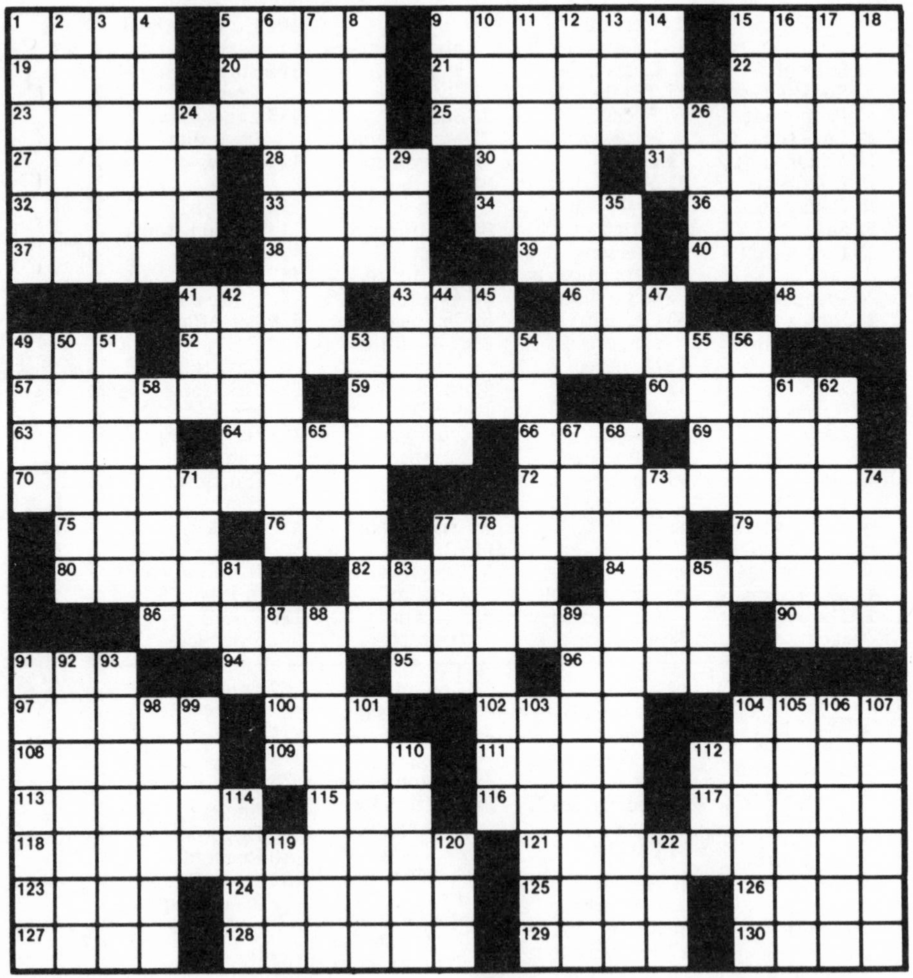

85 Silly one
87 City in Ohio
88 Fearless; bold
89 Signs a memo
91 Reunion groups
92 Adapts factory machinery
93 Small onion
98 Pilgrim couple
99 Cut grain
101 Moe or Curly
103 Kenyan secret society
104 Ravel classic
105 Resident
106 It's Supreme in Moscow
107 Purloins
110 Goose genus
112 Fordham's mascot
114 Big horn
119 Barber or Rurfing
120 Snaky curve
122 China, e.g.

73 Activists

By Richard Silvestri

ACROSS

1 Practice pedagogy
6 Anjou or Seckel
10 Live oak
16 Piece of needlework
18 —— the hills
20 Rode the Robert E. Lee
21 Evidence of error
22 Grip
23 Producing heat
24 Ex-Cub saves money
26 Winglike parts
28 Gagarin
29 "Buenos ——"
30 Friend of Larry and Curly
31 Good for plowing
33 Bill
34 Still
35 Emcee stops driving
38 Vacillate
40 Sun, at times
43 First sign
44 Grieg character
45 Charged particles
46 Hair net
47 Diamond "thief"
51 Sonnet part
54 Capital of Nigeria
55 Star-shaped
56 Movie heroes
57 Comedian is stifled
59 Col.'s boss
60 Unsettle
61 Helicon
62 Clumsy one's expression
63 Ilk
64 British verb ending
65 Poet gets angry
69 Booth item
70 Entered the lists
72 Waste maker
73 Canted
74 Earthworm, for one
75 Many-eyed monster
76 Bellow
77 Something to cast
78 American dogwood
79 Branch of physics
82 Sorrow
84 Showman went up in the world
87 Syrian weight
89 Serenade the umpire
90 Sonly or daughterly
92 Wrath
93 Olive genus
94 Bard's river
96 Cardinal point
97 Playwright digs
100 A fate worse than debt
102 Prefix with mural
105 In trouble
106 Small explosive
107 Reef material
108 Certain commuters
109 Confers upon
110 Tuesday
111 Molts

DOWN

1 Lingers
2 Flow forth
3 Orbit point
4 Aid for Miss Marple
5 Mace or sage
6 Kind of veto
7 Building additions
8 City SSE of Enid
9 Butter of a sort
10 Actress tends to her garden
11 Wedding-report word
12 Grant from Bristol
13 Safe from disease
14 Start of an Adams hymn
15 Comic's forte
16 Rundown
17 Gadgets for pipes
19 Activated
20 Use a shiv
25 Correlative
27 Girl for Lauder
31 Melodious
32 Art supporters
35 Inclination
36 Indications of hunger
37 Forster's "—— with a View"
39 Schnitzel ingredient
41 What Holmes gained
42 Pedal pentad
46 Philippine island
47 Rome's Spanish ——
48 Shallow bay
49 Forever, poetically
50 Let
51 Watergate judge
52 Famed patentee
53 Like a high mass
54 Adjective for some leaves
55 Stood out
57 Formed a hollow cylinder
58 Law-school subject
61 Comedienne plays shortstop
63 Puppeteer Lewis
65 Bull-pen assistance
66 Home-team home run, e.g.
67 Lox repository
68 Shylock's practice
69 Turf fuel
71 Foot: Comb. form
73 Run easily
75 Mongol or Tatar
76 Kane's treasured object
78 Sashes
80 Distorted a story
81 Runs through
82 Rule
83 Did thatching
85 Coarsely jocular
86 Stibnite, e.g.
88 Slackens
89 Merit ——
91 Recent
93 ". . . —— Tiger?": Stockton
95 One-billionth: Prefix
97 Inland sea
98 Javanese tree
99 Reckless
101 Detroit org.
103 Here's partner
104 Due follower

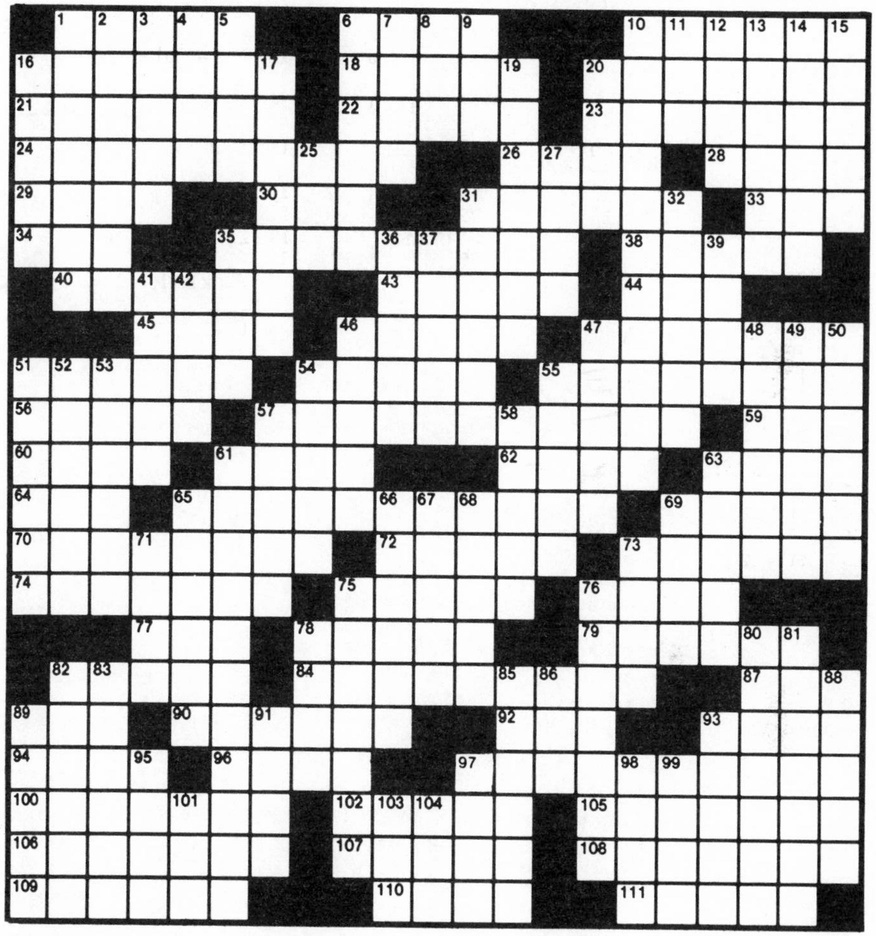

74 Exit Lines

By Edward J. Marchese

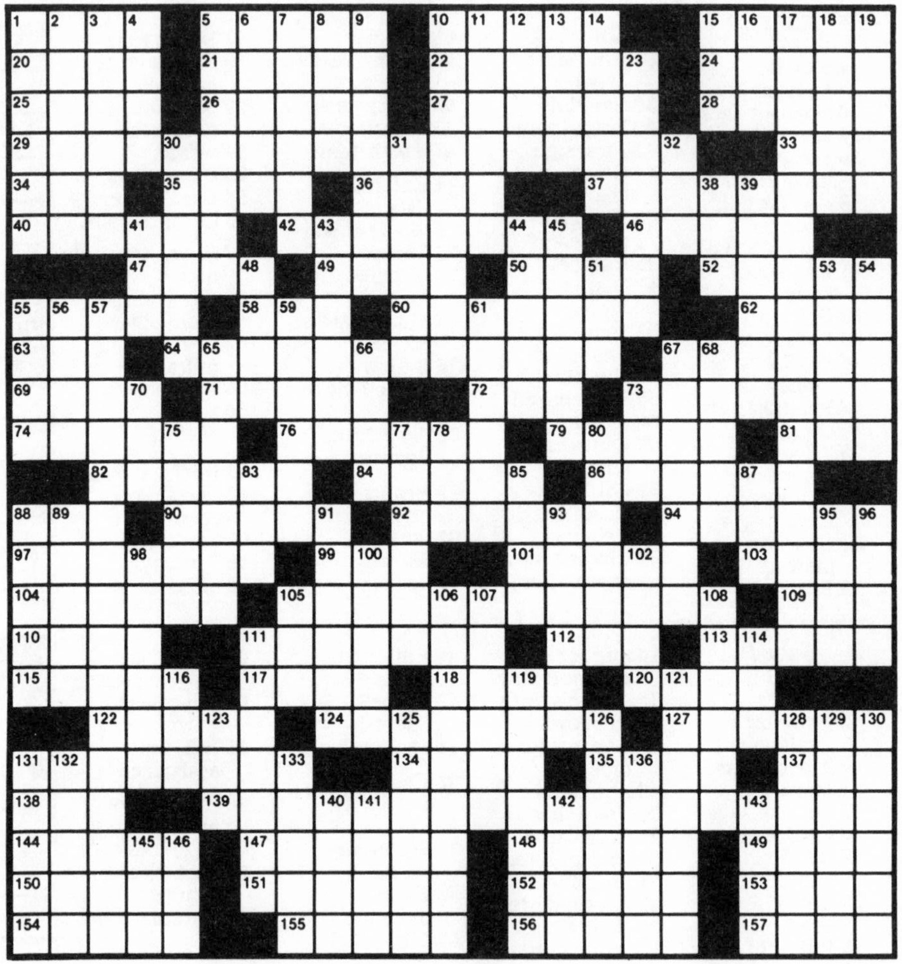

ACROSS

1 Barriers
5 Expenditures
10 God to a Meccan
15 Authoritative book
20 One of the Ages
21 Moslem units of weight
22 Corrupt
24 Ryan of Hollywood
25 King of the Huns
26 Singer Lanza
27 Regulate
28 Inner self
29 Last words of Robert E. Lee
33 Contemporary diarist
34 Before, to Byron
35 Toward the sheltered side
36 Head of an abbé
37 Shorthand notebook
40 Energy personified
42 Exhibits
46 Flooded
47 Core
49 Arabian Sea gulf
50 Winged
52 Doubly
55 Singing group
58 Kimono sash
60 Environmentalist's concern
62 Astringent
63 Expression of disgust
64 Epitaph Dorothy Parker suggested for herself
67 Remove, as by surgery
69 Dec. 24 and 31
71 Rubber city
72 Suffix for Finn
73 Jinni summoner
74 Arab's robe
76 Reddish-yellow dye
79 Mystical meditators
81 Objective
82 "Mansfield Park" author
84 —— operandi
86 Barfly's order
88 Hockey great
90 Opted
92 River bordering Manchuria
94 Having equal footing
97 Empty
99 Basic trio at school
101 Baffling problem
103 India butter
104 Low-I.Q. group
105 "Benjamin Franklin . . . lies here, ——"
109 Tiriac of tennis
110 N.Z. honey eaters
111 Model
112 Printing measures
113 Factory
115 Ruhr hub
117 Personal: Prefix
118 Arkin or Mowbray
120 Fencer's weapon
122 Depict
124 Faultfinding
127 Like a winning team
131 Retract
134 State bird of Hawaii
135 Kind of car
137 Miscue
138 —— standstill
139 End of Dryden's epitaph for his wife
144 Party in a money deal
147 Inventor of the phonograph
148 Fungus disease
149 At the peak
150 Given preference
151 Salt marsh
152 Ancestor
153 Betray
154 Light anchor
155 Hailey novel
156 Utter
157 Right

DOWN

1 Tuned in
2 Major thoroughfare
3 Liquefied by heat
4 Fit of pique
5 King Arthur's turf
6 Speak pompously
7 Oscar winner: 1979
8 Tinfoil for mirrors
9 Made grooves
10 Strong desire
11 Unbind
12 Rhythmic tune
13 Province of Saudi Arabia
14 Dupe
15 Woman's scarf
16 Auberge
17 W.C. Fields's epitaph: ". . . I'd rather ——"
18 Keats poem
19 Antelope
23 Source of honey
30 Descendant of a son of Noah
31 Be fitting
32 London suburb
38 Turner or Hentoff
39 St. Aidan's patron
41 Do likewise
43 —— d'être
44 Anklebone
45 Like wading areas
48 Part of a horse's leg
51 F.B.I. man
53 Interrupt
54 Castigate texts
55 Oil cartel
56 René's "Comment ——?"
57 Alleged last words of Rabelais
59 Russia's windstorms
61 Abhorrent
65 Achilles' talking horse
66 City in ancient Palestine
67 Synonym for 50 Across
68 "—— Street Blues"
70 Erwin or Udall
73 Mature
75 English track
77 —— force (clever creation)
78 Football stats
80 Prayer
83 Orion's beloved
85 Mgr., e.g.
87 Fall behind
88 Egg-shaped
89 Branch, to a biologist
91 Amatory
93 Ivanhoe's bride
95 Long time
96 Hire
98 Open
100 Helicopter part
102 Gaelic
105 A day's craze
106 Kind of twin
107 In a queue
108 Expedites
111 What Nolan Ryan does
114 Was ahead
116 Beak
119 "Aeneid" archer
121 Time before nightfall
123 Nose: Prefix
125 Chant
126 Capital of Angola
128 Roscoe
129 Imitation gold
130 Kind of crown
131 Author of "R.U.R."
132 "I could —— unfold . . ."
133 Malaysian state
136 Show scorn
140 Missile's home
141 Strange —— seems
142 Slant
143 Kiln
145 Cardiac perf. chart
146 Summer in Lyon

75

Those in Favor

By Alfio Micci

ACROSS

1 Rockfish
5 Word in Caesar's message
9 Chagall
13 Oat or corn follower
17 First garden
18 Sec. of the Treasury
19 —— by verdict
20 Horse's-mouth intelligence
21 Friendship emblems
23 Part of a table setting
25 Reconciliation expert
26 "—— thee sixpence . . .": Shak.
28 Coiffure protector
29 Unyielding
30 Turkish title
31 Anglo-Saxon lawsuit
33 Tend a furnace
35 Block up
37 Strengthen
41 Epsom ——
42 One not given due consideration
45 Seaman
46 Sioux
47 Spoil
48 At sea
49 Actor Moses
50 "I can get —— you wholesale"
51 Government department
56 Players at the right of dealers
57 Of a tribal spirit
59 Sampler verb
60 Prickly shrub
61 "Do I —— Waltz?"
62 Had in mind
63 Sch. official
64 Social beauty
65 Partner of room
66 Burma's capital
69 Water carriers
70 Leading the way
73 Mine yield
74 Nobel physicist: 1922
75 Med. school subject
76 Yak or chin
77 Hawaiian shrub
78 Mexican crested parrot
79 Uses a bit
83 Leaflet
84 Whip
87 Trencherman
88 Normand of silents
89 Omit
91 She had several fans
92 Costa ——
93 Ipse ——
95 Phileas's family
97 Bar orders
101 Service branch
103 Awaits
105 Bossy's home
106 Pledges
107 East or West
108 Author José Martínez
109 He wrote "A Death in the Family"
110 Cape
111 A few
112 Sicilian resort

DOWN

1 Improvement
2 Margin
3 Indigence
4 Daughter of Oedipus
5 Malice
6 Frankenstein's assistant
7 Mehitabel, for one
8 Discernment
9 Neighbor of Ia.
10 Mine entrances
11 Court whistler
12 Symbol of Turkish power
13 Ancient Cretan
14 Within: Prefix
15 Furnish
16 —— Sabha, India's lower house
18 Make a new knot
19 N.Z. tree
22 Report-card entries
24 Against
27 Liquor quantity
30 Future oak
32 Clean the blackboard
33 —— voce
34 Counting-rhyme phrase
36 Join up
38 Chinese-dinner finale
39 Rattan worker
40 Pelagic birds
41 Trifle
42 Ant genus
43 Joke
44 Soft shoes, for short
49 Auctioneer's word
51 Certain dances
52 Emerald Isle, once
53 Voodooism
54 Outburst
55 —— oneself (manage alone)
56 Snapshot
58 Certain fisherman
60 Cereal coat
62 Blotch
63 Kind of car
64 Yale marching song
65 —— B'rith
67 College at Oxford
68 Beside
69 Steeplejack's item
70 "The Lady ——"
71 Sea arm
72 Heyerdahl boat
75 Math process
77 Tuna
80 Sweater sizes
81 "The —— at eve . . .": Scott
82 Debate
83 Aspect
85 Hydrocarbon
86 Hipbones
88 Center
90 Exertions
92 Wash cycle
93 Boring one
94 Nagy of Hungary
96 "Rosenkavalier" baron
97 Where Anna taught
98 —— for one's money
99 Check
100 Italian statesman-historian: 1873-1952
101 Arab cloak
102 "Norma ——"
104 —— Locks

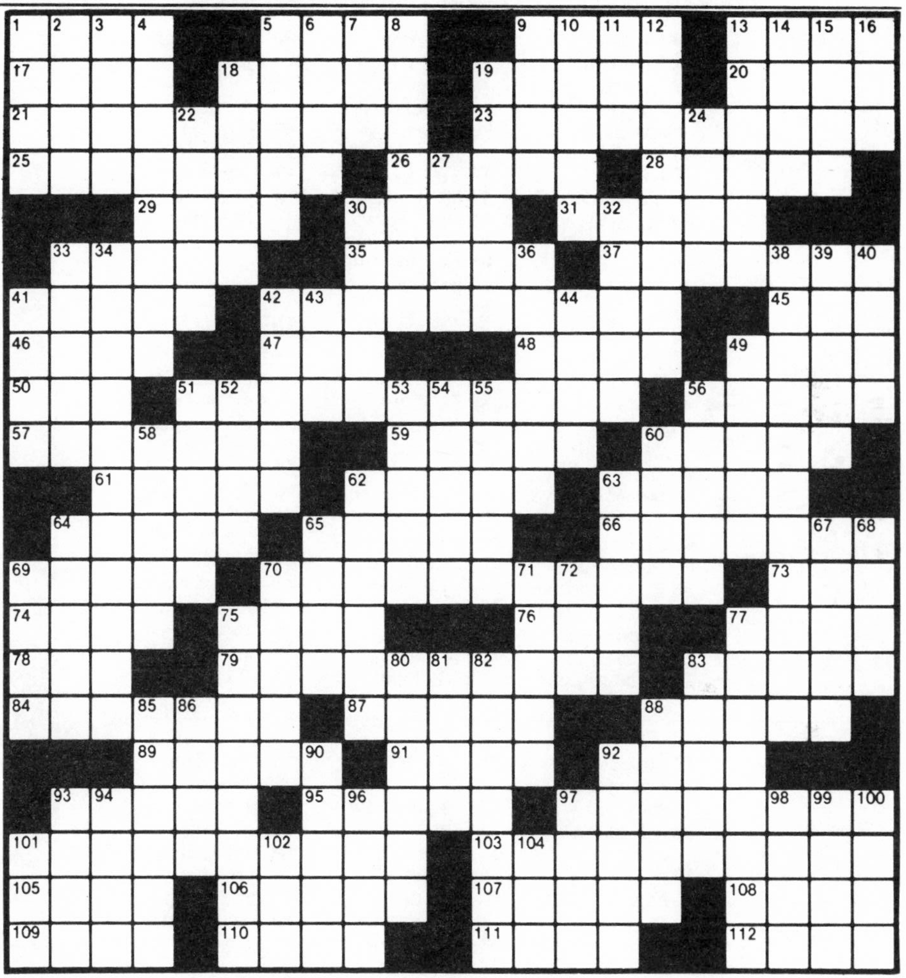

Relatively Speaking

By John M. Samson

ACROSS

1 Played the part
6 Retired N.C. senator
11 "God's Little ——"
15 Greek letters
19 Enfold
20 Kind of acid
21 An anagram for nail
22 "Let ——," Beatles hit
23 Brother of Peter Graves
25 Move slowly
26 Pelican's crop
27 Improper
28 Adam's son
30 Jezebel's husband
32 Individual
33 Keres people of N.M.
34 Via del Corso locale
37 Turkish border river
39 Frightened
41 Imbrown
42 Arturo Toscanini's son-in-law
45 Foxy
46 Ximena's husband
47 Scottish proprietor
48 —— -di-dah
49 Law deg.
51 Bring forth
53 Word of disgust
56 Served with gravy
61 Glows
63 Neighbor of Thailand
65 Lobster eggs
66 Growing out
67 City near Memphis
68 Kind of school
70 Kitchen utensil
71 Coolidge's third cousin
75 Vacuum tube
76 Makes a request
78 France's longest river
79 Queen —— War
80 You, in Québec
81 Myth
83 Nab
84 Nickname for a cousin of F.D.R.
85 Chemical suffix
86 Make merry
88 Gumshoe
89 Town on the Niger
92 Fountain treats
94 Cardinal points
98 Hallucinogen
101 Nobelist Max Born's granddaughter
104 Initials at O'Hare
105 Before daybreak
106 Type of sign
107 Plaintiff
108 ". . . but —— are chosen"
109 Collection
110 Alan or Cheryl
112 Fabric pattern
114 Picasso's "Dora Maar ——"
116 Suit adjunct
118 Diamond from Brooklyn
120 Barbara Hutton's cousin
123 Aphrodite's son
124 Genealogical diagram
125 Semblance
126 "The Golden Legend" heroine
127 Unit of force
128 —— spumante
129 Himalayan kingdom
130 Was foolishly fond

DOWN

1 Resolves
2 Of the skull
3 Noted Indian chief
4 Fencing weapon
5 Merit
6 Type of drum or ring
7 Loser to J.F.K.
8 Competes for
9 Tailor's concern
10 Naris
11 Prophet Mohammed's son-in-law
12 Miracle site
13 Franz Liszt's son-in-law
14 Adorn with a nimbus
15 Movie, for short
16 Herman Talmadge's second cousin
17 Novelist Blasco ——
18 Stitched
24 Lagoon enclosure
29 Bedevil
31 Wail
35 Davis or Hyman
36 "——, a dollar . . ."
38 Clipper, e.g.
40 Creek
43 Sluggards
44 Spoken
50 Bad, in Barcelona
52 Correlative
54 Prodded
55 Heterodoxy
56 Put the fizz in fizz
57 Concord
58 Playwright Jason Miller's father-in-law
59 Colorado tribe
60 Soil-bound slaves
61 Actor Tom Conway's brother
62 Edison's Park
64 Mubarak's famed predecessor
69 After strip or gold
72 Sift
73 "My Sister ——"
74 Brazilian port
77 Rower
82 Severn feeder
83 Scratched
87 Utopia
90 Help
91 Ellipsoidal
93 —— for (subbed)
95 Distress signal
96 "—— are the times that . . ."
97 Fleered
98 Radical
99 Hard playing marble
100 Loitered
101 Cantankerous
102 "—— girl . . ."
103 Promptly
105 Like some driveways
111 Daily sustenance
113 Easy task
115 Woody's son
117 Philosopher Lao-——
119 Garland
121 —— Khan IV
122 Brooks or Ferrer

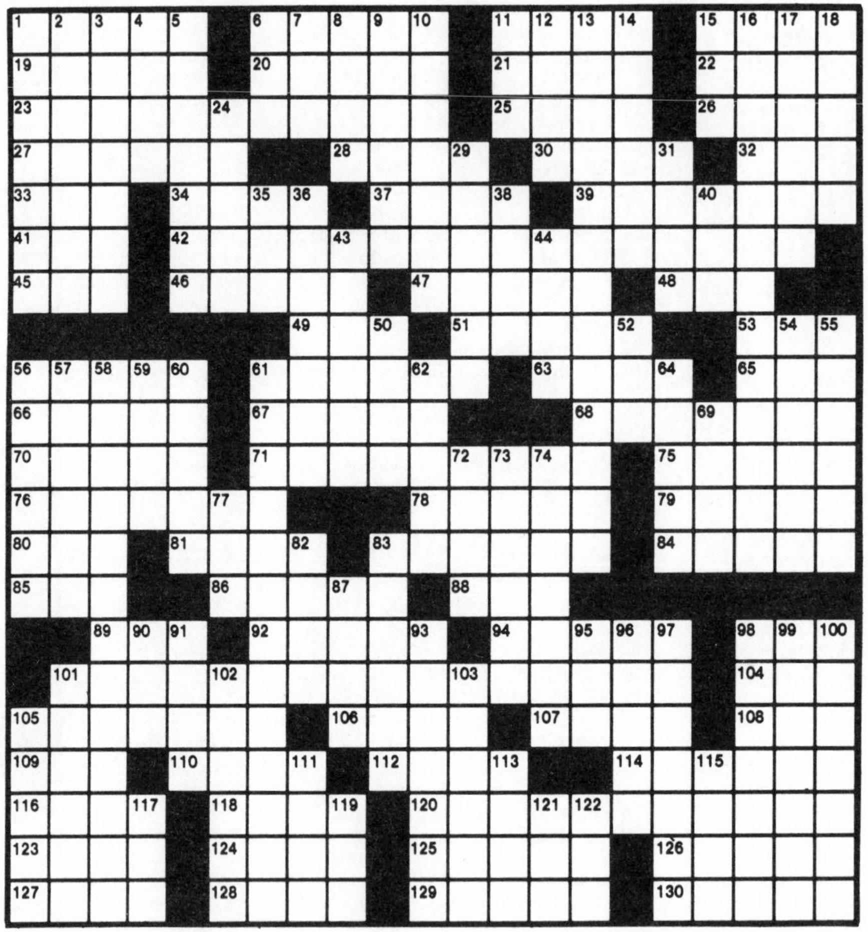

77

For a Loverly Day

By William Lutwiniak

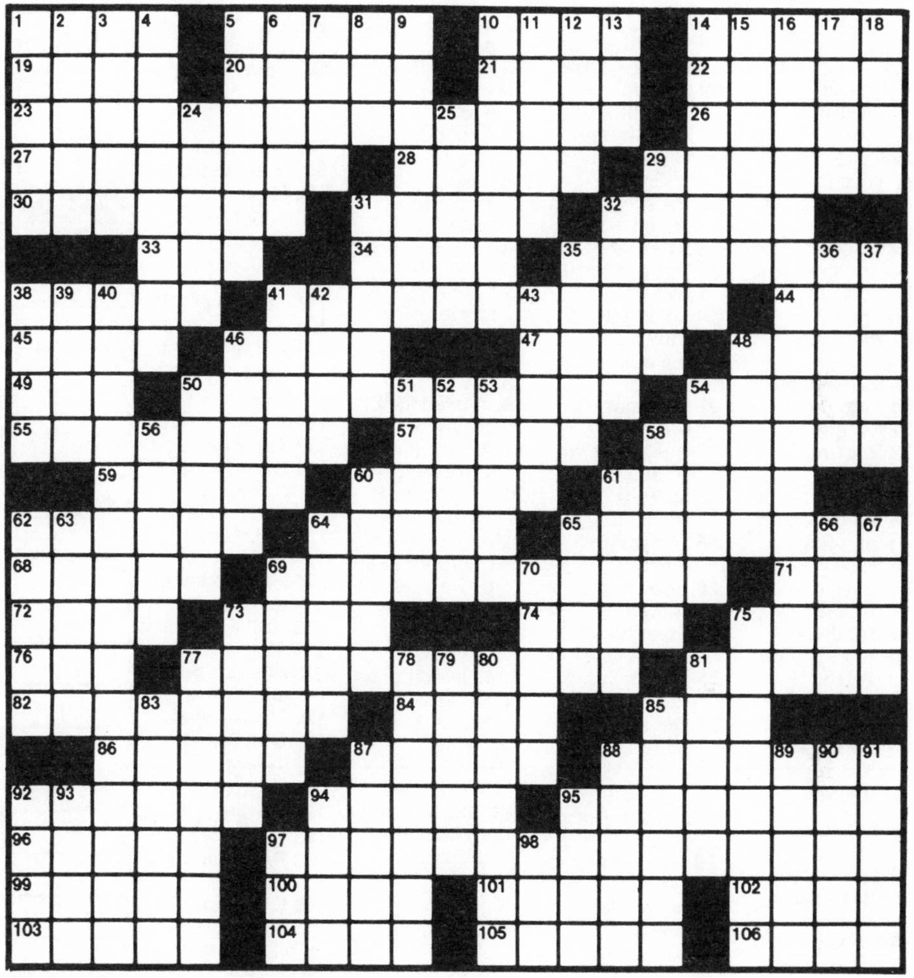

ACROSS

1 Jeanne et Marie
5 Ibsen's Gabler
10 Besought
14 Lesser Antilles native
19 Phnom ——, Cambodia
20 Saw
21 Singer Cantrell
22 Like lambkins
23 Phrase from Virgil
26 Meter fractions
27 Candor
28 Hop stems
29 Pavonine female
30 Chemical substance
31 —— de lune
32 Flora and fauna
33 Tired, in Tours
34 Attila's people
35 Silver medalist
38 Foyt or Yarborough
41 Victor Herbert operetta
44 Genetic initials
45 Famed publisher
46 Voyeur's look
47 Woos successfully
48 Twice LXXVII
49 Sound in a round
50 Garden annual
54 Composed a billet-doux
55 Erose
57 Fresh air
58 Sore
59 Awarded
60 Gypped
61 Oenology symbol
62 Pianist De Groote
64 Embark
65 Kowtowed
68 Arch-consumerist
69 Tennis score
71 Foiler of 40 felons
72 Israel's Abba
73 Shading
74 River to The Wash
75 Tall Asiatic tree
76 Brownie
77 Tony Bennett song hit
81 Gather
82 Knee jerks
84 Pointless
85 Hollywood or Murphy
86 Troubled
87 Dog's bane
88 Proverbial consenter
92 Put punch into the punch
94 Memorable Cairo V.I.P.
95 Oran native
96 Mall display
97 Naumachia spectacle
99 Common contraction
100 Sikorsky
101 Star of "Superman II"
102 Skin problem
103 Old hat
104 Crop
105 Whence beef comes
106 Draw close

DOWN

1 Track of a yak
2 City on the Salt River
3 Nine: Prefix
4 Roofing or haircuts
5 Asyla
6 Breathe
7 Commotions
8 Severinsen
9 Ethel Waters song hit
10 Hammer metal
11 Debussy opus
12 Biblical patriarch
13 Book by Nabokov
14 Allurements
15 Go gliding
16 Cavalier poet
17 Concerning
18 Noggin
24 Lend —— (hark)
25 Pitcher Luis
29 Certain bottles
31 Pierrette's friend
32 —— offering
35 Upcast
36 Wed
37 Did some road work
38 Campus org.
39 Height: Prefix
40 Consular V.I.P.
41 A natural at Reno
42 Lamb's-quarters, e.g.
43 J. R. in "Dallas"
46 Olive-green
48 Pancake
50 Samuel ——, Irish novelist
51 —— all (nohow)
52 Cerulean
53 Haut —— (chic society)
54 Interlace
56 Cleft
58 Validate
60 Pushover
61 Swinish
62 Deride
63 Gueridon
64 Hogties
65 Stick with this
66 O'Neill's mother
67 Mind-over-platter matter
69 Penalized
70 Items to be counted
73 Weighed down
75 City-council member
77 Radamès's adjective for his beloved
78 Where the Liffey flows
79 Beau ——
80 Isopods
81 Martinique peak
83 Compares
85 More important
87 Party gift
88 —— bracelet
89 She's more than nice
90 The Carmine Beauty
91 "—— the hero"
92 Bandy
93 Belém's state
94 Tale on a grand scale
95 "Permit Me Voyage" poet
97 Light bite
98 Bridal-veil material

78

Investment Opportunities

By Reginald L. Johnson

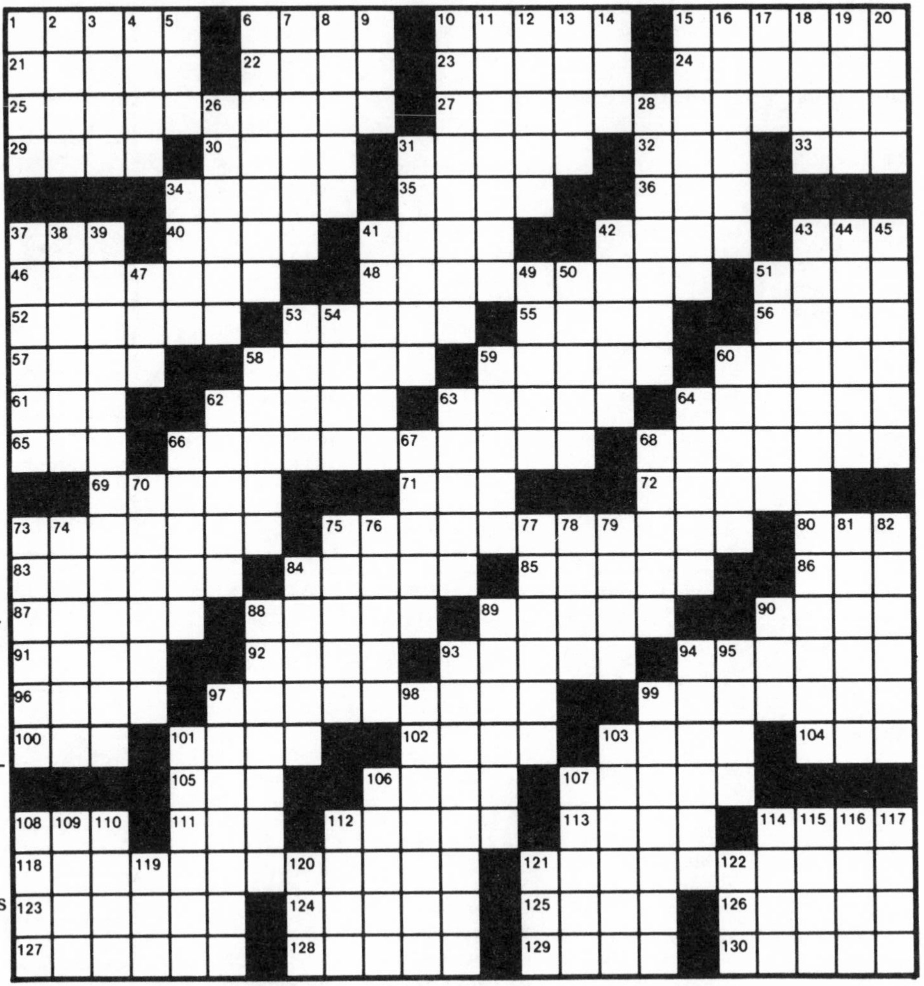

ACROSS

1 —— days (youth)
6 Interpret
10 Bore
15 Rude critic
21 Turn from
22 Airfield near Paris
23 Frightening
24 Preserve feed
25 Lots of terra firma?
27 Plebeian stores?
29 Extensions
30 Pomander
31 Lacquer
32 Hot time in Paree
33 'Tis, to Tacitus
34 Feed feasters for a fee
35 Fruity blends
36 Matelot's milieu
37 Bandicoot
40 Protector of Hector
41 Last of a litany
42 Towel word
43 Ullmann
46 Seeing red
48 Stupidity
51 Roses' partner
52 Looked searchingly
53 "—— intense young man": W.S.G.
55 Prefix for john or god
56 Salamanders
57 One of a Latin trio
58 Colette novel
59 Tiny locks
60 Ice-cold shower
61 Playmate of bro.
62 Business firm
63 Pungent
64 Surface mellowing
65 Inst. at Fort Worth
66 Pork-barrel contents?
68 Inventors' concerns
69 Gather, as money
71 Decalogue adverb
72 Extraordinary people
73 He pettifogs
75 Waterless pool?
80 Caucho
83 Encamped
84 Assail
85 Trunk in a trunk
86 Joplin creation
87 Like surf in a storm
88 Detection device
89 Saw
90 "Turandot" character
91 American suffragist
92 Neighbor of Wash.
93 Move furtively
94 Position taken by Palmer
96 "Twittering Machine" painter
97 In which E is ●
99 He wrote "The House of Fame"
100 Former univ. militants
101 Small sum
102 U.S. citizen, e.g.
103 Weight unit
104 Sinuous shape
105 Daughter of Cadmus
106 Raised
107 Stood
108 Corolla petal
111 Kind of cross
112 Extravagant
113 Boss of a first lieut.
114 Tasso's patron
118 Stock cars?
121 Bettor spots in N.Y.C.
123 Undivided
124 D'Artagnan's saddle
125 He raced with a Ford in 1976
126 Half a S.A. city
127 Stop
128 Meeting on the sly
129 Stowe novel
130 Dull finish

DOWN

1 F.D.R.'s mother
2 Asseverate
3 Plasterer's need
4 Isn't up to par
5 Painter Pres.
6 Took turns
7 Clears a tape
8 Modify
9 Woad, e.g.
10 Effete
11 Takes up again
12 La Douce et al.
13 Delineate
14 "—— the Lip"
15 Merry-andrews
16 Puts one's hat in the ring
17 Within: Comb. form
18 Shipment from Galveston
19 Wawaskeesh and wapiti
20 Music sign
26 —— stiff
28 Unbeatable rival
31 Gunpowder Plot target
34 Islanders' target
37 Gourmand's delight
38 Lacking pep
39 Memos from Sec. Regan?
41 Worshiped
42 Like abaca
43 Good will policy?
44 Rapt
45 Matches
47 Berenson's subject
49 Circus Maximus emcee
50 Haunts
51 Turmoil
53 Buzzing
54 Middle: Prefix
58 His star is rising
59 "But, by my sooth! she'll —— wee": Burns
60 Gratifies
62 Fought a fire
63 Pub order
64 Raccoon's relative
66 One who quotes
67 Prefix with lace or face
68 —— Vecchio
70 In —— (agitated)
73 Flues
74 Forerunner
75 Rivals of Persians
76 Customary action
77 Jacob's vision
78 Colt or filly
79 Press
81 Jousting needs
82 Moths harmful to trees
84 Vermont city
88 Extirpate
89 —— -camp
90 Birthplace of Henry of Navarre
93 English county
94 Kind of daisy
95 Zestless
97 Muezzin's perch
98 Trusts
99 Trimmed
101 Tall caps
103 Pinup girl in W.W. II
106 T.R.'s "Good!"
107 Man in a cast
108 Served perfectly
109 Single
110 Little subway makers
112 Supreme, in Stuttgart
114 English pen name
115 Winnow
116 Allowance for waste
117 To live, to Livy
119 "QB ——," Uris book
120 Adherent
121 Bizarre
122 Boss of the flock

Updating

By Bert Rosenfield

ACROSS

1 George C. Scott role
7 Hannah Van Buren, née ——
11 City with streets of song
17 Gives off
19 Plains man
21 Dumas's Chevalier d'Herblay
22 Grant another term
23 Building wing
24 Places for yachts
25 Bell, —— (ritual trio)
28 Words of confidence
30 A top female marathoner
31 Señora's cupboard
32 Asian holiday
35 Soothing agent
38 Leroy Anderson composition
44 Kind of wind
45 Symbol of Gov. McKernan's state
47 Tarpon Springs product
48 Drain off
50 Spoke harshly
54 Five-time P.G.A. champ
55 Spreads rumors
56 Rack one's —— (think hard)
58 No. 1 Norse god
59 RR depot
61 Hazard to paddle-wheelers
62 "—— Hey Kid"
65 Between fly and feather
68 Work unit
70 Golf-ball position
71 Nagana carrier
73 N.Y.C. subway
74 Patriarchs
77 Roman or Greek
79 Hawkeye's milieu
80 Man with a —— (Father Time)
82 Western elk
85 "Call Me ——"
88 Gemini star
89 North Sea sights
91 Menotti's operatic lady
93 Violet dye
96 "—— Clear Day"
97 Declaration signer
101 I.R.S. prospect
103 Moray
104 Shadow
105 Go quickly
107 Outstanding
108 Verdi opera
116 Bit parts
118 Contribute
119 Geometric figure
122 Interstice
123 Tubman and Turner
124 Musical interval
125 Abate
126 Auto pioneer
127 Pool person, for short

DOWN

1 —— se
2 Fell a fir
3 Item "mightier than the sword"
4 Hawk hooks
5 Shopping-list entry
6 Violin part
7 N.F.L. rest period
8 U.S.S.R. grain center
9 Kett of comics
10 Makes a beginning
11 Some consonants
12 "To —— and a bone . . ."
13 Precipitate
14 Sending forth
15 Kipling hero
16 Clandestine initials
18 Procyon, e.g.
19 Having a rhythmic fall
20 Therapy, to a G.I.
26 Pinocchio feature
27 Beachhead boat
28 In the same loc.
29 Judicial schedule
33 Betting advantage
34 Old comics character
36 Gibbons
37 Half a farthing
39 —— man (Scottish farmhand)
40 Whip marks
41 Cactus liquor
42 Greek officials
43 Niagara sound
46 Promontory
49 Scourge of serge
51 More Lilliputian
52 Golfer Lee
53 Small flounder
56 Rebounds
57 Make lace
58 Sash for Suzuki
60 Aquarium denizen
62 Item swapped for Richard's kingdom
63 Legal recipient
64 Slangy assent
66 Lawless state
67 Gull sound
69 Town on the Thames
72 African chief
75 Like some champagne
76 Kind of enemy
78 Service-record demerit letters
80 Insect feeler
81 Gaelic
83 Part of an ange
84 Cop a ——
85 Rodent's pathway in a lab
86 Pierre's girlfriend
87 Strips of honors
90 Red chalcedony
92 Skilled practitioner
94 Allen and Frome
95 "How sweet ——!": Gleason

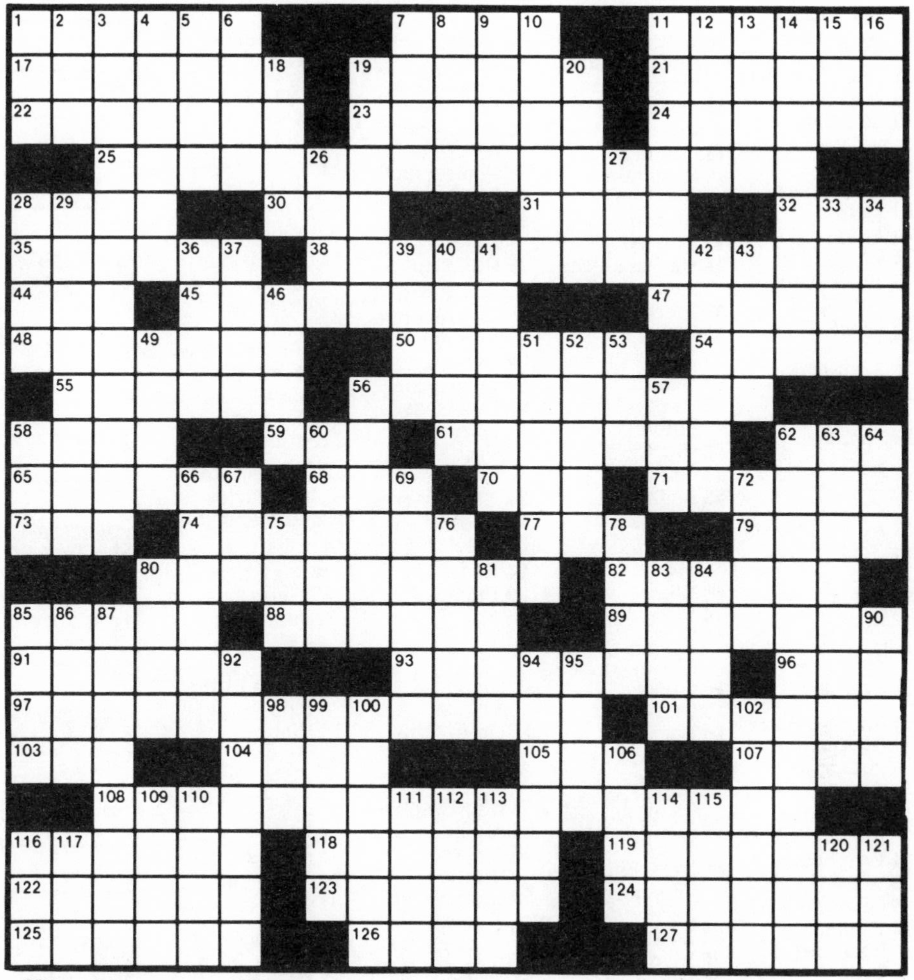

98 Lewisite, e.g.
99 Chandler's threads
100 Philippine city
102 —— Sunday of Advent
106 Genuine, in Gotha
109 The avant-garde
110 Big name in Hawaii
111 Suffix with class
112 Secret-police letters
113 Architect —— van der Rohe
114 Word on a towel
115 Thruway sign
116 "Silent ——"
117 Exist
120 Top golfer from Japan
121 Undev. film

Shades of Meaning

By Mary Virginia Orna

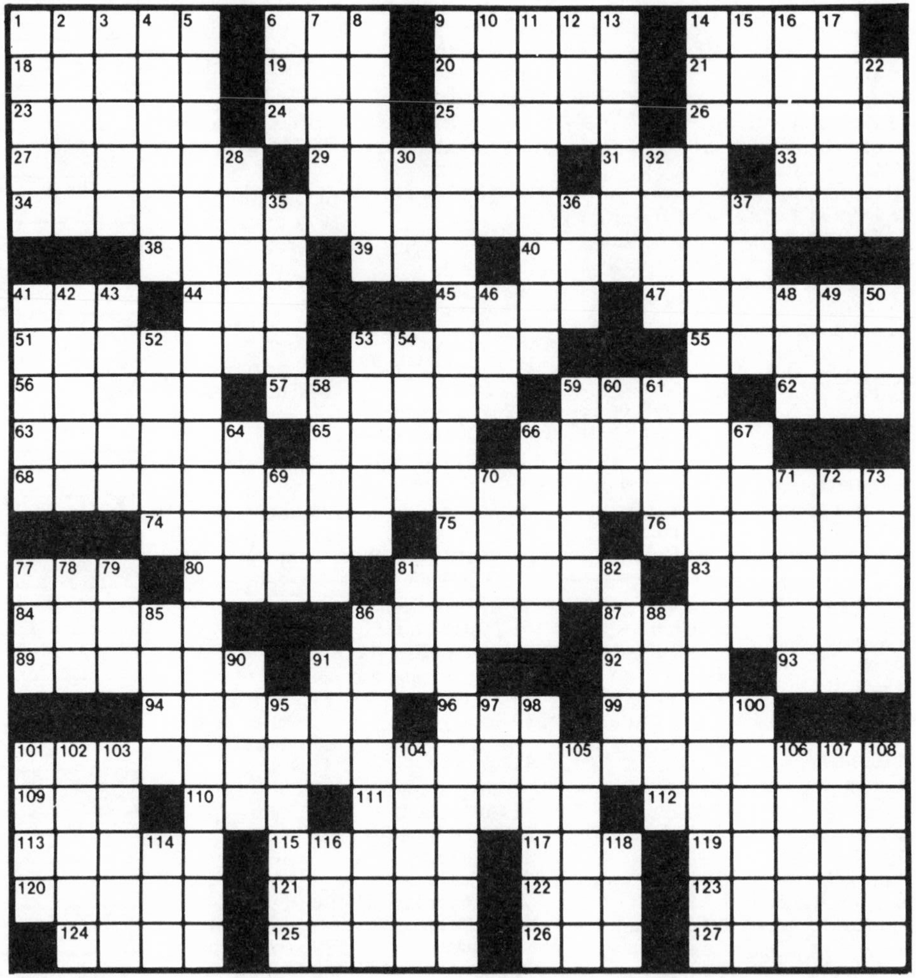

ACROSS

1 Sole of a plow
6 Vichy vineyard
9 Home of the slave
14 Rent
18 Of the blood
19 Layer
20 Alpine crest
21 Dragged in
23 Suffix with argument
24 Remnant
25 Mmes., once
26 Practical
27 S.A. tree or fruit
29 Popular science writer
31 Ervin or Rayburn
33 Again, to Bizet
34 Gold
38 Uttered
39 Artist —— Borch
40 Like some sentimental songs
41 Heckler's missile
44 Mamie Eisenhower, —— Doud
45 Bishop
47 Pickled
51 Unshackle the hackles
53 Piece of the pot
55 Wed
56 Edible tubers
57 Choice
59 Herds of humans
62 Handle clumsily
63 Beguile
65 Cutty ——
66 Aquiline abodes
68 Blue
74 "Popo" author
75 "Take —— Train"
76 Proportions
77 Little pocket
80 Bar owner's purchase
81 Perfect models
83 Meccan shrine
84 Architect Jones
86 Oar parts
87 —— storm (won over, as an audience)
89 Call it a day
91 Loud noise
92 Short word after long
93 Poet's monogram
94 Grate harshly
96 Roble
99 Gobs
101 Red
109 Burrows of N.Y.C.
110 Map abbr.
111 Game dog
112 Song made popular by Al Jolson
113 —— Gables, Fla.
115 Broadway musical
117 Goddess of dawn
119 Honshu seaport
120 Party boss in McKinley's day
121 Spokes
122 Indy 500 unit
123 Lacoste and Descartes
124 Romanov ruler
125 Filch
126 Pig's digs
127 Gerontius had one

DOWN

1 Catches flies
2 Gershwin's "—— Eat Cake"
3 Iranian prime minister in 1962
4 Boat hoists
5 White
6 Guevara
7 French historian: 1823-92
8 Author of "Jenny": 1911
9 Yellow
10 Russian noble house
11 Plushily covered
12 Summer in Sedan
13 Landlord
14 Green
15 Gnaw
16 Pretext, perhaps
17 Vestige
22 Vargueno, e.g.
28 Swiss poet: 1821-81
30 Nigerian university town
32 Bows
35 Nice notions
36 Rogers or Clark
37 Famed miler
41 TV's Barnaby Jones
42 Cum —— salis
43 Young sows
46 Women's service org.
48 Draw on a straw
49 Japanese outcast
50 Drop o' the mornin'
52 More withered
53 Blind's splines
54 Alpert
58 Aethelbald's thralls
59 Decoration
60 Pelf for Pizarro
61 Sawmill sound
64 Quarry
66 Sectors
67 Caterpillar parts
69 Garry Moore's "—— Got a Secret"
70 Attention-getting sound
71 Mirthful
72 Lynda Bird's in-laws
73 Violin virtuoso: 1858-1931
77 Evergreen
78 Cather's "—— of Ours"
79 Smidgen
81 Plato dialogue
82 Balance: Comb. form
85 Purport
86 Windy City border area
88 Culture media
90 Soprano Berger
91 Ebenezer's expletive
95 Aromatic chemicals
97 Holm on the Thames
98 Uses a prie-dieu
100 Brinker, for one
101 "Coffee Cantata" composer
102 One of Tirpitz's pack
103 Three-masted schooners
104 Anatomical meshes
105 Hulled grain
106 Silly
107 Site of a Herculean labor
108 Earthquake
114 Memorabilia
116 Vintner's vessel
118 Hale or Hari

Granary

By Fletcher Ingalls

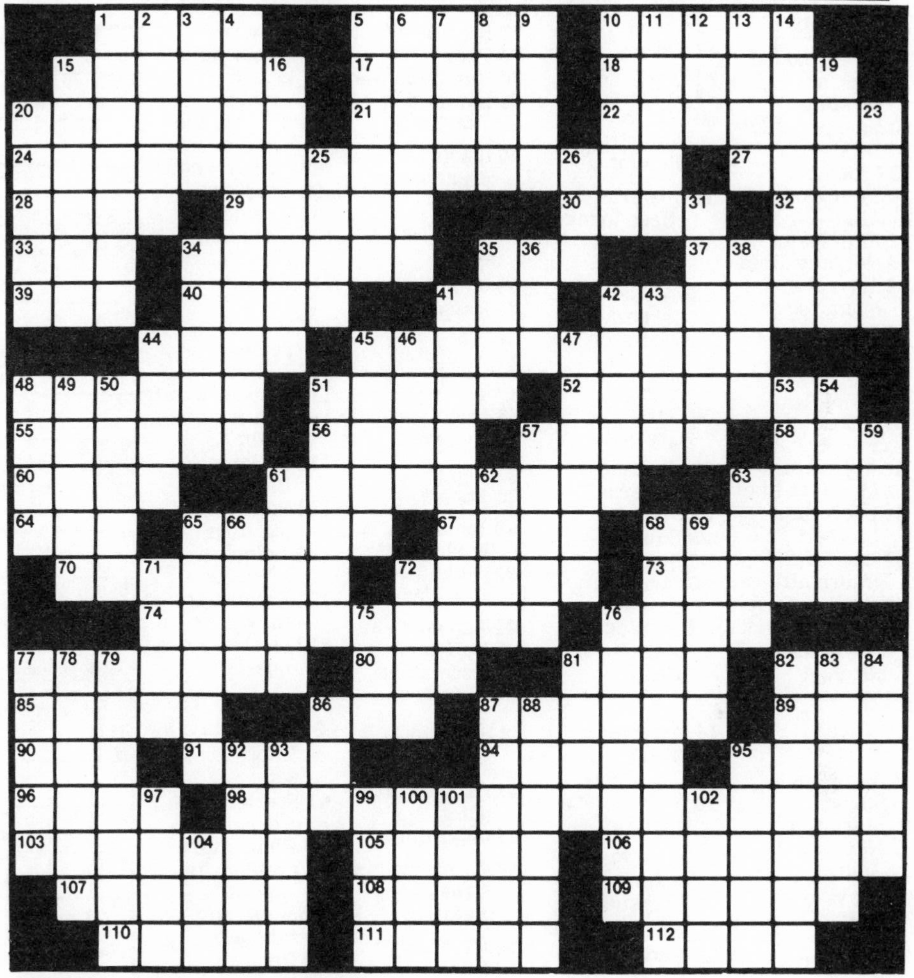

ACROSS

1 Black tern
5 "For —— waves . . .": Bates
10 Understand
15 Betake oneself
17 A Lyon river
18 Lido
20 Gest
21 —— rule
22 I.R.S. quarry
24 Words from ". . . Sixpence"
27 "Flee, feline!"
28 Plexus
29 Bowling unit
30 Spot of land
32 Mrs. McKinley
33 Palindromic word
34 Kent's Daily ——
35 Corn Belt animal
37 Kind of beam
39 Curve
40 Army missiles
41 Tapuyan Indians
42 Cgs unit of brightness
44 Julia Ward ——
45 Abundance
48 Acute food shortage
51 Faro cards
52 Warded off
55 Rubber
56 Signaled
57 "Luisa Miller," e.g.
58 Marvin
60 Ate's mother
61 Gruel, etc.
63 Bonzer birds
64 Hollywood nickname
65 —— card
67 Sidewalk superintendent
68 Cut in two
70 Guillemot
72 Meara and Jeffreys
73 Renée of the 1920's
74 Popish Plot fabricator: 1678
76 Kind of duster
77 White House family: 1853-57
80 Forage plant
81 Seed pod
82 Kernel-bearing item
85 Farrier's need
86 Three in Torino
87 Sports results
89 Número ——
90 Helm dir.
91 Apiece
94 Asteism
95 Roughage cereal
96 Revolution
98 Device in a Physics I lab
103 Interstices
105 Sacks
106 Sang lustily
107 Borate and oleate
108 Upbeats, in music
109 Gasket
110 Cultivates
111 Ensile
112 Genus of turtles

DOWN

1 Lowers, in a way
2 Quickly
3 Luxuriant
4 Commonly cultivated shrub
5 Feign
6 Polo player's need
7 Seethe
8 Within: Prefix
9 Riffle
10 Jane and Zane
11 Gloat
12 Happy —— lark
13 Swards
14 Explicit
15 Rodeo stars
16 Step into one's footsteps
19 Market figure
20 Peep show
23 Bolt
25 Blows chaff off
26 A threshing machine, e.g.
31 Where Mark Twain is buried
34 Disposed
35 Coop group
36 Big Ten letters
38 As blind as ——
41 Slopes
42 "—— Young Dream": T. Moore poem
43 Copycat
44 Steam sound
45 Quadrangle
46 Stettin's river
47 Shenanigans
48 Palpate
49 Gallico's Mrs. ——
50 Shade of yellow
51 Darts
53 Fudd or Gantry
54 Loser to a trey
57 Finishing strips
59 Punta del ——
61 Like Eleazer Wheelock
62 Unit of force
63 "Sour grapes" writer: Var.
65 Unresponsive one
66 Lavish affection (on)
68 Kiltie's whisky
69 Teraphim
71 Bell town
72 Rhine feeder
75 "—— the fields we go"
76 Zinkes
77 Durum yield
78 Cover, in a way
79 Earth's apex
81 Blessing
82 Uses rennet
83 Catapult
84 Filleted
86 Against —— grain
87 Flagpole ——
88 Pouched racquet
92 Edgar or Obie
93 Karpov's game
95 Melville's "—— Budd"
97 Foot follower
99 Lackaday!
100 Type of civil wrong
101 Run-of-the-mill
102 Meander
104 Author Deighton

82 Forget Your Troubles

By Henry Hook

ACROSS

1 Cavern sound
5 Tool for weeding
9 Beanery order
14 Secs
19 Globule
20 Guardianship
21 Alba ——
22 Anticipate
23 Not fully dried
24 Start of a quotation
27 Quotation: Part II
29 Singer-composer
30 System of worship: Abbr.
31 Apparatus
32 Meeting: Abbr.
34 Lucrezia's brother
37 Lacked, informally
40 Sand, to Chopin
42 Chaplain under William of Orange
46 Wallet fillers
47 Pinza
48 Whenever
49 Indian poet
50 "On the Waterfront" director
51 Quivering effect, in music
52 "6 —— Riv Vu"
55 —— personae
57 Carnera's successor
58 Cygnet's mama
59 Garlic, in Grenoble
60 Ulrica in "Ivanhoe"
61 Fosse
63 Equi-
65 Quannet
66 Quotation: Part III
71 Attraction at Rockefeller Center
72 Have an effect
73 Phony
74 Hampton ——
75 Inquired, in Ozarkese
76 Longest wholly-Swiss river
78 Asner's award in '80
80 Toothless
83 Harper Valley org.
84 Girl Scout's kid sister
86 Nutritionist's concern
87 Vogue
88 Boreal
89 Johansson, to boxing fans
90 Author Robert —— Warren
91 Aspen or Vail
93 Father of Ascalaphus
94 They're occasionally loaded
95 Vitiates
96 Bowlers and boaters
98 Author Wister
100 Gobs' org.
101 Wee'un
105 Quotation: Part IV
110 End of quotation
114 Polecat's defense
115 —— cotta
116 Bo-peep's staff
117 Wings for Amor
118 Ballet by Balanchine
119 Point in question
120 Amphora adjuncts
121 Croquet arena, maybe
122 Dart throwers' quaffs

DOWN

1 A work by Snorri Sturluson
2 Nebula in Taurus
3 "—— sum": Terence
4 Controverts
5 Scotland's —— Flow
6 Freelance photogs
7 A Nobelist in 1934
8 Scorn
9 Takes the rod to
10 Nancy's hubby
11 Quechua
12 Prominent Alaskan
13 Fell prey to quicksand
14 Masseter's locale
15 —— Jima
16 Author of the quotation
17 They do stoking
18 Elegance
25 Snick's partner
26 Pertaining to touch
28 Asian holiday
33 XX
35 Ireland's De Valera
36 "Sprechen —— Deutsch?"
37 Phone button
38 Zeno of Citium was one
39 Renowned fashion designer
41 Unpleasant, as air
43 Hymn by S. F. Smith
44 Ad —— (to the point)
45 —— a dime
47 Boccaccio's "The —— Heart"
48 De Witt and Pitt
50 "Louisiana Hayride" author
52 Postponement precautions, in sports
53 Significant event
54 Monoski
56 Robin Williams role
57 Nonsense!
62 Not so seldom
64 "Make —— Happy," pop song
65 Frosh-rushing group
66 Elementary problem for Watson
67 Seeresses' tableaux
68 Reticent
69 Words to live by
70 Lo-o-ong time
76 Scrap a project
77 Checks
79 Glee
81 ". . . let slip the ——": Shak.
82 Austrian town or river
85 Song from "Sunny"
86 When a partridge was given
88 "Delta of Venus" author
90 First woman, in Greek myth
91 Casements
92 Ralph and Nancy of sports fame
93 Janis Ian hit: 1975
94 Cartwright or Casey
95 —— -frutti
97 Left Morpheus's arms
99 Plied with the grape
102 Women's org. since 1866
103 Composer of 85 Down
104 Feb. 14 V.I.P.
106 "Hello!" in Honduras
107 Golden calf
108 Boom town in 1899
109 Mardi ——
111 Irish exclamation
112 Aberdonian's "unh-unh"
113 "—— Skylark": Shelley

Dramalgamations

By Tom Mixon

ACROSS

1 Breaches
5 Office corr.
10 Network
14 Covenants
19 Neglect
20 Duck
21 Raines from Washington
22 City on the Missouri
23 Weber opera introducing the Chief
26 Tropical plants
27 Previous
28 TV statistic
29 Organic compounds
30 Theatrical scenery
31 Boresome
32 —— time (soon enough)
33 Kind of drama
36 Minos' kingdom
37 Quechuans
38 —— up (fake it)
39 1966 musical backed by a star from Cincinnati
43 Wright wing
46 —— Reekie (Edinburgh)
47 King Arthur's lance
48 —— me tangere
49 Add to the scrapbook
50 Org. in Eden's sitcom
51 Star of the 50's is linked with a musical
56 Winter sight
57 "—— Lyricae," Watts hymn
59 These may form a fork
60 Put in stitches
61 Wherewithal for some Dutch treats
63 Indian lute
64 Canes; switches
66 Gabriel or Hruska
67 Legal help
68 "It's ——!"
69 Ellipse
70 Bellini opera taken in by Lucille Langhanke
74 Where Frankenstein wkd.
77 Sun. talks
78 River to Cairo
79 Lalo's "Le —— d'Ys"
80 They followed that star
81 Assay
82 Verdi opera in collaboration with U.S. dramatist
87 Top job in a bakery
88 Puccini hero
90 "Les Meules" painter
91 —— out (spiritless)
93 Majorca's capital
94 Where fans buzz
96 Judgment seat
97 Nice interjection
98 Loewe output
99 Fit for classifying
103 Jacket plated with steel
104 B'way flier linked with dancer-singer
106 Like an ingenue
107 Med. subject
108 Expiate
109 Bonnie bairn
110 Jackson and Bancroft
111 Bros., e.g.
112 Less stale
113 Editor's signal

DOWN

1 Boner
2 Early pulpit
3 "On the Waterfront" site
4 Accented
5 "Labyrinth" composer
6 Dale from Uvalde
7 "The —— Animal"
8 "—— Man Out"
9 Compact
10 Like a more dramatic role
11 —— marbles
12 Terms like "show biz"
13 Attach backdrops
14 Force
15 T. Williams character
16 1945 hit with Brooklyn-born star
17 Pin in a gunwale
18 Soprano Silvia
24 Cyma recta
25 Give —— (heed)
31 Vitro di —— (Venetian glass)
32 Suspended
33 Fellow
34 Chawbacon
35 Lone Star star latches onto a 1943 hit
36 Scoter
37 Slothful
40 Removes humidity
41 Of the mind
42 They fail to pass the bar
44 Light-flow measure
45 City on the Aire
49 First name of a superstar
51 O'Casey's land
52 Heflin or Johnson
53 Algerian city
54 Misanthrope
55 Having but one component
58 Some tests
60 Suffix with song or road
61 David, Robert or Jack
62 Troilus or Orlando
63 Popular playwright
64 Fixed relation
65 Annie of musical fame
67 Piece for Price
70 Water wheel
71 Words of disappointment
72 Medieval French kingdom
73 Grime
75 Pulitzer Prize author: 1958
76 Celtics' star
80 Names incorrectly
82 Stoats
83 Turkish inns
84 Artist's material
85 Spick ——
86 Bee, e.g.
89 Niche
92 Opposer
93 Large hickory
94 Prospect
95 Complete
96 —— bouche (tidbit)
97 "Give a —— horse . . ."
98 Rigging support
99 C. P. or Phoebe
100 Cry like a sheep
101 —— -majesté
102 Once, once
105 Spenserian hag

84

Playing the Angles

By Charles M. Deber

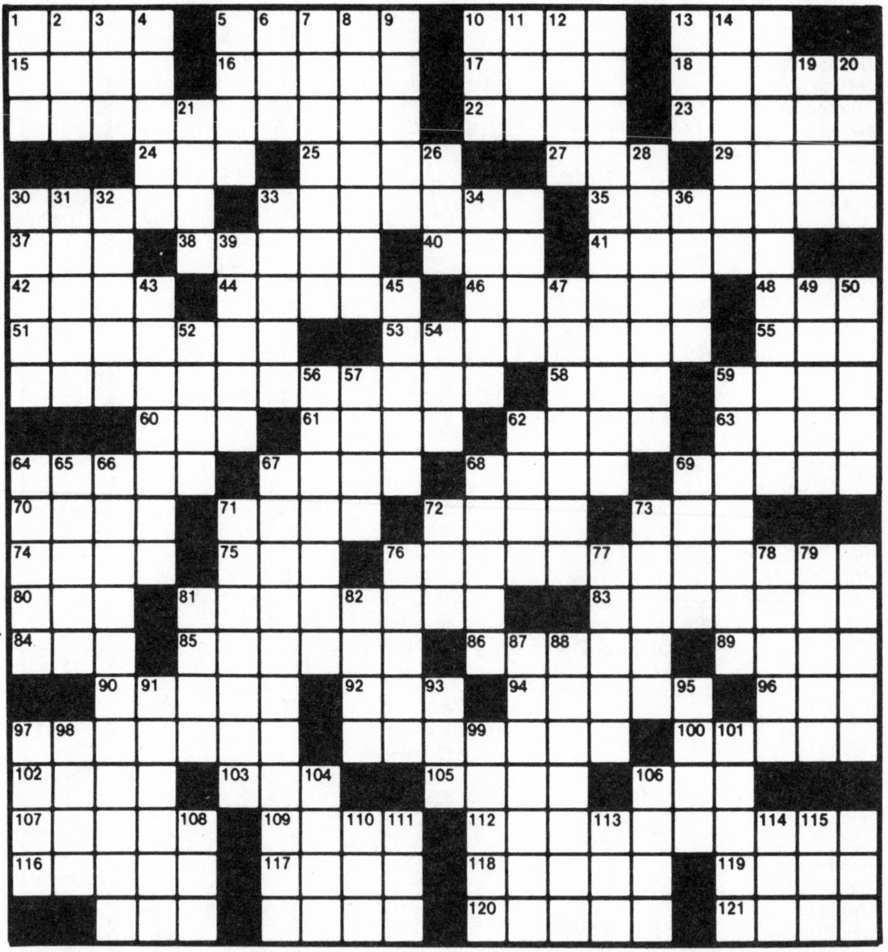

ACROSS

1 Quote
5 Exclude
10 Malthusian dilemma
13 Vertical
15 Ace
16 Marble
17 Assist
18 Box elder
22 Reminder
23 Cut of halibut
24 Be in debt
25 Cubes of chance
27 Watering place
29 Movie pioneer
30 Vestige or fish
33 Drivers' maneuvers
35 Toppled
37 Newswoman Lindstrom
38 Jags or cogs
40 Airport abbr.
41 Counterpart of lati-
42 Utah ski resort
44 Endures
46 Release a canary
48 Chi. time
51 Spelling system
53 Throbs
55 Japanese apricot
58 Type of grass
59 Coalition
60 Violinist Bull
61 Veronica or Swan
62 Cupid
63 Vow
64 Mild cigar
67 —— de vivre
68 A —— Able
69 Entices
70 Male red deer
71 Put out to sea
72 Stake
73 Prefix with fuse or fraction
74 Hebrew prophet
75 Logos
76 Thomas show
80 Inst. in N.Y.
81 Corrective
83 Ancient Roman province
84 Neighbor of Neb.
85 Coal-tar product
86 Sen. Kefauver
89 Clupeid fish
90 Like some stadiums
92 Tiny
94 Places of call
96 ". . . and Memories of ——!": Poe
97 Nightclub
100 Like the polo crowd
102 Eight, in Essen
103 Kind of story or sister
105 Gator's cousin
106 Ward heeler
107 Ancient monument
109 Flub
112 Nice way to end a pen-pal letter
116 "I will speak daggers —— . . .": Hamlet
117 Sicilian spouter
118 Corruptible
119 "—— Misbehavin' "
120 Ford flop
121 Fencer's blade

DOWN

1 Building blocks
2 Hostel
3 Golfer's gadget
4 Miscue
5 Appointment
6 Self
7 Outlaws
8 "Dinner ——," 1933 song
9 Colorado Rockies goalie
10 Electrical unit
11 Churchill's gesture
12 Shade givers
13 Afternoons
14 Gourmand's delight
19 Cluny ——
20 Barely managed
21 Hit a fly
26 Greek vowel
28 Orbital high points
30 In desperate straits
31 Thousandth: Comb. form
32 Twirler's tool
33 Come to
34 Strumpet
36 Chemical suffixes
39 Cream of the crop
43 Classifies
45 "Thus —— Zarathustra"
47 Flattop
49 Struck
50 Georgia and Cal
52 Normandy town
54 Caucho
56 Plaza dweller and namesakes
57 Banshee sound
59 Comic operas
62 Tasso's patron
64 Teacher's need
65 Vampire
66 From third to second to first base
67 Serried
68 Low-down joint
69 Delineate
71 Binaural systems
72 Shoe width
73 Biblical verb
76 A —— minute
77 Public
78 Second of two
79 Coins in Qum
81 Can. lawmen
82 Broke
87 Ladled
88 Big-billed birds
91 Stableboy
93 Ref. book
95 Boutique
97 Have, to W.S.
98 Eight: Comb. form
99 Motored
101 Pitchers for Pericles
104 The two
106 Weary
108 Osprey's cousin
110 Undivided
111 Distant
113 "Some —— meat . . .": Burns
114 Kennel sound
115 Compass point

Pro-and-Con Exchange

By Stanley Glass

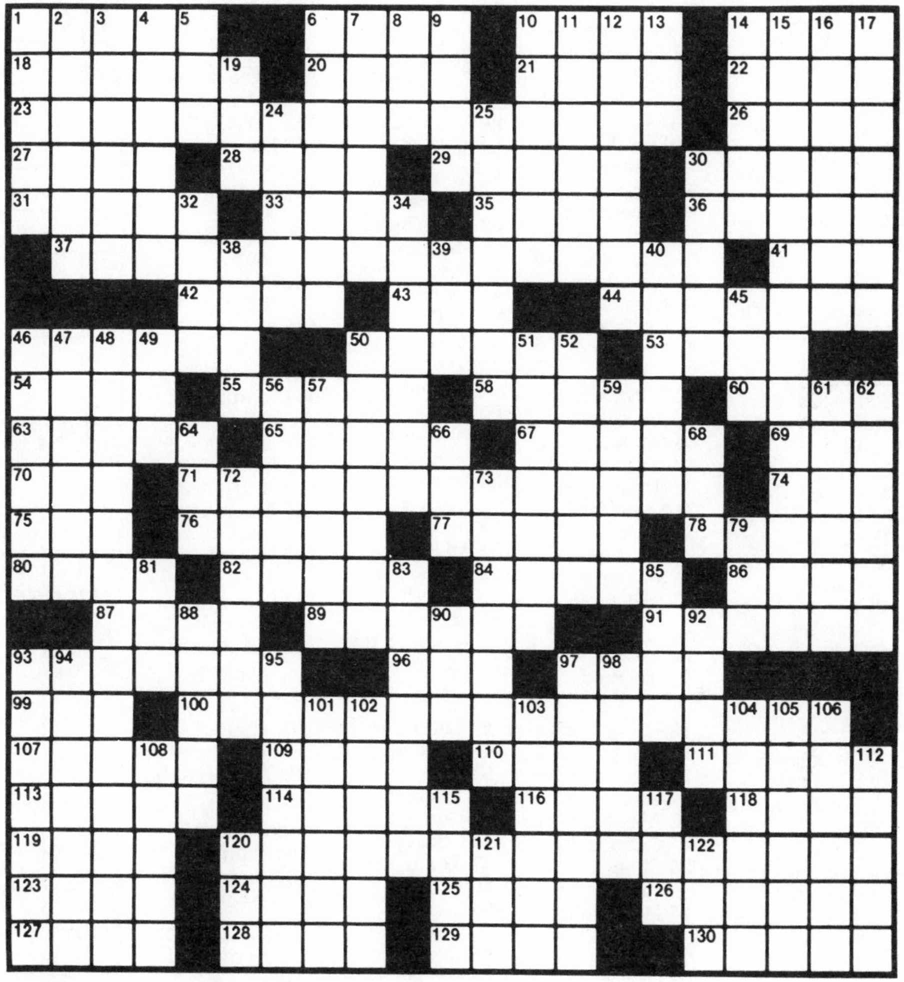

ACROSS

1 Stone carving
6 Taj Mahal site
10 "—— homo!"
14 Polish
18 Fancy
20 —— Man McGinnity
21 Zhivago's beloved
22 Type of type: Abbr.
23 Between-innings line at Shea
26 Where Vulcan forged
27 Geyserite
28 Gas station abbr.
29 Water barriers
30 Hesperus's fate
31 Pitch
33 "—— fan tutte"
35 Outlet
36 High flier's home
37 Cain's story
41 —— capita
42 Headlights time
43 Favorable to
44 Malicious tales
46 —— Zee Bridge
50 Credentials
53 Pacific aroid
54 Daughter of Cronus
55 Pandemonium leader
58 Diplomat Silas
60 Salamanders
63 Bouquet
65 City in SE Spain
67 Scribe
69 Swiss canton
70 Basketball tourn.
71 Atlantic City demonstration
74 José or Juan
75 Type of drum
76 Extremist
77 Left the reservation
78 Chicago soccer team
80 Masher's comeuppance
82 Cheats at hide-and-seek
84 Pithy
86 Sotto ——
87 A 1492 find
89 Bypass
91 Banker, at times
93 Least exsuccous
96 Many, many eras
97 Ooze
99 Vestment
100 Manufacturer's award
107 Opera by Handel
109 End of a hammerhead
110 One of Esau's fathers-in-law
111 One of the Moluccas
113 Make —— (get rich)
114 Wise men
116 Nautical bird
118 —— -ran
119 Eliot hero
120 Legislature at Plymouth
123 "Picnic" playwright
124 —— fixe
125 Chemical weapon
126 Trawler gear
127 Ending for mob
128 Jerk
129 —— Richard
130 Minute

DOWN

1 Areas in New York and London
2 Too much, in music
3 Involve necessarily
4 Served soup
5 Ike's command
6 Stoppage in a pump
7 Mato ——, Brazil
8 Legendary bird
9 Freshly
10 Janis et al.
11 Pyramidal rock piles
12 Double- —— puzzle
13 Suffix with nectar
14 Lager, in Lyon
15 Lots
16 Imaginary
17 Chip producers
19 Dart's partner
24 Treaties
25 Cut
30 "I —— Be Loved," 1933 song
32 A. Huxley work
34 Beginning
38 Phoenix team
39 Dandy
40 Westerns
45 Exist
46 Macbeth's rivals
47 Forward pass
48 Ponder the dummy too long
49 Jack of clubs
50 Share
51 Bounce back
52 Brook trout
56 Winged ant
57 Barnstormed
59 Requirements
61 Foggy state
62 Denver is one
64 —— Dhabi
66 Diary abbr.
68 Jumpy pieces: Abbr.
72 Border city
73 Capitol highlight
79 Power agcy.
81 —— the shot
83 Less easygoing
85 Before J.H.S.
88 Sire
90 A winner at tic-tac-toe
92 Cartel acronym
93 Roots relished in Japan
94 Neon is one
95 On deck
97 Harder to find
98 Race: Comb. form
101 Casino employee
102 Fixed prices
103 Cultural agcy.
104 Hilliard-Mann hit
105 Dahl or Francis
106 California peak
108 Cynical look
112 Antiquated
115 Nitwit
117 Future adm., perhaps
120 Kegler's target
121 "Little Red Book" author
122 Obtain

Hidden Baseball

By Caroline G. Fitzgerald

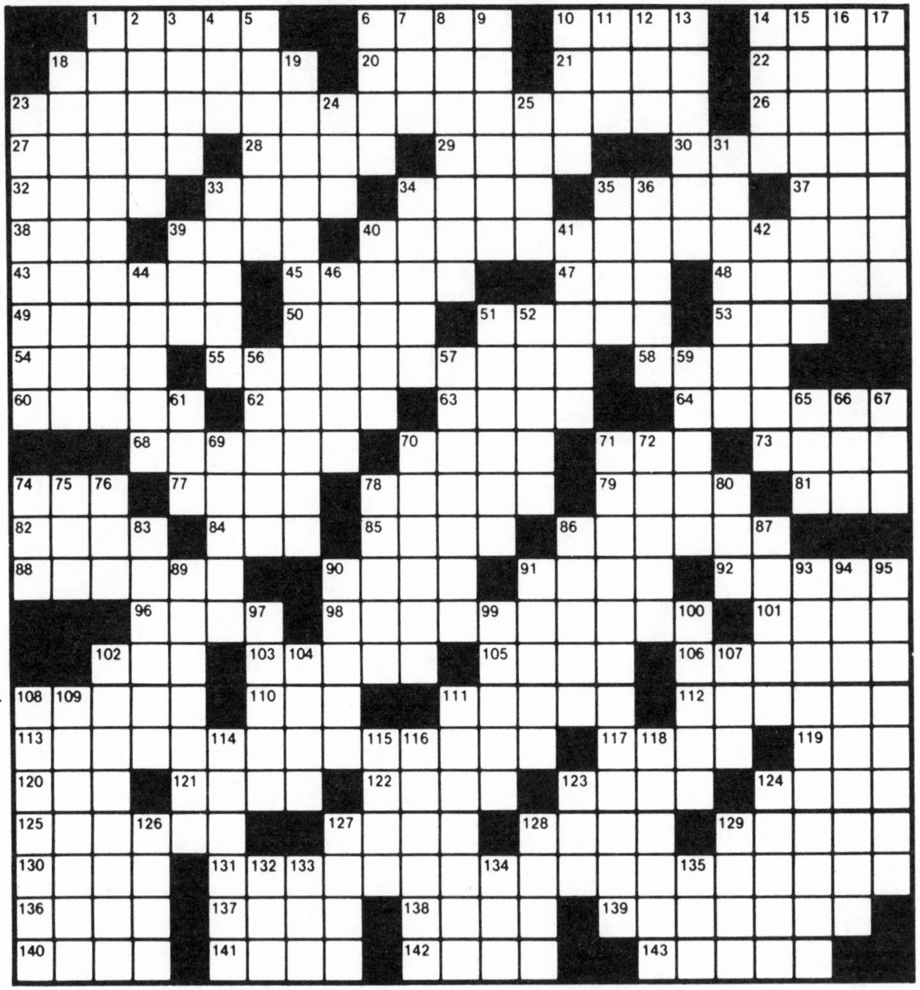

ACROSS

1 Quiet!
6 Pretense
10 Vault
14 Graham of N.F.L. fame
18 Scrap
20 Field measure
21 Wriggling
22 Poetic you
23 Novel of 1951
26 ". . . I do feel't and ——": Shak.
27 Overcharges
28 Encamp
29 Connery
30 Irish lakes
32 Refuges
33 Pith
34 Silo's neighbor
35 Gripe
37 Louis XIV, e.g.
38 Philip II, e.g.
39 Arafura Sea islands
40 Wrong; far off; senseless
43 John Paul II, in Roma
45 —— Dame
47 Corn or cycle leader
48 Godden's "In This House of ——"
49 Family members
50 Aleutian island
51 Fabric design
53 Own, to Burns
54 Pay, with "up"
55 Achieve results
58 Impudence
60 Prophets
62 Socks
63 Natural resources
64 Deviated
68 Lebanese port
70 British gun
71 School org.
73 Emulate Harpagon
74 Slip a cog
77 Crockett's quarry
78 —— forces
79 —— back (relaxed)
81 Arachnid's trap
82 Secular
84 Join closely
85 Anon
86 Ade's "—— in Slang"
88 Animalcule
90 Figure
91 Asian legume
92 Stingers
96 Tread
98 Hawk
101 Melt
102 Electrical unit
103 Nordland people
105 Nursery eloper
106 "—— for tennis?"
108 Make —— (transact)
110 Up: Prefix
111 Adventure tale
112 Rounded and smooth
113 Estimate
117 —— accompli
119 Formed a lap
120 "—— Ding Dong Daddy . . ."
121 Ancient town in Lucania
122 Certain
123 Dancer Bambi ——
124 Gudrun's victim
125 Language course
127 M.I.T. or R.P.I.
128 Bound
129 Stage part
130 Sponsorship
131 Maintain action
136 Skin spots
137 Work units
138 Hairy twin
139 Disembark at O'Hare
140 Robert Anthony ——
141 Seasoning
142 Cong. act
143 Arnold from Chelsea

DOWN

1 Cheap wine
2 Hayseeds
3 Poisonous sap
4 N.Y.C. is one
5 Tease
6 Trading center
7 Onassis
8 Perceived, in a way
9 "Lily of the Mohawks"
10 Observed
11 Gas: Prefix
12 Angler's gadget
13 Peephole
14 Honshu city
15 —— years (youth)
16 Slight advantage
17 Exterior
18 Water's edge
19 What bureaucrats give
23 Alexandra and Catherine
24 Chemical suffix
25 Meteorologist: 1839-1921
31 In error
33 Oafish
34 Edmund, the orator
35 Bolivian river
36 Nigerian people
39 Zoo favorite
40 Town on Hiroshima Bay
41 Guitars' kin
42 Yellow flags
44 Sour
46 Collins or Dryden
51 Lane, in Limerick
52 Correct
56 Great pain
57 Auxin, for one
59 Utilize
61 Like a vermouth
65 Uncooked
66 Second person
67 She comes out
69 Hawkeye
70 Drama critic Atkinson
71 Emulate Casanova
72 Parisian's smoke
74 High note
75 L.A. athlete
76 Bravo or Muni
78 Tin Pan Alley org.
80 Droplet on a petal
83 Oatmeal
86 Palm off
87 Bacchus attendant
89 Hangout for Ferdinand
90 —— Satan (brat)
91 Courage
93 Kind of potatoes
94 Commedia dell'arte character
95 Apple variety
97 Fierce look
99 Idolize
100 —— hand (abjectly)
102 Pertinent
104 Paul from Ottawa
107 Mesh
108 Young Ike's residence
109 Marred
111 Least prolix
114 Look- —— (twins)
115 Verbal contraction
116 Spouts
118 Gide and Previn
123 —— Abner
124 ". . . have —— in my mind . . .": Yeats
126 "The fat —— the fire"
127 —— dixit
128 Like a high wire
129 —— breve
132 Period
133 Leghorn's largess
134 Bleat
135 Decide upon

Out-of-Place Words

By Jeanette K. Brill

ACROSS

1 —— morgana
5 Implied but unsaid
10 Potato, for one
15 Having wings
19 Royal city of the Canaanites
20 Supreme Moslem deity
21 White poplar
22 Where Hyde once presided
23 Afghan road material?
25 Activity in a post-W.W. I free city?
27 Rivaled successfully
28 Rubbish
30 Fears
31 Field for Fabius
32 Ria
33 Kind of physician
34 Hercules, to Iole
37 Kind of lightning
38 Site of battles of Bull Run
42 Hair styles
43 Get squiffed in Formosa?
45 River in Wales and England
46 Bellow
47 Sassoon or Service
49 Stir
50 Holiday in Napoli
52 Dress (up)
53 Montana cosmetologist?
57 "—— Be," Beatles hit
58 Cantabs, Elis et al.
60 "Let's Make ——"
61 Greek moon goddess
62 One of the dryads
63 Fern leaf
64 Of yore
65 Full of chinks
67 Common contraction
68 Word game
71 Praying figure
72 Swimmer's motion in NW France?
74 Born
75 British buddy
76 Past
77 Yorkshire river
78 Tamarisk
79 Cuckoo
80 German sweets?
84 River, politician or cloth
85 Winks
89 Wash out
90 Ribs
91 Hebrew month
92 Pan-fry
93 Long and thin
94 Formulator
97 German engraver: 1471-1528
98 Berkeley's colleague
102 Know-how in SE France?
104 Error in chronology in Ohio?
106 Wading bird
107 Wildcats
108 Bronx warbler
109 Other
110 Swiss linear unit
111 "Last Case" sleuth
112 Over
113 Doyen

DOWN

1 Sham
2 Saroyan hero
3 Prohibition
4 Flatterer
5 Vintner's employee
6 —— ego
7 Oaf
8 Pop singer Janis
9 "—— Love . . .," 1924 song
10 Crisp woven fabric
11 Corvette's target
12 Mouth of a trumpet
13 Wapiti
14 Blush
15 Epic hero
16 Gershwin girl: 1929
17 Sere
18 Parts of divs.
24 Nigerian seaport
26 "But thou —— God . . .": Neh. 9:17
29 Tore
32 Cole Porter's "—— Men"
33 Puccini's "—— Lescaut"
34 Drays
35 In progress
36 Realistic in Czecho-slovakia?
37 Antitheses of deles
38 Of form
39 Nourishment in NW France?
40 Patty Duke ——
41 Ray
44 Water nymph
47 Football plays
48 Teutonic king
50 Feather an arrow
51 Sniggler for wrigglers
53 Truth, to Keats
54 Vetches
55 "—— Know Why," Wonder hit
56 Coppers
59 Bombinate
61 Quench
63 Refrigerant
64 —— about
65 Type of type
66 Man from Tabriz
67 Odysseus' smart dog
68 Get up
69 Wingding
70 Beginnings
72 Hubbub
73 René's aunt
78 Activated
81 Most proximate
82 Cerulean
83 Offend
84 —— one (betting odds)
86 Miss Marker in 1934
87 Nautical term
88 Gun mount
90 Smeared, in a way
92 Anthony
93 Delibes opera
94 Get on
95 Money in Meshed
96 Angle of a leaf-stalk
97 Desperately urgent
98 Piece of mail
99 Nettle
100 U.S. satellite
101 Govt. agents
103 Son of Odin
105 —— compos mentis

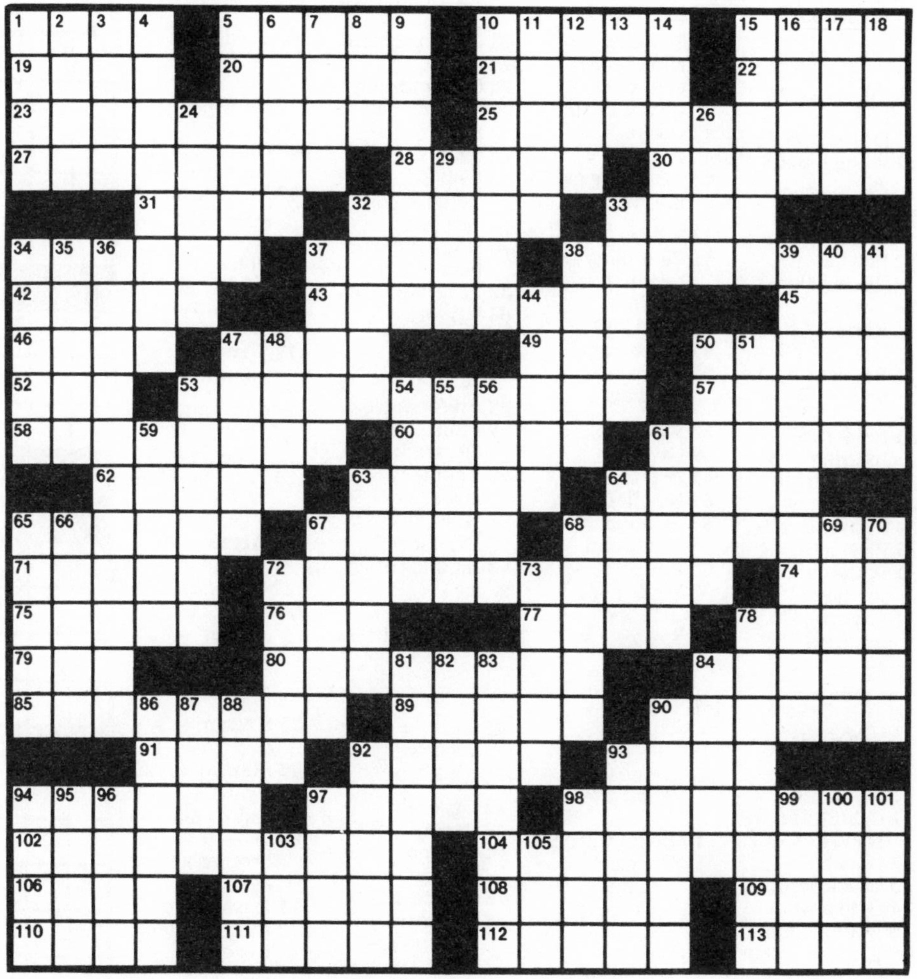

88 Title Roles

By William H. Ford

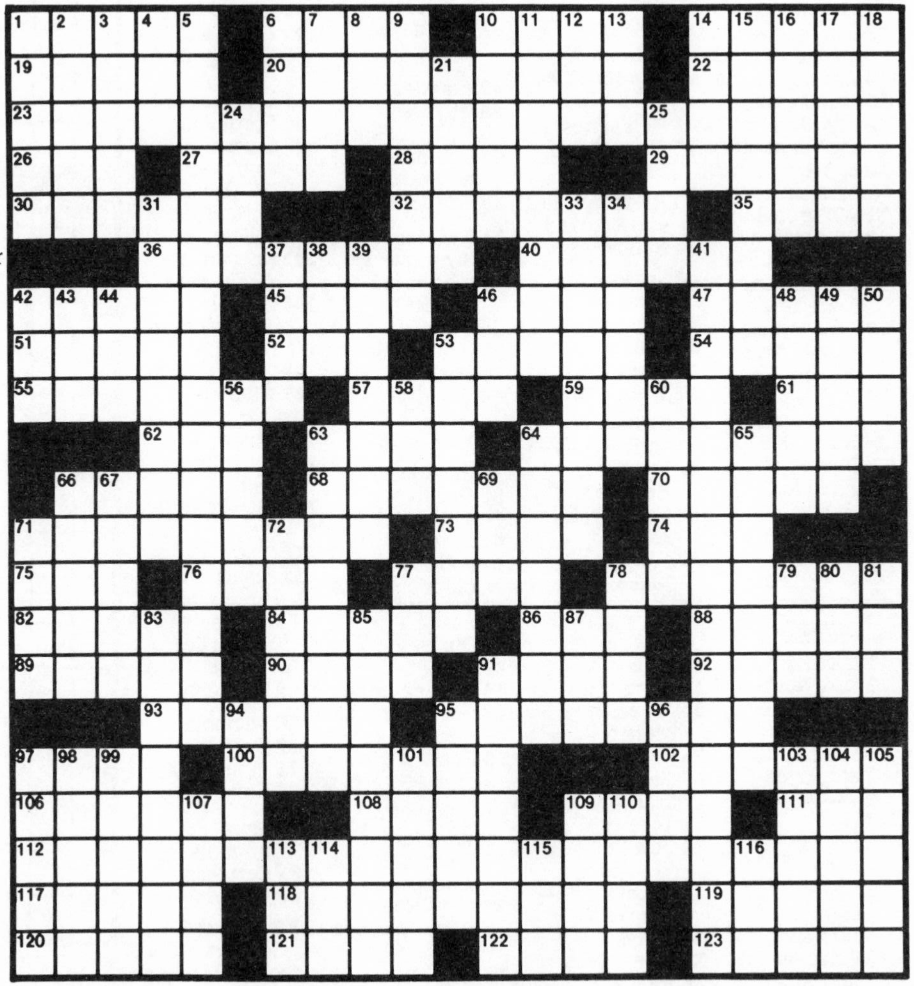

ACROSS

1 Put —— to (stop)
6 Dowels
10 Wang Lung's wife
14 Sweeting or greening
19 Powhatan's son-in-law
20 "Lillian Russell" star: 1940
22 Bounced by the boss
23 Jennet Jourdemayne
26 Charged atom
27 Resiliency
28 Had chits out
29 Pad sharer
30 Paths cut by scythes
32 Exporters' concerns
35 Swindles
36 Kin of corn pones
40 Closed chaise
42 Quay
45 Hideaway
46 "Evening out" memento
47 Mild cigar
51 Columbus's birthplace
52 Grain
53 Loud kiss
54 Macho type
55 Train or subway
57 What soaks do
59 Gypsum
61 Aspiration
62 Needlefish
63 Antitoxins
64 Oscar and Felix
66 White poplar
68 In proportion
70 Spicy stews
71 Joe Bonaparte
73 A Fed
74 O'er and o'er
75 Neighbor of Arg.
76 Spanish painter
77 Come a cropper
78 Highlander's purse
82 Lose one's cool
84 Driver's maneuver
86 Cumberland ——
88 Fit for ducks
89 Pioneer in electricity
90 Yakutsk's river
91 G.W., to Braddock
92 Dakota tribe
93 Roils
95 Non-biodegradable items
97 Fiddler on the reef
100 Put back
102 Jeremiad
106 City near the Rideau Canal
108 "Deutschland —— Alles"
109 Slay
111 Hawaiian ruler
112 Frankie Addams
117 Wreck completely
118 Skids laterally
119 Freud colleague
120 "—— of robins . . ."
121 Arthur Garfield ——
122 Eucalypt
123 Gulf south of Samar

DOWN

1 Gilmore of the N.B.A.
2 Not at all
3 Gluck heroine
4 Grid initials
5 Willie Loman
6 English author of 100 novels
7 Something —— (stunning!)
8 Schnapps
9 Small fry's transport
10 Amount bid
11 Ancient city in Phrygia
12 Port on Firth of Clyde
13 Tip
14 —— -Asian
15 Game with a 48-card deck
16 Boxer Carnera
17 Pravda founder
18 Selvages
21 Somewhat, in Berlin
24 Potion portion
25 —— Major
31 Jammed with people
33 Show-off boxer
34 Lucked out
37 Cluster
38 Auto-club letters
39 Portsmouth's neighbor
41 Lady Sneerwell, president
42 Kg. or lb.
43 Part of H.S.H.
44 Collected sayings
46 —— de Staël
48 Mexican timber tree
49 What Abe split
50 "Don't tread ——"
53 Dauntless
56 A Forsyte by marriage
58 Pizarro's pelf
60 Press coup
63 Army gunners' "eyes"
64 Earache
65 Extremist's doctrine
66 Main artery, in France
67 Doldrums
69 "—— my brother's keeper?"
71 Rush of air
72 Burned-over woodland
77 Brother, in a friary
78 Barracuda
79 Ebro or Mayo
80 S.A. herb
81 Greek goddess of night
83 River and state
85 Not durable
87 Newspaper items
91 With vigilance
94 Metric weight
95 Introductions to bks.
96 Nastase
97 Terra follower
98 Title for an Eng. peer
99 Tête- ——
101 Hautboys
103 Poet Dickinson
104 Group of nine
105 Argentine resort
107 Shoe part
109 H.E.W. was one
110 Tan liquor
113 Thirty-two qts.
114 Rocco's "Hurrah!"
115 Hawk parrot
116 Ike's initials

A Mother's Day

By Tap Osborn

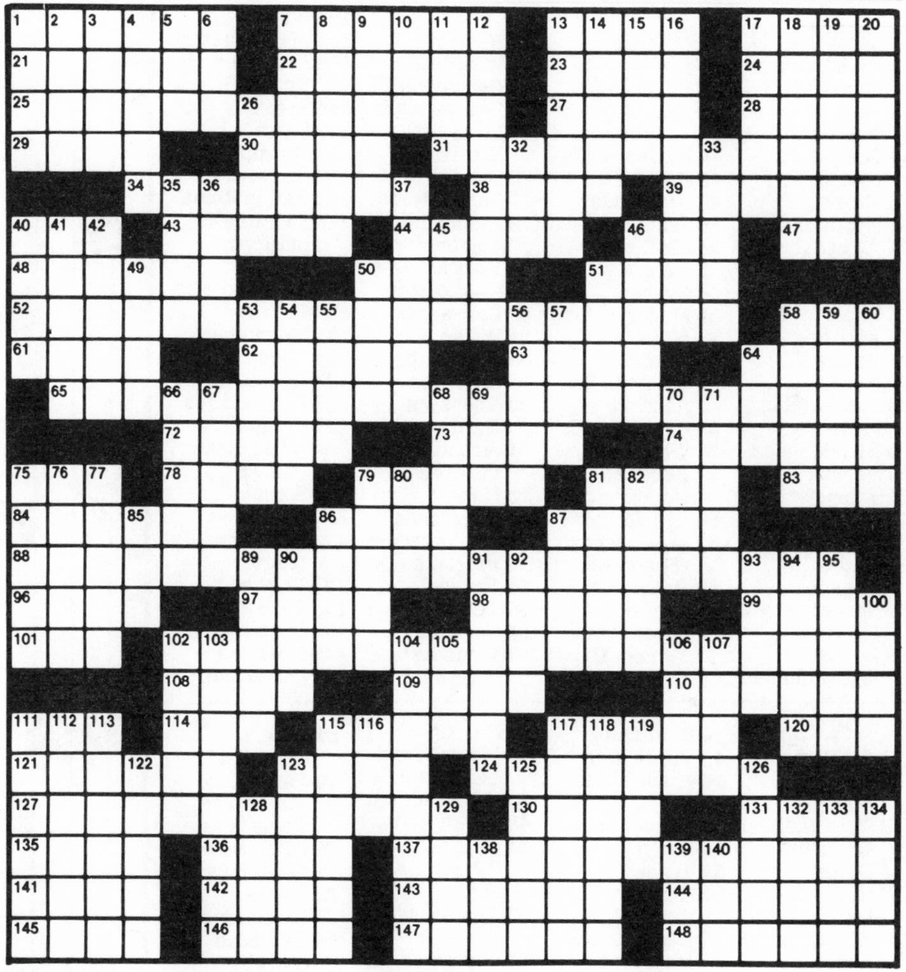

ACROSS

1 Robin's companion
7 Flimsy fare for Fido
13 Honshu ship
17 Myerson
21 One-seeded fruit
22 "... arm us 'gainst ——": Shak.
23 Verily
24 Uproar
25 6 A.M.
27 Sea hazard
28 Of soil: Prefix
29 Leander's lover
30 Sacred Egyptian ape
31 6:30-7:30 A.M.
34 Fortune maker for Thomas Watson
38 Dovecote music
39 Undersized
40 Within: Prefix
43 Old English coins
44 Singer John
46 German article
47 A Chaplin
48 Socialist of a sort
50 River duck
51 —— even keel
52 7:30-8:30 A.M.
58 Soupçon
61 Pedro's "Positively!"
62 Young beauty
63 Major follower
64 Boxer Tunney
65 9 A.M.-2 P.M.
72 Ephron et al.
73 Penance seeker
74 Interstice
75 Tennis stroke
78 Take —— the chin
79 Liszt
81 Valuable tree of India
83 Up to now
84 Words of relief
86 Imperfection
87 British India founder
88 2-4 P.M.
96 Amass
97 Winglike
98 "Do I —— Waltz?"
99 Electric force
101 Miscalculate
102 6 P.M.
108 Sicilian city
109 Dutch painter Frans
110 Fraud
111 Bedazzle
114 1 or 101, for short
115 Subject of an essay
117 Grain thresher
120 —— blanket
121 Body with two whips
123 Fabric maker
124 Incapacitated
127 8-10 P.M.
130 Huck's transport
131 Saarinen
135 Grandfatherly
136 Hatch cover
137 11 P.M.
141 Petrocelli or Carty
142 Fish-eating bird
143 Stupor
144 Conforming
145 Beaver skin
146 Hindmost
147 Surfacing machine
148 Kitchen tool

DOWN

1 Ablution
2 Pang
3 Wallace's "—— Documents"
4 Bordeaux wine
5 Memorabilia
6 Fresh
7 Midwest capital
8 Intones
9 Make a new knot
10 A cont.
11 Milne creation
12 Handpicked
13 Brando
14 In —— (tousled)
15 Emit fumes
16 Like a thankless child
17 Modified leaf
18 Regatta crews
19 In the extreme
20 Plastered
26 —— Valley, Calif.
32 Looby- —— (singing game)
33 Athapaskan group
35 Buccal
36 Starling's kin
37 Stay
40 Newts
41 Master, in Madras
42 Pinguid
45 Celtic Neptune
46 Bejewel
49 Footnote abbr.
50 Rail
51 Not fooled by
53 Brazilian dance band
54 Old Japanese gold coin
55 Smack
56 Sherry city in Spain
57 I use: Lat.
58 Kind of blind
59 Tarsus
60 Harass
64 "... the giftie —— us"
66 Kind of cake
67 "Theirs —— reason why"
68 Haggard
69 Coiffure style
70 Burst of cheers
71 Judge's role
75 Potter's wheel
76 Different
77 Misty
79 Botanist's concern
80 Indian novelist
81 On the ball
82 Minor prophet
85 Queen killer
86 Monks' titles
87 Lamb, for short
89 Ball-gown fabric
90 Alan or Robert
91 Wild dogs of India
92 Polanski film
93 A tide
94 Kind of grease
95 Pocahontas's mate
100 Skillful
102 Nobel physicist: 1925
103 Tamandua
104 They handle retorts
105 Beaked warship
106 Satie
107 Favus
111 Musical tone
112 Beetle
113 Weave together
115 Silk hat
116 Dance
117 Capet's domain
118 Thief
119 Wonder drug
122 Permit
123 Doone
125 Drift
126 Fraser of tennis
128 Reduce
129 Tiber tributary
132 Malevolent
133 Descartes
134 Kayo blow
138 Chattels mover
139 Start of a cheer
140 Chemical suffix

Metropolitan Tour

By A. J. Santora

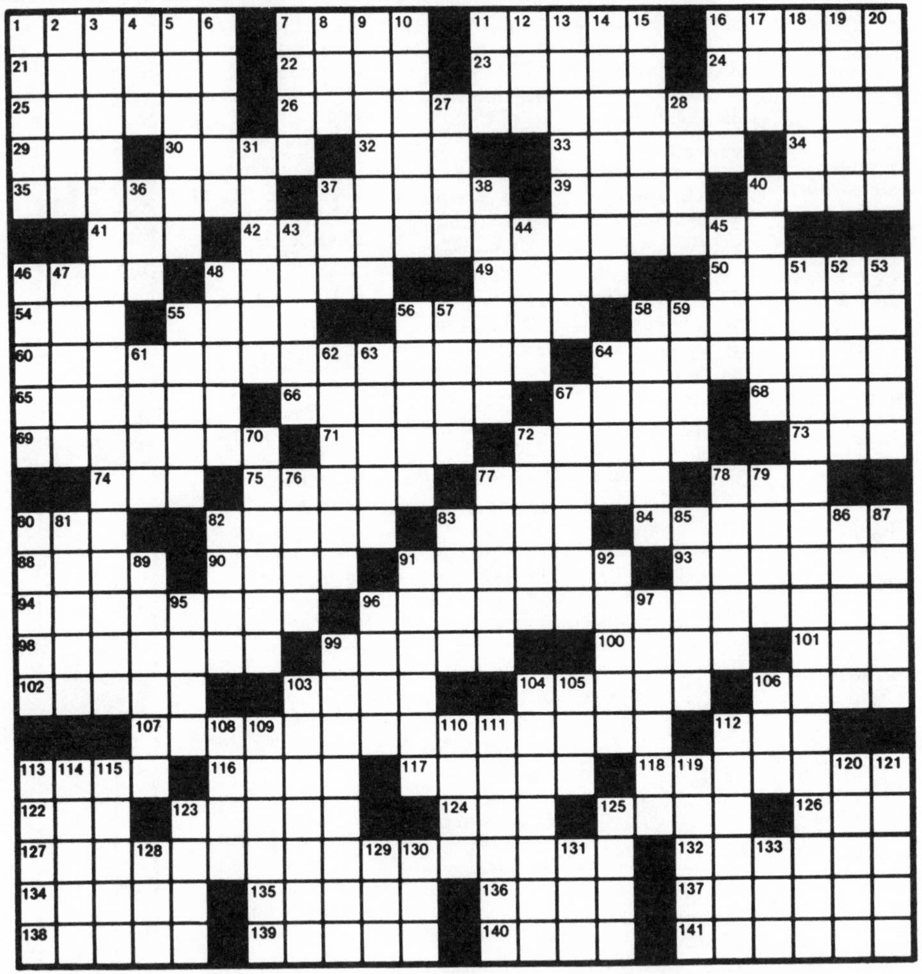

ACROSS

1 High Czech points
7 Japanese wrestling
11 Computing devices
16 Shrewd
21 Not injured
22 "When the frost —— the . . ."
23 Table fowl
24 Accustom
25 Bailey of comics
26 Swiss bidding system?
29 Blonde shade
30 Verve
32 Japanese carp
33 Overtrained
34 D-day craft
35 Of the breastbone
37 Shakespeare's Sir Toby
39 Lounge entertainment
40 Opinion
41 Lixivium
42 Chris Evert and ex-spouse at Wimbledon?
46 To live, to Livy
48 Rotates
49 Highlander
50 Seat the crowd
54 Medieval tale
55 Sage, e.g.
56 Cygnets
58 Macaroni for soups
60 First-aid bracer in SE Asia?
64 Cape off N.C.
65 Where Hacettepe Univ. is
66 Hijinks
67 —— mecum (handbook)
68 Pageantry
69 Leaflet appendages
71 Temporary stitch
72 He wrote "Games People Play"
73 Sonny's sibling
74 Loser to H.C.H.
75 Banal
77 Layer of skin
78 Ending for amateur
80 Easy as ——
82 —— couture
83 Lanyard
84 Bitter
88 Places, to attorneys
90 Rooney or Hardy
91 A concern of the chair
93 Noise
94 Brave man
96 He'll wheedle Fidel for news
98 Fringes
99 Tells all
100 Convene
101 What the dr. ordered
102 Bharat
103 Marine hazard
104 Emulates Robert Giroux
106 Speck
107 Swiss shrimps?
112 Sixty secs.
113 Rat, in Roma
116 Swimmer's platform
117 Flu shot
118 Compete with
122 Top card
123 Mountebank
124 Young one
125 Rabbit or Fox
126 Dec. and Jan.
127 Philippine roller coaster?
132 Prance
134 Stem
135 —— a beet
136 Salt Lake City team
137 Proviso
138 Take it easy
139 Percolates
140 Resort to
141 Dome team

DOWN

1 Big horns
2 "—— of robins . . ."
3 "Finlandia" in harmony?
4 Dull routine
5 Hollywood Dahl
6 Epitaph stone
7 Agree in writing
8 Consumption
9 Grivets
10 —— cat (sandlot game)
11 Here, in Honduras
12 College grad
13 —— Creed
14 Dominate
15 Fruitlessly
16 Movie house
17 Leaf cutter
18 Mutual-aid group
19 Jagged
20 Gossipy woman
27 Damone and Morrow
28 Odylic force
31 Adjective for Tony Dorsett
36 N.Y.C. suburb
37 Good, to Pierre
38 Navajo lodges
40 Marching perfectly
43 "The Balance"
44 Pointed tooth
45 Put out
46 Maxwell and Lanchester
47 Valentine, e.g.
48 Flower part
51 Film subtitled "Paris, Ah So"?
52 As a friend: Fr.
53 Grates
55 Rabbits' kin
56 Cut ham
57 Part of a candle
58 Ambling horse
59 Fit to ——
61 Yawn
62 Existence
63 Condition
64 Wrong
67 W.W. I battlefield
70 Fans' place
72 He hit 358 home runs
76 Discourteous
77 Condemns
78 —— ease
79 Croat, for one
80 Excuse at court
81 Element used in metallurgy
82 Crowning glory
83 Arrest
85 Throbs
86 Nine-part song
87 Incline
89 Spectrum color
91 Drinks
92 Pantomime
95 Connery from Edinburgh
96 Corn-oil product
97 Lower
99 Straddle
103 Gridiron "zebra"
104 Learned
105 Obscure
106 Cubic centimeter
108 Of speech
109 Manufacturers
110 Epsilon follower
111 Herschel's discovery
112 Wall décor
113 Tamerlane was one
114 Pigment for Opie
115 Jeopardy
119 Goal of a sort
120 Trunk
121 —— Park, Colo.
123 Bend, as an arm
125 Sit in the sun
128 "Life —— jest": Gay
129 Snooze
130 Scrolls: Abbr.
131 Shelter
133 Keeve

"Rose Is a Rose"

By Maura B. Jacobson

ACROSS

1 —— rosa (secretly)
4 Chow ——
8 Draw a bead on
11 Iranian coins
16 Change for a five
18 "The Velvet Fog"
19 Best of the movies
20 Jostler's weapon
21 Heart of the matter
22 Take up, as a cause
23 Drug dick
24 Uses a kettle
25 Rose
29 Caesar and Luckman
30 Electrical unit
31 Els, e.g.
32 Wheel shafts
33 Austen novel
35 Neighborhood
37 Pianist Gilels
38 —— de la Cité
41 Jason's ship
44 What a d.a. is
46 Maroon
48 Like otaries
50 Rose
53 Running in neutral
54 Everlasting: Poetic
55 Rosy feature
56 Amo follower
58 Villa d'——
59 Refuge for Valjean
60 Rose
64 Mason's item
65 He waited for Godot
67 Rolled tea
68 ". . . walk before thee like ——": Shak.
70 A daughter of Rose Kennedy
73 Rose
78 Certain Prado works
82 Soviet inland sea
84 Yeahs' opposites
85 Did catering
86 Freeloading fish
87 Rosy-cheeked
89 Rose
93 Salute of a sort
94 Vatican veils
95 Pronom
96 Highland refusals
97 Heretofore, to Herrick
98 Get one's goat
100 Wimbledon great
102 Cookbook abbrs.
104 Ply
106 "Winterset" hero
107 Genetic helix, for short
109 Anecdotal anthologies
112 Rose
117 Painter of "Olympia"
118 Bowler's aisle
119 Antilles Indian
120 Word with pittance
121 Absalom's initial
122 W.W. II alliance
123 Gives it a whirl
124 "Dukes of Hazzard" spinoff
125 "Beau ——"
126 P.T. place
127 Sultanas' chambers
128 Likely

DOWN

1 Gazpacho, e.g.
2 Monads
3 Dramatist-poet Ugo ——
4 Act the arbiter
5 Become weatherworn
6 Gazelle's kin
7 Holl.
8 Wives of Esau and Lamech
9 Anent
10 Ornamental knotting
11 Rose
12 "—— Lucy"
13 "—— Rose"
14 Lounge about
15 Vane readings
17 Rose
18 Thrash
19 Imbue with a wood finish
26 Credo
27 Vernon's vis-à-vis
28 Cato's 61
34 Role for Rosalind
36 Esteem
37 Oleoresin
39 Slow, in music
40 Trimmed the rim
41 Gibraltar beasts
42 Neural network
43 Rose gradually
45 Distant: Prefix
47 Lesion adhesion
49 Pub stock
51 Strip of tackle
52 Command to Rover
53 Coney and Catalina: Abbr.
57 "When I was —— . . ."
60 Yucca
61 Discoverer's cry
62 Devil-may-care
63 Hindu ascetic: Var.
66 1958 Presley hit
69 Rose
70 Do a grammar chore
71 Like a noisy crowd
72 Rosés
74 Busiest airport
75 W. Pt. enclave
76 Alouette's bill
77 Gouda's cousin
79 "I Never Promised —— Rose Garden"
80 Johnson of "Laugh-In"
81 Verbalizes
83 Film of 1967
86 Stats for Mike Schmidt
88 "—— Rose": S. Young book
90 May and Stritch
91 Add turf
92 Certifying officials
94 "You're a Grand ——"
99 U.N. agcy.
101 Wars of the Roses king
103 Pyrenees city
105 All thumbs
106 Part of a dram
108 Persian water wheel
110 Rose Bowl, in a way
111 Barber's aid
112 Kind of cabbage
113 Like tapers
114 VIII, to Virgil
115 Grid leaders
116 Gusto
117 Slick, e.g.

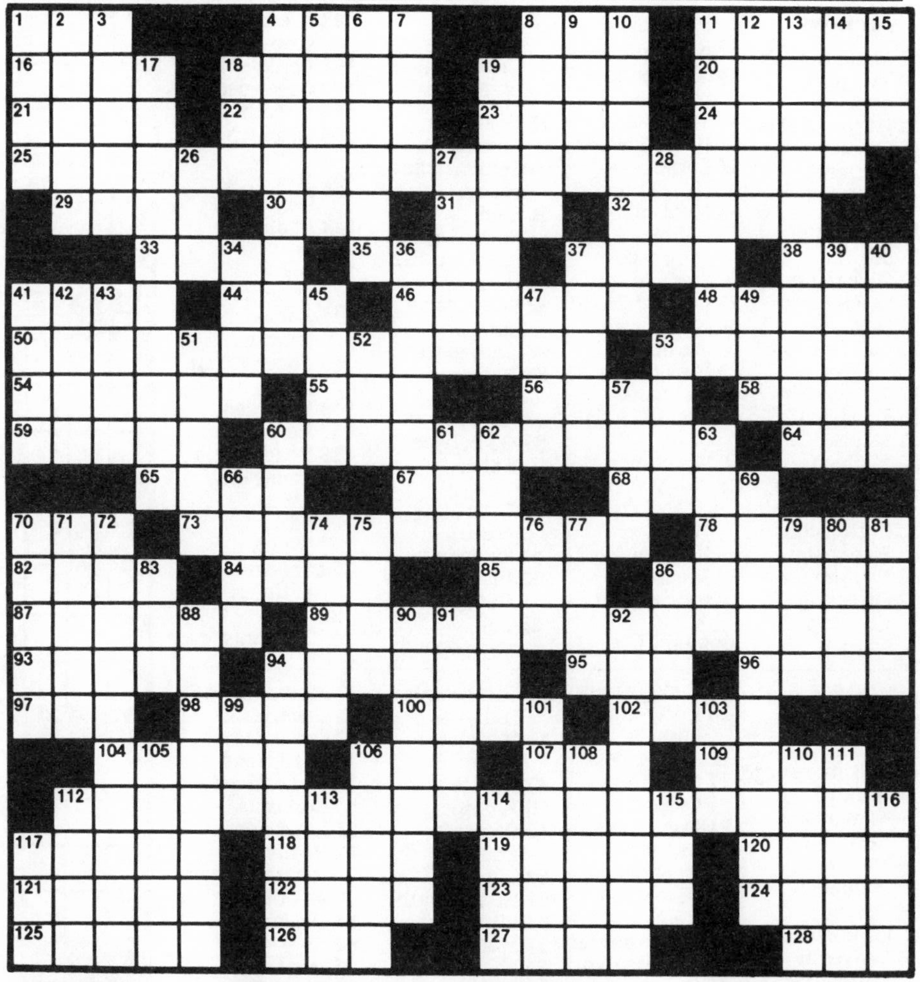

Bearding the Lions

By Alfio Micci

ACROSS

1 Mountain ash
6 Trattoria offering
12 Harbor sights
18 Piqued
19 Ancient Egyptian
20 Doubter of dogma
23 Give the sack to Foch and Ney
25 Call Franchot
26 Single
27 Mr. and Mrs.
28 Strong pulls
30 Struck out
31 Wallach
32 "—— kleine Nachtmusik"
33 Cab customer
34 Extirpate
35 Popular fabric
37 Directing Claude's course
43 Mike shields
45 Relative
46 Alphabetical trio
47 Trevi number
50 Bills collector
52 Corner —— (trap Irving)
53 Meat cut
55 Military command
56 Ziegfeld star
57 Lyricist David
58 Himalayan creature
59 Presidential nickname
60 "And what is —— . . .?"
62 Watchmen
64 —— May, in "Tobacco Road"
66 Russian John
67 Spooky-sounding city
68 Ready to swing
72 Divide geometrically
74 Cleaned the blackboard
76 Hokkaido, formerly
77 Semicircular recess
80 Sahl
81 Second word in a Wilder title
82 Shreds
84 Submissive ones
86 Bamboozle
87 Author of "Nausea"
88 Kind of code
89 Go-between: Abbr.
90 Give —— (care)
91 Salt trees
92 Flabbergast George
95 List components
98 Prefix for scope
101 Leeds's river
102 Greek peak
104 Wreath
105 Dispatch boat
107 Mrs. Leonowens
108 Appraise
110 Der —— (Adenauer)
111 Forsook Learned
113 Coach Edgar Lee
116 Detergent
117 Heroic verse
118 Road sign in Montreal
119 Like a hazardous wintry day
120 Shoemakers, at times
121 "—— Solemnis"

DOWN

1 Went through a safe
2 Baltimore or orchard
3 Admonishing Alexander
4 To —— (exactly)
5 Thread: Comb. form
6 Leaves in difficulty
7 Swiveling wheel
8 Davis Cup figure
9 Farrow and Slavenska
10 Chum
11 Case
12 Harass
13 Spartan king
14 Genetic inits.
15 Forty-niner's quest
16 Glycerides
17 Garb for Calpurnia
21 Don Juan's mother
22 Relinquish
24 Nice friend
29 Yen
32 Punch used in repoussé work
33 Demon
36 Small amount
38 Have reciprocal effect
39 Frenzied
40 —— honorables (reparations)
41 Frivolous
42 Cambodia's Lon ——
44 Mountain: Prefix
47 Article
48 Trumpery
49 Prefix for gram
50 Cyprinoid fish
51 Etc.'s relative
52 Little ones
53 Mutation
54 Vesicle
57 Event for Figaro
61 Italian rice dish
62 "Lost" item in a Milland film
63 Wristbones
65 Brain passage
69 Defeat Peter
70 Côte d' ——
71 Small shark
73 Mature insect
75 Once, once
77 Cutting tool
78 Island food
79 Something for Cerberus
81 Ladd role
83 Ready in Rennes
85 —— de mer
86 Parlor game
90 A —— apple
91 Posits
92 Typical of a holiday
93 Became nonproductive, as a well
94 Kind of derby
96 British measures
97 Forty winks
98 After-bath item

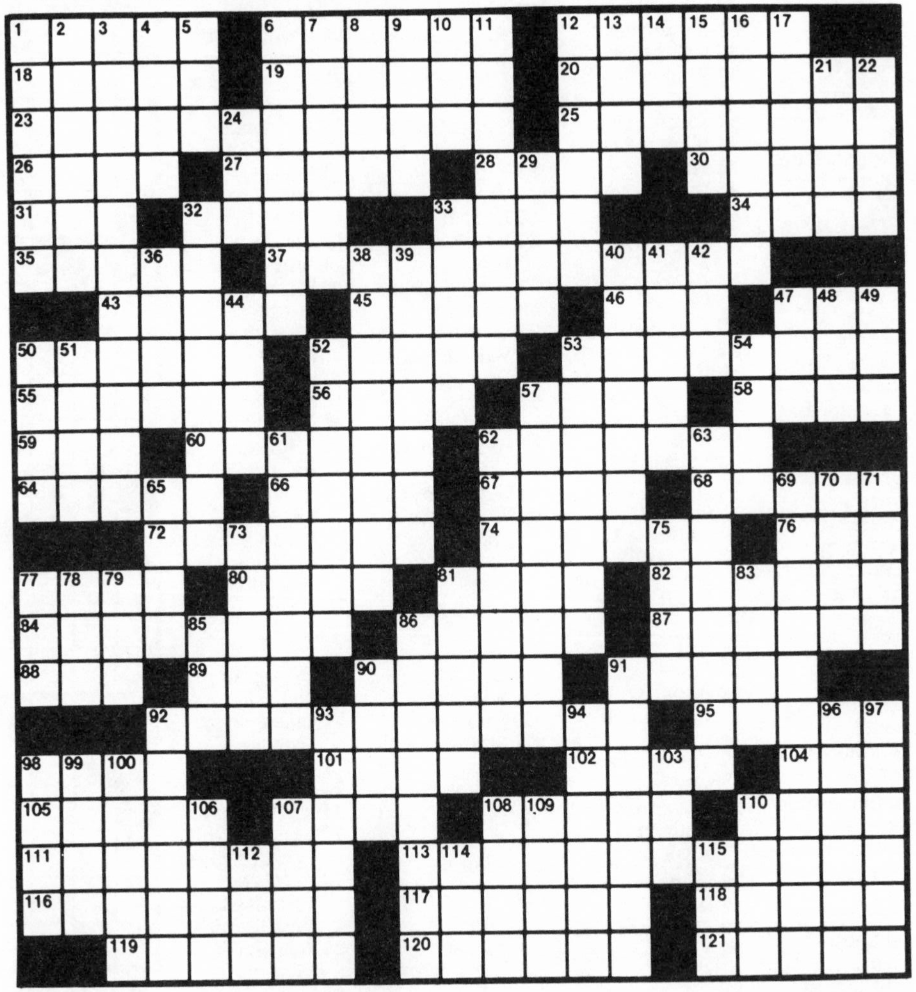

99 Knievel
100 "—— but a walking shadow . . .": Shak.
103 Plaice's place
106 Strauss's "Die Frau —— Schatten"
107 Dill of the Bible
108 Stringed instrument
109 Mont Blanc is one
110 Town near Teramo
112 Peer Gynt's mother
114 Postal abbr.
115 Penrod's playmate

Geoganagrams

By Richard Silvestri

ACROSS

1 Indian state
6 Mime
10 "—— steals my purse . . .": Iago
13 Emulated Gretzky
19 Whence testimony is given
20 Carnival attraction
22 Guarantee against loss
23 Michigan title
25 High-kicking dance
26 Tip
27 Acapulco gold
28 What money does
29 Waistcoats
30 The facts guide his acts
33 "In Reverse" painter
34 Before febrero
36 Like sea water
37 Oregon men
40 Agcy. aiding opera, etc.
43 Hermia's father
44 Units of loudness
45 Wagon follower
46 NCO
47 Rose, for one
48 Metric weight
49 Croc's cousin
50 Wind in rings
51 Maine shoe
55 March man
56 Crusader's foe
59 Transoceanic ship
60 Sparing
61 Flow forth
62 "Nothing could be —— . . ."
63 Alarm
64 Fable adjuncts
65 Kafka hero
66 Bound
67 S. Johnson drama
68 Wyoming predicament
71 Dravidian language
72 Carries on
73 Sulk
74 Matelot's milieu
77 Prefix with bar
78 Commedia dell'——
79 Perfume
81 Make baskets
83 Bill's partner
84 Ohio holy book
86 Pungent bulb
87 Bendix role
89 Building beam
90 Wear away by abrasion
91 Didn't possess
93 View from Bogotá
95 River island
96 Legal matter
97 Colorless, liquid solvent
99 Wisconsin realms
103 Like bright nights
104 Sham
105 Quickly
106 Covered with hair
107 Neighbor of Leb.
108 Bring up
109 Propelled a keelboat

DOWN

1 Vilifying villain
2 Prehistoric time
3 Wearing huaraches
4 Formicary denizen
5 16th-century opener
6 Kind of tie
7 Early invader of Britain
8 Author LeShan
9 Agama or anole
10 Former
11 Pan's foe
12 Confesses
13 Oft-bracketed word
14 Varlets
15 Lou Grant portrayer
16 Arizona nobility
17 Part of Q.E.D.
18 Iniquitous places
21 Intense looks
24 Chevet
31 Blackbirds of N.Y.
32 Electees
33 Demesne house
34 Singer John
35 ——-do-well
37 "Star Wars" captain
38 Emaciated
39 Rose essence
41 Long letter
42 Put fears to rest
44 Hasso
48 Winter wear
49 "But don't —— the water"
50 Rough
51 Split ingredient
52 Allan-——
53 Light aircraft
54 Laundry cycle
55 Bay duck
56 Arabic or Aramaic
57 Tenderly, in music
58 Texas hardship
60 Layer: Prefix
62 Secure
63 Walk proudly
65 —— Domingo
68 Lug
69 Slender stalk
70 Direct a helmsman
72 Casanova
74 Afflicted with paludism
75 Proof
76 Took a break
79 Amen
80 More vulgar
81 Kind of bond
82 Be human
84 Busy places in June

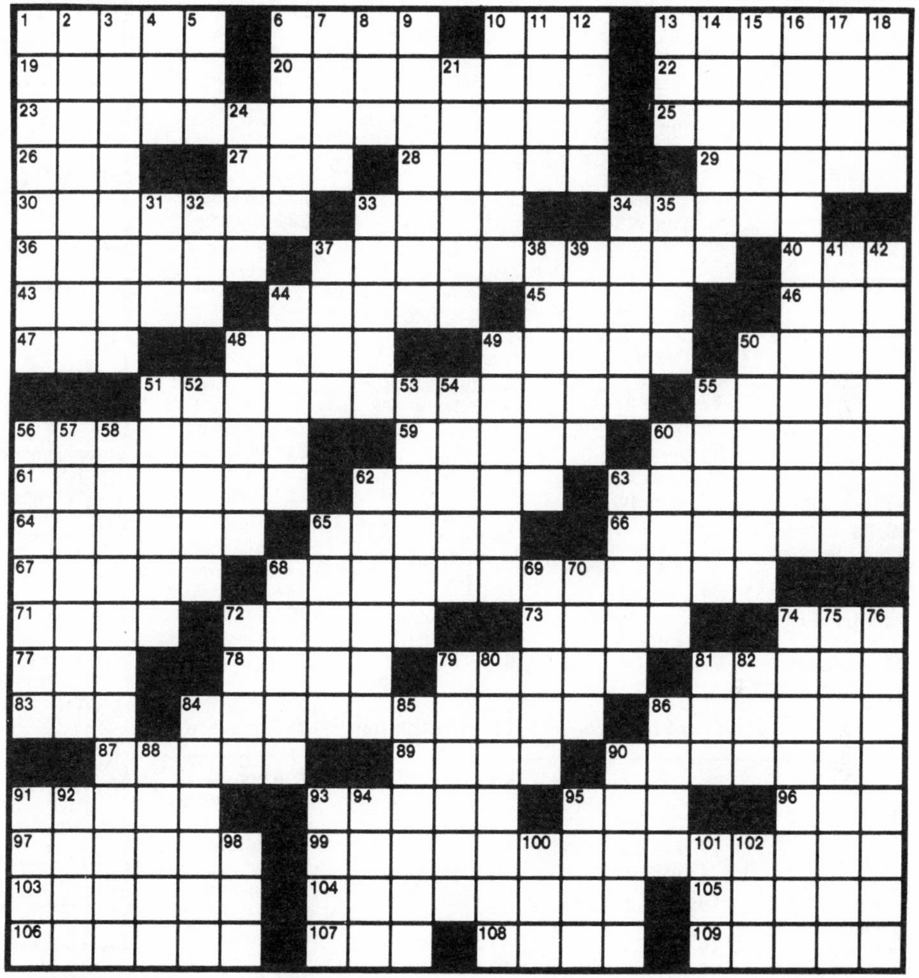

85 Joker
86 —— pieces
88 Musical passage
90 Fall beverage
91 Fastener
92 Overture follower
93 Elec. units
94 Not one, in Dogpatch
95 Amphora feature
98 Soap ingredient
100 A follower
101 Cartogram
102 Mil. address

94

Some Two-Steps

By Bert H. Kruse

ACROSS

1 Mess
6 Ark landfall
12 Appoint
16 Golf club
21 Different
22 Singer Vic
23 Arabian head cord
24 Mexican Indian
25 New York City
27 North African kingdom
29 Kind of plate
30 Begins
31 Fyodor and Alexis
33 Toscanini
34 Broke a Command-ment
35 House plant
36 Sioux
37 —— Mahal
40 Plural ending
41 Struck
43 Part of 70 Across
46 Deduced
49 U.S. Nobelist in Literature: 1938
52 D.C. tax collectors
54 Lofty
55 Vacation
57 Breaks a Command-ment
58 Fitzgerald forte
59 Kind of jaw
60 Bassanio's beloved
62 Miss Kett
63 Rossetti's "—— Beatrix"
64 The old sod
65 Demi follower
66 Actor Jack
68 Safari figure
69 Soviet rep.
70 Shakespearean tragedy
72 An Argonaut
73 Headliner: Aug. 6, 1926
75 Faith: Fr.
76 Emerson, —— Concord
77 Genetic offshoots
78 Ravel masterpiece
82 Surpass
85 Out-of-date
86 ". . . —— passion to tatters"
87 Noted Swiss poet: 1821-81
88 Resort east of Altdorf
89 Island group off Ireland
90 Beat pounders
91 Caught
93 —— code
94 Hogarth subject
95 Mount sacred to the Muses
97 Thug
98 Originate
99 Hot time in Paree
100 Hit song of 1912, with "My"
102 F. L. Wright's home in Wis.
105 "The Praise of Folly" author
108 Occupied
110 Spareable item
111 French possessive
112 Those born July 23-August 22
113 Hair style
115 Canyon mouths
117 Drenched
120 Playwright Tad
121 Erstwhile source of plumes
122 Anent
126 U.S. anthropolo-gist: 1901-78
128 Vodka drink
131 Cold period in Spain
132 Light a fire under
133 University board member
134 Sam or Toby
135 Island in Taiwan Strait
136 Imperative, e.g.
137 Talks back
138 Paravane

DOWN

1 Anderson's "—— Your Houses"
2 Roman emperor
3 Oates book
4 Give up
5 Charle-magne's dom.
6 Fatty
7 Blacksnake
8 Chemical compounds
9 Wallabies, for short
10 Tropical herb
11 Having left a will
12 Brazilian port
13 Money in Israel
14 Atlas material
15 Building part
16 Rose of ——
17 Doughboy's leg covering
18 Koolau Range site
19 Done
20 Notorious uxoricide
26 Scowl
28 The Sprats, e.g.
32 Luges
34 Paddock papas
35 Italian philosopher: 1822-1905
36 Florida city
37 Dyes
38 Chameleons
39 Bumppo's creator
42 Zero
43 Ticket
44 "Essay on Man" author
45 More incensed
47 Besides
48 Matelot's wheel-rope
50 County in Colo.
51 Cessation
53 Excel
56 Previously, previously
58 NATO's late cousin
60 Containers for liquids
61 Tilden in 1876
63 Plague
65 Trio
67 Keep —— (persevere)
68 Bialy's relative
70 Goes one's way
71 —— effort
72 Encrusted
74 Lorna of fic-tion
76 Knowing
77 Pharmacist's waxy prepara-tion
78 Seven: Comb. form
79 "Dondi" car-toonist
80 Shirt ruffles
81 Large pulpit-desk
83 Antipodean
84 Grooms
85 Bell the cat
86 Frogs' kin
88 Essence
90 Bag man
92 "—— Dei"
93 "Mikado" trio
95 Thackeray's "Henry ——"
96 "—— Ro-mance," 1936 song
101 Piscators
103 Halts
104 Unwilling
106 Kin of birches
107 So long
109 Holes-in-one, often
113 W. African an-telope
114 Inquired
116 Pickle
117 Noah's first-born
118 Chaplin's widow
119 Plankton col-lector
120 Spanish Super-realist
121 Roe
122 Pittypat in "G.W.T.W."
123 Conventicle group
124 Prefix for prompter
125 Humdinger
127 Kind of runner
129 Teachers' org.
130 Quid pro ——

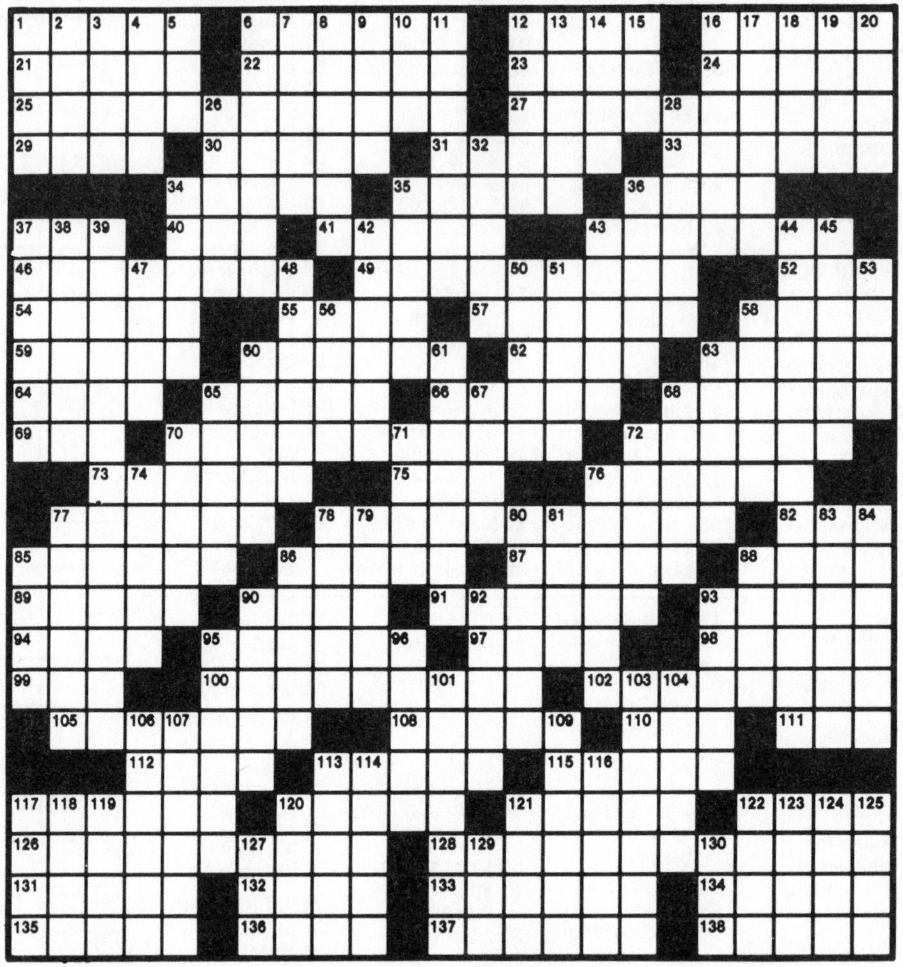

A Father's Day

By Tap Osborn

ACROSS

1 Flintlock musket
6 Gaff
10 Check
14 Bar at the bar
19 Centaurus star
20 Alleviate
21 —— Sound, Fla.
22 Like Behan's "Fellow"
23 6:15 A.M.
26 Loosen the bonds
27 Glass part
28 River into the Caspian
29 Forwarded
30 7:30 A.M.
38 Rich
39 Ribald
40 Shell adjunct
41 Nobelist Hahn: 1944
42 Lockup unit
43 Too smooth
44 Network
47 8:45 A.M.
53 Antic
54 Part of H.H.
55 Rain-forest vine
56 Cantankerous
57 Curt dismissal
58 Profound
59 ". . . had —— and couldn't . . ."
60 Cross or Ross
61 9 A.M.
66 Resemblance
67 Delon of films
68 Sapota or encina
69 Concord
70 Setting
71 Nitrite is one
73 In the style of
76 Swank
77 9 A.M. to 5 P.M.
80 Grimalkin
81 Epicist
82 Activist
83 Wahhabi, e.g.
84 Maa-saying ma
85 Occultism
88 Melodious
90 7:15 P.M.
96 Gypsy tongue
97 Male swine
98 Ungentlemanly one
99 Soap plant
100 11 P.M. to 6 A.M.
108 Take a reading
109 "The ——, Love . . ."
110 Spree or glee sound
111 Medium for some jockeys
112 Suckling's forte
113 King of Sodom
114 Scourge of serge
115 Bullet sound

DOWN

1 Kind of cat
2 Word of disgust
3 Interview
4 Victors at the polls
5 Honor
6 Sordid
7 Mary, in an old song
8 Bumbler
9 Car created by Olds
10 Prepares an egg dish
11 ". . . squander what he lived ——": Bierce
12 Poplar
13 Agree with
14 Buckingham officer
15 Moslem law
16 Architect Jacopo: 1486-1570
17 Sky hunter
18 Hammer parts
24 Luxor's river
25 Repentant one
29 Vapid
30 The clergy
31 Pliant
32 Aquatic mammal
33 Sheltered promenade
34 Great quantity
35 Bubble, to Luigi
36 Snow melter
37 Place mat
42 Leather pants
43 Mates for harridans
44 First Oscar film
45 Does a lawn job
46 A Capetown citizen
48 Like some hiemal days
49 Devoutness
50 Fuller in the face
51 Schenectady college
52 Actress Hildegarde
53 Recipient
57 Eloquent Roman
58 Godhead
59 Hawaiian tree
60 Kind of driver
61 Apia's locale
62 Squeeze out
63 Clubbed
64 Neon or gold: Abbr.
65 Total
66 Course
70 Virago
71 Kin of a lycée
72 Scotland's Sound of ——
73 City that tires Detroit
74 Realty contract
75 —— Day
77 Somewhat sorrel
78 Powell
79 Acid ——
81 Hash house
85 Refrigerant
86 Nova Scotian university
87 Cutting remark
88 A wife of Esau
89 Synge's "—— to the Sea"
90 Homeless one
91 Similar: Comb. form
92 Overact
93 Almost half the people

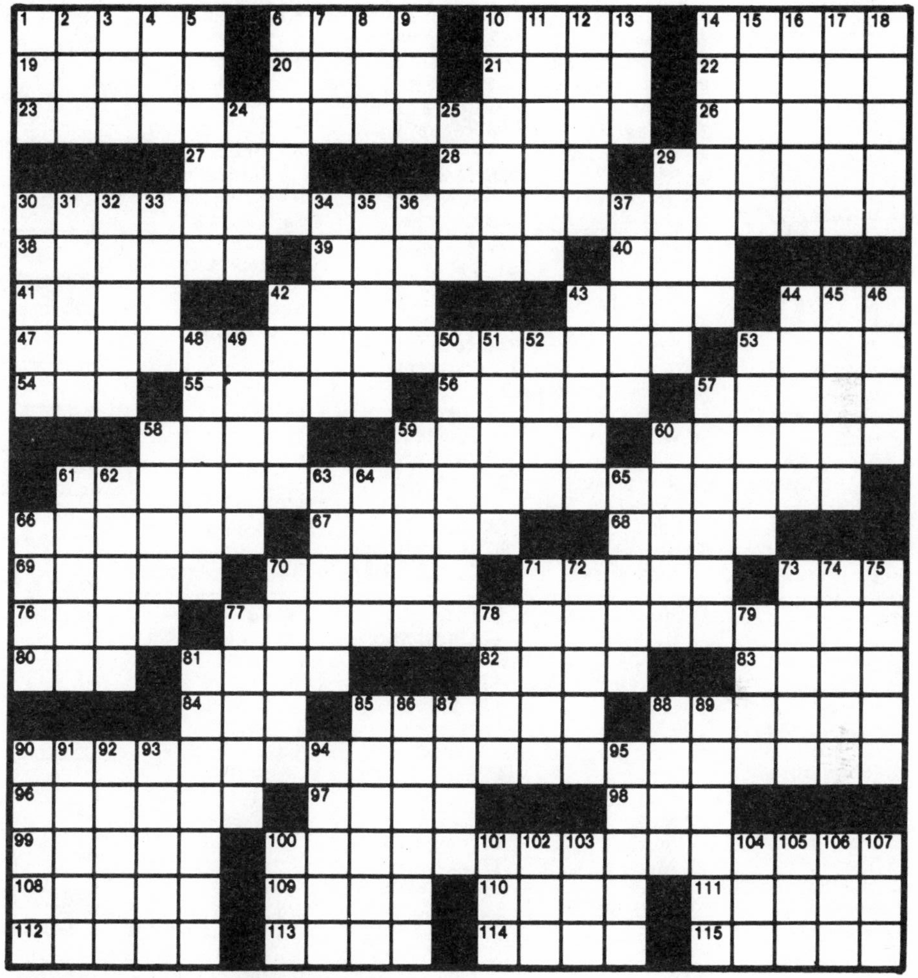

94 Hip part of cattle
95 Glee-club unit
100 Mischief
101 Hole maker
102 Its symbol is X
103 Knowledge
104 Dip bait lightly
105 Nabokov novel
106 Be A-1 at the Big A
107 Nailing block

All-American

By I. Judah Koolyk

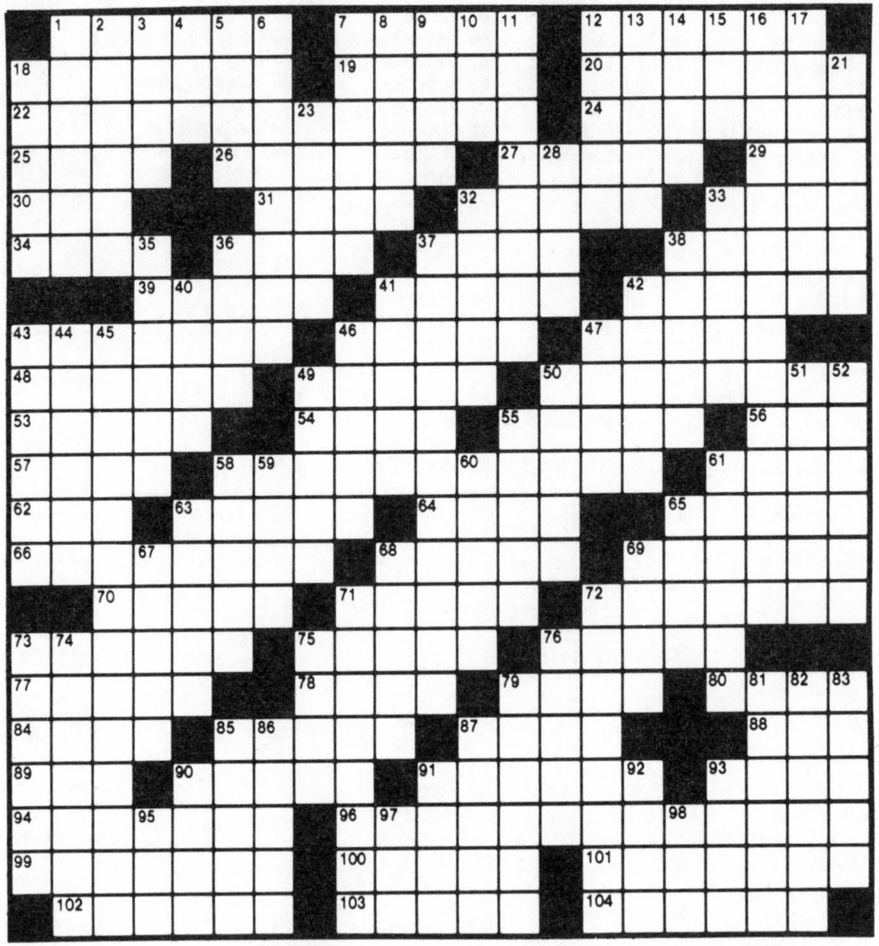

ACROSS

1 Haberdasher's item
7 Therapy, to a G.I.
12 XYZ —— of 1797
18 Hakka or Wu
19 Caribbean isle
20 Obscured
22 Visitors' cry at Detroit?
24 Mosaic piece
25 Steinbeck's Joad
26 Expresses love or hate
27 Persea and poon
29 Sine qua ——
30 A.L. player of yore
31 Hurok et al.
32 Toppers for the Brewers?
33 Draw's kin
34 Tense
36 Major ending
37 —— de combat
38 Rancor
39 Seeps
41 Zola heroine
42 Kitchen implement
43 Type of wrench
46 Became wan
47 Chamber instrument
48 Deter
49 Quotidian
50 Graceful ones
53 Noun suffixes
54 Admits
55 White Sox foundations?
56 Riv. project
57 Two of the Red Sox?
58 Northeast nuisances?
61 Small shoot
62 Compass pt.
63 First of 12
64 Roulette bet
65 Cause to be
66 Region's residents
68 Vessels for steaming
69 Ricochet
70 Word on a penny
71 Use a blast furnace
72 Rode with the Rangers?
73 Circus men
75 Cartels
76 Cookie pan
77 Vacuous
78 Australian ratites
79 Quid
80 Cummerbund
84 Distaff donkey
85 D.C. art gallery
87 Kipling's "—— Sea to Sea"
88 "The Gold Bug" author
89 Father of Phineas
90 On the qui vive
91 Man in a manse
93 Representative of Osiris
94 Appointed anew
96 Hot times in Cleveland?
99 Piney, e.g.
100 Prepares paint
101 Boot-camp G.I.
102 Rendezvous
103 Beethoven's "Für ——"
104 Break a union

DOWN

1 Stifled or strangled
2 Bench jockey's activity
3 Peruvian Indian
4 D.V.M.
5 Tarheel county
6 Semi man
7 Diamondback's warning
8 Iroquoians
9 Embraces
10 Honest one
11 Made a deal
12 Emulated Olivier
13 Lams
14 Trench
15 Indian rice
16 Metropolitan Stadium siblings?
17 Send by a new course
18 Elected
21 Hair particles
23 Comics heroine
28 Make incised marks
32 Apiculturist's product
33 Bicycle mishap
35 There
36 Israel's Weizman
37 Anaheim cyclists?
38 Wild plums
40 Numbers for the A's?
41 Wet
42 Garment gradations
43 Molded
44 Hydrocarbon from evergreens
45 Seattle senior citizen?
46 Karpov's octet
47 Singer Jerry
49 Cupolas
50 Travelers
51 Call forth
52 Weakened
55 Girl's garb
58 Girl's garb
59 "It —— Me, Babe," Dylan song
60 Carols
61 Characteristics
63 Cerulean
65 Sad, like the Jays?
67 Vernon's dancing partner
68 Chanson subject
69 Sprang up
71 Eventually
72 British prescription fillers
73 Arena officials
74 Selection from a literary work
75 One of the Royals?
76 Fleeced
79 Goalie's domain
81 Attach
82 Evening party
83 "Magister Ludi" author
85 Like a cheetah
86 Foxx's namesakes
87 Emulates the Orioles?
90 Aggregates: Abbr.
91 411, to Livy
92 Preserve, in a way
93 Gallic girlfriend
95 No matter which
97 None
98 Singer Davis

97

U.S. Songfest

By Anne Fox

ACROSS

1 Pilgrimage to Mecca
5 Wind
9 Rich soil
13 Manila hemp
18 Region
19 Cod's cousin
20 Physician: Comb. form
21 Ape
22 "Yankee Doodle" words
26 Jargon
27 Make tracks
28 Bugbears
29 Uris hero
30 Greek letters
33 Kind of cat
35 Term of endearment
36 Church calendar
37 Words by K. L. Bates
42 Fuss
43 Plat, e.g.
44 Vigoda
45 Herb of grace
46 Words by J. W. Howe
55 Calm; composed
56 Follower of Paul
57 Netherlands river
58 Syr. neighbor
60 Device for Walton
62 Shell adjunct
63 "From —— to shining . . ."
64 Purposive
66 Words by J. Hopkinson
72 Man with an army
73 —— Elum, city in Wash.
74 Guevara
75 Met extra
76 Beast of burden
77 Barrette
78 Early church desk
80 Football great
84 Key words
90 Wilde forte
91 Chemical prefix
92 Sgt.
93 Greek Aurora
94 "Stand ——" (words from Berlin)
103 Capital of Aisne
104 Henry ——, modern U.S. sculptor
105 Turkish title
106 White
107 Ossuary
108 City in Puerto Rico
110 Kind
112 Nullify
116 Words by G. P. Morris
121 Mortal
122 Employing
123 Lout
124 Kansas city
125 Scintilla
126 Tear
127 Mas that maa
128 Hole punchers

DOWN

1 Fastener
2 Greek gulf
3 O.T. book
4 Writer Timerman
5 Pure
6 Lout
7 Jack's predecessor
8 A wife of Jacob
9 New Guinea port
10 Other: Sp.
11 Properly
12 "Last of the Cocked Hats"
13 Writer Kingsley
14 Twice
15 Ethiopian province
16 Poet who wrote "As If"
17 Part of A.D.A.
20 Words by Walt Whitman
23 City on the Dnepr
24 Pet
25 Writer Van Loon
31 Vapor: Comb. form
32 Ghost
34 Helicon
36 Cassini
37 Access
38 Popular color
39 Abridgment
40 Suffix with cash
41 Equivoque
42 Jennet
47 Thickened areas of skin
48 Extract
49 A compass, for short
50 Pierce
51 Durrell novel
52 Piles up
53 Stew pot
54 Dresden denial
59 A-E connection
61 Spanish hero
63 Shack
64 Serving as a model
65 Resin
66 Windrow contents
67 Nejd native
68 Black
69 Cubitus
70 Alas!
71 Insignificant
77 —— Amiens (First Crusade preacher)
79 Roman Hades
81 Pulitzer Prize author
82 U.S. missile
83 Alts.
85 Duplicate
86 Played a child's game
87 Kind of dance
88 Ath. group
89 Meat cut
94 Palisades
95 Flap on a cap
96 "Moonlight ——"
97 Lovelace's greater love
98 Condone
99 Surrealist

100 Generous ones
101 Jug
102 Greek goddess of health
108 "Young Hickory"
109 Hibernia
111 Honshu seaport
113 Claim
114 William of Uri
115 Times
117 Needlefish
118 "Hansel —— Gretel"
119 Eleanor Smeal's org.
120 Howe, to G.W.

Breeding Reading

By William Lutwiniak

ACROSS

1 Jehu
6 Calendar period
11 Symbols of office
16 Heroic works
21 Stan's pal
22 Some Renoirs
23 Reconciled
24 Bring out
25 Vol. I
28 Ream fraction
29 Ditty
30 Pilfer
31 U.S. Indians
32 Duped
33 Catchall abbr.
34 Avocet's cousin
35 Piece of cloth
36 Palatial accommoda-tions
37 Proverbial septet
38 Plaints
40 Bread, in Brest
41 Vol. II
46 Lunar feature
50 MO imperative
51 Wroth
52 Mark well
53 Eared vessel
54 Storied batter
55 Ekberg
56 U.S. beef center
58 Man of Meshed
59 Lalapalooza
60 Jason's craft
61 Lacquered metalware
62 Up
63 Existed
64 Vol. III
69 Picador's target
70 Pyle of TV
71 Exploits
72 Vol. IV
77 Andrews or Maxwell, for short
80 Strayed follower
82 Perdition
83 Nat or Natalie
84 "Dove sono" is one
85 Goes for
86 Overindulges
87 Cancel a launching
89 Fencing gear
90 Maddened
91 Rights org.
92 Crash, to the R.A.F.
93 Natural-gas component
94 Dinero unit
95 Vol. V
99 —— were
100 Indo-European
101 City NW of Nîmes
102 Mexican statesman
105 Musical dir.
106 True-blue
108 Mil. man
111 Mystical formula
112 Squirrel away
113 Minh headquarters
114 Lariat
115 C'est- ——
116 Vol. VI
119 Dishes out
120 Kind of energy
121 Solus
122 Coronet
123 Till now
124 Men of letters
125 Nuclear particle
126 Elian piece

DOWN

1 Wooded area
2 Apply quotas
3 Mont ——
4 Luscious cherry
5 Hankering
6 Erect
7 Eye part
8 Part of a bird's bill
9 Part of a bird's bill
10 Lao- ——
11 Spanish mar-ried woman
12 Eager
13 Australian cry
14 Outfielder Slaughter
15 But, to Ovid
16 Spangle
17 Grown-up
18 Duplicity
19 Plantation
20 Spore
26 Will subject
27 Undo
32 Semblance
34 Sordid
36 Obese bag man
37 Bushelman
38 Protein source
39 Numerical prefix
40 Belittled
41 Republic on the Gulf of Guinea
42 Floribundas
43 River of Brazil
44 Before
45 Totally
46 Rates
47 Flooded
48 Descartes
49 "The Waltons" role
50 Old tub
55 —— self-defense
56 Different
57 Ballerina Shearer
58 Kind of verb: Abbr.
60 Home-run champ
62 Oise feeder
64 "Drake" poet
65 Nimble
66 Lazes
67 CINC's charge
68 Put up
69 City on the Maumee
72 Gags
73 Alpine house
74 In a dither
75 Image: Prefix
76 Sugar source
77 Of space
78 Old Nick
79 Scurrilous
80 Gaffe
81 Radial
84 Plant nuisance
86 Split: Prefix
87 Alms box
88 Berlin road
89 Hepburn role in "On Golden Pond"
91 In difficulty
92 Lover of Cupid

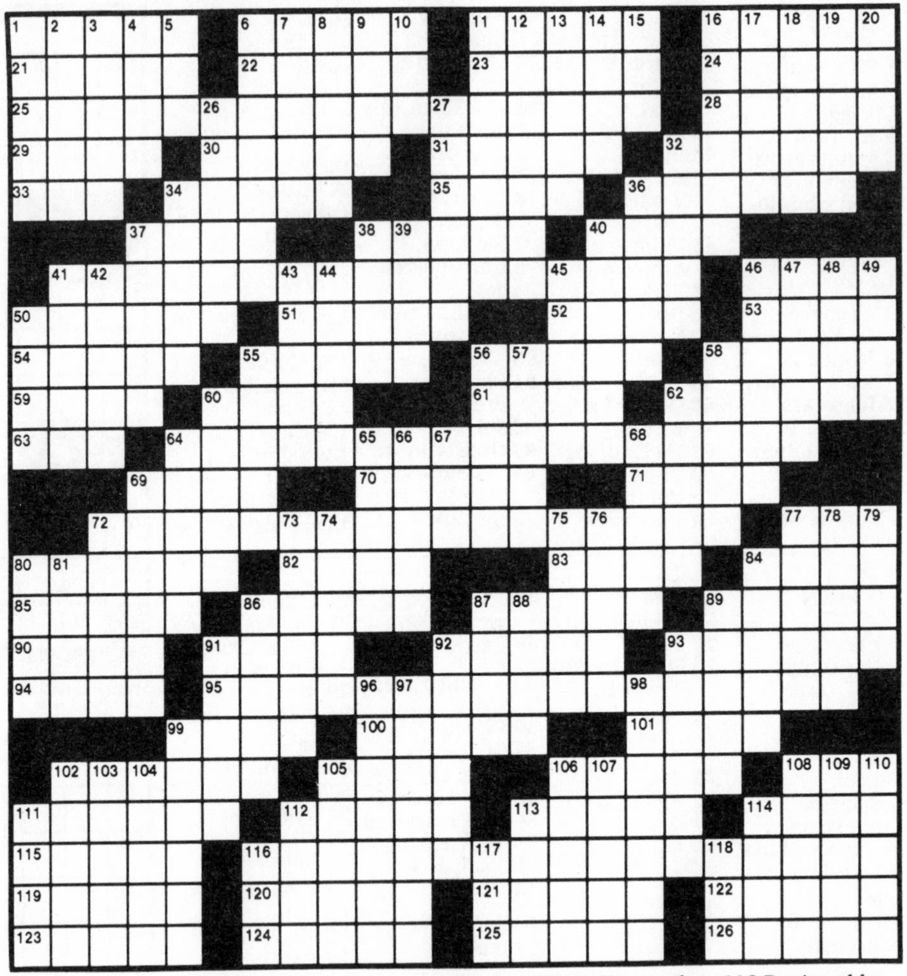

93 Bakery item
96 Drum beat
97 Utensils on pencils
98 Divulge
99 Stop
102 Green gems
103 Concord
104 Ending of a Kilmer poem
105 Memorial pil-lar
106 African capital
107 —— -trump (bridge bid)
108 Certain sodas
109 "Oberto" is one
110 Second SAC chief
111 Doll's word
112 Begone!
113 Robust
114 Box-score data
116 Recipe abbr.
117 For, to Fabius
118 Resident: Suf-fix

Space Trip

By Ruth N. Schultz

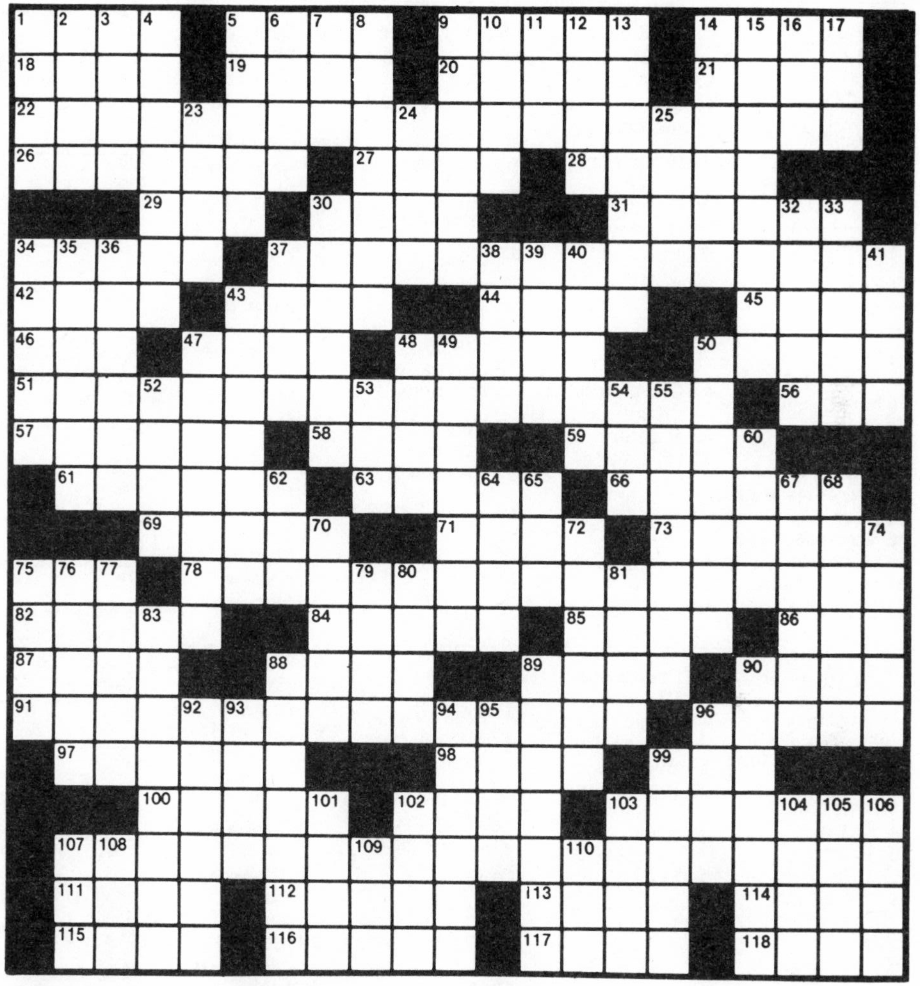

ACROSS

1 Bone: Prefix
5 Red planet
9 African language group
14 Inky
18 Derr Biggers hero
19 Seed coating
20 Squirrel's cache
21 Wool: Prefix
22 Huston film: 1957
26 Parts of clocks
27 Arouse
28 Bayard, for one
29 ". . . and Tyler, ——"
30 N.T. book
31 Consecrate
34 Some are moles
37 Esther Williams film: 1955
42 Golden, e.g.
43 Porcine abodes
44 Cries of disgust
45 Frown
46 Diminutive endings
47 Warp's partner
48 Muscat citizen
50 Davis or Midler
51 Como hit: 1958
56 Simpleton
57 Spatial
58 Droops
59 Galsworthy book
61 Reckoned
63 Ravioli or ziti
66 Legendary flier
69 Greek letters
71 Sow's sound
73 Verdi opera
75 "Angela ——," 1928 song
78 Plummer film in 1969, with "The"
82 Perfume base
84 Mob scenes
85 Learning method
86 Spanish relative
87 Rent
88 ". . . in corpore ——"
89 Beame and Burrows
90 Tenth part: Prefix
91 Weill musical: 1943
96 Termite, e.g.
97 Breastbones
98 Do a redacting job
99 Pacino and Capp
100 "Carousel" star
102 Ancient Syria
103 Obliteration
107 Time for K-K-K-Katy's rendezvous
111 A side of N.Y.C.
112 Kind of fig
113 Chinese: Prefix
114 London hero
115 Small roles
116 Anya the author
117 Buck heroine
118 Emulated Cordero

DOWN

1 Baron in a Strauss opera
2 Bandleader Fields
3 West German basin
4 Asked
5 Tropical fruit
6 Places of refuge
7 —— Tin Tin
8 Rush-hour headaches
9 Dr. J's target
10 Summit
11 Conjunction
12 "Desire," to the English
13 Takes off cargo
14 Glyn or Wylie
15 —— Day (July 14)
16 Yoko
17 Negative prefix
23 Cabell of baseball
24 Desert ravine
25 Type of moth
30 Groups seizing power
32 Bark of an E. Indian tree
33 Letter-shaped fasteners
34 Cheaters
35 Kind of race
36 Foot part
37 Mutt's pal
38 Abba of Israel
39 Telephoned
40 Crystalline rock
41 Ceramic stoneware
43 "And —— Mahmud . . .": FitzGerald
47 Shrill pills
48 First name of 72 Down
49 Crap-game loss
50 Murmur
52 Corn bin
53 Swathe
54 Thou, in Tours
55 U.S. literary family
60 Dryad's home
62 "Great ——," 1929 song
64 Pie plates
65 Kelep or emmet
67 Heavy overcoat
68 Valve or channel
70 Conductor Caldwell
72 Russian gymnast
74 Walking —— (ecstatic)
75 Marquand sleuth
76 Items in Watson's bag
77 Court decision
79 Printing machine, for short
80 Unguis
81 Grant and Lee
83 Personal influence
88 Denounces fiercely
89 With a lively beat: Mus.
90 Personnel file
92 Praying statues
93 Cadre, e.g.
94 Vile people
95 Dutch cheese
96 Bunk
99 A major crime
101 Word form with "vision"
102 G.I.'s pineapples, etc.
103 Sicilian resort
104 Destroy
105 Cattail
106 Medieval serf
107 Black widow's creation
108 "Bali ——," 1949 song
109 Lincoln Ctr. structure
110 Squeak squelcher

Hanky-Panky

By Alex F. Black

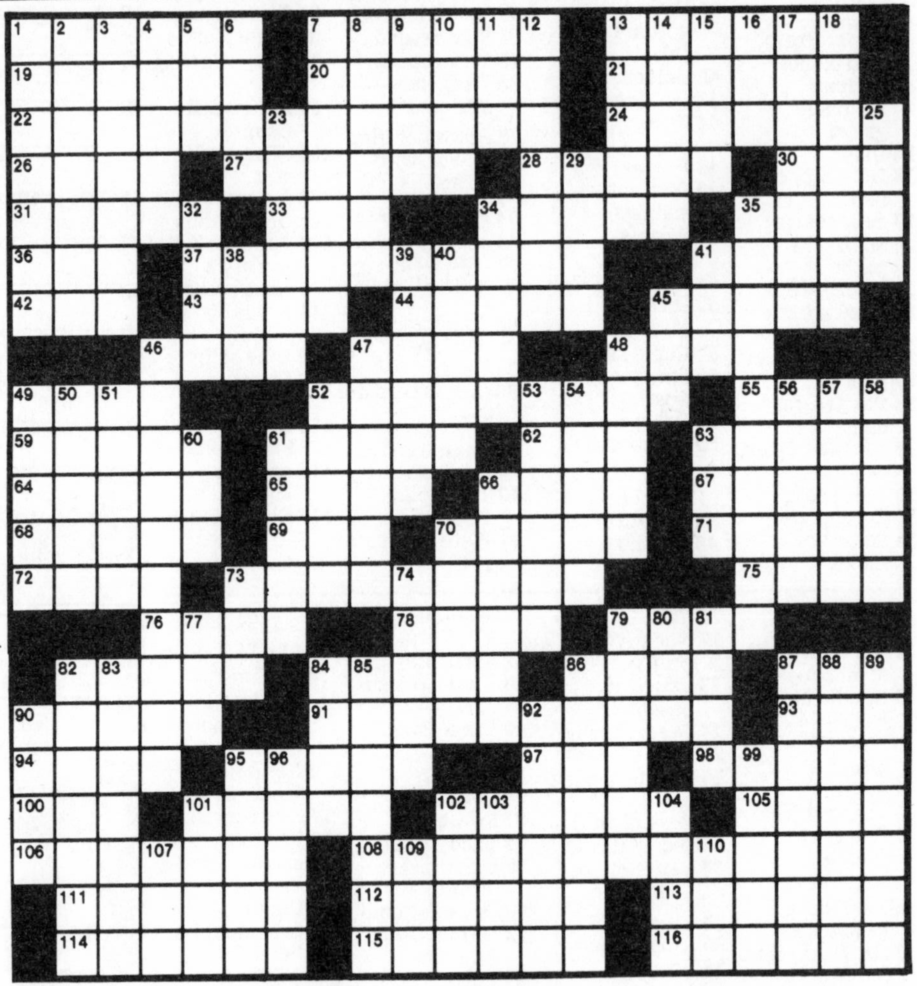

ACROSS

1 Prestige
7 Minuscule
13 Look
19 Bearlike
20 Sardou play
21 —— Beach, S.C.
22 Bilbao bottles
24 Melancholy merino
26 Stead
27 Most precious
28 Lowest Laconian
30 Séance sound
31 Author Hammond
33 Peat source
34 Chased woman
35 Ooze
36 Showcase for a Pavarotti
37 Oriental ship
41 Electronic device
42 McMahon and Asner
43 Unpaid sitter
44 Gas-company customers
45 Marriage notice
46 Dreary in Dundee
47 Pilaster
48 Pop
49 Box
52 Jack/Giant dialogue
55 One of Jubal's inventions
59 Pointer
61 Pâtisserie item
62 Grande or Bravo
63 Mystery writer's award
64 Pitcher at Monmouth
65 Border lake
66 "—— is the spur . . ."
67 Adriatic feeder
68 White poplar
69 Old Caen coin
70 Turns
71 Flips in a chip
72 Let
73 Reading for 46 Down
75 Fish dish
76 Regrets
78 Zhivago's mistress
79 Fellow like Othello
82 Teatime treat
84 Like London in 1666
86 Belts
87 Little, to Burns
90 Abzug or Spewack
91 Cuts family ties
93 Chum
94 "Life is ——!"
95 On the qui vive
97 Neighbor of Que.
98 Bitter
100 Trainee: Abbr.
101 Rage onstage
102 Starr player
105 Elihu's U.
106 Headgear attachment
108 Rainwear buyer
111 Cio-Cio-San, e.g.
112 Restricting rope
113 Special gift
114 Bevin or Seton
115 Wimsey's creator
116 Nocturnal noises

DOWN

1 "We can make our lives ——"
2 Worked out for a bout
3 Says yes
4 Tiny pest: Fr.
5 Burmese statesman
6 Divination is his vocation
7 Offend
8 Caucasian wagon
9 Harem rooms
10 Part of M.V.P.
11 Vex
12 Drum out
13 Padnag
14 Faulkner novel
15 Balkan boundary river
16 Printemps follower
17 Eagle depicted in heraldry
18 Bounties
23 Port Arthur's lake
25 Rapier's cousin
29 Makes mistakes
32 Hilum
34 Sly guy
35 Bird feeder
38 Vietnamese city
39 Crescent-shaped
40 Cordage fiber
41 Palindrome for pater
45 Dutch-born U.S. author
46 Funny Scandinavian creature
47 Family room, Roman style
48 Kin of bullaces
49 Visayan island
50 Investigate
51 "Stormy Weather" composer
52 Flesh: Comb. form
53 Shock
54 Evangelist McPherson
56 Type type
57 Fray, in a way
58 Basketball tactic
60 Forked shape
61 Youthful years
63 Waste watchers: Abbr.
66 City in Brazil
70 Square one
73 Order to Dobbin
74 "Felix Holt" author
77 "Faerie Queene" heroine
79 More debatable
80 Pick
81 Greek peak
82 Cause of losing by oozing
83 Bell part
84 Give a leg up to a yegg
85 Smokey's preserves
86 Daft
87 Tris or Tip
88 "Lilli ——"
89 Camus and Finney
90 Bric-a-——
92 J.F.K.'s favorite chair
95 Nanchang nannies
96 Steady Eddie of baseball
99 Circle: Comb. form
101 Different
102 Compassion
103 Molar malady
104 Accts.
107 Alewife's appendage
109 Where cows browse
110 John, to Jock

Body Language

By Jeanette K. Brill

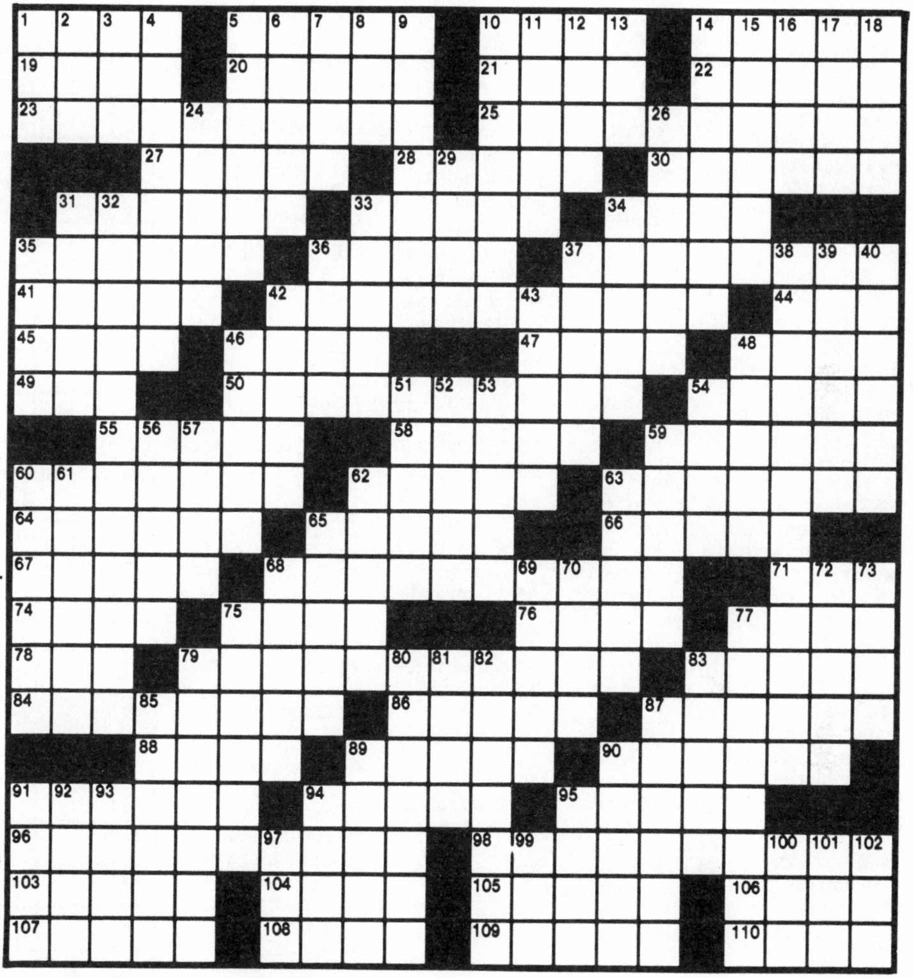

ACROSS

1 Secular
5 Discharge
10 Abound
14 At full speed, poetically
19 Church calendar
20 Lethargy
21 River or cartoonist
22 Annuity, to Pierre
23 Tec
25 Intimidated
27 Uneven
28 Normand of silents
30 Plenary
31 R.R. reading matter in the 40's
33 Geometric figure
34 "—— Swell," 1927 tune
35 Parts of a grand
36 Stylish shop
37 Furniture pieces
41 Monticles
42 Vigorous physical effort
44 Harper or Brenda
45 Small whirlpool
46 Pentacle
47 Artificial: Abbr.
48 Guide
49 Legal matter
50 Decisive conflict
54 Above: Prefix
55 Must
58 Set right
59 Seal
60 Illegal
62 Set of verses
63 Close friend
64 Habituated
65 Greek letter
66 Age
67 Sniggled
68 Kind of fern
71 Ammo material
74 See, in reference books
75 Contented sound
76 Iowa college town
77 On the briny
78 Noted painter of birds
79 Rosary bead
83 Shoot of a plant
84 Party game
86 Poplar
87 Leave
88 Extremities
89 Stair part
90 Gambols
91 Posture
94 Split
95 Arterial trunk
96 Insincere agreement
98 Daunt
103 Foyt rival
104 "—— a man with . . ."
105 Door sign
106 Beloved of Rochester
107 "Broom Hilda" cartoonist
108 Only
109 He played Belasco
110 Feat

DOWN

1 Cut off
2 Timetable abbr.
3 Aug. 13 in Italy
4 On the sly
5 Bars at the bar
6 "For whither thou —— . . ."
7 Flèche weapon
8 Oriental sauce
9 Organ device
10 Clerical chore
11 Slipped a cog
12 Organic compound
13 Grimace
14 Sandy
15 Natural body passage
16 Con
17 Where Caesar was borne
18 Hawaiian state bird
24 One sign of spring
26 Command
29 Down, to Drake
31 Sly and nasty
32 Snub
33 Native Israeli
34 Teach
35 Loire feeder
36 Duplicate event
37 Incubus, for one
38 Taro
39 Erected
40 Composed
42 Ceremonial citron for Succoth
43 Hogback
46 Glutted
48 Simoleons
51 Adjusted a loom for weaving
52 Gladden
53 Turkish royal court
54 Coarse hominy
56 ". . . lovely as ——"
57 Pung
59 Coconut fibers
60 Full-grown oxen
61 Iroquoian Indian
62 Bake eggs
63 Court officer
65 Vetches
68 Sordini
69 Misanthrope
70 Kind of corner
72 Approaches
73 Bakery purchase
75 Cater basely
77 Seemed
79 Grasping apparatus
80 Artlessness
81 Bone: Comb. form
82 Modern British poet
83 Partitions
85 More obtuse
87 Plucky ones
89 Kitchen utensil
90 Octavus Roy ——
91 Urban blight
92 Lilliputian
93 Vaulted church section
94 Winter sight
95 Italian wine center
97 Enthusiasm
99 "—— Mist," 1928 piano solo
100 Nautical chain
101 Prior to, to Prior
102 Sparks or Rorem

Latin Rhythms

By Mary Virginia Orna

ACROSS

1 Some of the Plain People
6 Mad. Ave. writer
11 Set of beliefs
16 Indian servant
20 Hawaiian island
21 Neutral shade
22 In any way
23 Wimbledon winner: 1975
24 Hit song of 1914?
28 Tristram's beloved
29 Item in a patch
30 Coagulate
31 Silvers and Harris
32 Slangy negative
34 Washer cycle
35 Stupefy
36 Hit song of 1931?
46 "Nature" author
47 Leopold and Mischa
48 Pull
49 Carlsbad feature
50 Director Wertmüller
51 Reap after a reaper
53 Vaunt
57 To —— (exactly)
58 Jackknife, e.g.
59 Styptic
60 Queeg's command
61 "Carousel" finale?
68 Romeo
69 Martin from Phila.
70 Lights
71 Dart's partner
74 "Amores" poet
75 Sailor's "Stop!"
76 Jahan's city
77 Compass point
78 Penang native
80 Kind of boom
81 Tempted
82 Foster favorite?
89 "Jailhouse Rock" singer
90 City on Lake Michigan
91 Natives of: Suffix
92 Forever —— day
93 Marine hazard
94 Long
96 Pip
97 Coerces
99 Attractive woman
100 Kings and queens, e.g.
102 Psychological school
103 Cole Porter hit of 1936?
110 Largest of the Cyclades
111 Identifies
112 —— -de-sac
113 Pivots
114 England, to Caesar
116 Livre relative
118 Think
124 Hit tune of 1924?
128 Bristle
129 Fiends
130 "Giant" ranch
131 Stable sound
132 Try
133 Oil source
134 Barracuda
135 Nobelist in Literature: 1946

DOWN

1 French cathedral town
2 Diamond great
3 "Long Day's Journey —— Night"
4 Mort from Montreal
5 Hurried
6 Father, in Arabia
7 Site of Pythian games
8 Blind ones of song
9 —— Mohammed Khan
10 Father of Abner
11 Dessert, e.g.
12 Blush
13 Turpitude
14 Met basso
15 Coronado's quest
16 Fermentable mixtures
17 Perugia neighbor
18 "Toil is —— of all": Homer
19 Ebullient
22 Suppresses
25 Flag
26 More aloof
27 Stern stroke
33 Once more: Abbr.
34 Ratite bird
36 Crumble
37 Neapolitan baritone: 1879-1942
38 Oncle's relative
39 Angler's basket
40 Neighbor of Syr.
41 More ingenuous
42 Grand worker
43 Swelling
44 Lingerie item
45 Managed
50 Was
51 Like stickum
52 Calm
53 Tropical isle
54 Brouhahas
55 Baxter and Jackson
56 Quinks or brants
58 Andy of filmdom
59 Head monk's office
60 Concordes' home
62 Lombard St. institution
63 Star in "Picnic"
64 Means
65 Former U.N. diplomat
66 Baghdad's river
67 Plume provider
71 Hard red wheat
72 Singer Crystal ——
73 Gage
75 Rivulet
76 "Fra Diavolo" composer
79 Arab's "A"
80 Top banana
81 Quidnunc's interest
83 Mystery writer Marsh
84 Gandhi was one
85 Estonian city
86 Atahualpa's people
87 Digger —— of radio and TV
88 Abominable
94 First word of "Lycidas"
95 Suffix with cook or rook
96 Grampuses
97 "But I must also —— as a man": Macbeth
98 Bear, in Bilbao
99 Marshal's men
100 Aromatic plants
101 Nautical term
102 Kokoon
103 Demand strongly
104 Famed crooner
105 Glories
106 Attacks
107 Hooflike
108 Marsh of a sort
109 Having a sharp point
114 Nagpur nursemaid
115 Part of N.B.
116 Sword for Athos
117 Derr Biggers hero
119 Cook's measure
120 Serf
121 F. F. Gosden role
122 Sea dogs
123 Commune near Padua
125 Road curve
126 Cen. parts
127 Turner or Hentoff

Bio-Synthesis

By Louis Baron

ACROSS

1 Llama's milieu
6 N.D. Indian
13 Card game
20 Zangwill's bio of Bessemer?
22 Unrepeated venture
23 Audie Murphy's bio of Orpheus?
24 Flying object
25 "—— Time," 1921 song
26 Become one
27 Irish: Abbr.
29 Short stalks
30 Ustinov's bio of Zsa Zsa?
32 Property seizer
35 Goddess of early risers
36 Gossip
38 Rabbi in "Winterset"
40 Rabat suburb
41 What a d.a. needs
42 Provo native
44 "Abdul Abulbul ——"
46 Cheka's successor
48 Abbot's subordinate
51 Natural film
52 Chekhov's bio of Jonathan?
54 Feat of Klee
55 Vote in
56 Isn't out of
57 Beach bonus
58 Phantoms
60 VI
61 Muppets' bio by Runyon?
64 Defrosting device
68 "—— diem"
69 Silly as ——
70 Dodo's bio by Michael Stewart?
72 Before: Prefix
73 "I had —— in Yucatan": Belloc
74 Collector's clock
75 Command
76 Caesar's last word
81 Ballerina's handrail
82 Poe's bio of Midas?
86 Oklahoman
87 Tolkien creature
88 Saarinen
89 Assents
90 Cipher clerk's job
91 Cagliari's isl.
93 Eve's "roots"
95 Glue
98 Tritons
99 Not neg.
100 Sly ones
102 Obeah's kin
104 Determinants
107 Pump gold
108 None: Comb. form
109 P.O. decision
112 Fairness
114 Thurber-Nugent bio of Kong?
118 Methusaleh
119 Papillon's bio by Hugo?
120 Have and hold
121 Calif. Indian
122 Poker expert

DOWN

1 "—— boy!"
2 Qui ——, Vietnamese port
3 Dry out
4 Highlander's uncle
5 Writer Lagerlöf
6 Sergeant-——
7 Annular
8 Gandhi's land, to Zola
9 A successor to 46 Across
10 Paraguay-Brazil river
11 Author Mazo de la ——
12 British "Tommy"
13 With: Prefix
14 Mot collections
15 Swimming: Comb. form
16 More pallid
17 Bligh's bio by K. Porter?
18 Colors
19 R-Roscoe of f-films
21 City in western Spain
28 Deli purchase
31 The Protestant ——
32 Kind of brain
33 Egyptian goddess
34 Italian stew
36 Patsy
37 Emph. in print
39 Encouraging yells
41 Polished, to Pedro
43 Picnic schnorrer
45 Order to a steno
47 Assurance
49 Lunar valley
50 Sad word
52 Strain
53 Mrs. Gynt
56 Bouncing Bess, e.g.
59 "Zip-A-Dee-——-Dah"
60 Churn
61 Provocative pest
62 Psychic Geller
63 Ointment
64 Critic-author Kenneth
65 Dr. DeBakey's bio by Martha Lear?
66 "—— Hassan," von Weber opera
67 Actress Dana
68 Flesh: Comb. form
70 Ruth or Herman
71 Like some tides
72 Metal casting
75 Washout
76 "Didn't say ——"
77 Site for lots of bucks
78 Without variation
79 Scenite's shelter
80 Desert regions
83 Slips
84 Hungarian statesman: 1803-76
85 Kalongs
86 Erasmus was one
92 Size up
94 McCartney, e.g.
96 Tear away
97 Actress Gray from Neb.
99 Veronese or Uccello
101 Pompeii's undoing
103 Alice's cat
104 Karate ploy
105 Renaissance family
106 Hagiography abbr.
108 Collar
110 Chinese weight
111 Other
113 Lots of mos.
115 Suffix for count
116 Metz Mrs.
117 Lower Nigeria native

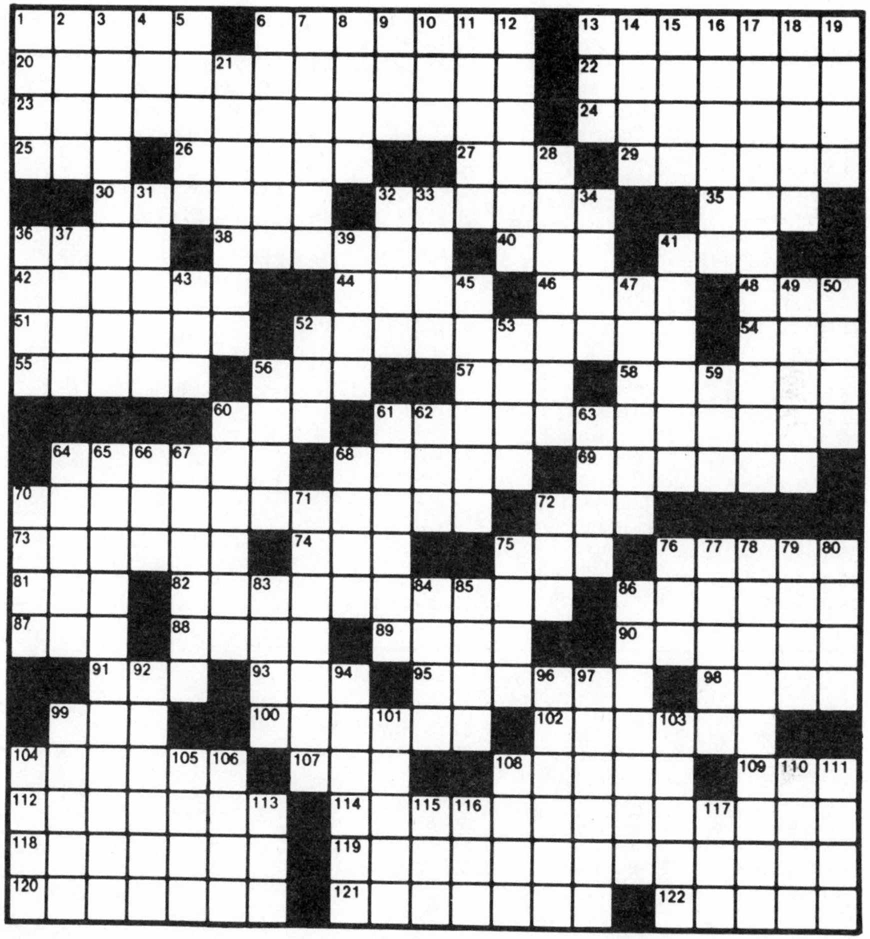

104

No Big Deal

By Charles M. Deber

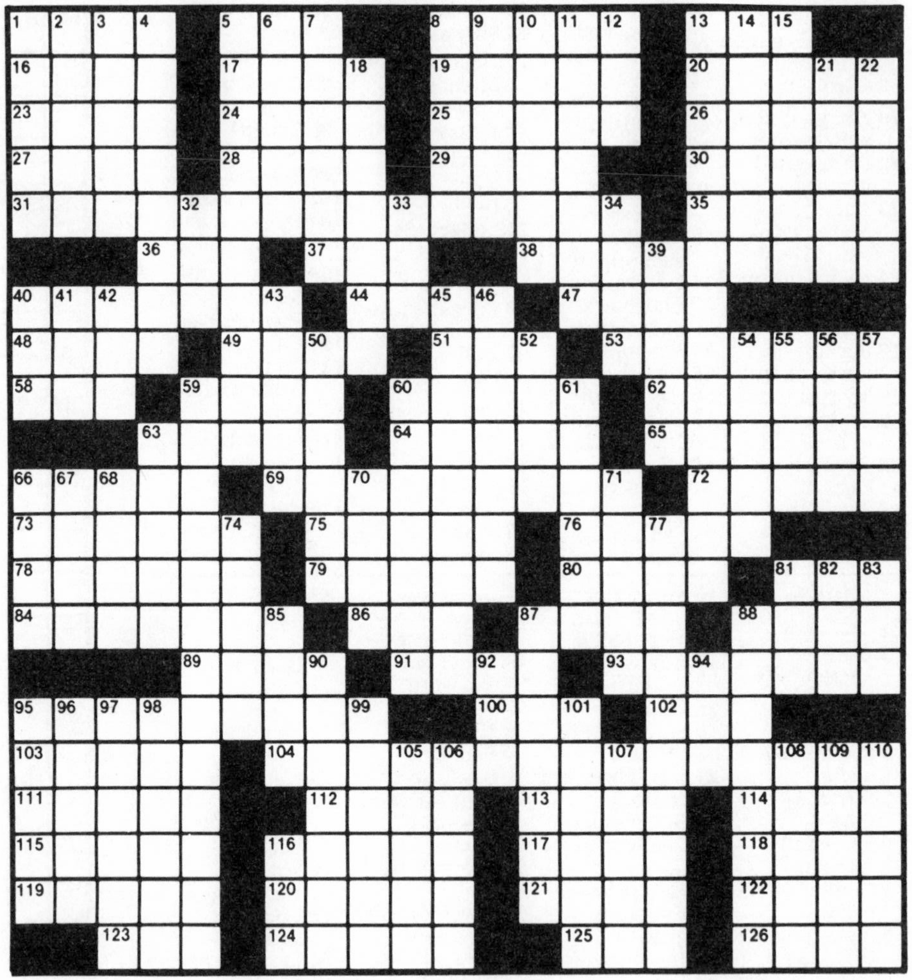

ACROSS

1 Something grand
5 Hebrew letter
8 Tart, in Toulouse
13 Luckman or Caesar
16 Nosegay
17 Greek resistance org.
19 Beam
20 Groom
23 Lively septet
24 Wee
25 Chimp's kin
26 Musical piece
27 Angry fit
28 Agitate
29 Vagabond
30 Unequal: Comb. form
31 Pair of queens
35 Exhausts
36 A title for R.W.R.
37 Upward: Prefix
38 Pair of kings
40 Moslem fasting period
44 Co-creator of "Charlie's Angels"
47 Be zetetic
48 Seed covering
49 Make an incised mark
51 Scrap
53 Conference
58 Hecht
59 Mt. Rushmore site
60 Those who tint
62 Nocturnal noisemaker
63 Trattoria's zuppa di ——
64 Suffix with fatal
65 Salad green
66 Hot drink
69 Pair of tens
72 Alleviates
73 Black Sea city
75 Scandinavian
76 Poor
78 Lariats
79 Pivoted
80 Deadly sin
81 Watering hole
84 Agrees
86 New Deal agcy.
87 To live, to Livy
88 Cross or last follower
89 Hall, in Honduras
91 Rigid ruler
93 Stoats
95 Pair of jokers
100 In medias ——
102 Sunbathe
103 Shining
104 Pair of threes
111 Level: Comb. form
112 Hautboy
113 Service tree
114 Picot feature
115 Krupskaya's spouse
116 B'way musical
117 Florence's river
118 "—— La Douce"
119 Echo, e.g.
120 Passover feast
121 Dam
122 The sun, for one
123 Thousands of lbs.
124 Some literature
125 —— U.S. Pat. Off.
126 Cistern

DOWN

1 Contraction
2 Doone of fiction
3 Moving
4 Based on intuition
5 Pair of nines
6 Choice
7 Type of envelope
8 Hawaii hi
9 St.-John's-bread
10 Yellowish-brown color
11 Indicates
12 Energy unit
13 Pair of Jacks
14 Wryly humorous
15 "Raging Bull" actor
18 Hospital device
21 Ford flop
22 "Out-to-lynch" item
32 Canton in Norway
33 Bronx attraction
34 Blood: Prefix
39 A.F.B. in Texas
40 Mortar beater
41 "—— You Lonesome Tonight?"
42 Gump's wife
43 Civil rights org.
45 Pair of sevens
46 Worried
50 Flocks of geese
52 Kingston, for one
54 Now
55 Yellow flag
56 Granular snow
57 French stoneware
59 Pair of fours
60 Break apart
61 Play parts
63 Band after bandits
66 Soft drink
67 Harem rooms
68 Luck of the Irish
70 —— contendere
71 Import
74 Take —— at (try)
77 Pair of aces
81 Trinity member
82 Evangeline's Grand ——
83 Commercials
85 Flat piece
87 "Able was I —— . . ."
88 Sommelier's offering
90 Everywhere
92 Estuary
94 Fairy queen
95 Single: Comb. form
96 One making eyes
97 Mars, e.g.
98 Eternal
99 Psychic energy
101 Sports official
105 Memoranda
106 "The Wreck of the Mary ——"
107 Banks of baseball
108 Main artery
109 Ear-lender to Antony
110 Pitch woo
116 Clairvoyance, for short

Transport Tie-Up

By Jim Page

ACROSS

1 Drillmaster's command
5 Mauna ——
8 Ling-Ling or Chia-Chia
13 Speech defect
17 Greek epic
19 Slip a cog
20 Liquid fat
21 —— en point
22 Strong glue
23 Onassis
24 Gets soaring contestants airborne
27 Contradicted
29 Bilko and Pepper
31 Robert Burns poem
32 Religious recluse
35 Muse of comedy
37 Anaconda
38 Aerial bombs
41 Fortification
42 Chemical endings
43 Tolkien creature
44 Debris, at sea
46 S.R.O. sites
49 Arm bones
51 Eliot's "—— Deronda"
52 Custard-filled pastry
54 Joy Adamson's charge
56 Packs citrus fruits
59 Actress Adams et al.
63 Inhabitant
65 J. B. Rhine specialty
66 Plato dialogue
68 PBS program
69 Men below a marquess
70 Elevates vehicles, as in a garage
74 Peaks
75 "Das Rheingold" role
76 Ending for cash
77 ". . . woman —— her way!": Holmes
78 Budd's beaters
80 Forks out
82 Emulates Sunny Jim Fitzsimmons
86 Rabbit ——
88 Supply oxygen
89 Perle's kin
92 Beanie wearer
95 Bearing
97 In a trifling way
99 Long, long time
100 Bash
101 Cordage fiber
103 Wood sorrels
104 King of Judah
105 "To ——": Burns
107 Resilient
109 Point or aim again
111 —— -majesté
113 An Iranian language
117 Sends out motorcycles
119 Erode
122 River in Brazil
123 "—— Tired," Beatles song
124 She created the Moffats
125 Prefix with cool or cook
126 Pool person
127 Hammer part
128 Eye fixedly
129 Diocese
130 Magi guide

DOWN

1 Darted
2 Mont Blanc, e.g.
3 He has his pride
4 Maneuvers grounded jets
5 Greensward
6 Ex-Bruin great
7 Awn
8 Size of paper
9 Cather's "—— Lady"
10 "I Love —— York"
11 Aloof
12 A Bantu language
13 Byron heroine
14 —— -European
15 A general in 1778
16 —— non grata
18 Textile worker
25 Medieval tales
26 Laps, perhaps
28 The old man: Ger.
30 Most lamblike
33 Queen Elizabeth's sis
34 —— fixes
36 Writer Lafcadio
38 P.O. category
39 Pay follower
40 An SST
45 Freshwater ducks
47 Sheep or swine
48 A-U connection
49 Part of N.A.
50 Gets Hawks and Doves aloft
53 Musical symbol
55 K-O connection
57 Whodunit first name
58 Bors, for one
60 Maid or cook
61 Ad infinitum
62 Soprano Silvia
63 Kues' predecessors
64 Holliday's pal
67 Frogner Park site
71 N.Y.C. transit
72 Rats of a sort
73 Aide-de-camp: Abbr.
74 Charm or poise
76 Negev locale: Abbr.
79 Ornamental bands
81 Morse-code signal
83 Rows
84 Lat. epic
85 Seven: Comb. form
87 Pitches woo
90 Pie —— mode
91 CBS is one
92 Hopes' companions
93 Vitamin C source
94 Stop ——
96 Least obtuse
98 Hirt and Pacino
100 Merganser

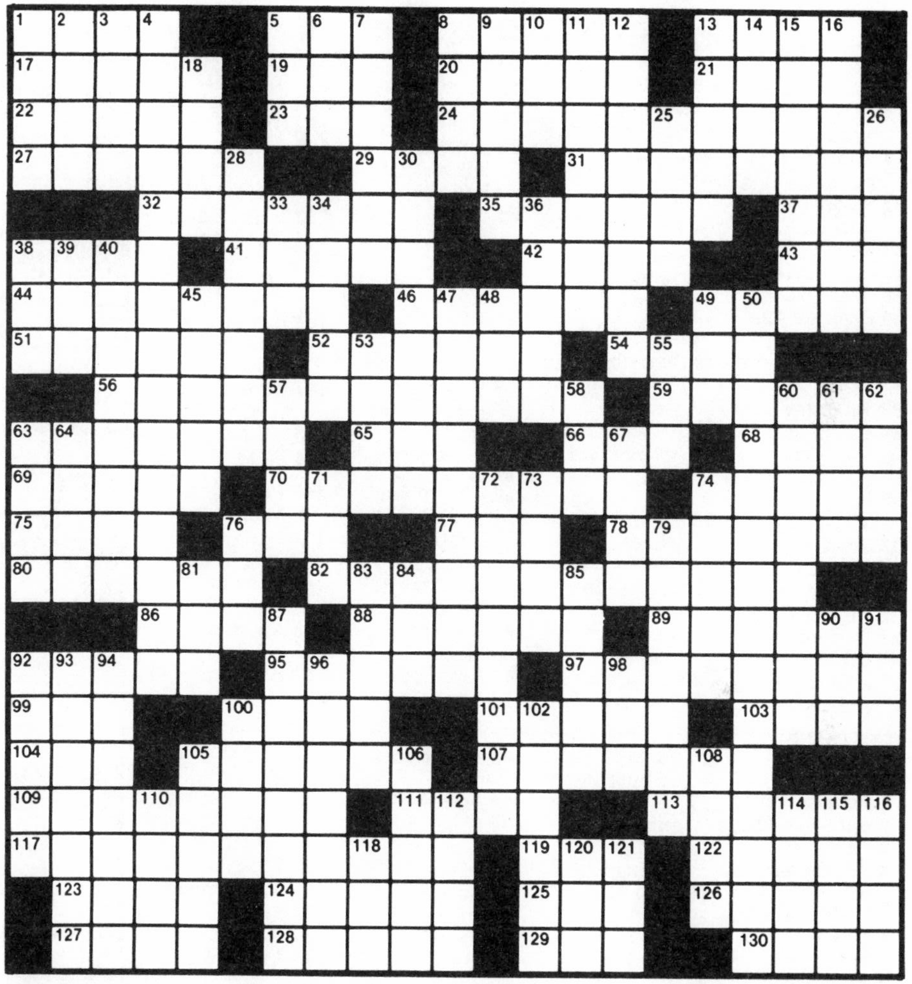

102 Hibernates
105 Torch's crime
106 Aunt in "Oklahoma!"
108 Fleming and Smith
110 —— dixit
112 Being
114 "—— a Kick Out of You"
115 Author Bontemps
116 Record-breaking horse
118 Letter from Greece
120 "We —— not amused"
121 Place for a driver

Menagerie

By Louise Earnest

ACROSS

1 Senate, e.g.
5 Pasty cement
11 Certain art works
17 Political position
21 Med.-sch. subject
22 Celia's alias in "A.Y.L.I."
23 Carried away
24 Ornamental case
25 Little Bighorn figure
27 Sellers vehicle
29 Entombs
30 Robe for Octavia
32 Item for Weiskopf
33 Scuffle
34 Assyrian's tongue
36 Pippin's heart
38 Dominant
40 Quite a different matter
47 Murray of silents
50 Legislate
51 Allison of TV
52 Sigma
53 See 61 Across
54 Ending for patriot or ideal
55 Seaport on Okinawa
57 Pierre's well-wishers
59 Describing the Holy See
61 With 53 and 100 Across, 1928 song
66 Chintzy felines, à la Field
70 Seaport on Panay
71 Bit of horn tissue
72 Imbue with new vigor
73 Sockeye and coho
75 Uncover
77 Moreno of baseball
78 Burgess's well-known first line
85 "—— Rhythm"
86 Public
87 ". . . from the lazy finger ——": Shak.
90 Crab or lobster
95 Recorded proceedings
98 Osage, for one
99 Locomotives
100 See 61 Across
102 Drain
103 Puerto ——
105 Stepped on
106 Hot time in Paree
107 Cooler
108 Meet
111 Soho bunk
113 Hanker after
116 Singer Acuff
117 Malicious hypocrite
123 Archons' kin
124 Brain tissue
125 Sonnet sections
129 Leopold III's bride: 1926
132 Engr.'s degree
134 Discourage
137 How banshees wail
138 Howard Hughes's seaplane
141 Diversionary tactics
143 Bellow
144 Meager
145 Physiologist Mosso: 1846-1910
146 Sing like Ella
147 Eurydice's abode
148 Approach collapse
149 Hard and cold
150 Pronoun

DOWN

1 Foundation
2 Cat-——-tails
3 Fact
4 Powder used in color TV tubes
5 O'Hara's Tara, for one
6 Trig cousin
7 Kinsmen
8 Native of Ger.
9 —— parentis
10 Cancel
11 Zip
12 "What's —— for me?"
13 Composer Bloch
14 "—— 'A' Train": 1941 song
15 Vol.'s supplement
16 Parts of turbines
17 Met fan's entreaty
18 Ordinal endings
19 Peat, e.g.
20 Flag
26 Dog —— manger
28 "—— Dimittis," old hymn
31 Macaws
35 Fussbudget
37 Town of Judah
39 —— judicata
41 Scotch fiddles
42 Code of morals
43 In the bag
44 World's highest capital
45 Emulate Cicero
46 Electrical units
47 Actresses Hines and Kennedy
48 Places of refuge
49 Surgeons' concerns
56 Curaçao's neighbor
58 Relish
59 Tammany man
60 Chemical prefix
62 Delineate
63 Tub plant
64 Banquet in Bologna
65 Remove money from an account
67 Like Dali's watches
68 ——-Turkish War: 1911-12
69 Attend to
72 The 21st Amendment
74 Stogie
76 It may be bum
79 Army missiles
80 It, too, may be bum
81 Like a diamond in the rough
82 Joker
83 Medical suffixes
84 Less ruddy
88 "—— prepare a place. . ."
89 "The School and Society" author
90 Statement of faith
91 Spur part
92 French article
93 Wall St. abbr.
94 In reserve
96 Like a stub-born hombre
97 Cancel a space trip
99 ". . . ere —— Elba"
100 Ran the show
101 Hell's Canyon is here
104 Egyptian Christian
108 Most derisive, in a way
109 Nfld. or Icel.
110 What not to rock or miss
112 Whites of the eyes
114 Sovereign's deputy
115 Word on a door
118 Ruler
119 Of the ego's source
120 Convoy
121 Hidden
122 Gaudy
126 Edwards or Lombardi
127 "King Olaf" composer
128 Networks of RR's
129 Staff mem.
130 Coast Guard acronym
131 Make plumb
133 Quiddity, in a way
135 Selvage
136 Syngman ——
139 Where to buy stps.
140 Ending for auction
142 Pipe joint

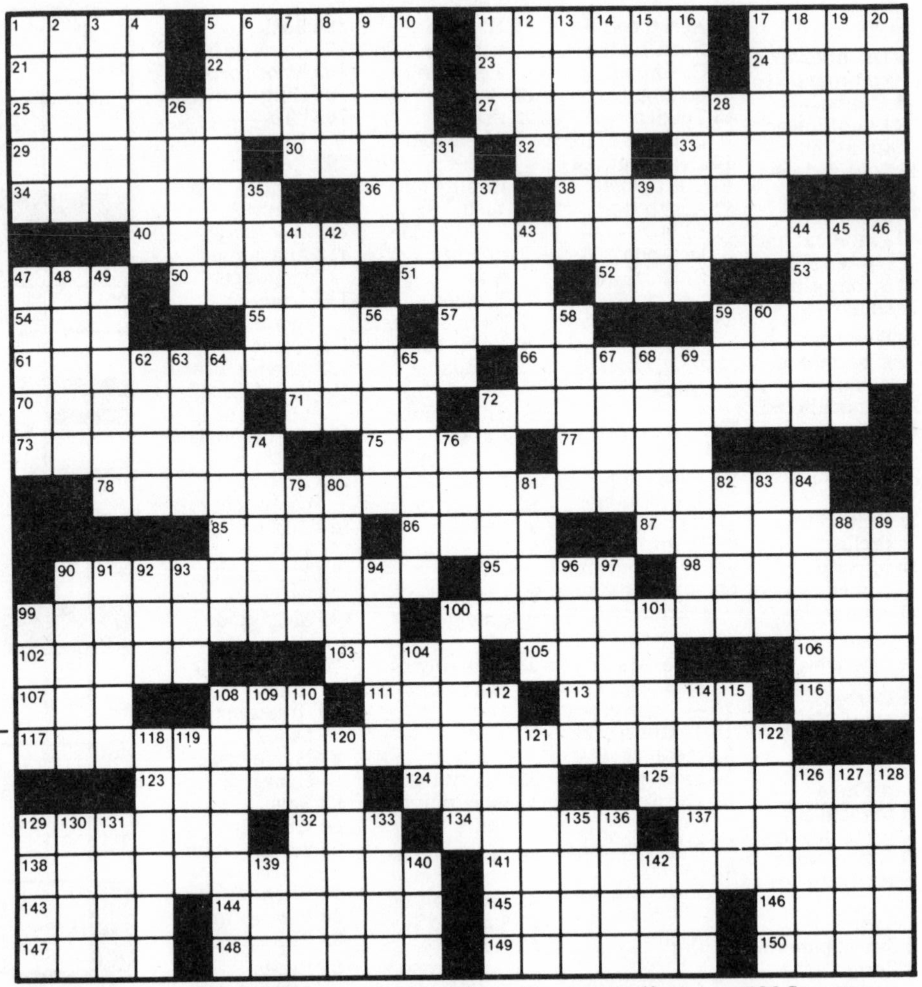

Katharine the Great

By Barbara Lunder Gillis

ACROSS

1 Martha or Randolph of films
6 Life raft
11 Gasconade
15 Set
18 Pentateuch
19 Fortified Portuguese city
20 Berra
21 Windmill sail
22 Symbol
24 Mariner's direction
25 Worried
27 The high cost of leaving
30 Witticism
31 Number of Disney Dalmatians
32 Capital of Okinawa
33 Original form of a word
37 Early bloomer
42 Gardner
43 City on the Vistula
46 Danube feeder
47 Shoshone
48 Companion of true
50 Violin for a virtuoso
51 Swift specialty
54 People of Ghana
56 Architectural disk
58 Leading lady
61 Kind of punch
62 Become a tar
63 Bone's basis
64 White House name
67 Jeanne or Cécile: Abbr.
68 Angled structure
73 Where to spend naira
76 Mining tool
77 Tough old bird
84 —— -run (baseball ploy)
85 "The gang's ——!"
86 Greek poet
88 —— di Bassetto (G.B.S. pen name)
89 Nastier
90 Bee chaser
93 Cry at Pan's parties
94 Chancel item
95 Gabor
96 Over sparkling water
100 "The Bicycle Thief" director
104 Old Irish capital
105 N-R connection
106 Stout
109 July elopement
115 Eden teaser
118 Last
119 Petty officer
120 Lemon
121 Sight on Oxford Street
122 Did roadwork
123 Expunge
124 Beastly place
125 Pintail duck
126 Rhonchus
127 Roman date

DOWN

1 What inspired Watt
2 Dance band
3 Sphere
4 Farfetched
5 Cool cat
6 Ornament
7 Sight at Como
8 City in the Ukraine
9 Lamour's apparel
10 Starry
11 From memory
12 Gad
13 Correspond
14 Colossus
15 Yak
16 Ma that says "maa"
17 Began
23 Anchor
26 Hordeolum
28 Conclusion
29 Mao associate
34 Havana casualty: 1898
35 She had a Hobby
36 Lowest point
37 Change significantly
38 Part of a palindrome
39 Org. established in 1949
40 Forbidding
41 "Crazy Jane" poet
43 Forbidden
44 Straws in the wind
45 Brings down the house
48 Antony's flame
49 Bolger
52 Joplin creation
53 Seth's son
55 Dress style
57 More fashionable
59 Polo Grounds hero
60 Sulla, to Marius
64 Type of room, for short
65 Acapulco gold
66 Almost
69 Narrated anew
70 Estranged
71 Windfall
72 Witch of ——
74 José or Buddy
75 Vigoda
77 Blathered
78 Oil source
79 Earthenware jars
80 Haggard's Ayesha
81 Worn
82 Cleave
83 Eight bells
87 Type of magazine
91 Raid site: 1976
92 Actor Richard
97 Lowest decks
98 Secular
99 Examination: Comb. form
101 Doctrine
102 Cods' kin
103 Relevantly
106 Capital of Jordan
107 Hire
108 Pelagic predators
110 Extreme
111 Counterclockwise
112 Dyer's device
113 Radio's "Vic and ——"
114 Subject of Katz's "Days of Wrath"
115 Cutting tool
116 Pair
117 Stir

Garden Varieties

By A. J. Santora

ACROSS

1 Hail on the ocean
5 Wimbledon winner: 1975
9 Glide
13 Lock
18 Leaping car
19 Appoint as an associate
21 Sickly
22 Great Lakes acronym
23 Growths in the Holland causeways?
26 Osmani, for one
27 What the fastidious farmer minds?
29 Oxford shoe
30 Cottage —— (country house)
31 Arrest
32 Gustav ——, German physicist
33 Utter
35 Small hooter
37 Gives a hoot
39 Disappoints
41 Plus
42 Outcasts in Osaka
43 "He's making —— . . ."
45 Mass. motto word
46 Juan Carlos I, e.g.
48 Greenville university
50 Snipefish
52 Clique in a club
57 Inquire into relatives' secrets?
62 Golden shiner
63 Venetian fishing boat
65 Tanning-material source
66 Groove
67 Epinicion
68 Peruvian gambling event?
71 Cockchafer
72 Singer Ronstadt
74 Inward
75 Actress Rowlands
76 —— colada
77 Johnson gets unnerved?
80 Best-planted garden?
82 Teacher's org.
83 Hangover helper
85 Pouch
86 Straighten
89 Makes wine from fruit
91 Labor
94 Saki
98 "Syne" predecessors
100 Soprano Mitchell
101 Fold
102 Map abbr.
103 Yoko
104 Where Meshed is
106 Groom, in India
108 Card
109 Sports headline?
114 Musician's transition
115 Rathbone goes barn-storming?
117 Part of Albert Hall
118 Particular
119 Mythical beasts
120 Of the dawn
121 Caucasian man
122 Sunbathes
123 Famed muralist
124 Terrier type

DOWN

1 Everyone
2 Brays
3 The Tyrones, actually
4 Sarlaks
5 Quaker gray
6 Sound
7 Difficult position
8 Hebrew bushel
9 Season
10 Caulking material
11 A Waugh
12 Summaries
13 Site of tomb of Seti I
14 Apple variety
15 "Nature" essayist
16 Teeters
17 Ukr., e.g.
20 Becomes edgy
24 Given a handicap
25 Insecticides
28 Type of pot holder
29 Scarf
34 Chemical ending
36 Strange
38 W.W. II fliers
39 Hookups
40 Fine pottery
43 Hussein's capital
44 Toy poodle, e.g.
47 Himalayan snowman
49 Nursery-rhyme start
51 To live, to Livy
52 Fallacies
53 Rock bottom
54 Fragrance
55 Man's slipper
56 Exceptionally fine
58 Empty
59 "Live Free ——" (N.H. motto)
60 International club
61 Gold measure
64 Enclosed, as a pupa
68 Guipure, for one
69 Alleviates
70 Dutch painter: 1632-93
73 Ate in style
76 Chinese unit of weight
78 Shade of brown
79 Without any doubt
81 Throws cold water on
84 Sticky stuff
86 Skater Babilonia
87 Frat men, at times
88 Shortages in containers
90 Star trekking
92 Conforming to proportion
93 Postpone
95 Dior creation
96 Track
97 A Giant at 16
99 —— first sight
100 Father of Eliasaph: Num. 3:24
104 He wrote "The Wild Duck"
105 French cathedral city
107 Surfer's surface
110 Old Norse poem
111 Information
112 Proverbial septet
113 Vous —— (you are, in Arles)
114 —— Paulo, Brazil
116 Wind dir.

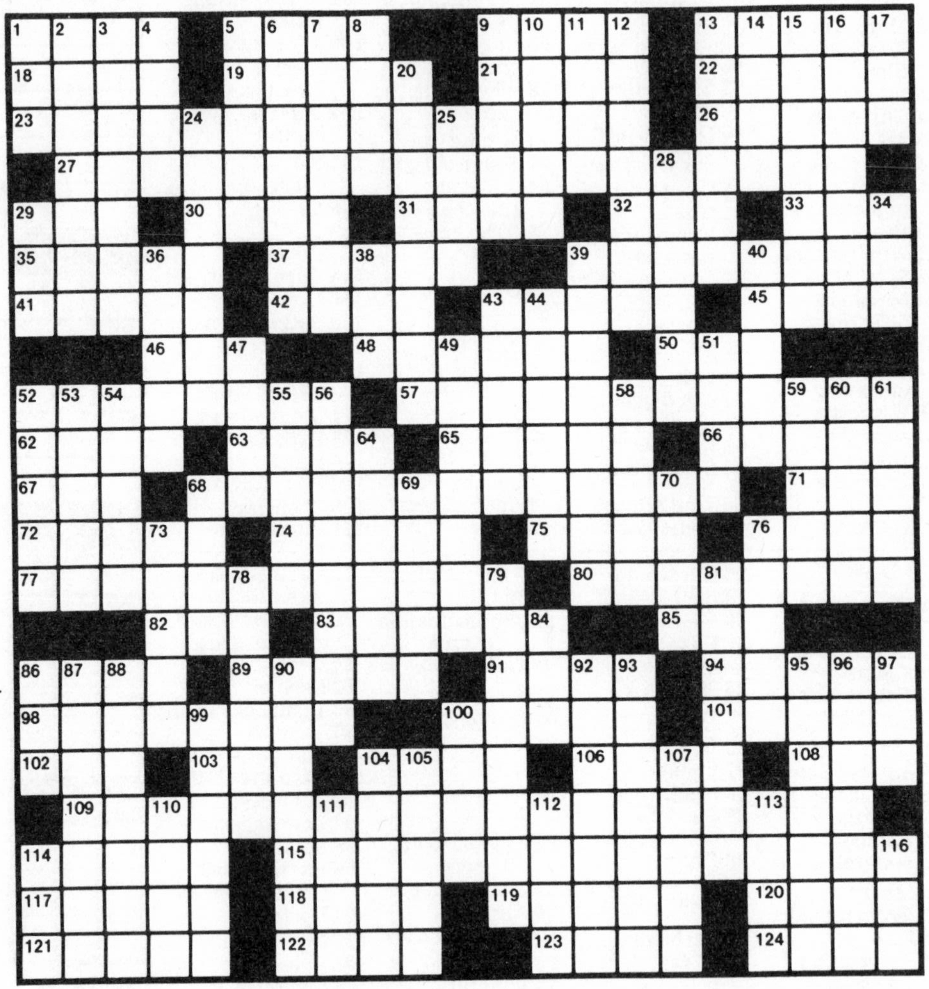

Tale Tails

By William H. Ford

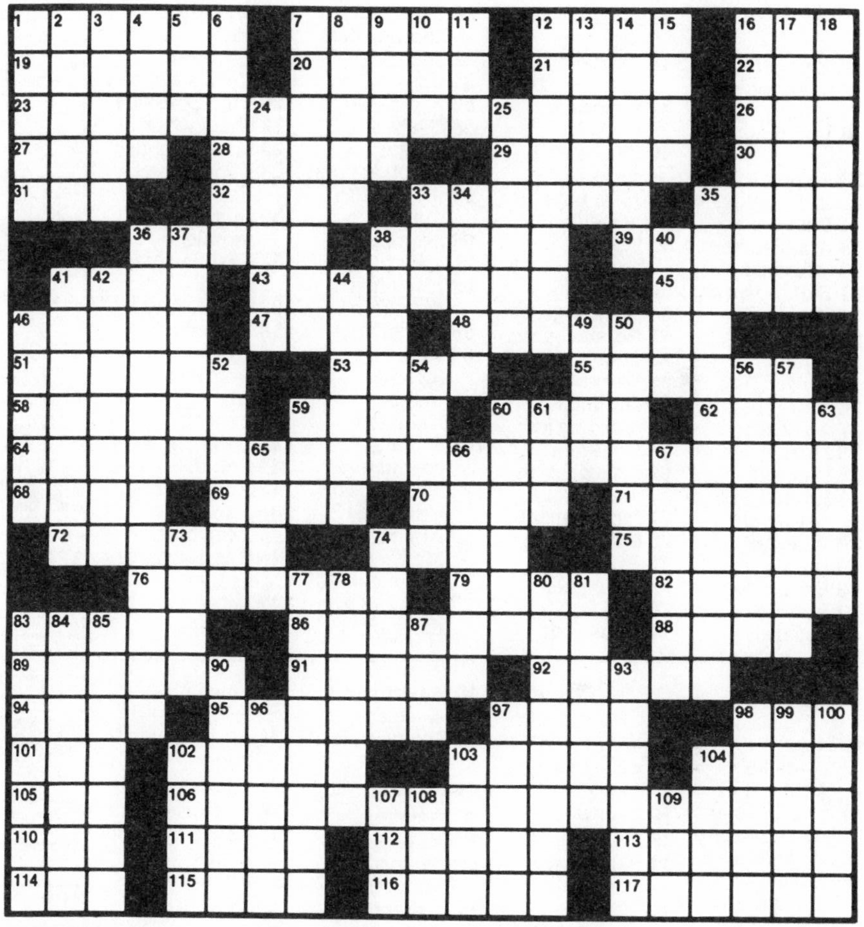

ACROSS

1 Rattigan's "Separate ——"
7 "Mr. Moto" star
12 And
16 Fragments: Abbr.
19 Fit like ——
20 Running berserk
21 Noon is one
22 This, to Virgil
23 Paton's "Cry" ender
26 Marne land
27 Demolish, in Sussex
28 Fear intensely
29 Rubber source
30 Hang limply
31 Nova Scotia time
32 SE Asia
33 Evita's successor
35 Whisper
36 Confessed, with "up"
38 Nonpareil in a "South Pacific" song
39 Squawker
41 —— au lait
43 Of a newborn child
45 Coquette's standby
46 Antony and Chagall
47 Name for an old dog
48 Sennacherib's domain
51 Just about
53 Warm Alpine wind
55 Made
58 Daydreamer, in a way
59 Like Cabernet
60 Offbeat guy
62 Legislative combine
64 Wells's "Mr." adherent
68 Leeds's river
69 Partner of kin
70 Kind of Nellie
71 ". . . alas, so —— far": Donne
72 Perfumed the air
74 Antinuke org.
75 Sings, Tyrolean style
76 Most shipshape
79 Grind, as teeth
82 Belgian princess
83 Aromatic plant
86 Bitterness of manner
88 Pulitzer winner: 1958
89 Eye-pupil border
91 Lorelei's abode
92 Not original
94 Getz or Kenton
95 Old dances in 2/4 time
97 Honolulu tec
98 Wee hour
101 Twitch
102 Large book
103 Vogue
104 Wagnerian goddess
105 Equal: Prefix
106 Forster's "Where" trailer
110 Nebraskan Amerind
111 Shaping tools
112 Topsy's partner
113 Name for Elizabeth I
114 Lepidopterist's trap
115 Spanish painter
116 Napoleon's Grande ——
117 Smollett's Roderick

DOWN

1 —— Mountains, Czechoslovakia
2 Turkish chiefs
3 Consecrated
4 It's below the tragus
5 Second person
6 Oxonian "Table Talk" author: 1689
7 Sachet filler
8 Hellenic haunter of hills
9 Fictional Lorna's John
10 Bird for a peri
11 W.W. II area
12 Poe's Lee et al.
13 Singer-actress Lenya
14 Of course!
15 Chalcedony
16 Spanish king called "the Handsome"
17 Silver-eagle wearer
18 Wand for Victoria
24 Whence Polo returned
25 Moslem theologians
33 Author Tarbell
34 Milton's antihero
35 Maugham's aftermath of "Of"
36 How Sayers finished "The Bone"
37 —— Islands off N Australia
38 "Tennis, ——?"
40 Province in SW Saudi Arabia
41 Of heat
42 Wardrobe
44 Lamebrained
46 African snake
49 Mon., on Tues.
50 On sudden impulse
52 Rode, kiddy style
54 Bestial laugher
56 To mourn for: Lat.
57 "Let sleeping ——"
59 Kg., e.g.
60 Chicago suburb
61 Pass or Peak in Colo.
63 Singled out
65 Spider nests
66 "—— your song, O!": W S. Gilbert
67 "—— the Top," 1958 film
73 Window part
74 Las Vegas feature
77 First
78 Kind of bus or year
80 Salinger's backer of "The Catcher"
81 Legree type
83 Bulwark
84 Prima ballerina, for one
85 Scoter
87 They got the votes
90 Anguish, for Pierre
93 Kind of games
96 He wrote more than 100 books for boys
97 Thirst for
98 ". . . just what —— in the papers": Rogers
99 Major Joppolo's post
100 Palindromic title
102 Rages
103 Duration
104 Banshee's bailiwick
107 Dep.
108 Baum marten, e.g.
109 Sound in a round

Ode on Fan Fare

By Charles Baron

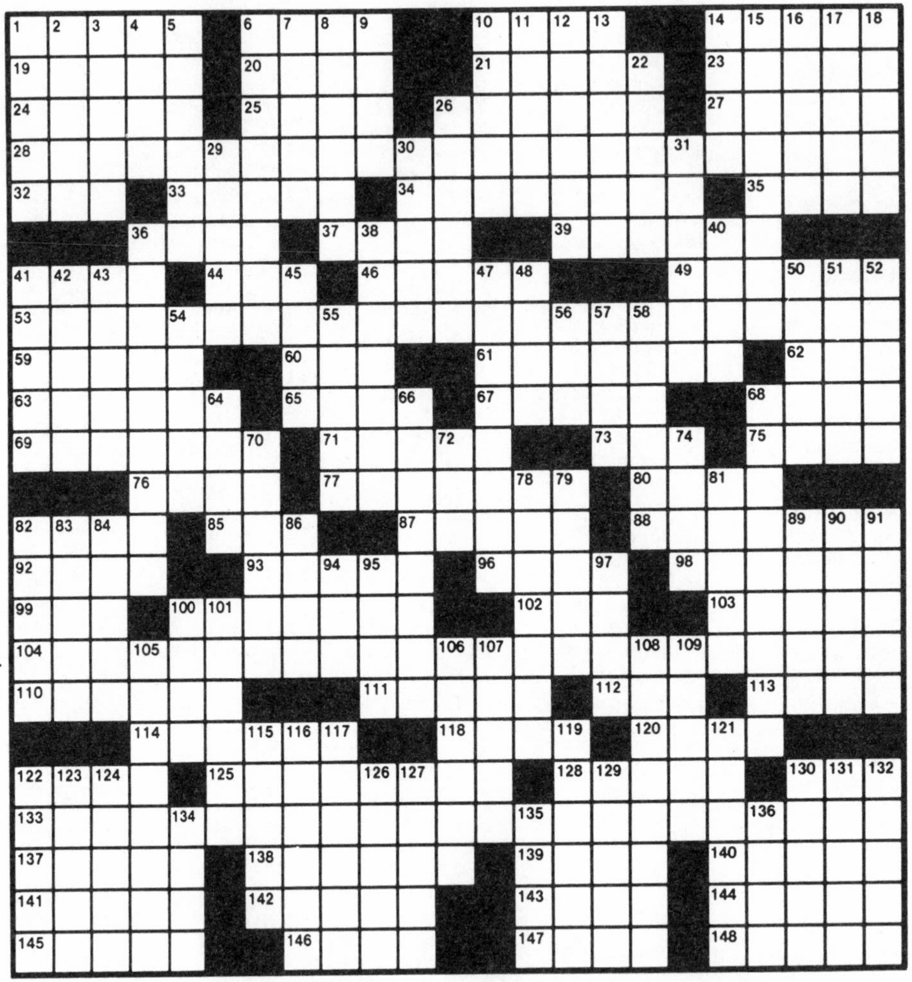

ACROSS

1 "Songs of Innocence" author
6 Triangular lyre
10 Airplane stairway
14 Big spender
19 U.S.S.R. hero
20 Stravinsky
21 Flotow work
23 Pirogue
24 Yens
25 Swinger in the garden
26 Actress Smith
27 Adak native
28 Start of a verse
32 Dash off
33 Famed Greek physician
34 Veteran
35 Does a takeoff
36 British dean
37 Puts on apparel
39 Republic since 1948
41 Bacheller's "—— Holden"
44 Wynn and Sullivan
46 Changes course
49 Altar boys' garb
53 Second line of verse
59 Picaroon
60 Hockey great
61 Persian green
62 Confucian way
63 Warns
65 Diminish
67 Morning hr.
68 Dollar bill
69 Issued, as an invitation
71 More logical
73 Court whistler
75 Prill and mispickel
76 —— facto
77 Thrust out
80 Teutonic demigoddess
82 Jupati
85 One —— time
87 Frost-covered
88 Grabs a bargain
92 Tropical plant
93 Prefix with mural
96 Depressed area
98 Albania's capital
99 O'Neill play
100 Retiree's income, maybe
102 Bar need
103 Famed conductor
104 Third line of verse
110 Allen and McQueen
111 Fusible resin
112 Ab —— (from the start)
113 Mid-March date
114 Come out
118 Koko's weapon
120 Big Apple side
122 Shadowbox
125 Made sluggish
128 "The Velvet Fog"
130 Buddhist temple
133 Last line of verse
137 Copland work
138 Regions, to Byron
139 Hebrides island
140 Beneath
141 Tatum or Ryan
142 Belief
143 Author Harte
144 Fancies
145 Deep blue
146 Russian press agency
147 Coteries
148 Vikings

DOWN

1 Mantle
2 —— Soleil (Louis XIV)
3 Personal slant
4 Ukrainian city
5 Naval officer
6 Half a synonym for topsy-turvy
7 Yawning
8 Plump
9 Honor in Honduras
10 Het up
11 "—— of robins . . ."
12 When James IV was killed
13 Crystal forms
14 Jazz term
15 Stanford site
16 Golfer's edge
17 Maquillage item
18 Hebrew letters
22 He played Lou Grant
26 Ready
29 Actor Conrad
30 Partitioned land
31 Vestiges
36 Hemingway book
38 Levy to excess
40 Great time spans
41 Wildcats
42 Former W.C.T.U. head
43 Ormandy, to a Berliner
45 Fawning admirer
47 Speakers' platforms
48 Marksman's —— trap
50 Pangloss, for one
51 Playing marble
52 Loafers
54 Colonist's Indian friend
55 Remove marks
56 Masefield heroine
57 A Bradley
58 French's "The —— Room"
64 Capital of Elam
66 Charm
68 Kind of organization
70 Porter's activity
72 Lincoln's "Cap'n ——"
74 Assortment of type
78 Like some inks
79 Reason out
81 Reach by radio
82 Aches' partners
83 Apportion
84 Lerner and ——
86 Part of Saturn's rings
89 Vegetarian's favorite
90 Loosen a knot
91 Couples
94 Conway
95 African big-game gun
97 Office circular
100 Can. official
101 Tired flops
105 Abroad
106 Evaluate
107 Aromatic U.S. herb
108 Gorges
109 Is nomadic
115 Respond to force
116 Stone chip
117 "Tippie" cartoonist
119 Baritone Bastianini: 1923-67
121 Gown ornament
122 Barber's gear
123 Dial a number
124 Legal help
126 Noted chair designer
127 Russian vetoes
129 French novelist-dramatist
130 Cautious bather
131 Land clusters
132 Concise
134 Hercules' prisoner
135 His ——, the V.I.P.
136 Ruin

Mark My Words

By Alfio Micci

ACROSS

1 Unbending
6 Reduce
10 Greek letter
13 Singular
16 Correct
17 Prospero's servant
18 One feted
20 Receipts of a kind
22 Cloakroom personnel
24 Ionian gulf
25 Mrs. Mahler
26 Streeter's "—— Mable"
27 Book of Hours
28 Honey buzzard
29 Fannie follower, in banks
30 Submerge
32 Type of skirt
33 Sow's pad
34 Make sure
37 Nuclear particle
38 "—— iron bars a cage"
39 "Israel in Egypt," for one
41 Cold
44 —— dimittis
46 Aromatic spice
51 Letter stroke
52 Prefix for date or cede
53 Legal matter
56 Leather worker
58 Champ in 1934
59 Riv. boat
60 Exhausted
62 Curb
63 Energy unit
64 Berlin divider
67 Greek under-grounders
68 Trap setter
70 Michelangelo masterpiece
71 Like: Suffix
72 Sra.'s daughter
73 Teacher's concern
74 For good, to Gray
75 Noted Jesuit lexicographer
77 Impenetrable
78 Near the back
80 Asther of old films
81 "Home, Sweet Home" author
82 Inclined
87 Scull
88 Aristocles
93 Game using marbles
96 Scale notes
99 Trooper's beam
100 Pequot sachem
101 Alphabetic trio
102 "Lead us not into —— Station"
103 Role in "Don Carlos"
104 Selvage
105 Actor from N.Y.C.
106 Biblical preposition
107 These have 64 squares
109 Supermarket feature
112 Like Simba
113 Not rented
114 Accumulate
115 Coterie
116 Debussy's "La ——"
117 Buddies
118 Brings home the bacon

DOWN

1 Summaries
2 Inn of Istanbul
3 The upper class
4 Quechua
5 Ike
6 Course for a future g.p.
7 Amonasro's daughter
8 Inspect again
9 Overhead transports
10 Casanova type
11 Table d'——
12 Contained
13 Passerine bird
14 Plant poisonous to fish
15 Part of F.D.R.
17 Historian Nevins
19 Old Irish alphabet
21 Truman's birthplace in Mo.
22 Greeting for Parton?
23 Witnessed
26 Obligation
30 Mass. city
31 Mao's successor
34 Homophone for Chekhov
35 Admonitory word
36 Sign the register
38 Rouge's counterpart
40 Win at an auction
41 —— as possible
42 Erudite
43 Pizza spice
44 Western alliance
45 Green
47 Sped
48 "Après —— le déluge . . ."
49 Getting on
50 Glutinous material
53 Gain further potential from
54 Alfonso's queen
55 Amble
57 Transformed
59 Coverlet
61 Agt.'s cut
64 Nixon's spaniel
65 Never, in Bonn
66 Tall tales
69 River in W. Germany
72 Hang-glide
76 Staff man
77 Evian and Dax
79 Permit: Abbr.
83 Quake
84 Engine knocks
85 Head of a tale
86 Tar's milieu
87 U. of Maine locale
88 Verify before proceeding
89 Stickers
90 Jeanne de la Fonte
91 Large hound
92 Hunter on high
94 Defeats in chess
95 Play the part
96 Coach
97 Hospital figure
98 Saws cords at night
102 —— Arenas, Chile
104 Marine flier
105 Choose what is choice
108 Objective
109 Medical examination
110 "—— Clear Day"
111 Function

Illegal Tender

By Bert H. Kruse

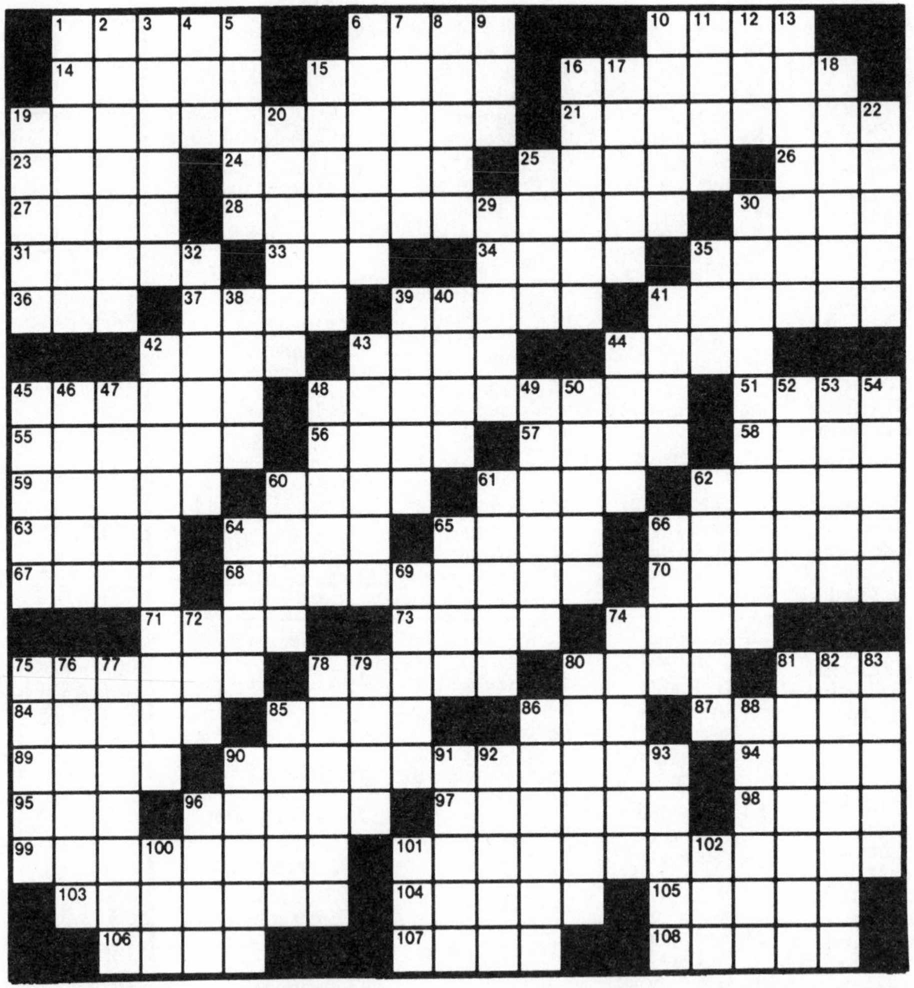

ACROSS

1 Fragment
6 Buss
10 City in Syria
14 Paradisiacal nymph
15 Ray
16 Type of type
19 Sorbonne site
21 Place for strays
23 Candid
24 Somewhat ordinary
25 Indigenous Japanese
26 Kind of hold
27 Midway attraction
28 Brief words from Greeley
30 Sage
31 Subject to ablation
33 Singleton
34 Late Yugoslav leader
35 North Sea feeder
36 Conjunction
37 Strobile
39 Stickers
41 Ritualistic formula
42 Cabbage
43 Duck
44 Dwarf: Comb. form
45 Inclination
48 Nobelist in Literature: 1938
51 Strong desires
55 Pixie
56 Tennis divisions
57 Kind of hemp
58 Ballet action
59 Pickle
60 Demonstrative
61 Cries of distaste
62 Middle, in law
63 Old tongue
64 Kubla of Xanadu
65 Molander's "Dollar": 1937
66 Like the rich
67 —— -do-well
68 Second-largest island
70 Cussed
71 Benefit
73 She sallied forth with fans
74 Looking good
75 Certain nun
78 Glass materials
80 Phonetically smooth
81 Stern
84 An Astaire
85 Align
86 Call for help
87 Word with alligator
89 Brötchen or kipfel
90 Salad ingredient
94 Relief in England
95 Divers information
96 Coat with an alloy
97 Shrimp
98 Porter's "I —— Love"
99 High-water point, usually
101 Woman's proverbial prerogative
103 Dopes
104 Nez —— War: 1877
105 Clamor
106 Retreats
107 "The —— 'e knows . . .": Kipling
108 Conventicle groups

DOWN

1 Poet Karl
2 Dijon is its capital
3 Spoiled
4 Prince Valiant's son
5 Inlaid
6 Self-defense system
7 Musical vamp
8 T-bone source
9 Patriotic org.
10 The ——, Netherlands
11 Sight at Innsbruck
12 "O sole —— "
13 Most discerning
15 Gyrene
16 Sherwood's "—— Delight"
17 John Todd's radio role
18 Stertorous one
19 Famed prisoner: May 1982
20 Defeated
22 Actress Paget
25 Indigo
29 Mountain-dew maker
30 Juvenile poultry character
32 Card game
35 Like Suckling's lover
38 Oenochoe's cousin
39 Exploits
40 Rows
41 Manufacture
42 W.W. I leader's nickname
43 Action at Pebble Beach
44 Sgt. and cpl.
45 Krupp works center
46 Seed
47 Jug for honey
48 Doggone it!
49 Dipped water out of a boat
50 Moslem brain trust
52 Venner of fiction
53 Forty- ——
54 Down at the heels
60 At that time
61 Lapps' neighbors
62 Tidbit
64 Sandpiper
65 Sanction
66 Mr. Mullins
69 Archangel
72 Glucide
74 Save
75 Corday's quarry
76 Male dreamboat
77 Put on cargo again
78 Hot dogs
79 Unwrought
80 Use a chaise
81 Democritus was one
82 Lynx and puma
83 Leaning
85 Pomme de ——
86 Golfer's concern
88 Like a biblical man
90 Inflames
91 A son of Ezra
92 "Like Niobe, all —— "
93 Collars
96 Govt. agent
100 Nigerian city
101 Navy off.
102 Adversary

Answering Service

By Frances Hansen

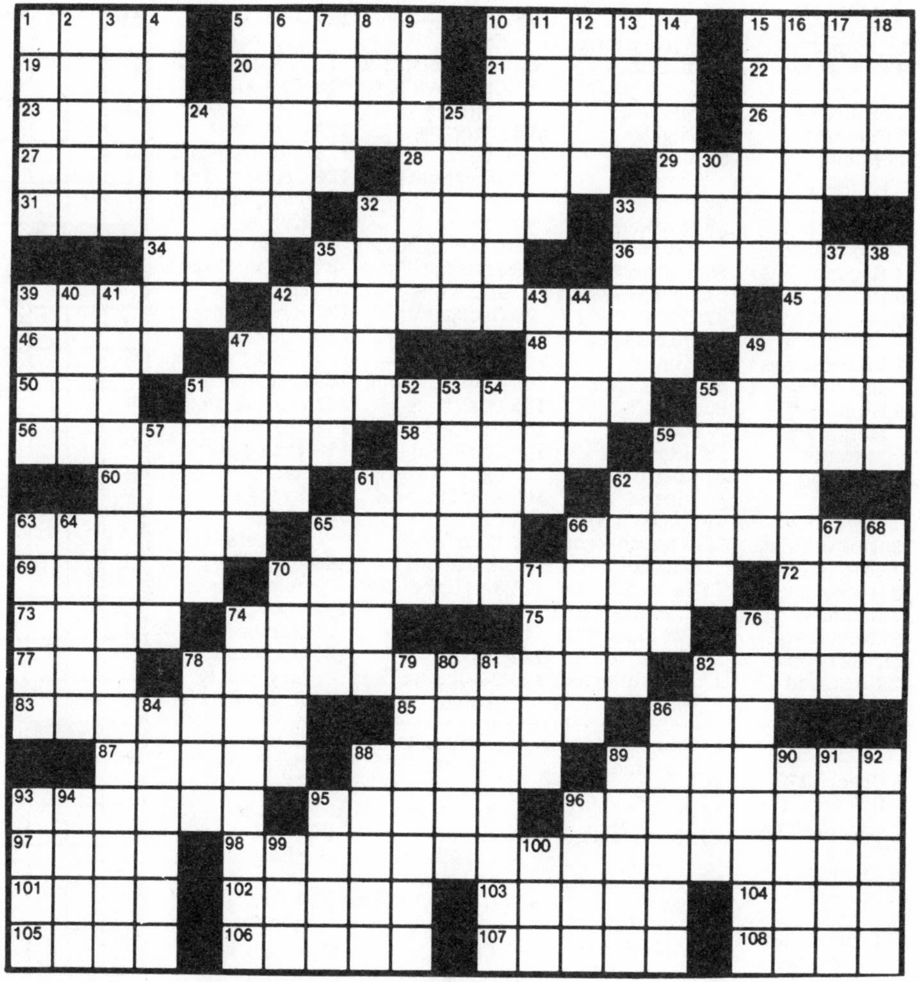

ACROSS

1 Brubeck or Garroway
5 "Horse Marines" captain
10 Name for cowboy Bill
15 Eskers
19 Kaffiyeh cord
20 One and all
21 Mercer-Raksin song
22 Tall follower
23 Chaste?
26 Black
27 Hot under the collar
28 "Them" author
29 Set
31 Legendary
32 Register
33 Swiss city (old spelling)
34 Wee drop
35 Sugar: Prefix
36 Bone formation
39 Six-Day War winner
42 Weight?
45 Botanist Gray
46 Cupid
47 Telegraphic speed measure
48 "The Censor"
49 "It's a —— brecht moonlecht necht": Lauder
50 "Who's on first?" questioner
51 Build?
55 Sheepish complaint
56 Port
58 Pay homage to
59 Memorable comedian: 1890-1958
60 Démodé
61 First American to orbit the Earth
62 Irish seaport
63 Rude bed
65 "—— say . . ."
66 "You said a ——!"
69 Pile up
70 So?
72 Singing syllable
73 Pedro's rock
74 Where Greek met Greek
75 Toward the mouth
76 Copper
77 One of the Three Stooges
78 Taut?
82 U.S. artist-inventor
83 Slightly aberrant
85 Hocus-——
86 Writer Deighton
87 Kind of day for ducks
88 Bombay bards
89 Poet May and family
93 Jog the memory
95 Actress Massey
96 —— away (hoard)
97 W.W. II losers
98 Sleigh?
101 Austen
102 Like windmills
103 Shinto temple gateway
104 Porter
105 Singer Ed from Boston
106 ——-Unis
107 Meanly nasty
108 Drop or gas leader

DOWN

1 "When —— Done," 1926 song
2 007, for one
3 Explorer da Gama
4 Freestone peaches
5 Social butterflies
6 Like old college buildings
7 Jerk
8 Long-tailed ape
9 Roget entry
10 Police unit
11 Atelier sight
12 Snubs openly
13 Bauxite, e.g.
14 Sea of weeds
15 Verdi opera
16 Minx?
17 Lily plant
18 Rip up
24 Kind of card or suit
25 Stuffed, in cookery
30 O.T. book
32 Strike out
33 Boxing events
35 Primitive dipper
37 Newton or Stern
38 Took care of
39 Farmer's place
40 Former Venezuelan copper center
41 Wear?
42 Mother-of-pearl
43 Squash type
44 Steak order
47 Toot one's horn
49 Mr. Christian's skipper
51 Aids in counting
52 —— Lama
53 That is: Lat.
54 Invigorating dose
55 Actress May from Sweden
57 Raft wood
59 Amenable to change
61 Reached
62 "The world is grown ——": Shak.
63 Toscanini's birthplace
64 "—— for the Misbegotten"
65 U.K. awards
66 ——-nest (hoax)
67 Coffee makers
68 Like George Apley
70 "The Boot" of Europe
71 Falconlike solar deity
74 Graceful pool entrance
76 Catch
78 Porter's "—— Love Again"
79 Supports
80 —— fro
81 Navigators' instruments
82 Kind of badge
84 Musters
86 Bonnie Annie of song
88 Cornflower
89 Fish bait
90 ". . . fame of friend ——": Riley
91 A wife in "Gianni Schicchi"
92 More foxy
93 Rani's mate
94 Quiz
95 Hebrides island
96 Indian title of respect
99 —— Tyler, English rebel
100 Style

114

Halloween Party

By John M. Samson

ACROSS

1 Comprehend
6 Bow who wowed 'em
11 Nonpayer
16 Conduits
21 Having rounded projections
22 Restrict
23 Kind of code
24 Record
25 Battery part
26 Lamblike
27 —— Ababa
28 Like Hermes' shoes
29 Humpty Dumpty's costume?
31 Sigmund Freud's costume?
33 Daw vehicle
34 100 to 1, e.g.
36 It's not nice
37 Brightens up
38 Remus, e.g.
40 Like poteen
42 He played Hopalong
43 Chatter
46 Early Roman monster
49 Czech river
50 Mama or Peggy
51 Montreal Canadien
54 Party hostess?
58 Roofing material
59 Likeness
61 Lounges about
62 Savor
63 He came as Klinger
64 Super stars
65 Vesta's vestment
66 Exploited
67 Lord of the theater
70 Alaskan port
71 What charcoal will do
73 Go back to the drawing board
75 She came with 135 Across
77 Hamlin's cave man
79 "Now I —— down . . ."
80 Watering place
81 Casanova's costume?
86 Detective Lupin
88 Where not to be led
93 Jot
94 Biennial herb
96 Stats for Walk and Waits
99 Occupation
100 Tiny Tom
102 Fit to be ——
103 Like Mr. Hyde
105 Push back
106 Entirety
107 Darjeeling, e.g.
108 How Dracula came
110 157.5° to a mariner
111 Salt Lake City team
113 Trickling
114 Hence
115 "—— Boot" (recent movie)
116 Reel backwards?
117 Boxing weight
119 Aphrodite's son
122 Debussy
125 Gift from Gina
126 Goodly amount
129 Thespians
133 Kermit's costume?
135 Shirley Booth's costume?
137 Indian state
138 Trick-or-treater's trick
140 Concluding
141 Durable wood
142 Take care of
143 Transparent
144 Lake NE of Ladoga
145 Indian princess
146 Düsseldorf's neighbor
147 "——, Wrong Number"
148 Utah's third-largest city
149 Rodeo animal

DOWN

1 Cheerful flowers
2 Singer-actress Blakley
3 Upstairs
4 Inhuman human
5 Type of student Bailey was
6 Oaf
7 Calf's ——
8 Fernando's friend
9 Phone
10 Gobbled
11 Controller, for short
12 Port, for one
13 Accuse
14 Corn color
15 Famous lioness
16 Singer Pride's costume?
17 Dump
18 Ship
19 Memorable Fields
20 What huskies haul
30 J.R. of TV
32 Vintage cars
35 Chisel and gouge
36 "The —— Thought of You"
39 India's first P.M.
41 Benedictine's costume?
42 Hogsheads
43 Conference site: 1945
44 Audibly
45 Ceramists' cookers
47 Anonymous Richards
48 Famed Canadian physician
50 Lesser Antilles native
51 Ruin
52 Old World lizard
53 Attack
55 TV-commercial award
56 Money held in trust
57 Soft clam's home
58 Hebrew "T"
60 Thelonious ——
63 Exquisite perfection
68 Like some excuses
69 —— Nui (Easter Island)
72 Betty of comics
74 Prefix with mutuel
76 One-time Washington Senator hopeful
78 What the Sprats cleaned
81 André, the pianist
82 Mores
83 Postman's rounds
84 Dressler movie
85 Fast-food food
87 Clear a tape
89 Journey
90 Swift
91 Author St. Johns
92 Hollers
95 Carson subject
97 Male ant
98 Papyrus
101 De Paul player's costume?
104 A neighbor of Tibet
108 James Bond movie
109 Pentateuch
112 —— off (angry)
113 More foppish
116 Crescent-shaped
117 Gondolier
118 Greenskeeper's job
120 Dark yellows
121 "—— Mater"
122 Hunt
123 Gets nosed out
124 Musical upbeats
125 He sings lays with a lei
127 Like a trident
128 Proscenium's locale
130 Pale-blue gas
131 Dancer Jeanmaire
132 More artful
134 Pravda provider
136 Clique
139 Shout
140 —— yong

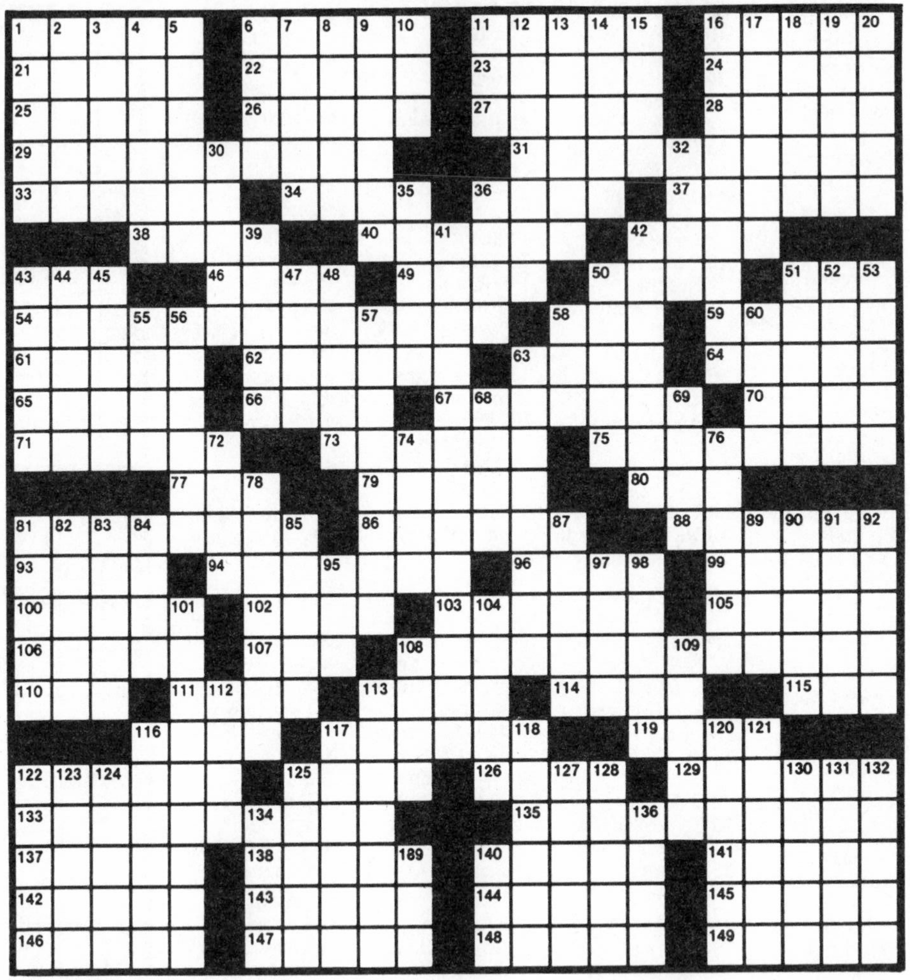

115

Animal Cracks

By Vincent L. Osborne

ACROSS

1 Sound
4 Con man's ploy
8 Main part of a mountain range
14 Site of St. Nicholas's tomb
18 "Kilroy was ——"
19 Break
20 Actress De Carlo
21 Black
22 Opposite of aweather
23 Sketch an African king?
25 Jewish month
26 Spiffy
28 Locales for crests
29 Equivoque
30 Trojan horse, e.g.
31 Refuge for wildebeests?
33 Quod —— faciendum
36 Remove surgically
38 Goddess of the moon
39 Roebuck's pride
41 He fought at Gettysburg
43 Essen name
46 Cranial cavity
48 Of —— (mediocre)
49 Calaveras County celebrity
53 Cinch
54 Line on a weather map
56 Hebrides dialect
57 St.-John's-bread
59 Headcheese
61 Eclat
63 Etoile
64 Some keys
66 Supple
69 Equines for the Continental Congress?
74 A snowflake is one
75 Sinew
76 Island of the Hospitalers
78 Profits from error
82 Shofars, e.g.
83 Wimbledon lane
84 Medieval silk fabric
87 Rum drink
89 June 13, e.g.
91 Raw
92 Crops
94 —— nach Osten
95 Funest
97 Hindu instruments
99 Passé
101 One of the Magi
106 Again and yet again
108 TV journalist
109 Hoary leporid?
111 Complain
112 Stout
114 Passage from a narthex
116 European finch
117 Ionian gulf
118 Stray wildcat?
122 Hill
123 Berliner's brew
124 Informed
125 "—— sanctorum"
126 Nob
127 River on The Broads
128 Coxswains
129 Parnassian
130 Exultant cry

DOWN

1 Ocelot or serval
2 Wroth
3 Undergo odontiasis
4 Yardstick: Abbr.
5 "—— diem"
6 In great haste
7 Whimper
8 Hind's lament?
9 Hail
10 Peruvian coin
11 Scrap
12 Hemingway's "—— Time"
13 African fox
14 Musts for Smokey?
15 Type of muscle
16 Certain turkeys
17 Anent
18 Is undecided
24 One of the Yalies
27 Doughboy
32 —— de société
34 Khan and MacGraw
35 Domingo is one
37 Newman's "Apologia pro Vita ——"
39 Horrify
40 Hick
42 Hwy.
44 Spontaneous
45 Do a Latin student's task
47 —— Joaquin
49 Agricultural loan agcy.
50 Grates
51 Correct: Prefix
52 Thugs vs. goons?
55 Brioche
58 Misrepresent
60 Emulated Niobe
62 Mrs. Flintstone
65 Chinese: Comb. form
67 Opening word
68 Banana oil, for one
70 Furniture style
71 Unmoored
72 Oscar winner: 1982
73 Small map
77 Pro vote
79 Dosimetry unit
80 Robert De —— of films
81 Still-hunt
84 Chemists' org.
85 Touchstones
86 Medical device
88 Time —— half
90 "Centennial," e.g.
93 —— Lanka
96 Wagers
98 Performs carelessly
100 ". . . —— fat hen"
102 Tenzing Norkay, for one
103 Ishmael
104 Awn
105 Zola heroine
107 He wrote "Gerontion"
109 Chemical prefix
110 Gallic income
111 "My Melancholy ——"
113 To live, to Livy
115 Cuff
119 Sault —— Marie
120 Cash follower
121 Totem pole

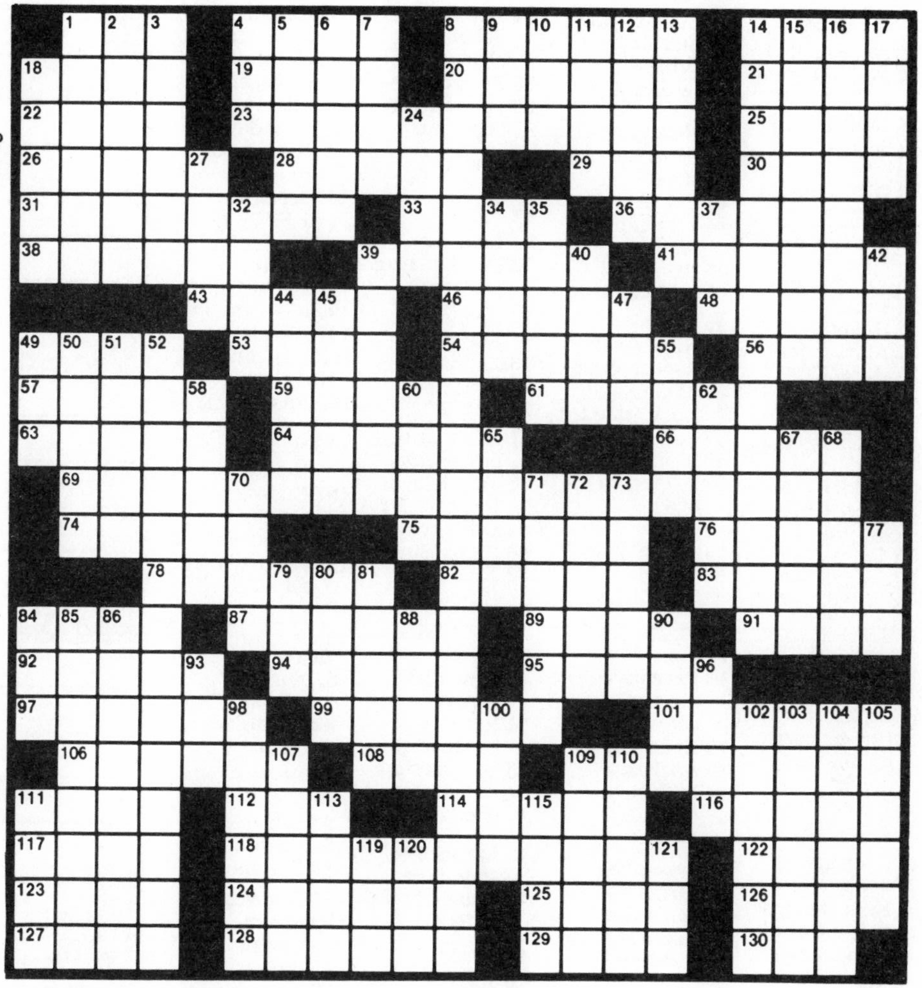

116

Role Call

By Mary Virginia Orna

ACROSS

1 Wherewithal
6 Feature in old serials
11 Embrace
17 Secular
18 Abrasive
19 Diospolite ruler
21 Interpreter of dreams
23 Freebooter
25 Snatch
26 Halos
27 Alaric's folk
28 Part of TNT
29 Gadzooks relative
31 Archery expert
33 Incline
34 Golden ——
35 Kind of glass or grass
36 Gainsay
37 Stein's "—— Lives"
38 Former ring master
39 Wide receiver
40 Fender bend
41 Prosit and skoal
42 Flycatcher
44 Jazz guitarist Montgomery
45 Brian ——, Irish hero
46 Shrank
49 Handyman
52 Suburban sight
56 "Dans la Loge" painter
57 Suffix with cell
58 Thun's river
59 Protected at sea
60 Collect
61 Choir leader
63 Loch of Argyllshire
64 Budd Schulberg character
65 Peau de ——
66 Ten concerns of podiatrists
67 Smeared
68 Stage
69 Actor
71 Bears
72 Dutch marine painter
74 Innuit or Yuit: Abbr.
75 Action
76 Skirt liner
79 Caprid
81 Historic town on the Lahn
82 March 15, in Italy
85 Salt's cry
86 Fatha Hines
87 Jazzman Brubeck
89 Hamartiologists' topics
91 German transcendentalist
92 Ropedancer
95 Enchilada relative
96 Letters at J.F.K.
97 Guides for augurs
98 Babbitt, e.g.
100 —— Bravo
101 Plunderer
103 Postcards collector
105 Analytical substance
106 Notions, in Nancy
107 Undoes
108 Gawks
109 Paludous place
110 H.r. and r.b.i., e.g.

DOWN

1 Nicaragua's capital
2 One concern of ophthalmologists
3 Friend, to François
4 Drug agt.
5 Snub
6 Kind of blonde
7 "New World" Symphony's key
8 Record again
9 Kind of coffee
10 Wolf: Comb. form
11 Nominate
12 First word of a 1968 movie title
13 Store
14 Periods
15 Watson concern
16 Horn players
17 Anchorite
20 W.W. II aircraft carrier
22 Wreathed
24 Groups of pheasants
27 Secluded vale
30 Table-talk adept
32 Oft-abbreviated Latin phrase
33 Magician
37 Anderson's "High ——"
39 Olpe
40 Canon-law expert
41 Hefty hardback
43 Sponsorship
44 Br. servicewoman
45 Aaron or Raymond
46 Rough, broken cliffs
47 Pardon
48 Silly
49 Flotilla
50 Kind of bread or thatch
51 New Mexico resort
53 Excuse
54 Dike
55 Yorkshire city
57 Author of "Trinity"
61 Hawaiian dishes
62 Recess
63 Merit
65 Long nap
67 Podium
70 Dominion
71 Revives
73 Myrmecologist's interest
75 Infernal
76 Quack
77 Belmont Stakes winner: 1975
78 Party favorites
79 Seafowl

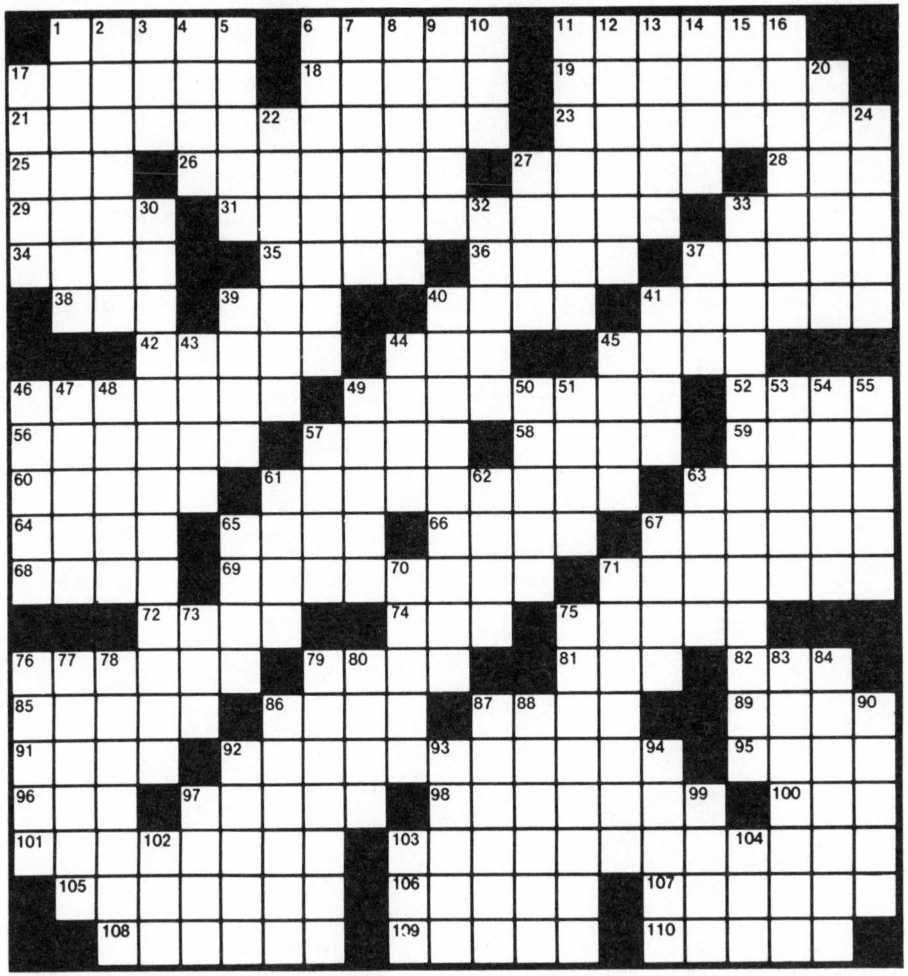

80 Old Danish coins
83 Evelyn, for one
84 Engraves
86 Field of poetic fame
87 Blade
88 Winged insects
90 Grimy deposits
92 Stoker or baker
93 Dutch town on the Mark
94 Exactions
97 Tale of heroism
99 Turnip or parsnip
102 Actor Hingle
103 Cloudy
104 Tibetan antelope

117

High Jinks

By Katherine Gould & Chris Remignanti

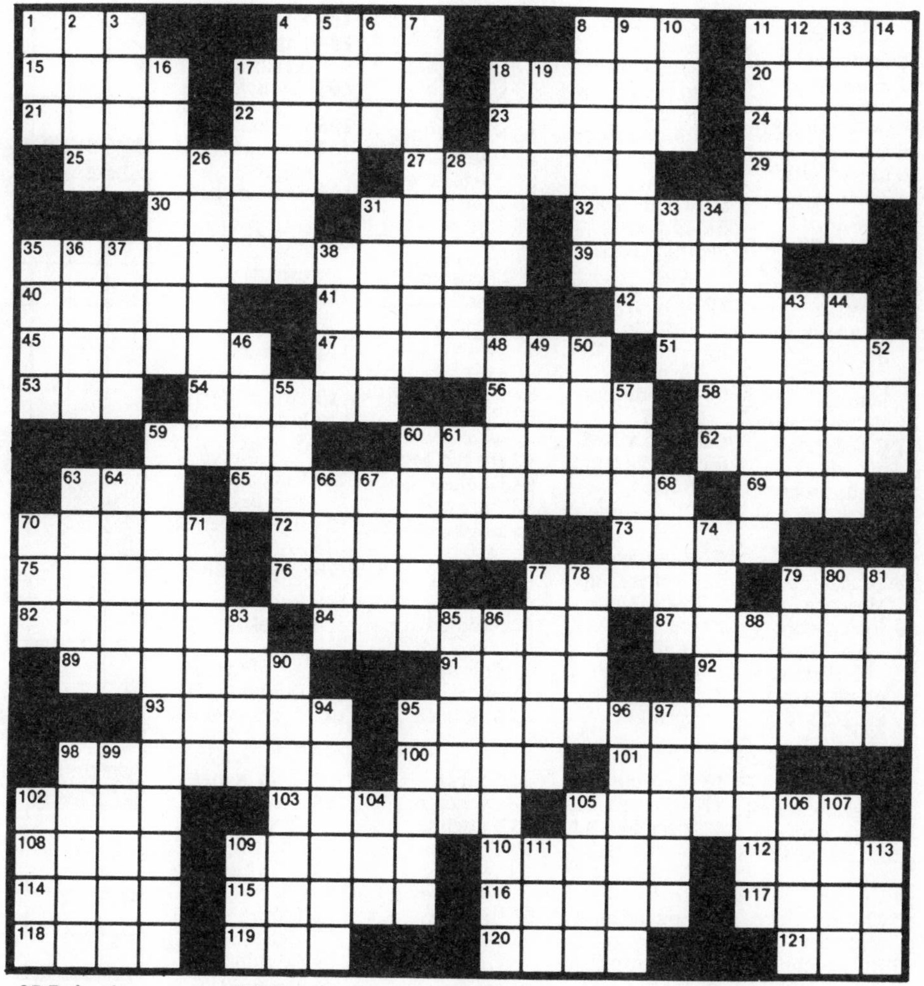

ACROSS

1 Half dollar?
4 March 15 fish?
8 Letters for letter carriers
11 Hardy lass
15 Word before fours
17 Z-z-z
18 "—— de Lune": Debussy
20 Fence good for a laugh
21 Tummy tightener
22 Festoon
23 Beds for Leo and Elsa
24 Fingal's land
25 Stanley's car
27 Somniferous fly
29 1,000-days queen
30 Maguey's kin
31 Greeting of a sort
32 Deadlock
35 Read between the lines
39 Actor J. Carrol ——
40 Beaverish
41 Fancy this
42 Naples, to Mario
45 This fits with fits
47 Having I problems
51 ". . . ditties of ——": Keats
53 A star-ry Knight
54 These have their bounds
56 Union collectors' items
58 Scent for Di
59 Houston "aspirin" server
60 Brahmins' bash
62 Lesser civet
63 Reb's govt.
65 Backwards and forwards
69 Her mate is ruff
70 Belle hops
72 Banquet
73 Father Time sound
75 Teed off
76 Bills often passed
77 Grand follower
79 It's "in one era and . . ."
82 Some human races
84 Expires like Nathan's kin?
87 A little, in León
89 Papers read on campus
91 Anagram for lire
92 Famed tale-teller
93 High costs of leaving
95 Run-on sentence
98 Rampart where el toro ambles?
100 Shot on the set
101 Outspoken Rev. Roberts?
102 Monkey not in the Louvre
103 Posers
105 Strive to equal
108 Draft at a bar
109 Stirring game?
110 Cradle rockers
112 Have a fling
114 Colorful duck
115 Tear-jerker
116 "—— with Me"
117 Riley's life
118 Chichi
119 Salt's course
120 Phooey!
121 Aurora's tears?

DOWN

1 Disco disks
2 Shelley's "Shucks!"
3 Oxidation's evidence
4 Undeniably
5 What to show intruders
6 Exhibit humanity
7 Figure on the watch
8 This is in rain, not sun
9 "Let us spray" fellow
10 No and J
11 A shot in the dark
12 Makes dough
13 Rise's follower
14 Playing with a full deck
16 Clip-joint actress?
17 Not a Lesser Island
18 Queenly monickers
19 Counterpart of long.
26 In nimble fashion
28 Hood's quiverful
31 Stashes in caches
33 Yaws (truly!)
34 —— as a church mouse
35 Something to pass
36 Broun's "Pieces of ——"
37 Edwardian euphemism
38 Baby talk
43 Gooselike?
44 Operating
46 Briny septet
48 Kind of card
49 Swell coming ashore
50 Lend an auricle
52 Prior, to Prior
55 Man: Comb. form
57 Wagnerian heroine
59 Rally round the flag
60 Type of buckle
61 Some connections
63 Weight for Diamond Lil
64 Cut prices
66 Descartes
67 Zenith
68 Indigenous Japanese
70 Auction action
71 Place for two
74 Jell
77 Cal of the P.G.A.
78 Key's little cousin
79 Pâté de —— gras
80 Peak
81 Capitol topper
83 Loren's evening
85 Of a region
86 Golfer in chains?
88 Bishop
90 Homilies
94 Chicago suburb
95 Relentless virtuoso?
96 Their lives are in tents
97 Vessel on a vessel?
98 This may have boughs
99 Eastern Christian
102 U.S.S.R. river
104 —— volente
105 Give off
106 Hopper
107 Being
109 Writer, partly poetic
111 Syrian sire
113 "As you ——, so shall you rip"

Dirty Tricks

By Warren W. Reich

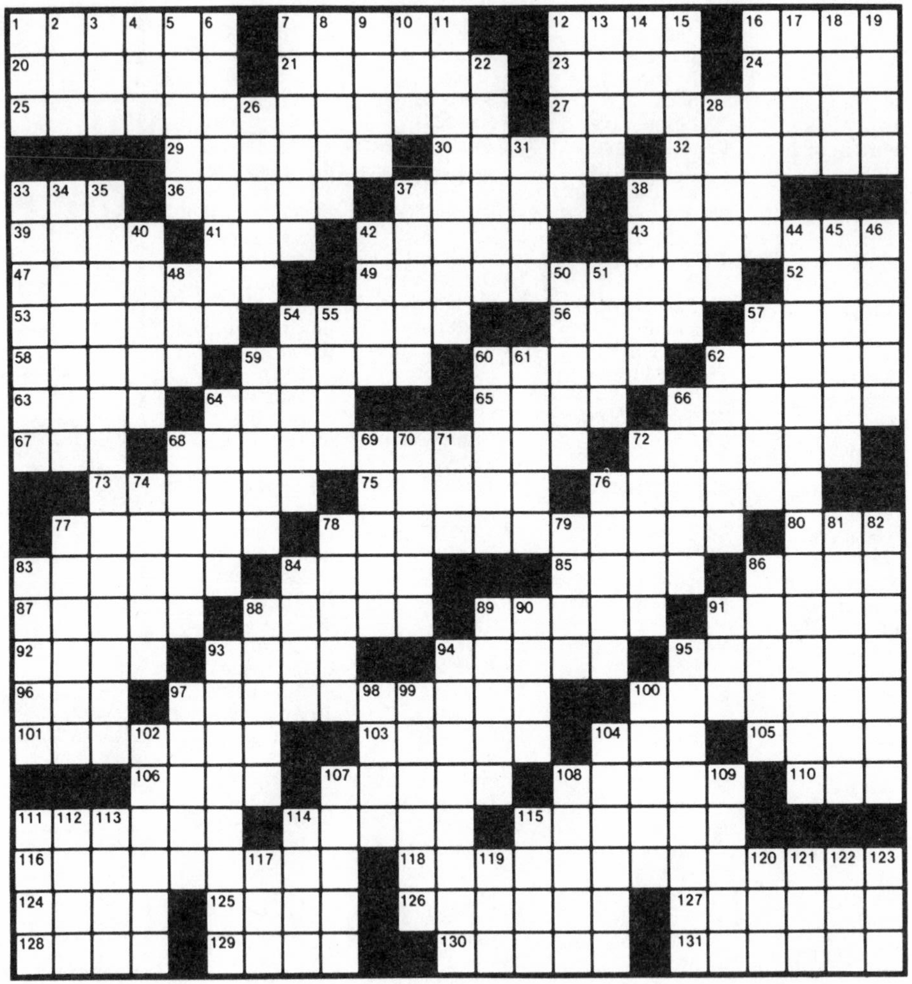

ACROSS

1 Function
7 Eastern bishops
12 —— spumante
16 O'Casey
20 Corner sitter
21 Tutti- ——
23 Image
24 Spot for gyring and gimbling
25 Sordid abnormality?
27 Raunchy music?
29 City on the Somme
30 Hebrew letter
32 Giants or dwarfs
33 Media control agcy.
36 Rivulets
37 Begot
38 Cenozoic and Mesozoic, e.g.
39 Byron work
41 Spread to dry
42 —— Manutius, printer-scholar: 1450-1515
43 Exercises
47 Split
49 Mud-covered impersonator?
52 Pile
53 "JR" author
54 Lee or Spencer
56 Faction
57 Woody's boy
58 Adipose
59 Jacques of song
60 Spot for swinging
62 Wind: Comb. form
63 Ecuadorean river
64 Term at sea
65 Martha from Butte
66 "Gentlemen —— Blondes"
67 Vane reading
68 Profits from porno?
72 Rouse
73 Henley's waterway
75 Part of a springe
76 Desert, as in a desert
77 Obliterates
78 Uncouth Pancho?
80 Nav. officer
83 Retarded
84 Adriatic wind
85 Love god
86 June 6, 1944
87 Grippers on horseshoes
88 Metallic disk
89 Welty's "Music from ——"
91 Copal or elemi
92 Pongo and wou-wou
93 Hit the books
94 Dodge
95 Burgage
96 Baton Rouge inst.
97 Ignoble athlete?
100 Saddle straps
101 "Ten Commandments" producer
103 Foamy drink
104 Lake in Kashmir
105 Tropical tree
106 Parson birds
107 Receive eagerly
108 Escritoires
110 —— de veau (sweetbread)
111 Places for frontals
114 Carman's "—— Airs"
115 Part of Berlin
116 Indecent dances?
118 Obnoxious approach?
124 Hindu peeress
125 Antic
126 Oder feeder
127 Redactor
128 Greek music halls
129 A Dutch treat
130 Inhibit
131 Alarm sounder

DOWN

1 Electrical unit
2 Opponent
3 Angelico, for one
4 Imaret
5 Closet material
6 Holy recluses
7 Off the right path
8 Husks of certain grains
9 "No ifs, ands or ——"
10 Panay tribe
11 With impassivity
12 Broadcast
13 Large amount
14 Kind of head
15 Coach
16 Gush out
17 Title between viscount and marquess
18 Arne oratorio
19 Loch ——
22 Bogged down
26 More contemptible
28 Event of '29
31 Coordinate
33 Vessels for liquids
34 Melons
35 Crass OPEC offering?
37 Golf flub
38 French chef's need
40 "—— to bed"
42 From a distance
44 Coarse sweetheart?
45 Pilgrim
46 Trace
48 "—— Walküre"
50 Belgian composer-virtuoso: 1858-1931
51 Plexus
54 Lock
55 Pawnees' cousins
57 Pico de ——, in the Pyrenees
59 Ice sheets
60 Partner of poesia
61 Weaker
62 Kind of squad
64 —— forces
66 Elfin beings
68 Xenon and krypton
69 Harden
70 E. E. Hale antihero
71 Tooth
72 Mehta's need
74 Atlanta five
76 Madame Curie
77 Pass
78 U.S. woman since 1920
79 Plumbum
81 Kenya's capital
82 Sense over syntax
83 Blanch
84 Reveal
86 Blue —— (dungaree)
88 Propounds
89 Coleridge's "gentle thing"
90 Motor sound
91 Soak flax
93 Pointed stake
94 Overwhelmed
95 Discuss
97 Rave notice
98 Relating to: Suffix
99 Hatchet woman
100 "Communism" author: 1927
102 Where Firenze is
104 More obtuse
107 —— salts
108 —— macabre
109 Nobel, for one
111 Hair style
112 Backpack
113 Harry Warren product
114 Robert or Alan
115 Varmint
117 Repressive force
119 Faugh!
120 Actress Ullmann
121 Follower: Suffix
122 Eur. land
123 Palindromic word

Displaced Persons

By Virginia P. Abelson

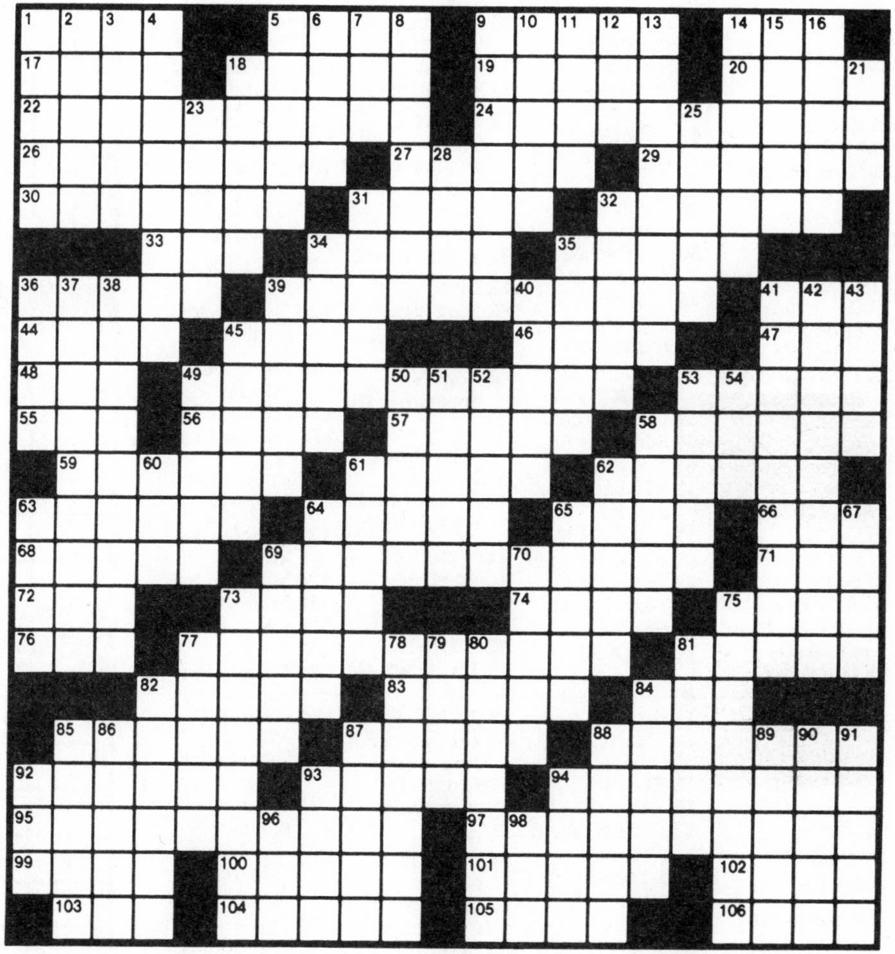

ACROSS

1 Shoe part
5 Soprano Lily
9 Actor Alan's college?
14 First letters
17 Suffix with comment
18 Enchantment
19 Cancel a space trip
20 French town once frequented by a writer?
22 Prima's beat?
24 Julie's bailiwick?
26 English polyphonic composition
27 Pupil of Socrates
29 Table wine
30 Home of Runyon's Nathan?
31 Once upon ——
32 Lean
33 Wallach
34 Verdugo
35 Seculars
36 Topknot
39 Dick and Mark's domain?
41 Pinguid
44 Charged atoms
45 Coconut fiber
46 Island in Taiwan Strait
47 Boxer from Clay Center?
48 Communication: Abbr.
49 Where Claire blossomed?
53 Room in a maison
55 Moray
56 Stunted plant
57 Did she go to Duke?
58 "Hedda ——," Ibsen play
59 Scenes of crimes
61 State flower of N.H.
62 Alehouse
63 Indian officials
64 Ax and adz
65 Caliber
66 Suffix with Bronx
68 Cather's "—— Lady"
69 Betty's sphere?
71 U.S.I.A. arm
72 Ziegfeld
73 First tiller
74 Piedmontese city
75 Morning moistures
76 Bandleader Weems
77 Van's hometown
81 Site of W.W. I battles
82 Portable craft
83 Pat's Iowa address?
84 Benign bump on the skin
85 Breed of sheep
87 Sharp ridge
88 City for cartoonist Young in the past?
92 Neighbor of a Kenyan
93 Cato was one
94 Belgian vassal?
95 Maurice's habitat?
97 Walter's settlement?
99 Bridle part
100 Buddy
101 Ninnies
102 —— B'rith
103 Foxy
104 Kin of movers and shakers
105 No longer new
106 Aussie town

DOWN

1 Sound
2 Make amends
3 Steed
4 Convent head
5 Coating
6 Stare amorously
7 Zero
8 Emblem of power
9 Long Islander's resort?
10 Subside
11 Picadores pick on him
12 Miscue
13 In a maudlin manner
14 St. ——, locale for Berg?
15 Rivulet
16 Wendell or Jeff
18 Year in Ethelred II's reign
21 N.C.O.
23 Young salmon
25 Spatula
28 Connection
31 Siren
32 Drawing room
34 "Romola" author
35 Cars for execs
36 Summits in Siena
37 Pete's stamping grounds?
38 Poet Paul's place?
39 Ring-tailed mammals, for short
40 Oracular
41 Whence Albert hailed?
42 Birthplace of Fred and Steve?
43 Row
45 Hints for Holmes
49 Hardest part
50 Dostoyevsky's "The ——"
51 —— prosequi
52 Clutch
53 Rescues
54 Vigoda
58 Bouquet ——
60 Nose: Prefix
61 Gird up one's ——
62 Hoity-——
63 Loony
64 Your, of yore
65 Sew loosely
67 Slack off
69 Kind of elm
70 Frankie or Cleo
73 Machinated
75 ". . . —— the light of the moon"
77 Bridewells
78 Margaret and Pat
79 Coward
80 —— -Nord, French dept.
81 Author Cornelia
82 Fissure
84 Hones
85 Plays in chess
86 Enamel
87 Luther or Larry
88 Quoted
89 "Give —— horse . . ."
90 Celebrations
91 "—— so near to another . . .": Job 41:16
92 Sun. discourse
93 Other
94 Canter's kin
96 Nigerian native
98 Romaine lettuce

Ornithology

By Bert Rosenfield

ACROSS

1 Rodgers and Hart's "—— in Arms"
6 Knout
10 LARK
16 It serves the telly
19 Animate
20 Fairy-tale opener
21 Branched
22 One-time Mideast initials
23 Tournament of Roses entry
24 French window
25 Consecrate
26 "Dio ——!"
27 CARDINAL
30 Uncivil courtroom acts
32 Seneca's foe
33 Whatever
34 Ab —— (from the start)
36 Libertines
37 Act as sommelier
39 SWIFT
45 Put the —— on (solicit)
47 Nobel Prize physicist: 1922
48 Power
49 November winners
50 Lamb-chop decoration
53 Liberty or Victory
55 Ineffective
58 Vehicles at J.F.K.
59 Driver's need
60 Scowl
61 Body muscle
65 "Rubáiyát" word
66 L.B.J. beagle
67 Made a wager
68 Put out
69 Bad or good
70 SNIPE
74 U.S. ancestral org.
75 Ponchielli's "—— mar!"
77 Precinct
78 Type of sack
79 Caesar's second announcement
80 Combiner meaning "nine"
81 Behind at sea
82 Blue
83 Participate
84 Bewitching charm
86 Fem.'s opposite
87 Rare treat, sometimes
88 Not dbl.
90 Author Santha Rama ——
91 Byzantine image
93 "Brute" antecedents
95 CRANE
99 Lively wit
103 In —— (hurried)
104 —— Annie of "Oklahoma!"
105 Fled
107 Apiece
108 Triple Cy Young Award winner
112 EAGLE
116 Police dept. alert
117 Not subject to a rule
119 Milnes role in "Otello"
120 Secant, for one
121 Stanley Cup org.
122 Flights by oiseaux
123 Tanglewood area
124 Make up for
125 Match the bet
126 SWALLOW
127 Flawless
128 Certain murals

DOWN

1 Lofted a golf ball
2 Entice
3 TV's "—— Woman"
4 DUCK
5 Caterpillar hair
6 Tyrolean fabric
7 Elia, e.g.
8 Glaswegian
9 Statue by Polyclitus
10 Auber's "—— Diavolo"
11 Animus
12 Melville work
13 Pork cut
14 Berlin's "—— This a Lovely Day . . ."
15 Et ——
16 JAY
17 Fishermen, at times
18 Baggataway stick
28 Dillon
29 Averse
31 Painter of "Odalisque"
35 Baron —— (Francis Bacon)
38 Asther of films
40 Nichols protagonist
41 Petty bribe
42 Medicates to excess
43 Rattail, e.g.
44 Tampa-to-Fort Myers dir.
46 Aromatic compound
50 GULL
51 "—— the new!"
52 Daughter of Cymbeline
54 In this vicinity
56 Levantine craft
57 San Antonio cager
60 CROW
62 Type of inspection
63 Maine national park
64 QUAIL
66 Step on it
68 Geometry letters
70 Secretariat, once
71 Mann's partner
72 —— beans (Mexican dish)
73 Cyrus or Philo
76 Ophidianlike
79 RAIL
81 Shanghai nurse
82 Judicial bench
83 Concordes, e.g.
85 Part of a trefoil
86 Country singer Bandy
88 Stanza

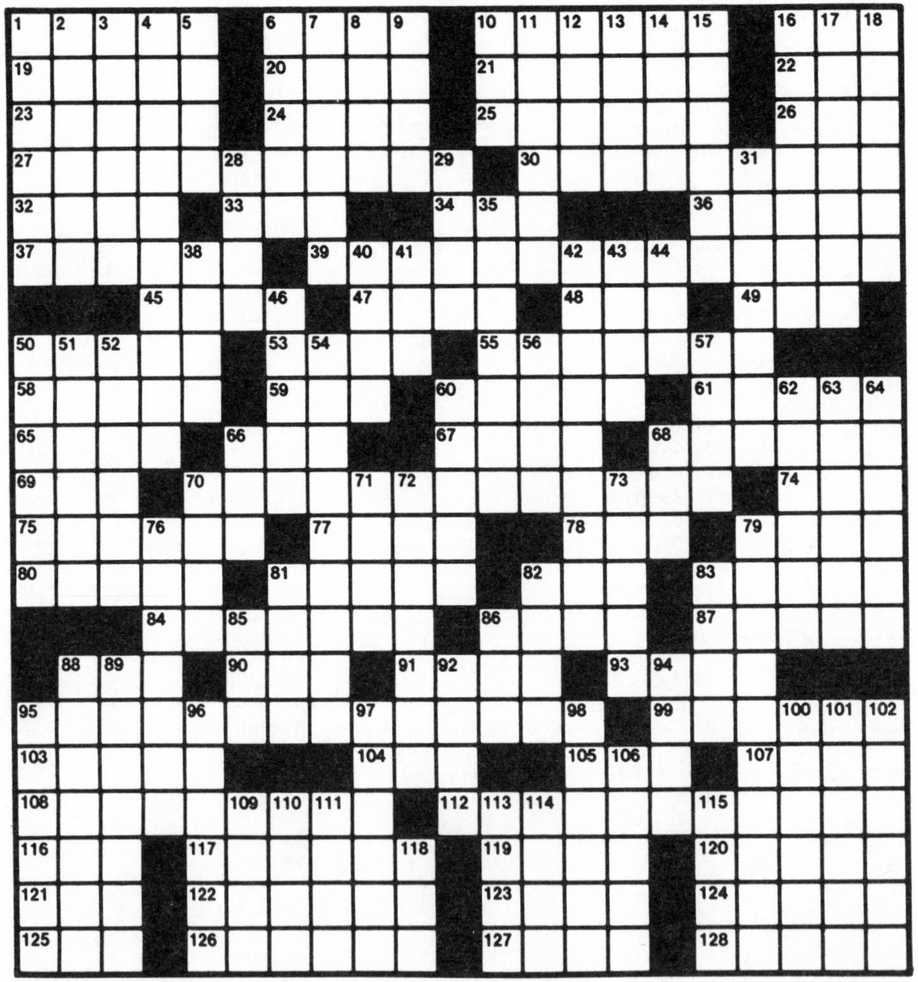

89 GROUSE
92 Granny is one
94 Watch over
95 Wicked people
96 "—— of St. Agnes": Keats
97 Novelist Lee
98 "Oom Paul"
100 Predacious flier
101 "—— Say No" (sung by 104 Across)
102 Anguish
106 Negative terminal
109 Neurite
110 South African grassland
111 Rhea's relative
113 Tenuous strip
114 Where Waialua is
115 Victorian and Edwardian
118 Monogram of Prufrock's creator

Sequential Seasonal Selections

By Anne Fox

ACROSS

1 In —— (hard pressed)
5 Recondite
9 Little angel
15 David, for one
19 Fixed course
20 Loaf
21 Roman Eos
22 Govt. agcy.
23 Words from an English carol
27 Actor Carl
28 Wind: Comb. form
29 Possessive pronoun
30 It's "sed" to Caesar
31 Spring mo.
32 Do a lawn job
34 Relative of Mrs.
35 Thus: Lat.
37 Cessation
39 Czechoslovak carol words
44 Source of betel nuts
45 Rat ——
46 —— havoc
47 N.Y.C. transit
48 —— Tuesday (day before Lent)
51 River isle
52 Greek letter
55 Words from Luke 2:7
61 Wind dir.
62 RR stop
63 Beldam
64 Haydn's "Consummatum ——"
65 Where Waterloo is
66 Medieval brocade
68 Residue
70 Tennis term
72 —— generis (unique)
73 Ho Chi ——
74 Toledo relatives
75 Creek
76 Chinese pagoda
78 —— -Magnon
80 Neckpiece
81 Words by Charles Sheldon
87 Kind of pole
88 One of the Orkneys
89 Former German state
90 Annoy
91 W.W. I group
92 Caron role
93 Some sculptures
96 Sussex carol words, with "The"
105 "—— a Grecian Urn"
106 French pronoun
107 Wash. V.I.P.
108 Press inits.
109 Constellation
110 Hind
111 Charpoy
113 Virginia willows
115 Deep sleeps
117 Words by Edward Throng
122 African tree
123 More suggestive
124 Jacob's twin
125 See 128 Across
126 Fret
127 Robust
128 With 125 Across, Civil War gen.
129 Utterance

DOWN

1 Ancient landing place
2 Crèche figure
3 Clothes
4 Intend
5 Unclothe
6 Old English letter
7 Famous pen name
8 A railroad, informally
9 Question by Ben Jonson
10 Quasimodo's creator
11 "—— tu," Verdi aria
12 Nickname for R.W.R.
13 Strawberry nettle
14 100 satang
15 Snooker stick
16 As snug —— . . .
17 Maltreat
18 Glib talk
24 "Sartor ——": Carlyle
25 Yesterday, in Roma
26 Cordage grass
33 Noel mo.
35 Tendon
36 Sign, in a way
38 Even one
40 Silent siren
41 Survive
42 Fund-raiser's verb
43 Actor John from Spokane
47 Gelid
49 A loser to R.M.N.
50 Genuine
51 Per se
52 Impala
53 Part of an elocution phrase
54 G.R.F. by birth
55 Scat!
56 Live oak
57 Begin
58 By far
59 Loser to D.D.E.
60 Lip
67 "—— was going . . ."
69 "Scots, wha —— . . ."
71 Weaverbird
77 The works
79 Item left out
82 "—— and Future King": White
83 Baths, in Brest
84 M.I.T. specialty: Abbr.
85 Ides cry
86 Math branch
91 Past
92 "—— Blas"
94 Columbus inst.
95 Tears a page from a book
96 Photographs
97 "—— choose to run . . .": Coolidge
98 Goad
99 London club: 18th century
100 Pour
101 Wild ass
102 Panay port
103 Church official
104 Had a snack
112 Sculls
113 Incensed
114 Middling
116 Dog-days word
118 Maul
119 Old French coin
120 Coniferous tree
121 Small quantity

Forth and Back

By Barry L. Cohen

ACROSS

1 Start of the 13th century
5 Puckerel
8 Plebiscite
12 Networks
16 Tennyson poem
20 Part of C.A.A.
21 Bishop
23 Anagram for Roma
24 CB word
25 Rover Boy saw mothers as goddesses
27 Place for an ICBM
28 Egypt's life-line
29 Jesse Stuart's "—— Heaven"
30 Patricia from Ky.
31 Median strip
32 Keynote
33 Choice
34 Memo abbr.
35 Rattling noise
36 Nero's tutor
37 French Lick is one
38 R.I.P. notice
39 "Do I dare to —— peach?": T.S.E.
40 "Woe is me!"
41 Peppy N.Y. nine beat bad guys
48 Hope
51 On the market
52 Medical suffix
53 Dupin's creator
54 Riley's life
55 Número ——
56 Dinesen offering
57 Weigh down
58 Blind alleys
60 Landlord
62 Jets' home
64 House of Lords cry
66 Like argon
67 Bars
69 Wave in la mer
71 Adolf's ally
74 U.S.S.R. range
75 Musial eliminated Wash. Senators
79 It's below the occiput
83 Heckle
85 ". . . leaven of ——": Byron
86 Kind of guest
88 Elicit
91 Davis Cup figure
94 Small village
96 Paradigms
97 Warden of a sort
100 Diarize
102 Bakery employee
104 Symbol of precision
105 Snarl
106 Deposed ring king
107 Jewish month
108 You gotta have miles of it
109 Underwater shocker
110 That guy sketches City Hall grass. Right?
114 Flèche weapon
115 Child, in Puebla
116 Take on
117 Part of an orch.
120 Plantation employee
123 London's "White ——"
124 Feme —— (spinster)
125 English essayist
128 Globular
129 Told all to the cops
130 Pond, in poesy
131 Sub
132 Con
133 First name in raga
134 Pilfer device for maintaining copter blade
136 Scarsdale, e.g.
137 "—— Rhythm"
138 Film coating
139 City in Sicily
140 Trireme features
141 Hart or Player
142 Strong wind
143 Minstrel tune
144 Arnaz

DOWN

1 Parts of cranes
2 Farrell's "Bernard ——"
3 Llamas' cousins
4 Up to one's ears
5 Dostoyevsky subject
6 Make peevish
7 Taro product
8 Any well-known entertainer
9 Ottoman Empire founder
10 Cape Dutch
11 Nav. rank
12 "When I ——": W.S.G.
13 Anatole's contemporary
14 Flax pod
15 Hit initials
16 Knotts performing; notices lack of approval
17 Akin to capric
18 Token
19 Betel palm
22 Gallic penny
26 Kind of clause
31 Mondrian contemporary
32 Five, nine or eleven
34 White poplars
35 Salad root
36 Realm of Somnus
38 Ellipsoid
39 Town near Padua
40 Bohr subject
42 Part of a Stein line
43 Harangue
44 Easter shrub
45 Still-life prop
46 Elbe feeder
47 For fear that
48 Gogol's "Taras ——"
49 Peggy of songdom
50 —— nova (Brazilian dance)
57 Hang
59 Islet
61 Little brat uses needles and wool again
63 Whets
65 Cousin of Saul
68 Mil. banner
70 Guidonian note
72 Kind of degree
73 Corresponding part
76 He sacked Rome in A.D. 410
77 Ancestors
78 Name in fashion
80 Sharp ridge
81 Martinique site
82 Car named for a tycoon
84 Shoe widths
87 Polaris
88 Forerunners of I
89 W.W. II rocket
90 Mouthward
92 Lifting with effort
93 Finis
95 Novelist Boulle
98 Leathermaker
99 Otherwise
101 Taxco treat
103 European juniper
108 Cab callers
111 Put on a Little act
112 Anserine quality
113 Huckleberry
118 Bivouacked
119 Decorated anew
120 Where to find Goyas
121 Ancient Greek colony
122 Cleverer
123 Advocate
124 Pyongyang's rival
125 Unfeeling
126 They have their pride
127 Chou ——
129 "Roots" or "Hawaii"
130 N.Y.C. art center
131 Portico
133 Gear
134 Part of a journey
135 Naphtha, e.g.

Compote

By Barbara Gillis

ACROSS

1 White cliffs feature
5 Sitology subject
9 Defiles
13 "Nabucco" is one
18 Floral emblem of Hawaii
19 Foot section
20 Medley
21 Intrepidity
22 Bakers' aides
23 Persian sprite
24 A "Hud" star
25 Nobelist in Literature: 1948
26 Morsel
27 Primly precise speech or behavior
30 Pinnacle
31 Mangel-wurzel
33 Varnish ingredient
34 Submit
36 Fetal membrane
38 —— linguae
43 Frangipani, e.g.
45 Sinecures for ward heelers
49 Peripheral
50 Lava
51 Stowe stuff
52 Expression of disgust
53 Tedious
54 Writer Joyce
56 —— and yet so far
59 Sloth, e.g.
60 Elevate
62 —— Flow
65 Attempt the impossible
71 Dam on 110 Down
72 Pacify
73 Expressions of inquiry
75 Gores
79 Actress Berger
80 English dramatist: 18th century
82 Paraphernalia
85 "Granada" composer
87 Who's sorry now?
88 He wrote "Philosopher's Quest"
89 Contention causer
93 Moslem lords
94 Nap, in Navarra
95 "Utopia" author
96 Redolence
97 Adler's —— Culture
101 Bearing
102 Swabbie
105 Singers' goals
111 Supported
113 Veranda
114 Juan's chamber
115 Sutter's place
116 Demote
117 Heath
118 Tupolevs, e.g.
119 Blackthorn
120 Davey of baseball
121 Woody, for one
122 Mountain in Thessaly
123 Perceptions
124 Join

DOWN

1 Plaster painting (from "dry": It.)
2 Small quahogs
3 Atmosphere
4 Bronx cheer
5 Immersed
6 Static
7 Beige
8 Spare
9 Refers to for information
10 New York city
11 Old Chinese weight unit
12 Former Italian coin
13 Imbricate
14 Language of Buddhism
15 Early Olympic site
16 Space
17 Some are fine
18 Roll
28 Ornamental case
29 Bore
32 English cathedral town
35 Natives: Suffix
36 —— arms
37 Boolean ——
39 We or us, e.g.
40 "Cogito, ergo ——"
41 Grid official
42 "Quiet!"
43 John Williams's group
44 Charioteer constellation
45 Designs
46 Electees
47 Murmur, in a way
48 Arista
50 Air
55 Spills over
57 Being, to Cato
58 Law
60 Before zwei
61 Kind of butterfly
63 Mae West line
64 Building stone
66 Spins
67 Strike out
68 Possession right
69 Execrated
70 Danube feeder
74 Buck book
76 Imp
77 Jot
78 Indian title
80 Fragrant perennial
81 Footnote word
82 Energy source
83 Finial
84 Mimic
86 —— wet hen
90 Annual, as some winds
91 Pledge
92 Young zebra
93 Metric unit
96 June passages
98 Actress Signe
99 Bridge declaration
100 Gaels
101 Extra dividend
103 Assault
104 Bonnet denizens
105 Entreaty
106 Warren or Holliman
107 Indigo
108 Contest
109 City in Siberia
110 African river
112 Hautboy

Echoes

By Louis Baron

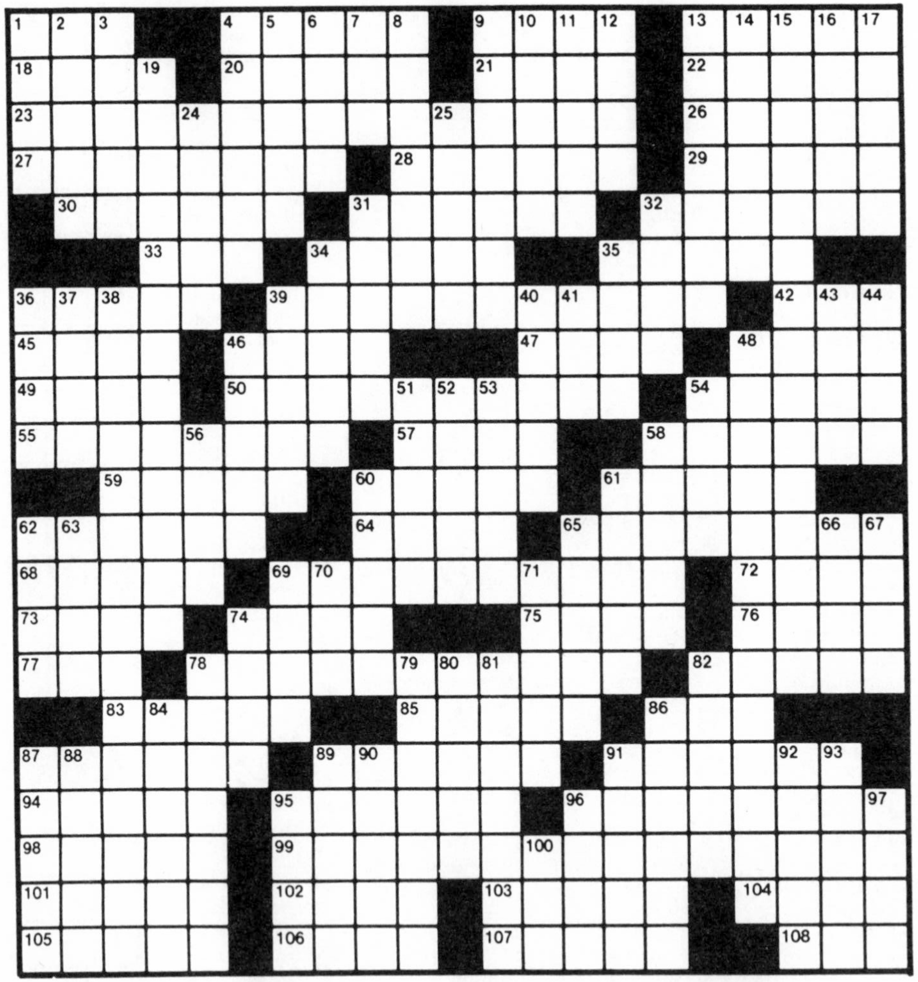

ACROSS

1 Start of many a book title
4 Ankara porter
9 Prot. sect
13 Appears menacingly
18 Like good books
20 Brier
21 Ai's cousin
22 Chief monk
23 Smart guy
26 Sad, in music
27 Refrigerates before shipment
28 African foxes
29 First: Comb. form
30 Noncombustible gases
31 Bowling-alley worker
32 Combined
33 "—— Dot," Maugham play
34 Down Under predator
35 Loafer
36 "I'll —— . . .": 1928 song
39 Burmese hood
42 Haggard's Ayesha
45 Gondola fare
46 Judicial seat
47 Debt memos
48 Square-ended transport
49 Moreno of baseball
50 Conventional bull
54 Ninnies
55 Maine symbol
57 Dudeen, e.g.
58 Diplomat Welles: 1892-1961
59 Calumniate
60 Proved viable
61 Small herring
62 Wirer's hook-in unit
64 Singular chap
65 Stated definitely
68 Van Gogh environs
69 Snake-house updater
72 Chapeau's milieu
73 Growl
74 Comfy
75 "African Queen" scriptwriter
76 About
77 Trinity figure
78 Vision of pink elephants
82 Was a histrio
83 Cape Cod resort
85 Nigerian group
86 Lilienthal's org.
87 Have ambitions
89 Cloppy shoes
91 Luck
94 Composer Robert Emmett ——
95 Desert salt
96 Wagnerian roles
98 Penless exams
99 Physicist's report
101 African language group
102 Classical "Whoopee!"
103 Receives rightfully
104 Second man
105 Bar legally
106 Hangouts
107 Resign
108 Like Vic or Bailey

DOWN

1 Alarm activator
2 Vieuxtemps or Wieniawski
3 Boccaccio's "The —— Heart"
4 Spartan serfs
5 Integuments
6 Soviet aircraft
7 Top of a suit
8 Uhlan exercise
9 Bête noire
10 Wind: Comb. form
11 Mindoro neighbor
12 Chiding words
13 Caricature
14 Von Weber opus
15 Inflation casualty
16 Woody copse
17 Lost a lap
19 Yesterday's Yule log
24 British truck
25 Valentino special
31 Do a cop's job
32 Watson, Holmes et al.
34 "Il Convivio" author
35 Billet-——
36 Icky eats
37 Book by E. E. Cummings
38 Repotted herb
39 In shorter supply
40 Thumbs-downed
41 Stickum
43 Water carrier
44 Basin adjunct
46 Cleansing agent
48 Pun
51 Offer a view
52 Cousteau crewman
53 "Lulu" or "Zaza"
54 Charismatic leader
56 Anacreon's birthplace
58 Reproductive body
60 Hogan
61 Heavy's look
62 Makes "it"
63 Pisa's river
65 Trims rims
66 Ecole verb
67 Owner's paper
69 Domini's partner
70 Fiasco
71 River in Morocco
74 Rainless
78 Angers
79 Kickbacks
80 Princess in Verdi's "Don Carlos"
81 Discerned
82 Skipper's order
84 "What news on the ——?"
86 Craving
87 Clay house
88 Marsh waders
89 Choiceless worker
90 Place that causes us to get tired
91 Skull: Comb. form
92 Chocolate source
93 Sumerian storm god
95 Did a Little skit
96 Duration
97 —— packing (fire)
100 Huon Gulf port

Comic Capers

By Frances Hansen

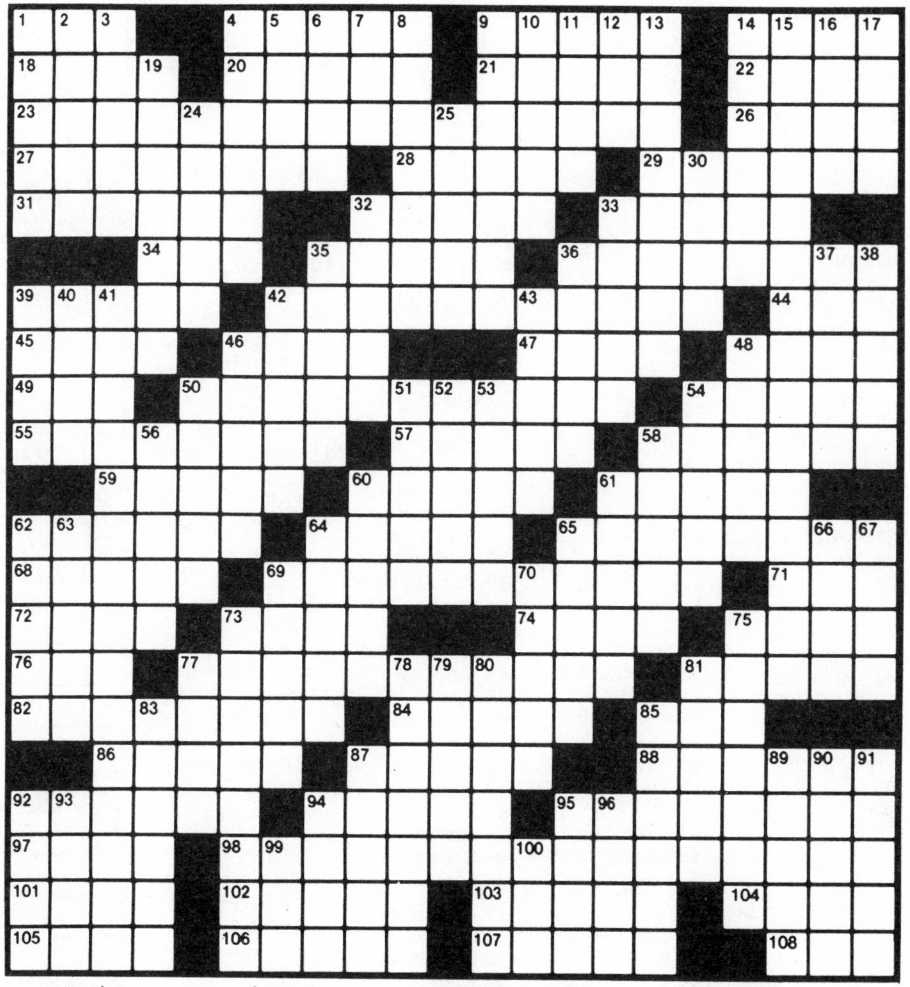

ACROSS

1 Vestment
4 Nahuatl
9 Fatty
14 Become warmer
18 Brian ——, early Irish king
20 Firenze cynosure
21 ——-doodle-doo!
22 "L'Espiègle Lili" artist, —— Giffey
23 McManus caper
26 N.T. book
27 Handel's "Messiah"
28 —— Novo, Benn's capital
29 Uproar
31 Despot
32 Tank part
33 Swiss city on the Rhine
34 Anthem author
35 Radio device
36 Expo '67 city
39 Start of a dicker
42 Goldberg caper
44 Baba
45 Legal claim
46 Amer. League rival
47 City in Sicily
48 Med. college subject
49 Huxtable or Rehan
50 Morley caper
54 "You ——," forerunner of "The Potts"
55 Whirlpools
57 Dodge
58 No sharps, no flats key
59 Aye-aye or maholi
60 Church society of Iowa
61 Sword, in Surrey
62 Capp's Lena et al.
64 "—— Want Your Kisses," 1929 song
65 Elastic
68 "La Bohème" stage prop
69 Messick caper
71 Town ESE of Little Rock
72 Anti: Abbr.
73 Take to one's heels
74 Frequent co-star of tot shots
75 Prearrange
76 Ump's relative
77 Willard caper
81 Flag background
82 One of a musical "76"
84 Parlor selection
85 To a man
86 "For her eyes were —— . . .": Arnold
87 Iloilo is here
88 Voyager Vasco
92 Firstborn
94 Simon ——, noted bass-baritone
95 Small singer in a loft
97 Café au ——
98 Browne caper
101 2900, to Nero
102 White poplar
103 Warehouse
104 Golda
105 "For Pete's ——!"
106 "The Velvet Fog"
107 Like a popular girl?
108 Football-field meas.

DOWN

1 Monastery head
2 London van
3 Pipe type
4 "Tobacco is —— weed": Hemminger
5 Pueblo Indian
6 Deli order
7 Ubiquitous puzzle bird
8 Director of "The Godfather"
9 Sweet potato
10 Diva Lehmann
11 Radarscope reflection
12 Mike's partner, in comics
13 "First Chief" of Mexico
14 Kind of bullet
15 Terry caper
16 Feed the kitty
17 TV's Batman
19 Not captured
24 Dead duck
25 Becloud, as a windshield
30 Dog star
32 "Un —— in Maschera," Verdi opera
33 Famed pioneer
35 Dagwood's "soaks"
36 Gambling game
37 Where Crockett died
38 Metric measure
39 King of Norway
40 One of Sandy's kin
41 Capp caper
42 Hen
43 —— dog's life
46 Connection
48 "Living is ——": A. Huxley
50 Ataturk
51 Dud
52 Svelte veldt animal
53 —— Kinte, Haley ancestor
54 "Forever" girl
56 Doctrine
58 Addition word
60 Revoke a legacy
61 Secretary of Commerce: 1969-72
62 Cupid's target
63 "Buck Rogers" Sunday artist: 1933-58
64 "Goodnight" girl
65 Age in the "Alley Oop" strip
66 Cure
67 "—— Cassius has a lean . . .": Shak.
69 Flaxen
70 Full of tang
73 "—— I was . . .": Dryden
75 Bunyan's Christian, e.g.
77 Business degrees
78 Out on a limb, in a way
79 Sir Gareth's lady
80 Under restraint
81 Aptitude
83 "—— in St. Louis, Louis"
85 Put on a pedestal
87 The 23d is comforting
89 Westminster, for one
90 Ocean sunfish
91 "Sgt. Fury" artist
92 Desirable trees?
93 The "one-L" priest
94 "Rome of Hungary"
95 Felix, in France
96 Dickinson's "thing with feathers"
99 Swedish name of Turku
100 Zeta-theta connection

126

What's in Two Names?

By Bette Sue Cohen

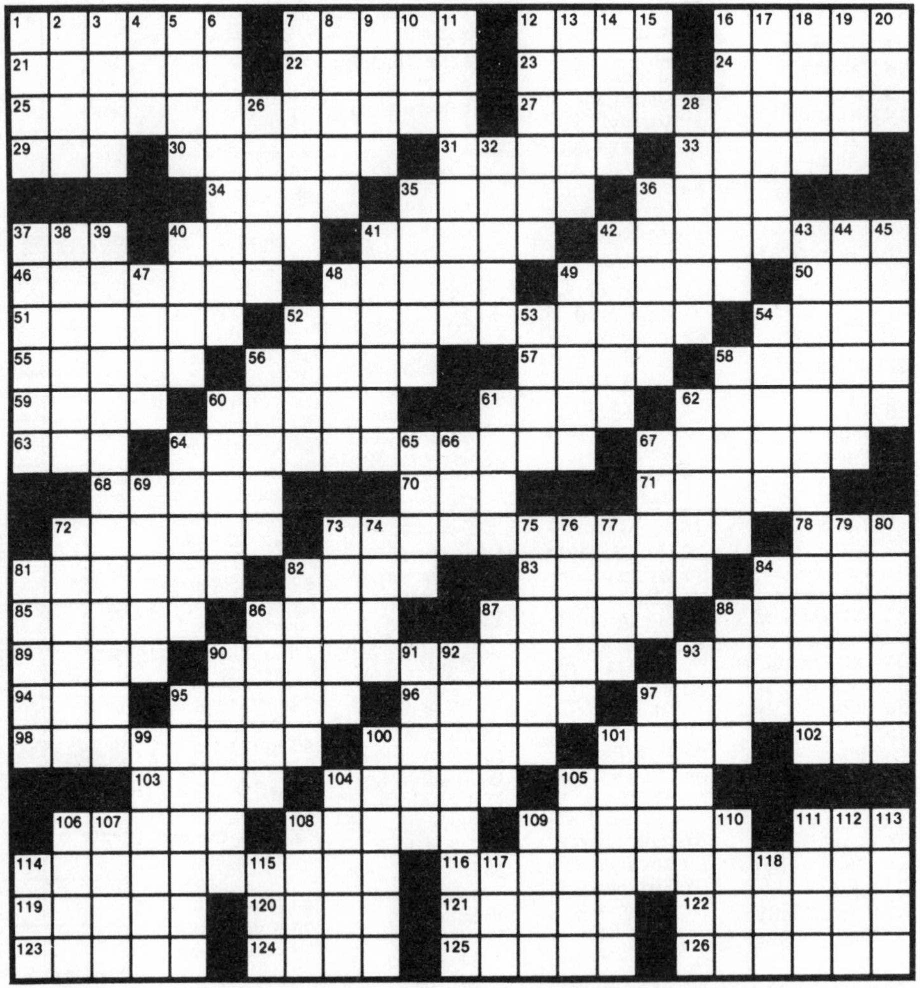

ACROSS

1 Fleet of warships
7 Stitched
12 Date of Columbus's last voyage
16 Rein
21 Jayhawker's neighbor
22 Impulse conductor
23 Very long time
24 Quantity of paper
25 Kubrick code word?
27 Cantrell gymnast?
29 Lacrosse team
30 French star
31 Certain lions
33 Two on the dial
34 Track
35 Garde predecessor
36 Kind of therapy
37 Cardiology chart, for short
40 Theorbo's kin
41 Poland Chinas
42 Concerns of coaches
46 West Germanic language
48 Writer Alexander
49 Recompense
50 Word with finch or thorn
51 Breakfast cereal
52 Segal seethes?
54 Bog
55 Expunge
56 Judicial writ
57 Trevi throwaways
58 Greene of "Bonanza"
59 Kind of photo
60 Ulrica, in "Ivanhoe"
61 —— Raton, Fla.
62 Straw-filled mattress
63 Airline abbr.
64 Ratoff measure?
67 Endorsed a passport
68 Holm
70 N.Y. time
71 All possible
72 Deepest, as thoughts
73 Fisher a liturgical singer?
78 Song syllable
81 Least restrained
82 Role for Liz
83 Upper-crust group
84 Baseball feature
85 Some gaits
86 Poe product
87 Leinsdorf or Korngold
88 —— Bay, N.F.L. team
89 Collections
90 Taylor pile at Las Vegas?
93 Contribute
94 Metal casting
95 Initiated
96 Condition
97 Discouraged
98 Like a stage setting
100 —— de visite
101 A star of "Cinderella Liberty"
102 Epoch
103 Bauxite and stibnite
104 Molding edge
105 Tinge
106 Campus orgs.
108 Friable
109 Corrigenda
111 Stole
114 Washington beach?
116 Wimsey products?
119 Typewriter type
120 All-conqueror
121 Poetic muse
122 Red-ink entries
123 What Sen. Dole does?
124 Hauls
125 Rent again
126 Long wooden bench

DOWN

1 Type of D.A.
2 Kyle of football fame
3 Lament
4 Bonnie Franklin role
5 Printer's delta
6 Nymph transformed by Artemis
7 Italic language
8 Glorify
9 Stirred up
10 Ethyl follower
11 Gathering by inference
12 Dorothy or Molly
13 Started a rubber
14 Atomic particles
15 Balin of films
16 This puzzle has 529
17 Stimulate
18 Crust
19 Hawk on Olympus
20 Form or fume prefix
26 Conrad short story
28 Burglaries
32 Mother of Perseus
35 Conscious
36 Fisherman's net
37 Decadent
38 Red Bordeaux
39 Chaplin attendant?
40 Ceil
41 Pushy person
42 Grain sorghum
43 Booth sanctuary?
44 Got rightfully
45 Pleasant
47 —— en scène
48 "—— evil"
49 Like winks
52 Rum drink
53 Political union
54 Bicuspid's neighbor
56 Royal celebrity
58 Device using light rays
60 Surfer's surface
61 —— noire
62 Central point
64 Sleekness
65 Old name for Tokyo
66 Plato's penultimate letter
67 Fodder plant
69 Widgeons
72 Like poetic justice
73 Burstyn from Detroit
74 Does
75 Unctuous preparation
76 Albee heroine
77 This goes to your head
79 Sword
80 Blake of "Gunsmoke"
81 Blinders
82 Intrigue
84 Spanker, e.g.
86 Judicial apparel
87 Les —— -Unis
88 Like Hammett's "Man"
90 Alcove
91 Nicholas and Boris
92 Ecdysiast
93 Property items
95 Frost subject
97 Muchachos' abodes
99 Make marginal markings
100 Muezzins
101 Bugs Bunny treat
104 Hood's missile
105 Minoan's land
106 Get one's goat
107 "Step ——!"
108 Lake or singer
109 Inclusive abbr.
110 Tropical plant
111 Outdo
112 Turgenev's birthplace
113 S. African fox
114 J.F.K. or H.S.T.
115 Abzug adornment
117 Before, to Spenser
118 Utah Beach craft

Truncated Titles

By Tap Osborn

ACROSS

1 Kind of gear or jacket
5 Town freed by the Allies: July 18, 1944
9 Legendary eagle rider
14 Teasdale
18 Where Waikiki is
19 Olympian blood
20 Undernourished lamb
21 Subatomic particle
22 "Metamorphoses" author
23 Countless
26 Lean
27 Watson flub
28 Decided on
29 Sicilian city
30 "—— newt . . .": Shak.
32 Borg boomer
33 Novel of 1847
34 Actress Joan: 1909-79
37 Lockout
43 Weaver and Campbell
44 Inkling
46 Zest
47 Burden, to Bardot
48 ——-eyed (angry)
49 Court dance
51 F.D.R.'s medium
52 Bandleader Fields
53 Substitutes
55 Far-from-frail male
56 Lee ——, former boxer
57 Strange
58 Spot for a shot
59 Big name in cameras
63 Bursts of energy
66 Kitchen utensils
69 Saw
70 Monotonous drumbeats
72 Eternally
73 Roman public-works head
75 Wave, in Avila
76 One of a pack at a track
78 Details
82 Flask size
84 Clayey
85 Chuddar
86 Singer Tennille
87 "And what —— rare . . ."
88 Monitor lizard
89 Facient
90 Arrested
91 Vanishing point
94 Stand
97 Golfer North or Bean
98 By way of
99 Pisces follower
100 Holly of Dixie
101 Duct
104 Future execs
105 Penitence period
109 Forgone
112 Grab-bag contents
113 Feudal flunky
114 Goal
115 Part of an arrow
116 The Storting meets here
117 Ship's minor officer
118 Subordinate
119 Brief sentiment
120 Carina

DOWN

1 Unsettled
2 Wall overhang
3 Amida Buddha sect
4 Summer squash
5 Grouper's group
6 Kill-joy
7 Countenance
8 Golden ide
9 Heroic poem
10 Hair dye
11 Stake
12 Exigency
13 Parabola
14 Corporate transfers
15 Clearinghouse
16 Hurdy-gurdy
17 Upward: Prefix
19 ". . . ring —— wed"
24 Glove leather
25 San ——, Italy
31 Jets' gains: Abbr.
32 Egyptian symbol
33 Wine: Comb. form
34 "—— good cheer": Matthew
35 Gull grouping
36 City on the Oka
38 Fruit squeezer
39 Robert or Alan
40 "The Age of Reason" author
41 Wintry
42 Develop
45 Dapper one
49 Polyhedron
50 Enzyme
51 Advert
54 Pollster Roper
55 Misogynist, e.g.
58 Spelunker
60 "—— of Divorcement"
61 N.Y.S.E. order
62 Downfallen
63 "Cut that out!"
64 Cultivation
65 Free-for-all
67 Confess
68 Ate out
71 Gay blade
74 Kind of lap
77 Word of distress
78 "—— Loves You," Beatles hit
79 A Chaplin
80 Fixed amount
81 Pitchfork part
83 Villagers
84 Active
85 High-protein staple
89 Practice
90 Caddoan
92 Redact
93 In an elliptical way
95 Through speech
96 Glossy, in Nice

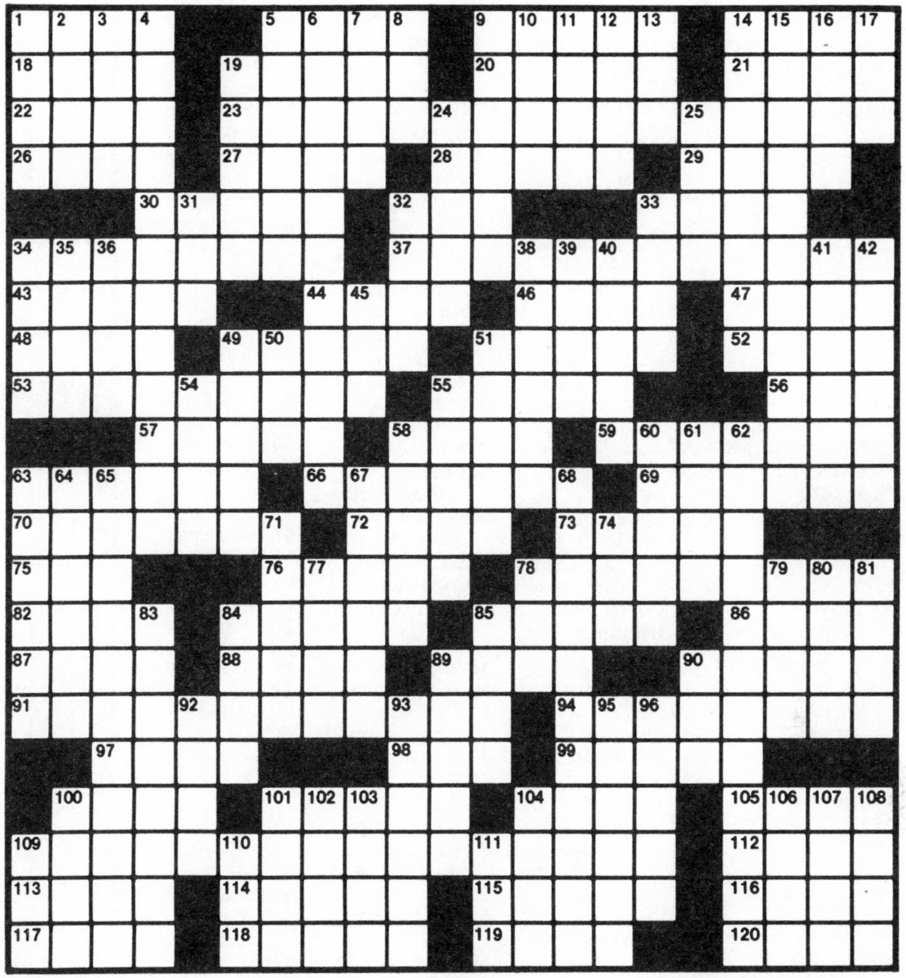

100 Words from Charlie
101 Give up
102 Aid an arsonist
103 Straight
104 Fictional detective
106 Other
107 Ludwig subject
108 Auger, for one
109 Network
110 Start of a cheer
111 Chef's meas.

Ess-capades

By Richard Silvestri

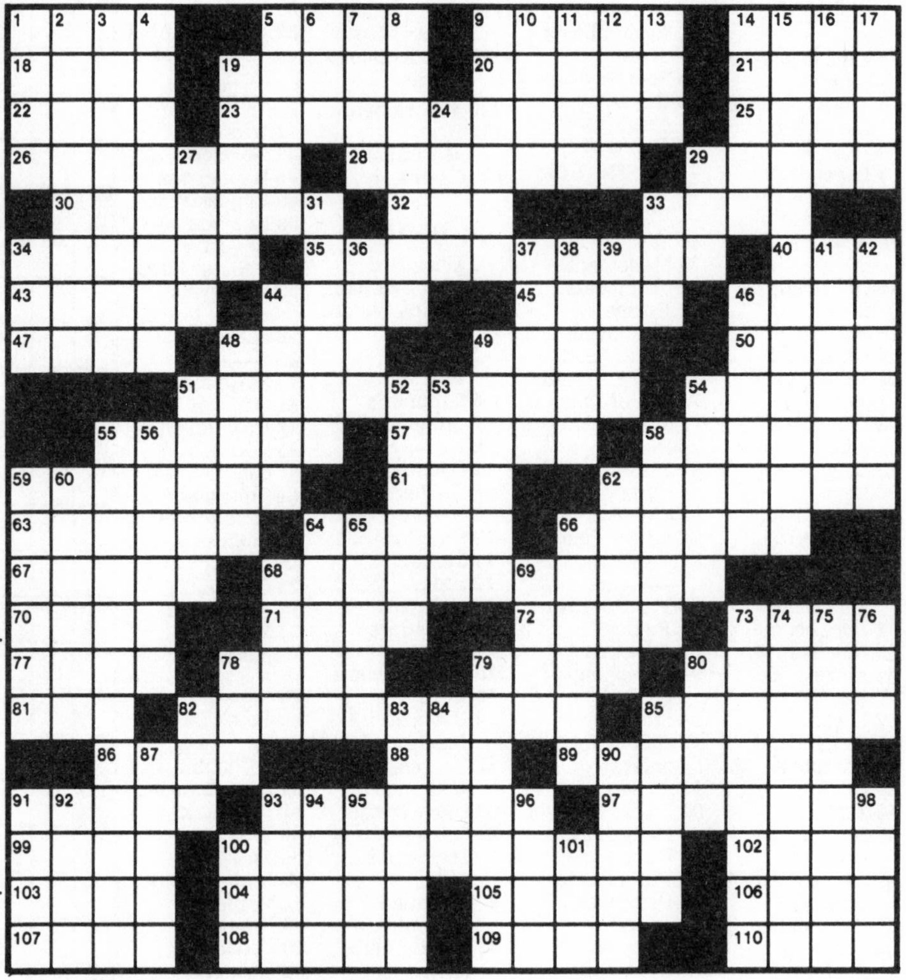

ACROSS

1 Rolling bones
5 Bric-a-——
9 Airs
14 Original sinner
18 Egyptian god of life
19 Largest city in Africa
20 Stringed playthings
21 Jungle swing
22 Surveyor's nail
23 Novelist's style?
25 Court proceedings
26 Dinner portion
28 Perturb
29 Sought information
30 Changes shoestrings
32 Yalie
33 Tiny earthmovers
34 Famed Italian sculptor
35 Violinist's bird?
40 Mack or McGraw: Abbr.
43 Data
44 Attica unit
45 Gaelic
46 Subject of "A Man for All Seasons"
47 High spirits
48 Can
49 Kind of wave
50 Take —— the chin
51 Actor's light?
54 —— as blazes
55 Opposite of nera
57 Code name
58 Raglan, e.g.
59 S. F. Smith air
61 Roadside rest
62 Boxed while training
63 Toothsome
64 Skirmish
66 "—— Restaurant"
67 General direction
68 Actor's course of action
70 Israeli port
71 Footless animal
72 Anne Nichols hero
73 Cur. units
77 Excise
78 Keep clear of
79 Ceramist's requisite
80 Winglike
81 English cathedral city
82 Comedian's drinks?
85 Songs from yesteryear
86 Jamie Green is one
88 Former times, in former times
89 Touching
91 Aptly named bird
93 Recreation
97 Adorned with nacre
99 It's played in chukkers
100 Actress's sense of humor?
102 Antitank device
103 Woody's boy
104 Show mercy
105 Likeness: Prefix
106 Amphora adjunct
107 Use a cupel
108 Prohibit
109 Euphemistic oath
110 Exigency

DOWN

1 Bespatter
2 Majestic
3 Grow together
4 Mine-shaft timber
5 Craft for Cleo
6 "6 Rms —— Vu"
7 La Scala solo
8 Clot
9 Obscure
10 I, to Plato
11 Small island
12 Zilch
13 Compass point
14 Nautical cry
15 Parent and in-law of a music-making comic?
16 Part of A.M.
17 Honey drink
19 Before seis
24 Monster of the Southwest
27 Smith and Fleming
29 Raggedy doll
31 —— Leone
33 "All the Things You ——"
34 Ger. coin
36 Weaving reed
37 Prognosticators
38 Minute amount
39 Baltic native
41 Channel
42 Let
44 About
46 Poverty, in Paris
48 Caprice
49 Social insect
51 Scottish landowner
52 Beamed
53 Paint ingredient
54 Word of woe
55 Soprano's misfortunes?
56 Pressed
58 Cardamom, e.g.
59 All the world, to Jaques
60 Proust
62 Done in
64 Finish, in a way
65 "—— and Ivory," 1982 hit song
66 Optimally
68 Hindu eclipse demon
69 Stat for Gossage
73 City board member
74 Principal highway
75 Sham
76 Method: Abbr.
78 Helios
79 Card game
80 Kelp
82 Hold a session
83 Bird dog
84 Completed a sky dive
85 "—— a customer"
87 In motion
90 Little activity
91 Young oyster
92 Lasted
93 "Wicked Wasp of Twickenham"
94 Spirited steed
95 Antitoxins
96 Grape disease
98 The Grateful ——, rock group
100 Hallucinogen, for short
101 —— ton soup

129 Of Clocks and Calendars

By Louis Sabin

ACROSS

1 About 17 million sq. mi.
5 Boards walker
10 Dig hard
14 Early victim
18 Roman clan
19 Title for Macbeth
20 Popeye's nemesis
21 Gad
22 Edward G. Robinson film: 1948
26 Puts out of mind
27 Face, militarily
28 Finances
29 Notice
30 Back a hand
31 Patron saint of France
32 Gen. Eaker
33 —— bonne heure
34 Deserve
35 Scarlett's place
37 Harper Valley org.
40 Comden and Green musical
47 Playboy
48 Onassis
49 Ad —— committee
50 Indonesian island group
51 Gershwin tune
55 Maxwell Anderson play
58 Switch words
59 Court segments
60 Con job
62 Outdistances
63 1, 66 et al.
64 Kind of ear
65 Twist
66 Progeny
68 Trigger or Champion
70 Solar disk
71 Farm sound
74 1940, 1980, etc.
76 "—— Rose"
79 Long times
80 Foe of Isr.
81 Needlefish
82 Buck's follower
83 Words from Berlin
91 Harvest goddess
92 Speeds
93 Counterpart of Rizzuto
94 Trap
95 Teen-ager
96 Japanese deer
97 D.A., e.g.
98 Coat-label abbr.
101 Used a radio
103 Circus member
104 —— de Troyes, 12th-century poet
106 Command-ment command
109 Rose Bowl, for one
110 Ever
111 Cache
112 Church calendar
113 Attic township
114 Golfing goals
115 Bristlelike parts
116 Incapacitate a hawk

DOWN

1 "—— Dei"
2 Net
3 Fireplace
4 Tennis celebrity
5 Pose —— (endanger)
6 Intone
7 Soviet news source
8 "—— Clear Day"
9 Hideaway
10 Mucilages
11 Strong brown
12 Hagen of the stage
13 Open-air blaze
14 Amphitheater
15 He played Hopalong Cassidy
16 Certain dates
17 A bandleader for Doris
20 Sluggish
23 Collection of numbers
24 Matisse
25 Roberto of the ring
31 Coarse cotton
33 Attention-getter
35 Leather strip
36 Ad-agency item
37 Cookbook word
38 Ponies
39 Tar's agreement
40 About
41 Midnight or dawn, e.g.
42 Snare beats
43 L.A. section
44 Goddess of discord
45 Water down
46 Jacques's cup
52 Prohibit
53 Long and slim
54 Met bass-baritone
55 Primes a timepiece
56 Terry or Burstyn
57 Ring unit
61 15-15 or 40-40
63 Oven item
65 Outburst
66 Kind of single
67 Monthly items
68 Seasons
69 —— -de-loup (military pit)
70 Make —— for (defend)
71 Gaby's spouse
72 Presently
73 "I had rather be —— . . .": Shak.
75 Buttoned weapon
77 Protection
78 Put up a swing
79 Jungian concern
84 "Butterfield 8" author
85 Rider's command
86 Chief
87 "Mene, mene, —— . . ."
88 Homes, so to speak
89 Thrust forward
90 Badgerlike animal
95 Dipper
96 Comedian Mort and kin
97 Now, in Tijuana
98 Vers ——
99 Crystal-lined stone
100 Sign up
101 Busy place
102 Term ender
103 Autocrat
104 Shoot the breeze
105 N.M. mecca for artists
106 Turf
107 Penn, for one
108 The hallux is one

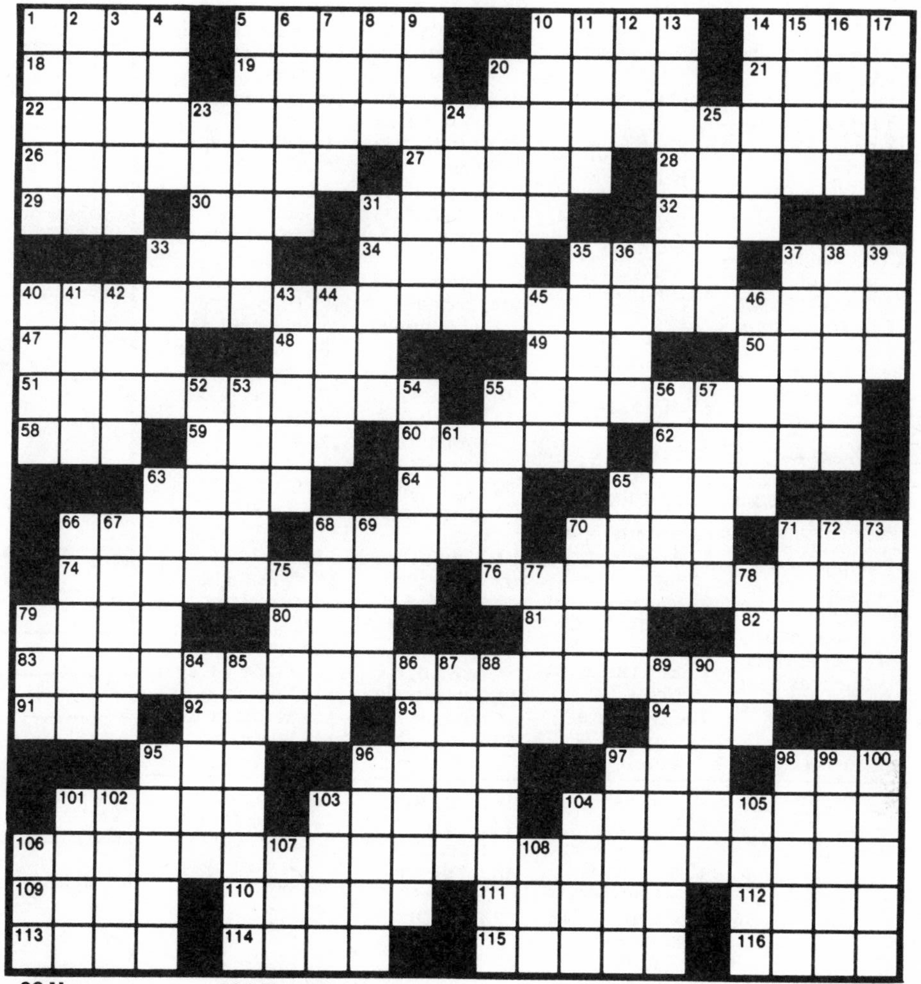

Global Situations

By Maurice J. Teitelbaum

ACROSS

1 He wrote "The Chocolate Soldier"
7 Rome Beauty
12 Kind of whale
17 Vola
21 Lindsay's partner
22 Cutting tool
23 Part of Pliny's wardrobe
24 Drought victim
25 German store employee?
27 Rook support
28 City east of Callao Bay
29 Lhasa ——, Tibetan dog
30 The "Splendid Splinter"
31 Libyan law enforcers?
34 Drupe
36 Trig
38 —— de plume
39 Former Hyde Park resident
40 Liech. neighbor
42 Feet: Fr.
44 Part of NATO
45 Dustin Hoffman role
50 New Jersey money changers?
55 Assigns
56 American Beauty
57 Sydney Pollack film: 1982
58 Hyson, e.g.
60 Omahas' homes
61 Place for an aspiring lt.
62 Fish trap
63 "Ode to ——": Collins
64 English scholar: 18th century
65 Fourth Estate
67 Angel's sign of joy
69 Farm adjunct
71 Basis of std. time
72 Bell ringer, at times
73 Enrapture
77 Vaudeville family
78 W. Hemisphere group
79 German U.N. employee?
81 Luckman of football fame
82 E. Indian herbs
84 Michigan entertainers?
85 Paste
88 French explorer
89 Cry heard at St. Andrews
90 Burns's always
91 Sageness
93 Entertain sumptuously
95 Bombast
98 Tec, at times
100 Use a Mason jar
101 Fidel's friends
102 Vein's glory
103 Member of some families
105 Sideswipe reminder
106 Certain alley buttons
107 Russian ranch hands?
110 Procedures before a deal
111 Clarence or Doris
113 Lucy Ricardo's friend
114 Norse underworld queen
115 Expressions of surprise
117 Nice friend
118 Reduce a fever
121 News feature
125 Ohio coachman?
131 Requisite for a good R.N.
133 Dippy or dotty
134 Hot spot
135 C'est- —— (that is to say)
136 Turkish hotel V.I.P.?
139 An element
140 Pitch
141 Theologian's principle
142 Strong
143 Sight from the Ponte Vecchio
144 Feather grass
145 M.I.T. grads
146 Wields or strives

DOWN

1 Row
2 Figure of speech
3 La Croce —— (Red Cross, in Italy)
4 Parade of a sort
5 Pvt.'s home away from home
6 Amish, e.g.
7 Start of a kindergarten refrain
8 Kabul currency
9 Most comely
10 N.Y. line
11 Light
12 —— Thurmond of S.C.
13 Snooker, e.g.
14 Meredith's "The ——"
15 Scaramouch
16 Verse form
17 Game having chukkers
18 Tamiroff
19 Vitamin C source
20 Picayunish
26 Author Kesey
32 Stance
33 Aggressive tyrant
35 Center of interest
37 Prone
41 Glossy fabric
43 Samuel's teacher
44 On the Marmara
46 Actor Ray
47 African entertainer?
48 Like some grasses
49 Aryan people of Caucasia
50 Author de la ——
51 English therapist, perhaps?
52 Cambodian family
53 Keystone —— of early films
54 Tpk.
55 Pulitzer Prize dramatist: 1967
56 Molders
59 Musical upbeat
62 Symposium topic, for Plato
63 Bloomery worker
66 Sch. groups
67 Small electronic organ
68 Deer playground
70 White House monogram
73 Apr. collectors
74 II x DXXV + I
75 Otic: Comb. form
76 Prefix for play or band
77 Type of fly
79 Impediment
80 Resolution time in Toledo
81 Pother

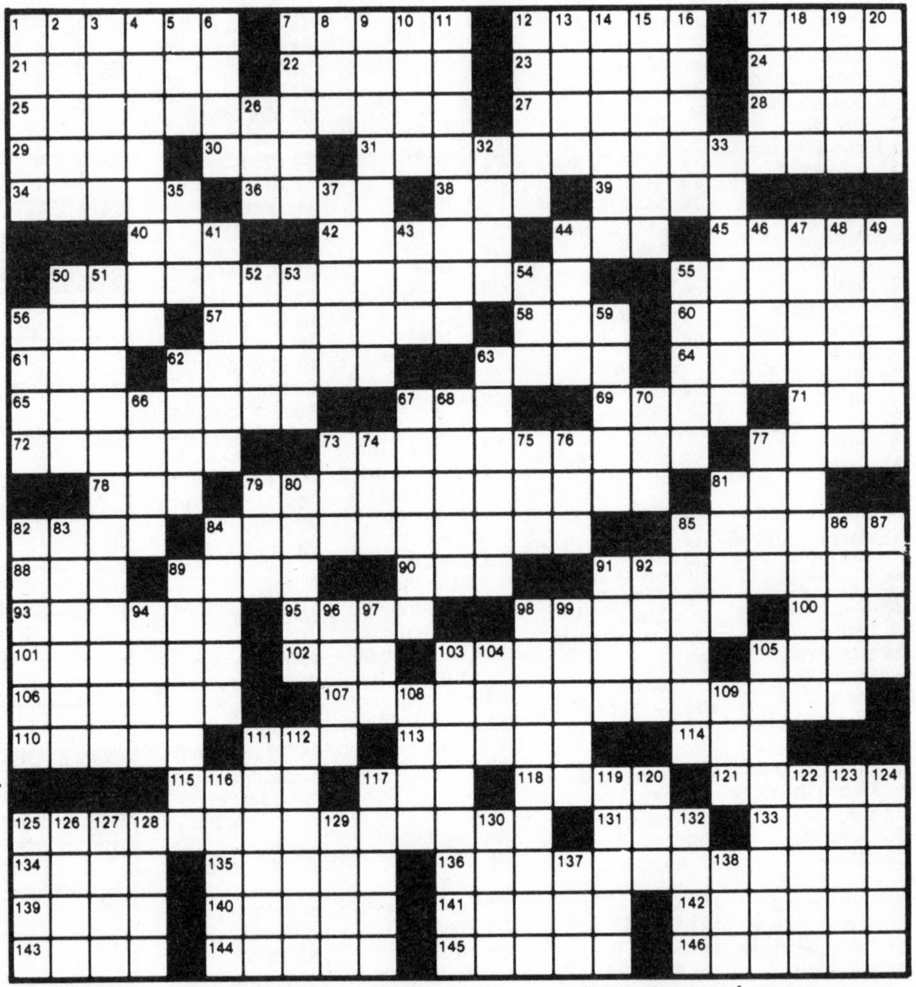

82 "—— -boom-de-ré"
83 Kitchen visitors of yore
84 Loamy deposit
85 Drama-school subject
86 Radar displays
87 Transmitted
89 Vagrants
91 In —— (in position)
92 Danish measure of length
94 U.S. author: 1909-55
96 Host
97 Avant-garde member
98 Bathroom fixture
99 Put to use
103 Cause to function
104 Scale note: Var.
105 Deputize
108 Trucking rig
109 Pronoun
111 "Sapho" and "Jack" author
112 Town near Perugia
116 Girders
117 Type of theater
119 S.o.'s and e.r.a.
120 Wahoo
122 Bird, e.g.
123 Mole, maybe
124 Widgets
125 Popular flavoring
126 Wireless word
127 Not pinguid
128 Ruin
129 Result when a tap isn't tip-top
130 A Churchill successor
132 Horn, e.g.
137 Suffix with law or saw
138 Associate of Luna

Group Dynamics

By Carol Dutting

ACROSS

1 Kitchen emanation
5 Nell of the Old Curiosity Shop
10 Fruits for Fabius
14 Ham's acknowledgment
19 Goddess of breezes
20 Jack roll
21 Caspian feeder
22 Expunge
23 The "family"?
26 Page of songdom
27 Vaisya is one
28 Take it all back
29 Had the flu
30 Scrubs the mission
32 Next to
33 Coe, Ryun et al.
34 Gloomy
35 Crazy as ——
36 Brave one
37 Where Kerman is
38 Calorie counters' kitty?
42 Adherent: Suffix
45 Catchall abbr.
46 Medic
47 Places
48 Wildebeests
49 Scottie's refusal
50 Shipshape
52 N.H. city
55 Ins. men
56 Grim Grimm characters
58 Selfless love
59 Struck
60 Shunt
62 Produce
63 One of the tunas
65 Atlas feature
66 Credulous
67 Wolfish looks
68 Common or proper word
69 TV device
71 Flit
72 Otho's dom.
75 Heidi's milieu
76 Army
77 Thrash
78 Hawk's delight
79 Séance signal
80 Jokesters' melee?
85 Relative of neo
86 Manifest
88 Mansard extensions
89 Did some road work
91 Hash mark
93 Pollen bearer
95 Annoy
96 He wrote "Marius the Epicurean"
97 Cucujo's cousin
98 Starchy roots
99 White poplar
100 7 A.M. stampede?
105 Tendrils
106 Feminine suffix
107 Weird
108 Italian town
109 Curves
110 At no time, to Tennyson
111 Discourage
112 Does

DOWN

1 Dolt
2 Half a quartet
3 Hockey great
4 Masked "bandit"
5 Ballroom dance
6 Schisms
7 Suffix with persist
8 Sgt. or Cpl.
9 Concerning that
10 Tosca's creator
11 Companion of Artemis
12 Seine feeder
13 Norwegian fjord
14 Garage sign
15 Divine revelation
16 Quilting bee?
17 Depside is one
18 Wallace and Whitelaw
24 Sites for drums
25 Do a lawn job
30 Trunk in a trunk
31 Two fans?
32 Lobbyist group
33 Bernstein heroine
34 Appearance
35 Energy source
36 Tenth part: Prefix
39 Keats was one
40 Run off
41 Elegance
43 All together, in music
44 City of the Ruhr
48 Winning hit: Slang
50 Waste allowance
51 Fun rm.
52 Cato's tongue
53 Century plant
54 Bird or Johnson
57 Shady spots
59 Avian feast
60 Libyan coin
61 —— Gay
62 André or Amaro
63 The voice of Porky Pig
64 Celtic sea god
66 Tammany Hall lampooner
69 "Rocky" actress
70 Mud hen
71 Place for a don
73 "Olympia" painter
74 Urge
77 Govt. agents
80 Hold down
81 Part of a partridge
82 Literary sketch
83 Glutted
84 One in a rage
85 Like a cardinal
87 Hurdy-gurdy: Fr.
90 Baseball family name
91 Modern frontier
92 Restraints discussed by Freud
93 Roof material
94 Sample
95 Successor to Bess
97 She was once bottled up on TV
98 Cause for a civil suit
101 Bee follower
102 Suffix with Annam or Assam
103 P.O. decision
104 Sun. talk

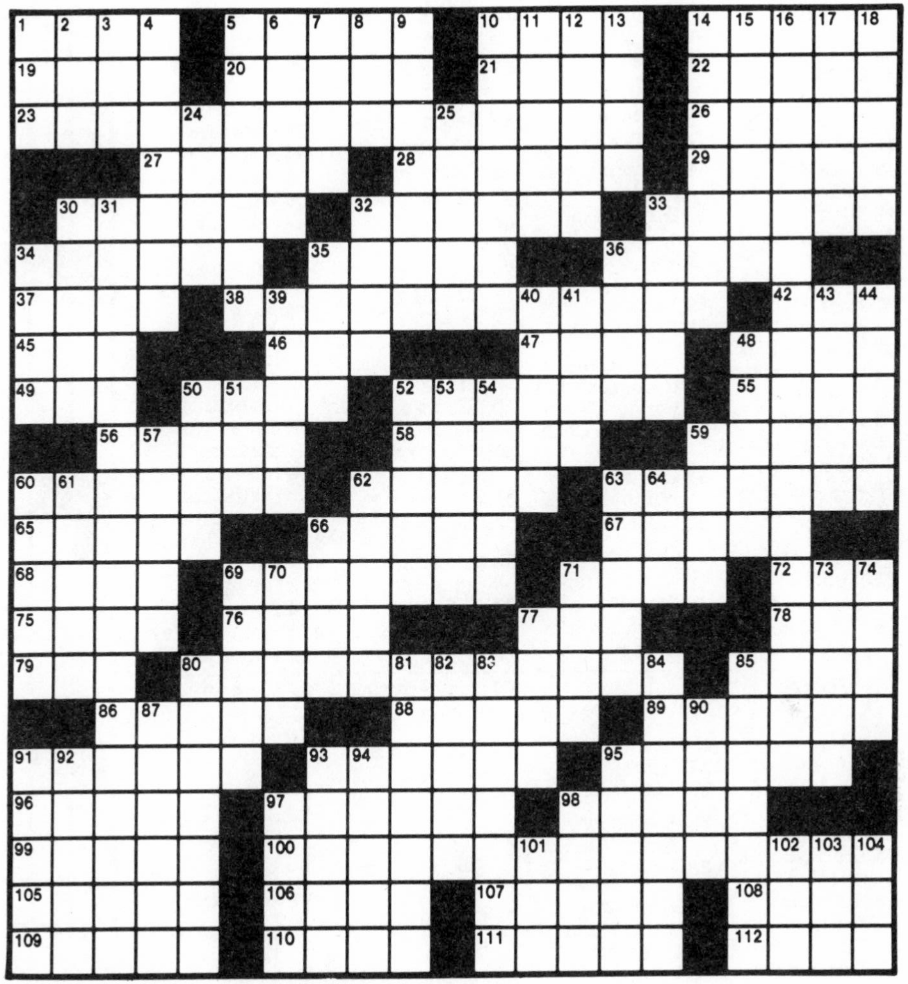

Socraticisms

By Robert H. Wolfe

ACROSS

1 Actor Clunes
5 Caterpillar, e.g.
10 Type of slipper
15 Cat sounds?
18 Yucatán Indian
19 Shun
20 Handsome man
21 Finial
22 Anatomical passage
23 Tropical fish
24 "—— Gurton's Needle"
25 Pithy bit of wit
26 What you do on the Aegean?
29 —— and all
30 Leaders at Sigma Chi
31 Colima coins
32 Summit: Comb. form
34 Valuable African tree
35 Humiliate
37 The nominees
40 Eccentric old chap
43 Object of adoration
44 Harvest goddess
47 Girl in "East of Eden"
48 Sigmoid moldings
49 Butter
50 Proof mark
52 Musical sign
53 Escapees from Pandora's box
54 What the Corfu ewe did?
57 Call at Wimbledon
58 "Nana" actress
60 Newscaster Seamans
61 Extorts
62 Assemble
64 Summoned, in a way
66 Broker's concern
67 Hades denizens
68 Fourth caliph of Islam
69 Forward
70 Youth org.
73 What the obese Athenian did?
77 Bakery implement
78 U.S. novelist: 1815-82
79 Daboia or jessur
80 100 square meters
81 Bristles
82 Insects' nests
83 N.Y. time, at times
84 Pitfall
85 Rose oil and neroli
86 Have —— for news
88 Out of dough
90 Hebrew month
91 Faiths: Sp.
92 Caesar, e.g.
94 Water bird
98 Pastries?
100 What Red Adair might do in Ionia?
105 Bill's possible future status
106 Pass
107 Super Bowl losers: 1983
108 Ancient Andean
109 Cry at Yankee Stadium
110 Interact realistically
111 Indo-European
112 Useful Latin abbr.
113 Omega
114 Betrays
115 Middle, in law
116 Potion portion

DOWN

1 Moslem princes
2 Batten
3 Keep an —— (look after)
4 Coaches
5 A.F.L.-C.I.O. member
6 Reluctant
7 She wrote "I'll Cry Tomorrow"
8 Don Corleone
9 Call it ——
10 Not dense
11 Jazz ensemble
12 Chilean timber trees
13 Kind of market
14 L.B.J. appointee to the Supreme Court
15 Isocrates?
16 Well versed in
17 Spot
20 Fevers
27 Fakes
28 A stone for Jimmy Carter
33 Affrays
35 West from Walla Walla
36 Complete failure
38 Aligns
39 Hugh O'Brian role
40 Helix
41 Oeillade
42 What the poker player did in Patrai?
43 Where Kurdish is spoken
44 Domesday Book money
45 Flintstone's daughter
46 Beene or Klein
50 Gugelhupf, e.g.
51 Sleeping
54 Course of a sort
55 Cook's exhortation
56 Kind of belt
58 Javanese vehicle
59 Ugandan pest
63 Feeling of uneasiness
64 Cram
65 Corolla petals
67 Blemish
69 Chirp
71 Wither
72 City in S France
73 Best of films
74 Falstaffian
75 Somber shade
76 Dies ——
77 Numbed with fear
81 Bronco's booth
84 Hoopla
85 —— Virginia Woolf
87 Glacial ridges
88 Explosions
89 Indian princess
90 Pithecanthropus, for one
92 Stone chip
93 Shock
95 Monte ——, Corsica
96 Son of Zeus and Callisto
97 Hymnist John Mason ——
98 Ashen
99 Image
101 Nautical term
102 Moslem prayer leader
103 Monza money
104 —— and means

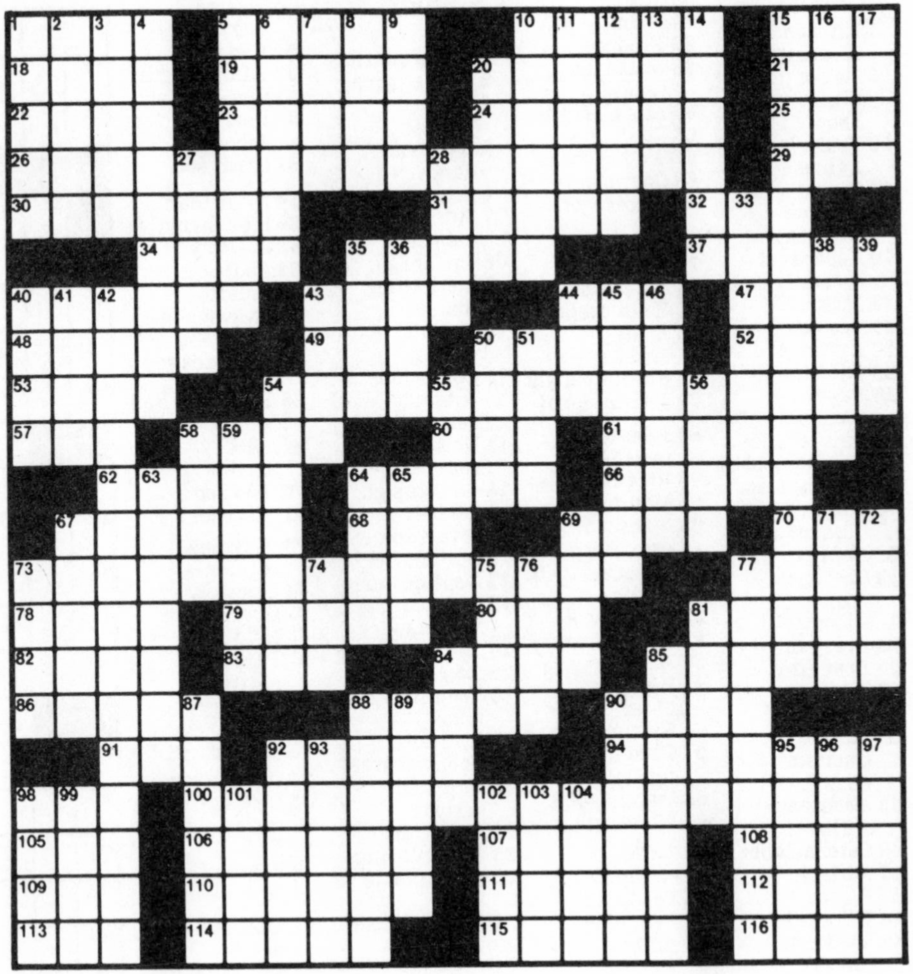

133

Openers

By Edward Marchese

ACROSS

1 Surface-to-air missiles
5 —— behind the ears
11 India's —— Plateau
17 Respiratory ailment
18 O'Neill was one
20 Take a breath
21 "... GETTING ON IN YEARS ..."
23 Wading birds
24 Weapon-makers
25 Ending for disrupt
26 Homeland of Ajax
27 Vestiges
28 Bored ——
32 Type of coffee
33 Roach or Chase
34 "THE DOOR OF HENRY'S LUNCH-ROOM OPENED ..."
37 Consumers' agcy.
40 Chekhov heroine
42 —— Tower, Chicago
43 Do finger painting
45 Iceberg part
46 Metric units
48 Demolish, in Devon
51 Accident
53 Kind of voice
56 "I WON'T GO TO BED ..."
59 Short melody
60 Cry of contempt
61 A former capital of Burma
63 Pebbly-surfaced fabric
64 Founder of New Harmony community
65 Primped
67 Malign
68 Musical suite
71 Kin of ophidiids
72 Cossack chief
74 French novelist: 19th century
75 Journey stage
76 Rib
78 "CALL ME ISHMAEL"
81 Sensitive: Fr.
83 Gusset
85 Booted one
86 —— clear blue sky
88 Asian festival
89 Biblical builder
91 Helpers
92 Show surprise
96 Time div.
97 "GRANTED: I AM AN INMATE ..."
101 School org.
102 Sun —— -sen
105 Dinesen offerings
106 Group of soldiers
109 "... —— of cloud": Browning
112 For shame!
113 He pops the question
115 St. Vitus' dance
116 "IT WAS LOVE AT FIRST SIGHT"
119 Firmly settled
120 Change into steel
121 Glasgow or Drew
122 Like Chippendale
123 Wane
124 Transfer

DOWN

1 Highlander's purse
2 Deviation of a sort
3 Bordeaux wine
4 Sword for Raglan
5 V.P. under G.R.F.
6 Room for a pres. or prin.
7 Bounty stopover: 1788
8 Twaddle
9 Annul
10 Mos. upon mos.
11 Limoges piece
12 Diarize
13 Spicy fare
14 "BUCK DID NOT READ THE NEWSPAPERS ..."
15 Utah ski resort
16 Promontory
17 Christie
18 Relig. discourse
19 Rheine's river
22 Referendum choice
28 Laconic
29 Approves
30 Sunfish
31 Mrs., in Córdoba
34 Start of a hole
35 Part of a lamp
36 "Zero- —— Society": Thurow
38 Double radius
39 Perquisite
41 —— Pasha
42 Pitcher Carlton
44 Tad
47 Lendl of tennis
48 Peruses anew
49 Italian fashion designer
50 Goad
52 Massé, e.g.
53 Strong urge
54 Lurched
55 "... I WAS BROUGHT UP IN PICTURES"
57 Grimes and Wynette
58 Knots in cotton fiber
62 "Giselle" composer
66 To exist, to Ennius
67 Pachyderm's pal, in pictures
69 Erskine and Mercer
70 Marine hazard
73 Hell
77 Fulmar's kin
79 Coconut fibers
80 African antelope
82 Xanthippe sort
84 A touch of rum
87 Pro ——
90 Words of delight
91 Cooler
93 Bartholomew or Simon
94 Disseminated
95 Benefactor
98 "... —— the odds": Housman
99 Eye ailment
100 Sister's son's sisters
103 Main artery
104 Aviary sound
106 Swindle
107 Chose
108 Games authority
109 Topmost: Comb. form
110 Turkestan salt lake
111 Bale
113 Troy meas. unit
114 Dakota Indian
116 Steinbeck character
117 Otto I's dom.
118 Shoe shade

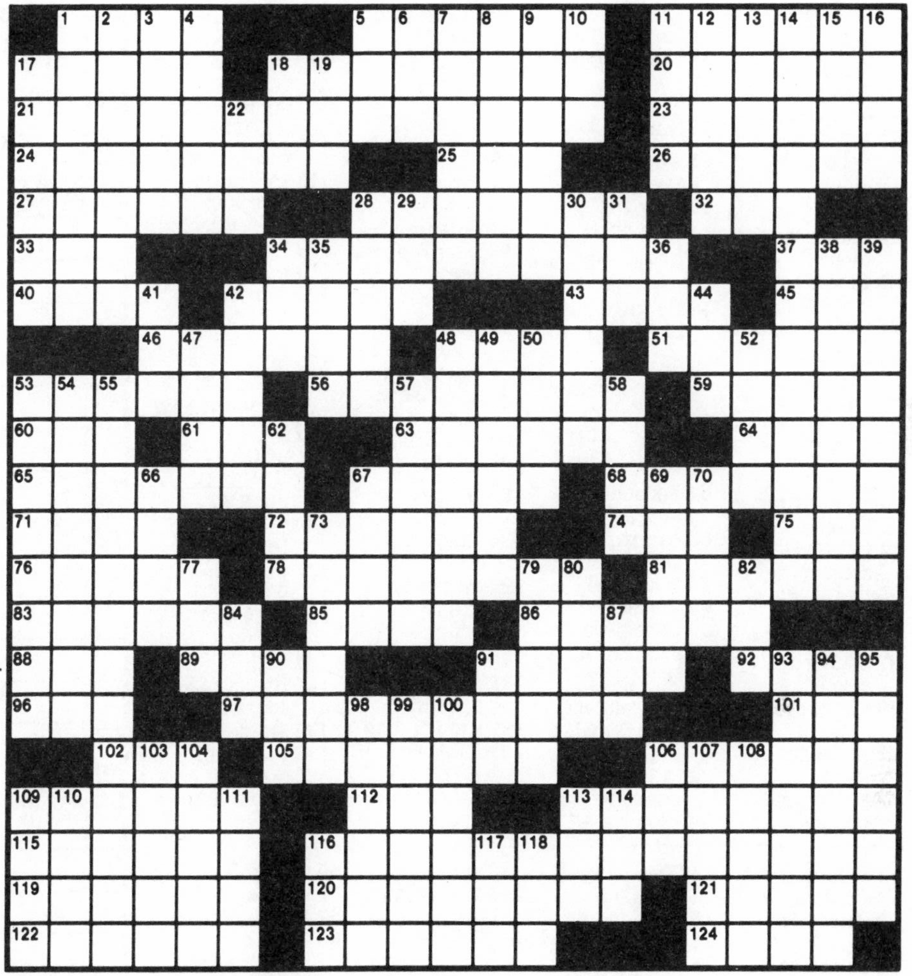

Now You C It . . .

By Judith C. Dalton

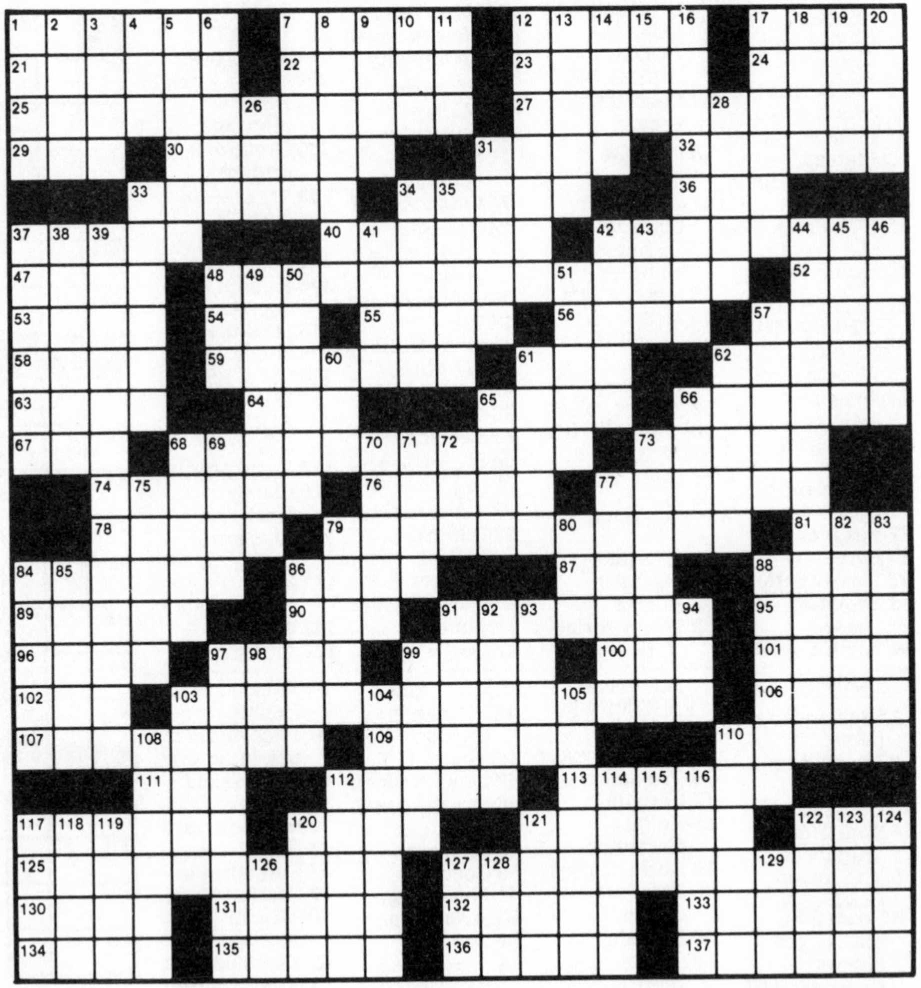

ACROSS

1 Take long steps
7 Render weaponless
12 Priest's neckcloth
17 Squeal
21 Like Pinocchio
22 Martinique mount
23 Pisces neighbor
24 German hall
25 LIONS, TIGERS, BEARS, etc?
27 BEAUTICIAN?
29 Golfer's gadget
30 Mandarin, e.g.
31 Corrals
32 Chewed the scenery
33 Lee or Starr
34 Separate
36 Anti
37 Sourdough's concern
40 Wicker's "A —— Die"
42 Arranges in twos
47 Shoots the breeze
48 BARD'S LAMENT?
52 Fla. neighbor
53 Away from the wind
54 Número ——
55 Airfield at Paris
56 Otaria member
57 Winter Palace resident
58 Political birds of a feather
59 Spanish painter called "El Divino": 16th century
61 Evergreen
62 Londoner's quart
63 Astern, to Drake
64 Headland
65 Former Congolese prime minister
66 Top kicks
67 Sch. subject
68 AGED BODY PART?
73 "Close ——," pop song
74 "Rock ——"
76 Hurdles for would-be Ph.D.'s
77 Richardson heroine
78 External
79 MONGOOSE?
81 Circular: Abbr.
84 Core groups
86 Derr Biggers hero
87 Corded fabric
88 Date of Columbus's last voyage
89 A Mousquetaire
90 —— Cruces
91 Too full
95 Grapevine disease
96 Heath for Heathcliff
97 Silvers or Harris
99 Sough
100 Parseghian
101 Preacher's sign-off
102 Kind of song
103 READY FOR EVEREST?
106 Zola heroine
107 Speed up
109 —— -order (tailored)
110 Trigonometry ratios
111 High, in music
112 Greek communes
113 Indulge in forensics
117 Fruity cocktail
120 "—— soit . . ."
121 Love song
122 Nonpro athletes' assoc.
125 SCRIPT DIRECTION FOR SALLY?
127 MUSIC, SCULPTURE, PLUS LOTS MORE?
130 "Rome of Hungary"
131 Power in "Star Wars"
132 Billy and nanny
133 Tell
134 Hyson and oopak
135 Staid
136 Pastrami order, often
137 Douay Bible's Ezra

DOWN

1 Catch a fly
2 Enameled metalware
3 Function
4 Marriage words
5 Spoil the shape of
6 —— nous
7 Topple
8 Former London prison
9 ". . . sin to tell ——"
10 Bro. or sis.
11 Fly type, for short
12 Charon's river
13 Intended
14 'Tis, in toto
15 Mongrel
16 Outstanding
17 Cuts of beef
18 Concupiscence
19 Lily plant
20 Alexander's men
26 Chinese dynasty: 202 B.C.-A.D. 220
28 Atlanta university
31 Fall guy
33 Do a lab division
34 Love, in Livorno
35 Decorticates
37 He played Tarzan
38 Lowland, to a laird
39 OPTIMISTIC ORANGUTAN?
41 Golden calf, e.g.
42 Feather: Comb. form
43 U.S. druggists' org.
44 KILN DEFENDER?
45 Fusee
46 Cabbie's arithmetic
48 Molasses distillate
49 Arranged neatly
50 Quagmire
51 Willow
57 Alpine region
60 Cinder
61 "The Way of All ——"
62 Hen
65 Otiose
66 Indefinite amount
68 She wrote "Angel of Light"
69 Sweater sizes: Abbr.
70 Namesakes of Chaplin's widow
71 Monitor lizard
72 "Mighty —— a Rose"
73 Finnish city
75 Rage
77 Assembly-line house
79 Commandment word
80 Sandy's plaint
82 —— Councils (A.D. 325 and 787)
83 Ross and Dors
84 Bivouacs
85 Go on —— (make merry)
86 Actor Eastwood
88 Villain
91 Meteorologist's device
92 Dinesen products
93 Module
94 Nabokov novel
97 Bishops
98 Chinese secret society
99 Don Shula's team
103 Bicuspid's neighbor
104 Editor, at times
105 Decorum
108 Eton boys' parents
110 Goggles
112 Musically smooth
114 Rub out
115 London's Big ——
116 Conductor Previn
117 Track event
118 Cherbourg cherub
119 Graceful tree
120 Thyme or sage
121 Sirius or Mizar
122 At a distance
123 "—— boy!"
124 Employs
126 Five score
127 In the past
128 Nessen or Ziegler
129 Borough council rep.

Colloquial Company

By Bernice Gordon

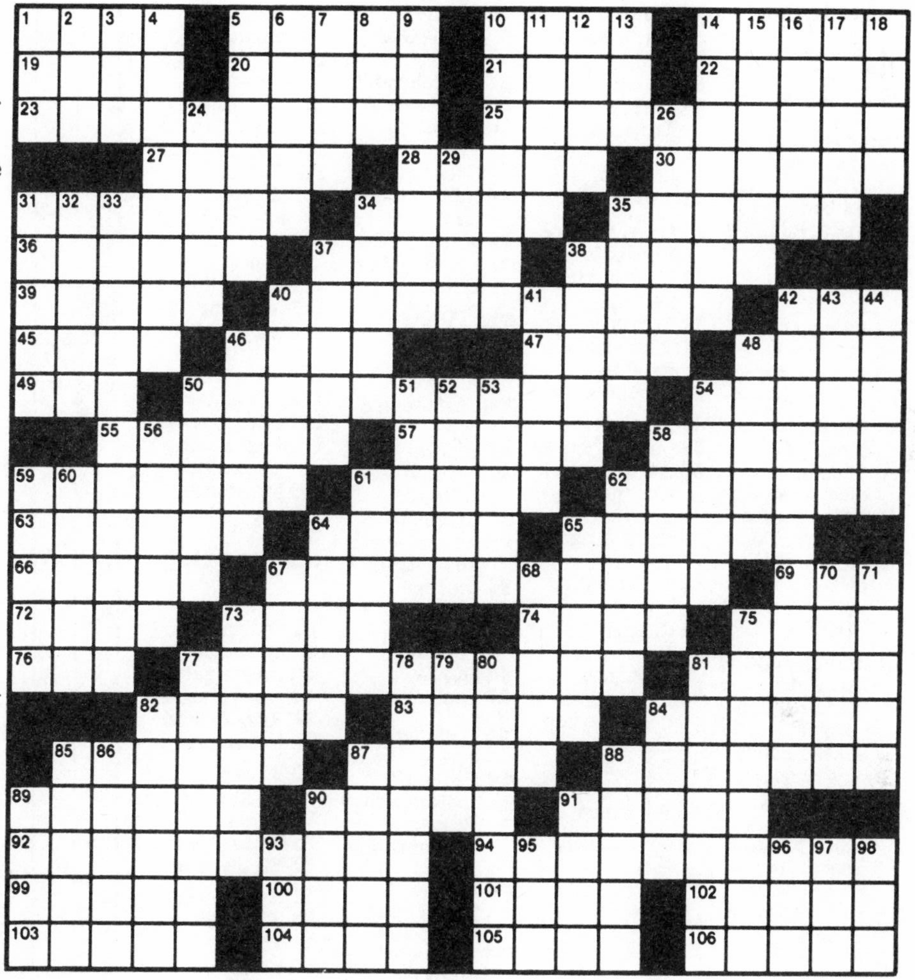

ACROSS

1 Move, in checkers
5 Onward in time
10 Sea lettuce
14 Burgeon
19 Novello
20 "Falstaff," e.g.
21 Source
22 Skin ailment
23 Carlo Maria Giulini
25 Warren E. Burger, at times
27 Spills the beans
28 Mother-of-pearl
30 Princes in Afghanistan
31 Pitiless taskmasters
34 A Monet contemporary
35 Overcharges
36 Companions of Pan
37 Skirt insert
38 British carbines
39 "Boys Town" won him an Oscar
40 Rona Barrett
42 Davis or Hyman
45 Legal wrong
46 Secular
47 Galley gear
48 —— bunting (a finch)
49 Y.M.C.A., e.g.
50 Burt Bacharach
54 Fixed relation
55 Applied cosmetics
57 Flat ring on a bit
58 Bandleader Stan
59 Checked
61 Frigid and Torrid
62 Winner at Wimbledon: 1925
63 Stories or crayons
64 Neural networks
65 Book of the O.T.
66 Guanaco's home
67 Joan Rivers
69 Religious letters
72 Property charge
73 Arrest progress
74 "—— bien!"
75 Kind of ball or bank
76 Buzzing beetle
77 Steve Martin
81 Line or twine: Fr.
82 Stable youngsters
83 Shriver, to Kennedy
84 Region in ancient Palestine
85 Manhattan garnish
87 Tradesman, for one
88 Site of a rock-carved lion
89 Fern leaves
90 Concert piece
91 Bridge ace
92 The Murrays
94 Tillie the Toiler
99 American dogwood
100 Further
101 Nothing, to McEnroe
102 Solo, in St.-Lô
103 Style of Vermeer's work
104 Unclaimed piece of property
105 North Sea feeder
106 He painted "The Great Forest"

DOWN

1 Arm of a crane
2 Grape
3 Witty saying
4 Lengthen
5 Author of "The French Lieutenant's Woman"
6 Menilites
7 Guns the engine
8 Pavarotti's three
9 Trompe-l'oeil painter: 1848-92
10 Accumulation of cinders
11 Grasp
12 Stage and screen star
13 Append
14 Light cotton fabric
15 Matures
16 Remove dowels
17 Jury members
18 Seamen
24 Wanting
26 Badgerlike animals
29 Access
31 Keno's kin
32 Slip
33 Mario Andretti
34 Produce a chemical change in
35 Kay or Bart
37 Started suddenly
38 Baronne de ——-Holstein
40 Beat
41 Fixed courses
42 Larry Holmes
43 Tumultuously
44 Progeny of a sort
46 Equipment used in Winter Olympics
48 Portage item
50 Cattails
51 Emulated Rice or Oates
52 Homer's tongue
53 Take an oath
54 Come up again
56 Frequently
58 Glacial ridges
59 Cook slightly
60 Character in "I Pagliacci"
61 Piquant
62 Nixon or Johnson
64 Brooklets
65 Kind of driver
67 Cox of "Mr. Peepers"
68 Volatile oil
70 Its capital is Chengchow
71 Borg is one
73 San Simeon resident
75 Roscoe attachment
77 Chef's garnish
78 —— sale and fare
79 Etats-——
80 With smoothness
81 Nimrod's need
82 He has a duel role
84 Assamese adviser
85 Water holder
86 —— armor (unwieldy ironclad)
87 Iranian dialect
88 Trained horse
89 Kermit of the Muppets
90 Soft palates
91 Shackle
93 Child's marble
95 Memnon's mother
96 Attila was one
97 They loop the Loop
98 Harm by exposure to moisture

Initial Drop

By John M. Samson

ACROSS

1 Massage
4 Evade
9 Medieval helmet
14 Nobelist in Literature: 1957
19 Gibbon
20 Kind of squash
21 Charter
22 Ammann's sect
23 Avoir. weights
24 Rent anew
25 Arterial trunk
26 Nouveau ——
27 English songbird?
30 Certain monuments
32 Half a snicker
33 Supreme Court member: 1955-71
34 Babilonia et al.
36 Command to a canine
37 Stable
38 Sheppard-Turpin gun
39 Incandescent linguist?
42 Overwhelm
45 Started a pool
46 Big endings
49 To scent, in Sevilla
51 Trip in a ship
53 Playwright Ionesco
54 Ascended
57 Invalidate
59 Cowboy's need
60 Designer with a young lady in mind?
62 He never grew up
65 Musical dir.
66 "Sometimes —— Goes By"
67 Apprehend
69 Habituate
70 Formerly
71 Pronoun
72 Greek
74 Nast uprooted him?
76 White poplar
78 Va. neighbor
79 Limit
80 Opposite of "exeunt"
82 Actress Allgood
84 Legionnaire's cap
85 Secret
87 "The —— See of You"
89 Originate
93 Actress who's misbehavin'?
96 Dull one
98 Highlands hillside
100 "—— Old Cowhand"
101 —— vu
102 Dieter's no-no
104 You, to Johann
105 Confesses
107 Clever actress?
109 Heat-resistant glass
111 Hilo hello
113 Atoll part
114 Song from "A Chorus Line"
115 Ham it up
116 Subsequently
117 Bête follower
118 Poetic preposition
119 Moistened
120 Trample
121 Flout
122 Irish golfer Smyth

DOWN

1 Bellamy and Edwards
2 Certain baton strokes
3 Scatter about
4 —— Hood, "Our Gang" actress
5 Lindy's hurdle
6 Looker
7 W.W. I
8 Hop the Orient Express
9 Beef —— mode
10 Speed Wagons
11 First First Lady
12 Admiration
13 Gunpowder item
14 Custody
15 Gaston, to Alphonse
16 Actress who deserved her Emmy?
17 Peck's early job
18 Radiance
28 Elbow-wrist link
29 Tartan wraparounds
31 Caine role: 1966
35 Silk filament
37 Odin's counselor
40 Fatuous
41 Entomb, in a way
43 "—— Flanders"
44 Satisfy
47 Tempts
48 "Gentlemen, be ——"
50 De Soto contemporary
52 Property incumbrance
54 Short journalistic addendum
55 Lawyer who made his mark?
56 A Khan
58 Defeat soundly
60 —— Islands, near Fla.
61 Sediment
62 Boz or Ouida
63 Investigate
64 "—— Fables"
68 Razzle-dazzle foursome
70 Have
72 Reddish brown
73 Foray
75 Clubs, e.g.
77 Hit the road
81 Protuberant
83 Will Durant's wife
84 Famous trailblazer?
86 Warmblooded group
88 Commands
90 Soprano Moffo
91 Sequoia
92 Apprentice
94 Scold
95 Altogether
97 Discourages
98 Man, e.g.
99 Nash forte
102 Cubic meter
103 Absolute
105 Fired
106 Noah's eldest son
108 Author Wiesel
110 Summer, in Somme
112 Dadaist Jean ——

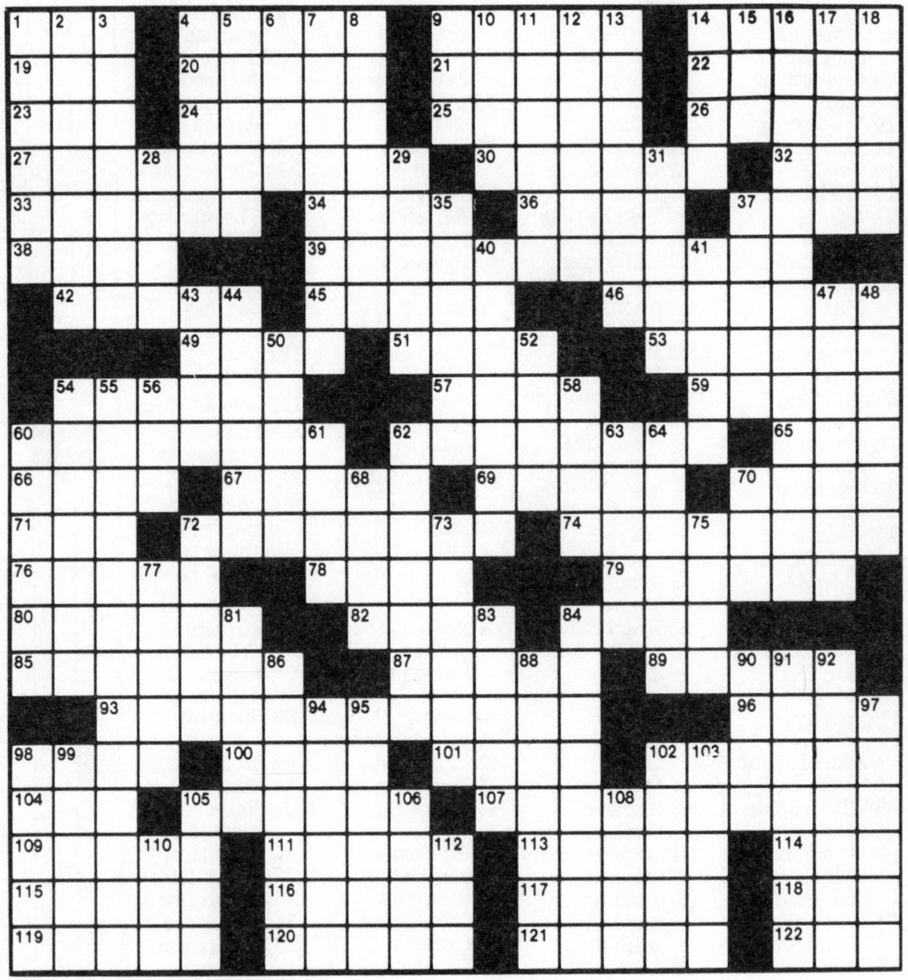

137

Diamond Chips

By Peter G. Snow

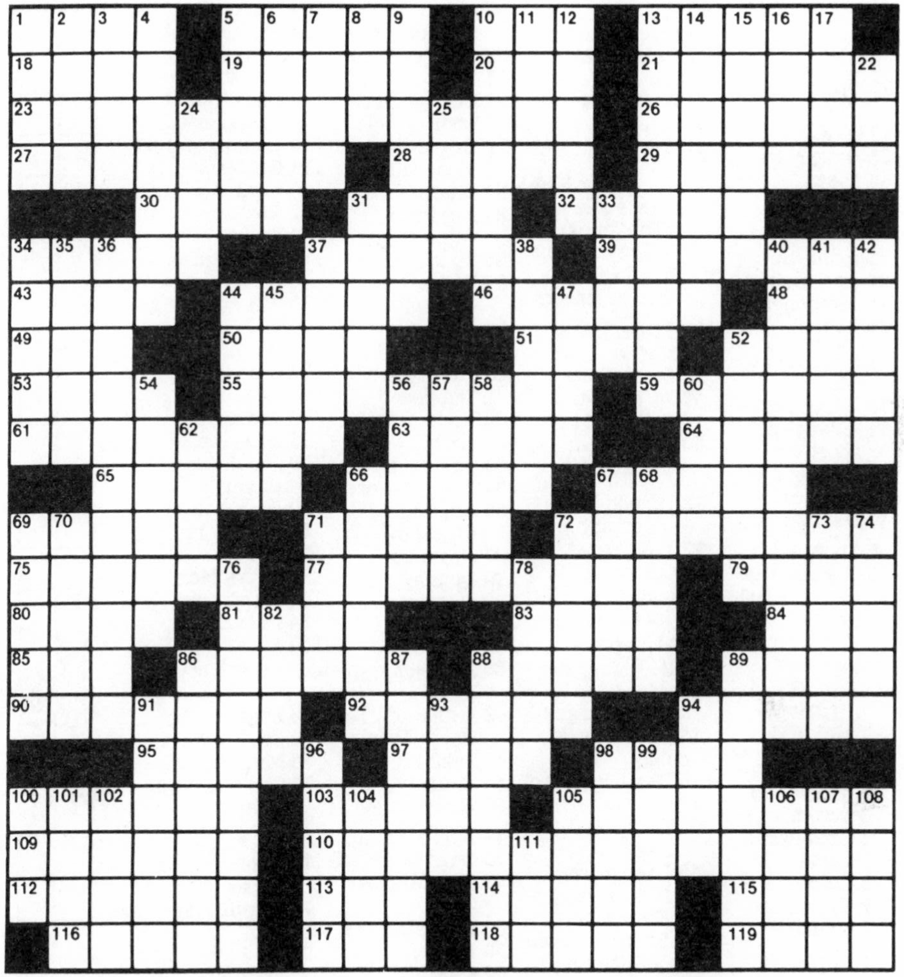

ACROSS

1 Secure
5 Postpone
10 Dowel
13 Swallows greedily
18 Fortas and Vigoda
19 M. Zola
20 Household god
21 Gluck products
23 Make a start
26 One of the weasels
27 Powell and Steber
28 Change type
29 Tulsan, e.g.
30 Wed.'s predecessor
31 Type of belt
32 A London suburb
34 —— up (gives info to)
37 Opposite of dynamic
39 Area of potential trouble
43 Titles of courtesy: Abbr.
44 Two-reel movie
46 West Indian Indians
48 General Eaker
49 Viral infection
50 Gas: Comb. form
51 Singer Simone
52 Merkel and O'Connor
53 North Sea feeder
55 Have a bull session
59 Stains
61 Jimmy and Gloria
63 Anglo-Saxon slaves
64 Titter or snicker
65 Dyer's "Your Erroneous ——"
66 Insults
67 Fatten
69 Antigone's uncle
71 Ear of grain
72 Constraining
75 River horses, for short
77 Type of accident
79 Aural
80 Escapees from Pandora
81 Role for Oland or Toler
83 —— Reekie (Edinburgh)
84 Overly
85 —— culpa
86 Tool for smoothing plaster
88 Hair plait
89 Cartoonist Lazarus
90 Souls or minds
92 Trigonometry term
94 Less desirable
95 Chopped
97 Units of acceleration
98 Flock talk
100 Collect in condensed form
103 Aptly named 19th-century novelist
105 Trust
109 Smallest quantities
110 Ridic
112 At the tip
113 Galena, e.g.
114 Prohibited
115 Steep, rugged rock
116 Relieve
117 Virginia Clemm's bridegroom
118 Sexist social gatherings
119 "—— Came Running": J. Jones

DOWN

1 Judicious
2 Explorer Tasman
3 Entertain
4 Shaker Heights sights
5 "Roxana" author
6 Eastern bigwigs
7 Sapins
8 Trio in Lilliput
9 Flag-lowering ceremony
10 Flexible
11 Slacken
12 Actress Nissen
13 —— for (defends)
14 Eradicates
15 Slot-machine items
16 School exec.
17 Sensible
22 Sun. talk
24 Blame
25 Habitual path
31 Narrow channel
33 Rap
34 Warp crossers
35 Key
36 Pressure of a sort
37 Classes
38 Film-festival site
40 Substitute in an emergency
41 Speak pompously
42 Demi follower
44 Buffalo hockey pro
45 Excites
47 Disencumbers
52 An arm of a worldwide org.
54 Pounces upon
56 Turned a lamp back on
57 Major Japanese seaport
58 Release
60 Passage for Pompey
62 —— Hegirae
66 Book parts
67 Soils
68 Imparts
69 J. Fred Muggs
70 Gets one's dander up
71 Famed Fabian
72 Vinegar container
73 Stringed instruments
74 René's school
76 Nut
78 Mends
82 Sprinkle
86 Type of underwear
87 Heir
88 Natural endowments
89 Inlays of tiles or stones
91 Superior
93 Moslem magistrate
94 Stray bit
96 Wilt; flag
98 Puzzle
99 Choir group
100 Japanese woman diver
101 Uses snuff
102 Minx
104 Large kangaroo
105 Midianite king
106 Lucius Domitius Ahenobarbus
107 Cherrystone, e.g.
108 Advantage
111 Long.'s partner

Breakfast Time

By Mel Rosen

ACROSS

1 Milquetoast
7 Caesar, for one
12 Trooper's beam
17 Rainbows
21 Have high hopes
22 Inspiration for Sappho
23 Accustom
24 Hat-trick component
25 Bacon
29 Adjust, in a way
30 Whittier's feet
31 Ways to go, shortly
32 Card game
33 Work unit
34 Old thralls
35 Shop tool
37 Greek letter
38 Georgia Tech grads
39 Comic actor Jacques
40 Printer's mach.
41 Relative of nifty
43 Rachel Carson target
44 Waffles
51 Salazar or Roe
52 He thought up "The Thinker"
53 Golfer Tommy
54 Word with shod or stream
57 Professional staff
58 Ostrich or emu
59 Suffixes for dull and tank
60 —— -Penh, Cambodia
62 Tuxedo accessory
63 Tea carrier
64 Conversational banality
65 Snacks in Sonora
66 Moray
67 Chianti, per esempio
68 More precious
70 "—— Fables"
71 Orange Juice
77 Charge
79 Bravery
80 Modernists
81 Blue
84 Big Ben's voice
85 Wainscot
86 Turner and Cantrell
88 Longfellow town
89 Sitar expert Shankar
90 Yield
91 Enter
93 Act of 1765
94 Folding money
96 Anger, and then some
97 Practice
98 Doughy pastries
99 Eggs
103 —— *favor*
106 Paid honor to
107 The last word
108 Clementine's shoe size
109 Dir. from Denver to Chicago
110 Explosive stuff
111 Gr. resistance force
112 Roster
114 Spree
117 Imposed, as a fine
119 Woodworking tool
121 Mr. Arden
122 Geometric surface
123 Toast
128 Nice depot
129 —— Jean Baker
130 Paints badly
131 Wood sorrel
132 "The —— of Laura Mars"
133 Disgusting
134 Out of order
135 Least experienced

DOWN

1 Social status
2 Assyrian's main deity
3 On the mark
4 Freshwater game fish
5 Common verb
6 Electrical device
7 "Come up and —— sometime"
8 Damascenes
9 Papa of TV's "Mama"
10 Homophone for eight
11 Leader of a small septet
12 French income
13 Ingredient in a pot
14 Club charges
15 The law's is long
16 Retracts an act
17 Taj Mahal site
18 Complained like Simba
19 Used a dray
20 Most sneaky
26 Kind of button
27 Bean produced in Burlington
28 —— mundi (opal)
34 Mansard extensions
35 Call
36 —— fell swoop
37 Dick and Schick
39 Like a harrow
40 Ushered
41 Creators of dins at inns
42 Author of "The Happy Prince"
44 Take out
45 Entirely
46 Wavy
47 Part of Spain
48 Dorothy's dog
49 Shame is his game
50 Fort Bliss site
55 Fickle
56 Kind of deck
58 Luxuriant
61 Pileup for an ed.
63 Oil-lamp feature
64 "Like —— not"
65 Oscar nominee: 1981
67 Sermon subject
68 Zygote
69 Sci-fi vehicle
70 Mil. addresses
72 Christening activity
73 Got even
74 Winless race horse
75 Result of six outs
76 Base; average
77 Summit: Comb. form
78 "—— is the question"
82 Medieval helmet
83 Kind of maniac
85 Put an end to
86 Master
87 Capital of Western Samoa
88 Make amends
90 An M.V.P. in 1980
91 Leaf pore
92 Puts in line
93 Postcard feature
95 Examined and filtered
98 Founder of a D.C. institution
100 Kind of machine
101 Biblical spy
102 Pass a bill
103 Animal fur
104 Arrowed street sign
105 Put on a pedestal
111 Pound and Stone
112 Setdowns
113 Fine-grained soil
114 Unit of energy
115 Those opposed
116 Decayed-rock material
118 April 13, e.g.
119 Sour, in Salerno
120 Portuguese titles
121 Word form with distant
122 Kind of hammer
124 Negative connective
125 Nabokov novel
126 Where some vets fought
127 Lizzie Borden's weapon

A Spell of Letters

By Alfio Micci

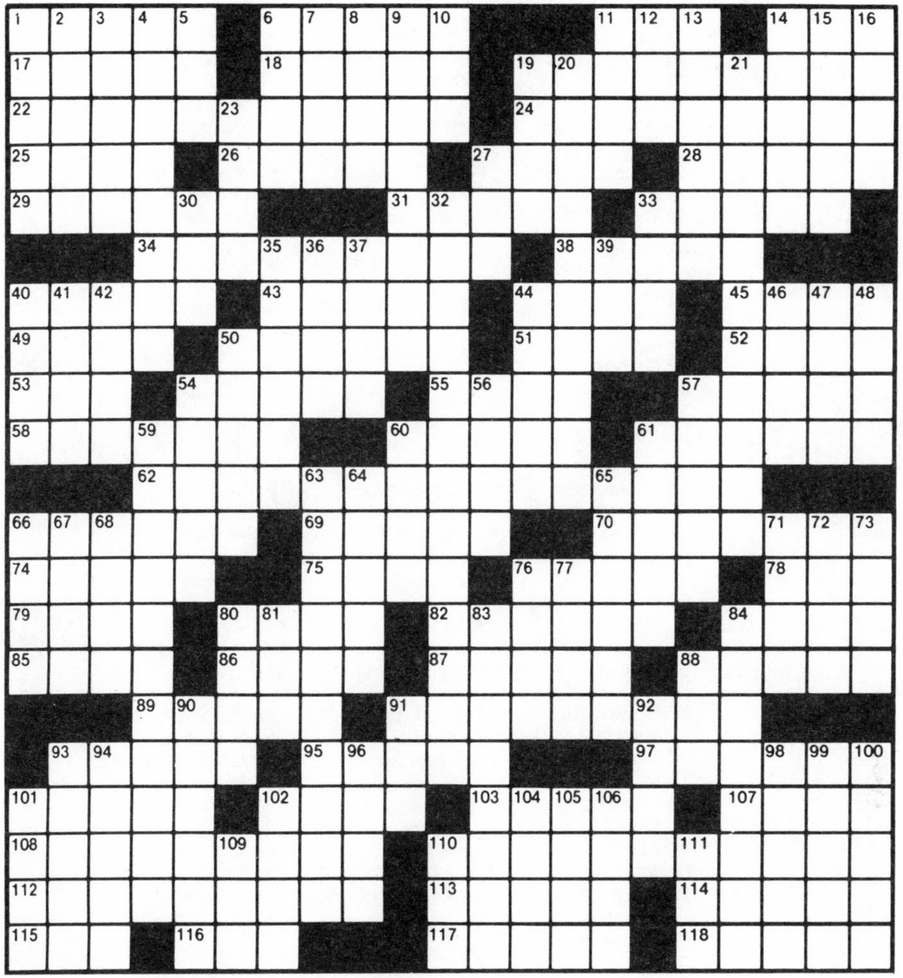

ACROSS

1 Name in an Inge title
6 Lawmaker
11 Highland precipitation
14 Shampoo additive
17 Macho types
18 Justify
19 Erudite
22 Party giver's req.
24 G.I. garb
25 Metrist
26 Unambitious one
27 "Giselle" composer
28 Ninny
29 Matriculate
31 Truman's birthplace
33 Batters
34 Youth org.
38 Commuters' haven
40 Bright stars that fade
43 Rice dish
44 Poisonous Tibetan plant
45 Skulk
49 "Green Mansions" hero
50 Alit
51 Loretta of "M*A*S*H"
52 Pa. port
53 Hubbub
54 Well-known
55 Bones, in Bologna
57 Nonsense
58 A Kennedy Center honoree
60 River of song
61 Crow, e.g.
62 Rights org.
66 Singer Smith
69 Tolls
70 A Carter
74 At —— (bewildered)
75 Playground for Pierre
76 Cooking direction
78 Corrida shout
79 Use shears
80 Little, for one
82 Plaza moppet
84 Argument
85 Cabbage variety
86 Wood quantity
87 Bridge positions
88 Upright
89 Moral
91 Govt. agency
93 Buckle
95 —— Soleil (Louis XIV)
97 Eloquent one
101 Copland ballet
102 Ardent
103 Himalayan land
107 Long vestment
108 Highway feature
110 Doctoral deg.
112 Garnished, N Italian style
113 Baseball statistic
114 Examined judicially
115 "The Gold Bug" author
116 Brynner
117 Together
118 Caucasians

DOWN

1 Mold
2 Bittern's kin
3 Moslem prince
4 Gift
5 Reply to a ques.
6 Tore
7 City on the Oka
8 Easy stride
9 Page's other side
10 Formerly named
11 Wedge
12 Fall mo.
13 Sour brew
14 Flynn or Fauntleroy
15 Word with spy or hour
16 Agree: Var.
19 Fountain treat
20 Dark-red color
21 Mil. truant
23 Unspeakable
27 "Today I —— man"
30 Soap ingredient
32 Workers' org.
33 Requirement
35 Monte ——, Ischia
36 Arachnid
37 Dull person
39 Clock numeral
40 Nothing, in Navarra
41 Cummerbunds of a sort
42 Opening
44 Soc.
46 Hindustani language
47 Latvian port
48 Wail
50 Avant- ——
54 The end
56 RR stops
57 Cyrus or Sally
59 Humane org.
60 Winged
61 Backbone
63 Elitist
64 Defy
65 Baton Rouge inst.
66 Support
67 Singer Logan
68 Besmirch
71 Hercules captured her
72 Templeton or Waugh
73 Undiluted
76 Autumn fruit
77 Stone: Comb. form
80 Grieve
81 South Seas staple
83 Livy lovers, e.g.
84 A Roe with a fishy pitch
88 Always, poetically
90 Vexatious
91 Fortify
92 Blockhead
93 Clown lashed by Nedda
94 Confuse
96 Gaelic
98 Popular morning show
99 "Martha" or "Louise"
100 Orchestra section
101 Meat cut
102 Bemoan
104 Saarinen
105 Peacock
106 River at Leeds
109 Hawaiian sarong
110 Kind of jacket
111 Slangy suffix with hot or got

Missing Links

By Mary Virginia Orna

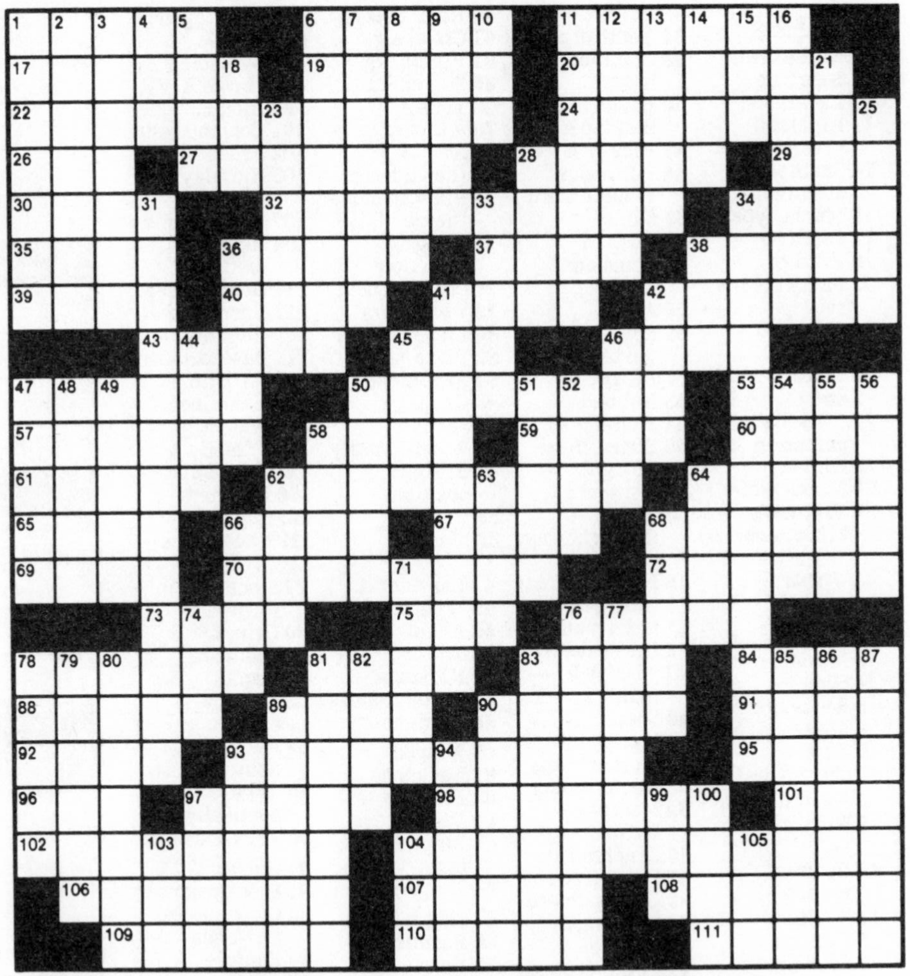

ACROSS

1 Not —— (mediocre)
6 Reporter's coup
11 Magnetic units
17 One who frankly admits
19 Nitrates-shipping city in Peru
20 Slow ballet dances
22 Unconditional Broadway hit: 1939-47
24 Lampoon
26 Suffix with press or fail
27 Infatuated
28 Fools
29 Word with play or pig
30 Rikki-tikki-——
32 Uncoordinated flag-bearers
34 "Flee, feline!"
35 Gershwin biographer
36 Skin layer
37 Empty
38 Elbow
39 Feudal slave
40 City on the Oka
41 John Irving hero
42 Frank
43 Roman household gods
45 Stake
46 Henry VIII's last wife
47 Neoteric
50 Ibo, for one
53 Vespid
57 Portuguese islands
58 Evanesce
59 Crocus, e.g.
60 Greek pitcher
61 Sculpture piece
62 Unexceptional English satirist
64 Arose
65 Star in Pegasus
66 Walesa is one
67 Sediment
68 Smelling like overripe apples
69 Lucy's Ricky
70 Used cars, sometimes
72 Wards off
73 Part of Q.E.F.
75 Period
76 Petruchio, for one
78 Doorframe parts
81 Rove on the wing
83 A Gardner
84 Former president of the U.N. General Assembly
88 Town house rel.
89 Rail
90 Symbol of slowness
91 Comeuppance spot for Gretel's witch
92 Furrows
93 Musical that allowed no speculation
95 River to the Gulf of Finland
96 Unclose, to W.S.
97 Bull and Bunyan
98 Stained
101 Costal bone
102 Off the track
104 Opera performed today, yet neglected
106 Trap
107 Suffix with form
108 Anglers' baskets
109 Magdalene, e.g.
110 West German steel center
111 Jockeys

DOWN

1 Greets
2 Subdue via fear
3 Nevertheless
4 Agcy. Elmer Davis headed
5 Asian holidays
6 Laws
7 Marsh plant
8 Pigments for Sargent
9 Upright
10 Norm for JoAnne Carner
11 Maine, e.g.
12 "Wizard" born in Milan
13 Austrian spa
14 Sponsorship
15 Ending for bishop
16 Trace
18 Physics unit
21 ". . . the ravel'd —— of care": Macbeth
23 Model's concern
25 Register
28 Off
31 Poem about a place farther away
33 Shaped like some leaves
34 Author not to boot
36 "The agony of de feet"
38 —— Huon, 1906 Derby winner
41 Novelist having no alternative
42 Baton
44 Martian: Comb. form
45 Soprano Sayao
46 Brace
47 Beat at chess
48 Aura pura
49 Nereids' mother
50 Identified
51 Gets one's goat
52 Angers
54 Revise
55 Emulate Old Faithful
56 Famed diarist
58 F.D.R. pet
62 Kind
63 Pre-Pasch period
64 Yield
66 Sch. adjuncts
68 Bactrian
71 A Bunker
74 Hudson contemporary
76 Drovers
77 Ballerina Markova
78 Boston delicacy
79 Headpiece
80 Clinic group
81 Collapse
82 Slew
83 Hemmed-in territory
85 Ate too much
86 Figaro's home
87 "Man is . . . a rope over ——": Nietzsche
89 Stick
90 Riyadh residents
93 Large gannet
94 Exams for aspiring collegians
97 Spirits of Islam
99 Catchall abbr.
100 Earl —— Biggers
103 So, in Spain
104 Banker's Fannie ——
105 Defendants, to Darrow

Human Equations

By Elaine Schorr

ACROSS

1 Light source
5 Corolla component
10 Latin-lesson word
14 Malcontent
18 Upolu town
19 Petrarch's beloved
20 Stephen V. or William R.
22 Berg's unfinished opera
23 Where Mae and Irving meet
25 Author and actor take on a builder
27 Fit for a silo
28 Unfledged
30 In sets
31 Raises the hackles
32 Horned creature
33 Make a case of it
34 Sported
37 Odorous
38 Newsy
43 Entity
44 Artist and historian stimulate growth
47 Oft passed bill
48 Deps.
49 Arrow poison
50 Sea creature
51 A noncom
52 Kipling title
53 Minnie and Asa form colorful combo
57 Attack
58 Pasture pealer
61 Sister of Ares
62 Fish workers
64 Bête ——
65 Bligh's "Halt!"
66 Less rubicund
67 Eos or Aurora
69 Couple
70 Pasadena coll.
72 Like Dracula's countenance
73 George and Gale cause turbulence
75 On the —— (busy)
77 Gun or actress
78 Egyptian queen of gods
80 Palm part
81 Beget
82 Actress Zadora
83 Ruth and Billie attend spectacle
87 Lohengrin's love
88 Heavy of heart
90 Jesse or Buck
91 U.S.M.A. member
92 Garb for a Bedouin
93 Kind of preview
94 What a caesura indicates
96 Official seal
99 Cather's "—— Lady"
100 —— to (woo)
104 Painter and botanist employ artisan
106 Monty and O. Henry summon up hotel attendant
108 Brittany's patron saint
109 Range
110 School, in Savoie
111 Toodle-oo
112 Braddock's 1935 opponent
113 Compulsory bet
114 Tied the knot again
115 Noah's heir

DOWN

1 Mosaic contribution
2 In —— (miffed)
3 Hatred: Comb. form
4 New England eleven
5 U.S.N.A. beginner
6 Some H.L. members
7 Marsh plant
8 "Exodus" name
9 Aeronautical pioneer
10 —— reo (defendant not present)
11 Apportioned
12 In a bit
13 Downing St. number
14 Bordeaux libation
15 "Too much rest is ——": Scott
16 Medicinal herb
17 Confederation
21 Small piece of tile
24 Place for a dance
26 Anthill
29 File's partner
32 Kind of berry
34 Ear covering
35 Gambado
36 Neil and Edith come to Oahu sight
37 "Love Story" actor
38 Like the start of "Hamlet"
39 Household implement, for short
40 Stephen and Julia take in waif
41 He wrote "FBI": 1976
42 Riga people
44 Ophidians
45 Anoints, old style
46 Gasconade
51 Battle royal
54 "Rosemary's Baby" author
55 Ten C-notes
56 Gambles
57 Pungent humor
59 Chief Teutonic god
60 ——-aimé (beloved)
62 ". . . Can You —— Dime?"
63 With serenity
65 Actor Delon
67 Expressions of shock
68 Whence Pompey sailed
70 Some B.A. earners
71 Percheron or Houyhnhnm
73 African village
74 Cerebrate
76 Turf for fuel
78 "Moonlight," etc.
79 Soul, in Sèvres
81 Tampico and Vigo
83 Medieval instrument
84 One who is feted
85 Is beholden to
86 Tan
89 Riser during a conniption
91 Hepburn role
93 Siestaed
94 Pension room
95 Used the black keys
96 Mop
97 Inner Hebrides island
98 Carried away
99 Rugby's river
100 Stag gang, e.g.
101 B. Young's state
102 Part of the epidermis
103 Vehicle going into an adit
105 NBC's parent
107 Connors coup

142 Opera-tion Tin Pan Alley

By Bert Rosenfield

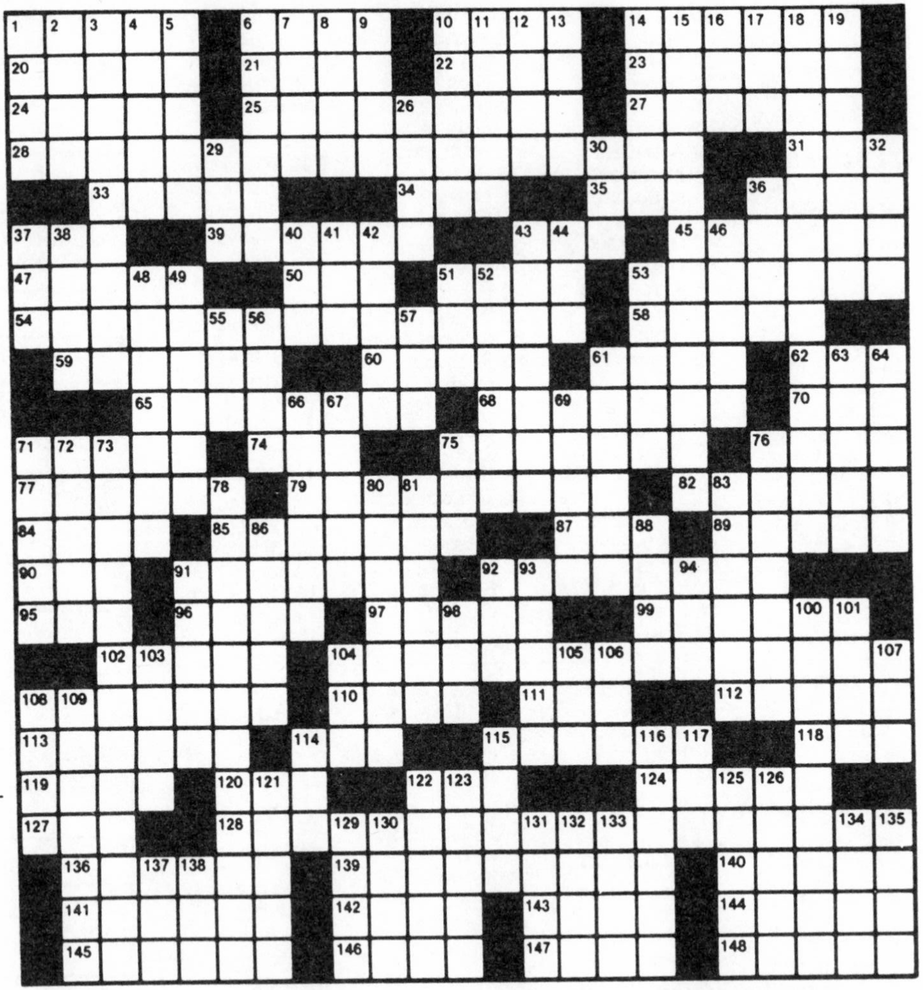

ACROSS

1 Deep sleep
6 Former film heavy
10 Rounded hill
14 Bridge bid
20 Antistrophe follower
21 Jack's adversary
22 Wolfe
23 Biblical plain
24 Joshua's fellow-survivor
25 Squabble
27 Natural animal trap
28 THE TALES OF HOFFMANN
31 Pts. of days
33 Stage direction
34 Author Whitten
35 —— Rio of silent films
36 Swain
37 Univ. degrees
39 Photographic light
43 Bounder
45 "—— Peace"
47 Deadly
50 31 gal.
51 Subj. in the news
53 Loud noises
54 LA TRAVIATA
58 Ethiopian battle site
59 Capital of County Kerry
60 Seine River feeder
61 Slayer of Castor
62 Under —— (afoot)
65 Broadway
68 Obstinate
70 S.E.C. member
71 Automotive blooper
74 Wild sheep of the Punjab
75 Very foolish
76 Bldg. maintenance man
77 Of sons or daughters
79 THE MARRIAGE OF FIGARO
82 Abridged, in a way
84 Word of approval
85 Musical instrument
87 Newscaster Pappas
89 Woodcutting tools
90 Sphere upholder
91 Rooted out
92 Yes man's forte
95 Parapsychological letters
96 Former Portuguese coins
97 Sebastian's twin
99 Absorb
102 Northern Chinese city
104 I PAGLIACCI
108 Music for a text
110 For a rectangle, length x width
111 Halloween sound
112 Growing out
113 Straightened
114 Homeless ones, for short
115 Member of the Five Nations
118 Fast jet
119 Melodic subject
120 Roscoe Tanner specialty
122 The Long March leader
124 In from the field
127 Second person
128 RIGOLETTO
136 Not forming an angle
139 Having an independent accent
140 Kind of bucket
141 Indian name of Mt. Rainier
142 Call to hunting dogs
143 Buckwheat tree
144 —— - out (inconsistent)
145 Puffs up
146 Certain dyes
147 N. C. college
148 Endures

DOWN

1 Dry, in Durango
2 Large ocean fish
3 Jacket material
4 Concert hall
5 Contradict
6 Klein or Young
7 City of the Taj
8 Sudermann's "—— Sorge"
9 Kind of caterpillar
10 Appellation for Mack
11 Flavored wine drink
12 Type of vaccine
13 Ward or James
14 Basketry fiber
15 SALOME
16 Bogey minus one
17 A Dada founder
18 DER ROSENKAVALIER
19 Starter
26 Blue or White
29 Egyptian pleasure god
30 —— man out
32 Beer, in slanguage
36 Forehead
37 Sternward
38 Thai monetary unit
40 Box-score stat.
41 Dictionary abbr.
42 Culpability
43 Enters
44 Grunhorn or Jagerhorn
46 Strike —— (model)
48 Montgomery of ——
49 Musical refrain syllables
51 Boot one
52 Kind of goose or lynx
53 Parts of circles
55 "Agnus ——"
56 Hankerings
57 Scotch bonnet
61 Type of valve
63 "Tiny Alice" playwright
64 Nautical spars
66 Navigational hazards
67 Nepalese goats
69 Verse foot
71 New Hebrides island
72 John D. give-aways
73 DIE WALKURE
75 "Rose —— rose. . ."
76 Garson co-star
78 LA BOHEME
80 1957 A.L. home-run king
81 Water nymph
83 Resemble some participles
86 Prompter's job
88 An Adams
91 Bert's Sesame St. sidekick
92 He won the Manila thriller
93 "Now It —— Told," 1938 song
94 Murder, ——
98 Harem room
100 Hakenkreuze
101 Explosives
103 Vulcan's forge
104 Vitiate
105 Bon —— (high style)
106 Straddler, e.g.
107 A race-starting word
108 Cloy
109 Ennoble
114 Mountain —— (hooch)
115 Part of London
116 Spelunking hazard
117 Mischievous child of Eris
121 Imogene et al.
122 Fable: Comb. form
123 Pseudonym in a Dumas novel
125 Perform a cook-out job
126 Yoga posture
129 —— bene
130 Tito
131 Major ending
132 Make turbid
133 Familiar with
134 Jalopy feature
135 Termini
137 Wood sorrel
138 —— a little (quite a bit)

Sound Effects

By Derrick C. Niederman

ACROSS

1 Voracious S.A. fish
7 Fellows
12 Tortures
18 He has pressing problems
19 Byron lass
20 Columbo's garb
22 Napoleon at St. Helena?
24 Protective covering
25 Jacob's brother
26 Utah's —— Mountains
27 Willie of boxing fame
28 Born
29 Puget Sound port
31 With 98 Down, 1974 Wimbledon winner
34 Colliery roof
36 Regal
39 Preseason?
41 Coffee container
42 Director Jules
45 Keelbill
46 Marine hazard
47 Faulkner's "—— Dying"
49 Nero's lang.
50 Shows compassion
52 Fitting
55 Worship
56 H.R.E. ruler: 962-73
58 Wall Street org.
59 Bedouin, e.g.
60 Yell
61 Wheel stoppers
63 Like Venus de Milo
65 Forbidden
68 100% pure beef?
71 Columnist Stewart
72 One who scatters things
74 Tanglewood locale
75 Expert
76 Devoid of interest
77 Blackstone's subjects
80 "Babaoua" author
81 Light-greenish colors
84 Disencumber
85 Greek beginnings
87 Pea dwelling
88 A spice
90 Canter's cousin
92 Equal: Comb. form
93 Prompt a blessing
95 "Ten thousand saw —— a glance": Wordsworth
96 I.L.A. influence?
100 "Gosh!"
102 Little sketch of a sort
103 Auto-engine category
104 Bob, for one
106 A Udall
107 —— Air, Md.
108 Evil spirit
110 Lett's neighbor
113 Sassoon job
116 Korean fish dish?
119 Competitors
120 Slur over
121 Stand-in
122 "—— is believing"
123 Dr. J's alma mater
124 "I have ——": King

DOWN

1 A.F.L. partner
2 "Rule, Britannia" composer
3 Homophone for rose
4 Prisoner
5 Indian swain on the hunt?
6 Suffix with east or west
7 Prospector's deed
8 Reddish dye
9 Start of a B'way title: 1978
10 Braid
11 Woebegone
12 Twerp's cousin
13 Genetic initials
14 Pretend
15 Local taxes?
16 Hoopster who was once Lew
17 Henry —— Commager
20 Swiftness
21 "You —— Lovely. . .": Rodgers-Hart song
23 Channel markers in harbors
30 Like some earth
32 Jalopy
33 Arrested
34 Philippine tree
35 Pronoun for a doe
36 Sine —— non
37 Major or Minor
38 Okla. city
39 Busy mound
40 D.C. art gallery
43 Tree-dwelling animal
44 Physician: Comb. form
48 Caused to go crazy
51 ". . . ere —— Elba"
53 El ——, Tex.
54 Recipe meas.
57 Flirted with
59 With maximum effort
62 Neurons' point of contact
64 Turf-roofed shelter?
65 Autocrat
66 Longfellow's bell town
67 Whence the reins came?
68 Shawl
69 Sentence divider
70 Iron ——
73 Viking great Carl ——
75 Armored, German style
78 Train warnings
79 Fresh
82 French girlfriend
83 Scorch
85 Mtg. with a doctor
86 Thick fog
89 Shipping wts.
91 Bauxite, e.g.
94 Mexican communal farmland
96 Fishy sign
97 Chant
98 See 31 Across
99 Shoot over
101 Affected person
104 Obeys
105 Starts playing poker
107 Cask stopper
109 Pelvic bones
111 What "être" means
112 Type of hoop or skirt
114 Pt. of T.G.I.F.
115 Strike out
116 Fire, in France
117 Agcy. watching provender and pills
118 Moon-vehicle unit

Countdown

By Sam Bellotto Jr.

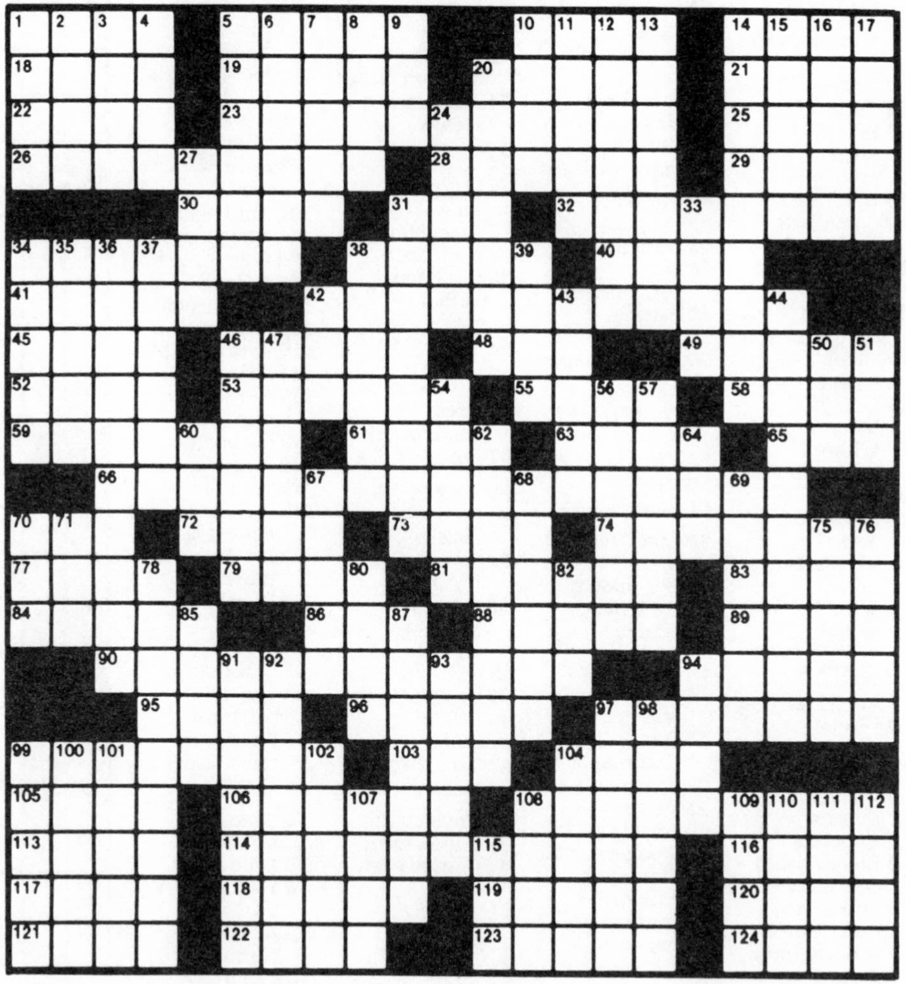

ACROSS

1 Charon's crossing
5 Domestic cat
10 Basilica part
14 Annie Oakley
18 Famed race horse
19 School for Siméon
20 Body: Comb. form
21 Moroccan district
22 Rockweed is one
23 Mets or Yankees
25 Stiff collar
26 Schoolyard chums
28 Successor to William II
29 Party popper
30 Needle for Calpurnia
31 Playwright James or Ronald
32 Parts
34 Perplexing situation
38 Dostoyevsky's "Little Mother"
40 Throaty notice
41 Ancient Greek colony
42 Faith, hope, charity et al.
45 Love-letter letters
46 1.0567 liquid quarts
48 Beaked ganoid
49 Leaves port
52 Abdomen: Comb. form
53 Put —— (be snobbish)
55 Limb's partner
58 Year in Nero's reign
59 One cause of absence
61 Library treasures
63 Run-of-the-mill
65 Wine cask
66 Welcome sound at a plant
70 I
72 Guthrie
73 Martha of movies
74 Mediterranean vessels
77 Bumpkin
79 Wall Street word
81 Maidservant, in Maidstone
83 Mosquito's cousin
84 Tether
86 Rio Treaty seq.
88 Declares
89 Give it —— (attempt)
90 "Let grievous . . . wounds / Untwine the ——!": Shak.
94 Lucy's landlady
95 Thin linen
96 Is zetetic
97 Bridge ploy
99 End of a countdown
103 B.&O. and L.I.
104 Gina's darlings
105 Gradient
106 Polo implement
108 Shine
113 "Urbi et ——" (papal benediction)
114 This deserves another
116 Dispatch
117 Calcar
118 Skiddoos
119 Very, to a virtuoso
120 Garage job, for short
121 Viking target
122 Kinski role
123 Thermae
124 Ratites

DOWN

1 Crisp cookie
2 Motorist's duty
3 Hindu asceticism
4 Bony photo
5 King-jack combination
6 Vinegar
7 Major —— of radio fame
8 Robert and Nellie
9 River in England
10 Where Pres. Schmidt works
11 Arabian peers
12 Time-study unit
13 "Dinner ——," 1933 song
14 By dribs and drabs
15 "Flow gently, sweet ——"
16 Quick quaff
17 Submerges
20 Distorting
24 It meets the Saône at Lyon
27 Legal offenses
31 Speed-regulating device
33 My, to Marius
34 Fish: Comb. form
35 Spur part
36 Meekly creeping
37 A-test atoll
38 Episodic
39 Grandfatherly
42 Dep.
43 South Bend team, for short
44 Semiquavers
46 Also-rans
47 Shoe part
50 B'klyn campus
51 Break a Commandment
54 Bags for Blasco
56 Circumventer
57 Emerson works
60 Walk in space, for short
62 Frolics
64 Baseball's Master Melvin
67 Kind of guard
68 Entwines
69 Ambassador
70 Chi. transportation
71 Caught
75 Nostrils
76 Art Deco, e.g.
78 Barnstormers' stunts
80 Colleen
82 Fin
85 Junior's exam
87 Binaural systems, for short
91 "Poet and Saint! . . . The —— sacred names": Cowley
92 Childhood, in Cherbourg
93 "Leave —— heaven": Shak.
94 Chisholm Trail town
97 Actress Fawcett
98 Natives of Isfahan
99 Besom, e.g.
100 Pupa predecessor
101 Brownish yellow
102 Fido's tormentors
104 Audacity
107 Illum. devices
108 "—— deal!"
109 Wight or Man
110 Styptic stuff
111 Ban
112 "Hungry ——," Twitty hit
115 Flounder

For Zel-ous Fans

By A. J. Santora

ACROSS

1 Relinquish
6 Studied
10 Signal the doctor
14 Elderly
18 Writer Calvino
19 Made goo-goo eyes
21 Kind of chord
22 Pedro's parlor
23 Floral bunch
24 Veal cutlet style
27 Certain majority
28 Caesar's bad day
30 Occupied
31 Money on a grand scale?
32 Overboard goods
34 Pilar
35 Flower part
36 Lotions for bruises
39 Detroit boo-boos
41 Cancel an undertaking
42 Faulkner hero
43 Memorable stage duo
44 Airport abbr
46 Sever
47 Actor Dullea
49 Japanese native
50 Swiss capital
51 Hosp. people
52 Announcer for Burns and Allen
56 —— St. Lawrence (G.B.S. residence)
57 Coat with plaster
58 "En —— Natt," Ingrid Bergman film
59 Nap-raising plants
61 Run out
64 Pseudologists
65 With enthusiasm
66 Snack food
68 Sand's "—— et Lui"
69 Living-room piece
71 Pledge
72 Beet used as fodder
75 Haircut
78 Tints
79 Kind of reckoning
80 Burnsian turndowns
81 Wife of Zeus
82 Ending for mountain
83 Sales pitch
85 Decline
87 Labyrinths
88 Pinned, in a way
90 Birds called "dippers"
93 Greek letters
94 Emulate Zayak
96 Atelier stand
97 Caseous
99 Battle with sickness
100 Against
101 Went out front
104 Subject of a Milford biography
107 Mubarak's city
109 Competent
110 Unicorn fish
111 Sad Sack's girlfriend
112 "Tomorrow" girl
113 Bent
114 Dress meat for cooking
115 Norman of TV fame
116 Light beer

DOWN

1 Prank
2 Preppy English school
3 Certain expressions of good wishes
4 Elba, to Napoleon
5 Time when "we love"
6 "Ivanhoe" lady
7 Sponsorship
8 Hood's drink
9 Refutations
10 Officious
11 Behold, to Pilate
12 Numerical ending
13 Complete treatise
14 Starlike
15 Having lustrous, expressive orbs
16 Kind of sch.
17 "Portrait of Gala" artist
20 Darcel of films
25 Robots of literature
26 Bits
29 Telegrapher's dash
33 Israeli port
34 One of the Morgans
35 Next-to-last syllable
36 Cordial
37 Footnote abbr.
38 Third-world nation
39 Finnish poem
40 Constitutional
43 Minnelli et al.
45 All hopped up
47 —— Abdul-Jabbar
48 Work unit
49 A brother-in-law of Diana
50 Sink
52 Mountain chain in Germany
53 Hidden
54 —— fours (creeping)
55 Fall pickup
57 Soft centers
60 Of grand-parents
61 Lyric composition
62 Examined, in a way
63 Pro football V.I.P.
64 Kind of tender
67 Start of a speech
69 Hang in loose folds
70 Ending for material
73 Destitution
74 Connect
75 Making a slanted edging
76 Russian grain market
77 Lake fish
81 Harass
83 —— trap (prepares to snare)
84 Frolicsome
85 Shaping tools
86 N.F.L. play
87 "Evita" is one
89 Did some gardening
91 Submit
92 Kind of grass
94 Glazed, in a way
95 Pub item
97 Emperor
98 Goddess of youth
99 Waken
100 Inter ——
102 Coloratura Mills
103 Active one
105 "—— Mist," 1928 piano solo
106 He wrote "The College Widow"
108 A follower of Santa

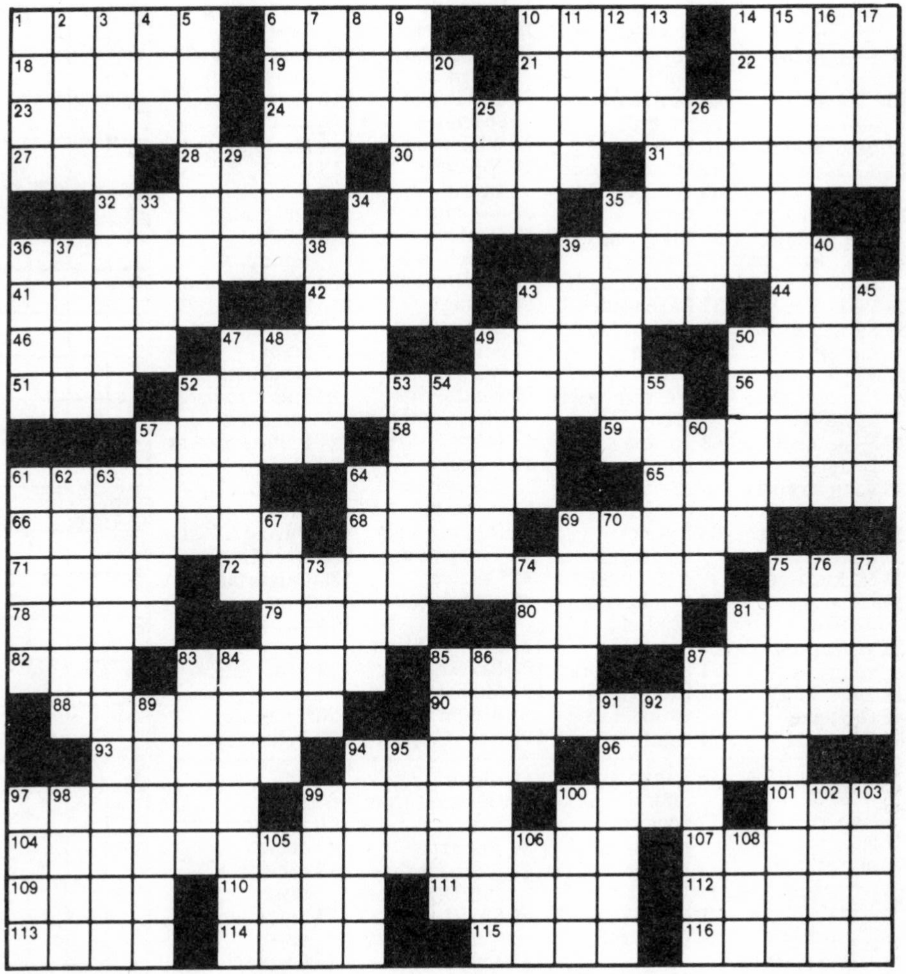

146

Weights and Measures

By Warren W. Reich

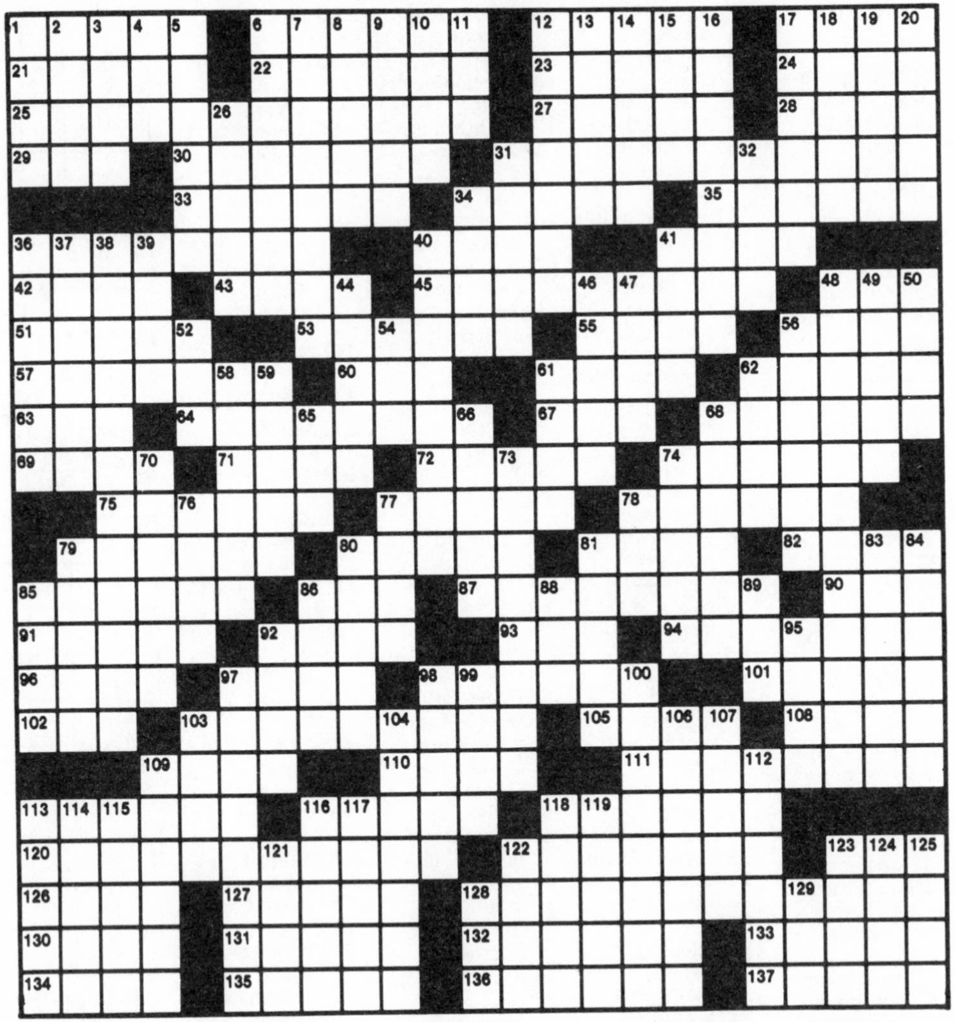

ACROSS

1 —— gin fizz
6 Plant fibers
12 "I'll Walk ——"
17 Bard's product
21 Soprano Lucine
22 Ammonia compounds
23 A.L. team, for short
24 Vedic fire god
25 Standing measure?
27 Egg-shaped
28 One of three squares
29 "—— Walks in Beauty"
30 John McGraw was one
31 Pope's eight quarts?
33 Makes amends
34 Other, in Auteuil
35 Warm and snug
36 Sage field?
40 Gardner
41 Common Vatican name
42 Early Cuzco citizen
43 Coil
45 Lustrous length?
48 Patriots' org.
51 Side nuisance
53 Touches of color
55 Crazy one
56 Town in Normandy
57 Bareheaded
60 Ribbed fabric
61 Range of frequencies
62 Western resort area
63 Cockney tailor's infernal measure?
64 Extinct measure for a roll of cloth?
67 Compass pt.
68 Ranted
69 Bring up
71 Chinese port
72 Hungarian national hero
74 Southern beauties
75 Patriarch
77 Quarterback, at times
78 Von Braun specialty
79 Whirlpools
80 Japanese sword
81 —— qua non
82 Dexterous
85 O'Neill's "—— the Horizon"
86 Chinese dynasty
87 Setter's weight?
90 Kind of dye
91 Sky: Comb. form
92 Fortune's partner
93 "Vive le ——!"
94 Reporter, e.g.
96 Trunk item
97 Uncover
98 John Jacob Astor, for one
101 Spot for birds
102 British letter
103 Medium weight?
105 —— -majesté
108 Portuguese cape
109 Soviet news source
110 "Arrivederci ——"
111 Board weight?
113 Oyster pond
116 Actor Walter and family
118 NCO's command
120 Gun measure?
122 Whining person
123 Scroll repository
126 Measurement standard
127 Pale as a ghost
128 Short measure?
130 Only
131 Part of AWOL
132 Branding iron
133 Calabrian's land
134 —— -in-the-bone
135 Procrastinator's word
136 Trinities
137 Bells the cat

DOWN

1 Knocks
2 Nanking nursemaid
3 Grown-up filly
4 Mork's planet
5 Finnish lake
6 Title for Loren
7 Intrinsic
8 Rossini's "The —— of Corinth"
9 Puts in at a table
10 Wanton look
11 Kazakh, e.g.
12 Canceled a space flight
13 Casanova
14 Kind of orange
15 Well-known, in Napoli
16 Laborious effort
17 Gaucho's milieu
18 Moldings
19 Perform
20 —— Way
26 Of course: Slang
31 Mews
32 Berlin's "—— Be Surprised"
34 Islands off New Guinea
36 Shrivel
37 Sniff
38 Some distance north of England?
39 —— of Sandwich
40 Moussaka ingredient
41 Incite
44 Durward from Ky.
46 Antelope
47 Word for the 1940 Olympics
48 Small gain to Tony Dorsett?
49 Icy sheets
50 Like some dorms
52 Browning's "—— Bratts"
54 Avant-gardist
56 Used a cat
58 Installed in office
59 Greek island
61 Bill
62 Substitute for action
65 Buzzing bug
66 Word on a 1775 flag
68 Fresh
70 Changed, as décor
73 View from a tower
74 Something extra
76 Chinese: Comb. form
77 Compos mentis
78 —— Bravo
79 Creepy
80 Small role
81 Sales pitch
83 "The Creation of Adam," for one
84 Black Watch garb
85 Sec. of Agriculture: 1971-76
86 Spy name
88 Word with hood or head
89 Women's org. founded in 1890
92 Fashions
95 Bisect
97 Clubs on diamonds phenomenon
98 Sing lustily
99 Los Angeles team
100 Canceled
103 Adjective for cerium
104 Like the neighbor's grass
106 Severe critics
107 Item for Hurd
109 Inclined
112 Thetis, e.g.
113 Bit
114 Grease pencil
115 Flaming
116 Buddhist monk
117 Musical note
118 Asian range
119 Small aquarium fish
121 On a cruise
122 Oktoberfest quaff
123 Culture medium
124 Measuring device
125 Florida features
128 D-day craft
129 —— loss

Wordplay's the Thing

By Arnold Moss

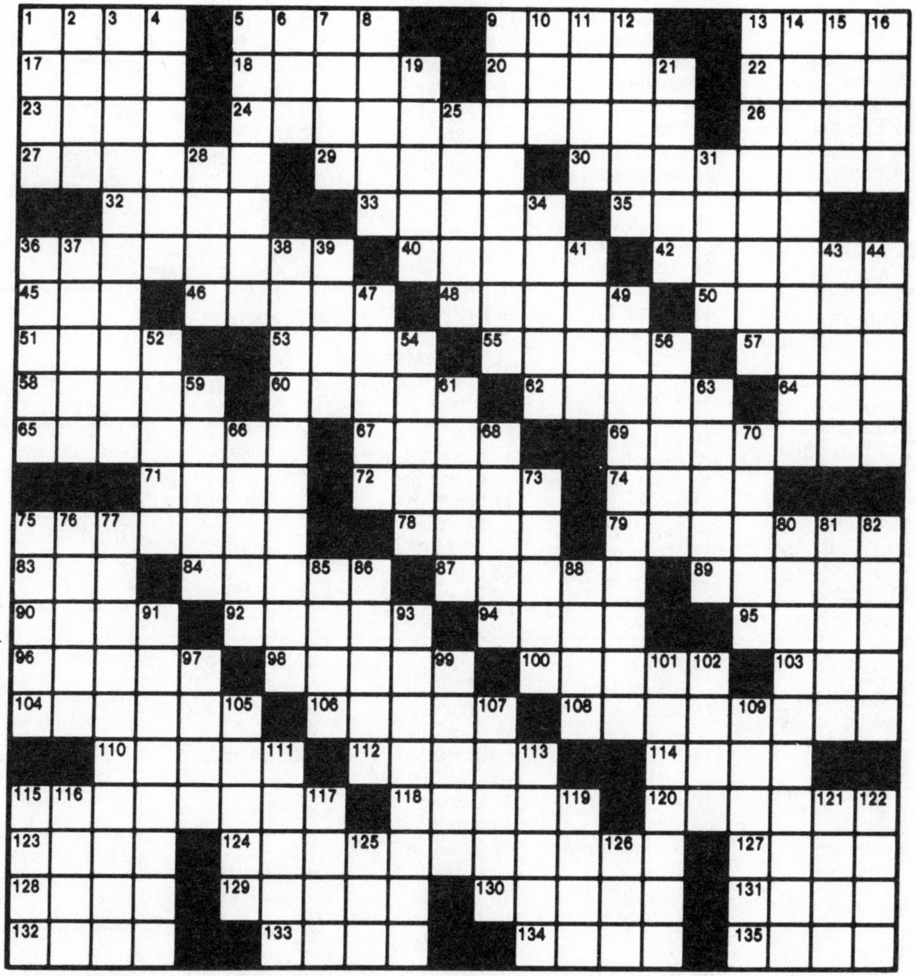

ACROSS

1 Flower plots
5 Snares
9 Paterfamilias
13 Birthright salesman
17 Ambler or Knight
18 W.W. II beach
20 Chemical compounds
22 Cuckoo
23 Wood strip
24 Belly dancer's movement?
26 W.W. I admiral
27 Acropolis resident
29 "Measure for Measure" constable
30 Crusaders' foes
32 Mythical Norse giant
33 Albacore and bluefin
35 Lethargy
36 Miserly
40 Liquefies
42 Memorable esthetic dancer
45 —— carte
46 A.k.a.
48 "Sore labour's bath": Shak.
50 —— Flow
51 Incline
53 An iris, for short
55 What Shankar plays
57 Makes a boo-boo
58 —— vitae
60 Toast starter
62 Peter and a Wolfe
64 Actress Scala
65 Like the worst of gossips
67 Templeton
69 Deli item
71 Appear
72 Auditioned
74 Plummer role
75 Bright star in Auriga
78 Slammer
79 Alumni groups
83 Brugg's river
84 Semiprecious stones
87 An oil man
89 Take a case to a higher court
90 Bolster
92 Laughton role in 1953
94 Site of Vance A.F.B.
95 Luxembourg neighbor
96 Gowns, in Granada
98 Kind of resistance
100 Tumbler
103 Heat meas.
104 Stagnating
106 Lithium, e.g.
108 Twaddle
110 Scale
112 Where matzohs are eaten
114 Dinesen product
115 Sea-ears
118 Sensations
120 Some steamers
123 Grant or Lee: Abbr.
124 What Juno saw with?
127 Secular
128 Mahler's "Das Lied von der ——"
129 Germ cell
130 European quart
131 Kahn or Preminger
132 Lat. catchall
133 Mild expletive
134 Passing grades
135 Gist

DOWN

1 Bartók
2 Eram, eras, ——
3 Lisping shepherd's giddy male sheep?
4 Outline
5 Albany's wife
6 "—— Dreamer . . ."
7 Cathedral part
8 Command-ments word
9 Breakwaters
10 "Airways, ——": Dos Passos
11 Decomposes
12 Inventor Howe
13 Place securely
14 Shipload of gold ingots?
15 Egyptian symbol
16 Functions
19 Stamp book
21 Boston fish
25 Flat and sharp
28 E. Indian palm
31 Bird of Paradise constellation
34 She wrote "Tender Buttons"
36 Food wrapping
37 Mild cigar
38 Female equines that run after dark?
39 Novelist Zona
41 Port in S France
43 Bliss Carman's "—— Airs"
44 Twangy
47 "The Divine ——"
49 Hero on the Rue de Rivoli?
52 Composure
54 Strikes out
56 George Brett, e.g.
59 Fishing devices
61 Former treaty org.
63 Backwoods cheroot
66 Biblical word
68 Campaign issue
70 "Everything's Coming Up ——"
73 Sturm und ——
75 —— pants
76 "The Green Pastures" role
77 Respectable male goose?
80 Steadfast spouse?
81 Love-poetry inspirer
82 Pancake additive
85 Sixty grains
86 Heels' forerunners
88 Silents' actor Asther
91 Match; equal
93 Hindered
97 Form of wrestling
99 He succeeded Nasser
101 Brooding Rhode Island Reds
102 Train in a ring
105 City near the ruins of Carthage
107 Like some holidays
109 Challenge for Stenmark
111 Sun Devils' home
113 Vestige
115 Pulitzer Prize novelist
116 Parks or Wheeler
117 L.A. nuisance
119 Developer's concern
121 Fiber used for cordage
122 Burns, for one
125 "—— pro nobis"
126 A B C's end

Biblical Offshoots

By Jeanette K. Brill

ACROSS

1 —— code
5 Aver
10 Coarse hominy
14 Emerald ——
18 Platter of sorts
19 Fleshy fruit
20 Place for a frontal
21 Anagram for atom
22 Tall yucca
24 Ship's strong piece of timber
26 Quechuan Indians
27 English philosopher: 1632-1704
29 Detest
30 To hurl, in Le Havre
31 Indian princess
32 Reiner or Bernstein
33 Wash
34 Portent
35 Certain spars
39 Some standardbreds
41 Seeds used as beads
43 ". . . a man —— mouse?"
44 Grandson of Eve
45 Colored
47 Blackthorn fruit
48 Side dish
49 Apprehend
50 British bassinet
54 English potter
55 Find out
57 Depside, e.g.
58 Harmonized
59 "——, Come Back to Me"
60 Flavor
61 Hispanic blonde bombshell
62 Perplex
64 Capital of Crete
65 Nightingale
68 Less polite
69 Rose of Sharon
71 Mrs., in Mexico
72 Swirl
73 Provençal love song
74 Lab heater
75 French copper
76 Ripen
77 The constellation Columba
81 Witch in Goethe's "Faust"
83 Car barn
86 Busy place
87 N.M. neighbor
88 —— now (at this time)
89 Edible mushroom
90 Ornate
92 Dickens protagonist
95 Banker's pet
96 "Mother ——," 1903 song
97 Crape jasmine
99 Medicinal part of a S.A. plant
104 Japanese general: 1885-1948
105 Took a stab at
106 Enraged
107 Lake that sounds weird
108 Smell —— (be suspicious)
109 Many centuries
110 Takes out
111 One farmer's habitat

DOWN

1 Modifying word: Abbr.
2 "—— Rita"
3 Tee predecessor
4 Gains
5 Modern frontier
6 Turkic language
7 Spring mos.
8 Inventor's monogram
9 Young female sheep
10 Quench
11 "Ma, He's Making Eyes ——"
12 Postgrad degrees
13 Slip out of place: Med.
14 African antelope
15 Pollution factor
16 Attack verbally
17 Major follower
20 Rise
23 —— den Linden
25 Standard
28 Wallet fillers
30 Plant of the phlox family
31 Crucifixes
32 Painter of "Une Matinée . . ."
33 Veranda
35 Former German coin
36 Black calla
37 Swap
38 Fiddled furiously
39 Remain unsettled
40 Colliery tool
41 Deride
42 Sandy ridge
46 Gas-company customer
48 Steeple
50 Man with a van
51 Relative of bingo
52 Poplar
53 Porticoes
54 Ceramic fragment
56 Small flock of quail
58 "——" Symphony (Beethoven's Ninth)
60 Mother of Isaac
61 Family group
62 —— Dane
63 "Barnaby ——"
64 Plot
65 Lavish party
66 One of Plato's dialogues
67 Every's companion
69 "Half —— . . ."
70 Slant
73 Furnish explanatory comment
75 Bloomed
78 Jostled
79 Extreme
80 Went to extremes
82 Sacred pictures
84 Burrowing rodent
85 Egyptian goddess
89 Fathers and sons
90 "God shall —— thee": Acts 23:3
91 Secretes
92 Computer fodder
93 Aroma
94 Indian prince
95 Rotate
96 Face shape
98 Player or Barber
100 "Butterflies —— Free," 1969 play
101 Pay dirt
102 Black gold
103 —— Aviv

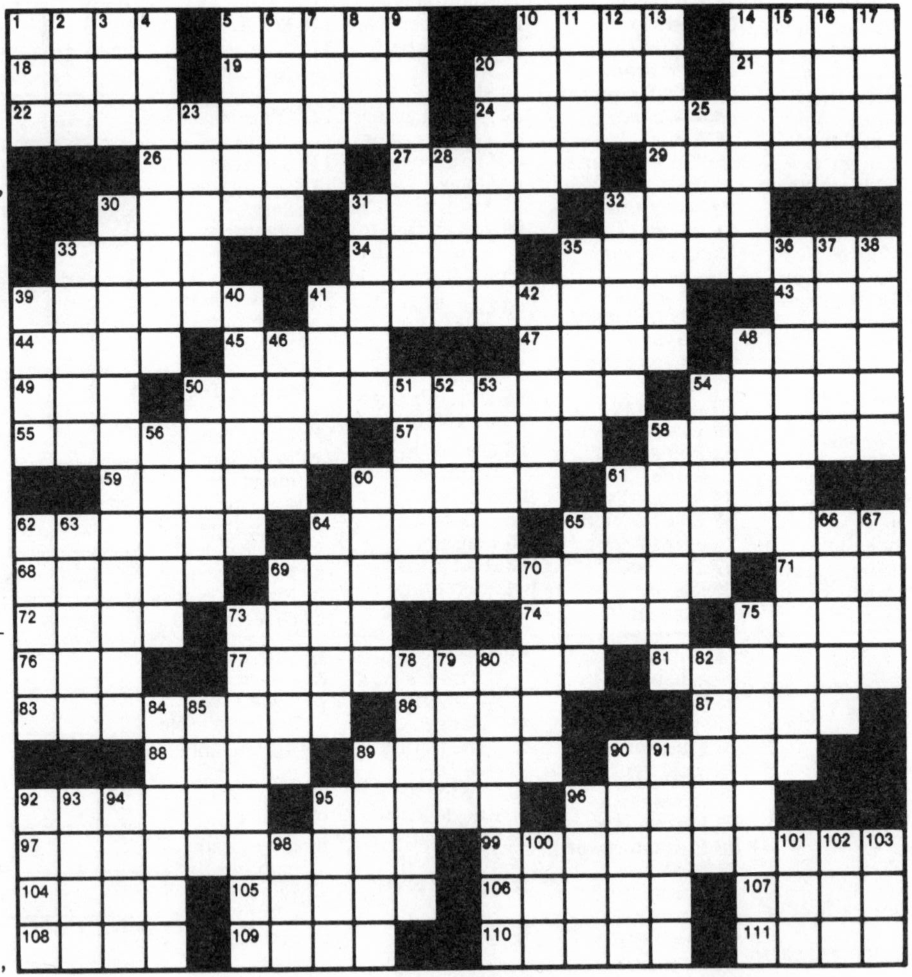

Playing with Matches

By Jim Page

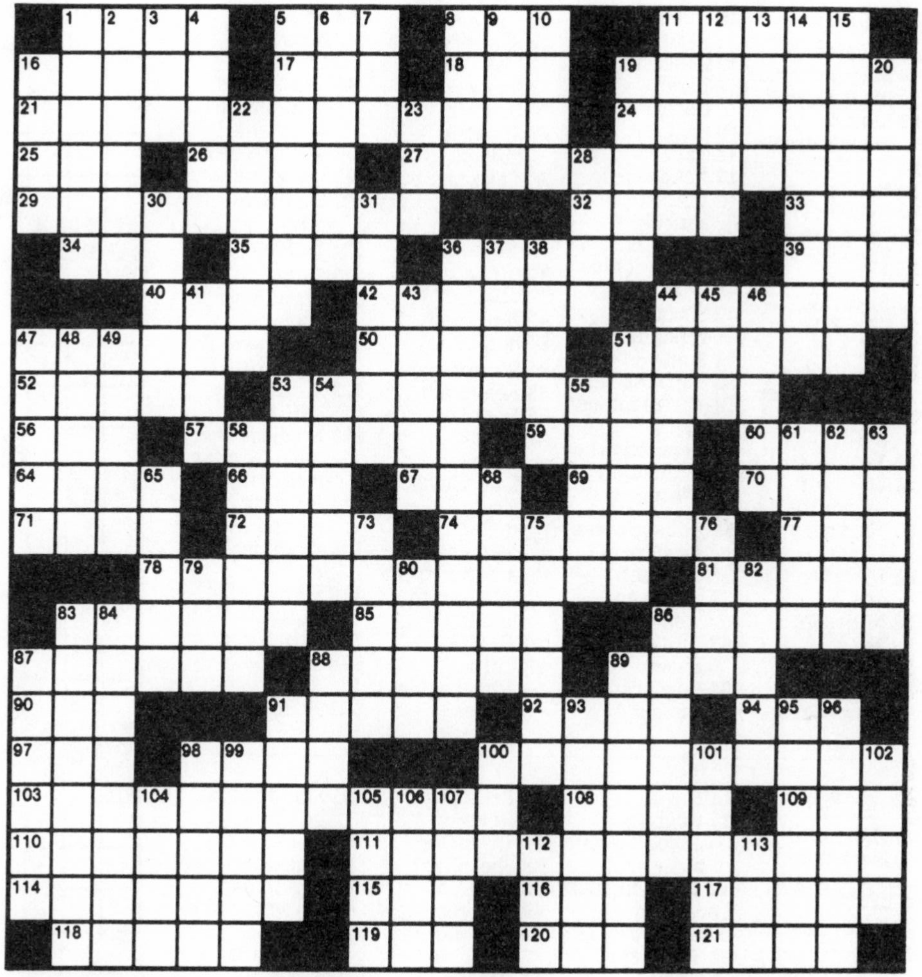

ACROSS

1 Sailors' saint
5 Warp yarn
8 Part of R.S.V.P.
11 Draw out
16 Foreign
17 $5 bill
18 Chemical suffix
19 Shadowboxed
21 Tuskincisor
24 Presidential hopeful
25 Sesame
26 Vega's constellation
27 RaymondKelly
29 Throwshag
32 Inspires wonder
33 A Gershwin
34 Brace
35 Midianite king
36 Loam deposit
39 —— Shams University, in Cairo
40 Fill the bases
42 London insurance company
44 Used a dory
47 British statesman and family
50 Clare Boothe and Henry
51 Beats
52 Rub clean
53 Platterdisk
56 Ho of Hawaii
57 Shallow-draft vessel
59 Profit's opposite
60 Blind as ——
64 Same, to Seneca
66 Three-time champ
67 Rickover was one: Abbr.
69 Book by Dos Passos
70 Korean border river
71 —— Verde National Park
72 Cornea irritant
74 Barrel-binding group
77 Sohrab, to Rustum
78 Dynegravity
81 Straighten ranks
83 Aaron specialties
85 "—— Chan," T. N. Page book
86 "—— Restaurant"
87 Hilliard-Mann song: 1950
88 Weedy rye grass
89 Feds
90 Blotter target
91 Siberian holes
92 Grim Grimm character
94 Rheine's river
97 Memphis-to-Mobile dir.
98 Mil. units
100 Carboniron
103 Beannoodle
108 Diamond from Brooklyn
109 One of a comic trio
110 Small spaces
111 CarrySenecas
114 Pipe smokers' devices
115 —— Tin Tin
116 Cat has one to cross
117 Makes an incised mark
118 Dates set for attacks
119 Bullring shout
120 Slip up
121 Pteroid

DOWN

1 Win ——, former radio emcee
2 Stay in hiding
3 Kingsley's "—— in White"
4 "Mon ——," Tati film
5 Declared
6 Smear
7 Big A venture
8 Trickle through
9 Worldwide: Abbr.
10 City near Utah Lake
11 Pindar's last stanza, e.g.
12 Euphemistic expletives
13 Like some heraldic crosses
14 Having a skull
15 Where congers congregate
16 Pituitary-gland hormone
19 Mergansers
20 Rid of grit
22 Freshwater polyps
23 Hairpin turn
28 Squire in "Silas Marner"
30 Trees bearing valuable nuts
31 Pollster of note
36 Saxantler
37 —— and terminer
38 Ford's lemon
41 A sawbuck has 10
43 St. —— (Windward island)
44 College treasurer
45 Outworn
46 Ore analysis
47 Obscure
48 Wear away
49 Roosters on spires
51 Peace officers, oater style
53 Arty parties
54 Like a cliché
55 Creamy dessert
58 Tuareg or Berber
61 Fundamental
62 Byrd book
63 Cahn-Styne products
65 Barbara or Hoople
68 Common code
73 He wrote "Philosopher's Holiday"
75 Black-spotted cat
76 Event on G.W.'s birthday
79 Quebec affirmative
80 Diet
82 Material from flax
83 Showed disapproval
84 Hoover Dam formation
86 Novel by Fielding
87 Expel a lawyer
88 Spode piece
89 Like some pastures
91 F.H.A. concerns
93 Neuter, for one
95 The sensitive plant
96 Squatter in 1889
98 The Hoosier poet
99 Growls from Fido
100 J.F.K. sight
101 Excessive
102 Stack TV role
104 Fruits for Virgil
105 Kind of dollar
106 Indigo
107 Eat in style
112 Juin, juillet et août
113 Suffix with baron or manor

People You Can Count On

By J. Samuel Smart

ACROSS

1 RICH MAN
6 Member of the lily family
10 Indian mountain pass
14 U.S.S.R. river
18 Betel palm
19 Lymnaeid
20 Deep-sea diving pioneer
21 Cordial flavoring
22 DOCTOR
24 CHIEF
26 Resident of Green Gables
27 "Gasoline ——"
28 Twilled fabric
29 Word with scandal or iron
30 Marshal at Waterloo
31 Steve Ovett is one
32 Milieu for Drew
33 More agile
34 Eastern Europeans
35 Italian violinmaker
36 Concerning
37 Less impassioned
40 SAILOR
42 Calloway
45 Acknowledged
46 Furniture stuffing
47 Phone button
48 Shade of blue
49 Defamation
50 Shoot randomly
51 Spin
53 Cuttlefish ink
54 Thrice minus twice
55 Reputed to be
56 Without, in Würzburg
57 Photographic equipment
58 For each
59 One of an identical pair
63 Au —— (in the know)
64 Concurs
67 Bucolic
68 Graduates
69 Kind of tire
71 LAWYER
73 Snooze
76 Go over
77 Scottish hillside
78 Take care of
79 London gallery
80 Region south of the Sahara
81 "If seven ——. . ."
82 Hammett detective
84 Western lake
85 Leave out
86 Poet Teasdale
87 "I —— Freedom": Kravchenko
88 Useful metallic element
89 A period from late Apr. to late Oct.
90 THIEF
93 Carp
94 Whence sherry comes
96 Thin layer
97 Daisy Mae, to Li'l Abner
98 Van Gogh's "The Potato ——"
100 —— as a beet
101 Integuments
102 BEGGAR-MAN
105 Sudden
106 Sully
107 Cardamom, e.g.
108 Drink used in Vedic rituals
109 SOLDIER
111 DOCTOR
113 Königsberger —— (German meatball)
114 Hoisting machine
115 Kramden's mate
116 Sudra or Vaisya
117 Unsubstantial
118 Sioux
119 Style
120 At bay

DOWN

1 U.S. naval historian
2 "Goodnight, ——"
3 Actor Reginald ——
4 Measure of area
5 Shakespearean lord
6 Tarsi
7 Section of a cake
8 Unctuous
9 Old cloth measure
10 Brown girl
11 Ambiguous statement
12 Busy as ——
13 Atlas abbr.
14 Ravel
15 Hogback
16 Jacob's eighth son
17 Their, in Tours
19 Vendor
20 Slight breeze
21 Squirrel's tidbit
23 In the calaboose
25 Loom in the future
28 Arrangement of chips
31 Edible mushroom
32 Loose outer garment
33 Fish-line attachment
34 Flycatcher
35 Presently
36 Revere
37 Shropshire
38 Sheeplike
39 POOR MAN
40 Suppress
41 ESP pioneer
42 SAILOR
43 Peregrine
44 Aesop character
46 Moves swiftly
48 Long
50 Handled clumsily
51 "He who can call —— his own": Dryden
52 Submerge; engulf
53 Urban-renewal target
55 Stand one in good ——
57 Use a pestle
60 Angst
61 Inveigles
62 Go wrong
63 Genetic duplicate
65 Welcome
66 Scottish dance
68 Stage direction
69 Fix up the lawn
70 Profs' concoctions
71 Cassandra's father
72 Collect
74 Coral isle
75 Calvin of the P.G.A.
77 Magnate
79 Watered silk

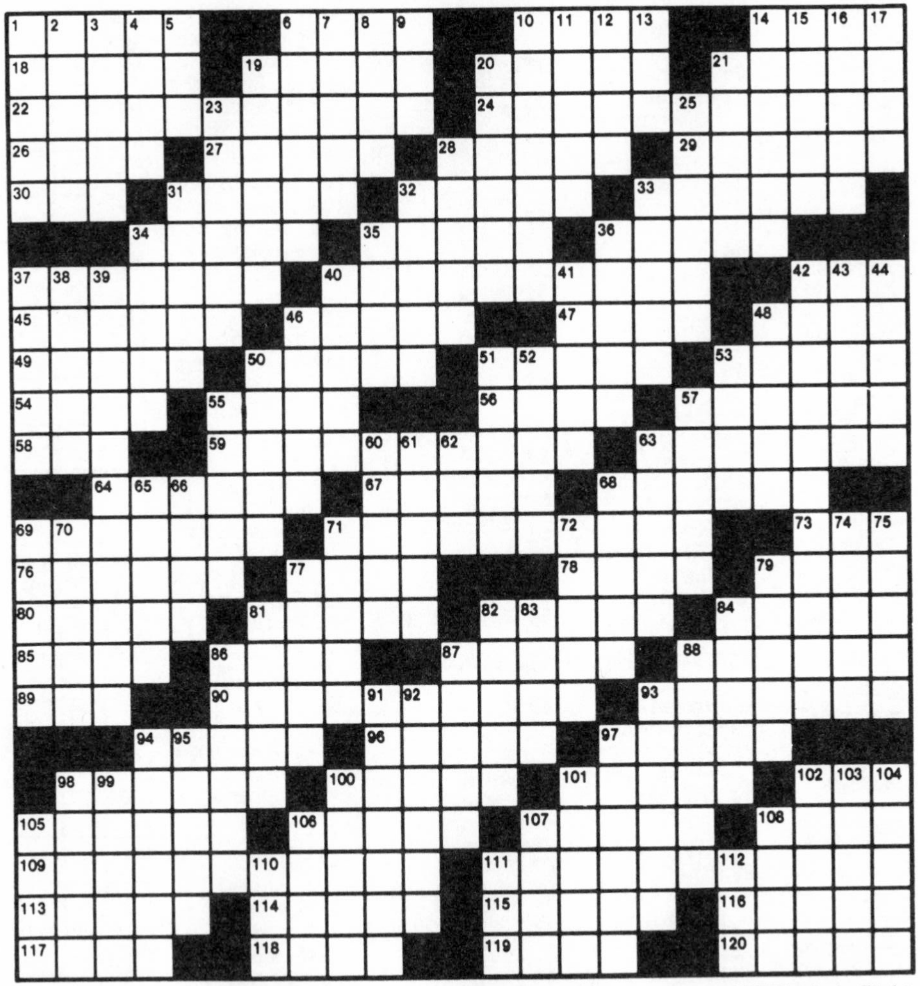

81 One of three Dutch painters
82 He wrote "Muhammad Ali"
83 Sulk
84 "Sous les —— de Paris," René Clair film
86 Ancient capital of Laconia
87 Joy
88 Shore bird
91 Basic nature
92 Beat
93 —— Lorraine
94 Short and thick
95 Restoration recorder
97 Fine fellow
98 Mezzo-soprano in "Don Carlos"
99 Protection
100 —— acids
101 Plant pest
102 Hustlers after rustlers
103 Ham it up
104 Dwindled
105 Aleutian island
106 Short play
107 Finale in flight training
108 Betelgeuse, for one
110 Company, proverbially
111 Obstruct
112 Pretend

AlphaBetiC Clans

By Tap Osborn

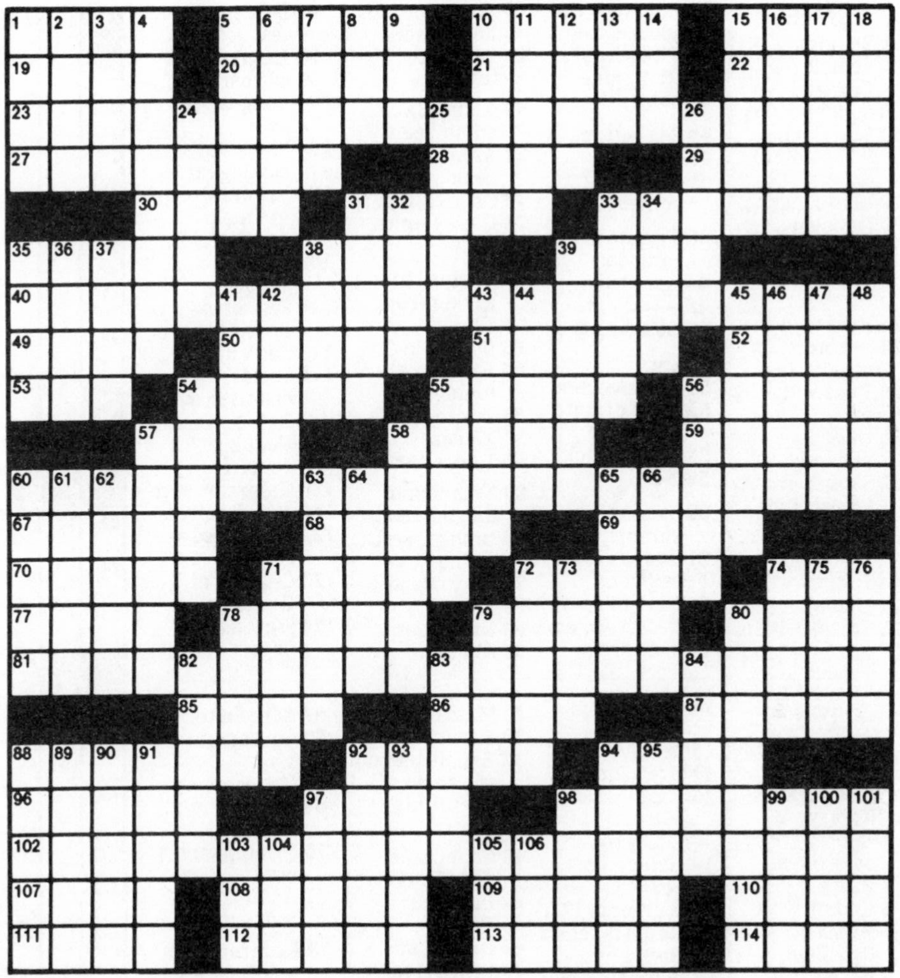

ACROSS

1 Plagiarize
5 Sock exchange
10 Unisonally
15 Counterfeit
19 This may have an aglet
20 Forgo
21 Composer Anderson
22 Foofaraw
23 Davises
27 Event for Figaro
28 De Soto or Hudson
29 Far from popular
30 Occupied with
31 Nickname of a famous warship
33 Précis
35 Skirmish
38 Tops
39 King, for one
40 Johnsons
49 Lampshade wearer
50 Physician from Pergamum
51 Induct
52 Lapse, in Lisbon
53 Queen before Sofia
54 Orchard product
55 Cold
56 Lips
57 Actuate
58 Harry's back-up man
59 Legislate
60 Washingtons
67 One of the Starrs
68 Charged
69 Get out of control
70 Colliery accesses
71 Korean port
72 Set a value on
74 Former chess champ
77 Sheltered nook
78 Stud
79 Ice-cream flavor
80 Cleaning agent
81 Williamses
85 Grist for Cholly
86 Enfilade
87 O. Henry device
88 Barbarians
92 Like a kook
94 One of the Trimurti
96 Figure of speech
97 Decapod's weapon
98 Lounged clumsily
102 Russells
107 Nevus
108 Defeat
109 Wild calla, e.g.
110 Differently
111 Maraud
112 Awkward
113 Gloves for Fisk and Cerone
114 Legislative body

DOWN

1 Stolid one
2 Prince in Punjab
3 Culinary specialist
4 Help
5 Diaphoresis, commonly
6 Freight
7 Happen
8 Macao coin
9 Swan or hutch
10 Beatles' "Abbey Road," e.g.
11 Take care of
12 "—— take arms . . .": Hamlet
13 Gershwin's "But —— for Me"
14 Cyclone center
15 Ermine, at times
16 Book genre
17 Revoke a legacy
18 Pierre's world
24 Amerced
25 Roll
26 Henry Luce's birthplace
31 Leafy retreat
32 —— instant (immediately)
33 Heston film: 1961
34 Kind of master
35 A spice
36 Joie de vivre
37 Constellation for Orpheus
38 Qualified
39 Cold-war activity
41 Gothic arch
42 D.C. gadfly
43 Lyle or Nita
44 Gardener's tool
45 Selfish person
46 Papal name
47 Heath
48 Reluctant
54 Fountain drinks
55 ". . . —— and hungry look"
56 Shelf
57 Liquefied by heat
58 Paternal kinsman
60 Philippine fiber
61 Make spangly
62 Oil source
63 Obvious fact
64 —-Terre, Guadeloupe capital
65 Segal or Fromm
66 Hide away
71 Propounds
72 Bothersome
73 Chastise
74 Dog that went to Oz
75 Arabian seaport
76 Windermere, e.g.
78 Leap by Massine
79 Maximum
80 Hastily recorded
82 Bruce of films
83 Donnybrook
84 Giant, to a Dodger
88 Semipostal, for one
89 Ann ——, Mich.
90 Cotton fabric
91 Fictional Bostonian
92 Type of steak
93 Fat
94 Alley woe
95 Crocus and gladiolus
97 Masticate
98 Watt or Adam Smith
99 Actress Damita
100 Smooth
101 Fishing device
103 Flaw
104 Auditor, for short
105 Greek W.W. II resistance movement
106 —— Lanka

Hometown Hokum

By Stanley Glass

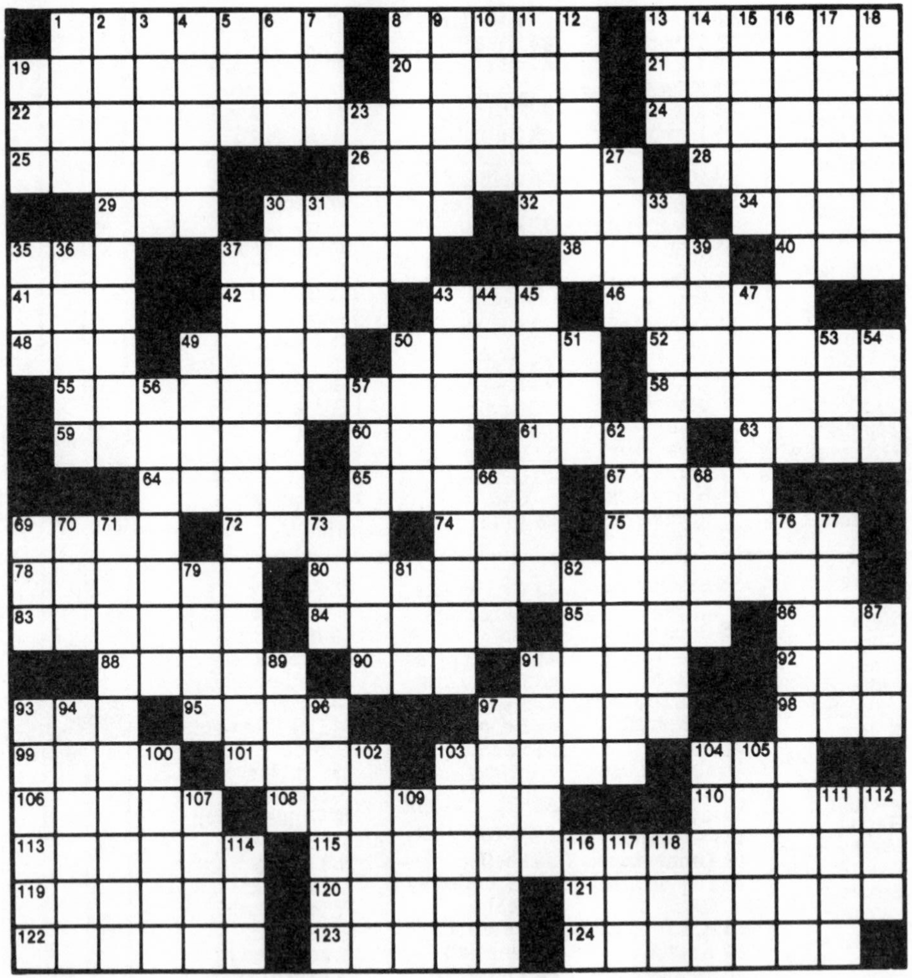

ACROSS

1 Shavian vehicle for Cornell
8 Sudden flurry
13 Van Gogh's "The Potato ——"
19 Like a leaf
20 Delicious
21 "Rose of ——"
22 President out of Pa.?
24 Kind of verb
25 Segments of insects' legs
26 Typewriter parts
28 Initiated violently
29 Song from "A Chorus Line"
30 Up the ante
32 Blackthorn fruit
34 Undercooked
35 Small British isle
37 Fontanne and spouse
38 Fiber from a Philippine palm
40 Sea bottom
41 Bizarre
42 Stuttering comedian
43 Tribute to a toreador
46 Love feast
48 —— diem
49 Cobbling gear
50 Spry
52 On cloud nine
55 Head of state out of S.D.?
58 Had a snack
59 Beat
60 Soissons summer
61 Je vous —— (I beg you)
63 Pinball no-no
64 Secret society of a sort
65 Containers for holy water
67 "—— fan tutte"
69 Young Capitol employee
72 Area of a bird's beak
74 Once called
75 Glossy finish
78 Luck
80 Former first sacker from Fla.?
83 County in Ga.
84 Fermentation fomenter
85 Taken, in Toulon
86 Dart's partner
88 Neighbor of Saudi Arabia
90 Biblical verb ending
91 German port
92 Teachers' org.
93 Utility agcy.
95 Alliance
97 De Lesseps feat
98 Essay
99 Old cars
101 Long-tailed apes
103 Male seal's contingent
104 Printers' org.
106 Act melo-dramatically
108 Lively, to Verdi
110 Did some flooring
113 Show up
115 Social historian out of Ohio?
119 Goalie's domain
120 Gantry or Rice
121 —— -Lautrec
122 Conducted a roundup
123 City NW of Grenoble
124 Sign, as a payee

DOWN

1 Small salmon
2 Home of the first great library
3 Hebrew month before Iyar
4 Passé
5 Ending with Bronx or Brooklyn
6 Berg's "—— Wein"
7 "Bleak House" heroine
8 Emphasis
9 French poodle's paw
10 Tennis star of the 70's
11 Dazes
12 Periwinkle, e.g.
13 Zeta follower
14 Overcute
15 Early resident of the Caucasus
16 Ruler from N.J.?
17 Warner of 1775
18 Rated in tennis
19 Body governing TV
23 Mine entrances
27 Carolina rail
30 Lincoln's fiancée
31 "—— of robins . . ."
33 Playwright out of Ore.?
35 Mass of hair
36 Expert
37 Bandleader out of Kan.?
39 Beautiful: Prefix
43 Comic poet from Utah?
44 Fabulize
45 Passed
47 Diversion
49 Pisa's river
50 Hudson or Essex
51 A cont.
53 Slippery one
54 Banned pesticide
56 Understanding between nations
57 KO counter
62 Cold comfort
66 Yurt
68 Undermines
69 Controversial chemical
70 Triumphant cry
71 Actor from Ind.?
73 Rogers or Acuff
76 Toothless
77 Pilsen product
79 Search thoroughly
81 Mother of Fr., Sp., etc.
82 State a viewpoint
87 —— Nineties
89 Kaye of ballet fame
91 Pope John Paul II's given name
93 Moralize
94 Always, on a score
96 Annul
97 Provides provender
100 Frame for a fourposter
102 Asinine
103 Sort of port
104 Balbo or Tajo
105 Indonesian island
107 Alleviate
109 Exec's note
111 Gaelic
112 Tint
114 Ryder of comics
116 Daughter of Eris
117 —— sequitur
118 Flop

Sounds Familiar

By Jim Modney

ACROSS

1 West Coast naval air base
8 Absquatulates
13 Worthless rock, in mining
19 Lets down one's hair
20 Ace place
21 Quercus fruit
22 What analgesics are to pain
23 Frenzied regattas on the Shannon?
25 Hide
27 Unseats
28 Episcopacy
29 In re
31 Flanders river
32 SANE targets
33 Antiwar demonstrators' org.
34 Koala ——
35 Vapor
38 —— diem
39 Drivel
41 Horse's armor
44 Cookie-jar pilferer
46 Pendergast partisan, e.g.
50 Declare
51 Like Schönberg's early work
53 Statue spot
54 Smashing events
57 Peter of the 88's
58 Fabulous
59 Benign bump on the skin
62 Violinist Morini
64 More like the Magi
66 Ruler ousted on Jan. 16, 1979
67 Lode finds
69 The Dark Ages?
72 Place for a chapeau
73 English poet laureate: 1715-18
74 Assyrian chief deity
75 With full force
77 Turner or Sorensen
78 Checkmates, in a way
81 Seasoned
83 "Ragged Dick" author
85 Package-deal features
86 Schliemann find
88 Comical TV show
92 Routs
95 Square one
97 A vacuum tube
98 Maxwell's cousin
99 Prefix with cycle or form
101 React to the heat
103 Icky stuff
104 Rheine's river
106 Grafters' items
108 Others, to Octavian
110 Raven's haven
111 Like Leroy Brown
112 Prussian nobleman's glass
114 —— boy (Mel Ott)
116 Times to put one's foot down?
119 Closes again
122 Lipase or amylase
123 Hard red wheat
124 Takes a breath
125 Transferred property legally
126 Poet Lizette Woodworth ——
127 Dixon or Leek

DOWN

1 Focus of a Spielberg thriller
2 Pearl Harbor remembrance
3 Athletes' athletes
4 Special delivery from a dating service?
5 Boardroom biggy
6 Orangeman's city
7 Size up
8 ——-fi
9 Something easy to catch
10 "The Age of Anxiety" poet
11 Leave without a leg to stand on
12 Caressed
13 Range fuels
14 Leipzig laments
15 Eur. land
16 Wall Streeter predicting pay dirt?
17 Not hitched
18 Slalom path
23 Common contraction
24 Rhone tributary
26 Asian holidays
29 Swedish rock group
30 "... snarled and yelping ——": T. S. Eliot
36 Long long time
37 Where parades are held to lionize heroes?
39 Ward heelers
40 Greet abruptly
42 Feeder of Maumee Bay
43 Voiceless bird
45 Unit of fineness for gold
47 Fannie follower
48 Emulate Howard Hughes
49 Dotty
52 Collected sayings of Christ
55 Turner and Louise
56 What a kanone does
58 Of a region
59 Defeats
60 X-rated
61 Holiday hangover?
63 Istanbul brass
65 Madame Bovary
68 Babylonian or Phoenician
70 Downs and Carey
71 Tour highlight
76 Poetic negative
79 Involved with
80 Compass pt.
82 Type of poker
84 King's waterproof coat?
87 Oneirocritics' field
89 Quantity bargain at a donut shop?
90 Fusses
91 Cried
93 Regretting
94 Juicy-tidbit seeker
96 Powder-puff covering
100 Outgo's opposite
102 Baghdad's river
104 Waned
105 W.W. I pivotal battle
106 Shaped tires
107 Hypocrite in "Little Orphan Annie"
109 Actress Rich
112 Marceau, e.g.
113 Chemical suffixes
115 Davis Cup captain
117 Shakespeare contemporary
118 Uno + uno + uno
120 Guitarist Paul
121 Draft agcy.

Literary Sobriquets

By George Rose Smith

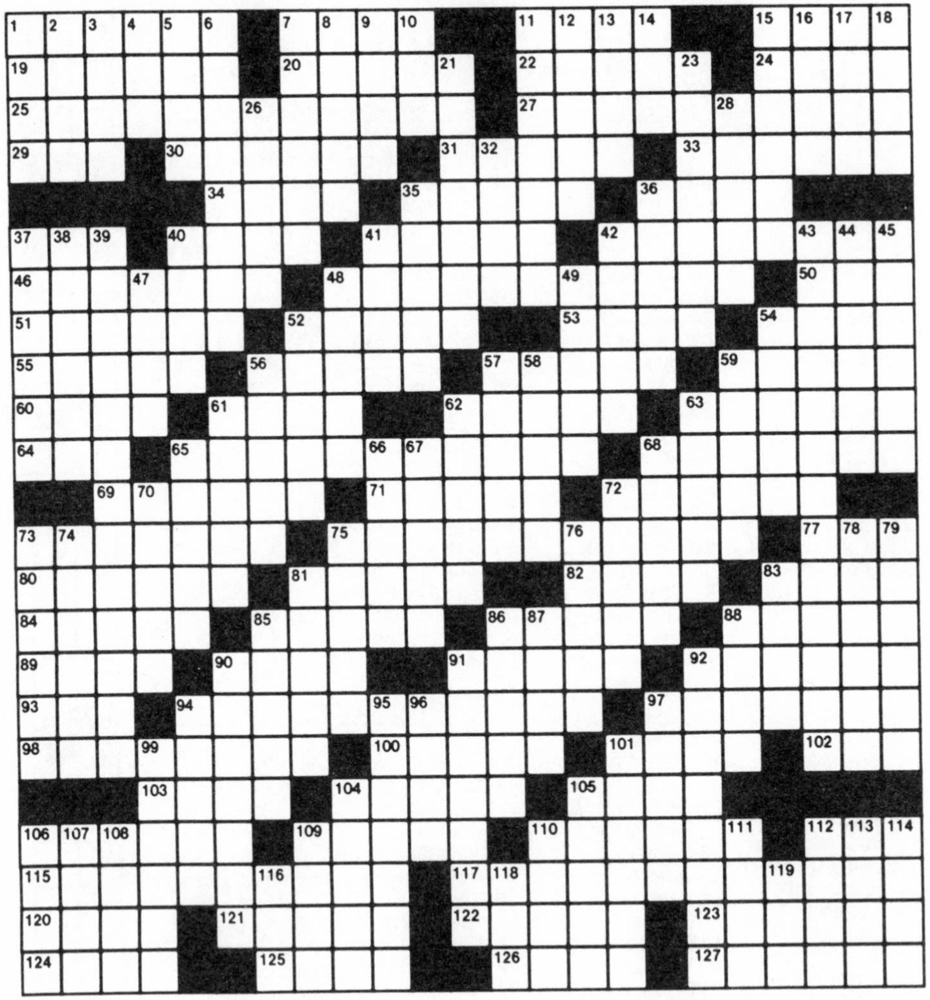

ACROSS

1 Fabricated report
7 Spike the punch
11 Calif. county
15 Navy rank equal to Col.
19 Thoroughfare
20 "The —— of Greece . . .": Byron
22 Elsinore courtier
24 To shelter
25 Barrie's "Little Minister"
27 Bolt's "Man for All Seasons"
29 Top of a gamut
30 Colored
31 —— as a beet
33 Jonathan's cousin
34 Capital of Calvados
35 Cross: Comb. form
36 Procreator
37 Golf or tennis term
40 Felix Krull's creator
41 Calorie
42 Marine shipping cost
46 Wail
48 Hale's "Man Without a Country"
50 Nut, for Nero
51 Treat
52 Listless
53 Bowl
54 Quick cut
55 Kind of act
56 Natural talent
57 Small amount
59 Luigi's foot
60 Tear
61 Goalie Peeters
62 Mark of literature
63 "Laura" lyricist
64 Onassis
65 Steele's "Man Who Saw Through Heaven"
68 China, Japan, etc.
69 Mature ones
71 Very much
72 Prepared
73 Shelters of a kind
75 Chesterton's "Man Who Was Thursday"
77 D.C. monogram
80 Washed away
81 Home of Petruchio's bride
82 Air: Comb. form
83 Key letter
84 Philanthropist
85 Left Bank chapeau
86 Patrick of films
88 Decree in Canada
89 Bombs that bomb
90 Middle East resident
91 Interdict
92 Ina of stage and screen
93 Vane dir.
94 Hubbard's bearer of "A Message to Garcia"
97 "Now, —— and Vixen!"
98 Study of immunity
100 Met basso
101 Kin in Barcelona
102 Boxers' stats.
103 "Battle Hymn . . ." composer
104 Creator of Alice the Goon
105 Stirs to activity
106 Potassium source
109 "Whither thou —— . . ."
110 Most delicate
112 Layer or thickness
115 Welty's "Optimist's Daughter"
117 Scott's "Lady of the Lake"
120 Bombeck
121 Permitted
122 Rhone tributary
123 Brought to nought
124 Tissues
125 Female equine
126 Foxx from St. Louis
127 Bed's canopy

DOWN

1 Bingo device
2 Of grandparents
3 Russian river
4 Black bird
5 Midget
6 Devote
7 Lend an ear
8 White with fright
9 Not nude
10 Suffix with auction or profit
11 Bridge bid
12 Jacob's eighth son
13 Jab
14 Purpose
15 Room on wheels
16 Unbalanced
17 Elf
18 Youngster
21 Impressive
23 Jolly good
26 Fatuous
28 Seductive one
32 Hindu attire
35 Lustrous
36 Chef's creation
37 Dawn
38 Resourceful
39 A. C. Doyle's "Veiled Lodger"
40 Beer ingredient
41 Son of Odin
42 Produced on a loom
43 Wilkie Collins's "Woman in White"
44 Cicerones
45 Skillful
47 Cooking staple
48 Proverbial corrupter
49 Water wheel
52 Cornea irritants
54 "Yes ——!"
56 Word on a dollar bill
57 Mystic
58 Medieval guild
59 Intrinsically
61 Whined
62 Papal headdress
63 Swedish seaport
65 More gigantic
66 Swap
67 Opening
68 "—— to the Moon"
70 Grooves
72 Fall flower
73 Barbara Bel ——
74 Excite
75 Avant- ——
76 Some sunken goods
78 Music buff's purchase
79 Spuds
81 Victor at Lake Erie
83 Breakfast dish
85 U.S. tennis champ: 1937
86 Gull or kitten
87 Gallic rebel's word
88 Soliloquy opener
90 Wiseacre
91 Does one's bit
92 Cancel; dele
94 Set apart
95 Cajole
96 Controls dishonestly
97 Brooded
99 Family in a 1936 novel
101 Thumped
104 Detector at sea
105 Buff
106 Lammed
107 Bern's river
108 Feeling nothing
109 Nutty
110 Arctic sight
111 Air
112 Gunpowder, for one
113 Abbe or Lois
114 Battle site: Oct. 1914
116 —— and haw
118 Small ape
119 Mdse.

Question Box

By Peter Swift

ACROSS

1 Kind of squad
5 ". . . you'll be ——, my son!": Kipling
9 Cumulus
13 Slough
16 Violinist Stern
18 Dugout
20 Perfume
22 Biblical high priest
23 Sure thing
24 Foster father of King Arthur
25 Fret
26 Infant's garb
27 "What ——?" (query of 1929)
31 Chase away
32 City in Georgia
33 Dealt successfully
34 Asian food source
38 Pretend not to see
41 Jockey Turcotte
42 "When ——?" (query of early 1600's)
48 Lose interest
49 Raise
50 Clear
51 Backward
52 Faro card
53 Badgers
55 Punts
58 Butt or butter
59 Sponge
61 Hoofed animal
62 Yahoo
63 "Where ——?" (query of 1948)
69 Bull, at times
70 Sweet wine
71 Wound up
72 Stigma
73 A symbol of thinness
74 Out of —— (vexed)
76 Crucifix letters
80 Dactyl or hallux
81 Suffer
82 Baritone Gobbi
83 This may be over your head
84 "Who's ——?" (query of 1962)
92 Dieter's abbr.
93 French historian and family
94 Puckered
95 Bluenose
98 "Virumque" follower
99 Checkmate
100 "Why ——?" (query of 1638)
109 Elec. current unit
110 Bring out
111 Scottish landowner
112 "Schwanda the Bagpiper," e.g.
113 The quiet side
114 The O'Grady lass
115 Bat
116 Oases
117 Mary Quant's style
118 Swab's supper
119 Look of a rake on the make
120 Where a padlock goes

DOWN

1 One of a trio by Caesar
2 Fertility goddess
3 Lean
4 Anagram for ache
5 Paint remover
6 Virile
7 Prefix with body
8 When both hands are straight up
9 Road surface
10 Olympian
11 Horse house
12 Under lock and key
13 Jazz style
14 Oil producer
15 Heckled
17 Flimflam
19 Unit of work
21 Who obeyed Howe?
28 He played the mark in "The Sting"
29 Kind of walk
30 Hanker
34 Fleet fliers, for short
35 Where the Miami flows
36 Almost a meter
37 Lightens
38 Least bit
39 Bothers
40 Mary Lincoln, —— Todd
41 Tpks.
43 "Procrastination is the —— time": Young
44 Starter
45 In a tangle
46 In high dudgeon
47 Celebrated
53 Pkg.
54 Fast and stirring, musically
55 Nursery-rhyme opener
56 Make a choice
57 Airplane part
58 Spot for a flea-flicker
60 Gas: Comb. form
61 ". . . this —— golden time": Shak.
62 Dorcas Society meeting
63 "—— One Track Mind," 1945 song
64 What ibn means
65 More faithful
66 Monogram of the "Mood Indigo" man
67 Feather's partner
68 QB's objectives
73 Joins
74 Leo is one
75 Outfielder Amos
77 Recess
78 Brioche
79 Full of uncertainties
81 Candidate for a suit
82 Musical sound
85 Alan or Robert
86 Dancer in a 1921 song
87 Buyers
88 "—— pronounce you . . ."
89 "—— What's Become of Sally," 1924 song
90 Saharan
91 Cricket-bat wood
95 Sacred song
96 Benvolio's friend
97 Increased
98 Mainspring
99 Shape
101 Land of Esau's descendants
102 Liturgical tunic
103 Kingdom loser in a refrain
104 Minute
105 Red-fleshed fish
106 Hindu writings
107 Mother of Ate
108 Speak harshly

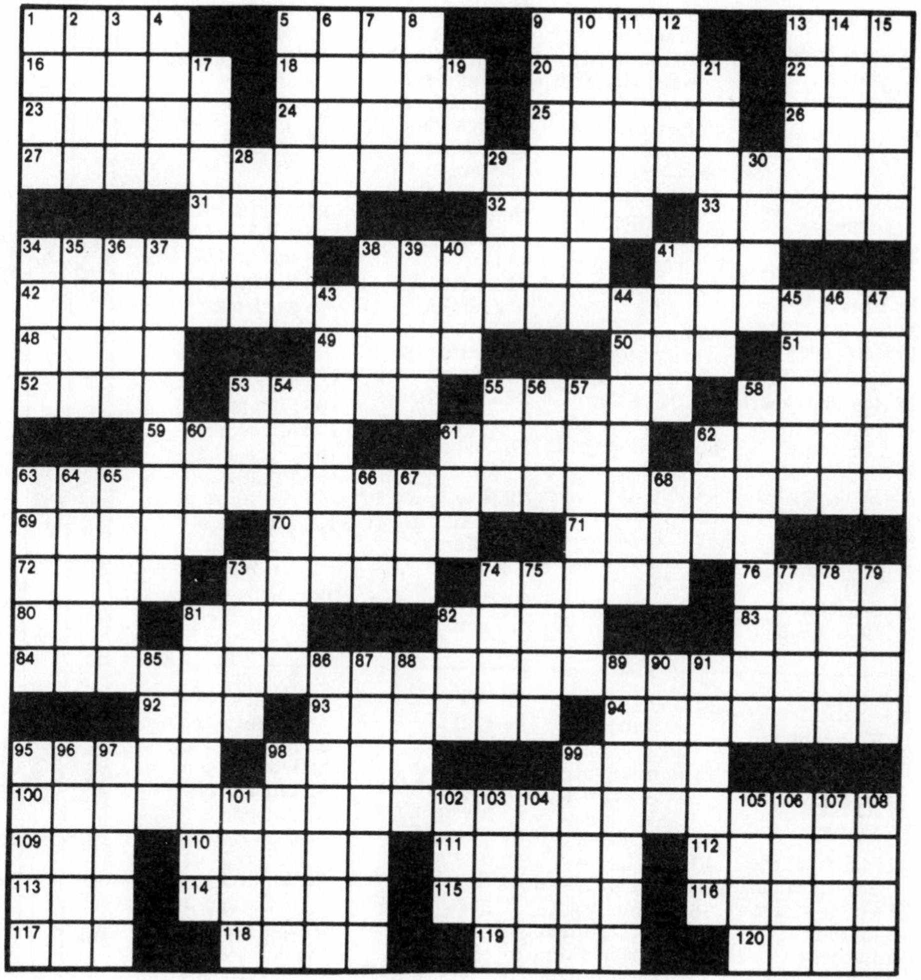

"... Quite Contrary"

By Frances Hansen

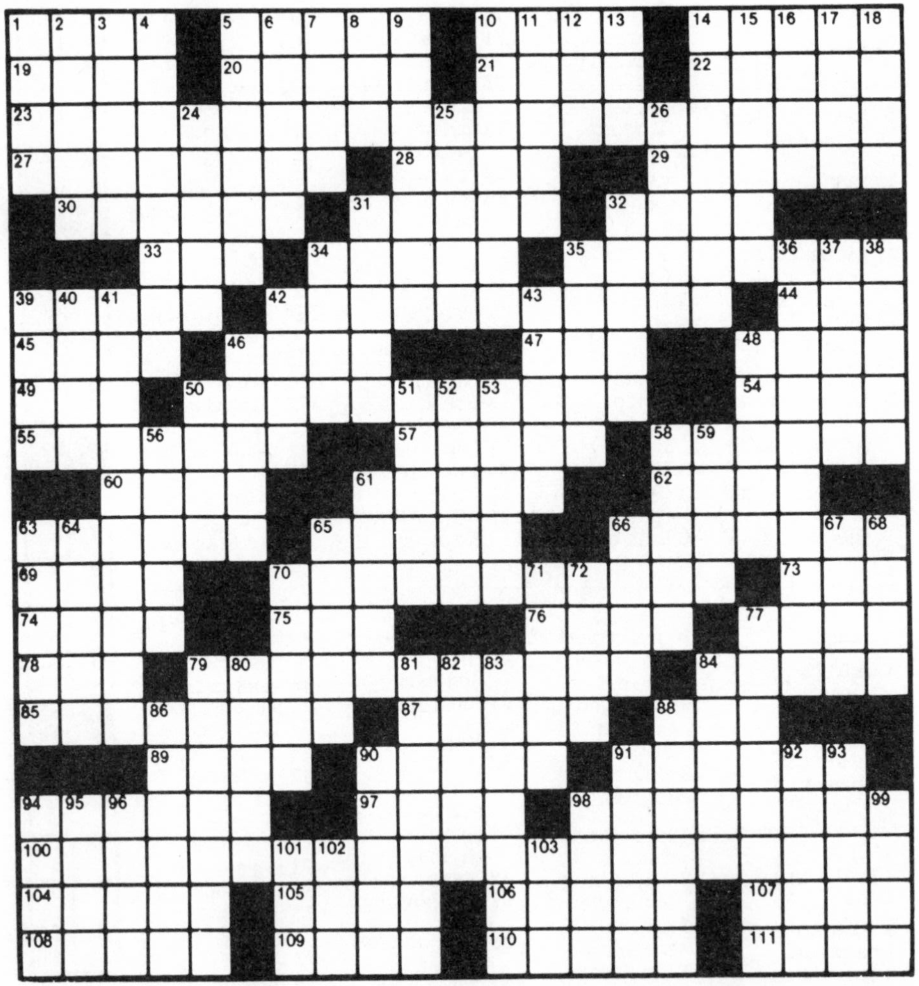

ACROSS

1 Came to rest
5 Alaskan seaport
10 N.Y. museum acronym
14 Domicile
19 Sudanese people
20 The 23d is comforting
21 Yemenite
22 Caused yawns
23 How does your garden grow?
27 How does your garden grow?
28 Vol's state
29 Sleeve type
30 Cash-register reading
31 French governing body
32 Do a cotton-picking job
33 Possessive pronoun
34 Jeanne d'Arc was martyred here
35 He dyes for a living
39 —— Lama
42 How does your garden grow?
44 —— toot (carousing)
45 Arabian Sea gulf
46 Later, alligator
47 Castor, for one
48 904, to Nero
49 Baron's color
50 How does your garden grow?
54 Dog star
55 Whenever
57 "Down —— the Sugar Cane," 1908 song
58 Treatise on plants
60 Pop
61 Pepys's penwork
62 Fragrance
63 Pieceworker
65 Stickum
66 Abscam concern
69 Hautboy
70 How does your garden grow?
73 Goal
74 Medieval crucifix
75 Before, poetically
76 Shave an apple
77 Lien on one's house: Abbr.
78 Last month, in a bus. letter
79 How does your garden grow?
84 "Merry Widow" man
85 Go awry, as a plan
87 A Page from Okla.
88 Distinguished dict.
89 Agog
90 Put in a piggery
91 Carryings-on
94 Of a feather
97 A P.M. under George III
98 How does your garden grow?
100 How does your garden grow?
104 Talk gibberish
105 Isinglass
106 Mirador
107 Little monkey
108 Prodded
109 Hamill stunt
110 Mr. Bruce (memorable Dr. Watson)
111 Shrine Bowl team

DOWN

1 Elec. units
2 Navigational device
3 Rainbow: Prefix
4 Man from the Barbary Coast
5 Witches' stock in trade
6 Progeny
7 Russian news agency
8 J-N connection
9 Dilettante
10 Actress Anna of "The Rose Tattoo"
11 Praying figure
12 Deface
13 Beame or Burrows
14 Double this for a Faulkner book
15 Inimitable Scarecrow at Oz
16 Viva voce
17 Ten: Comb. form
18 Definitely not Mary's garden
24 Raccoon's kin
25 Magazine plea
26 Singing syllables
31 Plumb the depths
32 Seethes
34 Fischer's castle
35 Hold fast
36 How does your garden grow?
37 Louise or Loos
38 Part of U.S.N.A.
39 Mrs. Copperfield, née Spenlow
40 "You said it, brother!"
41 How does your garden grow?
42 In a pet
43 Daft
46 Third largest of the Philippines
48 St.-John's-bread
50 Sojourn
51 Reach by radio
52 Cremona name
53 Bridge is his long suit
56 "And so ——" (see 61 Across)
58 Silver, for one
59 Work on copy
61 Librarian's gadget
63 Great vessel for grog
64 Small change in the agora
65 Dodge
66 Spinning-wheel sound
67 Capital of Latvia
68 Norse giant
70 Caught wind of
71 Assigned to a post: Abbr.
72 Where to climb Haleakala
77 Ply with healing potions
79 Attacked brutally
80 Beadlike pellet
81 Most favorable
82 Actor Ralph of "The Waltons"
83 Cowboy's hat
84 Pretend
86 Danish king of England: 1016-35
88 His moon was for "the Misbegotten"
90 New "Age"
91 Shaded walk
92 Papal court
93 Leopard's immutable markings
94 "Hair" (and other hits) producer
95 Cio-Cio-San's set of boxes
96 Neighbor of Minn.
98 Few: Prefix
99 Loretta of "M*A*S*H"
101 Singer Sumac
102 Social reformer Dorothea
103 "Exodus" hero

157

Sentencing the Celebrities

By Maura B. Jacobson

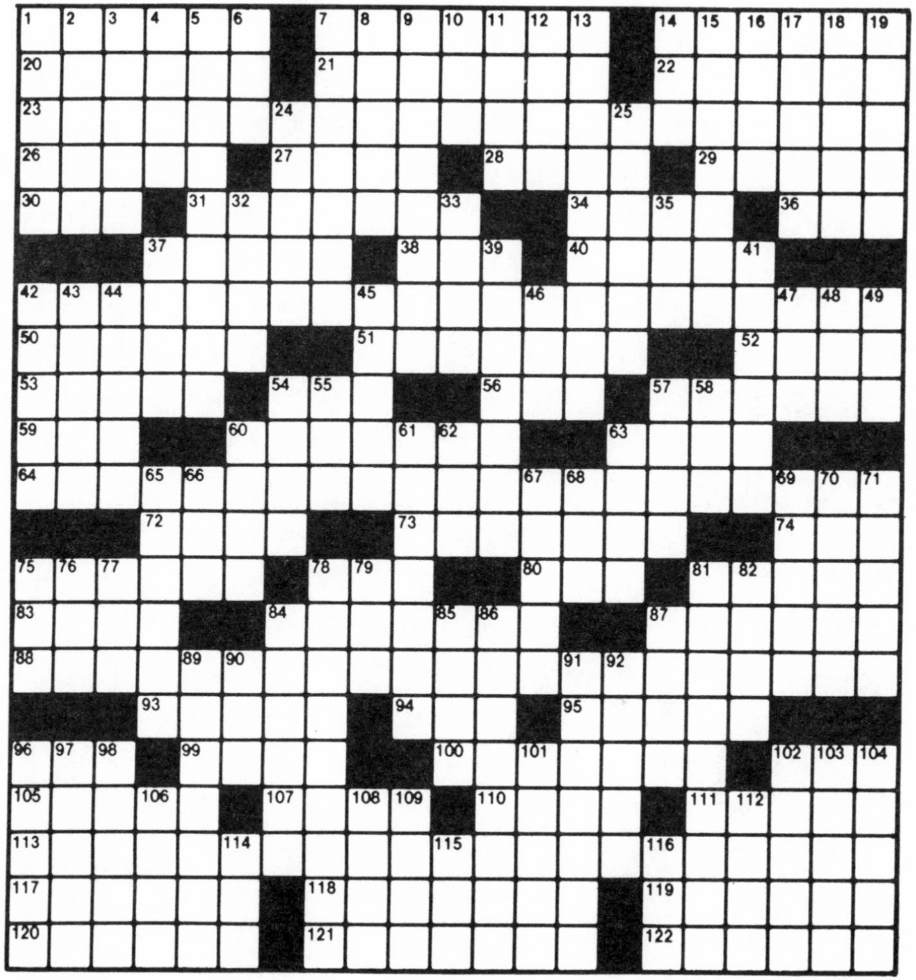

ACROSS

1 Twain is buried here
7 Minx's specialty
14 Becky Sharp's friend
20 Ease up
21 Composer Salieri
22 Parlors
23 Fred Jim Tom Edna
26 "The Lady ——"
27 Rat-——
28 Cyrano's problem
29 Less noble
30 Kiltie's refusal
31 Neck of land
34 Part of T.A.E.
36 El stop
37 City on the Mohawk
38 Caddy contents
40 Lowed
42 Lola H. L. Teresa
50 Annual period
51 Swimmer Williams et al.
52 Pouting grimace
53 Lazy or black-eyed one
54 Verdi's "La Forza —— Destino"
56 Nanny has three
57 Hit with a ray gun
59 Go-aheads
60 Bring up on charges
63 Turnpike levy
64 Alistair Robert Jack George
72 Linguist Chomsky
73 Cry of praise
74 Sleep phase, familiarly
75 Unbend
78 L.B.J. beagle
80 Rotating piece
81 Architect Jones
83 Western Samoan city
84 Skulnik of the stage
87 Kind of garage
88 Oscar Thomas William Dean John
93 Stalk: Comb. form
94 Roman hearth deity
95 Hornet's nest
96 Monterey's Fort ——
99 Do pruning
100 Languid speaker
102 Barbary beast
105 Shortchange
107 Vincent Lopez theme
110 Babylonian war god
111 The Bulbul Ameer
113 Ronald Lou Karen Dan
117 Apprehensive
118 Slattern
119 Pass
120 Eosin
121 Free of iniquity
122 More soppy

DOWN

1 Fey
2 Liza's sister
3 Watered silk
4 Peekaboo words
5 Version
6 Plus
7 "You can —— again!"
8 Region in Indochina
9 Ordinances
10 Cry out loud
11 Privy to
12 Actor Robert De ——
13 Filmy items
14 "—— was going to St. Ives . . ."
15 Boxer turned actor
16 Exile island
17 Wind-borne soil
18 Map detail
19 "Ad —— per aspera"
24 Gate closure
25 Casabas, e.g.
32 Poster
33 Posted
35 Pledge
37 She-bear, to Octavia
39 Dry fruits
41 Cheek dent
42 Org.
43 White: Prefix
44 Chaliapin, for one
45 Black: Prefix
46 Barbie's beau
47 Rep. group
48 Artist's concern
49 Spread hay
54 Type of table or major
55 Miscalculate
57 Novelist Gale
58 Castor or Pollux
60 As blind as ——
61 "Moby Dick" narrator
62 Nanty ——, neighbor of Johnstown
63 Chinese society
65 Works dough
66 Many eras
67 Large parrot
68 L-P connection
69 Heath
70 Juridic
71 Atlanta campus
75 Inexperienced
76 Finial
77 Mae West role
78 Whirlybird sites
79 Mil. branch
81 Suited for safeguarding
82 Beatty and Calmer
84 Acting droopy
85 One source of roe
86 Like Hagar of the comics
87 Word with shoppe
89 Rapture
90 Pallid
91 Swathes
92 Fragrant bush
96 Come about
97 Avignon's river
98 Opposite of stetted
101 Guthrie namesakes
102 Learn to fit in
103 Race-track prize
104 Church functionary
106 "Diary of —— Housewife"
108 Asiatic lemur
109 Radio-controlled bomb
112 Tempo
114 Comedian Louis
115 The works
116 Site of the Royal Botanic Gardens

Directory

By Mary Virginia Orna

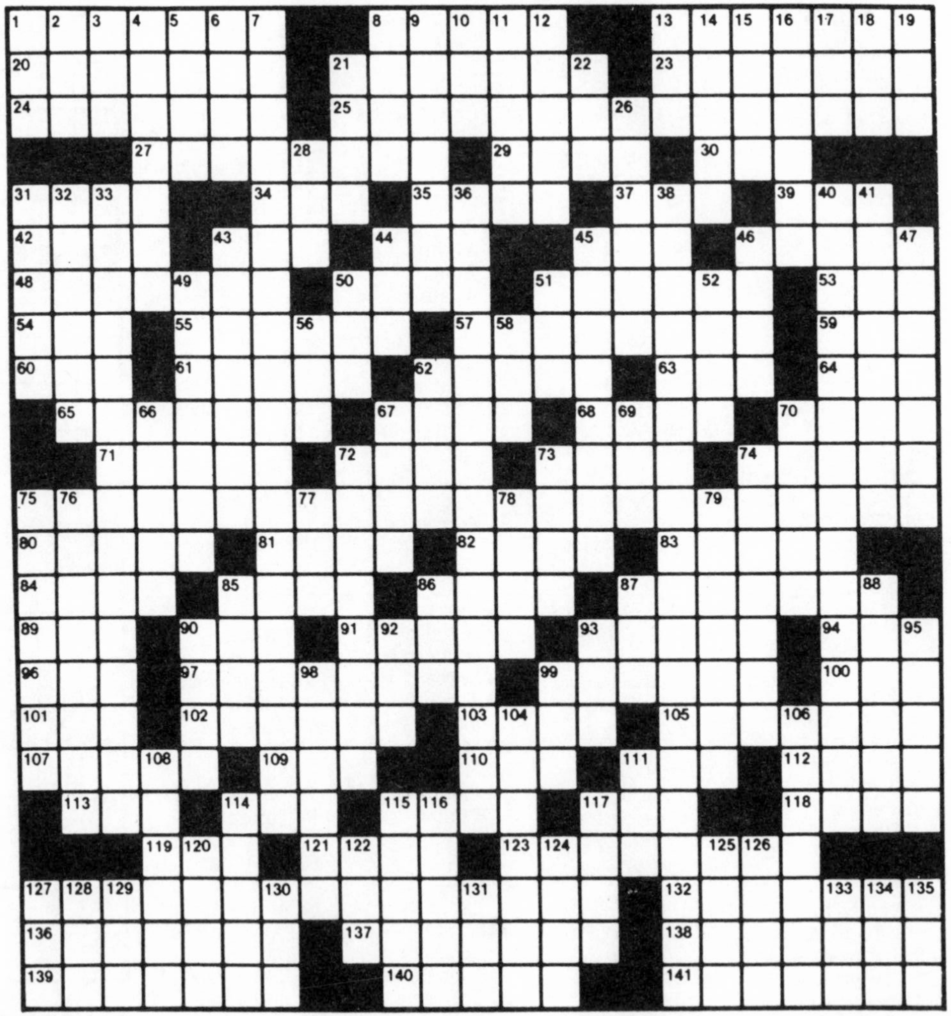

ACROSS

1 Painted carelessly: Slang
8 Notions
13 Histrionics
20 Portuguese poet: 1482-1552
21 Walpole's "The Castle of ——"
23 Cluj's country
24 "—— us our friends . . .": R.L.S.
25 Bass-baritone at Covent Garden?
27 Like some female elephants
29 Holm oak
30 Very long time
31 Malay short jacket
34 Shoe width
35 Mets' milieu
37 Opposite of trans
39 Nigerian native
42 U.S., Can., etc.
43 —— Sarah Siddons
44 Arthur or Lillie
45 Impair
46 Northern porgies
48 Hebrew day of rest
50 Hum of a motor
51 Of an insect's stage
53 G.O.P. member
54 Author Fleming
55 Sadat and others
57 Employee's extra hours
59 Refrain syllable
60 Pen point
61 "A rose —— other name . . ."
62 Like a kook
63 Blynken pal
64 Wimbledon call
65 Most ashen
67 River-pollution problem
68 A Diamond who was rough
70 Star of "Mon Oncle"
71 God, in Gaziantep
72 Heifetz's teacher
73 Habit
74 Ray
75 Soprano on Wilshire Boulevard?
80 Rigel's constellation
81 Cosmo or astro follower
82 Heal
83 Rope for Red Ryder
84 Chaney Jr. and Sr.
85 On a par in Paris
86 Actor Bruce ——
87 A cause of absenteeism
89 Gautier's "—— Nuit de Cléopâtre"
90 Outside: Comb. form
91 Heart chambers
93 Taco topping
94 —— Aviv
96 Marble or river in England
97 Western showdown
99 Hitchcock film: 1964
100 Stowe girl
101 Ransom —— Olds
102 Reflect
103 Off
105 Of the stomach
107 Rather dark
109 —— Plaines, Ill.
110 Conducted
111 Hideaway
112 Foil's cousin
113 Start of the 12th century
114 Fall mo.
115 "The Maja Nude" painter
117 Larch
118 Masefield's "—— Harker"
119 Potok hero
121 Salty drop
123 Pool event
127 Soap-opera character at S.M.U.?
132 Expert performer
136 Policy that pays off
137 Item in the street scene
138 Skittler's target
139 Certain courses
140 Onset
141 Hankered

DOWN

1 Grads' successors
2 Sass
3 Attorneys' org.
4 Disquiet greatly; agitate
5 Prie-——
6 Crafts' partner
7 Educator at the White House?
8 Inhabitants: Suffix
9 Worker in lead
10 Site of the incus
11 Actress Dickinson
12 Memorial marker
13 Beautician Westmore
14 Fashions
15 Predecessor of "Mardi"
16 Kind of acid from gallnuts
17 Suffix with opal
18 Pianist —— y Castellano
19 Line for Gleason
21 Molding or arch
22 Comedian Olsen
26 Dray
28 Bandleader Brown
31 Vessel for washing
32 R. W. Reagan's first Sec. of State
33 French playwright in the Midwest?
36 Composer at the Colosseum?
38 Songwriter on the Unter den Linden?
40 Actor in Amish country?
41 Lehár specialty
43 Worker's time unit
44 Word with school or tour
45 Where Backbone Mt. looms
46 Travois or luge
47 Steric
49 Hammurabi's city
50 Peep
51 Albanian coin
52 F. F. Gosden role
56 Myrmicid
58 Anatomical vessel
62 Peat, e.g.
66 Glee-club group
67 Kugel ingredient
69 Minute part of a joule
70 Esthetic judgment
72 Overpraises
73 He wrote "The High and the Mighty"
74 Villains
75 Scroll-shaped
76 Mineral called halotrichite
77 Motorists' org.
78 Body fluids
79 Playwright Hellman
85 She loved Narcissus
86 Actress Joanne ——
87 German pronoun
88 County, lake or river in Utah
90 Spot
92 Anderson's "High ——"
93 Hudson or Nash
95 Spiked the punch
98 Folk singer from Birmingham
99 Rabid
104 A —— a famine
106 More snappish
108 Geraldine's boyfriend in Flip Wilson shows
111 Faint
114 Elliptic
115 Balls, e.g.
116 Praying figure
117 Idée ——
120 Word in an ultimatum
122 Guernsey or Jersey
124 Whip mark
125 Coloratura Mills
126 Erupter in 1983
127 Haggard novel
128 Word with long or short
129 Tolkien creature
130 Abnormal: Comb. form
131 "—— Na Na"
133 Biol. lab item
134 Bond
135 Remnant

Sins of Omission

By Alfio Micci

ACROSS

1 "The Consul" heroine
6 —— Gay
11 Prefix with light
14 Knight's garb
18 Wickerwork material
19 Skirt inserts
20 Leather from sheepskin
21 Church calendar
22 Art letter
24 Focal point
26 Full of gusto
27 A for sore eyes
29 "On —— Boat to China"
32 Musical sense
34 Blue Eagle meas.
35 Monotonous life style
36 Sideways
37 Worried
39 Roi's mate
43 Part of the Pacific
46 Ger.
47 Less lenient
49 Curr. unit
50 Patterns
52 Footless
53 Homeless one, for short
54 Fleet
57 "of All Flesh"
59 Copter's relative
60 Windflower
62 Laconic Pres.
63 Road shoulder
64 Type of prof
65 Roastmaster Martin's nickname
66 Like some silks
68 "I am monarch of —— survey"
70 Report-card foursome
72 Redolence
74 "Dolce —— niente"
75 Was far from cordial
78 Cotton quantity
79 "A in time . . ."
82 Ravel's "La ——"
83 Explorer Johnson
84 "When I was —— . . ."
85 Japan's largest island
86 Agcy. Eric Johnson headed
87 Be bratty
89 Eke Crater locale
90 Municipal officials
94 Succeed
95 Short narrative
96 Unreasonable
97 Postal abbr.
99 Take an unfair share
100 Serling or Laver
103 In agreement
104 "Tell, in mournful numbers": Longfellow
109 "—— evil . . ."
111 American inventor
112 "upon a time . . ."
118 So be it
119 Eternally
120 Wild hogs
121 Dissimulation of a sort
122 Wagnerian tetralogy
123 Glowing
124 White-plumed bird
125 Perfume the air

DOWN

1 P. Wylie's target
2 "—— was going to . . ."
3 James Jones heroes
4 —— Moines, Iowa
5 Site of Horse Mesa Dam
6 Fowl products
7 Nick of films
8 Indic language
9 Actor Cariou
10 Invites
11 Astaire-Rogers film: 1935
12 Bide one's time
13 Bring on oneself
14 Chiller heavy
15 TV's Johnson
16 Brainstorm in Brest
17 Bereft, old style
20 Emulate Miss Otis
23 Tritons
25 Habituated
28 Flood
29 Cinders collector
30 "A Touch of"
31 County in Sweden
33 Sound heard in a parade
36 Kin of the sunfish
38 "Then I like some watcher of the skies": Keats
40 "A for All Seasons"
41 Approaches
42 Bane of grain
44 Haste, in Hanover
45 Fuss
47 Box
48 Busy Yuletide person
51 Steep slope
52 In wonder of
55 Chemical compound
56 Pasquale or Giovanni
58 Germany's first First Family: 1919-25
59 Emperor after Nero
61 Kind of soup
66 Artist Grant
67 Mount or Prince
69 Murray Schisgal play
70 Domicile
71 Street of songdom
73 Cart
75 Synagogue
76 Early ascetic
77 Silas ——, U.S. patriot
80 Yoruban deity
81 Half or third of a dance
84 Poplars
88 Book by Philip Roth
89 Dog that barks at Luna
91 A Keaton
92 Relating to insects
93 Army V.I.P. in charge of provisions
95 Masticated
98 Second of two
101 Levant or Hammerstein
102 Steel-plow pioneer
104 Dread
105 Noted Italian film director
106 Zilch, to Pierre
107 Budge
108 Start of a famous solilo-quy
110 Once, once
113 Ale's cousin
114 Mispickel or bauxite
115 Otto —— Bismarck
116 Em followers
117 Recolor

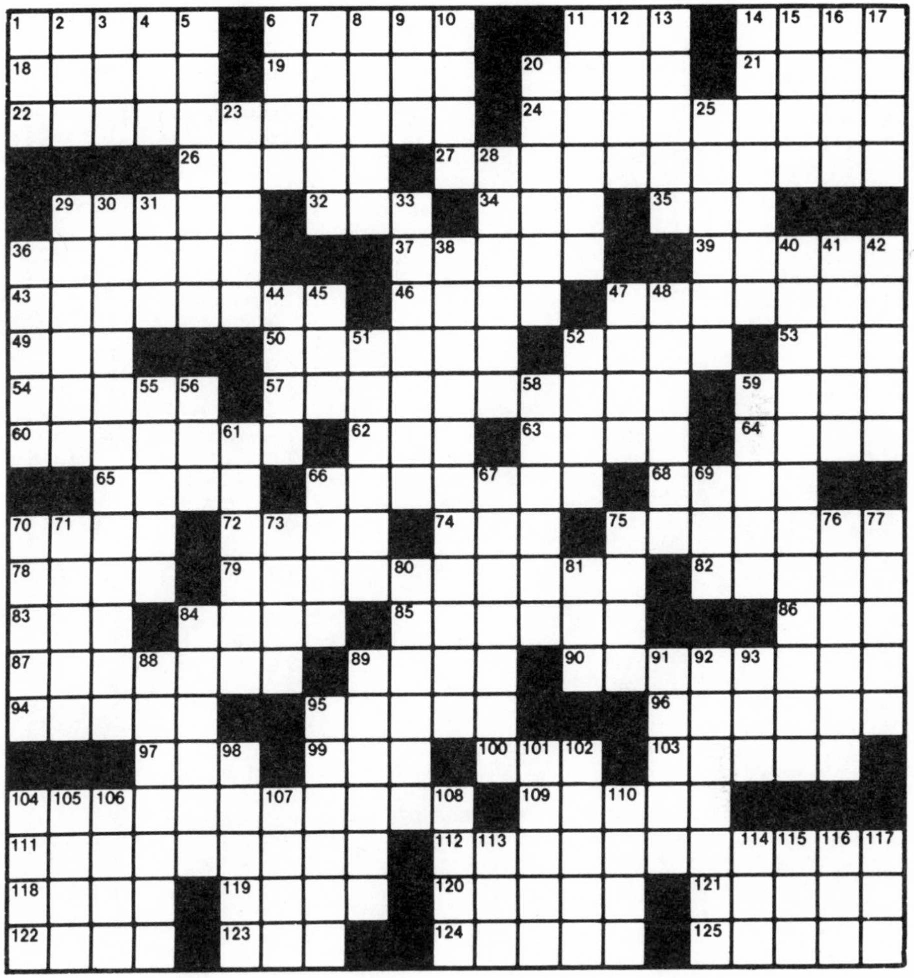

Cosmos

By Bert Rosenfield

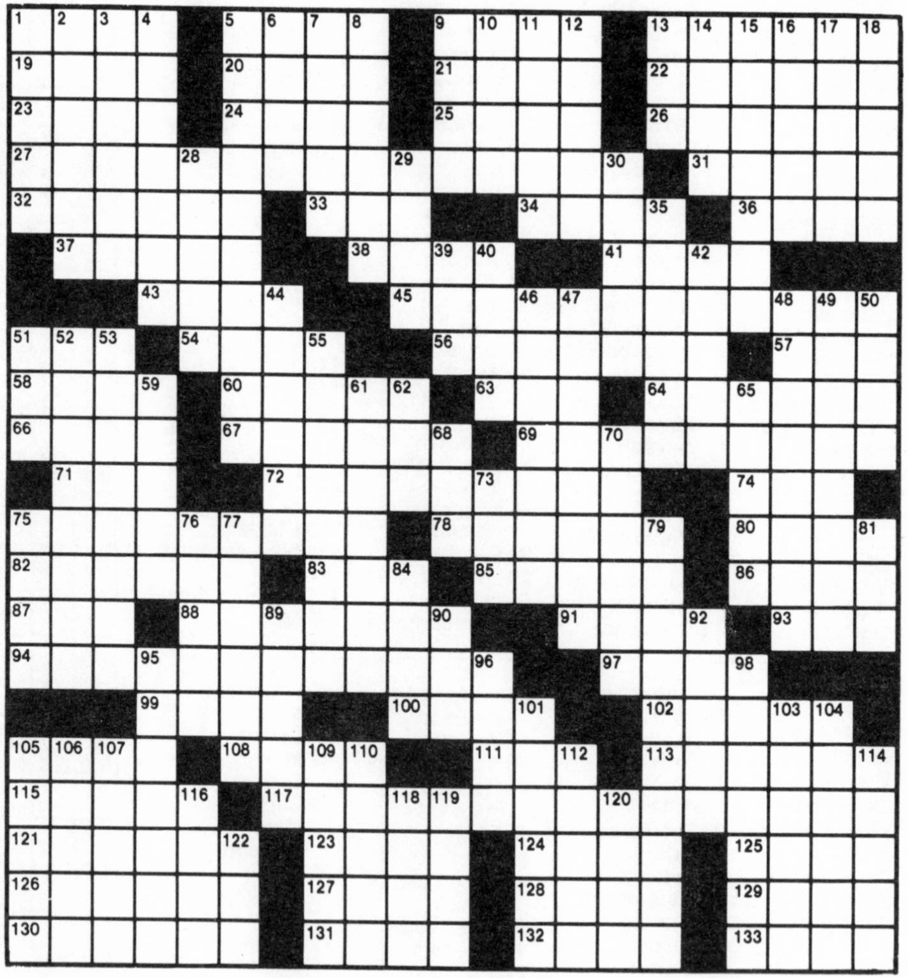

ACROSS

1 Stillage or spillage
5 Con man's ploy
9 Roe source
13 FATHER OF ONE-EYED SONS
19 Statue by Polyclitus
20 One of the Guthries
21 Do port work
22 Cocktail-party item
23 Forbear
24 Trumpet
25 Hussein, for one
26 Up
27 WEILL MUSICAL
31 Paramour in Paris
32 Posher
33 Screw pine
34 N.K.V.D. antecedent
36 Robert or Alan
37 "Student Prince" prop
38 Indian groom
41 Notation in an M.D.'s book
43 Hunk of pie
45 METEOROLOGY OR GEOPHYSICS
51 Biblical verb ender
54 Ship's berth
56 Electrician
57 General Eaker
58 Worm of Assam
60 "Of Thee ——"
63 Tappet mover
64 Tizzies
66 Leo, for one
67 Virgilian opus
69 FINANCIAL MOGUL
71 Bd.-of-director's head
72 Renowned Met basso
74 Make lace
75 RODGERS-HART OPUS
78 Entire membership
80 Amos of baseball
82 Eyepiece
83 Abet's companion
85 Canonic mark
86 "Le ——," Massenet aria
87 European salamander
88 —— the Admiralty (U.K. naval brass)
91 Shipment to a hospital
93 Aberdeen's river
94 NORTH AMERICAN WHELK
97 U.S. mil. decorations
99 Where Sikkim is
100 Port ——, Egypt
102 Potsdam pronoun
105 Minn. neighbor
108 Rowing gaffe
111 Have being
113 Sulky
115 —— in (receptive)
117 CALOMEL
121 Grape seed
123 Worms get-together
124 Ab's follower
125 Partaking of
126 Soirs' antitheses
127 Ferber
128 Fad
129 A billionth: Comb. form
130 Kent's Daily ——
131 Time's Thomas
132 Anne and Cécile: Abbr.
133 Kind of plaid

DOWN

1 New growth
2 Aegean island
3 —— Express
4 Little pies
5 WINGDING, ROMAN STYLE
6 Zambezi denizen, for short
7 Hilo hello
8 Traverses the turnpike
9 Serb or Croat
10 Pika's cousin
11 Hersey's W.W. II town
12 Spray a vine
13 Fiddler-crab genus
14 —— avis
15 Do a Disney job
16 Twangy
17 Topple
18 "Flying Dutchman" soprano
28 —— -de-boeuf (oval windows)
29 Alice of films
30 Burst of energy
35 Directed aloft
39 Cornfield sound
40 Sevareid
42 Tex's mount
44 Split a circle
46 —— John of TV
47 Ups and downs of fashion
48 Treated chemically
49 Ingenious
50 Shrine Bowl team
51 M.I.T. degrees
52 Type of landing gear
53 L.A. event in 1984
55 Small minnows
59 Invalidate
61 Rather miserly
62 Hodges or McDougald
65 Plummer, e.g.
68 Short swim
70 New
73 Nadelhorn, for one
75 Jovial
76 Stake, to Sulla
77 Wry
79 REVERSIBLE COTTON FABRIC
81 Match the bet
84 Sylvan denizens
89 Build up matériel
90 Ala. neighbor
92 —— acids
95 Gulled
96 Mendacious one
98 Employing a springe
101 Basement appliances
103 Town on the Moselle
104 Fixed over
105 Act of 1765
106 Almost princely
107 Singer O'Day
109 Dangerous mosquito
110 June walker
112 Dash
114 Wood-joint component
116 Cape Cod feature
118 Copper, once
119 Its motto is "Industry"
120 Titanic
122 Orly-Dulles transp.

161

Role 'Em!

By A. J. Santora

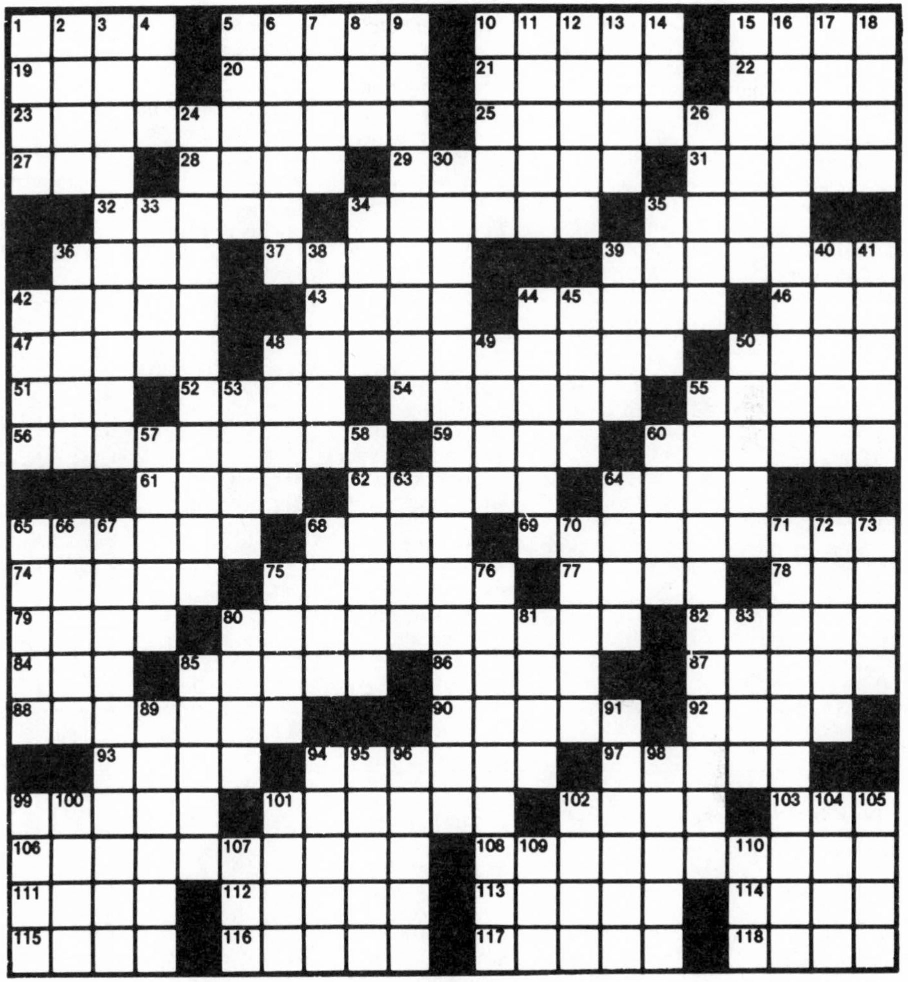

ACROSS

1 Feast at Waikiki
5 Cook on a grill
10 Florida city
15 Portmanteau word
19 Elec. units
20 Viking chieftain
21 Italian "Cleopatra": 1954
22 Setting for Leigh and Gable
23 Charles Boyer: 1938
25 Clint Eastwood: 1971
27 With 48 Down, Sinatra film: 1957
28 Always
29 Surgical instrument
31 Plant of the parsley family
32 Enthusiastic
34 Request
35 Like some screens
36 Soviet news service
37 Think
39 Lamb stew
42 Bearded, as barley
43 Biographer Leon
44 Piquant
46 Merkel of films
47 Mount climbed by Moses
48 Robert Duvall: 1972
50 V.P.'s boss
51 "—— Love You"
52 G.I. on French leave
54 Looked cheerful
55 Developed motion-picture film
56 Most vaporous
59 Sheep genus
60 —— vivre
61 Like some R-rated films
62 Loss of breath
64 Tape erasures
65 Complain
68 Rosebud of "Citizen Kane"
69 Guest at the club
74 "—— New York"
75 Ravel hit
77 "Rosemary's ——"
78 Prefix with spore or sphere
79 Field mouse
80 Cary Grant: 1946
82 —— Bell (Emily Brontë)
84 "Knute Rockne, —— American"
85 Fashion-show attendee
86 Jacks of clubs
87 Barbra Streisand: 1969
88 Like a wedding cake
90 Follower of knock or weak
92 Curved arch
93 Bad guys in W.W. II films
94 Allot
97 Deep void
99 Provide
101 Mall
102 Chemical suffix
103 Beige's kin
106 Gert Frobe: 1964
108 Rosalind Russell: 1958
111 Kind of club
112 Newman-Redford film, with "The"
113 Meetings
114 Syria, once
115 Compound
116 Scuffle
117 Notched, as a leaf
118 Thereabouts

DOWN

1 Arctic nomad
2 Swedish port
3 Bette Davis: 1961
4 Kind of tax
5 Musical note
6 Doc Holliday: 1939
7 Swan genus
8 Type
9 Laxity
10 Silent film, e.g.
11 Spirals
12 Word on a Montreal stop sign
13 Baltic citizen
14 Some of a sum
15 Locus —— (right to be heard)
16 Greer Garson: 1943
17 Stowe's "The Pearl of —— Island"
18 Marvin of recording fame
24 Ray Danton: 1960
26 Comous
30 Bob Hope: 1951
33 On the Celebes
34 Contract proposals
35 G.I. Janes of W.W. II
36 Jackie Coogan: 1922
38 Strips
39 Colored
40 Upright
41 Art appreciation
42 Kin of daboias
44 Of a Frankish people
45 "Peyton Place" denizen: 1957
48 See 27 Across
49 Hipster's patter
50 Polyhedron
53 Litz, e.g.
55 Gene Hackman: 1971
57 Nimble
58 More up in the world
60 Door-frame piece
63 Coop sound
64 Growl
65 Compete with
66 —— Gay, famed plane
67 Shelley Winters: 1964
68 Fish entree
70 Like Arbuckle
71 Jane Russell: 1951
72 Banishment
73 Cheerful
75 Hopalong Cassidy: 1935
76 Soft drink
80 What directors give
81 Agents, in some films
83 Firewood
85 Like a trailer from Hollywood
89 Oozed forth
91 Robert Donat: 1934
94 Potter's clay
95 Film shot
96 Title for Silvers in "You'll Never Get Rich"
98 Capital NW of Salt Lake City
99 Like omelets
100 Lopez theme song
101 Pay for a hand
102 "Journey —— Fear," 1942 film
104 Latin lover's word?
105 James Mason: 1954
107 Doctrine
109 Erstwhile Arab rep.
110 Little Red Book author

Echoes

By Richard Silvestri

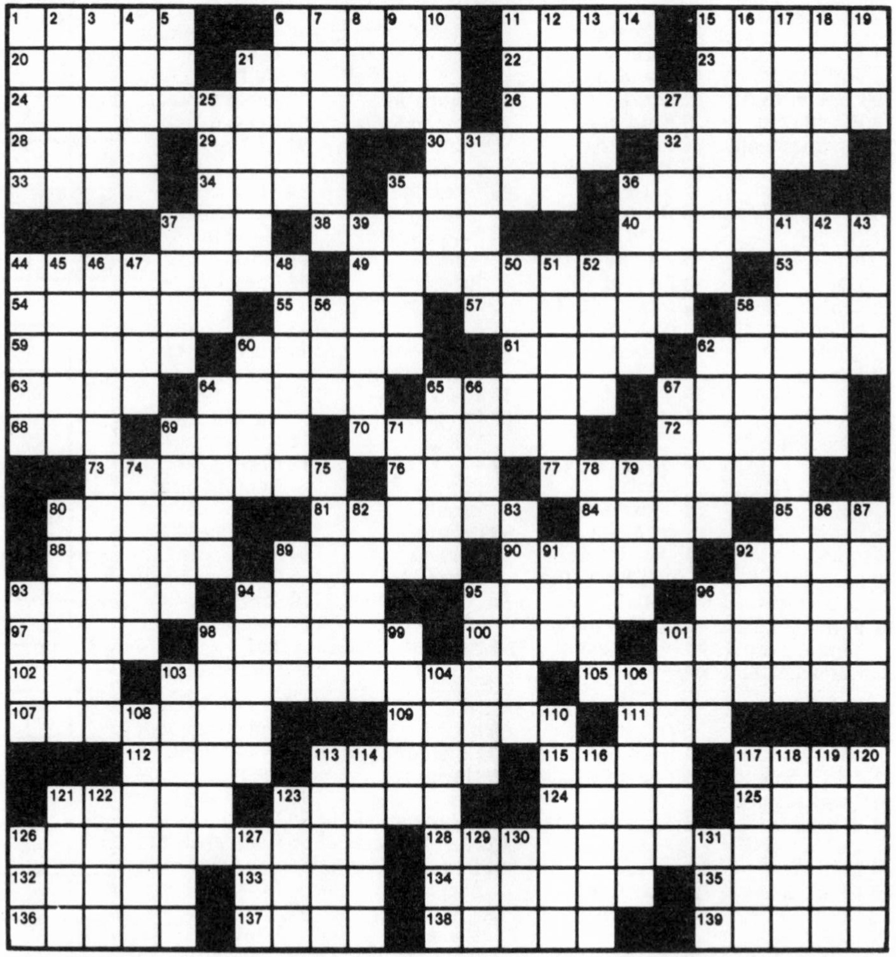

ACROSS

1 Mendacious
6 Walk through puddles
11 Agile
15 Bogart role
20 Expect
21 Lacedaemon
22 Creator of Mrs. Sarah Battle
23 Calumets
24 Film-festival dance?
26 Crazy stratagem?
28 Son-in-law of Elon
29 Pop singer Clapton
30 Leave in the lurch
32 Targets for Ness
33 The one here
34 Strike location
35 Hooch holder
36 Dispatched
37 Ginger
38 Hawthorne's birthplace
40 Die face
44 Calculated
49 North African-Scottish accent?
53 Grand —— Opry
54 Belong to
55 Woeful cry
57 Sudatory
58 Kind of jerk
59 Idolize
60 Just picked
61 Eastern European
62 Alternate of a sort
63 Burg
64 Mussolini portrayer in a 1940 film
65 It was good for Buck
67 Uses shears
68 Parabolic path
69 Part of A.M.
70 Think up
72 Conn man
73 High-tails it
76 Showed the way
77 Opposite of de jure
80 Anatomical trunk
81 Bordeaux product
84 Trevi throwaways
85 "—— we but world enough . . .": Marvell
88 Pounce
89 Contaminate
90 Ho predecessor
92 Capital of Western Samoa
93 AMPAS give-away
94 Additional
95 Mountain spur
96 Crop killer
97 German valley
98 Diamond measures
100 Hue
101 One of the Pelican State natives
102 Latin I verb
103 German candy?
105 Covered old ground
107 This ends via time or use
109 Ready for battle
111 Kindled
112 Netman Nastase
113 Ancient astrologer
115 Overlook
117 Church alcove
121 Mideast capital
123 Choir division
124 Art style of the 20's and 30's
125 Declared
126 Farewell to a Hoosier Democrat?
128 Prison social event?
132 Dipper
133 Century plant
134 Renan or Seton
135 Coppers for Copperfield
136 Drew back
137 Sea swallow
138 Long and thin
139 Mink's cousin

DOWN

1 Gem surface
2 Flooded
3 Hawaiian porch
4 Antrum
5 Tours season
6 Sixteenth-century power
7 Lists weapons
8 Grampus
9 RR stop
10 Boxing second
11 Denominations
12 Grit
13 In the chips
14 Tibetan ox
15 When he botched words, he watched birds
16 Ornamental loops
17 Snake, for one
18 —— ex machina
19 Second sight, for short
21 Difficulty
25 Moon goddess
27 W. S. Porter
31 Metrical feet
35 Pound sought by Shylock
36 Bottom of the map
37 Skin opening
39 Cast down
41 Deride Winnie?
42 Firstborn
43 Eye drop
44 Cowboy's rope
45 Witch of ——
46 Dog food?
47 "Show Boat" composer
48 Shade in
50 Washstand appurtenances
51 Took five
52 Balneal activity
56 Souvenir of Hilo
58 Marsh bird
60 Lot
62 In the bag
64 At hand
65 Turn inside out
66 Staff member
67 Ten in two on an alley
69 First woman to sit in Parliament
71 Verve
74 Bellowing
75 Deified beetle
78 Noisy beetle
79 Quitting time, for some
80 Take for granted
82 Rest at anchor
83 Royal roost
86 Bridal path
87 Behind the times
89 Riven
91 Dusk, to Donne
92 Father of Hippolyte
93 Algerian port
94 Parsonage
95 Molecule constituents
96 Sigma Chi, e.g.
98 Trigonometry word
99 Catches
101 Agora wear
103 Fastened, nautically
104 Bully or boxer
106 Draw out
108 Mentally quick
110 Sidestepped
113 Burgomaster
114 Cinereous
116 Not shipshape
117 Plus factor
118 Canvas covering
119 Inasmuch as
120 Garden tool
121 Indian maid
122 Middle: Prefix
123 Cotton unit
126 Librarian's deg.
127 Cave dweller
129 High dudgeon
130 Compass point
131 Where ltrs. come and go

Coining Phrases

By Louis Baron

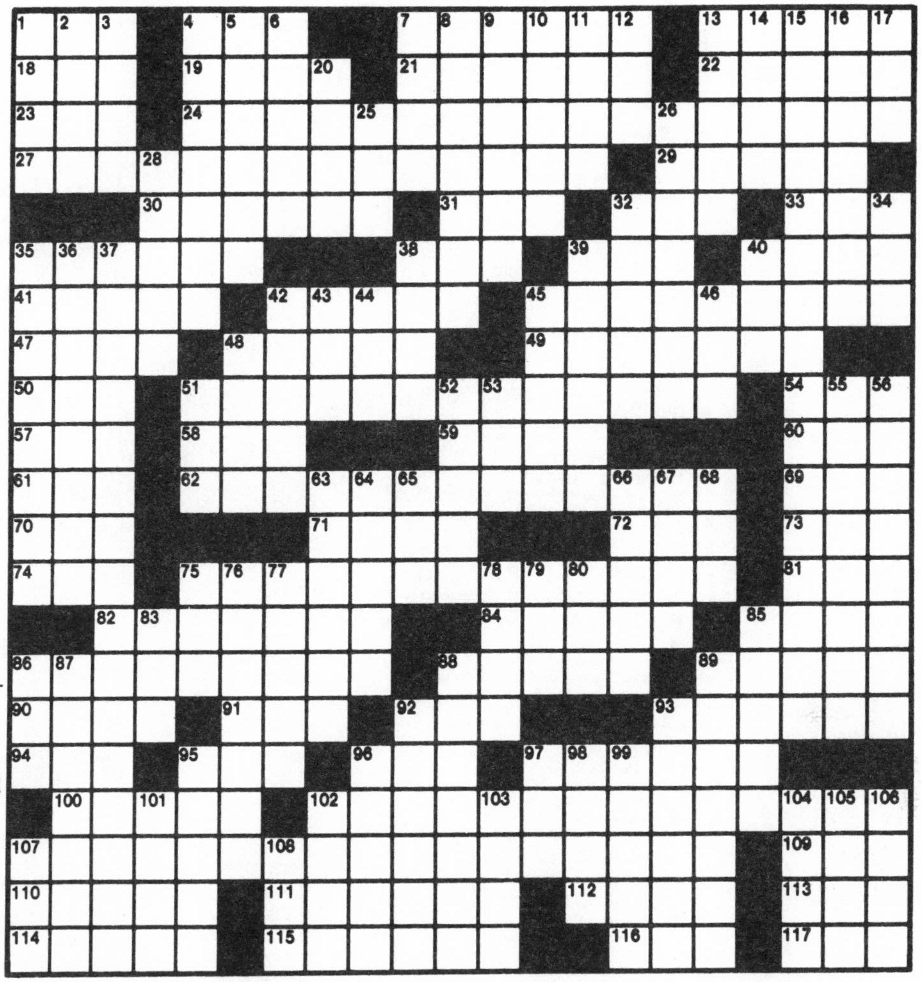

ACROSS

1 Short of
4 Popular promise
7 Color: Comb. form
13 City that once tired the U.S.
18 Old lyric poem
19 Lopez theme song
21 Titubated
22 Sheer linen
23 Cleo ender
24 Schizoid biblical economist?
27 Wellsian telephone?
29 Port of Israel
30 Poet —— Maria Rilke
31 Connective word
32 Miguel's aunt
33 Pitcher part
35 "... rare as a day ——?"
38 Use credit cards
39 Sonny's sibling
40 Dracula's pet comb. form
41 Othello's people
42 Loses ardor
45 London borough
47 Rubicund's opposite
48 Remembered ship
49 Where Emily Dickinson lived and died
50 Mil. bigwig
51 Complicated Russian contraption?
54 Exclamation in Aachen
57 Flu shot, e.g.
58 Zoological suffix
59 Assamese hill dweller
60 Refrain opener
61 Taboo-free, in Hawaii
62 Phrase from an OPEC butler?
69 Keatsian contraction
70 Port. coin
71 French director Clair
72 Palindromic Amerind
73 Polynesian beverage
74 —— gratias
75 Exchequer business?
81 Rap; chin
82 "—— the Night," 1941 song hit
84 Uhlan's gear
85 P.O.W. in England
86 Unreflecting
88 Intrinsically
89 All nerves
90 Sailing vessel
91 Pipe joint
92 Beach top
93 Rasped
94 Ottoman title
95 N.T. book
96 Consult with
97 Cop's arrest
100 Thrusting sword
102 Peon's partnership dream?
107 Where to find Washington?
109 She-bear: Sp.
110 Sleipnir or Bucephalus
111 Area above a bumper
112 Inner: Comb. form
113 Author Beigel
114 Has coming
115 Family of a German philosopher
116 Sov. state
117 Peruvian coin

DOWN

1 Blind feature
2 Hodgepodge
3 Complain shrilly
4 Wickiup occupants
5 Ahead, in golf
6 "Hellzapoppin" star
Housing in a O.T. eng.
12 Poe's Angel of the ——"
13 Open courts
14 Eastern cosmetic
15 Propertied Saudi?
16 Of yore
17 Formerly called
20 Disyllabic sigh
25 Lobed organ
26 Goethe's "Wilhelm ——"
"Advise and sent"
36 "——, jolly red ...": Ravenscroft
37 Turkish fur merchant?
38 Kiev was his capital
39 Large Asiatic deer
40 Many mins.
42 Room on a steamship
43 Canvas
44 —— and the same
45 Shield
46 Cgs unit
"Scarface"
52 "Being ——, sail": Herbert
53 Some notes
55 Glacier hazard
56 Heckled
63 Show up
64 Gallic royal personage
65 Lodging
66 Domingo asset
67 Ecole verb
68 Allowables
75 Ending for cheer or tear
76 Auber opera: 1834
77 Willow for baskets
78 Fido's "uninvitee"
long way off
80 Pt. of a test
83 Director Jean-—— Godard
85 Courage
86 "Life —— jest ...": Gay
87 Purplish red
88 Warm up
customers via ads
89 Farm machine
92 Uang or elater
93 Endocrinologist's concern
95 Some Yalies
96 Bit of mistletoe
97 Off. document
98 River to the Elbe
99 Blum and Trotsky
101 Now's partner
102 Interlaken's river
103 Smeltery piles
104 Chits
105 Kon-Tiki Museum's city
106 Spike's relative
107 Simple sugar
108 Cry of disgust

Occupational Hazards

By Charles M. Deber

ACROSS

1 "Choice" fellow
7 Bos. or N.Y.
10 Memorable Belgian musician
14 Reckless
18 Boo-boos in a book
19 Parseghian
20 Legal
22 Scat singer
23 Pride member
24 Admiral's nightmare?
27 He raised Hel
28 ". . . —— her curds and whey"
29 Regatta and poet William E.
30 Engineer's downfall?
34 Reverse of verso
35 African lake
36 Tomato blight
38 Scents
42 Bowl call
44 Quagmire
47 Bad time for an auto mechanic?
49 French saint: Dec. 1
51 Buttons on dryers
53 Lair for Leo
54 Marie or Anne: Abbr.
55 Kind of ray or globulin
57 Snide remark
58 Referee's predicament?
63 Haberdasher's headaches?
65 Andrea ——
67 Type of sleeve
68 "Tribute" playwright
70 Reuters' rival
71 Northern forest
72 Shipment to Kennedy
74 Set starter
76 Peril for a veterinarian?
80 Mattress salesman's affliction?
83 Sprite
85 Prepared
86 Chip off the cold block
87 Mouths, to Marius
88 Incantations
91 Pickle spice
92 Plumber's fantasies?
97 Guarantee
99 Peggy or Pinky
100 Wonder of songdom
101 Whale spray
103 Baseball's Rusty
105 Follow
107 Electrician's worry?
112 Comes forth
115 Type of type
116 Doer: Suffix
117 Watchmaker's woe?
119 Darcel or Levertov
121 Burden
122 Witnessing clause, in law
123 Huxtable or Rehan
124 Dangerfield
125 Robin's residence
126 Flagmaker
127 Belgian-French river
128 Prevailing procedures

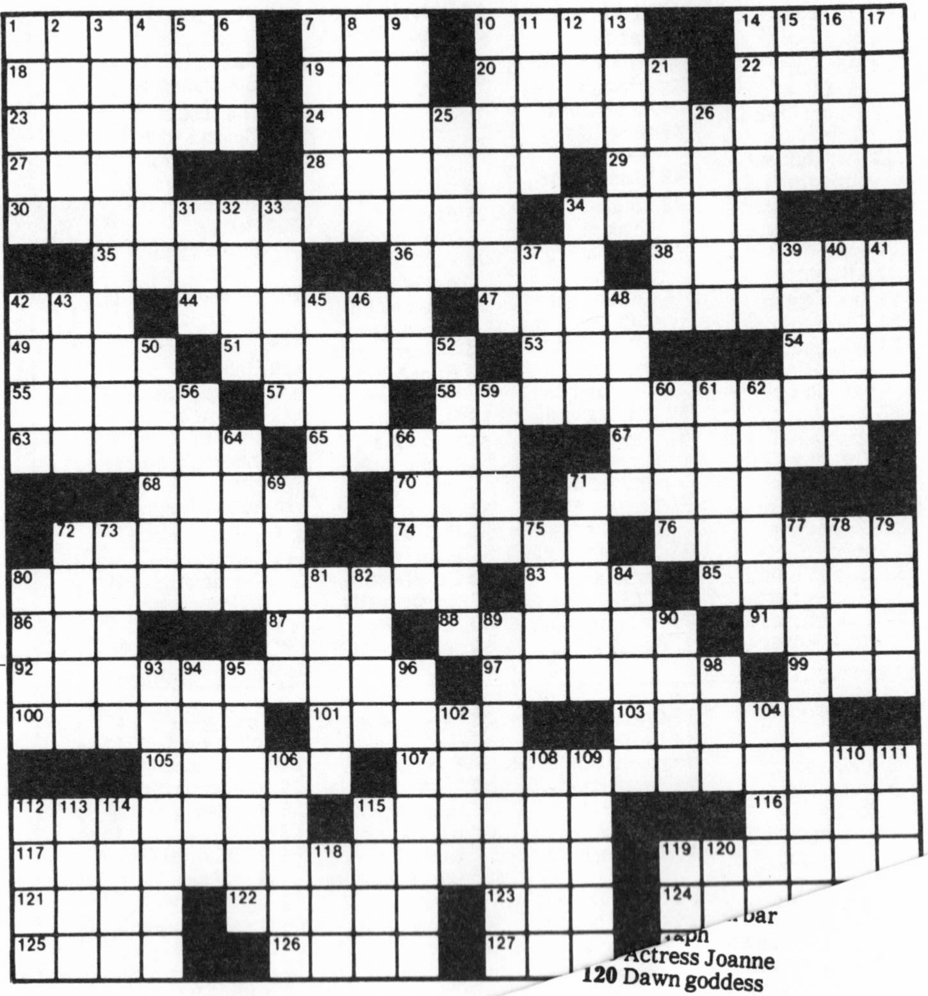

...bar
...aph
Actress Joanne
120 Dawn goddess

DOWN

1 Cry of surprise
2 Celestial hunter
3 Problem for a real-estate agent?
4 Mental health
5 Suffix with Capri
6 Author Hentoff
7 Hebrew letter after nun
8 Famed Trojan
9 Most delectable
10 Bridle flap
11 Where socks are exchanged
12 Hosp. test
13 Limber
14 Perennials do this
15 Maguey's relative
16 Do in
17 Toppers
21 "My Mother ——," TV series of yore
25 Pakistani region
26 —— nous
31 Batter or butter
32 Hebrew lyre
33 Was solicitous
34 Judges
37 Middle: Prefix
39 One-time Perle of society
40 Chekhov
41 "That's one small —— . . ."
42 Mil. group
43 Jai ——
45 Dramatic device
46 Perennial herb
48 Prefix with mural or muscular
50 "—— will, I can . . .": Sheridan
52 Petty thieves
56 "A man, —— . . ."
59 Pelage
60 Secular
61 Actress Samantha
62 On the schedule
64 Emulated Stratas
66 Trick
69 Crusoe's creator
71 Legendary Uri family
72 Footnote abbr.
73 Pancake
75 Victory signs
77 Carpenter's bad habit?
78 Inactive
79 Gomer or Howard
80 Drinks a little
81 Rub out
82 Bara role
84 Poker hand
89 Fat...
90 Mlle., in Madrid
93 Bleak peak
94 Dog found in the Outba...
95 Ta...
104 Kampala is here
106 ...
11...

165

Three-in-One

By Derrick C. Niederman

ACROSS

1 Seized firmly
8 Christmas spirit
14 Hummingbird sound
18 W.W. I battlegrounds
19 Flog
21 Top-notch
22 Two generals and an actress
23 Two Presidents and an actor
25 Lurches
26 Flick
27 Like cookie flour
28 Bandicoot
29 In an ignoble manner
30 Spot for a house plant
31 "Coal-ition" initials
34 Simple organism
36 Dud
38 Cheese city
42 Uncluttered
44 Two actresses and a trumpeter
47 Gums
48 Islet: Sp.
49 Balzac work
50 —— de plume
52 Lulu
53 Related through males
56 —— Zee
59 Golfer Bert
61 Transvaal capital
63 Three times CCCLI
64 Moreno
65 Sun. message
66 Two authors and another author
69 Loc. of Sydney
72 Grampuses
74 About
75 Kidnap, in a way
77 Jamaican musical form
79 Lacking consideration
81 Song girl
82 Coordinate markers
83 Mad. and Lex., e.g.
85 Unit of heat
87 —— years (elderly)
88 Shock
89 Two patriots and a historian
93 —— noire
94 Neth. port
96 Nimbi
97 On the move
99 Neighbor of Jord.
100 Publishing name
102 First-aid device
105 "—— Town"
107 Chatterer
110 Tartan wearers
111 Harsh, rasping sound
115 Two football greats and an author
118 Two former Yankee southpaws and a director
119 Home of Octavius
120 Amble
121 V.P. and family: 1877-81
122 Combat flies
123 Abhor
124 Sides

DOWN

1 Spanish linen
2 Lascivious look
3 Fury
4 Horror-film sound
5 Apparition
6 Poetic dusks
7 Result of "spring forward"
8 Characteristic beliefs
9 Serious
10 Thug
11 Famed 1961 defector
12 Navy agcy. like 101 Down
13 He played Gen. G.S.P.
14 Vacillate
15 Campsite sound
16 Concerning
17 Comedian Foxx
18 What R.N.'s provide
20 Cousin of indigo
24 Aught
26 Succeeded
29 Like a tired tire
30 Fair
31 Opens a beer can
32 Like a char's wages
33 Two cowboy portrayers and an actor
35 Thiamine's kin
37 Pearl and Mouse
39 Two dancers and a gourmet
40 Nautical term
41 Lamb owner or a Lamb
43 Precisely
45 Beacon, e.g.
46 Hypocritical cunning
51 Countless
52 Can. province
54 Puccini work
55 Pupil regulators
57 Piscatorial carnivore
58 Ache
60 Oise tributary
62 Plaintiff
67 Author Yutang
68 Abruptly, in comics
70 Soundness of judgment
71 Frank
73 Grid blockers
76 Semisolid lump
77 Indian bigwig
78 Tchr.'s concoction
80 Within, in Dijon
84 Hence
86 Catamaran
90 Embryonic
91 Well supplied
92 Nurse or yes man
95 Astaire hit: 1935

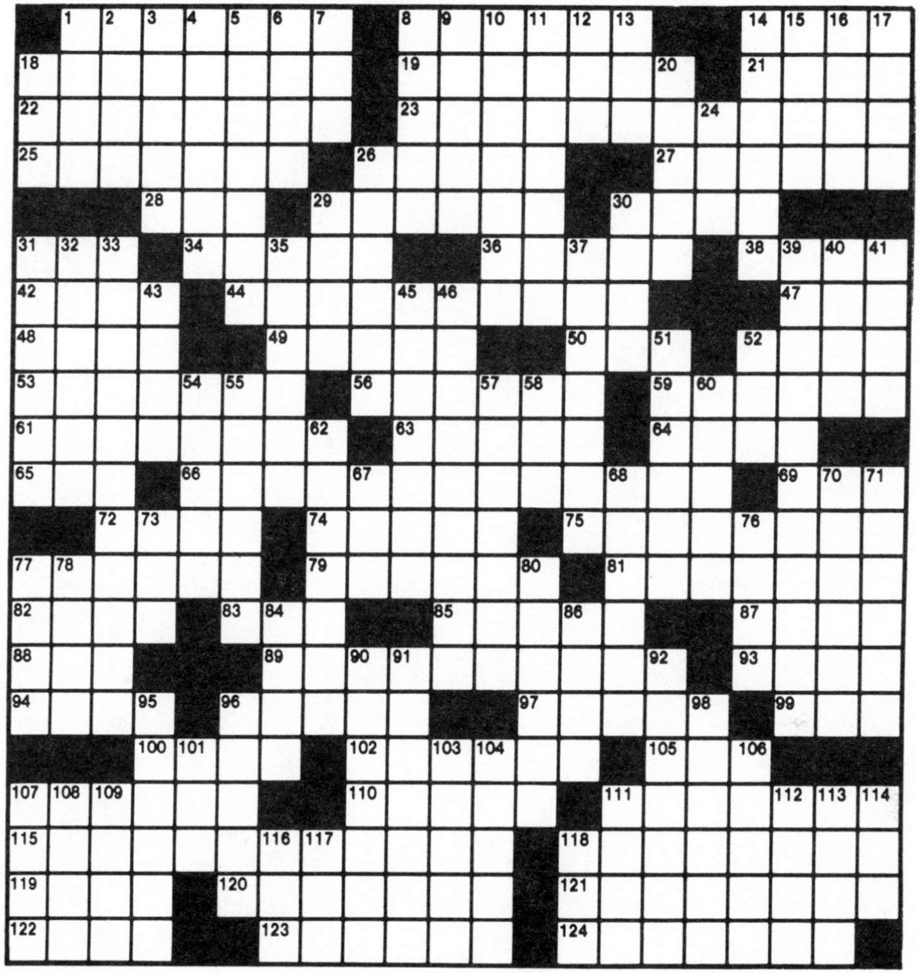

96 Throat-clearing sounds
98 Curdled
101 Bush's old org.
103 Highway divisions
104 Exanimate
106 Browning, for one
107 Diamond V.I.P.'s
108 Lined up
109 Vasco da ——
111 London district
112 Active one
113 Stowe's "The Pearl of —— Island"
114 Hwys.
116 Traipse
117 Repent
118 Monogram of an 1865 assassin

Madison Ave. Leftovers

By Barry L. Cohen

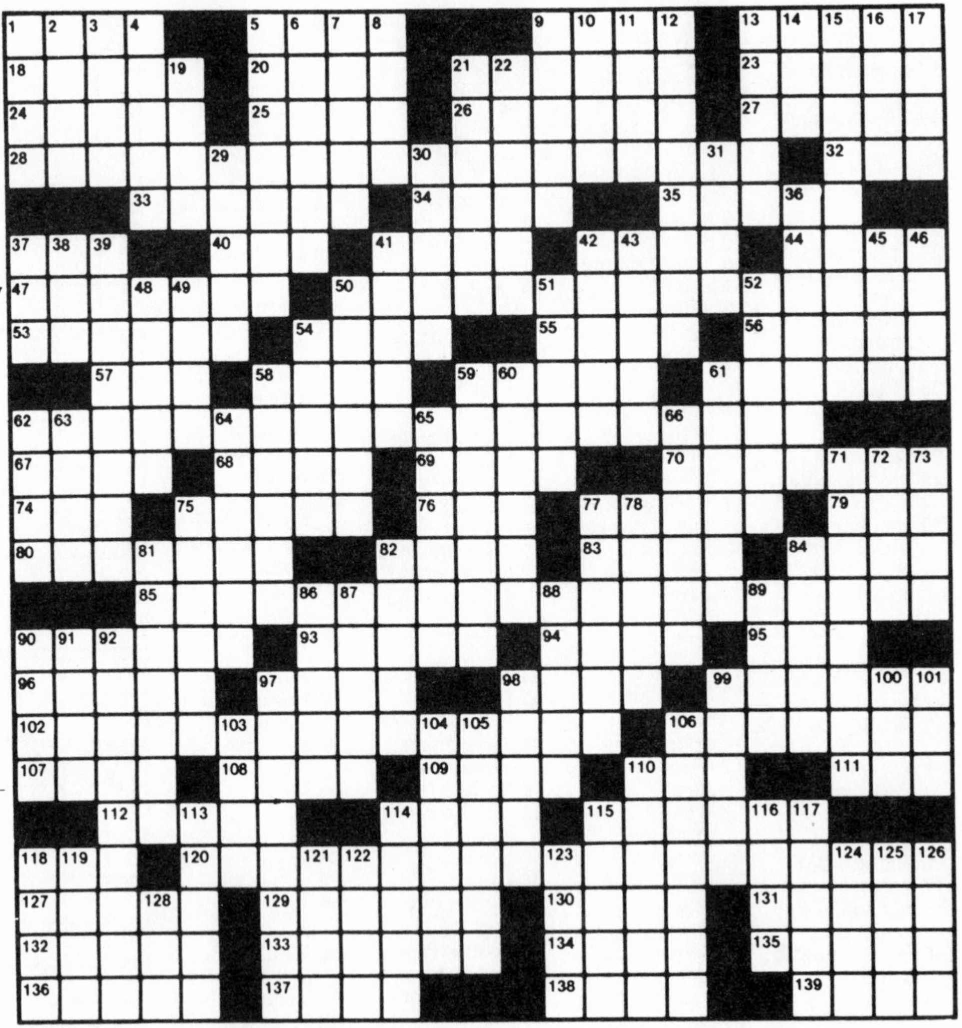

ACROSS

1 —— de Boulogne, Paris
5 Prefix with medic
9 Flaccid
13 Grant
18 Sports news
20 Nile bird
21 "... a bone and a hank ——": Kipling
23 Lorna of fiction
24 Philippine island
25 Sandy's utterances
26 Bobby Thomson's victim
27 Prefix with state
28 Sales slogan of certain spice vendors
32 "Leave —— to Heaven"
33 Yiddish gossips
34 —— Major
35 "Irma la ——"
37 Priest's robe
40 T-man, e.g.
41 Opponent of Muhammad: 1978
42 Reputed to be
44 Broadway's Ellis
47 Wheedle
50 Slogan of a rosary vendor?
53 Adman's come-on
54 Cockboats
55 Monticle
56 —— barrel (at one's mercy)
57 Basketball pos.
58 Yawn
59 Circus Maximus official
61 Like street talk
62 Fedora-industry slogan?
67 Hebrew measure
68 Sharp
69 Infinitive in Finistère
70 Charleston forerunner
74 Follett's Needle, e.g.
75 Fitted with a glass sheet
76 Island garland
77 Fine fiddle
79 Actor Vigoda
80 —— of Baltimore (H. L. Mencken)
82 Put on a Little act
83 The Great Commoner
84 Ruy or Gil
85 U.S.M.A.'s polite invitation?
90 Products of a certain boom
93 Diamond wear
94 Disraeli, to Arliss
95 —— Gatos
96 Type of U.S. radar plane
97 Kelly character
98 Whimper
99 Nemesis of The Joker
102 Baking firm's gift-wrap slogan?
106 Not cerebral
107 Gridiron's Rote
108 Vinegar: Prefix
109 Therefore
110 Helios
111 Find fault often
112 Put up
114 Zoological suffix
115 Braid, in a way
118 Drs.' group
120 Hotel contractor's lure?
127 Presidential reception
129 Longfellow hero
130 Intertwine
131 Courtyard
132 Nigh
133 Emended a manuscript
134 Tied
135 Attends Choate, e.g.
136 Powders
137 Casa part
138 Actor Frobe
139 Sybarite's delight

DOWN

1 Turkey
2 Silvery fish
3 Doctrinaire
4 Sordid
5 Turkish coin
6 Twain's "A Tramp ——"
7 Jazz figures
8 Kind of dir.
9 Holy city
10 Fleming and McKellen
11 Timid souls
12 Of dinner
13 Ta-ta, in Tours
14 Put on
15 Passé
16 As to
17 Lachrymose drop
19 Kind of surgeon
21 Fairy king
22 California city
29 Deduce
30 Long namesakes
31 Famous scout
36 Ties
37 Fitting
38 Town north of Port Moresby
39 Shiner
41 German pistol
42 Overturned a milk can
43 City on the Rhone
45 Titanic sinker
46 Asinine sound
48 Composite flower
49 Exceedingly
50 Rumbled, as a gang
51 Complain childishly
52 Drooped
54 Chili's partner
58 Kind of hen or pig
59 Regards highly
60 Ridicule
61 Where whips keep watch
62 Part of M.V.P.
63 Abbr. for a frog or newt
64 "Rock ——"
65 Moray trap
66 "Two —— Seesaw"
71 Charm
72 Israel's Abba
73 Gadfly or aphid
75 Most wan
77 Winds thread
78 Kind of search, in realty
81 More piquant
82 Words before war or God
84 Kipling opus
86 Hit
87 Shell crew, at times
88 Cape Cod town
89 Draft
90 Enjoy a beach
91 Off
92 Popular seasonings
97 Imagines
98 Sound of the West
99 Misrepresent
100 One —— time
101 Darkroom prod.
103 Jane Russell film: 1966
104 Poe maiden
105 Waxed eloquent
106 In the black
110 Printer's device
113 Witnesses
114 "—— Kick Out of You"
115 Figaro's specialty
116 Creator of Marryin' Sam
117 Finnish lake, to Swedes
118 "When I Was ——": G. & S.
119 Waiter's presentation
121 Hindu scripture
122 Malefic
123 Cassini
124 Willow
125 Pinches
126 Cyrano's outstanding feature
128 Erode

167

Second Meanings

By Bert H. Kruse

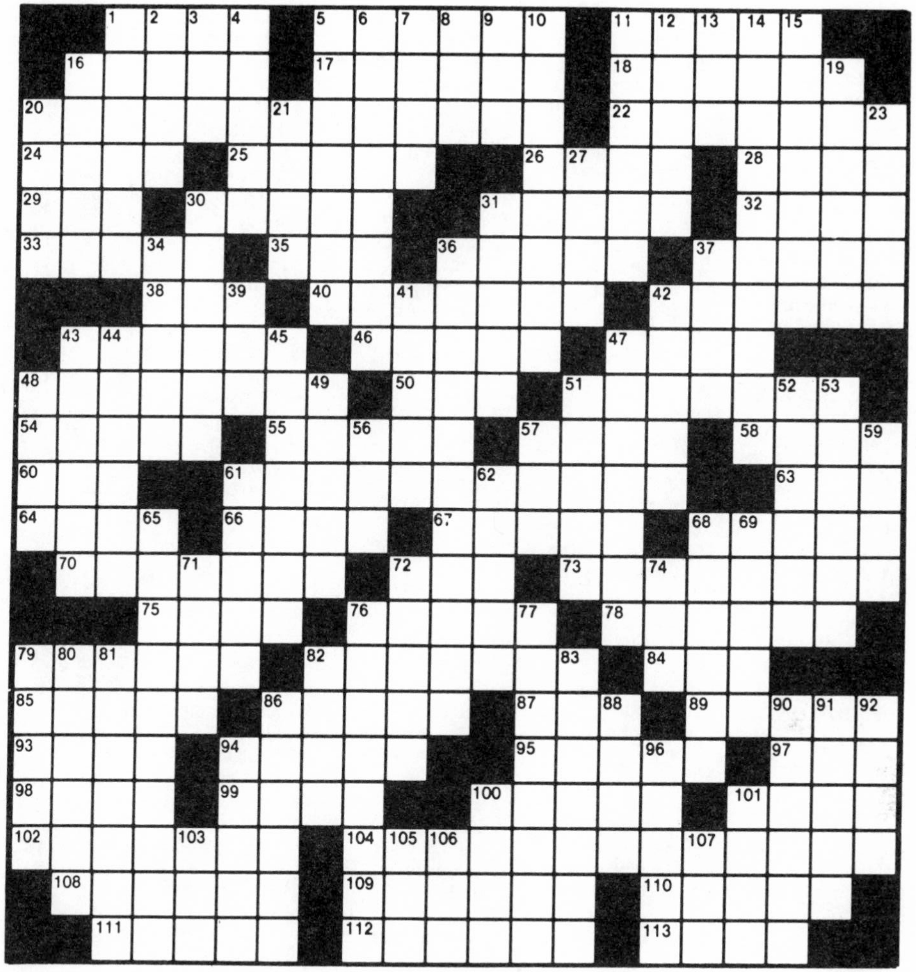

ACROSS

1 Stronghold
5 "On —— Day. . ."
11 Lily type
16 Motherless calf
17 Author Smith of "Topper" fame
18 —— Belt or Sword
20 Flock of sheep?
22 Center of New York
24 Duck, in Düsseldorf
25 Daunted
26 Land area
28 Greek-Roman theaters
29 One, to a Scot
30 Be dishonest
31 Smidgens
32 Bearing
33 Speeder's nemesis
35 Mexican Mrs.
36 Detection apparatus
37 —— Rica
38 Name with Abner
40 Interstate rte.
42 British chums
43 Yalta's location
46 Flower part
47 Kind of cure
48 Dance for dodos?
50 Sword beater
51 Valuable fur
54 Some French clerics
55 Fluff
57 Gutsy
58 "Boola boola" people
60 Wrath
61 Parties one shouldn't go to?
63 "—— Got You Under My Skin"
64 Etruscan title
66 Fix the carver
67 Total
68 Jeanmaire of ballet
70 Recording sites
72 Likely
73 Wristwatch?
75 Main mass
76 T-bone producer
78 Power checkers
79 Ohio-Indiana river
82 Had the lead
84 Kind of dance
85 New York island
86 Certain shavings
87 Skilled person
89 Rhone tributary
93 Ins, in France
94 Spirit or gazelle
95 Notorious Vichy prime minister
97 Moon vehicle's unit
98 Russian chess champ and family
99 No ifs, ands or ——
100 More sapient
101 Lincoln bill
102 Moved like Shakespeare's schoolboy
104 Aware of a truck-trailer?
108 Fred —— of court fame
109 Patriots, e.g.
110 Speechify
111 Bitter follower
112 Dinner courses
113 Bonkers

DOWN

1 Paid, as a bill
2 Look of desire
3 Dress
4 Emulate Socrates
5 Crosswise
6 Fast felines
7 Nobleman
8 Silkworm
9 Sothern or Sheridan
10 Like some sportscasts
11 Gorget, e.g.
12 Ram aloft
13 Author Yutang
14 Crazy reason for doing something?
15 Subject to electrolytic action
16 Prima ——
19 Like some precipitation
20 Endure
21 Heels' opposites
23 Nursemaids in Nottingham
27 Jib guy
30 Orts of sorts
31 Sioux City Sue, e.g.
34 "What ——!"
36 The best con men?
37 Moslem judge
39 —— culpa
41 Correct a cribbage score
42 Darns
43 Some are kings
44 Playwright Sherwood
45 Canal Zone airfield
47 Mayflower passenger
48 Author Sheehy
49 Fish-eating birds
51 Impressionist painter
52 Novelist Glyn
53 Comedienne Joan
56 Compass pt.
57 Kind of role
59 Observed
61 During
62 "Wind in the Willows" character
65 U-boat assignment?
68 Follow again?
69 Jugs
71 Union concerns
72 In any respect
74 Gull
76 Emphasizes
77 Put back
79 Athletic events
80 Poe's foster family
81 Wail
82 Satisfy
83 Ollie and Fafnir
86 More coarse
88 Pizzeria necessity
90 George and T. S.
91 Musical
92 Uncles in Dundee
94 Poplar
96 Firebug's crime
100 High Hindu god
101 Official sanction
103 Law deg.
105 Guidonian note
106 Tormé or Brooks
107 Claret-yielding area

168

X Y Z Paper

By Diana Sessions

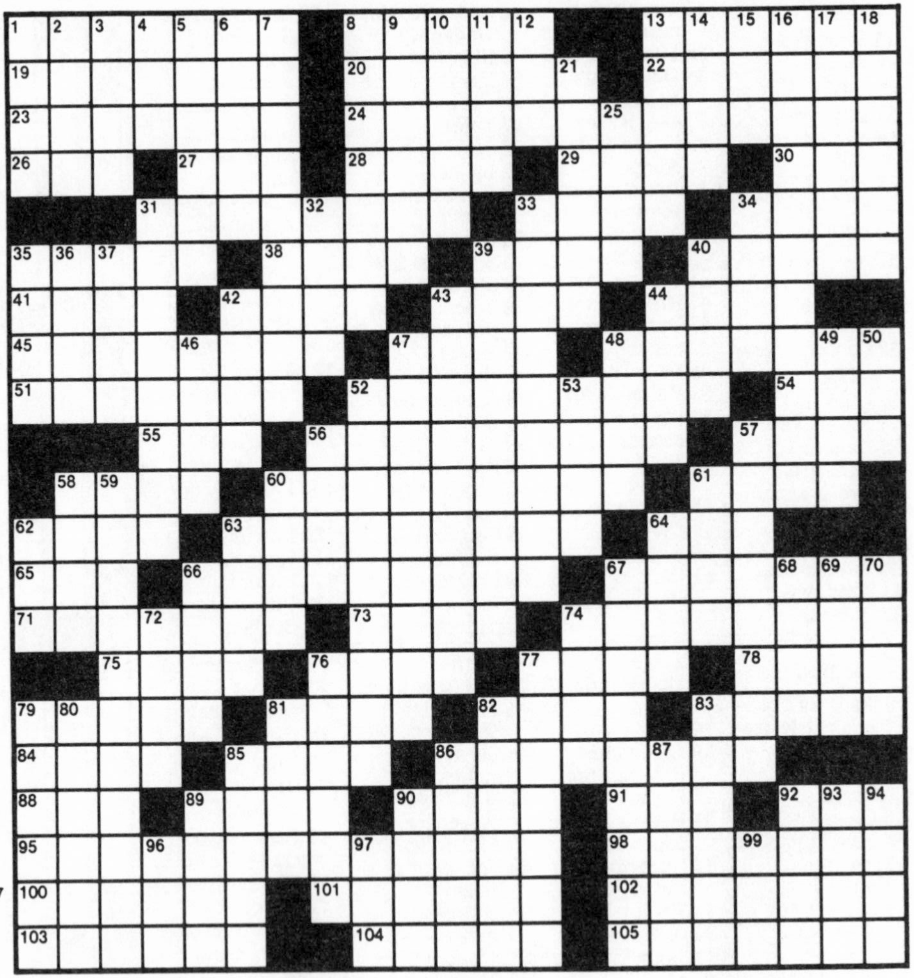

ACROSS

1 Fortunes
8 Words on Alice's cake
13 Squirrel or magpie
19 Platonism subject
20 Visionary project
22 Dorotea's dollar
23 Upper limit
24 Frank Morgan role
26 Bon ——
27 Nursery item
28 Brazilian money until 1942
29 A son of Cronus and Rhea
30 Taylor nickname
31 Vibrant
33 Pottery, e.g.
34 Soccer's Edson Arantes do Nascimento
35 Kitchen tool
38 Dip
39 Cicero's shorthand man
40 Under a strain
41 Eager
42 "—— -Dee-Doo-Dah"
43 True grit
44 Albanian king: 1928-46
45 Appoint as an assistant
47 Color
48 Change of residence
51 Treat nonnaturally
52 Adroitness
54 Father of Phinehas
55 Cutting tool
56 Cartago is here
57 Mum's distant cousin
58 Nimble
60 Setup for eavesdroppers
61 Bribes
62 Fabric's diagonal
63 Adopt Teutonic customs
64 "Sketches by ——": 1836
65 Samovar
66 Dupe
67 Gagged
71 N.J. resort
73 La ——, site of Iron Age remains
74 Unwavering
75 Historic Italian commune
76 Kind of defense
77 Snazzy
78 Hindu land grant
79 Mind: Comb. form
81 "Bird thou never ——": Shelley
82 Croaker's kin
83 Eurasian range
84 Plumbum
85 The number called
86 Nutritional necessities
88 Pacino and Hirt
89 Partial: Comb. form
90 Social group at a un.
91 Hosp. workers
92 Gretzky's milieu
95 Small Liberian animal
98 Think-tank specialist
100 Consecrate
101 Porky Pig's trotters
102 Denmark's largest island
103 Fine wool fabric
104 Bowling or trolling
105 Scopes

DOWN

1 Writer Bombeck
2 Wrinkle or ridge
3 Type of dancer
4 "Open sesame" lad
5 Logger's call
6 Ornamental cases
7 Typify
8 Erik of TV
9 Part of a strawberry
10 "—— Girl" (Clara Bow)
11 British royal stables
12 —— Watanabe, Olympics figure skater
13 Dross
14 Knight and Turner
15 Bear: Sp.
16 In an introspective way
17 Markova was one
18 Gave the bird to
21 Champ between two Joes
25 Baltic island
31 Career soldiers
32 Nucha
33 Prepare for Jack Frost
34 Double this for a Samoan port
35 Pops
36 "—— a Kick Out of You"
37 Reproduce
39 Torment
40 Poe's "—— Mother"
42 Umph; vim; wallop
43 Mets' miraculous year
44 Sixth Greek letter
46 Antimacassar
47 Will
48 Jambalaya ingredient
49 Cry of woe
50 Official curb
52 Certain quarters for dollars
53 Russian hemp
56 Sulky
57 Cars with low m.p.g.
58 Dam's mate
59 Source of troubles
60 Large quantity
61 Guy
62 Clinging weed
63 Lollobrigida
64 George of Washington
66 Fruitless
67 Spellbind
68 Large moth
69 And elsewhere: Abbr.
70 Reps.' rivals
72 Reared
74 Beat badly
76 Babbitt's home town
77 Sit-in, e.g.
79 Marketplaces
80 Western capital
81 Put on guard
82 British dry-goods dealer
83 Remove from office
85 Thought-provoking
86 City in Utah
87 Catalogue
89 Tonio Kröger's creator
90 Turkey
92 "—— Old Cowhand"
93 Argot
94 Some are tight
96 —— Bravo
97 Orion's beloved
99 Stout

City Fathers

By Elaine D. Schorr

ACROSS

1 Denpasar is its capital
5 Cinch
9 Commandment word
14 Shetland land-tenure system
18 One of Hollywood's Jacks
19 "You —— mouthful!"
20 Bernstein hit song
21 Fuselage part
22 Old Norse poetry collection
23 Actor Patrick
24 —— ease (uncomfortable)
25 Perdition
26 ——, Washington; ——, Arizona
29 Stamping ground of 42 Across
30 Dirty trick
31 One-time Genoa magistrates
32 Ding-dong
33 Drains
37 Feast
38 Farm fodder
41 George Eliot's real surname
42 ——, Nebraska; ——, Kansas
46 Part of A.S.P.C.A.
47 Fine spray
48 Province of modern Greece
49 Mind-boggling period
50 Kind of American
51 Fish ailment
52 ——, Kansas; ——, Montana
56 Madame de ——
57 Leaf adjuncts
59 Decked out
60 Trigonometric function
61 Transient traveler
62 Less furnished
63 Not so deceptive
64 Puts up to
66 Shaitan
67 Like some typing paper
70 Load lugger
71 ——, Mississippi; ——, Vermont
73 Rhone feeder
74 Marksman of myth
75 Christie's Miss Marple
76 Grow dull
77 Part of V.M.I.
78 Type of strike
79 ——, Indiana; ——, Wisconsin
83 A joint
84 Fluffs
86 Disposition
87 Tedious talker
88 Occult character
89 Coconut-oil source
91 Levantine ketch
93 Sorcery session
95 ——, Maine; ——, Texas
101 Mohammed descendant's title
102 Iraklion's locale
103 Vacancy sign
104 One-—— (superior to)
105 —— Blanc
106 Nixies or pixies
107 —— Canyon, on Idaho's border
108 Constance or Louise
109 Walt Kelly character
110 Some horses
111 It, in Italy
112 Expression of relief

DOWN

1 Skittles sidekick
2 Italian cinematographer
3 Windermere, e.g.
4 Mosque bigwig
5 Kingsley's "The —— of Dee"
6 Electra, to Menelaus
7 A wife of Esau
8 Peer of Charlemagne's court
9 Iota
10 City on the Saale
11 French site of Roman ruins
12 Pseudologist
13 Use a shuttle
14 Chimerical
15 ——, Georgia; ——, Alaska
16 Tigers' milieu
17 See-through item
19 Noise, to Nero
27 Hockey great and family
28 Zilch
29 Glasgow's "—— of Iron"
32 Wood for masts
33 Trailer types
34 Dislodge
35 ——, Missouri; ——, Texas
36 Tolkien creature
37 The vat man
38 Type of battery: Abbr.
39 Charles of the cards
40 Gallic school
42 Knocked 'em dead
43 Candlenuts
44 W.W. II Air Force general
45 Henbit or knawel
48 O'Flaherty's Gypo in "The Informer"
50 Bewildered
52 Frame of mind
53 Peele product
54 An element
55 Herr's evening
56 Pickling brine
58 Hard nut to crack
60 Swimming stroke
62 Pará state capital, in Brazil
63 Folklore figure
64 ——-Unis
65 City N of Kiev
66 Contravene
67 Inclusive abbr.
68 Kind of thread
69 Make a note
71 Malayan gibbons
72 Gyre
75 Make sport of
77 Stepmother of Helle
79 Moses of the movies
80 China's —— tree
81 To laugh, in Le Havre
82 —— riot act (reprimand severely)
83 Given to deviltry
85 —— Vallarta, Mexico
87 Ancient people of Britain
89 Conductor Fausto ——
90 Customarily
91 "Bubbles" of opera
92 Defective: Comb. form
93 —— David
94 "Typee" sequel
95 Woody's boy
96 Hannah Van Buren, née ——
97 Robert of the reels
98 Moonfish
99 Fuel variety
100 ". . . I —— him, Horatio"
102 Wax: Comb. form

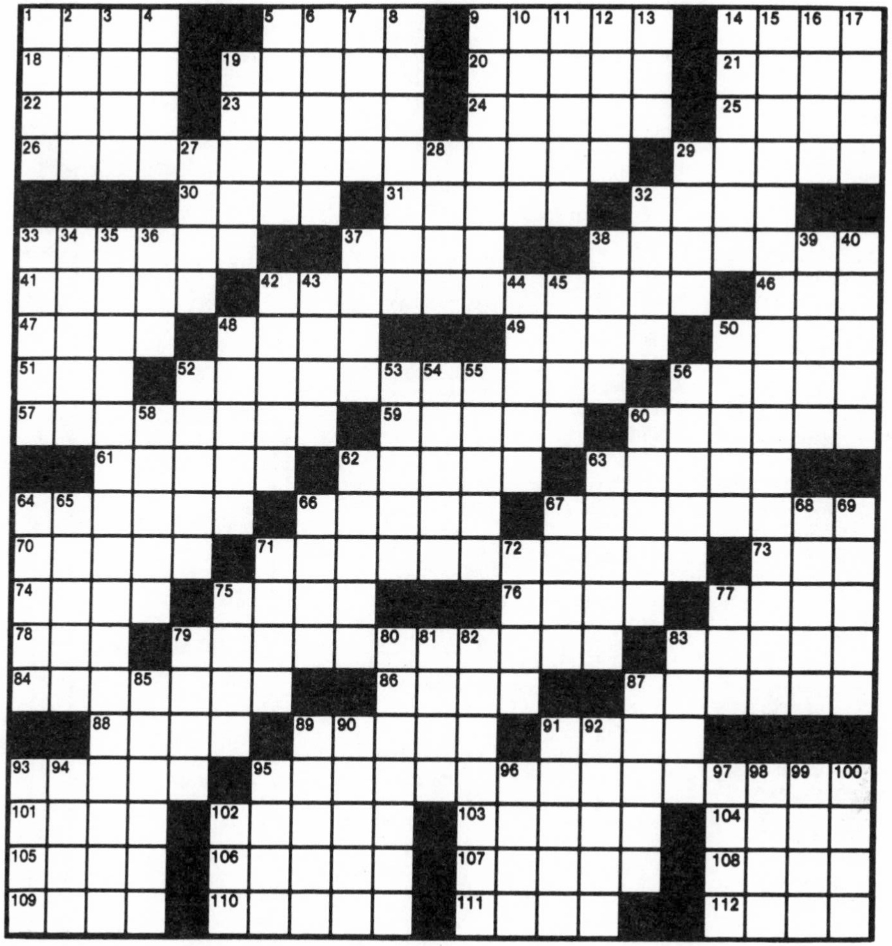

"... in the House?"

By Jack R. Harnes, M.D.

ACROSS

1 Homes
7 Dr. ——, Anne Page's suitor
12 Luck of the Irish
16 Pretense
20 Street shows
21 Sinuses
22 N.M. colonizer
24 Silkworm
25 Monster maker in movies
27 Noted bandleader
29 Explosives
30 Gyle or mum
31 Sellers role: 1963
32 Relative of TM
33 Doris and Dennis
34 Sleuth's companion
36 Lloyd's ratings
37 Jackson or Farrell
39 French Sudan today
40 Ruhr rivet
43 —— salad
44 Helix
46 Alexander's group
47 Festive
51 Thurber's secret surgeon
54 What Jocko Conlan did
56 Marcus of TV
60 Jot
61 Dill of the Bible
63 Upper crust
64 Of grand-parents
65 Gull or its sound
66 "The Cabinet of Dr. ——," 1919 film
70 Done in
71 Portuguese navigator
73 Foreign
74 Don Pasquale's physician
76 One born a serf
78 Long coat
80 Annexes
81 "L'Elisir d'Amore" quack
85 AC-DC experts
86 Spice
90 Approves
91 Current
93 "—— the season . . ."
95 MX
96 Of frogs
97 Ado
98 "High ——"
100 Ireland's ancient name
101 Legal extract
103 Hero of a TV series
108 Exigency
109 Velez
111 —— Rico
112 Covered way
117 And
118 Bacchanalia
119 Tots' favorite retailers
120 Dr. ——, famed horse
124 Springes
127 —— production
130 Wall St. clippings
131 O.R. figure
134 Engagement
135 Quality, in Québec
136 Groucho role
137 "Amazing" E. G. Robinson role
141 Alaskan island
142 Back of a book
143 Large vessel
144 City SE of Rome
145 Heather's place
146 —— -do-well
147 Mom, to a Harrow boy
148 Estimate

DOWN

1 Sandy's sound
2 Mozart or Rossini physician
3 Shipment from Ocala
4 Certain pajamas
5 Cartoon squeals
6 Reno-to-Carson City dir.
7 Ben of TV fame
8 Stakes
9 Anatomical passage
10 Locale of "William Tell"
11 José or Juan
12 Shoppers' concerns
13 Don's January
14 Plain
15 British gun
16 Edison's Park
17 Malicious firing
18 "Jumblies" craft
19 Helen and Citizen
23 Work unit
26 Bullets, Rockets et al.
28 "I earn that ——": Shak.
31 Leg extension
32 Illum.
33 Arp's art form
34 Friendly
35 Jai ——
38 Moist
39 Dr. ——, Hoffmann magician
41 Purposeless
42 Graduate deg.
44 Pack
45 Favorite
46 Sobriquets
47 Lionel Barrymore role
48 Domingo specialties
49 "—— Be," Beatles song
50 Town in Ohio
52 Golf position
53 Label
55 Mortar's companion
56 Roll of money
57 A Gabor
58 Loiter
59 Doc ——, famed Army fullback
62 Stat for Doc Medich
65 Mutilate
67 Troubled
68 Byron heroine
69 Map within a map
72 Tapeworm larva
73 Hungry-sounding mineral
75 Pennines, e.g.
77 Marlowe hero
79 View on some postcards
81 Poet Mark Van ——
82 Decree
83 "Festina ——"
84 Acct.
87 Pedro's "—— favor"
88 German article
89 Caviar
92 Hockey great
93 Japanese leader executed in 1948
94 Mythical princess
99 Org. sponsoring vocational training
100 Geisha's receptacle
102 Wholly
104 Seaman's direction
105 Unalloyed
106 Parts of violins
107 Bowler and dicer
110 Stance
113 Dr. ——, Dekker role in 1940
114 Vial
115 Actress Darcel et al.
116 U.S.N.A. graduate
117 Commedia dell'——
120 Parisians' tea substitute
121 Red dyestuff
122 Tropical lizard
123 Glacial ridge
125 Stockholm gnome
126 —— Lev, Potok hero
127 Dull finish
128 Rose oil
129 View
132 100: Abbr.
133 Black
134 Gossip
135 Triumphant cries
137 Wheel projection
138 Mauna ——
139 Yeast-acid initials
140 Ar follower

Homophony

By Mary Virginia Orna

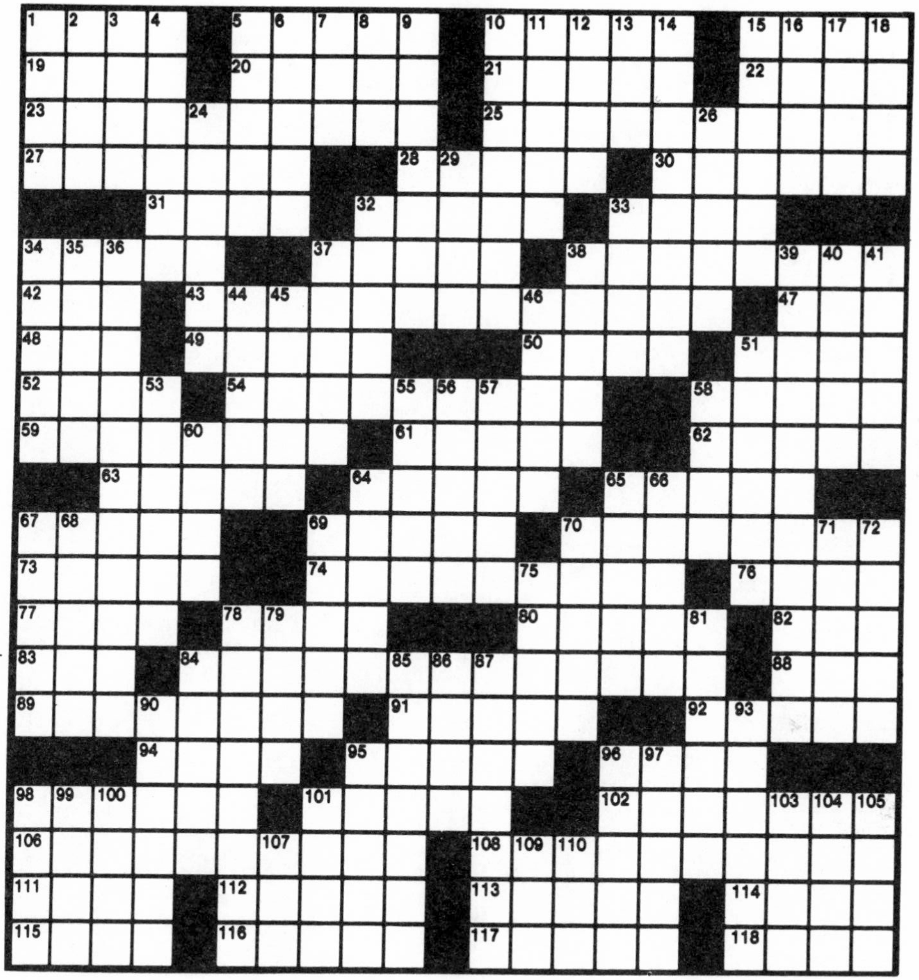

ACROSS

1 Risky biz
5 Tyrian contemporary of Solomon
10 Philadelphia suburb
15 Anjou or Bosc
19 Dolphin's predator
20 Writer Rogers St. Johns
21 Dynel relative
22 River to the Laptev Sea
23 Arlene's puppets?
25 Disney's dance?
27 Impassive
28 Protozoan
30 Singer-actress O'Shea
31 Broadway musical
32 London lane
33 Author Stoker
34 Hoople's rank
37 Personal assurance
38 Four-in-hand kin
42 —— Dhabi, Arab emirate
43 Composer's coins?
47 Peppery
48 —— Aviv
49 Psalm ending
50 Elizabeth II, to Lady Sarah
51 Lay at anchor
52 Type of eng.
54 Lew's lilts?
58 Symbol of a sort
59 Asset
61 Gore
62 Bigwig in Kabul
63 Violinist Laredo
64 Debussy's "—— de lune"
65 Nicholas and Alexander
67 Furthers
69 Star of "The In-Laws"
70 Laments
73 Lapwing
74 Madison's makeup
76 A Copperfield
77 Mars, to Menander
78 "Comus" composer
80 —— prosequi
82 Short word after long
83 Doing poorly
84 Sprite's sensors?
88 January on the links
89 Breathes
91 Carthaginian
92 Dough
94 English architectural style
95 Best seller in 1924
96 Hershfield's "agent"
98 One of six Vatican leaders
101 Pivots
102 Drew or Lester
106 Harlow's heritage?
108 Sin of one of the Finns?
111 Peak
112 Storehouse
113 Glorify
114 Scenery changer
115 Antarctic sea
116 Univ. divisions
117 Strikes out
118 Gives the once-over

DOWN

1 Repairs the lawn
2 Low trick: Scot.
3 A feature of this puzzle
4 Printed cotton
5 Attacked
6 Fans' favorites
7 Electrical unit
8 "—— These Women," 1964 Bergman film
9 First president of Czechoslovakia
10 —— attorney
11 "The Sheik of ——"
12 Pot, in Potosí
13 Oft-drawn item
14 School
15 Transfusion infusion
16 Fish dish
17 Prefix for septic or social
18 Demolish
24 Mufflers
26 Whip marks
29 Rumple
32 Chapeau designer Lilly
33 Beethoven's birthplace
34 "Stabat ——"
35 A poplar
36 Massenet's marquises?
37 Springe
38 Gounod opera
39 Cecil's streets?
40 Sidestep
41 Cowpoke's charge
44 Fortify again
45 Type of clover
46 Less common
51 Muzzle stuffer
53 Mexican tree dwellers
55 Describing armozeen
56 Author Nin
57 "Of Thee ——"
58 Jezebel's god
60 One of the Hebrides
64 Unrelenting
65 Edison contemporary
66 Hex
67 "—— of star-cross'd lovers": Shak.
68 A Milton who found paradise in TV
69 Choreographer de Mille
70 Chemical suffix
71 Cereal blight
72 Rhone feeder
75 Strip a ship of tackle
78 Put in order
79 African's leather thong
81 Sighting
84 Roles for sopranos
85 Consorts
86 Champagne department
87 Isolated
90 Tom and Robert Treat
93 Charge with gas
95 Was dormant
96 Sweeting, e.g.
97 Surpasses
98 Open a bit
99 Art ——
100 L.A. team
101 Pushover
103 Agile
104 Baritone Hawkins
105 Fiber clusters
107 Summer, in Saumur
109 "Whacks-work"
110 Buddy

Take It From the Top

Bert Rosenfield

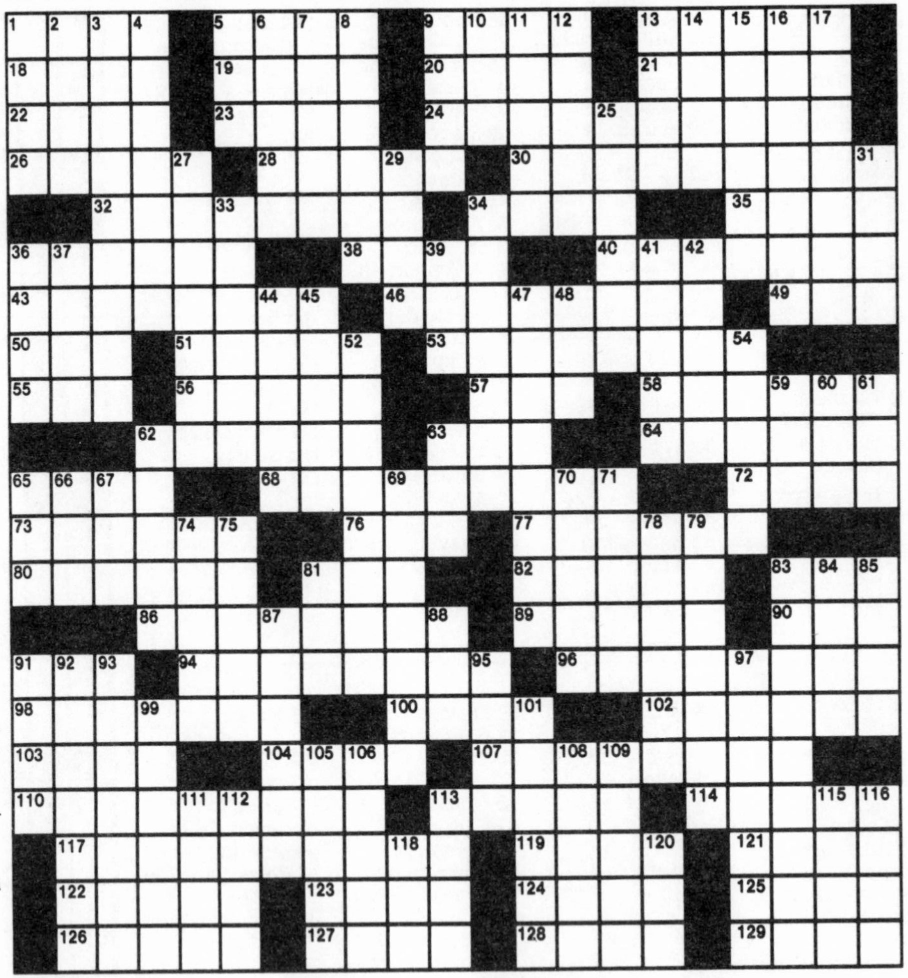

ACROSS

1 Bhang or ramie
5 Soapstone
9 One-third of ML
13 Card for Carmen
18 —— Mts., in Kirghiz
19 Mudfish genus
20 Nimbus
21 "—— Louisa," 1931 song
22 Rotate
23 Lansbury role
24 Plunger becomes embezzler
26 Singapore —— (gin drink)
28 —— de café (cup of coffee, in Chambéry)
30 Feeling odium
32 Disciple becomes master
34 Comme ci, comme ça
35 Port on the IJsselmeer
36 Surgical instrument
38 Tohubohu
40 Volatile chemical compound
43 Contemptibility
46 Early publication becomes late one
49 Novelist Deighton
50 Turkish chieftain
51 Works on a bone
53 Medieval verses
55 —— Tafari (Haile Selassie)
56 Girl's nickname
57 Scale notes
58 Where two dozen merls wound up
62 Anglers' baskets become their spools
63 Cardboard bx.
64 Cryptographers
65 ". . . —— of troubles": Hamlet
68 Hateful act becomes joyous one
72 "—— Ideas," 1951 song
73 Performer becomes nonperformer
76 G.I. cops
77 Excite
80 Easternmost Great Lakes port
81 Witty saying
82 Soup made with okra pods
83 Dallas campus letters
86 City inside Houston
89 Indian, for one
90 Cough: Sp.
91 Dec. 24, 1983
94 Calumnies become columnist
96 Certain rear seats
98 Henchman
100 Main St. brightener
102 Cotton-mill employee
103 Moreover
104 Famous nom de plume
107 One ballplayer becomes four
110 Electrical-circuit devices
113 Prefix with cede
114 Utensil for bolting
117 Tactician becomes musician
119 Sans —— (matchless)
121 Ski resort in Colo.
122 Tailward
123 Coxswain's command
124 Red Sox second sacker
125 U.S. sky eye
126 Three-striper, familiarly
127 Fox or dog follower
128 Montand from Monsummano
129 Word from Gromyko

DOWN

1 "—— off!"
2 Jewish month
3 Opahs and sego lilies
4 Ship's boat
5 Headgear at St. Andrews
6 Teacher of Stradivari
7 Big beans
8 —— Rodney, Declaration signer
9 Ablative or dative
10 Ryder or Stanley
11 Start of Iago's Act II aria in "Otello"
12 Intertwines
13 Mah-jongg counter
14 Lackaday!
15 Unappealing person becomes appealing animal
16 Egg-shaped
17 One of the Moluccas
25 Never-never land
27 Farm worker becomes Garden player
29 Smarty-pants
31 Federal fuzz
33 Monte Carlo's ——-et-quarante
34 Cat man's requisite
36 Skier's uphill assister
37 Hindu musical form
39 Neptune or Pluto
41 Language branch including Sanskrit
42 Combiner meaning "comb"
44 Stuffs
45 Refuse
47 Roadside weed
48 Monogram of J. Silver's creator
52 Bone shaped like a certain seed
54 Hawkins or Thompson
59 Cribbage item
60 Wrath
61 Id adherent
62 Joshua's co-survivor
63 Abbr. re ergs, etc.
65 Amas preceder
66 Lucy, to Linus
67 Son of Geo.
69 Favorable economic sign
70 Behave like Krakatoa
71 Slayer of Paris
74 Relative of 70 Down
75 Psychologist May
78 River on Zaire's boundary
79 Young boys
81 Aristotle's "political animal"
83 Command from Montgomery
84 Grimace
85 Kazakh, Uzbeck et al.
87 Lie-detector inventor becomes a crime
88 Hamlet's "before"
91 Mosel feeder
92 Start of a famous palindrome
93 Mosaic piece
95 Distributed
97 Animate
99 Vassal becomes vessel
101 Supper club
105 Cant
106 Very red heavenly body
108 Desert in Israel
109 Bowler's "inning"
111 Dross
112 Flag
113 R.P.I. is one
115 Saw-filer's need
116 Gulf of Aqaba port
118 "—— y Plata," Montana's motto
120 Battle of the ——: 1918

"Bah! Humbug!"

By Martha J. De Witt

ACROSS

1 Stack
5 S.F.B., the inventor
10 Impofo
15 Octagonal sign
19 Maumee Bay feeder
20 He wrote "The Hollow Men"
21 Of the cheek
22 Buzzy place
23 Nonsense
25 Nonsense
27 Piths
28 Complete
30 Recoil
31 Suffix with hip or tip
32 Foxx
33 Placebo
34 Walking on air
37 Gibes
39 Pug's vulnerability
44 Having rounded projections
45 Its capital is Khartoum
46 Wearying time
47 Opposite of dep.
48 Jeune fille
49 Nonsense
51 Shelter: Fr.
52 Southern constellation
53 Not bright or clean
54 Tots
55 Euphoniums, e.g.
56 What a weak battery needs
58 Wine variety
60 Enthusiastic
61 —— Semple McPherson
62 Apollyon
63 —— obscure (chiaroscuro)
64 Dipped out
66 Metric measure of capacity
67 Put a tail on
70 Menilites, e.g.
71 Andrews from Miss.
72 Goggle
73 Wood sorrel
74 Spiny-finned fish
75 Nonsense
78 Acidity
79 Drop a fly
80 Simile or metaphor
81 Kind of cow
82 Tarsus
83 Sci-fi movie
85 Sudra, for one
86 Entreated
87 German article
88 Hoover and Roosevelt
89 One means of travel
90 Post again
93 Compendious
94 Possible victim of xenophobia
98 Nonsense
100 Nonsense
102 Players, in the cat's absence
103 "Like it ——!"
104 Dogma
105 Toward the center
106 Part of U.S.N.A.
107 Comes close
108 Tinker's target
109 Medical subj.

DOWN

1 Ganymede's predecessor
2 Time periods
3 Is not in the pink
4 Hero's spot
5 Yosemite river
6 Senior
7 U.S. radio station in Berlin
8 Mayday's cousin
9 Delicate
10 Fixes firmly
11 Scotch landowner
12 Confederate
13 Carp
14 Horse-training art
15 Sings above true pitch
16 Monkey, marmoset or tree
17 Pizzeria's sine qua non
18 Freshen, with "up"
24 Put in a ledger
26 Sayers's "—— Body?"
29 Early sci-fi author
34 "Pomp and Circumstance" composer
35 Nantes's river
36 Nonsense
37 Deem
38 Nelson, the singer
39 Lightheaded
40 Cobb and Marvin
41 Nonsense
42 Island off Scotland
43 Carpus
45 Char
46 Kind of chair
49 Lit
50 Senegal's capital
51 Complement of video
53 "South Pacific" group
55 Kind of mark or wind
57 Having grades
58 Medieval invader of eastern Europe
59 Suffix with Capri
60 Wing-shaped
62 Subsequently
63 Cautious
64 Theater sections
65 Opposite of "to starboard"
66 Illuminators
67 Cordwood measure
68 College, in Calais
69 Belled the cat
71 Fashion name
72 Part of a revue
75 Enos, to Adam
76 Smith and Bede
77 Tape holder
78 Asiatic Turkey
80 Package security
82 Betel palm
84 Staggered

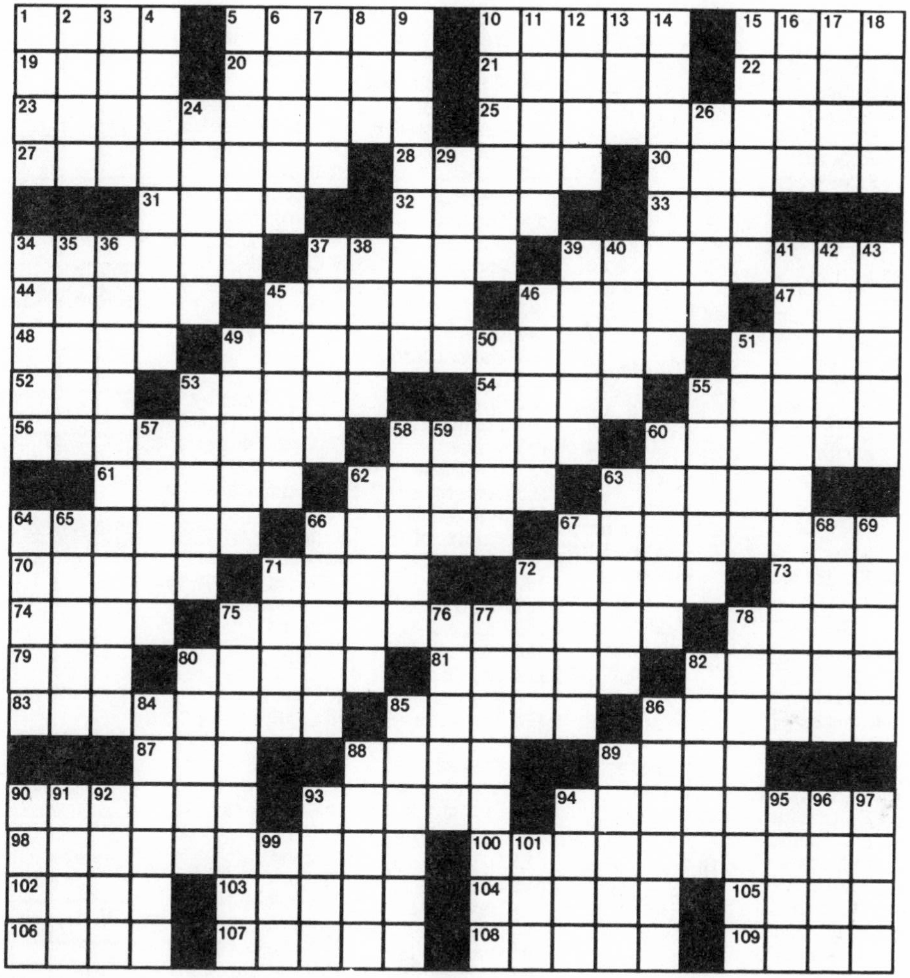

85 Proofreaders' marks
86 Phoebes
88 Ornamental scheme
89 Temperature over 98.6 degrees
90 Hindu hero
91 Monumental
92 Humane org.
93 Kind of sandwich
94 Number of inches in a span
95 Where H.H.H. lived
96 Cartoonist Hulme
97 Indian peasant
99 "Chances ——," Mathis hit
101 Preacher, familiarly

Yuletide Excerpts

By Anne Fox

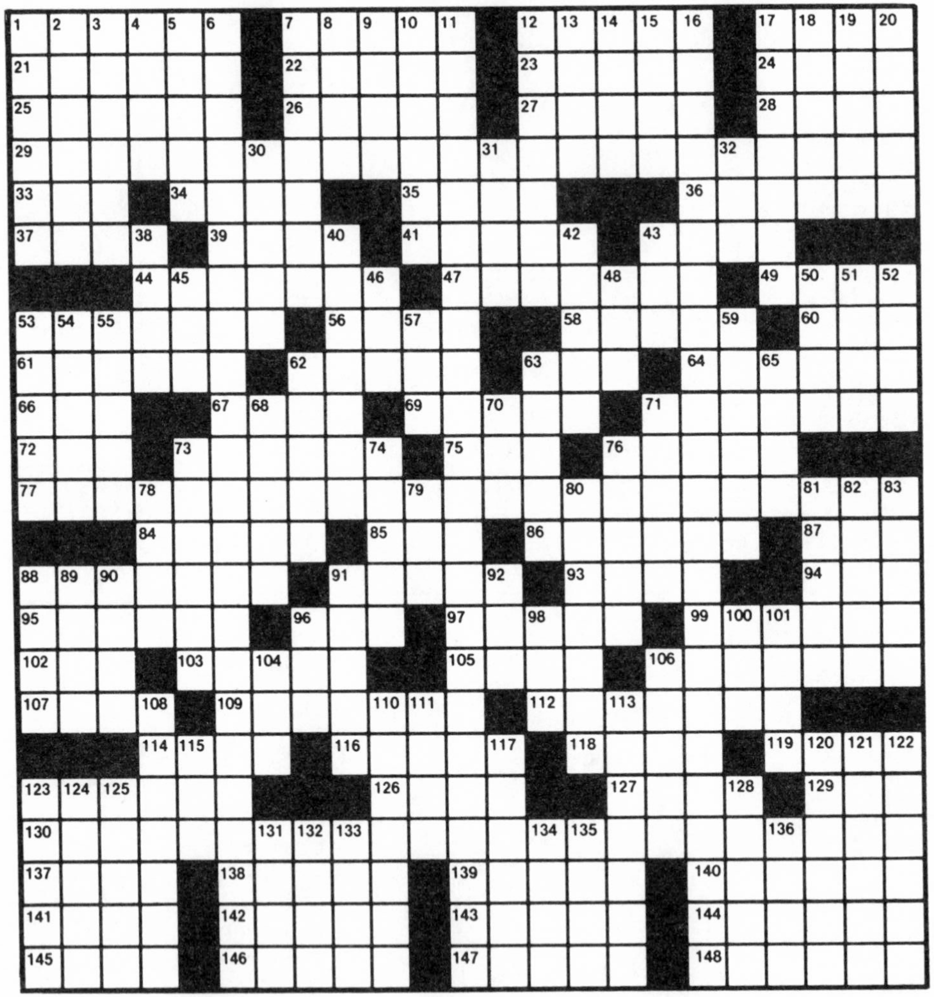

ACROSS

1 Kiddie's foot
7 Oodles
12 Cases for small articles
17 Sagan or Sandburg
21 Hangnest
22 Commandment verb
23 Traffic sign
24 Margarine
25 "—— Talk," Doris Day film
26 Board for a medium
27 Roi's mate
28 Marquand's sleuth
29 Words by Edward Caswall
33 Mass. cape
34 Kind of glass
35 "Betty ——," 1930 song
36 Three-legged stand
37 Labels
39 Check
41 Grand —— (Rocky Mt. peak)
43 Grovel
44 Granted
47 Ninth Islamic month
49 Attracted
53 Like a bull
56 Colorless
58 Composer of "The Seasons"
60 Former U.S. agcy.
61 Possessing
62 Dodge
63 "—— armes, citoyens!"
64 Of milk
66 U.S.A. member
67 Chaplin prop
69 Fiddle with a guitar
71 "—— Road," Caldwell novel
72 Atlas abbr.
73 Alecto, for one
75 Punch
76 Enjoy
77 Words from a Czechoslovak carol
84 Old calculators
85 Shubert or Strasberg
86 Kind of pace
87 MOMA offering
88 "He that —— his rod . . .": Proverbs
91 Zero
93 Sole
94 Cheer
95 Ancient scrolls
96 Explosive
97 Pitchers
99 Basswood
102 Actress MacGraw
103 Gemstone
105 Monastic
106 Painter of "Guernica"
107 Fling
109 Some colonists
112 Calms
114 Gone
116 City on the Missouri
118 Fast time
119 Dostoyevsky's "—— Youth"
123 Ancient Italians
126 Have —— for (wish evil to)
127 A Dumas
129 Topsy's playmate
130 Words from a Sussex carol
137 Connect
138 Manlike ape, for short
139 Early father of twins
140 Wife abandoned by Paris
141 All the same: Fr.
142 Remove a ship's upper deck
143 Scandinavians
144 Adjective for intransitive verbs
145 Over
146 Long for
147 Punkies
148 Some Fords

DOWN

1 Formal wear
2 Epithet for Elizabeth I
3 Lubrication
4 Kind of booth or bridge
5 Slow animal
6 "—— now proclaim Messiah's birth"
7 Scrubbed
8 Autosuggestion pioneer: 1857-1926
9 Tel ——
10 Dishearten
11 Words from a Polish carol
12 Eden's domain
13 Bumbo or cacao
14 "Exodus" author
15 Charged particles
16 Words from "Song of the Crib"
17 Order
18 Throw for —— (flabbergast)
19 Type of rocket
20 Bats
30 Eccentric
31 Greek letter
32 Mountain —— (moonshine)
38 Draped garment
40 Potpourris
42 Book of the Bible
43 Fairy
45 Prevail
46 Actress Joanne
48 French spa
50 Campus org.
51 Heroic
52 Site of Baylor U.
53 Namely
54 Overflowing
55 Family member
57 Certain personals
59 Gomer Pyle's real name
62 This is not joie de vivre
63 Kissel and Marmon
65 Singer Vikki
68 Gee follower
70 Edge
71 Dravidian language
73 Colo. peak
74 French greeting
76 Nixon's first Sec. of Commerce
78 Not one, country style
79 Triangle side
80 Breather of a sort
81 Compounds
82 Highlanders' hillsides
83 Race: Comb. form
88 Lovers' quarrel
89 —— Alto
90 Bee genus
91 Beachhead of W.W. II
92 Word with step or time
96 Young one
98 Naval off.
100 Rosalynn Sumners's milieu
101 Space org.
104 Half a motorboat sound
106 Kind of button
108 Scintillate
110 Little bit
111 Bye-bye
113 Mars
115 Some
117 "Dombey ——"
120 Far off
121 Family name in Scott's "The Monastery"
122 Baseball's Big and Little Poison
123 Flirted, in a way
124 Irish county
125 Middle name of author Doyle
128 Charger
131 Anglo-Saxon coins
132 Where Samson died
133 Standout
134 State of Brazil
135 Cardinal point
136 Obligation

Cheers!

By Alfio Micci

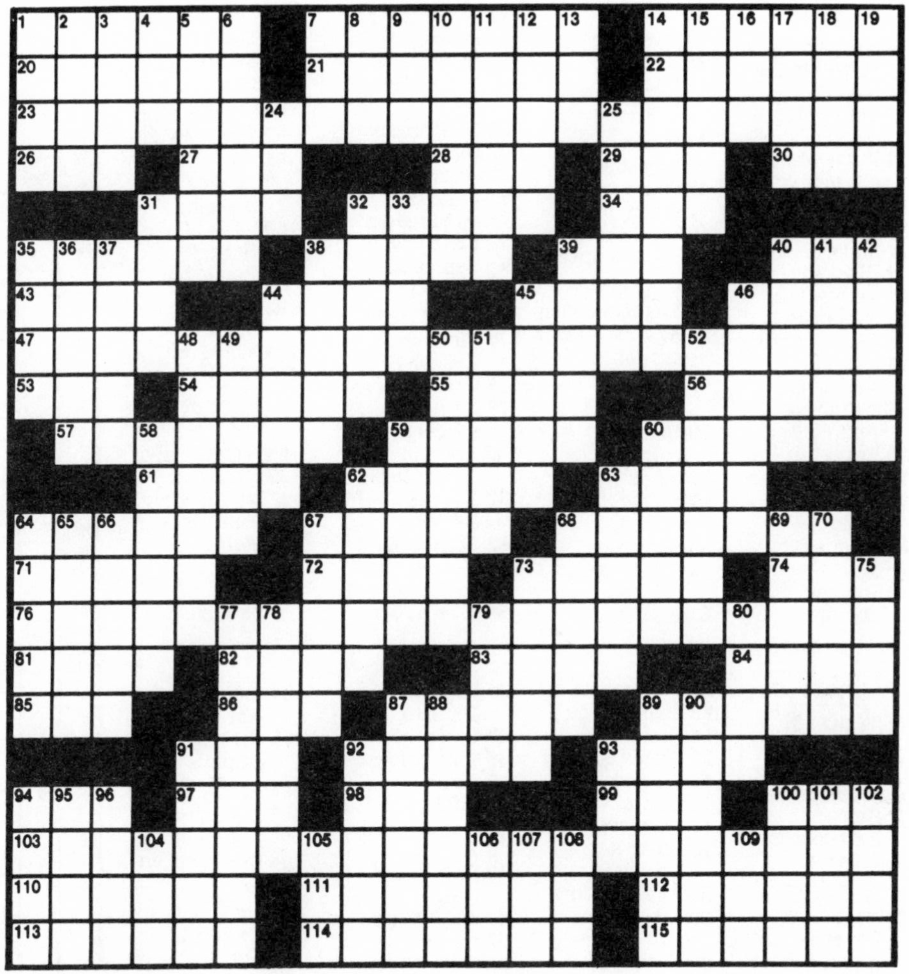

ACROSS

1 Say it is so
7 Fixed a recording
14 Author of "Pensées"
20 Gob
21 Crimson Tide
22 Grand Canal bridge
23 Start of a verse
26 Psychic initials
27 Ship-shaped clock
28 Eastern holiday
29 Burrows or Beame
30 For shame!
31 Castle's protection
32 Uncalled-for display
34 Biological duct
35 Firecracker
38 Composer of "The Planets"
39 Kinsman
40 Drop bait lightly
43 A king of Judah
44 Capital of ancient Edom
45 Mil. truant
46 Mazo —— Roche
47 Second line of verse
53 Successful politicians
54 Rigel's constellation
55 —— Corleone, Puzo's "Godfather"
56 Asp's weapon
57 Like Kirk Douglas's chin
59 Wonders number
60 Expunge
61 Greek Mars
62 Less adorned
63 Actor Richard from Phila.
64 Cloth for draperies
67 Doctrine
68 Potter's-wheel part
71 Embellish
72 "By the Time —— to Phoenix"
73 Mollusk deposit
74 Eccentric
76 Third line of verse
81 Vicinity
82 Tweed twitter
83 A heap
84 Shoal
85 Wash. V.I.P.
86 Piggery
87 Rocket stage
89 After-dinner quaff
91 Town sprouting near Brussels
92 Friendliness
93 Sullen
94 Road for Romero
97 Flesh: Comb. form
98 A Johnson
99 Headland
100 Producer of royal jelly
103 Last line of verse
110 Stalagmites site
111 Native to a region
112 Regal headwear
113 Author Lin ——
114 Bestow a fixed look upon
115 Ancient Italic tongue

DOWN

1 Wimbledon winner: 1975
2 Grazing areas
3 Northern European
4 Domain: Abbr.
5 Janet or Mitzi
6 Group of nine
7 Immature
8 English cathedral town
9 Monogram of a famous inventor
10 Eases up
11 Source
12 Chew the scenery
13 La-di-——
14 To all appearances
15 Features of anges
16 Bank abbr.
17 Treble or tenor
18 Longfellow's bell town
19 Come in second
24 Salamander
25 Redeemer
31 Bison's locks
32 Fish-eating bird
33 Kind of pigeon
35 Polynesian canoe
36 Correct
37 Sculptors' creations
38 Salome's stepfather
39 Faint
40 Revolutionary patriot
41 Distribute
42 Vichy victory symbol
44 Smiley's people
45 Miller's "—— the Fall"
46 Fought for one's honor
48 Price, for one
49 Van Gogh painted here
50 Actor Chad
51 Emulate Rosie of W.W. II
52 Including everything
58 "I'll —— landlord's daughter": Lamb
59 Less deranged
60 Steel-plow pioneer
62 Sired
63 Up for ——
64 Calls from nurseries
65 Antarctic cape
66 Senior member
67 Intoxicated
68 Seed integument
69 Oscar winner: 1961
70 Moved sidewise
73 Garden bloom
75 Challenge
77 Discomposed
78 Cronkite's successor
79 "—— a Song Go..."
80 Composer Khachaturian
87 "Glass Menagerie" character
88 Kind of ale or beer
89 Explosions
90 "From —— with Love"
91 Quercus fruit
92 ——-garde
93 Fido's warning
94 Piquant
95 Two-toed sloth
96 Mag. insert
100 Italian province
101 Dash
102 If not
104 Truly
105 "For —— a jolly..."
106 Kipling's "Follow Me ——"
107 By way of
108 Outside: Prefix
109 Fairy queen

Piecework

By Richard Silvestri

ACROSS

1 Gremlins
5 Something to tend
8 Throw off course
14 Put two and two together
19 Delhi wear
20 Afore
21 Make clear
22 Blockade
23 Very small
25 Picked up
26 Glossy fabric
27 Ardent supporter
28 "Winnie —— Pu"
29 Best
30 Motion picture
31 S-shaped molding
32 Ham's O.K.
33 Thy: Fr.
34 Ran into a doctor?
38 Whitney invention
41 Rank
43 Baseball's Rose
44 Storm preceder
45 Spacewalk, acronymically
46 Blackthorn
47 At a distance
49 Long green
50 L-Q connection
51 Against lateral portions?
55 Canterbury headdress
56 Onager treading insect?
57 Ray of the screen
58 Stylish
60 Sight from a crow's-nest
61 Fabrication
62 A scoreboard listing
63 Grand instruments
65 Ornery
66 Dad's track records?
70 Sidewalk scam
71 Finance a mind reader?
73 Ye follower
74 Pennines pinnacle
76 Rams' dams
77 Punta del ——, Uruguay
78 Greek letter
79 Name in spydom
80 Arabian watercourse
82 Promenade for Pericles
83 Forage plant
84 Restrain auto people?
89 45 or 78, e.g.
90 Cornered
92 Cutlet meat
93 Before secundus
95 Contract
97 Filmy piece
98 —— a doornail
99 Canvas covering
100 "—— of Honey"
102 Pointed up
105 Clear the board
106 Yule airs
107 Chess champion: 1960-61
108 Western lily
109 Removed from a manuscript
110 Pamper
111 Half a blackjack
112 Move cautiously

DOWN

1 "The Lady —— Tramp"
2 Doorway accessory
3 Golf instructor's dreams?
4 St. Peter, originally
5 Developed into
6 Highest spot in Turkey
7 Trust
8 Great pleasure
9 Bewitching stare
10 Springfield and Mauser
11 Chip in a chip
12 Refrigerate
13 Took charge
14 Designate
15 Woody co-star
16 Discourage blokes?
17 Auspices
18 Bump a Durant
24 Agenda entry
29 Like surf or soap
30 Orchestra section
31 Where the Marxes spent a night
32 Get one's goat
33 Puccini heroine
35 Separated
36 Likeness: Comb. form
37 Gives the ax to
39 Kind of tower
40 Scruff
42 Lifeless
47 Hersey locale
48 Parries
49 Province of Italy
50 SALT topic
52 Nonsensical
53 Gift
54 Homeric work
55 Devilfish
58 Sleepy Hollow victim
59 Forbidden desires
63 Diametrically opposite
64 Indian river test?
65 Nickelodeon output
66 Lapwing
67 Corroded by a fine spray?
68 Obstructs, in law
69 Invisible vapor
70 Speck of dust
71 Seedless plant
72 Olympics reward
74 Impudence
75 Commando action
80 Try for a pin
81 Dactyl's relative
84 Was a tenant
85 Dispatch boats
86 Creeping S.A. plant
87 Delphi V.I.P.
88 Pheasants' nest
91 Hairdresser's application
94 Parsonage
95 Made haste
96 Tortoise's rival
97 "Star ——"
98 Information
100 Banking abbr.
101 Confucian truth
103 It may have come first
104 Buck's mate

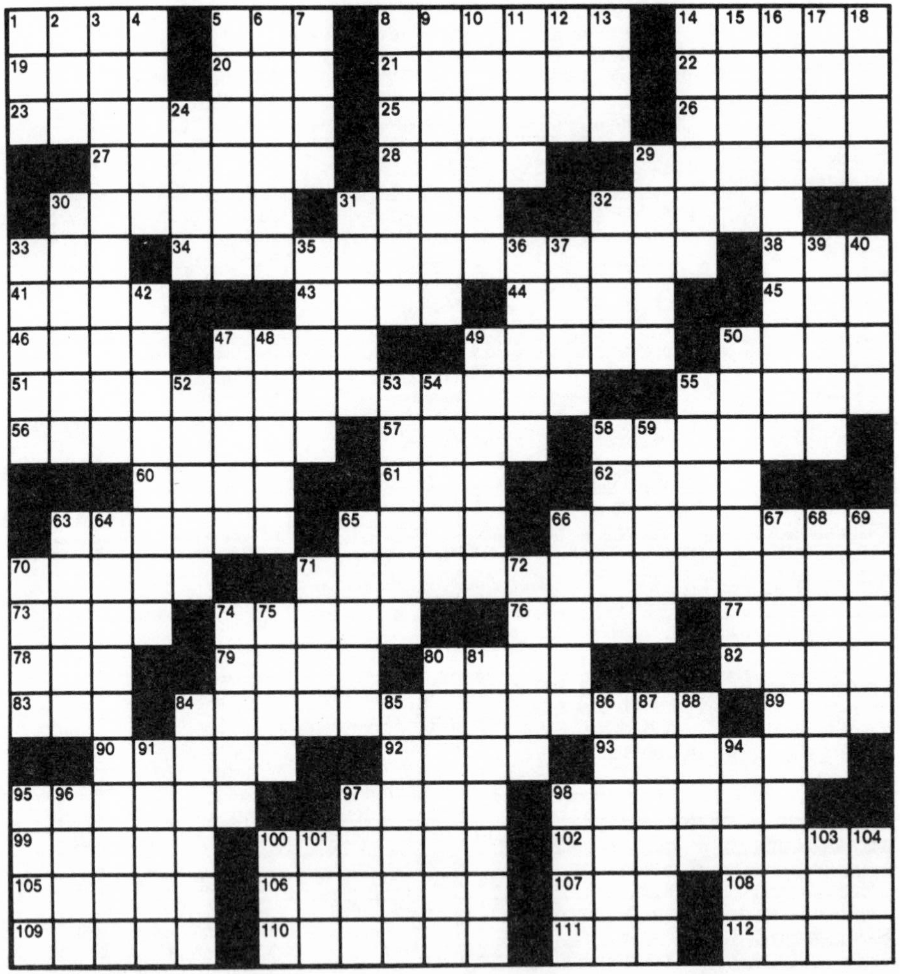

New York Trip

By A. J. Santora

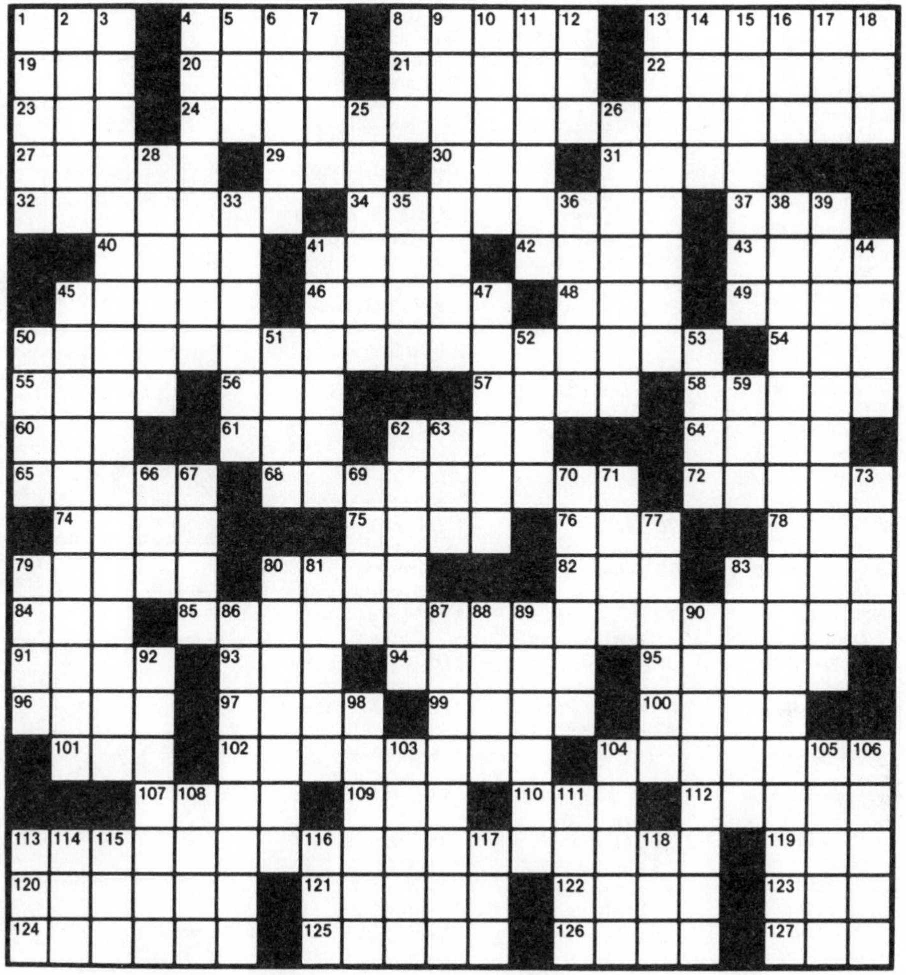

ACROSS

1 Gold, to Cortés
4 Dandies
8 —— plume
13 Kind of acid
19 Corral
20 Germ for a Madison Ave. product
21 French spa
22 Stupid behavior
23 Hill "carpenter"
24 Where to see Atlas
27 Annealing ovens
29 Natural resource
30 Gramps, e.g.
31 Sphere preceder
32 "Ida, —— Apple Cider"
34 Pickle maker's purchase
37 Kin of Mr.
40 Ingredient of some muffins
41 Violent Adriatic wind
42 Ditto
43 Throwaway found on 42d St.
45 W.W. II guns
46 Keynote
48 Light ammo
49 Asian weight unit
50 TV variety show: 1950-51
54 Triborough starter
55 Cross
56 Wallach from Brooklyn
57 Fire Island hues
58 Better
60 Animator's need
61 In medias ——
62 Pianist Gilels
64 Without
65 Hybrid primrose
68 Subject of a 1906 hit song
72 Ben Adhem's group
74 Cell: Comb. form
75 Sojourn
76 Spaceman Solo
78 Sight from Long Island
79 —— Penh, Cambodia
80 Arrived
82 Self
83 What a treas. accounts for
84 Toady's reply
85 Huber's TV show: 1950-51
91 Shelton of "Annie"
93 Memorabilia
94 Fiber plant
95 Canned fish
96 Calendar used at St. Patrick's
97 The Tombs, to a con
99 Koppel and Nugent
100 Bacon part
101 Moynihan or D'Amato from N.Y.
102 Inducted one
104 With the exception of
107 Summit
109 Gotham beginner
110 Chit
112 Tomato blight
113 Dos Passos novel
119 Beam
120 Quantity
121 Rubber basis
122 Father
123 Letter before sigma
124 Strike out
125 —— France
126 Part of U.S.M.A.
127 Penn ——, N.Y. resort

DOWN

1 Milky gems
2 Freshen
3 Bowling term for a hit
4 "The —— wisest . . .": Milton
5 French king: 888-98
6 Bill of cowboy renown
7 Munro
8 Old salt's clock
9 Regard too highly
10 Coe or Ovett
11 Cowboys' home
12 N.Y.-to-N. Eng. dir.
13 Gentility
14 Footnote word
15 Most petite
16 Decay
17 Surface for the Ranger sextet
18 Minsky's Lili St. ——
25 Marine air station in Calif.
26 Geometric figure
28 Scan a page again
33 Retort
35 Not care ——
36 African land
38 Famed N.Y.C. vessel
39 Boxing's Marquis of —— rules
41 Like a stripling
44 Extorted
45 Razzes at Yankee Stadium
47 Being
50 Con —— (mus. dir.)
51 Actor Clunes
52 Gloriole
53 N.Y.C. river
59 Deface
62 Joins
63 Pasture sound
66 Westernizer of Japan
67 Apple: Comb. form
69 "Woe —— !"
70 Hailey book
71 Slow horses
73 Affluence
77 Cosa ——
79 Heat: Comb. form
80 Environment
81 Make use (of)
83 Importuned, in a way
86 Tape cartridge
87 Giggled
88 Conversational cliché
89 Words on some Japanese imports
90 Trembled
92 TV show host
98 Kingly
103 French demonstrative
104 Of ascetic Islamic mysticism
105 Birthplace of G.R.F.
106 Smooth fabric
108 Gasp
111 Greek peak
113 Hopping ——
114 Soul, in Amiens
115 Lon ——, Asian leader
116 Winner at Madison Square Garden: Sept. 1977
117 Tool for Ali Baba
118 Seaver stat.

Kerchoo!

By Frances Hansen

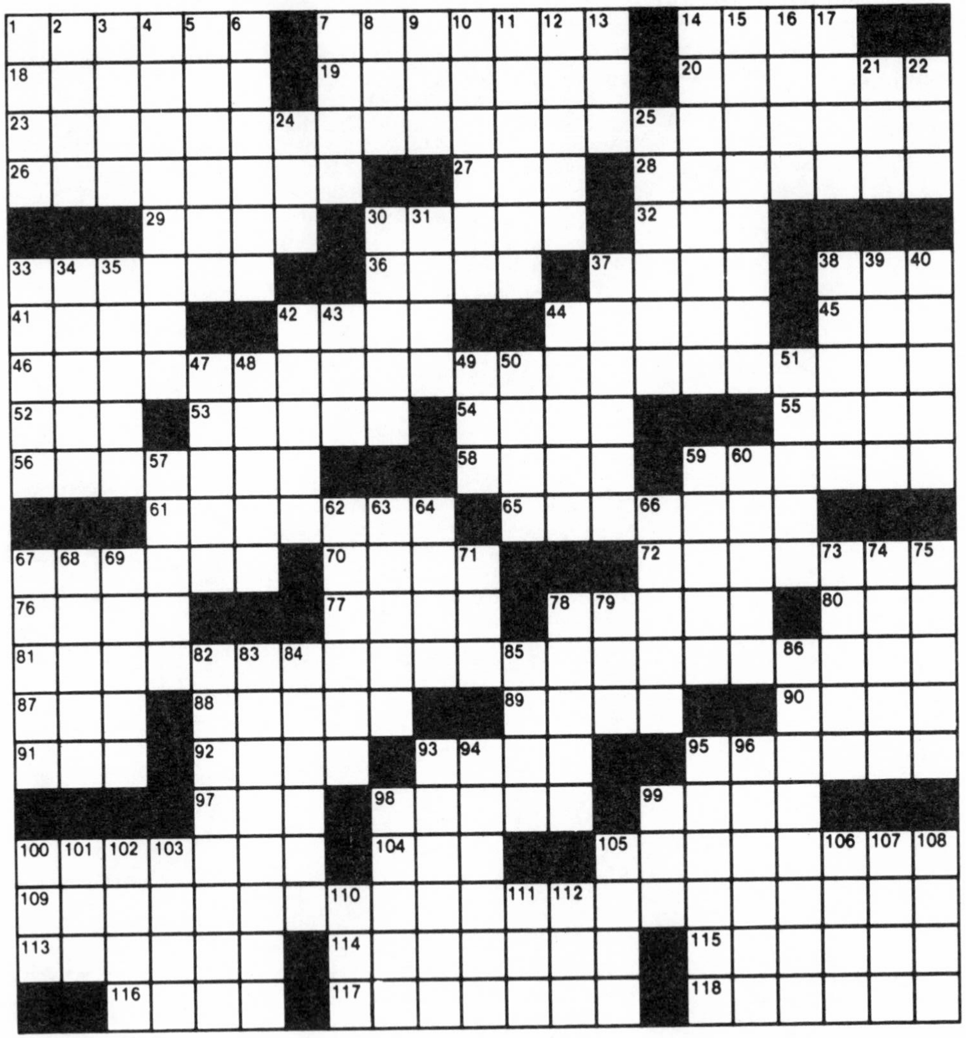

ACROSS

1 Happens
7 Higher than any other
14 Flemish painter Frans
18 Barnum's Wild Man of ——
19 Site of U.S. naval base in Cuba
20 Silverware city of New York
23 Start of a verse
26 "—— in the kitchen with Dinah"
27 Incur coryza
28 Inane
29 Rhythmic Hindu music
30 British verse measure
32 Pro —— (for the nonce)
33 Gets the better of
36 To —— (exactly)
37 Revived art style
38 "I —— lone lorn creetur . . .": Dickens
41 Gen. Robt. ——
42 Actuality
44 Island in the Firth of Clyde
45 For each
46 Verse: Part II
52 Fell for a joke
53 Feather: Prefix
54 Use the grinders
55 Mine entrance
56 Reconnoitered
58 Take out
59 Ketcham's Dennis
61 Sun parlors
65 A Dietrich
67 Naïve
70 Little Sir of song
72 Think-tank group
76 Lamb's pseudonym
77 Celestial twinkler
78 Legendary Jewish robot
80 Yoko —— Lennon
81 Verse: Part III
87 Hiss seeking silence
88 Spicy hot drink
89 Husband of Hera
90 Fountain of fame
91 Last word of "Ulysses"
92 Terrier type
93 Wolmirstedt's river
95 Matter for the Met and Mets
97 An O'Neill
98 Pussyfoot
99 Roman goddess of hope
100 Noisy
104 "Tarzan" Barker
105 —— the seams (gives way to pressure)
109 End of verse
113 Down —— (shabby)
114 Recent Broadway hit
115 Punta ——, Chile
116 Jug handle, to Jeanette
117 Yellowstone spouters
118 Abandon

DOWN

1 Cio-Cio-San's sashes
2 Hepburn role on Broadway
3 Bone up
4 Like the milieu of the chambered nautilus
5 Colorful grain
6 Noted Chinese sisters of yesteryear
7 Flip a coin
8 Alsatian abstract painter
9 52, to Fabius
10 Vatican representative
11 Whole
12 Shoulder wrap
13 Mystery writer Josephine
14 Pet puss
15 Metallic element used in alloys
16 Uris or Trotsky
17 Moslem title of respect
21 Duryea or Dailey
22 Affirmative vote
24 Hyson, e.g.
25 Westerns on TV
30 He-man type
31 This makes Henri a girl
33 Fervent Fabians Beatrice and Sidney
34 Derived from oil
35 Right-hand page
37 Bureau division
38 Footless lot
39 Mil. first-aider
40 Mountain ridge
42 "—— cold and starve a fever"
43 Tune
44 Writer Rogers St. Johns
47 Author Sinclair
48 Stone pillar
49 A-E connection
50 Polite interruption
51 City in Crete
57 Customary
59 Role for Judith Anderson
60 Front de Boeuf, to Ivanhoe
62 Save
63 Rhythmical stress
64 The Pequod's captain
66 Sings gaily
67 Landing pier
68 "Für ——," Beethoven bagatelle
69 Leaves waiting at the church
71 Globe
73 Suburbanite's purchase
74 Related on Mom's side
75 "The Highwayman" poet
78 Zorba, for one
79 Univ. at Columbus
82 Places in office
83 Inflame anew
84 Of Mubarak's land: Comb. form
85 Pound or Stone
86 —— Creed
93 Kind of street
94 Groups of six
95 Western ranch
96 Singer Siepi
98 Primordial mud
99 U-boat
100 Lingerie item
101 Afire
102 Turkish title
103 Now's partner
105 Top honcho
106 Unit of loudness
107 Jewish month
108 Assay
110 Jokester
111 Sandra or Ruby
112 Pigeon pea

Matchmaking

By John M. Samson

ACROSS

1 Hold
5 Part of T.A.E.
9 Final part of a pas de deux
13 —— pudding
18 Daredeviltry name
19 Manicurist's charge
21 Prognostic
22 Brutus's burdens
23 Actress-novelist match
26 Stair post
27 Actress Stritch
28 Kind of jaw
29 Bunyan's Babe, e.g.
30 —— de guerre
31 Cooking banana
33 For shame!
34 Progenitor
35 Fine point
37 Comedian-actress match
40 Parallel passes
42 "It's —— than you think!"
43 Migrate
45 Loren's birthplace
46 Surfeit
47 Candied items
51 Biblical book
53 Deadened
55 Excited
57 Loser to Braddock: 1935
59 Punty
60 36th U.S. Pres.
62 He's below a marquess
64 Dreamy composition
66 Call —— day
67 Actress-tennis star match
70 Yelp
71 Prufrock's air
73 Speck
74 Aristotle's Aurora
75 Low
76 Director Buñuel
77 Terra ——
79 It's made backwards?
81 Novae, e.g.
83 Rec. measures
85 Boxer O'Grady
86 500 sheets
88 Highlands language
89 More frigid
91 Most mirthful
93 Actress-painter match
98 Implant
100 Mr. Bones
101 Apt. particulars
102 Makes hay, in a way
103 Homophone of neigh
105 Aramaic translation of the Old Testament
106 Main
109 Themes
111 Anew
112 Comedienne-camera bug match
114 Sledded at Lake Placid
115 Taxi
116 Seasons lumber
117 Countertenor
118 Looks of a rake on the make
119 Malts
120 New England grid team
121 Swill

DOWN

1 Herculean ones
2 Arthur's island paradise
3 Actress-jazz musician match
4 She out-wrestled Thor
5 Echidna or pangolin
6 —— -de-dah
7 Stringed instrument
8 Soprano Gluck
9 End of an O'Neill title
10 Bongo of Gabon
11 For, in Frankfurt
12 Actress Sheridan
13 Type of degree
14 On —— keel
15 Needlework
16 Vingt-neuf follower
17 Mythical beast
20 World's greatest coffee port
24 Start
25 Ticket part
29 Bundle
32 Pianist-singer match
34 Ballplayer-entertainer match
36 Word before walk or mix
37 Mame's critic
38 Norway's patron saint
39 Eucharistic plate
41 —— Darya, Asian river
43 Delight
44 Dig up
46 West Point greeting
48 —— Dhabi, Mideastern land
49 Actress-comedian match
50 Privileged students
52 Sunday clothes, for some
54 West role
56 Imitator
58 Rest
61 "—— good cheer . . ."
63 Greek letter
65 Mrs. Tracy
68 "Sing all —— willow": Shak.
69 "When the —— Robin . . .": Woods song
72 Geller's gift
78 Where trades are made
80 Gas: Comb. form
82 Assay
84 Freudian names
87 Foolish
90 Stuff
91 Unlike a rolling stone
92 Industrial hub of the Ruhr
93 It may be major or minor
94 Madden
95 Less at ease
96 Destroys
97 Atlanta arena
99 Shed
102 Actress Shire
104 Prohibit legally
105 Lofty
106 Nuncupative
107 University in N.Y.C.
108 O.K. Corral fighter
110 Arts degs.
112 Borrioboola-——, locale in "Bleak House"
113 Service call

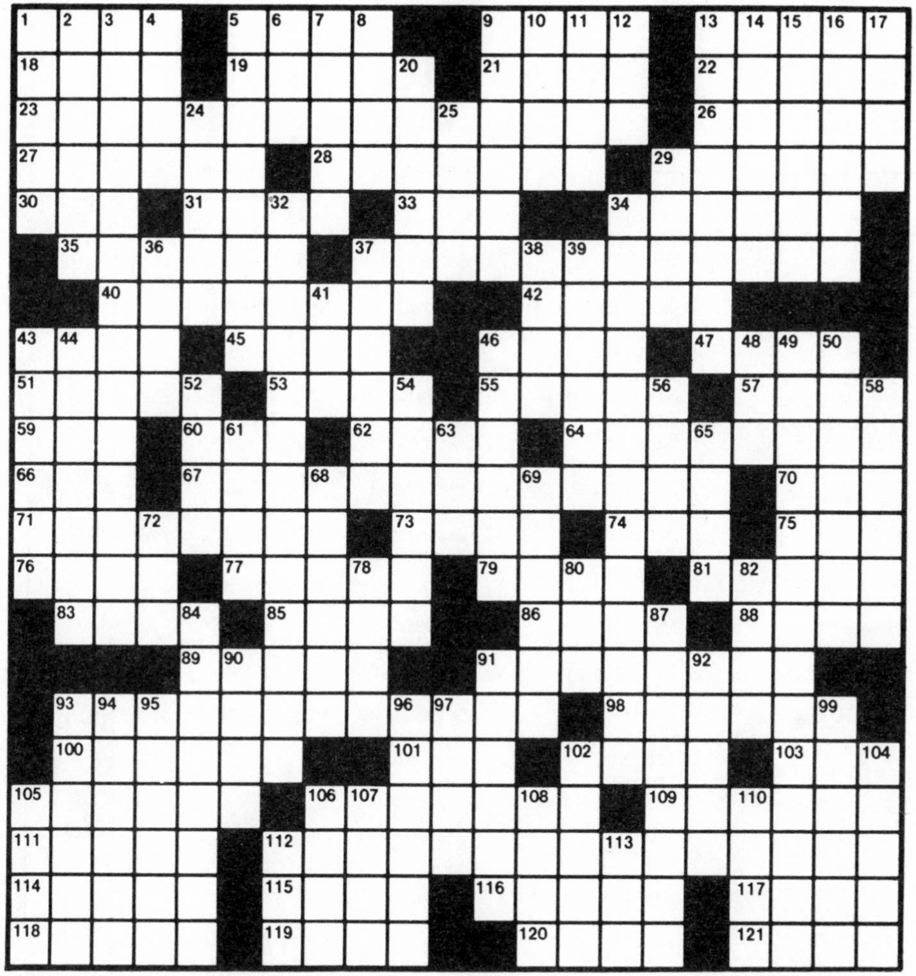

Beastly Assembly

By Henry Hook

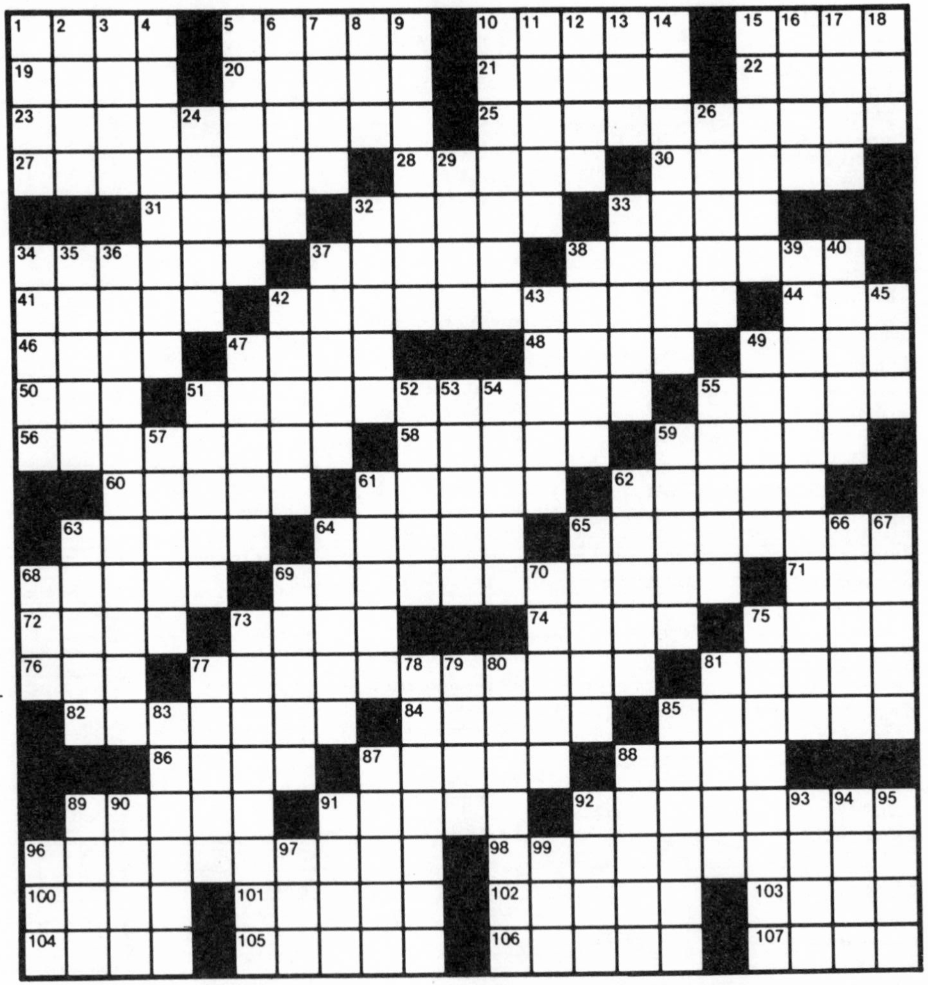

ACROSS

1 Amazon estuary
5 Mid-February toxophilite
10 Extracted stibnite
15 Oscar-winning costume designer
19 Opposed, in the Ozarks
20 "——, fair sun . . .": Romeo
21 "See if ——!"
22 Nervous
23 Michael Bond's bear
25 Turtle owned by Eloise
27 Battle of the Bulge site
28 Hayseed
30 Daisy type
31 Negro and Bravo
32 Fields of snow
33 Sale stipulation
34 Strong man
37 Chauvinist
38 A Freudian
41 Actress France ——
42 Beatrix Potter's hedgehog Mrs. ——
44 Org. with a taxing job
46 Tool for Kite or Hite
47 Half-seas over
48 Goose eggs
49 Supplication
50 A handful
51 President Nixon's puppy
55 Collapsed, with "in"
56 Investigation culmination
58 Piggyback periods
59 Ersatz backyard swings
60 Bat
61 Cue to the band
62 Proprietary
63 Out of cabbage
64 Bright star in Cygnus
65 Barkeep's rocks
68 Cheaply ornate
69 Orlando's charger
71 Hammarskjöld's predecessor
72 As soon as
73 Leads up to a proposal
74 Cloverleaf egress
75 Parakeet suite
76 Randy's rink-mate
77 Black cat who inspired Yeats
81 Threw for a loop
82 Major French newspaper
84 ——-Detoo, of "Star Wars"
85 Highland music makers
86 Reo's eponym
87 Violin virtuoso
88 "—— Want for Christmas . . ."
89 Org. co-founded by Victor Herbert
91 Varnish ingredient
92 Is dilettantish
96 Bountiful boar of Valhalla
98 Duke of Wellington's steed
100 Joyce's —— Livia Plurabelle
101 Pe-Pe or Xeng-Li
102 Singer Frankie or Cleo
103 "Cabaret" Oscar winner
104 Disagreement
105 Supporter of the arts?
106 Expressionist artist Max
107 P.D.Q., on a memo

DOWN

1 One of the Three Bears
2 Late-show actor John
3 Blackmore hero
4 Danny Kaye portrayal
5 Zumbooruk or culverin
6 Twists one's arm
7 Watermelon residue
8 Equi-
9 Renunciative
10 Have the facts wrong
11 F.D.R.'s Interior Sec.
12 Tooth's partner
13 Marshall Plan initials
14 Evictions of kings
15 Marcion's opinions, e.g.
16 MacDonald's co-duettist
17 "The Morning Watch" author
18 Red 1 is one
24 Back of the skull
26 Philip Nolan's fate
29 Where to hear "Evoe!"
32 Option in Polk's slogan
33 Daring display in the Gay Nineties
34 Show scorn
35 Old Roman coins
36 Westminster's Best-in-Show: 1940-41
37 Maggie's Mr.
38 Negatively charged particle
39 Race horse in an A. C. Doyle tale
40 1913 poem, set to music in 1922
42 Modicum of color
43 —— water (on the carpet)
45 Blue
47 Be contingent (on)
49 Polynesian loincloth
51 Curly's kin
52 Hockey infraction
53 Motorist's stopover
54 Evidence for the defense
55 Half of diez
57 Tube type
59 Nebbish
61 "—— great observer": Shak.
62 Carol opener
63 Hackneyed
64 Bombinate
65 Only state never under a foreign flag
66 "The —— Sanction," Eastwood film
67 Acorns, e.g.
68 Understood
69 Recommended wartime purchases
70 Pyromaniac's crime
73 Trachea
75 "Art . . . with an earnest soul and a ——": Roche
77 Dental concern
78 Type of pass
79 City near Provo
80 Saclike part of the ear
81 Moral corruption
83 High-grade coffees
85 Orrery item
87 Transparency
88 Congregation's cries
89 Texas —— M.
90 Dispatch
91 Danube tributary
92 Joy ride
93 Sponsorship
94 Mohammed —— Pahlavi
95 Child's play
96 —— Paulo, Brazil
97 Calf laugh?
99 What a thole supports

Cryptically Speaking

By Derrick C. Niederman

ACROSS

1 Open-mouthed
6 Not sing.
9 Sault —— Marie
12 Barrie dog
16 Nobelist in Economics: 1981
17 Capital of Calvados
18 Drooping
20 Kitchen gadget
21 Like a computer that could put Reagan into office, I see. You see?
23 Rhyme scheme
24 In any way
25 His business is blooming
26 Does place for horses make L.I. quite secure?
29 Start of a vowel sequence
30 Classes in biology
31 "Play It As ——": Didion
32 Ink-lined plane used by lottery commission?
37 Half of CDXXII
39 Dye used in cosmetics
40 Bête ——
41 Actor Carroll
42 Farming abbr.
45 Words of protest
46 Shabby
47 Pests get on Aaron's brother around Ecuador's capital?
50 Less disturbed
52 Balkans dweller
54 Experience
55 Medical suffix
56 Ludlum's "The —— Circle"
59 Within the law
60 Quill
62 Shrimp cock-tale?
65 Corrida cheer
66 Sturdy as ——
68 Moving furtively
69 ". . .bring forth ——": Matt.
71 Soil enhancer
73 Bewail
74 Kane, e.g.
77 Isn't Nicklaus a card?
79 Fashion name
81 Emblem, for short
82 Many secs.
83 Slots spot
84 Emulate a cat
86 Nat and Natalie
87 Eleanor's successor
88 Complete a toll road?
90 Playground fixture
94 Selfishness
96 —— culpa
97 Ex-Yankee wearing a Disney cape?
99 Héloïse's beloved
103 Girl watcher
104 "Thanks ——!"
105 A Southern belle's esteem for her man?
108 Genghis et al.
109 Attic township
110 Coffee makers
111 Poetic possessive
112 Diminutive suffix
113 Mann's "—— Zauberberg"
114 Pop
115 Arty party

DOWN

1 Devoured
2 Player's forte
3 Early victim
4 One trillionth: Comb. form
5 Board the 20th Century Limited
6 Hyperventilate
7 Wreath of welcome
8 Hazy
9 Worked for Legree
10 Roman flower
11 Hugs
12 Brazilian port
13 Ankara cab
14 S. Foster heroine
15 Gauguin's "The Women of ——"
17 Borrower's backup
19 Compensate
20 Singer Page
22 Nothing, in Nice
27 Concerning
28 Holster occupant
30 "—— Out of My Head," 1964 song
32 Socialites' five-time candidate?
33 Does he rue? Ay!
34 What a mixed-up "moon-starer" really is
35 —— up (gets smart)
36 Nile green
38 Eye the guys
41 —— -a-mist
42 To —— (exactly)
43 Medusa poses with Emile. Say cheese!
44 Kingly
46 What gears do
47 Deep-sea catch
48 Most slothful
49 Only
51 In the —— time
52 Some pool people
53 Sri —— (Ceylon)
56 Year in Louis VII's reign
57 With hands on hips
58 Silver abbr.
60 S.A. rodent
61 Father of Methuselah
63 Tropical fibers
64 Kodiak's home
67 Possessive mark: Abbr.
70 —— turpentine
72 Off one's rocker
74 Visionary in the 15th century
75 Elbe tributary
76 Kind of guard
78 Opened a lettre de cachet
79 S.M.U. housing
80 —— Jima
84 Alger's fiddler
85 Floral growth
86 Alpine sights
87 Heavyweights Max and Buddy
88 Be unsteady
89 Actor Will: 1902-78
90 "Summer and ——": Williams
91 Figure for Fleming
92 Fame
93 Structure for a Euripides opus
95 Aphorism
98 Coward's "—— About the Boy"
99 Texas —— M.
100 Moslem official
101 Position at Aqueduct
102 Early Bond nemesis
106 Stat. for Guidry
107 Cozy room

Minority Report

By Bert H. Kruse

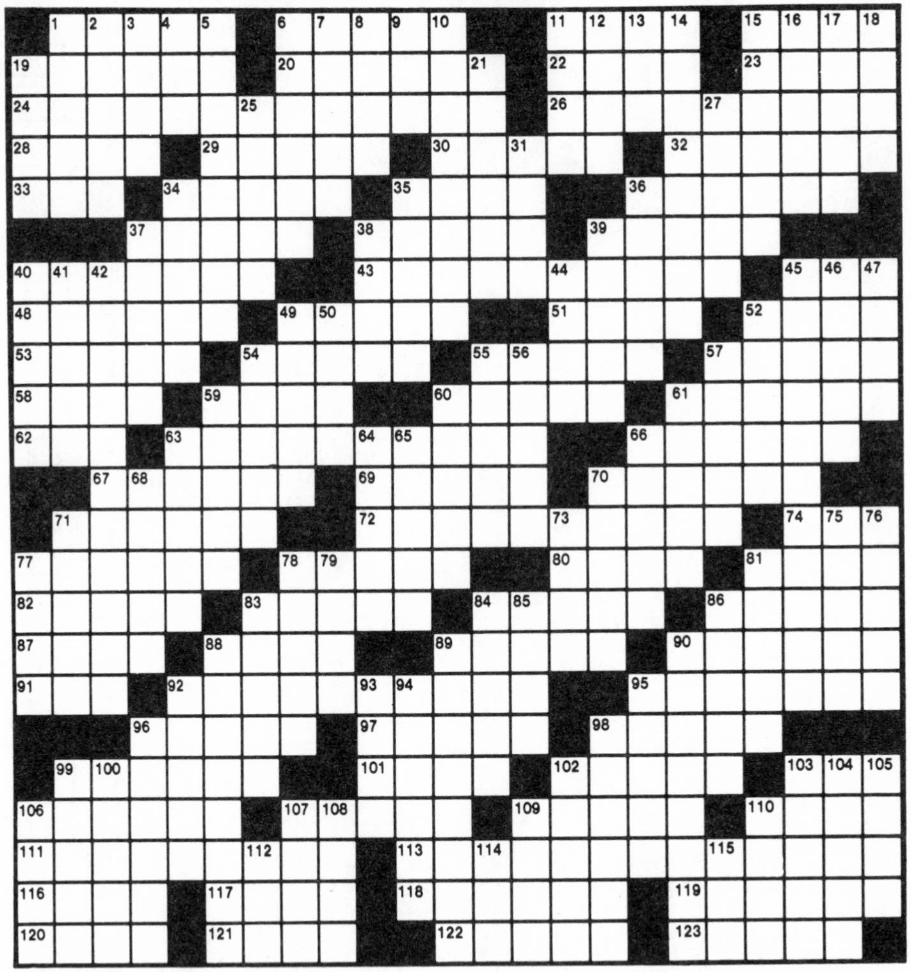

ACROSS

1 Ice pinnacle
6 Violin's sire
11 Drive down lightly
15 Brotherhood Week theme
19 Shakespearean deputy
20 Athenians' market centers
22 Asian sitter
23 District
24 Hero of a national holiday starting in 1986
26 Jackie and Bojangles
28 Fencer's weapon
29 Blue part of Old Glory
30 Twain's brother
32 "—— your heart be troubled": John 14:1
33 TU-144, e.g.
34 Singer Bailey
35 Blueprint
36 Ski race
37 Famed Rialto couple
38 Buonarroti work
39 Nonprofessionals
40 Seeks lofty goals
43 Famed labor-brotherhood organizer
45 Bulge in a billfold
48 A concern of Cal Peete
49 Chummy, in Cheshire
51 Diamond units
52 College founder —— Bethune
53 Abolitionist Sojourner ——
54 Inheritance items
55 Aqua ——, gold-dissolving liquid
57 Law group
58 Raise one's hackles
59 Blessing
60 Persians' contemporaries
61 Kind of acting
62 Crewman
63 Memorable N.A.A.C.P. director
66 Bayard ——, Washington March organizer: 1963
67 Vehicles for Price and Bumbry
69 "—— Allen," by Gwendolyn Brooks
70 Lafayette is here
71 Stands
72 Diplomat-editor-orator Frederick and family
74 Scout org.'s former name
77 Greek nymph
78 Happy tunes
80 Train or plane info
81 Bandleader Kenton
82 Welles or Bean
83 Jolly Roger figures
84 Cheered
86 Electrical problem
87 High time
88 Activist
89 More with it
90 Rough shelter
91 Rutledge or Jillian
92 Olympic great
95 Presidential hopeful: 1984
96 A Nobelist of 1957
97 Persona non ——
98 Part of a Dante work
99 Sockeye, for one
101 Kids
102 Twinges
103 Turner or Cole
106 Attribute of Marian Anderson
107 Muralist Rivera
109 Presages
110 Rhine tributary
111 N.A.A.C.P. co-founder, historian-sociologist
113 Underground Railroad leader and Union spy
116 Geraint's wife
117 Medieval serf
118 Hooky player
119 Get one's bearings
120 Brace
121 Ellington
122 Impressions
123 Food, clothing, etc.

DOWN

1 Sinecures
2 Plume bearer
3 Neural network
4 The Greatest
5 Award winner
6 Fall guys
7 Völund's brother
8 Civil-rights leader Julian
9 Work unit
10 Wheedler's forte
11 Tropical food source
12 King in Kings
13 Shelley subject
14 Wendell ——, Anti-Slavery Society president
15 At the end
16 Maine campus site
17 Spite
18 Cardinal point
19 Iowa college town
21 Printers' mistakes
25 Mythomaniacs
27 Under, in poesy
31 —— instant (right away)
34 Fish or roost
35 Pan's music makers
36 Board game
37 Alex Haley hero
38 Strasbourg export
39 The Brown Bomber
40 J. R. Richard was one
41 Tiny groove
42 Memorable actor-singer
44 Venetian chief
45 Booker T.'s family
46 Hot crime
47 Tinted
49 Catty remarks
50 Noted opera costume designer
52 "We Shall Overcome," e.g.
54 Prado sights
55 Err at cards
56 Old car
57 Spray candidates
59 Feeling ennui
60 Calculator key
61 Thought
63 Fortification
64 Serve soup
65 Grannies, e.g.
66 Flattened a flat
68 Tree having edible seeds
70 Glacial-stream deposit
71 Hammerin' Hank
73 Big name in tennis
75 Andrea del ——
76 Chekhov
77 Actress Freeman
78 Fine soil
79 Regarding
81 Military dress hat
83 Petty officer
84 Carries on
85 Handle for Brutus
86 Faiths
88 Discharged, as from the R.A.F.
89 Atlantic coast, e.g.
90 Poet-dramatist-novelist Hughes
92 —— and Kashmir, Indian state
93 Monster
94 Creator of Bigger Thomas
95 Leigh or Gaynor
96 Like plowed but unharrowed acres
98 Fellow graduates with Gen. Benjamin Davis Jr.: 1936
99 All in
100 Iowa coal center
102 Pencil part
103 Dubbed
104 Isles off Ireland
105 Something to pitch
106 Dumbfounds
107 Drop shot for Noah
108 What "video" means
109 Breakfast food
110 Nichols suitor
112 Columbus inst.
114 Regret
115 Yorkshire river

Association Game

By Peter Swift

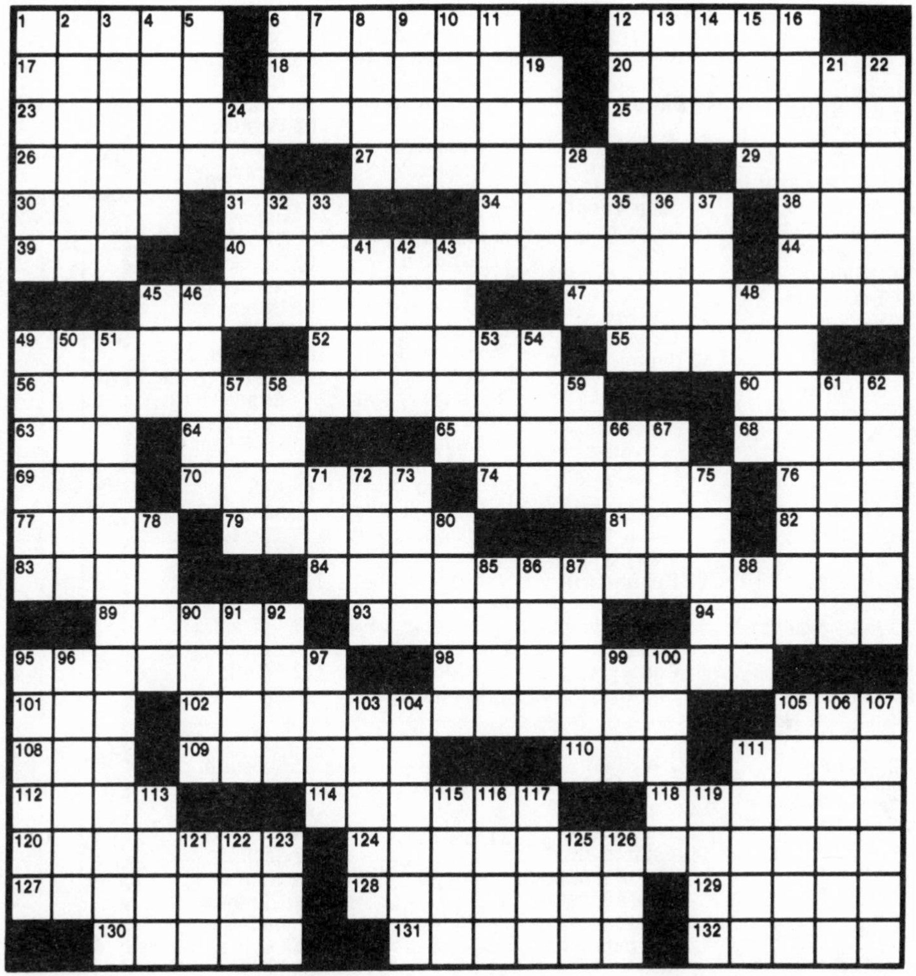

ACROSS

1 Behind, at sea
6 Drool
12 Foolhardy
17 Book size
18 Makes effervescent
20 Overly optimistic
23 Grain grinders?
25 Cleaves
26 Driven in a group
27 Roofer or critic
29 Copy, for short
30 Some are fine
31 Actress MacGraw
34 Underwater "wolf pack"
38 Botanist Gray
39 Denials
40 Shavers?
44 Clear
45 Goldsmith's "—— of Wakefield"
47 Be noncommital on an issue
49 Passionate
52 Father of Andromache
55 Hall and ——, musical duo
56 Nones?
60 "Up and ——!"
63 Fitting
64 Hit sign
65 Pretentious art or writing
68 Change the décor
69 Bird of prey
70 Home of maroon-and-white Leopards
74 Converts chips
76 Equivoque
77 Abbrs. on maps
79 Safari participant
81 A Dadaism founder
82 "Some —— meat and canna eat": Burns
83 —— Jahan
84 Cold spells?
89 Knobs
93 Vito Farinola
94 Cocktail garnishes
95 Pyrenees dweller
98 Intertwines
101 Fall mo.
102 Fox hunts?
105 Trim
108 Wayne Gretzky's milieu
109 Wooden mallet
110 Workshop, for short
111 A Delano
112 Baltique et al.
114 Bad-tempered person
118 Jason Robards role
120 Weaken
124 Stags?
127 Legendary
128 Bluish gray, as a fur
129 Scorch
130 Bard's preposition
131 Pressed
132 In pursuit of

DOWN

1 Hound or shawl
2 Dance or jacket
3 Puts on guard
4 Exercises serendipity
5 Style
6 —— Jacinto
7 Emulated Ozawa
8 Word with length
9 Ski resort
10 Cartoonist Hulme
11 —— oculi (muscle of the eye)
12 Bandeau, for short
13 Gat
14 Volcanic emission
15 Calls, in poker
16 Rails' kin?
19 Ancient Arabian country
21 Thistlelike plant
22 Patrimony
24 Antarctic cape
28 Male gypsies
32 Bulgarian's coin
33 "I wander'd till ——": M. Arnold
35 Oakland, for one
36 Japanese monastery
37 Trellis item
41 Served perfectly
42 Archibald of the Bucks
43 Negus, e.g.
45 Part of TNT
46 Nobelist in Literature: 1946
48 Treasured
49 Summers
50 Quart, to a gallon
51 Chessmen?
53 Chemical suffix
54 Naldi of the silents
57 Damascene, e.g.
58 Lie detector on Pinocchio
59 Draft agcy.
61 Statesman Benes
62 Louvre display
66 Niger neighbor
67 Münster mister
71 Bit
72 Mouthward
73 Shade of green
75 Genetic mutation
78 "Out, damned Spot!"
80 Encrusted, in a way
85 Therefore, in Dijon
86 Flowerlike: Comb. form
87 Staircase feature
88 Twice
90 Fragment
91 A Gardner
92 Advantage
95 Hostility
96 Harmful
97 "En Enda ——," Ingrid Bergman film: 1938
99 Marsh elder
100 Important Disraeli book
103 "His word burned like ——": Ecclus.
104 Perfumery oil
105 Threnody
106 Princely European house
107 Armored, German style
111 Letter stroke
113 Wizened
115 Autocrat
116 Concerning
117 Give profusely
119 —— Nostra
121 Inlet
122 J. Herriot, for one
123 Old English letter
125 Lisbon-to-London dir.
126 Pop

Double Takes

By Jack L. Steinhardt

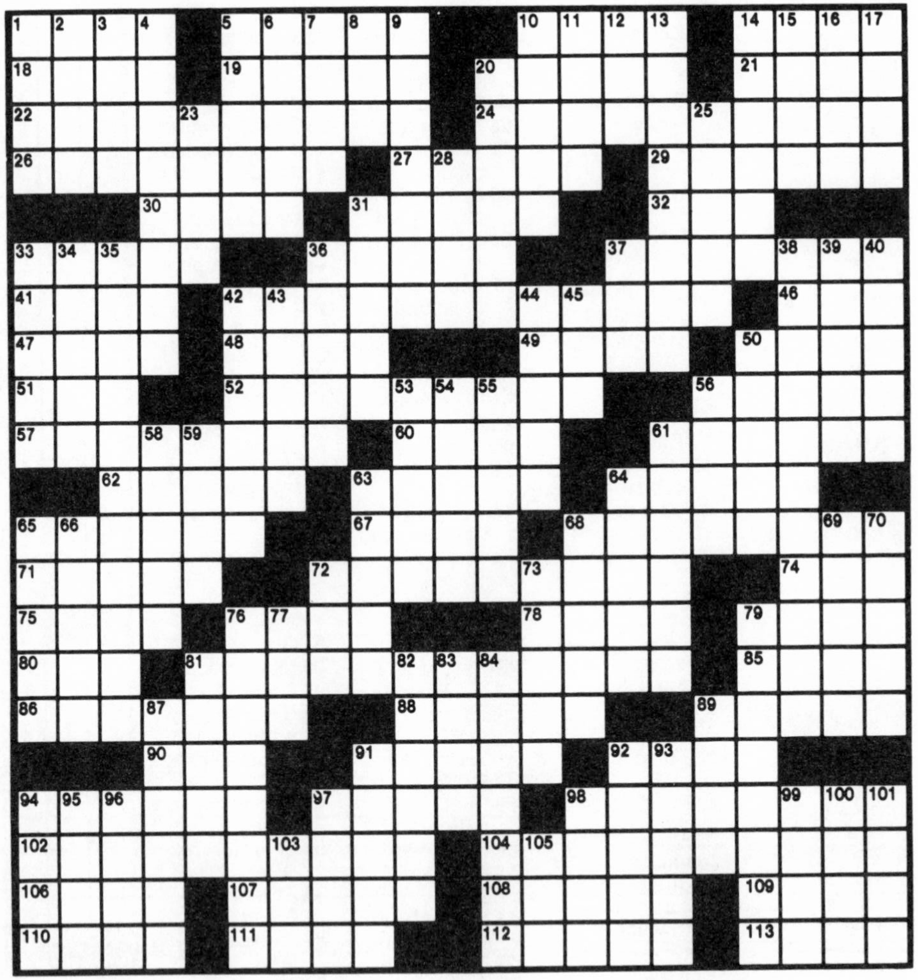

ACROSS

1 Canaanites' deity
5 Son of Jacob and Zilpah
10 Venetian traveler
14 Rolled steel
18 Rounds for a certain fighter
19 Permission
20 Mosquito
21 Transcribe
22 Harlow's inheritance
24 Vessel for oarsmen
26 Earthworms
27 Docent's relative
29 Moslem decrees
30 Kenny Rogers hit
31 Wisent
32 Dandy
33 Author-columnist Joseph
36 Spy's necessity
37 Lab tube
41 —— bene
42 Koussevitzky's crescendos
46 Butter
47 Mideast diplomat
48 Kirghizian range or valley
49 Disgusting person
50 Diva's delight
51 Word of dissent
52 Pygmy power
56 Wolfe's creator
57 Detailed exposition
60 Fillet border
61 Carr's "The —— in the Waxworks"
62 Regimen, in Reims
63 Precursor of a reaper
64 Corday's target
65 Sec. of State after Vance
67 Speaker of the diamond
68 Like many a saint
71 Russian workers' collective
72 Vista on a tourist's postcard
74 Mined find
75 —— -Carlo Menotti
76 Possessor of Mjollnir
78 Itinerary abbr.
79 Star of "Scarface" in 1932
80 "Agnus ——"
81 Rubs V.I.P.'s the wrong way
85 Sacred Egyptian bull
86 Actor from Pen Argyl, Pa.
88 His magic helped Prospero
89 Frozen wintry coating
90 Like Leroy Brown
91 Fluffs
92 Together, in music
94 Symphony originally named "Bonaparte"
97 Greek name for Orcus
98 Hampers
102 Peak pip
104 Pot cover, e.g.
106 Higher-pitched English horn
107 Its capital is St.-Etienne
108 Not the others
109 Hebrides island
110 Absolutely not, poetically
111 They can be tight or loose
112 Auricularly appendaged
113 Smaller amount

DOWN

1 —— California
2 Kind of corner
3 Galsworthy's "—— of Devon"
4 Individual's request at a bank
5 Cold
6 Rundown
7 Late actor Conried
8 Conductor Queler
9 Impatient
10 Noted Argentine name
11 Carpathian river
12 Comedian Lehr: 1896-1950
13 Ultra-conservative
14 Minor to-do
15 Kind of mouth or speaker
16 Chevet
17 Tournament slots
20 Young and Mature
23 Cuff
25 Short riding whips
28 Exploits
31 Strong truck or cart
33 In connection with
34 Having rounded projections
35 Remained decorous
36 Box
37 Links org.
38 Acting Boy Scouts
39 Cliff slope
40 Emulate Cabotin
42 Heavy silk fabric
43 Molière character
44 Father of Excalibur's owner
45 Trumpery
50 Deviate
53 Victor or Roger
54 Apollo 15 astronaut
55 Sharon of "Cagney and Lacey"
56 Catalogue
58 Senlin's creator
59 European linden
61 Loving gesture
63 Cordwood measure
64 "Olympia" artist
65 One of the Gabors
66 An archangel
68 Bismuth, e.g.
69 Pyle or Banks
70 Jefferson was one
72 Fuddler
73 Montana Indians
76 Fit for barter
77 Timothy produces it
79 Knight's protection
81 Decorate
82 Respectful gesture
83 Fortitude
84 Snappy comeback
87 —— dictum
89 Amounts
91 Speaks carelessly
92 Developed
93 Threw down the gauntlet
94 Poetic dark hue
95 Agrestic one
96 An Amerind
97 Indemnified
98 Former name of Kalinin, U.S.S.R.
99 Cry at Pan's parties
100 Meniscus
101 Mmes.' Latin counterparts
103 Geologic time
105 Eureka!

Non Personae

By June A. Boggs

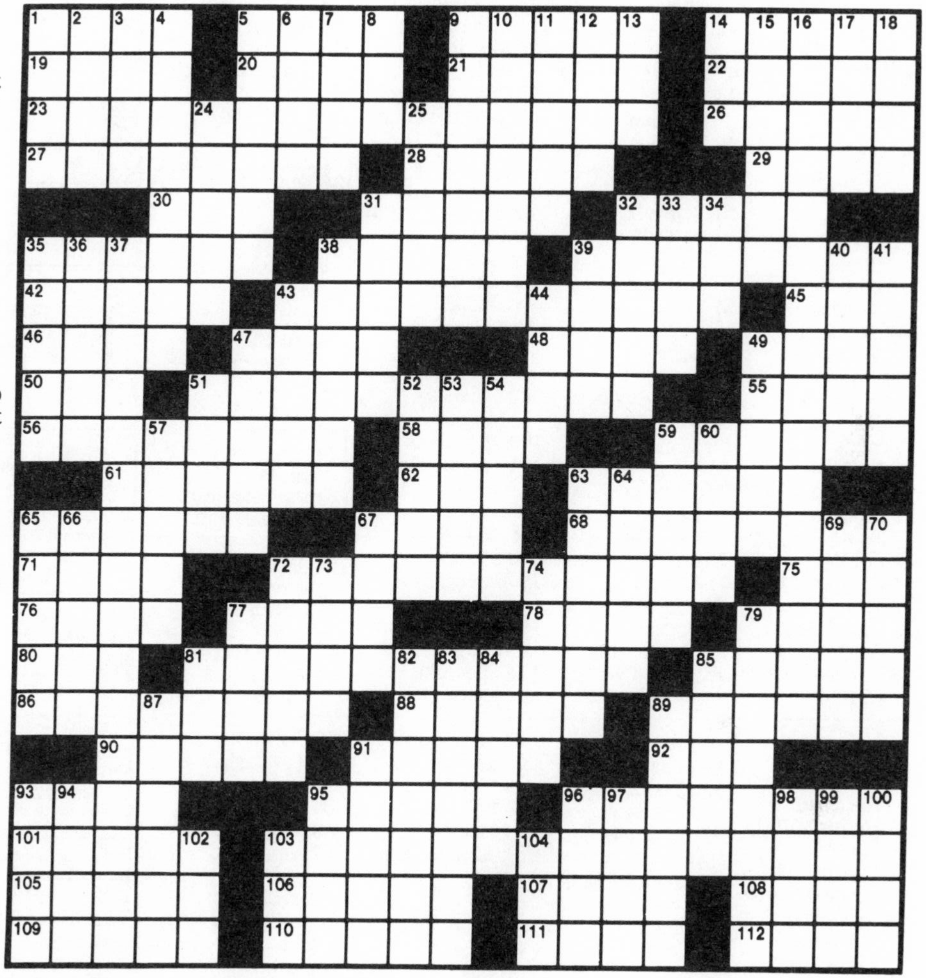

ACROSS

1 Capp's —— Iggle
5 Wild goat
9 Bay State town
14 Cogwheel item
19 Lulu
20 "It's ——!"
21 TV's —— Na
22 Shade
23 HARRY
26 A Peace Prize winner in 1908
27 "Etude ——": Swinburne
28 Amsterdam
29 Uriah
30 Rumanian coin
31 Trunks
32 Glacial mass
35 European thrushes
38 Danton colleague
39 Sylvan
42 Mortimer of radio fame
43 SUE
45 Fatima slept here
46 Call it ——
47 Locale
48 Phoenician letters
49 Out yonder
50 Comprehend a joke
51 FRANK
55 "Thus with a kiss ——": Romeo
56 Citizen of Asmara
58 Annapolis inst.
59 Kraits
61 Family of dynamite's inventor
62 Derisive interjection
63 More cunning
65 Used a ketch
67 Aggrieved
68 Neglecting
71 Love song
72 SALLY
75 Antiaircraft missile
76 Signet
77 —— Raton, Fla.
78 European linden
79 Auspicious
80 Utter
81 BOB
85 Cathedral section
86 Toward the center
88 Zeena's mate in a Wharton book
89 Voguish
90 Sent to Elba, e.g.
91 Minor prophet
92 Highly timely
93 Four noggins
95 Support for Manet
96 Copper smelting center
101 Reach an ultimate point
103 JEAN
105 Sand did this
106 Even
107 Father of Ahab
108 News, for short
109 Conduit
110 Professed opinion
111 Kringle's burden
112 Sheep shelter

DOWN

1 Adonis's killer
2 Last Stuart ruler
3 Harold Teen's leaping car
4 Whimsical humor
5 St. Paul's birthplace
6 Sanction a crime
7 Expectancy
8 Deli choice
9 Elaine's bailiwick
10 ". . . that serveth ——": Num. 3:36
11 Pluto
12 Just
13 Minstrel's offering
14 Place for three men
15 Sioux
16 MARK
17 Ailanthus, e.g.
18 Part of a lamp
24 Harvest
25 Love, in Lucca
31 Overdoes it on the beach
32 Fathom
33 Goofs
34 Soak hemp
35 Inedible orange
36 D. Thomas's "—— Milk Wood"
37 CAROL
38 Morning prayer
39 Pâté de —— gras
40 Robin of balladry
41 Galba's ghostly guardians
43 Kind of basin
44 Soprano Lisa Della ——
47 Golfer Ed
49 Brass helpers
51 The City, Rome: It.
52 Geologist Arnold: 1807-84
53 Shark's crime
54 Printer's roller
57 Kind of loss
59 "It's ——!"
60 Record
63 Inducement
64 Forcefully, in poesy
65 Cheek and Foldi
66 City on the Allegheny
67 Corset part
69 Prosaic
70 Grinding substance
72 Humanity
73 Cloyingly sweet
74 Besides, to Brutus
77 Eliot hero
79 Bombast
81 Monogram of the author of "The Biglow Papers"
82 Afflicted with rubella
83 Moor who suspected amour
84 Greenland air base
85 Italian philosopher: 1866-1952
87 Wily
89 Id est
91 Ingenuous
93 Seats for parishioners
94 Concerning
95 Pitcher
96 Weapons, for short
97 Not any, in Dogpatch
98 Lad, in León
99 Bonkers
100 Drug-yielding plant
102 Through
103 What an R.N. gives
104 Punctum

Collectives Collection

By Bert Rosenfield

ACROSS

1 Central American rodent
5 Declines
9 —— Pendragon
14 Key fruit
20 Junior and senior events
22 Verdon in "Damn Yankees"
23 Bland
24 —— Doctrine
25 Conductor Caldwell
26 Musical collective
29 Cornmeal cakes
31 Graf ——, scuttled in 1939
32 Gloucester's cape
33 Foreign
34 Composer of over 40 operas
35 Gal of song
37 Skirt insert
39 Race-starting word
40 Automotive collective
46 "The ——," Midler film
47 Rubbish!
48 Waters of Avignon
49 Painter Veronese
50 Dust-up
52 Type of current
55 Sleep destroyer
57 Peak: Comb. form
58 Levee accessory
61 Ivory-tower collective
66 Dockers' org.
67 Mirliton
69 Foreign Legion headgear
70 Seat, in Sonora
71 Guinness title
72 Problem with horns
74 Tokyo, once
76 Manon's lover —— Grieux
77 Partlet
78 Of gums: Comb. form
79 Sartorial collective
86 Count beginner
87 Summer time in N.Y.C.
88 Regulus's constellation
89 Thumb, for one
90 Do the room over
92 Starter for classic
93 Retired, as a female professor
97 V.I.P.'s location
100 Wine disorder
101 Ship-shaped clock
102 Juvenile collective
105 Stems
107 River in England
108 King or Bean
109 Play
113 Shoe-box letters
114 "Hard ——!"
116 Contralto in "Siegfried"
118 —— culpa
119 Jezebel's deity
121 Adolescent collective
126 Extension
127 Formal mall
129 Tennis term
130 Top grade, almost
131 Clique
133 Break bread
136 Bird of no return
139 Musically pleasant
140 Motel collective
144 Epithet
146 American sable
147 Part of a joint
148 Garden spot
149 Chou ——
150 Ancient ascetic
151 End of a Stein line
152 Heraldic beast
153 Bucky of baseball

DOWN

1 Letters below the letter
2 Plains buffalo hunter
3 Companions for kind hearts
4 Mrs. Prynne of "Private Lives"
5 Qua —— (here and there, in Italy)
6 Lancelot's nephew
7 Radar-screen image
8 Most logical
9 Org. founded in 1941
10 Geyseral deposit
11 Goldie from Washington
12 Good news
13 Place to dep. cash
14 An Allen
15 Court decree
16 Alaska's —— Glacier
17 Religious collective
18 Royal Indians
19 —— cross (ankh)
21 Aoudad, for one
27 Paraphernalia
28 Loses concentration
30 Black haw
34 Moss once flourishing on Broadway
36 Steady Eddie of baseball
38 —— Grande, Mojave Desert town
41 Plaintive Portuguese song
42 Memorable impresario
43 Chemical compound
44 Retreat Brezhnev had
45 Mother of the Nereids
46 Postal Service letters
50 Item made by a queen
51 —— many words
53 Use the hammock
54 South American constrictor
56 Vigilius and Sisinnius
58 Perceptive device
59 Property recipient
60 Granary
62 Gambol
63 Towser's friend
64 Nests
65 Singer Howard
67 American plover
68 Property collective
72 Chaperon
73 Michael and Harold
75 Frequently, to Keats
80 Saarinen
81 "And —— goes"
82 Brouhaha
83 Victor of tennis
84 Customary, in Châlons
85 Freshet
91 Y.W.C.A., e.g.
93 Facility
94 They have lots of mdse.
95 "And the same ——"
96 Southwest winds
98 Key
99 —— up (find)
103 South Africa's Prime Minister
104 French Riviera comber
106 Vinegar —— (worm)
110 Responsive
111 Azure
112 Russian wire service
114 Close margin
115 Cat or pigeon, often
117 Med school subj.
119 Fitted
120 Hilo hellos
121 Beth preceder
122 Ye —— Gift Shoppe
123 Like Raggedy Ann
124 Blind as ——
125 —— tonic (bar drink)
127 Types, in Tubingen
128 Lyon, to Vittorio
132 Town SW of Padua
134 —— Domini
135 J. Louis specialties
137 Comte —— Fère (Athos)
138 Roberts
141 Thus, to Tacitus
142 Syracuse-to-Utica dir.
143 Sault —— Marie
145 Wagon- —— (Parisian Pullman)

Pairaphrasing

By Jim Page

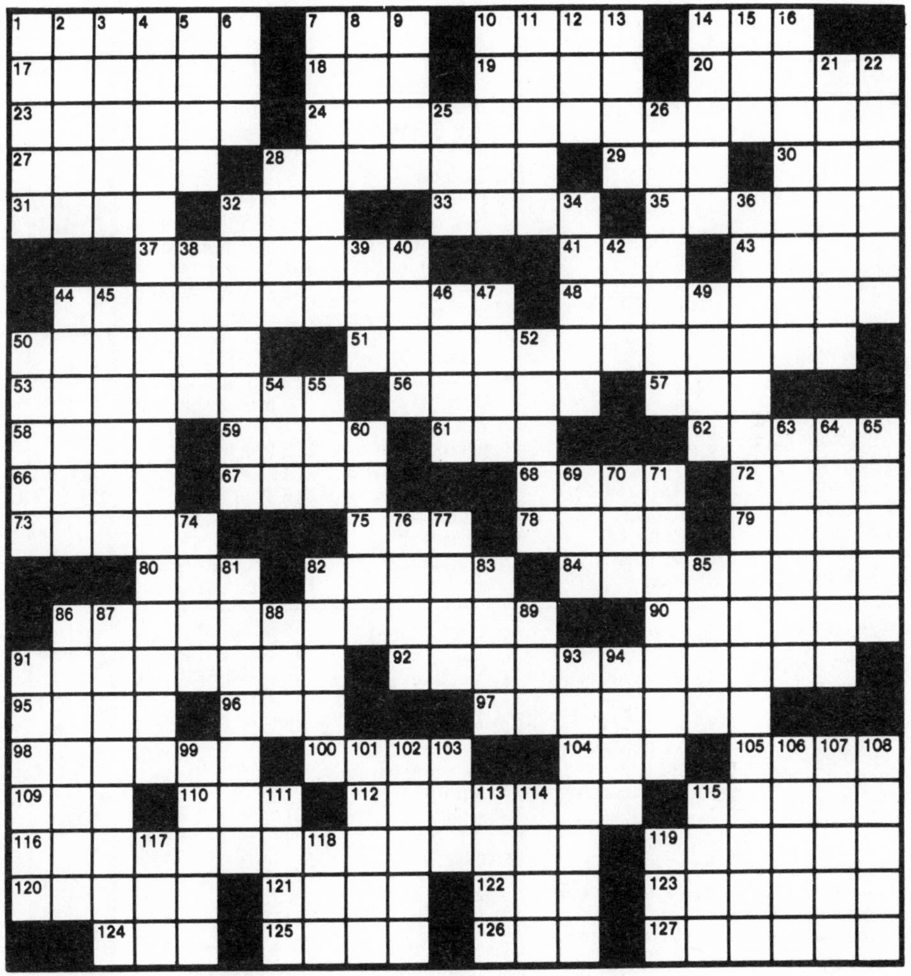

ACROSS

1 Crèche setting
7 Pol. union: 1958-61
10 Diamond item
14 Paleozoic or Victorian
17 Ill will
18 Hoopsters' org.
19 Half a seaport name
20 Skin flick
23 Make the scene
24 007's protection
27 Finger-bowl accessory
28 An A.F.C. player
29 506, to Nero
30 Author Santha Rama ——
31 Etc. kin
32 Debussy's "La ——"
33 Jumble
35 In full court
37 Quarantine
41 Miscalculate
43 Pierre's guardian
44 Ezra's meter
48 Went over galley proofs
50 Battle standard
51 Archie's mouth
53 Like lawmakers
56 Klemperer and Kruger
57 Brain tracing, for short
58 Taunt; jeer
59 Present times
61 Beethoven's Ninth, e.g.
62 Twist; squeeze
66 City ESE of Bergen
67 Jollity
68 Sound measure
72 It followed "Typee"
73 Shoplifter's crime
75 It's concerned with rtes.
78 Lagomorph
79 —— no good
80 Fixed
82 Oak tree
84 Actor-singer Harve
86 Comedy
90 Moore of "Arthur" fame
91 Activity of some demons
92 "Fire and Ice," e.g.
95 "Rule, Britannia" composer
96 Bishopric
97 Fall, as the market
98 One of the finches
100 Dick or Schick
104 Buzzing insect
105 Glory
109 Bull ——, Citation's sire
110 "We —— robbed!": Joe Jacobs
112 Dress material
115 OPEC vessel
116 What a "midnight ride" horse earned
119 Mountain crests
120 Dexter, e.g.
121 Braves' pitcher of yore
122 MacLaine, to Beatty
123 "Honor Thy Father" author
124 —— Plaines
125 Mountain: Comb. form
126 Thickwit
127 Guitarist Segovia

DOWN

1 Reduce price a bit
2 Seeress's card
3 Trajan's courtyards
4 Fulton's oratory
5 Impose a tax
6 Netherlands town
7 Take off a belt
8 Busy as ——
9 "The —— is to the swift"
10 Bender
11 Resting places for Leo
12 Ins. salesman, e.g.
13 He played Cassidy
14 Finally, in France
15 Chafe
16 Iglesia attendee
21 "Look Back ——": Osborne
22 Drew out
25 City in Baden-Württemberg
26 Late, as a train
28 —— -portrait
32 Harbor activity
34 Helots
36 Sally's childhood environment
38 Printer's term
39 Add up
40 Prefix for dollars
42 Jewish complimentary title
44 Exile
45 Make possible
46 Former A.L. team
47 Sheriff's rep.
49 Once more
50 Sired
52 Pizazz
54 One of a Tenn. eleven
55 Homophone for you
60 —— Tranquillity
63 Starts rolling
64 "I will —— thee go . . .": Gen. 32:26
65 Aussie's stone
69 Henry Harley Arnold's sobriquet
70 Ice-hockey great
71 "I have no —— tongue": Roethke
74 —— off (irate)
76 47 Down is one
77 Jai ——
81 Hero of an Old French romance
82 Thesaurus name
83 Guernsey and Jersey
85 Sea swell
86 Most agile
87 Feathered
88 Ending for ethyl
89 Appomattox figure
91 Rooms, in Lyon
93 Age; antiquity
94 Expanse of ice
99 Water pitchers
101 Spookish
102 Pool person
103 Hebrew letter
106 Change; vary
107 Presidential adviser
108 Irish Gaelics
111 Fair-to-middling
113 —— Verde National Park
114 Goddess of the rainbow
115 Algerian seaport
117 Shoe width
118 Word with East or West
119 —— standstill

!PU SMOTTOB

By Frances Hansen

ACROSS

1 Carpenter's friend
7 Like fattening foods
14 Second-largest Syrian city
20 "—— Necessarily So"
21 Done with
22 Club soda, branch water, etc.
23 !PU SMOTTOB
26 Use a wiretap
27 High dudgeon
28 Spring bloomers
29 Norm: Abbr.
30 Bundle of sticks
32 Not gross
33 Cloister head
37 Storage problem
38 Save
39 Mine car
43 King Hussein's wife
44 Popular pickle
45 Seemly
46 Chaplin's widow
47 !PU SMOTTOB
53 "——was saying . . ."
54 Architectural style
55 Flying prefix
56 Billiards shot
57 Hat for J. R. Ewing
59 Repute
60 Dreiser's Carrie
61 Tenor role in "Don Pasquale"
65 Street game
67 Jolson hit
70 Six: Comb. form
72 Tagged
76 Poet H.D.'s first name
77 Price addenda
78 Moonshiner's device
80 Soul of St.-Cyr
81 !PU SMOTTOB
86 "—— Do Is Dream . . ."
87 Peak of perfection
88 Auld lang syne
89 Minute amount
90 Stable pet
91 Jersey or Manhattan trailer
92 Boss, in darkest Africa
94 Dry table wine
96 Arafat's org.
97 Ship to remember
98 Writer Brofeldt's pseudonym
99 Lax little shepherdess
102 007, e.g.
103 Shallow-water transport
108 !PU SMOTTOB
112 Samantha's mother on "Bewitched"
113 Pep up
114 Lassie, for one
115 Tempest container
116 Mean, cowardly cad
117 Make beloved

DOWN

1 Heir's concern
2 Thine, in Noisy-le-Sec
3 Prince Souphanouvong's land
4 Schism
5 Provided
6 Is frugal
7 —— Andy of "Show Boat"
8 One —— time (singly)
9 New Guinea seaport
10 In heaven
11 Certain rockets
12 Map feature
13 B-F connection
14 Little cherubs
15 On the up and up
16 They've been "Reno-vated"
17 Marquette, e.g.
18 Corp. head
19 Kirghizian oblast
24 Disencumber
25 Stately court dance
30 Kind of acid
31 Tamarisk salt tree
33 Writer Seton et al.
34 Blow one's own horn
35 Alamo name or knife
36 Suffix for trick or witch
37 Rodolfo's love
38 In front
39 Go —— (become worthless)
40 Shake out of bed
41 By —— (barely)
42 Louis B., the "star-maker"
44 "Go and catch a falling star" poet
45 City in Argentina
48 Interpret wrongly
49 Not a soul
50 Leader of the Long March
51 Go back to the drawing board
52 Good-natured
58 Plant's clinging part
60 Milan's La ——
62 Doubting Thomas's demand
63 Up-tight
64 Former name of the Amu Darya
66 Like peas in a pod
67 Bundle of stalks
68 ——-the-wisp
69 Spurious wing
71 G.I.'s address
73 One of the Days
74 Ham it up
75 Coup ——
78 Tea accompaniment
79 Neighbor of Twelve Oaks
82 Reviled
83 Denizens of the deep
84 Tatum's father
85 Inlet
92 They're locked in with lox
93 Hip

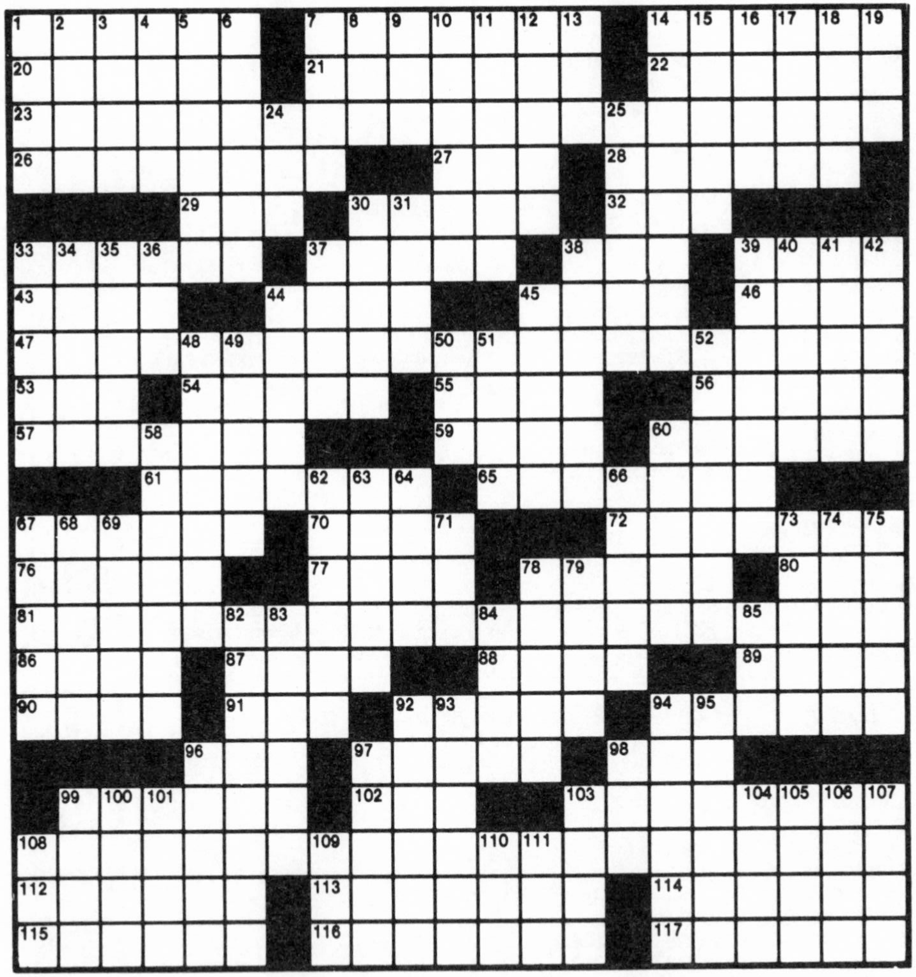

94 Risk
95 Relief for dishpan hands
96 Rock: Comb. form
97 —— Carta
98 High-school math
99 Cause of distress
100 Strange-sounding Norwegian canton
101 A deck
103 Part of UNICEF
104 Forward
105 Make eyes at
106 Author Lieblich
107 Stadium feature
108 As —— (until now)
109 Buttons
110 Tenn. power project
111 For each

189

Play Ball!

By Jeanette K. Brill

ACROSS

1 Burgomasters
7 Chilean river
10 Kind of fiddle
14 Part of a lamp
18 Turkish inn
19 Pervading atmosphere
21 "—— Ben Jonson!"
23 Soundness of mind
24 What Musial wore on his jersey
26 Gravelly ridge
27 Synagogue
28 Fields
29 D.D.E.'s command
30 Verve
32 Little, for one
34 Teased
36 Hasten
38 Houston N.L. team boo-boos
43 Swiss river
44 Word with rear or tight
45 "Did You —— See a Dream Walking?"
46 Beget
47 He wrote "The Old Town"
48 Castle on a square
50 Col. Tibbets's mother
53 Whilom
56 Id adherent
57 Flowering shrub
59 New York, home of Shea's tenants
63 Daft
65 Tanglefoot
66 Banderilla
67 Old Dominion V.I.P.'s
70 Stage-light color sheet
72 Kind of bore
74 Thug
76 Prior, to Prior
77 Eager
79 Tenor in "I Pagliacci"
81 "—— the Dark," 1941 musical
82 Ostracized Arlington Stadium player
84 Eldritch
85 Sesame
88 Soft mineral
89 Beefsteak blight
92 He's no yes man
93 Triangle ratio
94 Get on
97 Essex or Mercer
99 G.W. in '76
100 Sandy's barks
101 Reese, once
105 Due follower
106 Quitclaim
108 Malefic
109 Nests
111 Jehoshaphat's father
112 Cretan king
115 Pelvic bones
117 She wrote "Memories of a Star"
120 Atlanta, to H. Aaron: 1966-74
123 Informal bookmark
124 Olfactology subject
125 Pangolin
126 Card game for two
127 Jean Stein best seller
128 No longer visible
129 "—— tu," Verdi aria
130 Put studs on a shield

DOWN

1 Writ of right
2 Second of a Latin paradigm
3 Steinbrenner scribble
4 Mirador
5 Go over again
6 Porker's pad
7 Resins
8 Nebraska Indians
9 Curt
10 "—— Mir Bist Du Schoen"
11 Soprano Moffo
12 Steep cliff
13 Plato's Luna
14 Provide shelter
15 Hand holder
16 Alcofribas Nasier
17 A past tense
20 Flâneurs
22 Molders
25 Glaswegian negatives
31 What a narthex leads to
33 Reine's spouse
35 Bell the cat
36 Grass
37 Seriatim
39 Lacrosse team
40 Fragrance
41 Kind of sch.
42 A king of Judea
49 Caffeine-rich nut
51 For fear that
52 Region dominated by Athens
54 Scoriaceous lava
55 Alpine region
58 Bismuth, for one
60 Fortification
61 "A Clockwork ——," 1971 film
62 Barn bedding
64 Fairway clod
67 Detroit team in first place
68 Coquette
69 Pen name of Philo Vance's creator
71 Jazz singer Simone
73 German song
75 Start of an invention
78 Glazed pottery
80 Mountain nymph
83 Can. air group
85 Tedious
86 Made more intense
87 —— - majesté
90 Shaver's vessel
91 Egyptian solar deity
93 Bernhardt and Caldwell
95 Regret
96 "—— Madigan," 1967 film
98 River in Venezuela
101 Quasi
102 Tenant's fee
103 Swell
104 Lionel Bart musical
107 Soap plant
110 Painter of "L'Absinthe"
113 Words of dismay
114 Units for Lendl
116 Air: Comb. form
118 Fixed price
119 Angered
121 Father of Phinehas
122 Hialeah action
123 Gal who "comes out"

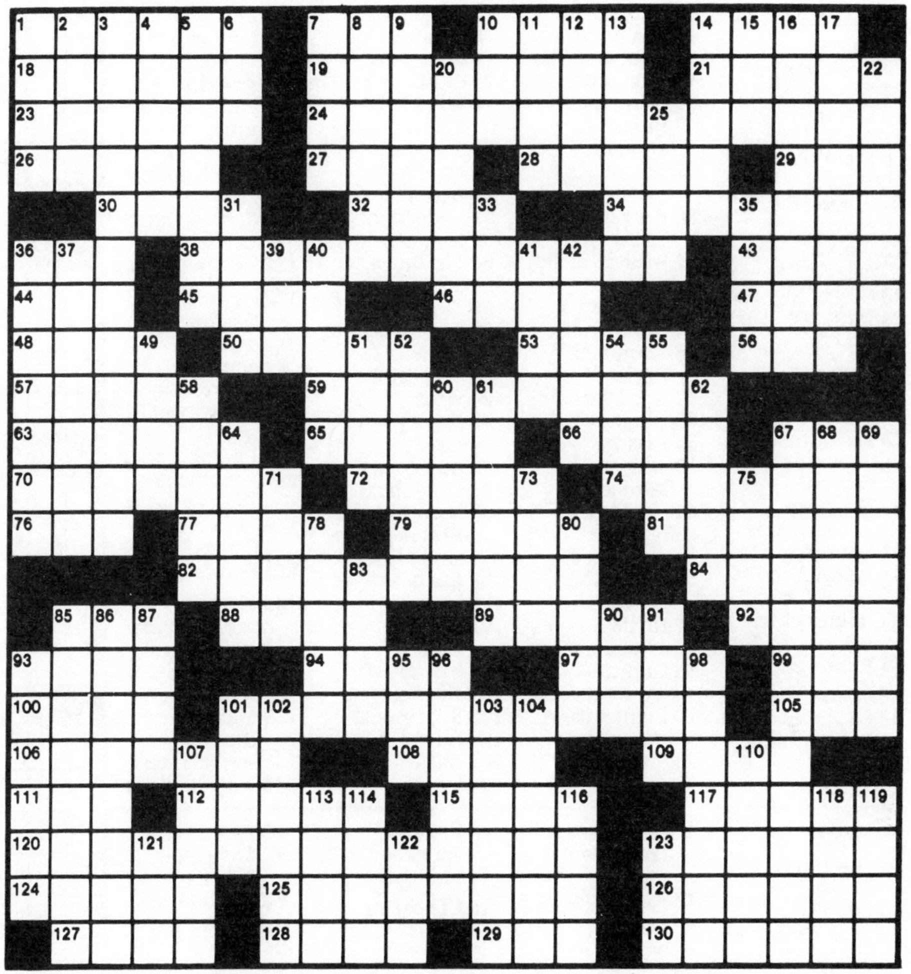

Unreal People

By A. J. Santora

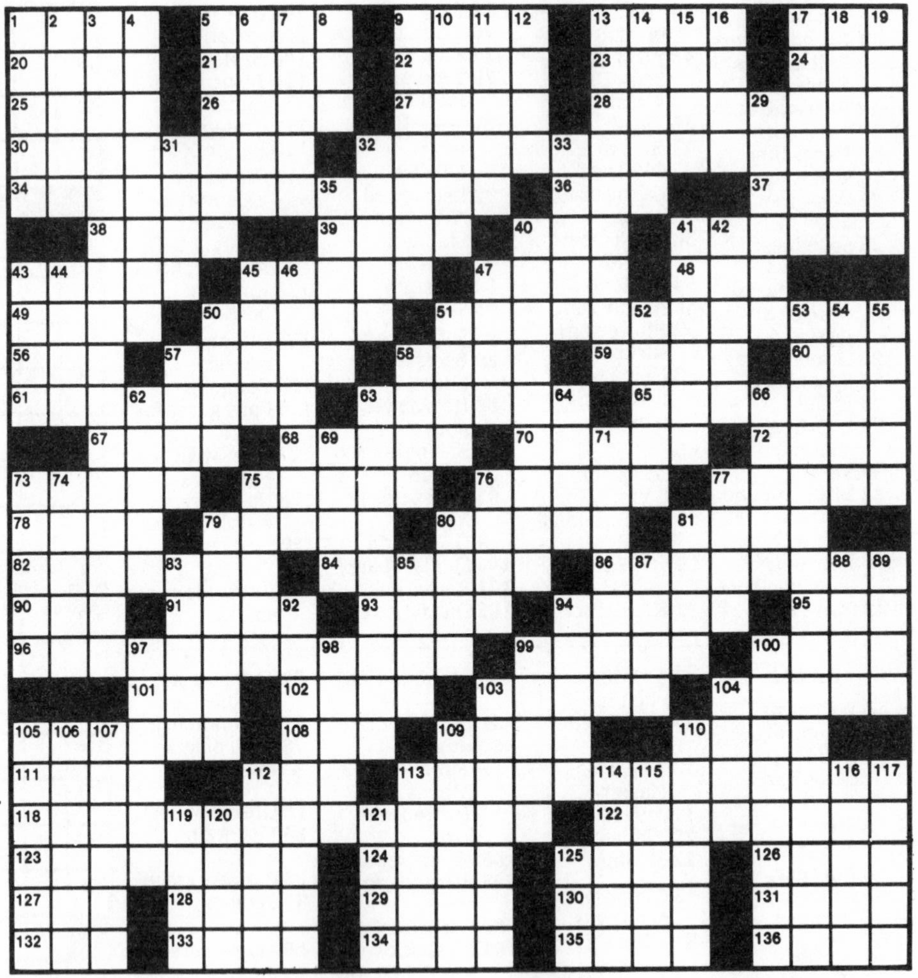

ACROSS

1 Sacks
5 Headlong
9 "—— boy!"
13 Creeks
17 Alley of comics
20 Field of an E.E.
21 Ending for citron
22 Walked heavily
23 City in Nigeria
24 Initials in 1933
25 About
26 Prune
27 Navajo's neighbor
28 Rayburn's Japanese strings?
30 Decorate Asner's skin?
32 Fans Mays, Stargell and Randolph?
34 Holden of an actors' org.?
36 Ram's mate
37 Concerning
38 Capture
39 Bear on high
40 Abbr. at Kennedy
41 Spoils
43 Composer's notational sign
45 Kind of den
47 Oversupply
48 Japanese apricot
49 Not quite a meter
50 R.b.i. and e.r.a.
51 What Elsa did at Mrs. Adamson's command?
56 Clamor, in Paris
57 Bob follower
58 Glory
59 Fissure
60 A feast —— famine
61 Go offside
63 Most distressed
65 Kin of "My goodness!"
67 Hirt's companion
68 Guthrie namesakes
70 Light musket
72 Part of A.D.
73 "Ave —— vale"
75 Sly guy
76 Gone up
77 Chauvinist
78 Closed
79 Wrapped a present
80 Suppress quietly
81 Active
82 Watertight chamber
84 The moon, to poets
86 Time saver
90 Where lts. are made
91 Cool drinks
93 Wrong
94 Having a salty taste
95 Initials at Columbus
96 Escort writer Bracken to the street floor?
99 Rundown
100 Feds
101 Never, in Essen
102 Habitat of a chamois
103 Reprimand
104 Edwin of D.C.
105 Baffles
108 Layer
109 Biblical name for Tanis
110 Viscount's superior
111 Marquisette
112 Finial
113 Escorting a nice "country girl"?
118 Carney and Linkletter?
122 Heating device
123 Cartoonist Gardner's unlisted number?
124 Puerto ——
125 Buckwheat tree
126 Pumpkin seed
127 Andaman or Tasman
128 Tints for Downs?
129 Bard's river
130 Have —— in one's bonnet
131 Philbrick's "—— 3 Lives"
132 Bizarre
133 Mailed
134 Disavow
135 Predicament
136 Wall St. place

DOWN

1 —— retreat (fall back)
2 Capp's degree? Horse feathers!
3 Sending Gossage to an early shower?
4 Caledonia
5 Flinch
6 Poet Ginsberg
7 Chute
8 Chance
9 Godlessness
10 Liz of TV news
11 Stowe girl
12 Colliery opening
13 Billy's "Aquacade" pool?
14 Stand —— of (revere with fear)
15 African gazelle
16 Loess or loam
17 —— million
18 Like mean critters
19 Annie Oakleys
29 Deli machine
31 Medley
32 Indian teachers
33 Hopping mad
35 Very
40 Salvo from pollster Roper?
41 Coarse woolen cloth
42 Overplay a scene
43 Indian stableboy
44 Merit
45 Of hearing
46 Applause for Boone?
47 —— of August (1st of that month)
50 Indo-Chinese native
51 Shakes up
52 Host's suggestion at dinner
53 "Tonight Show" host in 1962?
54 Gasket
55 Mississippi river
57 Had on
58 Pan's foe
62 Complete defeats
63 Insult Mrs. Rockefeller?
64 Ivory source
66 Oft-watched line
69 Sign on for another hitch
71 Takes in Skelton's act?
73 Usher's tie
74 "They went ——-way"
75 Tendon
76 Dee or Keeler
77 Panel
79 Fogies
80 Ice mass
81 Osseous
83 Rainy-day girl?
85 Has obligations
87 Cache
88 Takes advantage of
89 "Elmer's" is one
92 Most like Dapper Dan
94 Person
97 "... the —— perfect day"
98 Dog-tired
99 Former Iranian rulers
100 Marylander
103 Soft
104 Famed biblical trio
105 Sun Bowl site
106 Looked like Marvin and Buttons?
107 Illiterate
109 Matura diamond
110 Whirled or purled
112 W. German seaport
113 Forgo
114 African antelope
115 Of a cereal
116 Uses a jigsaw
117 Eat away
119 Famed publisher
120 Dissolute dandy
121 Alum
125 Check for Hunter?

Workman's Compensation

By Tap Osborn

ACROSS

1 Esparto grass
5 Treasury worker
9 Decline
14 Join into a whole
19 Unable to decide
20 Broadway actress Mary
21 Waugh's "The —— One"
22 Agatha's award
23 Sulky driver's dessert?
25 Game warden's dish?
27 Jackie's second mate
28 One touch of Venus
30 Estuary
31 Wood ibis
32 Goes over old ground
34 Detect and expose
36 Dot, in Lisbon
37 Freshens
38 Start of a D. H. Lawrence title
39 Night crawlers, e.g.
40 Unctuous speech
43 Property held for others
45 Banker's breakfast?
47 Cairo lizard
48 After
49 Ormoc's locale
50 Plumber, at times
52 Habituates
54 Like many a hoopster
56 A.F.B. in Texas
57 Mies van der ——
58 The Greatest
59 RR train
60 Secret explosions
61 Croupier's comestibles?
66 A Siouan
71 Call from a columbary
72 Rain and snow mixt.
73 Use a letter opener
77 Baseball's Banks
78 Change a bit
80 Ancestral link
82 Beatty, for one
84 Editing mark
86 Lexiconizing physician
87 Stickiness
88 Complaint manager's meal?
90 Naught, in Nottingham
91 Put it to
92 Ganges platform
93 Holy statue
94 Aspect
95 "—— hell": Sherman
97 Tricolore part
98 Singer Natalie's side dish?
101 Enter, as a crowd
103 Grand ——, Nova Scotia
104 Zanuck
106 Where Tell did his thing
107 Violinist's veggies?
110 Sanitary engineer's treat?
112 Pyromaniac's crime
113 TV role for Linda Lavin
114 When Casca struck
115 Porgy
116 Shoddy
117 Doctrine
118 Opera by Handel
119 People generally

DOWN

1 Stock term
2 Peter of "Casablanca"
3 Boxer's beverage?
4 Blyth
5 Hard blows
6 U.S. slalom greats
7 First sign
8 Siestas
9 Zermatt sight
10 Like Stanley Kowalski
11 Make use of
12 Mexican Indian
13 Dead letter
14 Bluestocking
15 G.I.'s dog tag
16 Psychiatrist's supper?
17 Bingo device
18 Whilom
24 Old card games
26 He has "I" trouble
29 Muzzle
33 Deliverance
35 Padre's pastry?
36 —— Mink, Hawaii's first Congress-woman
38 Certain legumes
39 Poppycock
41 Explanatory phrase
42 Penates' partner
43 White Russian ruler
44 Petrocelli of Red Sox fame
45 Resign
46 Beethoven's last symphony
47 Not aweather
49 Tibeto-Burman group
51 J. S. Copley's forte
53 Bark cloth
55 Circle segment
60 Concerning
62 Astringent
63 Fashion
64 Cut off, in a way
65 Novelist's need
66 River triangle
67 Court star
68 Critic's snack?
69 Message from the pen
70 Lunar New Year in Vietnam
73 Klammer's arena
74 Electrician's repast?
75 Curare's cousin
76 Four: Comb. form

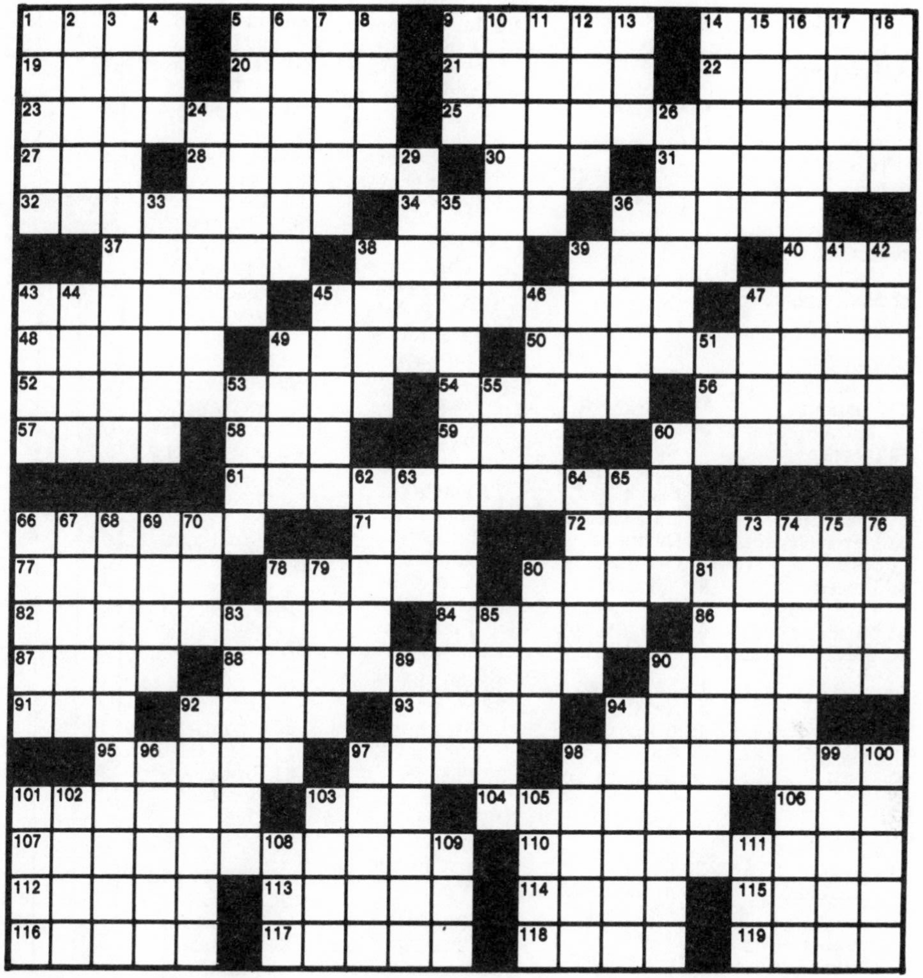

78 Hog plums
79 Gist
80 Cleanse of oil
81 Battery type
83 Heartsore
85 Not sotto voce
89 Golden intangible
90 Belafonte's forte
92 Like the Cheshire Cat
94 Previous
96 Out of control
97 Smart one
98 Unfinished
99 Contend
100 Nebulous
101 H.S. junior's exam
102 Norwegian river
103 He kicked to conquer
105 Tennis term
108 Lost weekend
109 Young plant
111 Adherent

Game of the Name

By Louis Baron

ACROSS

1 Pine for
5 Beats
10 Boxer, e.g.
13 Gone
17 Top Ferrara family
18 Detestation
19 Gaper's state
20 Obeyed the sentry
22 Shakespearean fox?
25 Polished
26 Double trio
27 Virtuous jazzman?
29 Incenses
30 Kind of drama
31 I use, to Nero
32 Sierra Nevada resort
35 Voiced
37 Talk foolishly
41 Muscat's land
42 Erewhon's Ruggles?
45 Shoulder: Comb. form
46 Needlefish
47 ". . . all my fame for —— of ale": Henry V
48 Films' Calhoun
49 Flèche weapon
50 Say more
51 Former grouch at the opera?
55 Less green
56 Versatile legumes
58 Lake Geneva resort
59 Some clerks
60 Drying chamber
61 "McSorley's Bar" painter
62 Gen. Bradley
63 Barrio sauces
65 Divested; fleeced
66 Event for Salazar
70 Colonists' newscaster
71 Labor heavy before 1980?
73 Poetic palindrome
74 Guns Lizzie
75 ". . . Bounty" narrator
76 Imprison
77 Purviance of silents
78 Parisian's "eine"
79 Young Gig's opposite?
83 Colliery approach
84 Doctor in "The Marriage of Figaro"
86 Fixes front ends
87 Headline word in 1929
88 Mini-powerhouse
89 Nerve-cell process
90 Razz
92 Film magnate who fired an old comic?
97 Headset part
101 Londoner's thyroid problem
102 Wastrel of the poetic world?
104 Cereal grass
105 Guess wrong
106 Play to the cheap seats
107 Tough
108 Be without
109 Difficult: Prefix
110 Washer button
111 Roman clan

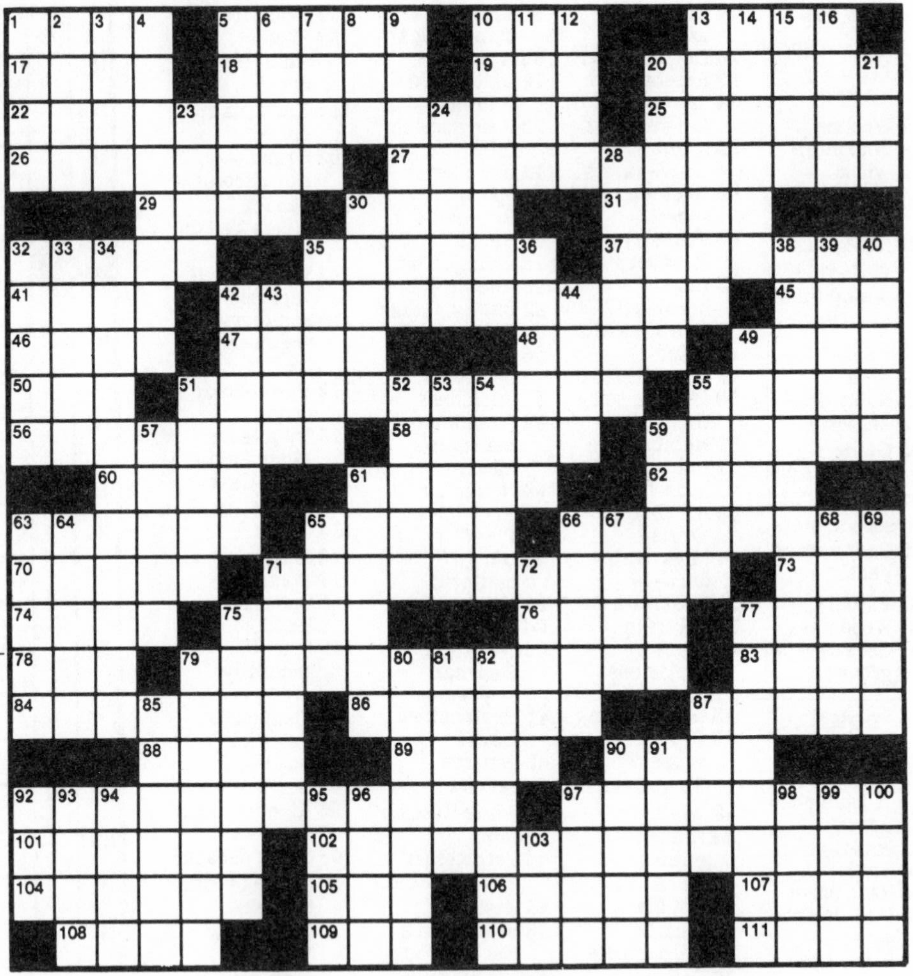

DOWN

1 Snafu
2 Dordogne feeder
3 Charon's crossing
4 Divisions
5 Baker's goodie
6 Trims for a deadline
7 —— en scène
8 Take's opposite
9 Coca
10 Southern hollies
11 Due
12 "Bug"
13 Cook partly
14 Walt Kelly's alligator
15 Bandsman Kenton
16 It's north of Ga.
20 Brinkley's old pal
21 Susan ——, TV actress
23 Roll-call reply
24 Antithetical
28 Alabama's Tigers
30 Undergoes ecdysis
32 Judges' wear
33 Novelist Jorge from Brazil
34 Slapstick survivor?
35 German sculptor-wood carver: 1440-1533
36 Kilt cloth
38 Memorable jitterbugging columnist?
39 Pasha's colleague
40 Old African rifles
42 Pacific squalls
43 Atop
44 Kayo's "brudder" in comics
49 Israel's leading oil port
51 Franck or Cui
52 Pepo
53 Eburnean hue
54 Old Chinese weight
55 Anatomical fissures
57 First, second and third
59 Whom a teller might tell on
61 Bronze Age city Ras ——
63 Clean up
64 Action site
65 Pottery pail
66 Castle protectors
67 Classical vessel
68 Avifauna
69 O'er's opposite
71 ". . . no inscription upon ——": Emmet
72 Off center: Abbr.
75 Hokum
77 Aardvark, literally
79 Drove
80 Snapping beetles
81 Shrew
82 "Set thine house ——": Isa. 38:1
85 Spill the beans
87 Wearily make do
90 A source of mistakes
91 Clone's origin
92 MVD follower
93 Auroral
94 Leeds's river
95 Owned previously
96 Peppy
97 Psyche's love
98 Karlovy Vary's river
99 Garish sign
100 Austria's first chartered city
103 Burnsian kin

Geographic Jingles

By Beverly Tivin

ACROSS

1 These may be bald
6 Three, to Tomás
10 A language in Bangkok
13 Vivaciousness
19 Expiate
20 What flattops carry
22 Stipend
23 Venezuelan instruments?
25 Inquiry into lost goods
26 Worldwide workers' org.
27 Hwy.
28 Admission
29 Liqueur ingredient
30 Doral sight
33 Certain wise men
34 Table fowl
36 Like certain sports
37 Italian metal?
40 Twilight
43 Situation
44 So
45 Site of Honolulu
46 Largest of the Truk Islands
47 —— de mer
48 Max, Buddy or Bugs
49 Austrian author Marie von —— -Eschenbach
50 Toltec capital
51 South African headgear?
55 Shawl
56 Regimental commander
59 Ellipses
60 Xenophobe's fear
62 Disposed to love
63 Jar for oil, etc.
64 Mercury or Mars, in Marseille
65 Scold
66 Ancient Greek council
67 Brought into agreement
68 Shake —— (high-tail it)
69 Southwestern manor?
72 ". . . ye better reck the ——": Burns
73 Drug fighting infections
74 In a skillful way
75 Concorde
78 W.W. II post for Ike
79 "Questa o quella," e.g.
80 Nobelist in Chemistry: 1934
81 Dull finish
83 Quiet!
84 Some New York traffic sounds?
87 Fruitless
88 Root used in perfume
90 Cleopatra attendant
91 Alighieri admirer
92 Man's slipper
94 Miller's "—— the Fall"
96 Switz., Ger. et al.
97 Ending for function or budget
98 Captivate
100 Island sleepwear?
104 Announcement
105 Belief
106 "—— Psyche": Keats
107 Pledges
108 Sun. talk
109 A ruminant
110 Bridge expert

DOWN

1 Quaker tenet
2 Legendary Greek heroine
3 Doughnut-shaped
4 Former Spanish queen
5 Dry, as champagne
6 Toothsome
7 Coleridge creation
8 Period
9 Yells
10 Strategy
11 At a distance
12 —— -bitsy
13 Part of i.e.
14 Mexican's woolen blanket
15 Flat: Comb. form
16 Midwestern soup bowl?
17 Angers
18 Londoner's radial
21 Scope
24 Sandarac tree
31 Decay
32 Misfortune
33 Grieve
34 Comedian Myron
35 Sino-Russian border river
37 S.A. ostrich
38 Limp
39 Hindu princes
41 With light rapidity, in music
42 Slipped by, as time
44 Board
48 Judicial writ
49 Cancels
50 Moral pang
51 Feeble, childish condition
52 Single quantity
53 Yeastlike fungus
54 Palate part
56 Nightclub
57 Brunch dishes
58 Texas beefsteak?
60 Relieve
61 Secular
63 Grant's first Vice President
64 Adjective for buddies
66 Actress Ina
69 Spanish coins
70 Hyde and Regent's
71 Vigoda et al.
73 Item for Indira
75 Banner
76 An ester used in ointments
77 "Idylls of the King" poet
80 Without protection
81 Staff
82 Bonsai or origami
84 Ornamental pin
85 To this place
86 One of Pan's companions
87 Theda of silents
89 Put off
91 Miami's super receiver
92 Schism
93 —— about (time-setting phrase)
94 Rudiments
95 Subway token
96 Verb suffix
99 Legal matter
101 Chemical ending
102 Emulate James F. Fixx
103 Stir

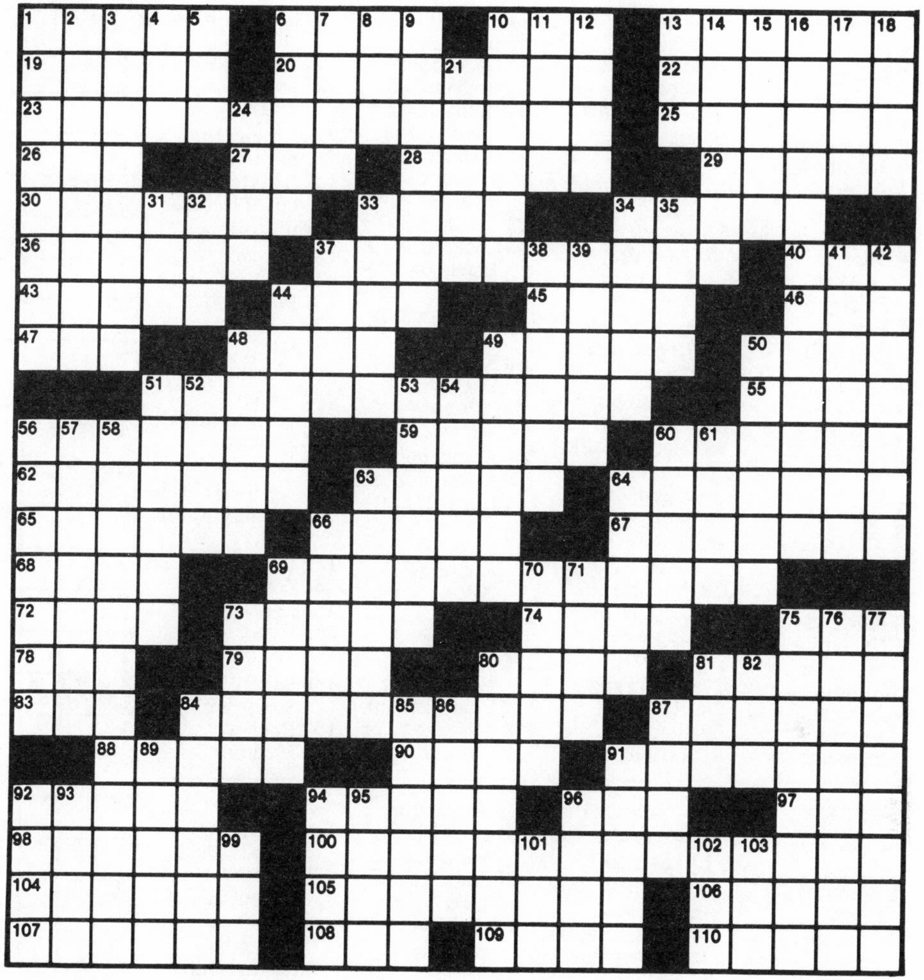

Also-Rans

By Richard Silvestri

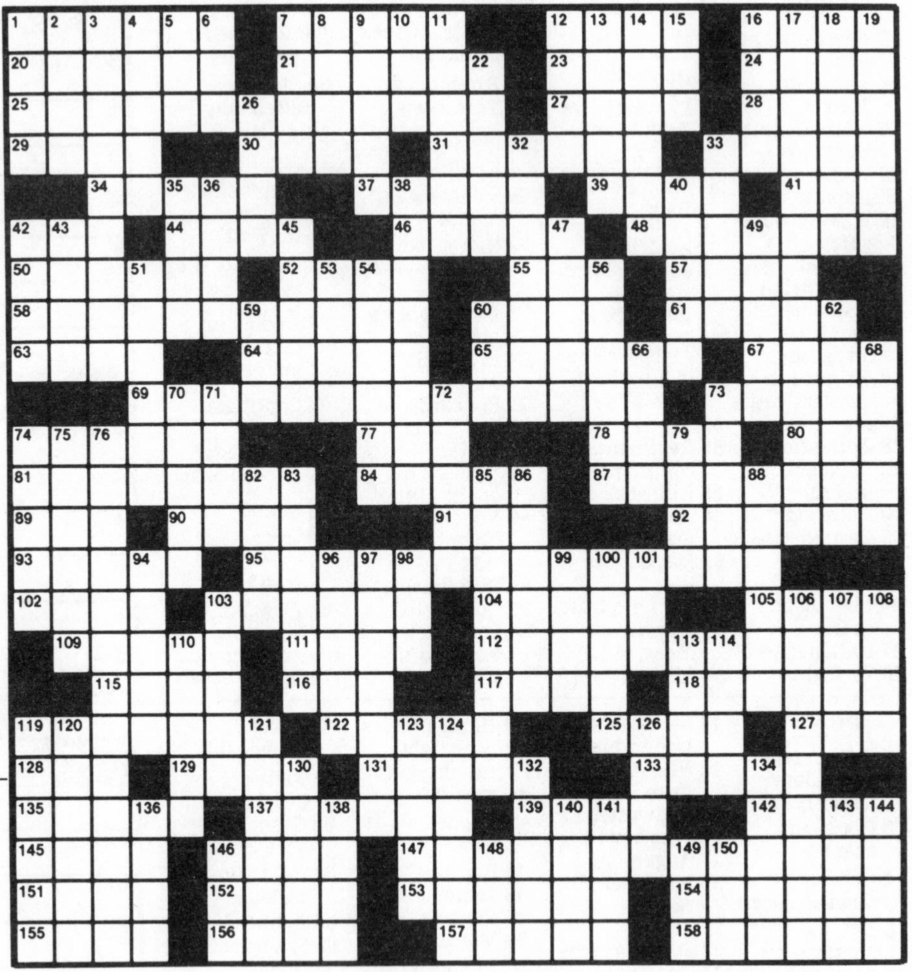

ACROSS

1 In
7 Wanted-poster listing
12 Bare
16 Citrus drinks
20 Full of eddies
21 Covered carriage
23 Ellipsoidal
24 Big rig
25 Loser to Pierce: 1852
27 One of Salome's seven
28 "Heads —— . . ."
29 Within: Prefix
30 Diamond Head site
31 Matures
33 Marsh bird
34 Ed Norton's milieu
37 Clamber
39 F or C reading
41 Overtime producer
42 Baseball stat
44 Ancient Hebrew measure
46 "Oberon" is one
48 Muscle that expands another part
50 Bighorn
52 College in N.C.
55 A neighbor of Ga.
57 Record
58 Loser to Buchanan: 1856
60 Anthracite
61 Steps over a fence
63 D.A., for one
64 Long hill
65 Short bandlike sleeve
67 Bubble and squeak, e.g.
69 Loser to Grant: 1868
73 British coppers
74 Opposite of aboard
77 Simple sugar
78 Run amok
80 Shooter
81 Kern musical
84 Mends hose
87 Letter holder
89 DeSoto or Hudson
90 Holm
91 Absent
92 Attended to pressing business
93 Conform
95 Loser to Eisenhower: 1952 and 1956
102 Somewhat, in music
103 Kellogg- —— Pact
104 "Do I —— Waltz?"
105 Actual being
109 Piece of cheese
111 Layer of the eye
112 Loser to Roosevelt: 1904
115 Bestows, in Dundee
116 Nun's predecessor
117 Polanski film
118 Evaluate
119 Clergymen
122 Shaped like a cupola
125 Blue-pencil
127 Omaha Beach craft
128 First of the cardinals
129 A state carved out of Deseret
131 Wall recess
133 Old-womanish
135 Go on all fours
137 Moon goddess
139 Vientiane's land
142 Alaskan island
145 Battery compartment
146 Siamese
147 Loser to Truman: 1948
151 Avails oneself of
152 Linen marking
153 Zoo man
154 Lent
155 Eye inflammation
156 Snorri Sturluson opus
157 Rocket stage
158 Muddles

DOWN

1 "—— forgive those . . ."
2 Romulus or Remus
3 Second-guesser's forte
4 Part of a sentry's query
5 Roman 1,051
6 Scrutinize
7 Hawkeye portrayer
8 Scourge
9 Anvil
10 Hubbub
11 Subordinate official
12 Arouse feeling
13 Part of a meet
14 Put up
15 Type of extension
16 —— were (so to speak)
17 Loser to Madison: 1812
18 Pucci
19 Geyser deposit
22 Serviceable
26 Body of knowledge
32 Emulate Olivier
33 Disunite
35 Prokofiev character
36 Moslem prince
38 "The Barefoot ——," 1954 film
40 Center
42 Indian V.I.P.
43 Bremen bread
45 Pardon
47 Cottonwood
49 Private line
51 Notwithstanding
53 N.J. or Calif. city
54 —— terms (friendly)
56 Entice
59 Historical time
60 Winslow Homer's "Rum ——"
62 Galsworthy play
66 One of TV's Grays
68 Took an ax to
70 Pluto's path
71 Antique autos
72 Namesakes of Saarinen
73 Feather: Comb. form
74 Org. for Cahn and Kahn
75 Feb. 2 omen
76 Loser to Grant: 1872
79 Sheep genus
82 Winglike
83 Wearisomeness
85 Titmouse's relative
86 An Isaac Bickerstaff
88 Anchorites
94 Places for conductors
96 Washed
97 Windflower
98 Mrs. McKinley
99 Large casks
100 Uneven
101 Palindromic name
103 Attack on all sides
106 Halloween rattlers
107 Mtg.
108 First, in Frankfurt
110 Duds
113 Stitch
114 Piedmontese province
119 Spherical bacterium
120 Turmoil
121 Wearing an obi
123 Byelorussian capital
124 Summer cooler
126 Sprint
130 Learned
132 Run away, in a way
134 Actor Lorenzo from L.A.
136 Additional
138 Dame ——, Jurgen's wife
140 Congregational comeback
141 Norwegian river
143 Rather low joint
144 Enlarges
146 Beverage for Bardot
148 Command of a col.
149 Einstein's birthplace
150 Sturgeon product

J.S. Filmfest

By John M. Samson

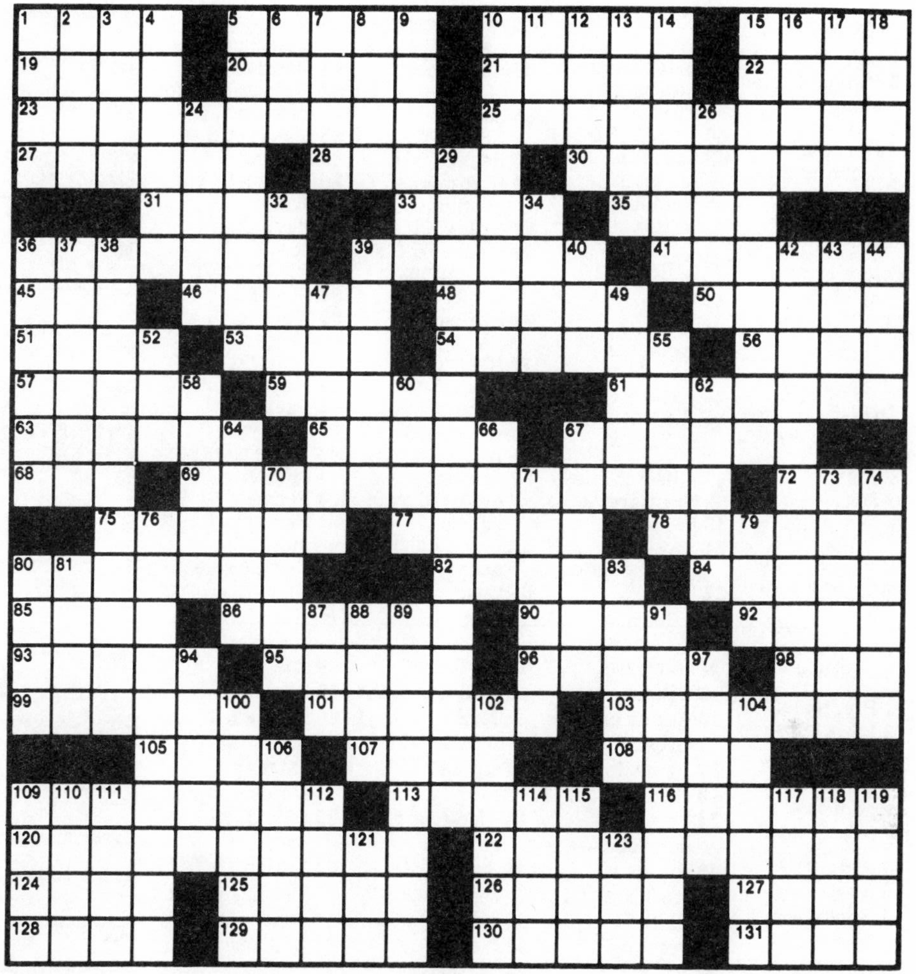

ACROSS

1 Ogden or Beau
5 Book of Psalms word
10 Haycock
13 Swenson of "Benson"
19 Whale-of-a-film: 1977
20 Wine taster's concern
21 Firth of Clyde sight
22 He pulls in pushers
23 Peeping Tom's favorite J.S. film?
25 Gambler's favorite J.S. film?
27 Captain drawn by C. C. Beck
28 Tabriz native
30 Small, black flies of the South
31 Magdeburg's river
33 Dane of the Cardinals
35 Actress Carter
36 Wonder of the World site
39 "Gloria" painter
41 Sluggish ones
45 Gold, in Guanajuato
46 Fry, in a way
48 Turkish port
50 "Some Like ——"
51 Celtic flier
53 Triplet
54 With "with," encounter
56 Melodic subject
57 Shaped like a strobilus
59 Actor Hyman
61 "—— Each Other," 1939 film
63 Kind of lamp or crown
65 Corallic barriers
67 Engross
68 Racer Fabi
69 Godiva's favorite J.S. film?
72 Theory
75 Martian moon
77 Rockies' feature
78 Elijah's disciple
80 Biased
82 Crunching sound
84 Nibbler
85 Hunger sign
86 "—— My Lou"
90 Prefix for trooper
92 Cartoonist Walker
93 Ghana's capital
95 Teller's hidden helper
96 Concerning
98 Actor Fernando
99 Vaporizes
101 Shows reverence
103 Maverick
105 Suffrage
107 Judge Hardy's son
108 Suffix with scan
109 Ambitious one
113 Actor Ritchard
116 Ricochet
120 Virginian's favorite J.S. film?
122 Fleming's favorite J.S. film of 1939?
124 Strong flavor
125 Use a thurible
126 Movie barbarian
127 Reo's father
128 They get threshed
129 Puccini's second opera
130 Drum type
131 Jollity

DOWN

1 Average
2 Belt
3 ID mark
4 Actor Keitel's favorite J.S. film?
5 Yawl or cat
6 Eagle of Greenland
7 City near Milano
8 Mid-February celebrity
9 Cook's discovery
10 Emulate Swift
11 Princely letters
12 City on the Oka
13 Southwestern box canyon
14 Jacks
15 Stationery item
16 Malayan chevrotain
17 Drink on the drink
18 Luke book
24 "War of the Worlds" author
26 Instruments for Yo-Yo Ma
29 Vincent Price's favorite J.S. film?
32 Habituate
34 Fan fare
36 New Cub Scout
37 Songlike
38 Gene Kelly's favorite J.S. film?
39 Madagascar mammal
40 Kind of wit
42 Hoover's favorite J.S. film?
43 —— sapiens
44 J.S. for five decades
47 Coronets
49 Lively Cuban import
52 Hugo van —— Goes, Dutch artist
55 —— chat (ballet leap)
58 Small crane
60 Princess Organa
62 Lonnegan in "The Sting"
64 Fruit from the Keys
66 Plaintiff
67 President of Mexico: 1946-52
70 Screwdriver part
71 Buddhist shrines
73 Actress North
74 St. Stephen, e.g.
76 Mint plates
79 "—— a Camera"
80 Wells for the well-to-do
81 Milk: Comb. form
83 Journalism
87 Class
88 Central Illinois city
89 Ditchdigger
91 Sophocles tragedy
94 Mishna interpreter
97 Angler's spoon
100 Golfer's concern
102 Sammy Cahn's forte
104 Kind of computer
106 Wrapped up
109 Skippy's role
110 He played 62 Down
111 Ivy League team
112 Chinese clan
114 Sacred picture
115 Actress Nyman
117 Will I, —— I
118 Bow to Fischer
119 Chimney, in Köln
121 Botanist Gray
123 Remote

Nursery Performers

By Ernst T. Theimer

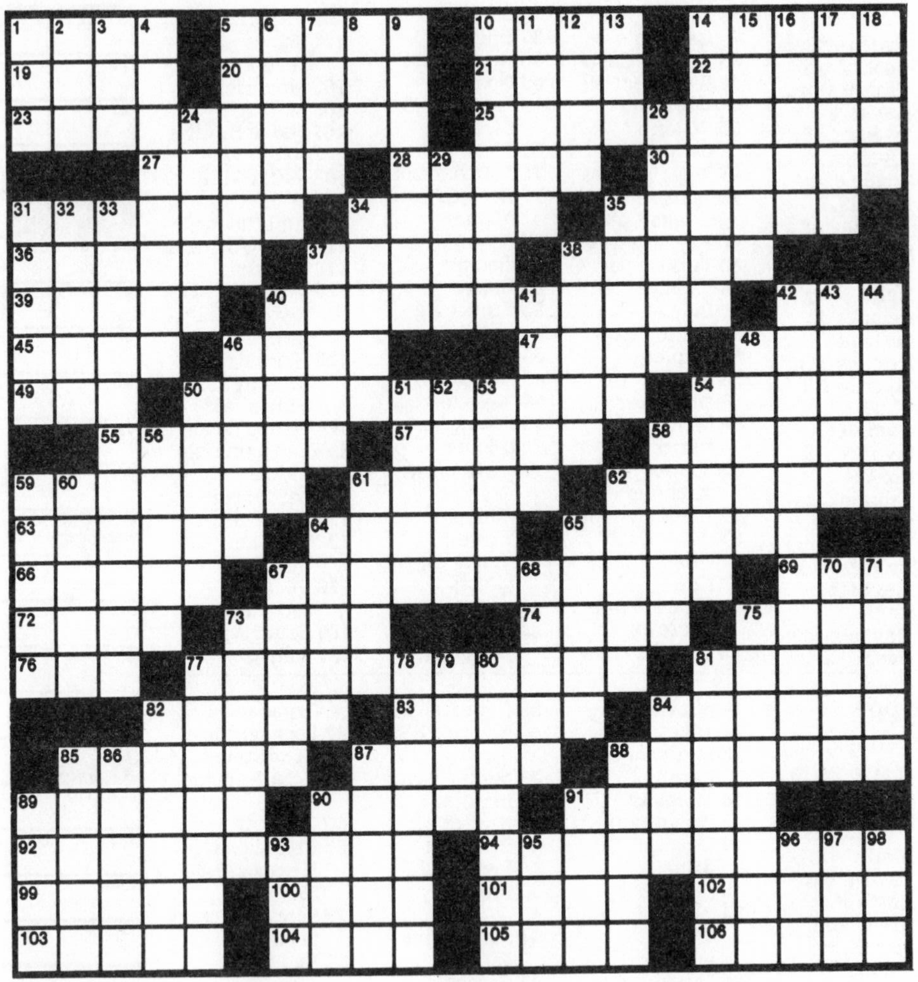

ACROSS

1 Soft mineral
5 Rips or rips along
10 Repetition
14 Quickly
19 Melville opus
20 Apportion
21 Equal, to Henri
22 Saw of a sawfish
23 COW
25 HORNER
27 Records of sorts
28 City on the Rhone
30 If not
31 But
34 Disdainful smile
35 Passionate
36 Sports locales
37 Thesaurus man
38 Black-ink item
39 City on the Aire
40 HUBBARD
42 Sounds of laughter
45 Nomologists' forte
46 Its capital is Denpasar
47 War god
48 An NCO
49 Epinicion
50 JACK
54 Tosca's lover
55 Runs away, à la Jessica
57 Milers' milieus
58 Transgressor
59 Denounced
61 Ray ——, country singer
62 Valid
63 Victimized by a scam
64 "When you —— tulip . . ."
65 She wrote "Black Beauty"
66 High-ranked netman
67 OLD WOMAN
69 Where R.N.'s sometimes work
72 Haruspex
73 Helot's lot
74 Head start
75 Exchange
76 Go astray
77 KNAVE OF HEARTS
81 Crater explored by Apollo 17
82 Great Lakes acronym
83 Own
84 Music-shop offering
85 Maori people
87 Former Indian currency
88 Make rougher
89 Sparing
90 Baclanova and Korbut
91 Navigator's need
92 FINE LADY
94 BO-PEEP
99 Whence Caesar embarked
100 Singer Cantrell
101 Facility
102 A Forsyte
103 Unpleasantly difficult
104 Former French prime minister
105 Vargueno, e.g.
106 River of Kenya

DOWN

1 Pig stealer
2 Latin I verb
3 Looby-——, children's game
4 Vies
5 Mole grays
6 Gantry
7 Eiger and Jungfrau
8 Kind of deer
9 Curtis of the P.G.A.
10 Surfeited
11 He eyes with sighs
12 Greek crosses
13 "Spoon River" poet's monogram
14 Into parts
15 BB, for one
16 Author of "The Green Hat"
17 Pinnacle
18 Nubbins
24 Certain domestic fowls
26 Puckers
29 Reduce a sail
31 Call of greeting
32 Mt. Ida maiden
33 ONE LITTLE PIG
34 Kind of boom
35 Jacob's eighth son
37 Brötchen, etc.
38 Sight at Tara
40 Bundled hay
41 Postpone
42 THE COCK ON THE WOODPILE and LITTLE BOY BLUE
43 Afro-Asian gazelle
44 Fern's reproducer
46 Man, for one
48 Waterway
50 They go to blazes
51 Greenstreet associate
52 Like some college walls
53 Large parrot
54 U.M.W. member
56 Kind of eclipse
58 Stitched
59 Demean
60 Shaman, at times
61 Suburban status symbols
62 Of bodily tissue
64 Tittles
65 Driving hazard
67 Tender spots
68 N.Y. island
70 Indian princess
71 Dish's companion in flight
73 Mexican dish
75 Snorers' acts
77 Kind of traffic zone
78 Chinese puzzle
79 Mrs. Stengel
80 Piled up
81 Like a cloudless night
82 Scottish pudding
84 Product of saponification
85 Rebel
86 Shrimps
87 Jewish prayer
88 Brass
89 Out of
90 Viva-voce
91 Tax, Irish style
93 Rochet's kin
95 "Some —— meat . . .": Burns
96 Beaufort or Weddell
97 Place for stps.
98 Essex contemporary

197

Nuptials

By Barbara Lunder Gillis

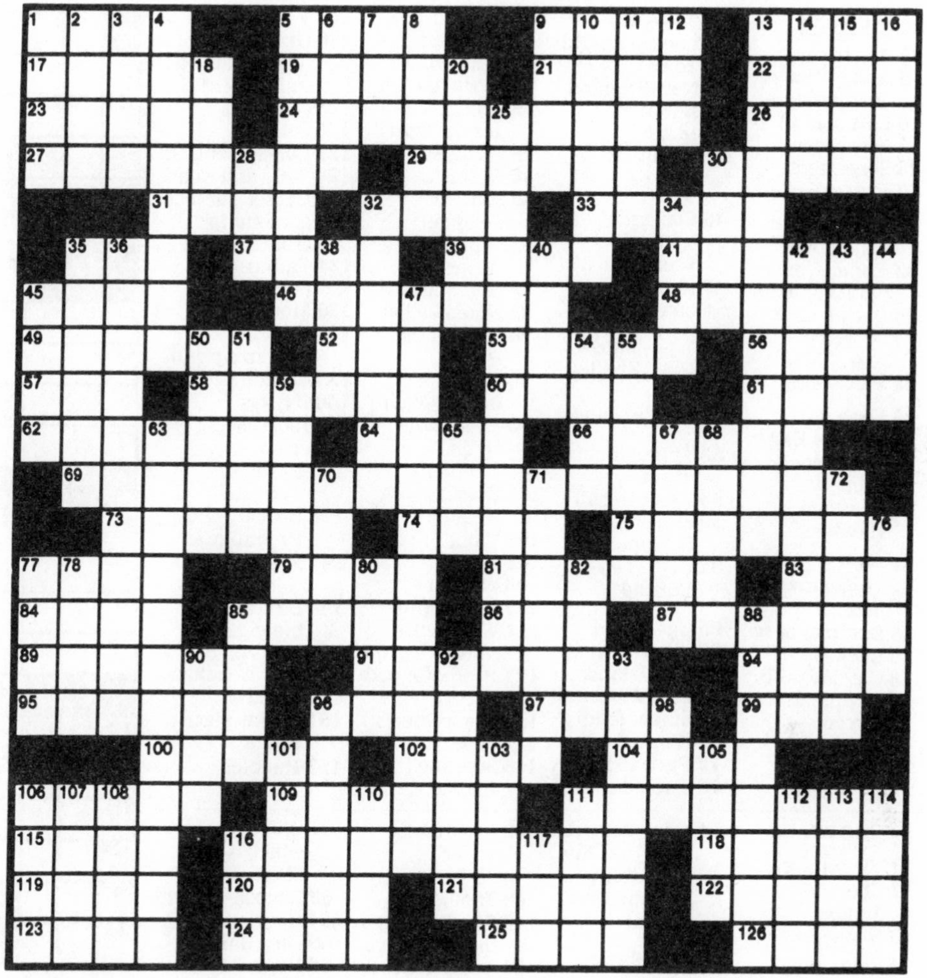

ACROSS

1 Casino game
5 Information
9 Clergyman
13 Dalai ——
17 Meshed native
19 Organic compound
21 Valley
22 Wild goat
23 Painting on plaster
24 Happy days
26 Compartment
27 Stage dance
29 About three nautical miles
30 Davis or Midler
31 African republic
32 Language of Buddhism
33 Harsh
35 —— Jima
37 A memorable Bugs
39 Best seller by Jean Stein
41 Piston-packing ring
45 Humdinger
46 Marked, as a manuscript
48 New York's geographical hub
49 Least rubicund
52 Heine's sigh
53 Approaches
56 Greek letters
57 Ga. capital
58 Russ Westover's heroine
60 Feat for Pete Peeters
61 Mil. vessels
62 Valises
64 Merganser
66 Palindrome part
69 Waugh work
73 Too
74 Subsequently
75 One way or another
77 Lily plant
79 Beowulf is one
81 Francis from Boston
83 Period
84 Cook book
85 He painted "Christina's World"
86 Bauble
87 Lively wit
89 Soprano
91 Greek vase
94 Epinicia
95 Enclosed, as a pool
96 Wings for Amor
97 Like Kareem Abdul-Jabbar
99 Scheldt feeder
100 Absolute
102 Keystone ——
104 City near Phoenix
106 Arabic dialect
109 Eyeball covering
111 Pampers
115 Carte before the course
116 December 31 activity
118 Mosaicist
119 Window section
120 Snead's needs
121 City in Turkey
122 Mothball
123 Lover's quarrel
124 At loose ——
125 Actor Clunes
126 Desires

DOWN

1 Exchequer
2 —— code
3 Draw off wine
4 "—— unto the breach"
5 Showy flowers
6 One way not to run
7 U.S. import
8 Daughter of William the Conqueror
9 Eager
10 Part of an ensemble
11 Pulitzer Prize poet: 1929
12 Annapolis grad.
13 Car necessity
14 Incite
15 Thaw
16 Mandrel
18 Waterloo is here
20 Grommet
25 Perennial herb
28 Relative of a dalmatic
30 Cereal
32 Exact
34 Psyche components
35 "Three men ——"
36 Neat and clean
38 Lat. phrase
40 Prelude to an invention
42 Some of Nelson's last words
43 Emulate Harold Ross
44 Soviet wire service
45 Oculus mundi
47 Wilder subject
50 Geological time period
51 Blake beast
54 Tel ——
55 Release via a deed
59 Actress —— - Anne Down
63 Pay a compliment
65 Old English letter
67 Unanimously
68 Annual marchers
70 Issue a sensational promo
71 Establishes
72 Strays
76 Opponents of the 18th Amendment
77 Heading on a playbill
78 Forsaken
80 Romance lang.
82 Northern constellation
85 "Bird thou never —— ": Shelley
88 Trend in a specific direction
90 Louis Marie Julien Viaud
92 Bradley U. site
93 Annual source of information
96 Curved
98 Permit
101 Ruhr city
103 Zoo attraction
105 Congeals
106 Evil spirits
107 Harvest
108 Soprano Moffo
110 Excluding
111 Motion picture
112 Blackthorn
113 Darr
114 Pyrite and galena
116 Shoshone
117 "Sleepy-time ——"

Plant-ers

By Mary Virginia Orna

ACROSS

1 Antitoxins
5 Abbey Theatre dramatist
10 Lots of land
15 Nile green
18 Speedlight
20 Fracas
21 Consumer of eucalyptus
22 Ending for planet or aster
23 One of "Twelve Angry Men"
25 Stud stakes
26 Fashion
27 Actress Hagen
28 Old French coins
29 Baritone Hawkins
31 "It Happened Tomorrow" actor
33 Decimal base
34 Cuckoopint
36 Catchall abbr.
37 Frequently, to Byron
38 Snoop
39 H. James novelette
43 "—— a Lonesome Old Town"
44 New England sculptor: 1825-61
45 Feminine suffix
46 Constellation south of Scorpio
47 Keatsian container
49 "—— Shook Up," Presley hit
50 Stable sound
53 Type of pine or grain
56 Essential oil
59 Site of first Olympics
63 Orff's "—— Burana"
65 Chessmen
67 "Wolf!" crier
69 —— Islands, in Bay of Bengal
70 Singer from Kentucky
72 Pat and Debby
73 Excludes
74 —— -ed-Din, Ottoman statesman
75 Librarian's aid
76 Glinka's "—— for the Czar"
78 Mangles
80 Resource
85 Soul, in Sologne
86 Diplomat Welles
89 Give the nod
95 Noted violist
98 Gene of the P.G.A.
99 Opposite of phenomenal
100 First mayor of N.Y.C.
101 Needlelike
102 Ko-Ko's weapon
103 Valor or virtue
105 Noble
108 Washer cycle
109 —— gestae
111 Word with time or weed
113 Prefix for pod or corn
114 Gloucester's cape
115 Soprano Lucine
118 Vacation spot
120 Grocery clerk who became a millionaire
125 —— acid
126 Owns
127 Colony denizen
128 Weld and woad
129 Carson subject
132 Ex-Senator from Indiana
134 Tamarack's kin
136 Moue
138 Year in Trajan's reign
139 Corolla petals
140 Bypass
142 Increase's scion
145 Baseball's Penguin
146 Book by D. S. Freeman
147 Resort on Lake Geneva
148 Bahrain bigwigs
149 Units on N.F.L. fields
150 Macaw
151 Floral-piece fillers
152 Handles crudely

DOWN

1 Virginia, e.g.
2 Chore for Junior
3 Nonsense
4 Solomon Levy's son
5 Singer from Peru
6 North Sea catch
7 Further
8 Bristly plant
9 Descend-*Ant* of Noah's eldest
10 TV's "—— Pablo"
11 United
12 F.A. Hartley's collaborator
13 Picks
14 Prov. between Man. and Alta.
15 He betters most bettors
16 Slicker
17 Calculating vipers?
18 Plant disease
19 House or box
24 —— Saint Edmunds, in England
26 A founder and editor of Punch
30 Beige
32 Geyserite, e.g.
35 Spanish Surrealist
40 Floyd Bennett was one
41 "A stitch ——"
42 Architect under Jefferson
48 Tabula ——
49 Expanse fed by the Syr Darya
50 Defective spot on a plant
51 Billionth: Comb. form
52 Word on a dollar bill
53 —— Juan Hill
54 Matter, to Matteotti
55 Gardener
57 Maxwell or Zachary
58 Northwest "passage"
60 The Swedish Nightingale
61 ". . . a dagger which ——": Macbeth
62 Charon's river
64 Houston org.
66 Dist. units
68 Hugh Capet was one
70 Pass along
71 Kind of show
73 Mark on Miss Marker
77 Truman's birthplace
78 Godets or gussets
79 Mediterranean sailboat
80 Barley beards
81 London college
82 Swamp
83 "Street Scene" dramatist
84 Bond
86 Dallas campus
87 River to the Caspian
88 Prefix with plane or tone
90 Breastbones
91 Sequence
92 Verve
93 Clears
94 Famed English actor-manager
96 Collections of anecdotes
97 Notion
98 Secular
104 More worthless
106 Stowe novel
107 Mrs. Andre Kostelanetz
110 Apiece
112 —— Spee
114 Take for granted
115 Head monk's jurisdiction
116 Engaged in drudgery
117 Decks out
118 Lad
119 Graft of a sort
121 Org. created in 1946
122 Tried hard
123 Author Uris
124 Shun
130 Tinker's target
131 Mannerisms
133 A vamp of the silents
135 Child directive
137 Pack firmly
141 Venus or Minerva
143 Thrash
144 Congou, e.g.

Not on the Map

By Charles M. Deber

ACROSS

1 Taj ——
6 Near, in poesy
10 "Magic Mountain" man
14 Slayer of Castor
18 Easter event
19 On a cruise
20 "Ill wind"
21 Noon, in Nancy
22 What a spot!
25 Experts
26 Suspect
27 Overindulge
28 Dig they must
29 Over: Prefix
30 Raft wood
31 Famed portrayer of Lincoln
32 Where drivers play?
38 Hostel, in Anatolia
40 Old-womanish
41 Carrie and Louis
42 Kind of date
43 "Norma ——"
46 Niche
48 Bald bird
51 Voracious insect
53 Holiday spot for soda jerks?
56 Keys state
57 Cry of derision
58 Error
60 Part of aspirin
61 "—— and the Detectives": Kästner
65 Where dentists sail?
69 Lips in sync
70 Fort ——, in the Canal Zone
72 Repeat
73 Former Portuguese colony
75 Anti-macassars
77 High anxiety locales?
85 Che, more formally
86 Let up
87 "I have ——": M. L. King Jr.
88 Group of RR's
89 Director Sidney
91 Twitches
94 "A Majority ——": 1961 film
95 Certain fighters
97 Stop on Cook's tour?
100 Calm
102 Loses fur
104 Egg: Comb. form
105 Rust, for one
106 "The Wreck of the Mary ——"
107 Localized
113 Crossbar
114 Charitable address?
117 Defeat narrowly
118 Previously
119 Den denizen
120 Issued temporarily
121 "—— is more": Browning
122 Honey bunch
123 Boundary
124 "Oklahoma" aunt

DOWN

1 Skirt length
2 Electrical discharges
3 "Stop!" from a cop
4 Hebrew month
5 King of Massa
6 How Dapper Dan dresses
7 ". . . meet it —— set it down": Hamlet
8 Prefix with graphic or logic
9 Home for a jet
10 Othello's kinsmen
11 Second First Lady
12 Bar follower
13 Word with drag or hair
14 Obtrude
15 Location of last resort?
16 Cherish
17 Spacek
18 Foot: Comb. form
23 Quaker in a grove
24 Jackson protégé
28 Where the Rolling Stones landed?
30 Type of reader
31 Luzon port
32 Role
33 Freshly
34 "Little Caesar"
35 Actor Guinness
36 ——-majesté
37 Chick's expression
39 Put out of humor
42 West African republic
44 Hardy and Rooney
45 And others: Abbr.
47 Curved plank
49 D'Artagnan and friends
50 Actress Kedrova
52 ". . . —— saw Elba"
54 Ralph Rackstraw, e.g.
55 Crispin's product
59 Pedro's payment
61 Georgia university
62 Good place to unwind?
63 Loaf
64 A way, for Superman?
66 Eight of a kind
67 Companion of Artemis
68 —— Nol of Cambodia
70 Fruit drinks
71 Fix the piano
74 "I —— Camera"
76 About
78 Paving stones
79 Pertaining to units of living matter
80 Scent
81 Turkish city
82 An 1898 discovery
83 Zest
84 Hook's first mate
90 Soul
92 Rockette, for one
93 Dicer's natural
96 Shelves
97 Actress in "The King and I"
98 Paragons
99 Carp
100 French historian: 1842-1906
101 Give off
103 Pluto, to Plato
106 Sand pile
108 Lion
109 Buccal
110 Broadway hit of 1982
111 Assert
112 Guided
114 Little pocket
115 A crowd, to Tiberius
116 Turf

Personal Possessions

By Alfio Micci

ACROSS

1 Footlike part
4 Diced
9 Kite adjunct
13 Writer Santha —— Rau
17 "Vissi d' ——," Puccini aria
18 Fred's sister
19 Type of Greek architecture
21 Plant form
22 British actor's factories
24 Tennessee auto
26 Criminal activity
27 Covenants
29 Hardy sidekick
30 Free
31 Country house
32 Belli's concern
33 Blue Eagle measure
34 "Mattinata" composer
35 Actor-director Martin
36 Quickly
39 Redcap on Tin Pan Alley
41 Mil. decoration
44 Stet's opposite
45 Throe
46 Is left on base
47 Stable youngster
48 Greek vowel
49 Moppet in the kitchen
53 Toscanini's birthplace
54 Wash. bigwig
55 Ambler or Knight
56 Folklore creature
57 Certain marquis's activity
58 Spectral type
60 Golden-egg producer
61 Lock
62 "Catch-22" star and family
63 Richard or Daniel
64 Ballet movement
66 Double agent
68 Marks and crowns
69 Piece of land in Hollywood
71 "—— Rheingold"
72 "—— It Romantic?": 1932 song
73 Something easy to catch
74 "—— a Song Go . . ."
75 Exhaust
76 B.A. or M.A.
77 Chef on a tour
81 Hen
82 I.o.u.'s
83 Courage
84 Comedian Conway
85 Strands
88 Riches
89 Devil: Comb. form
93 Pied-——
94 "Flying Dutchman" girl
95 Signifies
96 Legume that sprouted in Vermont
98 Mr. Leach's subsidy
100 Zilch, in Toulouse
101 Flood tide
102 Popular poplar in puzzles
103 Sponsorship
104 Theta follower
105 "—— Cassius . . ."
106 Pittsburgh export
107 Years upon years

DOWN

1 Delve
2 Lucy's TV friend
3 What a judge passes
4 Embroidered blouse
5 City northeast of Venice
6 Neth. neighbor
7 House extension
8 Loathe
9 Popular gift for a man
10 Corporeal channel
11 Travelers' havens
12 Deck count, for a Latinist
13 Fill the tank again
14 Future oak
15 Stable creatures
16 Confuse
17 "A door is not a door when it's ——"
20 Island near Borneo
23 Gape
25 Wallace colleague
28 Hgts.
31 River of song
32 Passé
34 Pick-me-up
35 Cross-examine
36 Summer quaffs
37 Rambler owned by Charlie Hustle
38 Comedian's ruler
39 Colombian city
40 "Swan Lake" role
41 Miss von Kappelhoff's diary entry
42 Tool in a private eye's digs
43 Silent one
45 Sounds contented
47 Evanesce
49 What a teen-ager pants for
50 Kind of pigeon
51 Chum
52 They go to blazes
53 Denuded apples
57 Wading bird
59 Change the color
60 Role for Ingrid
62 Kind of test
63 Healing ointments
64 Conn man
65 Scallion's kin
67 North Sea feeder
69 "—— me" (chimney sweep's O.K.)
70 Firenze bloom
73 Certain checkers
75 Boy Scout event
77 Annoyance
78 Steered clear of
79 Faction
80 S.A. capital
81 Tael

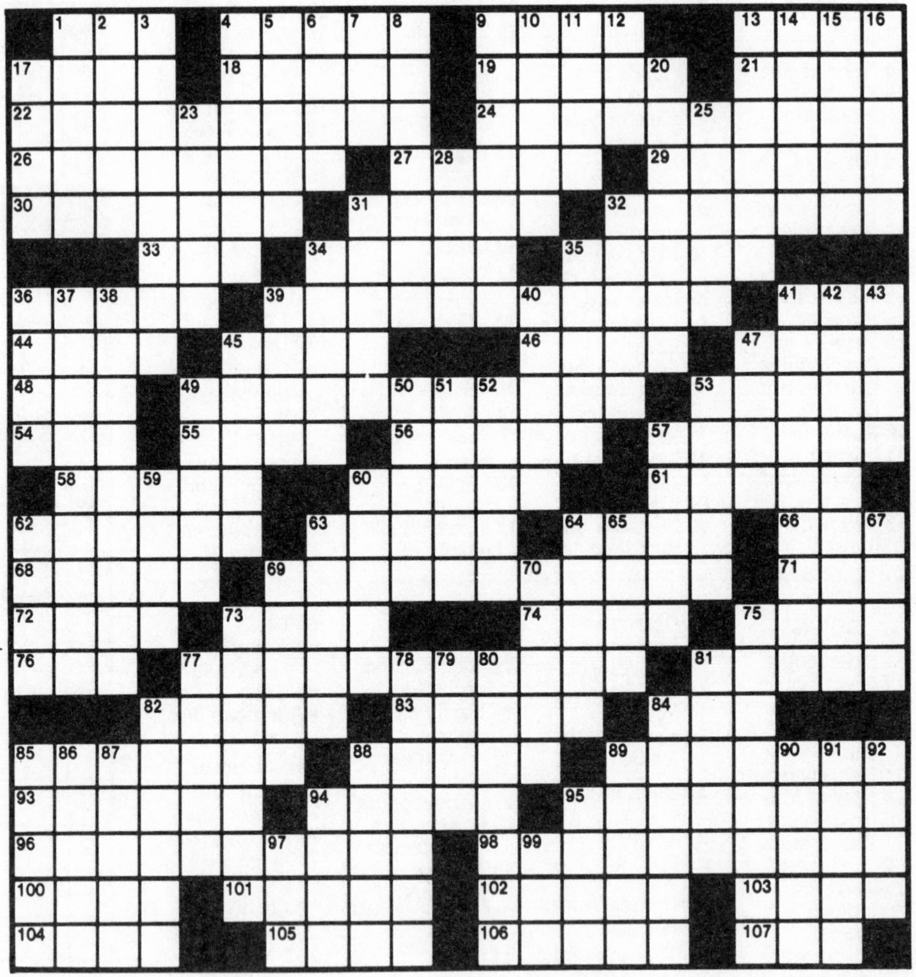

82 Halo
84 Pre-Yule purchase
85 The rainbow fish
86 Valley between volcanic cones
87 Adjust the clock
88 Hear of
89 Moriarty's creator
90 N.Z. university
91 Figure in "Reds"
92 Kilns: Var.
94 Utah lily
95 An Algonquian language
97 Botany is one
99 Browning's "—— Vogler"

TIMES BOOKS CROSSWORD ORDER FORM

L.A. Times Sunday Crosswords

Witty, contemporary puzzles from the pages of the Los Angeles Times.

VOL	ISBN	QUANTITY	PRICE	TOTAL PRICE
1	91910-6	______	$7.50	_____
2	91911-4	______	$7.50	_____
3	91915-7	______	$8.00	_____
4	91916-5	______	$7.50	_____
5	91917-3	______	$7.50	_____
6	91918-1	______	$7.50	_____
7	91919-X	______	$8.00	_____
8	91920-3	______	$7.50	_____
9	92227-1	______	$7.50	_____
10	92228-X	______	$7.50	_____
11	92229-8	______	$8.00	_____
12	92230-1	______	$8.00	_____

Washington Post Sunday Crosswords

N.Y. Times-quality puzzles from the nation's capital.

VOL	ISBN	QUANTITY	PRICE	TOTAL PRICE
1	91933-5	______	$8.00	_____
2	91934-3	______	$7.50	_____
3	92109-7	______	$7.50	_____

N.Y. Times Daily Crosswords

America's favorite mental exercise!

VOL	ISBN	QUANTITY	PRICE	TOTAL PRICE
27	91879-7	______	$7.50	_____
28	91899-1	______	$7.00	_____
29	91937-8	______	$7.00	_____
30	91997-1	______	$7.50	_____
31	92043-0	______	$8.00	_____
32	92082-1	______	$7.50	_____
33	92183-6	______	$7.50	_____
34	92209-3	______	$7.50	_____
35	92270-0	______	$7.50	_____
36	92340-5	______	$8.00	_____

N.Y. Times Sunday Crosswords

The standard by which other crosswords have been judged for more than 50 years.

VOL	ISBN	QUANTITY	PRICE	TOTAL PRICE
10	91083-4	______	$7.50	_____
11	91115-6	______	$7.50	_____
12	91166-0	______	$8.00	_____
13	91191-1	______	$7.50	_____
14	91681-6	______	$7.50	_____
15	91781-2	______	$7.50	_____
16	91839-8	______	$7.50	_____
17	91878-9	______	$7.50	_____
18	92268-9	______	$7.50	_____
19	92083-X	______	$7.50	_____

N.Y. Times Toughest Crosswords

The "toughest of the tough" from the Times puzzle page.

VOL	ISBN	QUANTITY	PRICE	TOTAL PRICE
1	91694-8	______	$8.00	_____
2	91828-2	______	$8.00	_____
3	91912-2	______	$8.00	_____
4	92178-X	______	$9.00	_____

Crossword Omnibus Volumes

Your best puzzling values—each with 200 crosswords, at a great price!

VOL	ISBN	QUANTITY	PRICE	TOTAL PRICE
Will Weng Sunday Crossword Omnibus				
1	91300-0	______	$10.00	_____
2	91645-X	______	$10.00	_____
3	91935-1	______	$10.00	_____
N.Y. Times Daily Crossword Omnibus				
1	91094-X	______	$10.00	_____
2	91018-4	______	$10.00	_____
3	91066-4	______	$10.00	_____
4	91117-2	______	$10.00	_____
5	91708-1	______	$10.00	_____
6	92124-0	______	$10.00	_____
N.Y. Times Sunday Crossword Omnibus				
1	91139-3	______	$10.00	_____
2	91791-X	______	$10.00	_____
3	91936-X	______	$10.00	_____

N.Y. Times SkillBuilder Crosswords

The first crossword series in three levels of difficulty—specially designed to teach beginners the "rules of the game" and improve puzzlers' skills.

VOL	ISBN	QUANTITY	PRICE	TOTAL PRICE
One-star Beginner Level				
1	92302-2	______	$8.00	_____
Two-star Apprentice Level				
1	92303-0	______	$8.00	_____
Three-star Strategist Level				
1	92304-9	______	$8.00	_____

Acrostic Puzzles

Change-of-pace puzzles with a literary flavor that reveal interesting quotations when completed.

VOL	ISBN	QUANTITY	PRICE	TOTAL PRICE
N.Y. Times Acrostics				
3	91116-4	______	$7.50	_____
4	91302-7	______	$7.50	_____
N.Y. Times Acrostic Omnibus				
2	91994-7	______	$8.00	_____
3	92362-6	______	$8.50	_____
L.A. Times Duo-Crostics				
1	92225-5	______	$8.00	_____

GAMES Magazine Crosswords and Word Games

Lively, solver-friendly puzzles from America's most fascinating puzzle magazine.

VOL	ISBN	QUANTITY	PRICE	TOTAL PRICE
World's Most Ornery Crosswords				
	92081-3	______	$13.00	_____
Giant Book of Games				
	91951-3	______	$13.00	_____
Will Shortz's Best Brain Busters				
	91952-1	______	$11.00	_____
Games' Best Pencil Puzzles				
	92080-5	______	$11.00	_____
Brain Twisters from the First World Puzzle Championships				
	92146-1	______	$11.00	_____

Puzzles For Kids

Start your favorite youngster on a lifetime of brainbuilding fun! (For ages 7 to 14)

VOL	ISBN	QUANTITY	PRICE	TOTAL PRICE
GAMES Magazine Kids' Giant Book of Games				
	92199-2	______	$12.00	_____
GAMES Magazine Riddlers for Kids				
	92385-5	______	$11.00	_____

Cryptic Crosswords

Sophisticated puzzles in the British style, using American English.

VOL	ISBN	QUANTITY	PRICE	TOTAL PRICE
GAMES Magazine Cryptic Crosswords				
	91999-8	______	$8.00	_____
Crosswords from The Nation				
1	92012-0	______	$7.50	_____
2	92013-9	______	$7.50	_____
3	92031-7	______	$7.50	_____
4	92032-5	______	$7.50	_____
5	92033-3	______	$7.50	_____
6	92034-1	______	$7.50	_____
N.Y. Times Puns and Anagrams				
1	92271-9	______	$7.50	_____

N.Y. Times Crossword Dictionary

The revised edition of the classic reference book for crossword fans.

VOL	ISBN	QUANTITY	PRICE	TOTAL PRICE
	91131-8	______	$21.00	_____

Additional Times Books crossword puzzle books are available through your local bookstore, or fill out this coupon and return to:

RANDOM HOUSE, INC., 400 HAHN ROAD, WESTMINSTER, MD 21157. ATTN: ORDER PROCESSING

TO ORDER CALL TOLL-FREE
1-800-793-BOOK

☐ Enclosed is my check or money order payable to Times Books

☐ Charge my account with: ☐ American Express ☐ Visa ☐ MasterCard

☐☐☐☐☐☐☐☐☐☐☐☐☐☐☐☐ ______________ EXP DATE (MO/YR)

Price applies to U.S. and territories only.
In Canada write Random House of Canada, 5390 Ambler Drive, Mississauga, Ontario.
(Prices subject to change.)

____Total Books

Total Dollars $________

Sales Tax $________ (Where applicable)

Postage and Handling $ 2.00

Total Enclosed $________

Please send me copies of the crossword books I have checked off, in the amounts indicated.

Name (please print) ____________________ Signature ____________________

Address ____________________ City ____________ State ________ Zip ________

1

2

3

4

5

6

7

8

9

10

11

12

13

14

15

16

17

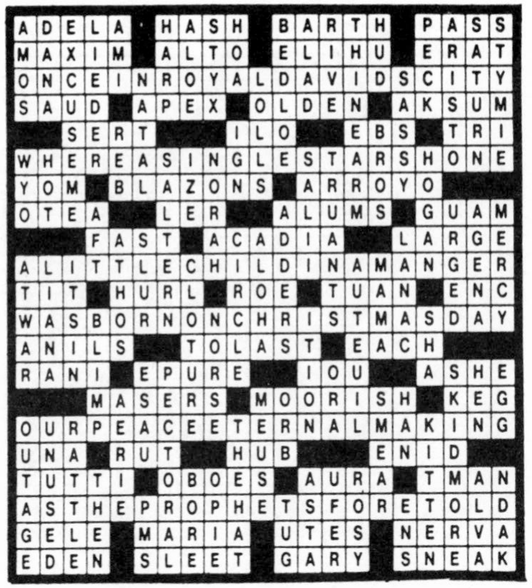

18

19

20

21

22

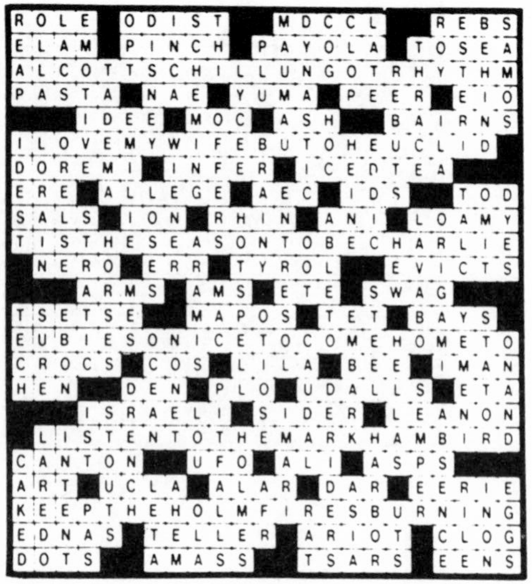

23

24

25

26

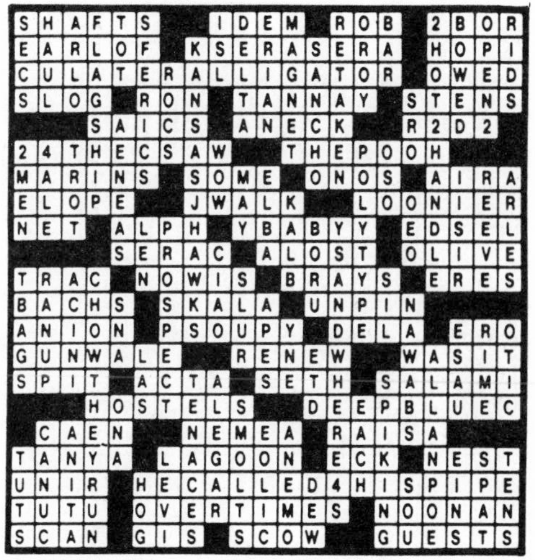

27

28

29

30

31

32

33

34

35

36

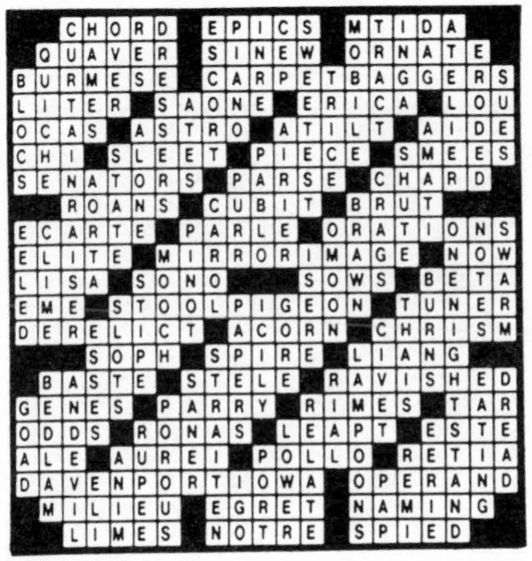

37

38

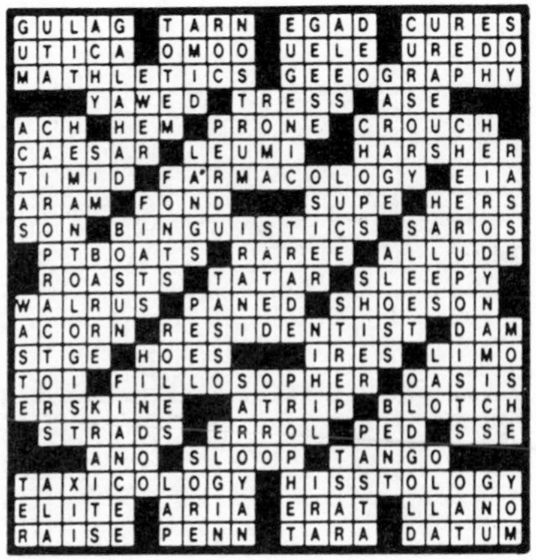

39

40

41

42

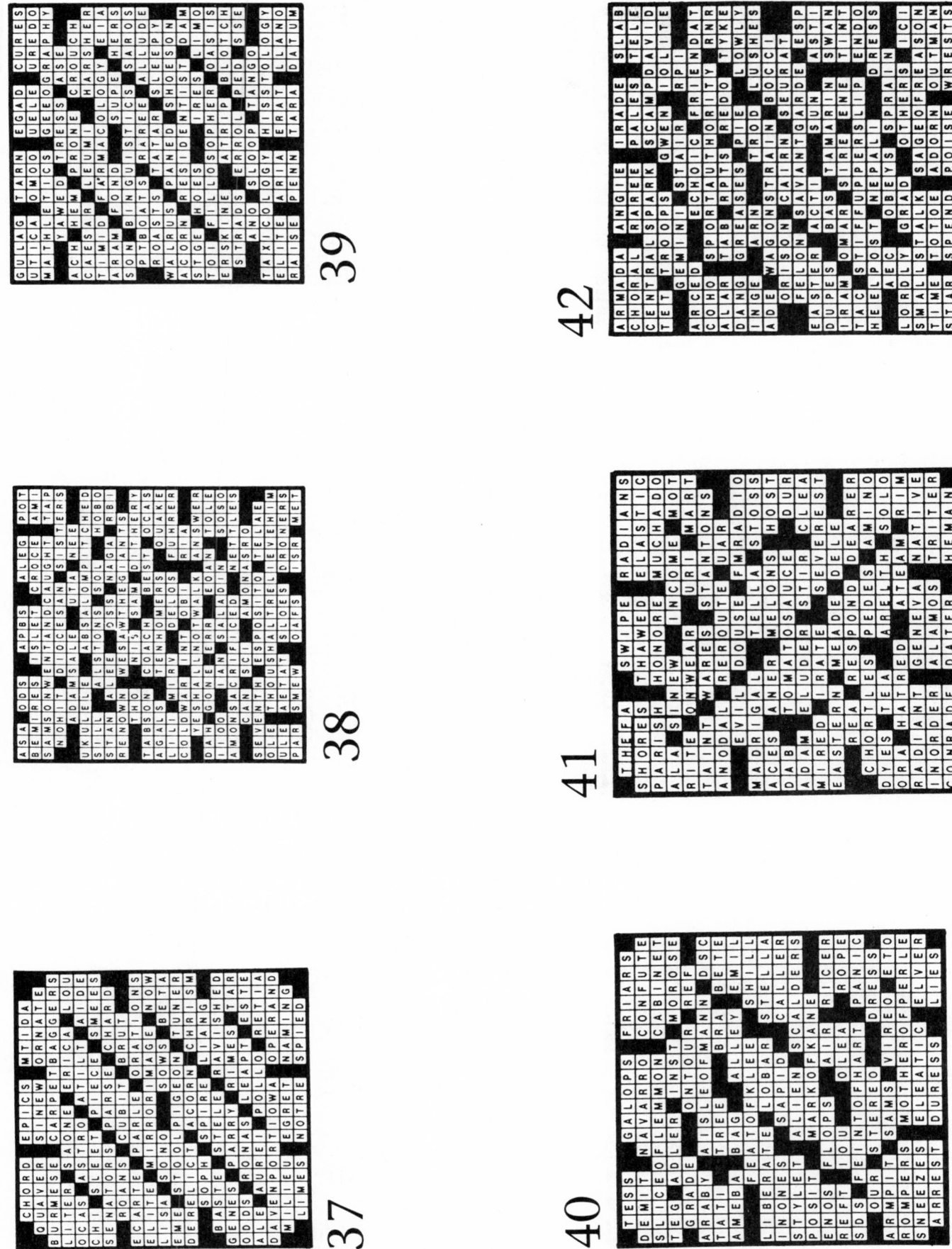

43

44

45

46

47

48

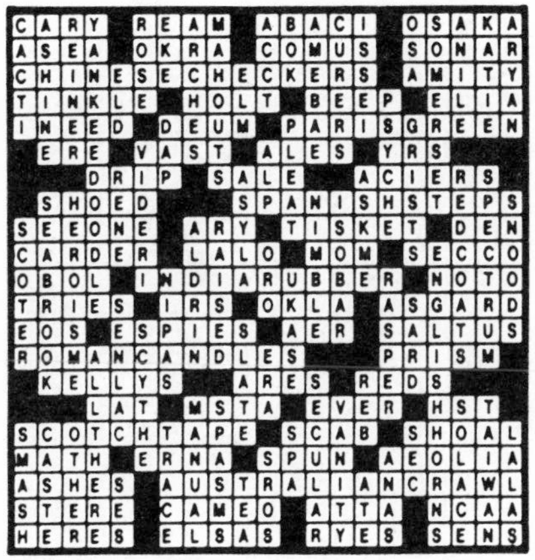

49

50

51

52

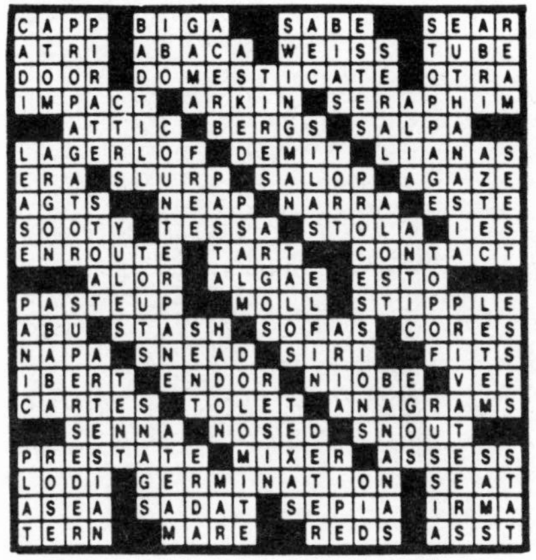

53

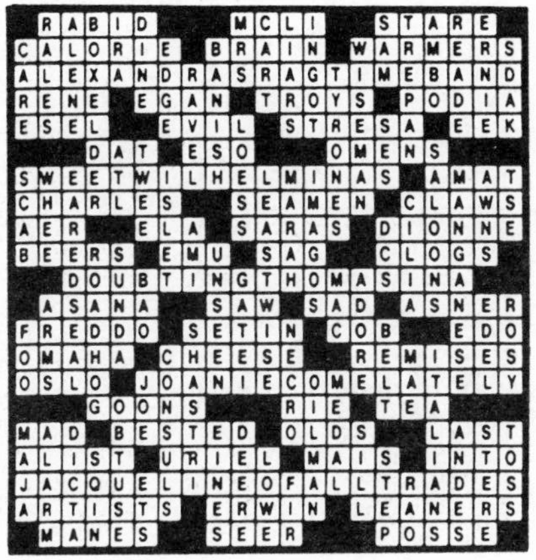

54

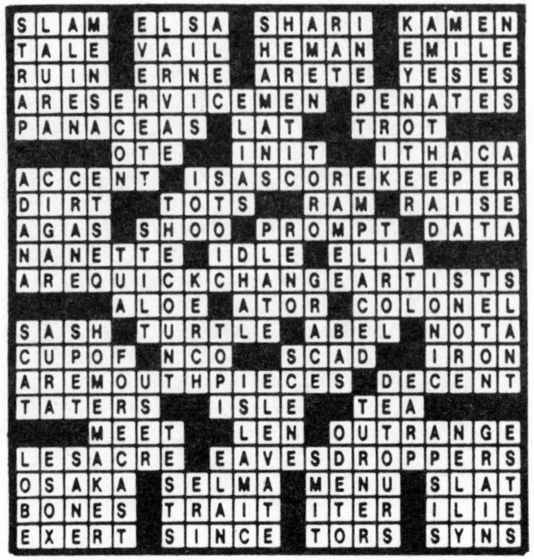

55

56

57

58

59

60

61

62

63

64

65

66

67

68

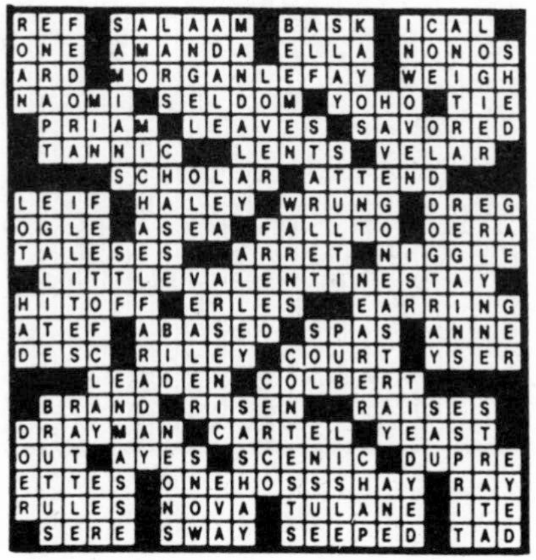

69

70

71

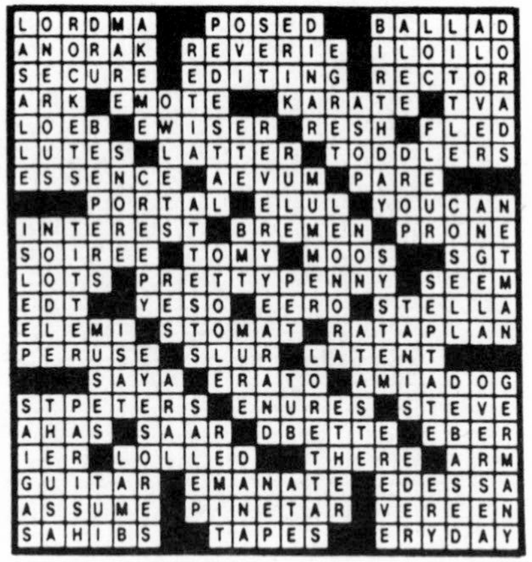

72

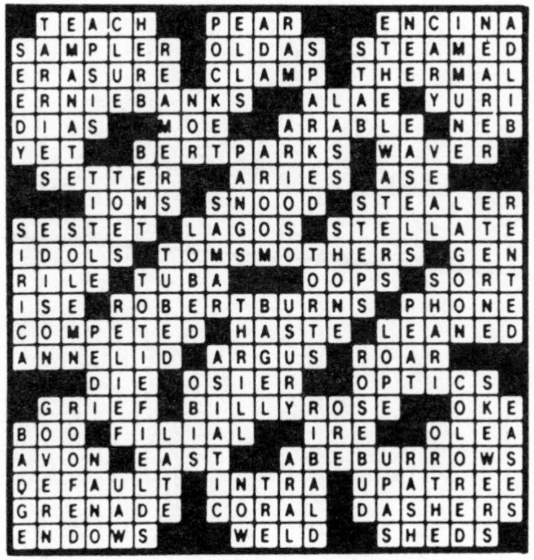

73

74

75

76

77

78

79

80

81

82

83

84

85

86

87

88

89

90

91

92

93

94

95

96

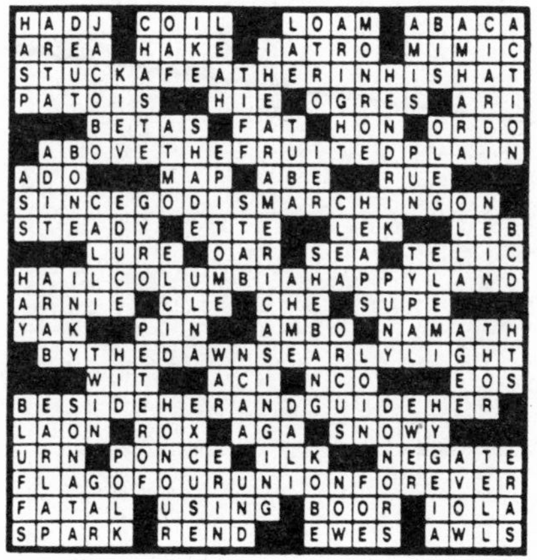

97

98

99

100

101

102

103

104

105

106

107

108

109

110

111

112

113

114

115

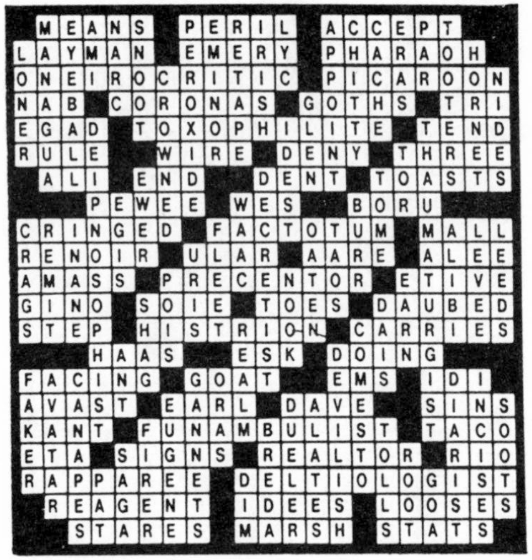

116

117

118

119

120

121

122

123

124

125

126

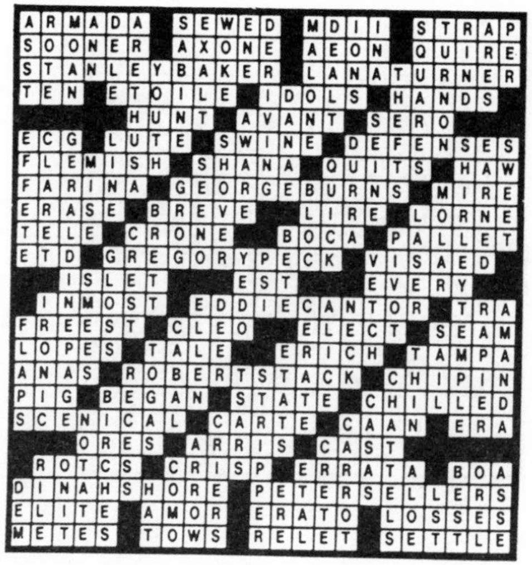

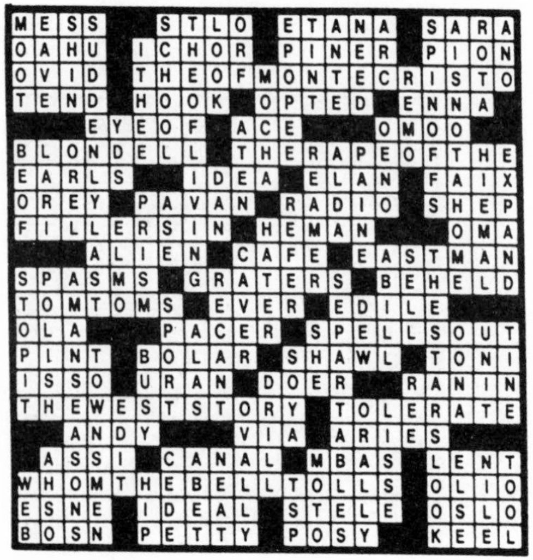

127

128

129

130

131

132

133

134

135

136

137

138

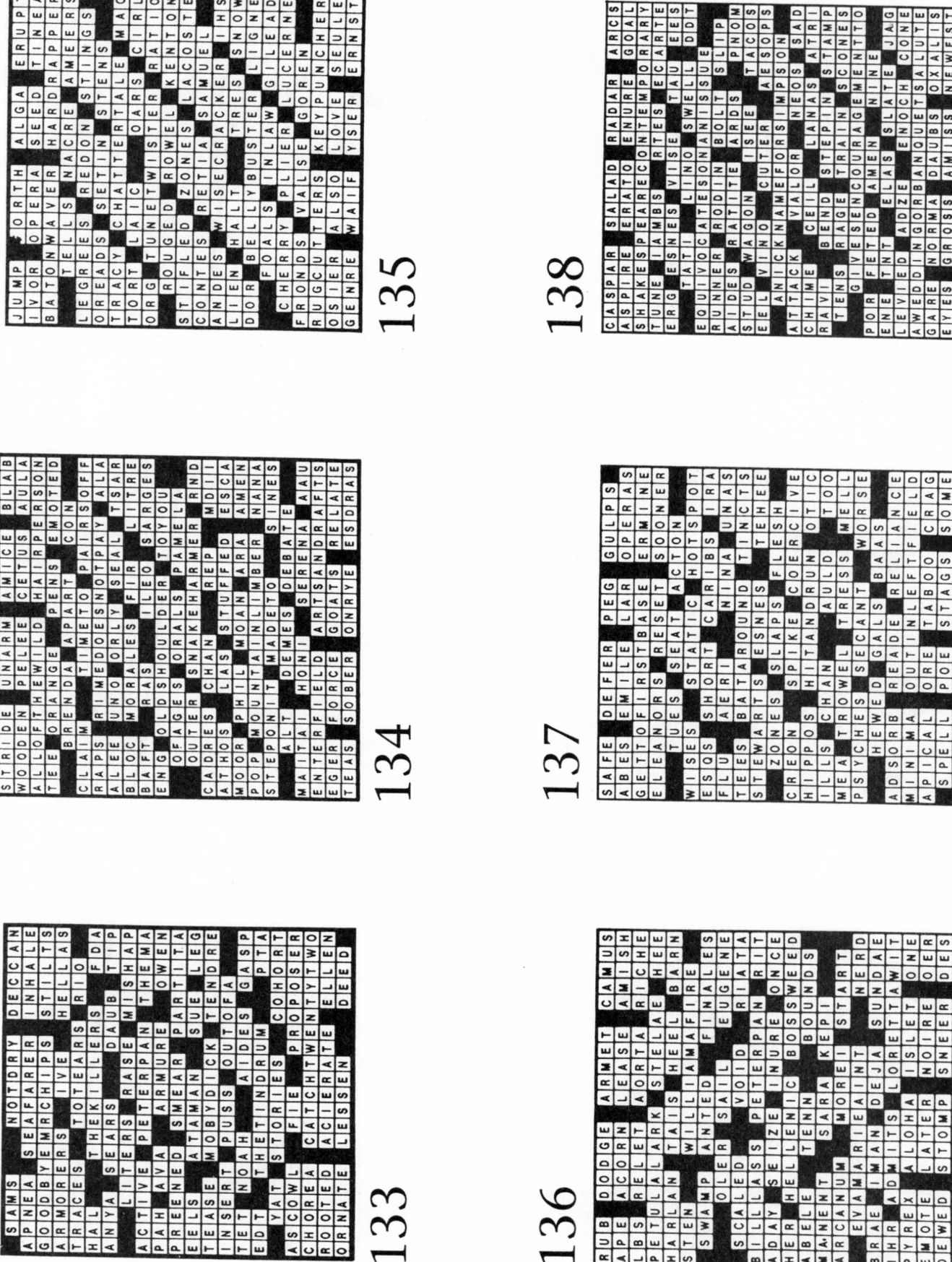

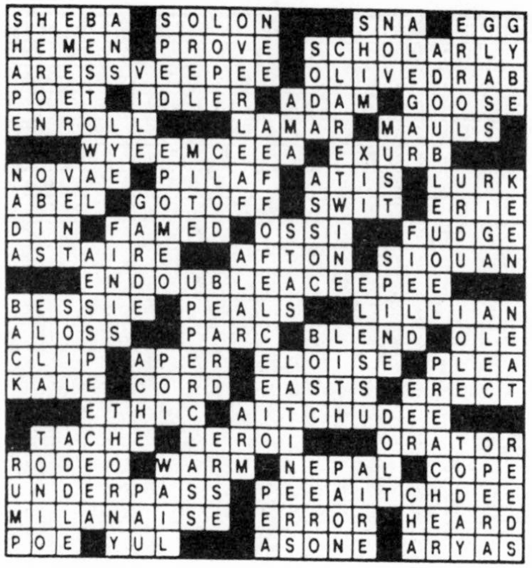

139

140

141

142

143

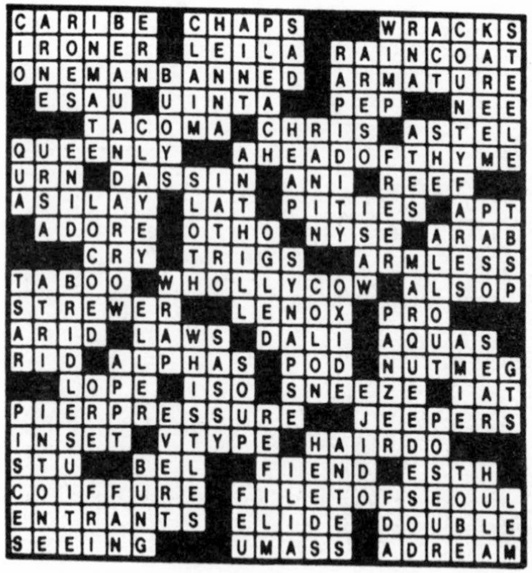

144

145

146

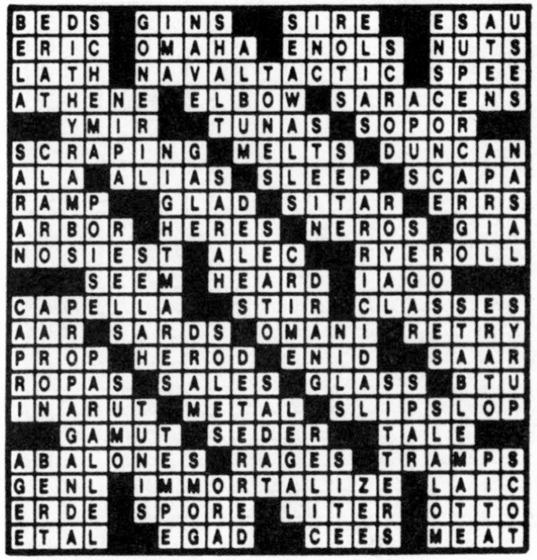

147

148

149

150

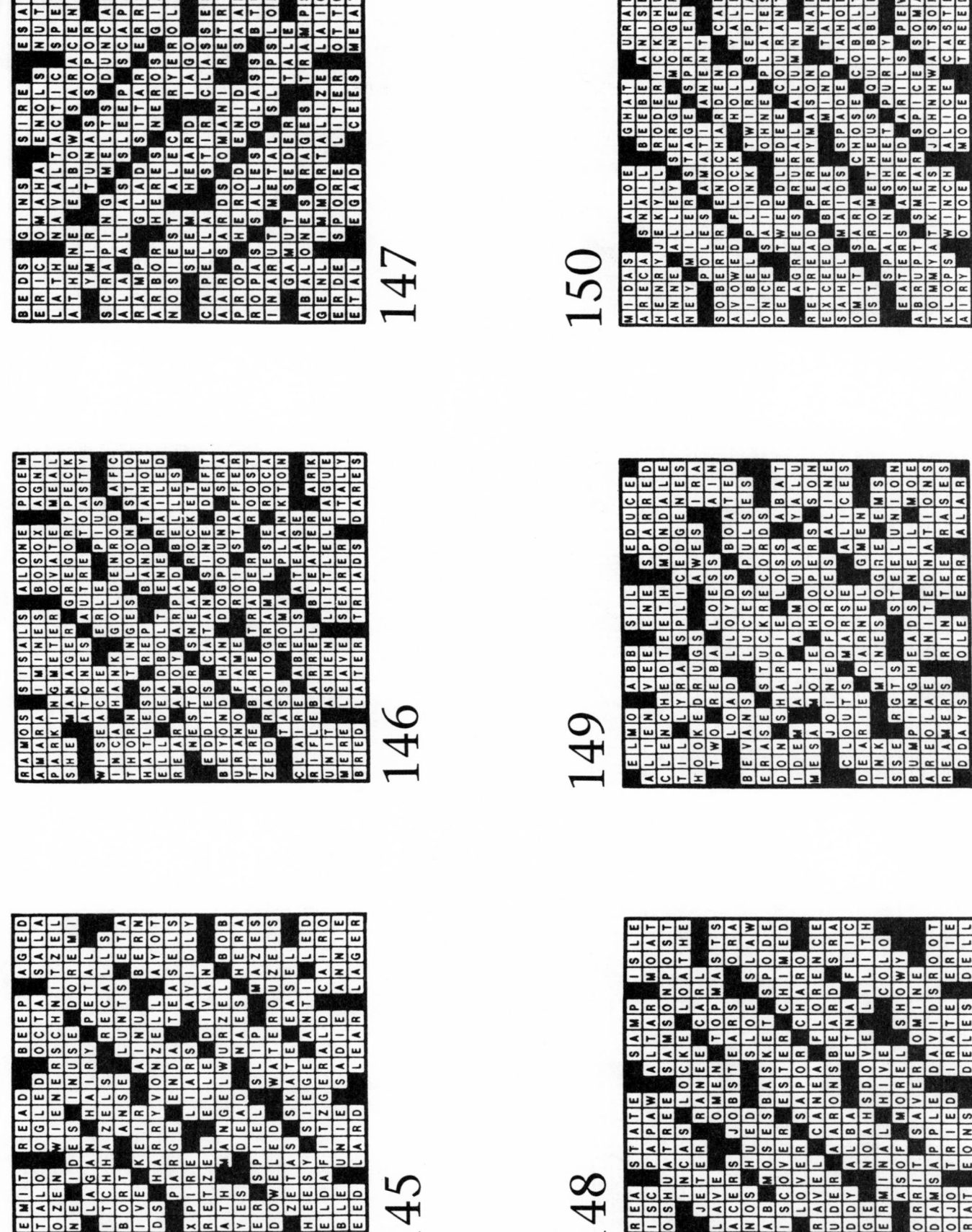

151

152

153

154

155

156

157

158

159

160

161

162

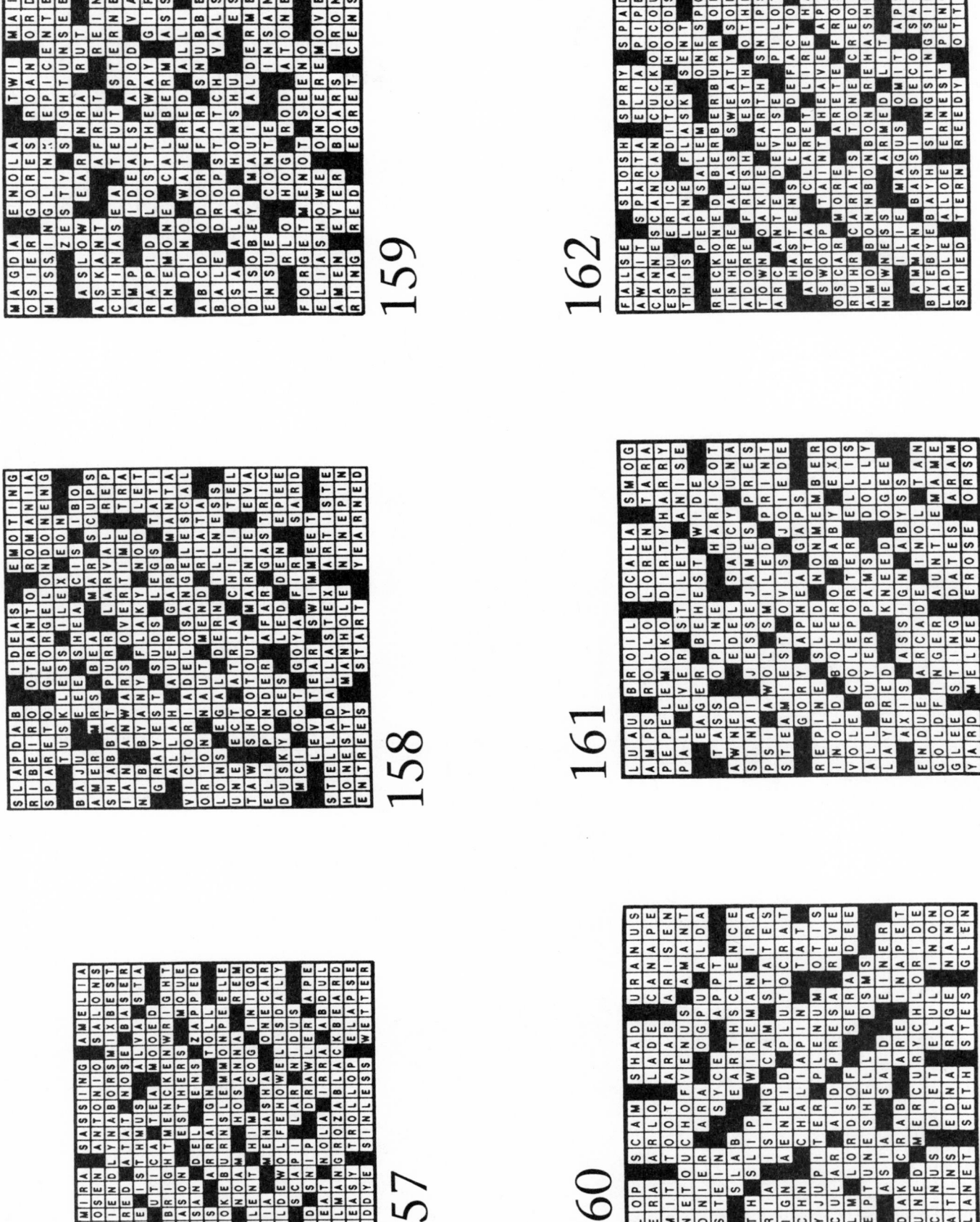

163

164

165

166

167

168

BALI SNAP SHALT UDAL
ELAM SAIDA MARIA NOSE
EDDA ONEAL ILLAT RUIN
RAYMONDCHANDLER VEGAS
RUSE DOGES PEAL
SEWERS DINE SOILAGE
EVANS WAYNENEWTON SOC
MIST NOME AEON AFRO
ICH HOWARDBAKER STAEL
STIPULES ROBED COSINE
NOMAD BARER TRUER
EGGSON DEMON ERASABLE
TOTER LELANDSTOWE AIN
AMOR JANE PALL INST
TEN GARYMERRILL ANKLE
SLIPUPS MIEN PROSER
RUNE COPRA SAIC
COVEN ALFREDHITCHCOCK
AMIR CRETE TOLET UPON
MONT ELVES HELLS LAKE
POGO ROANS ESSO PHEW

169

ABODES CAIUS CESS MASK
RAREES ANTRA ONATE ERIA
FRANKENSTEIN SEVERINSEN
TNTS BEER STRANGELOVE
LOGO DAYS WATSON AONES
GLENDA MALI NIET
TOSSED SPIRAL BAND GALA
WALTERMITTY UMPIRED
WELBY IOTA ANET ELITE
AVAL MEW CALIGARI SLAIN
DAGAMA ALIEN MALATESTA
NEIF PELISSE ELLS
DULCAMARA ELECS PEPPER
OKEHS UPTODATE TIS IOIO
RANAL STIR NOON IERNE
ESTREAT TRAPPERJOHN
NEED LUPE PUERTO ARCADE
ALSO ORGY TOYMEN
FAGER SNARES MASS CPNS
ANESTHETIST DATE ALOI
HACKENBUSH CLITTERHOUSE
ATKA DORSE AORTA NAPLES
MOOR NEER MATER ASSESS

170

SPEC HIRAM PAOLI PEAR
ORCA ADELA ORLON LENA
DAHLSDOLLS WALTSWALTZ
STOICAL AMEBA TESSIE
CATS DRURY BRAM
MAJOR SAYSO FOULARDS
ABU FRANCKSFRANCS HOT
TEL SELAH AUNT RODE
ELEC AYRESAIRS BADGE
RESOURCE INSET AMEER
JAIME CLAIR TSARS
ABETS ARKIN DEPLORES
PEWIT GUYSGUISE DORA
ARES ARNE NOLLE AGO
ILL ARIELSAERIALS DON
RESPIRES PUNIC PASTE
ADAM SOBIG ABIE
ADRIAN SLUES PEARSON
JEANSGENES LAPPSLAPSE
ACME ETAPE EXALT TRIP
ROSS DEPTS DELES EYES

171

172

HEMP TALC CCCL TAROT
ALAI AMIA AURA ILOVE
TURN MAME SPECULATOR
SLING TASSE DETESTING
PARTISAN SOSO EDAM
TROCAR RIOT PICRATE
BASENESS PREPRINT LEN
AGA GNAWS BALLADES
RAS ETTIE LAS INAPIE
CREELS CTN CODERS
ASEA SLAUGHTER IGET
MIDLER MPS AROUSE
OSWEGO MOT GUMBO SMU
BELLAIRE OCEAN TOS
SAT SLANDERS TONNEAUS
ABETTOR NEON GINNER
ALSO SAND WINFIELD
RESISTORS INTER SIEVE
WELLINGTON EGAL VAIL
AREAR OARS REMY ESSA
SARGE TROT YVES NYET

173

HEAP MORSE ELAND STOP
ERIE ELIOT MALAR HIVE
BALDERDASH BILGEWATER
ESSENCES EVERY SHRINK
STER REDD SOP
ELATED JEERS GLASSJAW
LOBAR SUDAN SIEGE ARR
GIRL FIDDLEDEDEE ABRI
ARA DINGY ADDS TUBAS
RECHARGE TOKAY ARDENT
AIMEE SATAN CLAIR
LADLED LITER SHADOWED
OPALS DANA STARE OCA
GOBY GIMCRACKERY ACOR
ERR TROPE DAIRY ANKLE
STARWARS CASTE PRAYED
EIN DAMS FEET
RESEND TERSE NEWCOMER
APPLESAUCE TRIVIALITY
MICE ORNOT TENET INTO
ACAD NEARS EVERS ANAT

174

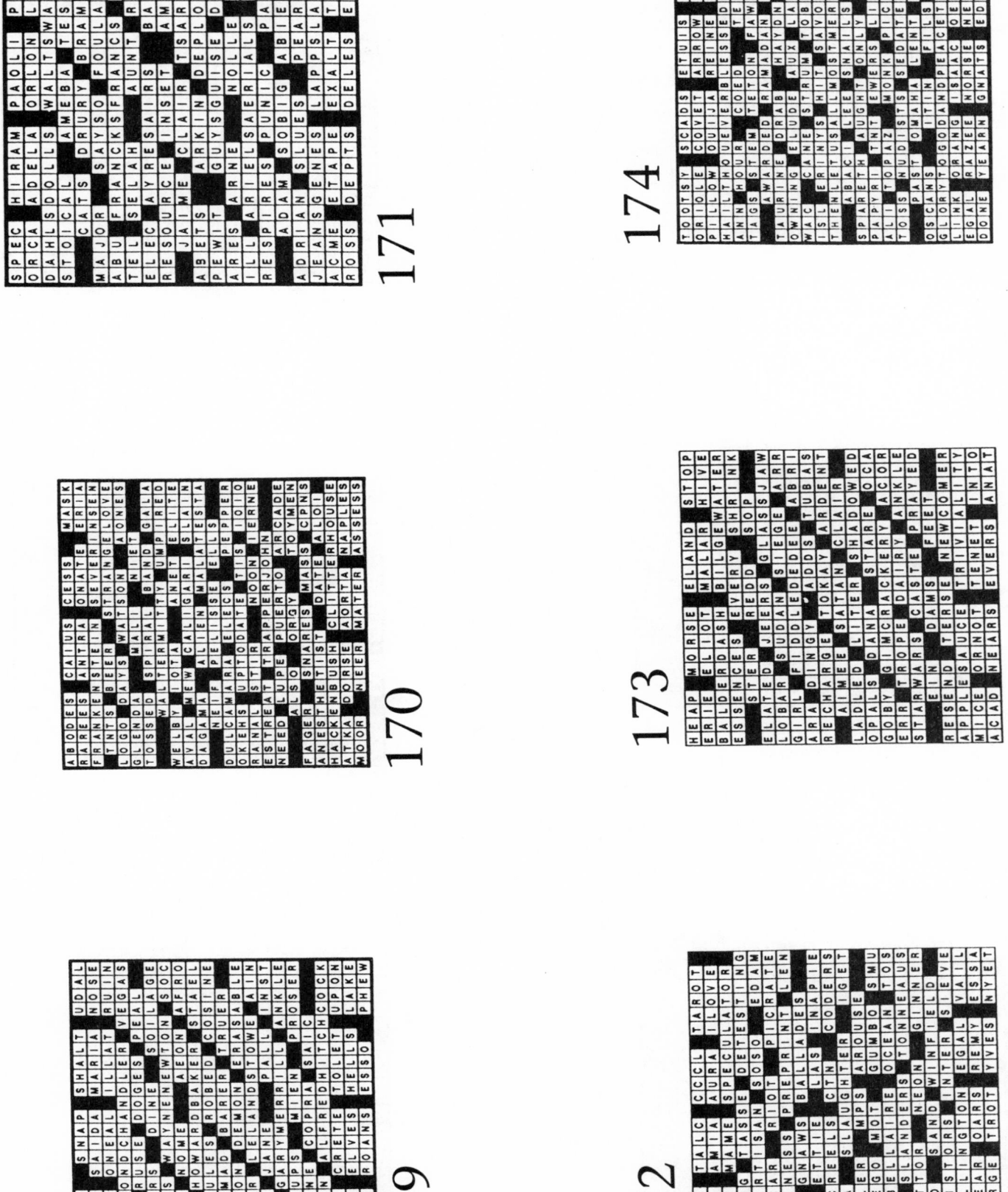

TOOTSY SCADS ETUIS CARL
ORIOLE COVET ARROW OLEO
PILLOW OUIJA REINE MOTO
HAILTHOUEVERBLESSEDMORN
ANN HOUR COED TEAPOY
TAGS STEM TETON FAWN
AWARDED RAMADAN DREW
TAURINE DRAB HAYDN OPA
OWNING ELUDE AUX LACTIC
WAC CANE STRUM TOBACCO
ISL ERINYS HIT SAVOR
THENLETUSALLMOSTMERRYBE
ABACI LEE SNAILS ART
SPARETH AUGHT ONLY RAH
PAPYRI TNT EWERS LINDEN
ALI TOPAZ MONK PICASSO
TOSS NUDISTS SEDATES
PAST OMAHA LENT ARAW
OSCANS ITIN FILS EVA
GLORYTOGODANDPEACETOMEN
LINK ORANG ISAAC OENONE
EGAL RAZEE NORSE NEUTER
DONE YEARN GNATS EDSELS

175

176

177

178

179

180

181

182

183

184

185

186

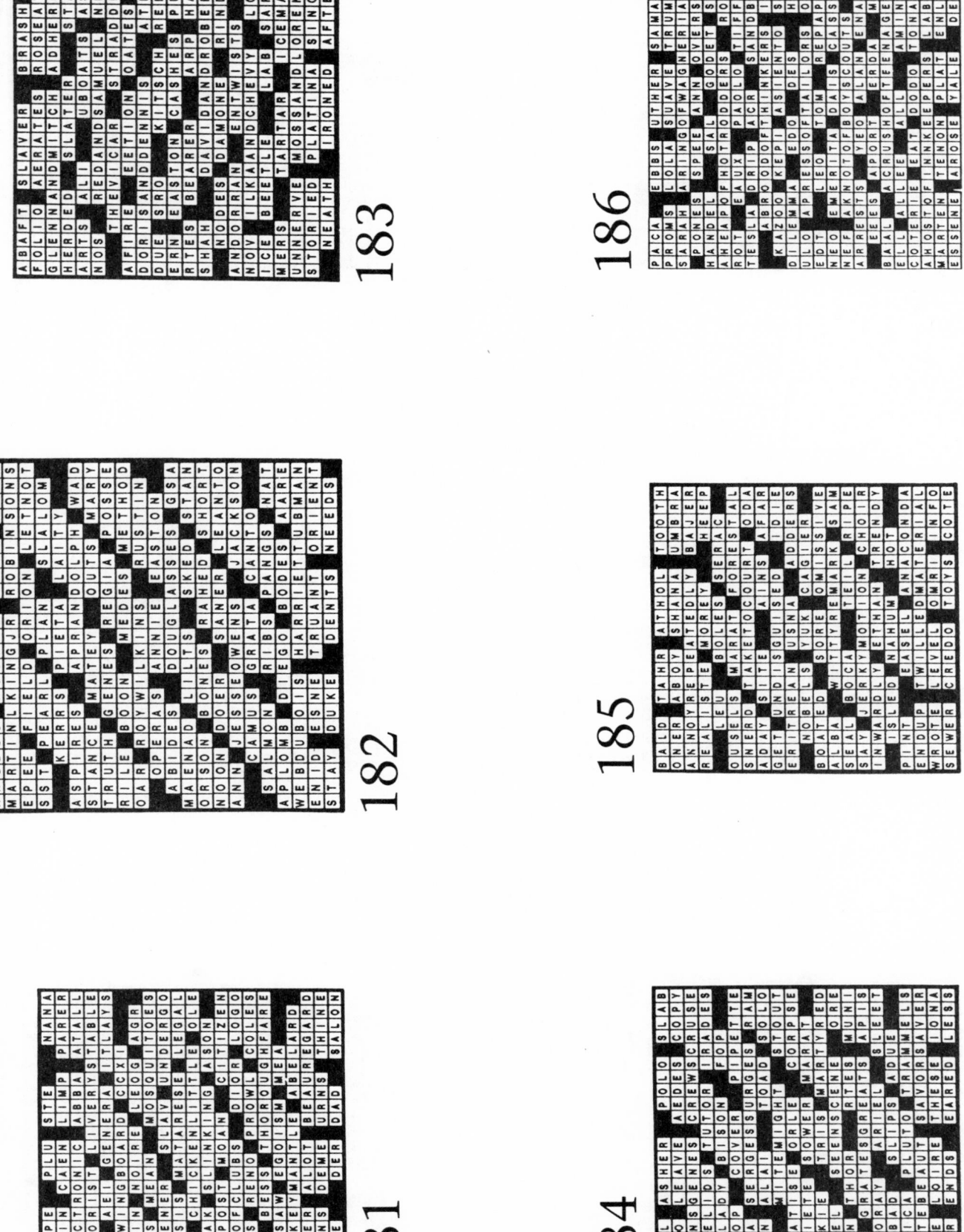

187

188

189

190

191

192

193

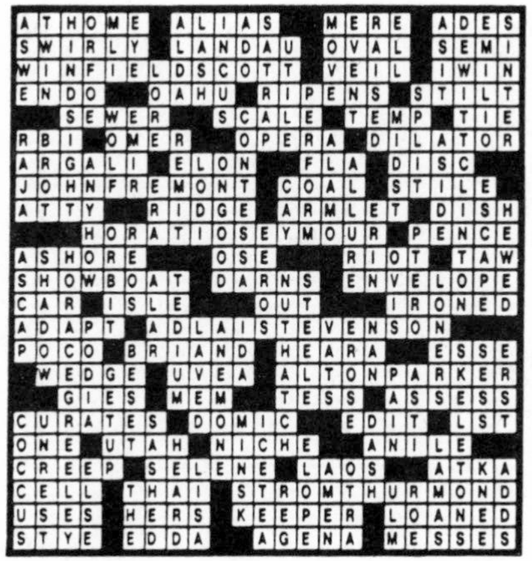

194

195

196

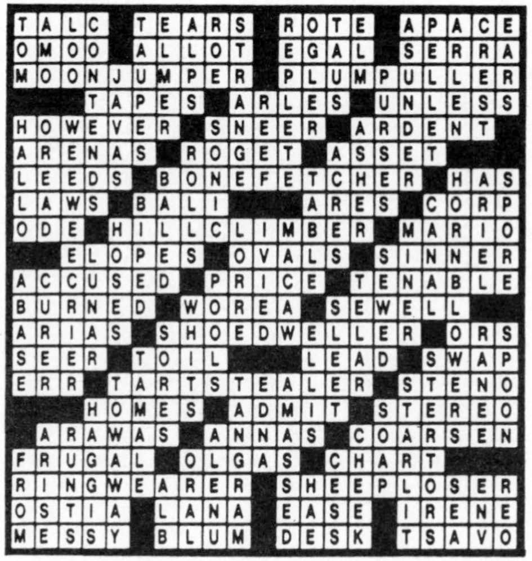

197

198

MAHAL NIGH MANN IDAS
PARADE ASEA OBOE MIDI
EXCLAMATIONPOINT PROS
DISTRUST GORGE HOERS
EPI BALSA MASSEY
PARALLELPARK IMARET
ANILE NYES BLIND RAE
RECESS EAGLE FIREANT
TWOCENTSPLAIN FLORIDA
YAH SLIP ACETYL
EMIL ROOTCANAL KISS
AMADOR ECHO GOA
DOILIES TENSIONMOUNTS
ERNESTO EASED ADREAM
SYS LUMET TICS OFONE
PLANES KITCHENRANGE
SERENE SHEDS OVI
OXIDE DEARE REGIONAL
RUNG FUNDRAISINGDRIVE
EDGE ONCE LION LOANED
LESS BEES SIDE ELLER

199

PES CUBED TAIL RAMA
ARTE ADELE IONIC ECAD
JOHNSMILLS ERNIESFORD
ABETTING PACTS LAUREL
RELEASE VILLA DEFENSE
NRA TOSTI GABEL
APACE COLESPORTER DSC
DELE PANG DIES FOAL
ETA JULIASCHILD PARMA
SEN ERIC TROLL SADISM
SSTAR GOOSE TRESS
ARKINS BOONE PLIE SPY
COINS SALLYSFIELD DAS
ISNT COLD ILET JADE
DEG THOMASSCOOK LAYER
CHITS HEART TIM
MAROONS LUCRE DIABOLO
ATERRE SENTA CONNOTES
ORSONSBEAN CARYSGRANT
RIEN EAGRE ABELE EGIS
IOTA YOND STEEL EON

200

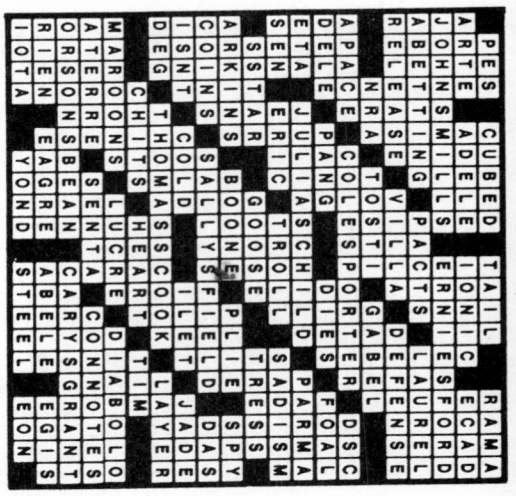